Abnormality

Abnormality

Experimental and

Steven Reiss
Rolf A. Peterson
Leonard D. Eron
Maggi Musico Reiss

[C]linical Approaches

MACMILLAN PUBLISHING CO., INC.
New York

COLLIER MACMILLAN PUBLISHERS
London

Printed in the United States of America

Macmillan Publishing Co., Inc.
866 Third Avenue, New York, New York 10022

Collier Macmillan Canada, Ltd.

Library of Congress Cataloging in Publication Data
Main entry under title:

Abnormality : experimental and clinical approaches.

Bibliography: p.
Includes index.
1. Psychology, Pathological. 2. Psychiatric research.
I. Reiss, Steven. [DNLM: 1. Psychopathology. WM100
A155]
RC454.A26 616.8'9 76-8474
ISBN 0-02-399300-6

Printing: 1 2 3 4 5 6 7 8 Year: 7 8 9 0 1 2 3

To the memory and creative spirit of my father, Ben Reiss, who taught his children to love to learn almost as much as they loved him.

To my parents, Richard and Amy Peterson, my wife, Sandra, and my children, Bradley and Pamela, for their support and understanding.

Preface

A textbook in abnormal psychology is a major summary of the substantive work in the field and as such should have several important functions. First, it should be educational. It should present the basic facts accurately and the theoretical concepts clearly. It should stimulate critical thought and serve as a model of scholarship and good writing. Second, a textbook in abnormal psychology is often a major reference source for psychologists and graduate students seeking basic information. Thus, textbooks should provide sufficient literature citations to enable the user to begin research on a particular topic. Third, a textbook should provide an overview of the field. It should serve as a statement of where the field currently is, how the study of abnormal psychology reached its current state, and what its probable future directions are. Thus, the historical context of current ideas should be presented, and the major trends of recent decades should be identified.

Accomplishing these purposes is difficult for any textbook writer. Inaccurate and misleading statements in textbooks have in some cases become influential myths in our field. One reason for the occurrence of inaccurate statements is that there really are no experts covering the entire area of abnormal psychology. No single person could possibly have expertise in all the topics in this book; no single expert could possibly keep up with the thousands of publications in abnormal psychology each year. One solution to this problem is to enlist expert writers, but previous attempts to do this have encountered difficulties in presenting a consistent and well-organized book. To fulfill our responsibility of keeping the statements in this book as accurate as possible we enlisted the expert help of colleagues in the writing of five of the twenty chapters. To maintain a consistent viewpoint and writing style, the chapters written by others were rewritten, edited, and returned to the original author for careful review.

A writer's responsibility includes a concern that statements not be misleading, even though they may be technically accurate. At the very least, writers should be careful to ensure that their statements are socially responsible. In addition, the impressions created by various sections of the book should be consistent with the book's major themes.

IMPORTANT THEMES OF THIS BOOK

1. *Abnormal behavior is not necessarily unusual and occurs in almost everyone in varying degrees and forms at various points in their lives. Furthermore, people who exhibit abnormal behavior have many areas of psychological strength.* To emphasize this theme, this book includes a chapter entitled "Abnormal Behavior in 'Normal' People."

2. *A review of the relevant literature indicates that very little is known about the biological causes of most disorders and that even less is known about the psychological causes. In contrast, in recent decades demonstrable progress in the treatment of abnormal behavior has been witnessed. Contrary to popular opinion, progress and theory in abnormal psychology have typically followed, rather than preceded, advances in clinical psychology. In fact, much of what* *we currently think of as abnormal psychology is a reaction to advances in clinical psychology.* An unusual feature of this volume is that it presents relatively extensive coverage of clinical psychology and does so prior to a presentation of the research on the various types of abnormality. This is appropriate because many theories of abnormal psychology were originally constructed to explain the effects of a clinical treatment or to provide a justification for such treatment.

3. *Theoretical diversity within abnormal psychology has always been basic and profound, and this continues to be true. Such diversity has increased in recent decades perhaps because, for the first time in history, many people are engaged in the study of abnormal behavior who have not received formal training in physiology. There are two types of theoretical divergence. First, psychologists approach the study and treatment of abnormal behavior in different ways. Second, psychologists have proposed different specific hypotheses about causation of particular disorders.* Five approaches to abnormality (biological, psychoanalytic, social learning, phenomenological, and community) are presented in Part II of this book, which includes an entire chapter for each approach. The decision to provide extensive coverage of the approaches was based on two beliefs: (1) that it is as important to learn ways of thinking about and studying abnormality as it is to acquire factual knowledge and (2) that theoretical diversity is and always has been an important characteristic of the field.

Different approaches to abnormality are typically concerned with the study of different aspects of abnormality. The disagreement among adherents of the various approaches is often a reflection of different interests rather than a disagreement over the accuracy of any particular set of facts.

Knowledge is precious and scarce. The five approach chapters were written in the belief that no single approach has a monopoly on knowledge or truth and that each approach has made its own unique contribution and will continue to do so.

4. *With regard particularly to the delivery of mental health services, the historical perspective of this book does not depict inevitable progress. Recent hopeful developments are noted but are presented in a context of similar developments in previous centuries. Emphasis is given to the transient nature of reforms and to the tendency of mental health care to revert to old ways after a reformer dies or when economic recession occurs.* The doctrine of progress has obscured the social reality—Pinel and Dorothy Dix accomplished far less than we like to believe. For example, Pinel was neither the first to free the insane nor the last. If history teaches us anything, it is that there is a continual need for people like Pinel; that is, there is a continual need for vigilance regarding the quality of mental health care because of social attitudes and the general difficulty of obtaining adequate funds.

CREDIT FOR EARLY INVESTIGATORS

As a major summary of a field, a textbook should not be unduly influenced by recent "in press" articles reporting research that has yet to be replicated. Often recent studies fail to replicate, or the findings turn out to have implications much different from initial impressions. Moreover, an increasing number of recent, seemingly exciting discoveries are really old findings and old issues expressed in a new language; the difference is purely semantic, arising from a relabeling of old phenomena. Textbooks should not contribute to this growing amnesia of our history. The present volume focuses on research findings for which attempts at replication have been made, strives to credit early investigators whenever possible, and presents the most recent research without giving undue emphasis to the latest possibility.

CONTENT AND ORGANIZATION OF BOOK

This book is organized around three basic questions: "What is abnormality?" "How is abnormality studied and treated?" and "What has been learned about abnormal behavior?"

Part I ("What Is Abnormality?") begins with a chapter on classification. The DSM-II system is presented, in part to provide the student with an overview of the types of behaviors that constitute the subject matter of the field and in part to provide an example of a classification system. The DSM-II system is critically evaluated and other classification systems are noted. General issues pertaining to classification are reviewed, and the now famous Rosenhan pseudopatient study is critically evaluated. Chapter 2 presents the history of the subject matter, first from the perspective of the scientist and then from the perspective of the client. The review focuses in part on the historical development of theoretical diversity within the field and emphasizes the fact that the study of abnormal behavior is 4,000 years old. Legal issues are discussed at the conclusion of the history chapter. Part I concludes with a chapter on the concept of abnormal behavior; this chapter critically evaluates the major definitions of abnormality and emphasizes the point that there is nothing true of all abnormal behaviors that is false of all normal behaviors.

Part II ("How Is Abnormality Studied and Treated?") contains six chapters that can be read in any order. Moreover, instructors wishing to focus on a particular theoretical orientation may assign only some of these Part II chapters without impairing the student's ability to comprehend the Part III chapters on the clinical syndromes. The first chapter in Part II is on psychological assessment. The next chapter is a comprehensive discussion of the biological approach to abnormality; one of the themes of this chapter is that many biologically oriented investigators have been concerned with the discovery of biological correlates of abnormality rather than with the discovery of biological causes. The chapter also includes a discussion of ethical issues pertaining to the use of biological treatments. The next chapter is a comprehensive presentation of psychoanalytic theory, particularly as espoused by Freud. A major theme of this chapter is that psychoanalytic theory contains different levels of hypotheses that are relevant to different types of evidence. The chapter on social learning theory presents the behavioral approach in its broader aspects, covering material pertaining to symbolically mediated behavior. A distinctive aspect of this chapter, moreover, is its incorporation of some recent advances in animal learning theory. For almost a decade now, animal learning investigators have been broadening the focus of their research. Theories have appeared that predict behavior to complex stimulus situations as a function of learning to stimulus components of that situation. Pavlovian conditioning, moreover, has been expanded to include learning resulting from circumstances in which a CS predicts the absence of a US. Unfortunately, these advances have been largely overlooked by social learning theorists, who continue to present learning theory much as it was during the 1950's and in terms of only a few basic principles that often do not have the generality that was once assumed. The chapter on phenomenology presents this approach as a science, a philosophy, and an attitude. The discussion includes humanistic philosophy and ethics. Part II concludes with a chapter on community psychology and community mental health.

Part III ("What Has Been Learned About Abnormality?") consists of ten chapters on the various syndromes of abnormal behavior. Some of these chapters focus on detailed presentations of clinical concepts and clinical descriptions; other chapters include extensive introductions to the various lines of research on the classification, etiology, and correlates of the syndrome under discussion. The chapters on the neurotic syndromes, personality disorders, and organic brain syndromes are primarily clinically oriented, even though basic research is covered. The chapters on psychophysiologic disorders, sexual variance, affective disorders, schizophrenia, mental retardation, abnormal behavior in "normal" people, and aggression and fantasy are primarily research oriented, even though extensive clinical descriptions are also provided. Generally the purpose in covering research is to introduce the student to the different types of investigations that have been conducted.

ACKNOWLEDGMENTS

Gershon Berkson, Alexander Rosen, and Leonard W. Sushinsky reviewed portions of the manuscript.

The contributions of Charles L. Gruder, Sharon Gurwitz, Alfred W. Kaszniak, Patrick O'Neill, and Leonard W. Sushinsky are noted in the contents.

Macmillan's editor for this volume was T. P. McConahay.

S. R.
R. A. P.
L. D. E.
M. M. R.

Chicago, Illinois

About the Authors

Steven Reiss received his A.B. degree in 1968 from Dartmouth College and his Ph.D. degree in 1973 from Yale University. He completed an internship in child clinical psychology at the Massachusetts General Hospital and at the W. E. Fernald State School. In 1972 he joined the faculty of the University of Illinois at Chicago Circle, where he is currently an associate professor. His research to date has focused on application of behavioral personality theory to clinical and educational problems and includes studies on conditioned inhibition, symbolically mediated generalization, intrinsic motivation, and open education.

Rolf A. Peterson received his B.A. degree in 1964 from Wisconsin State University, Oshkosh, and his Ph.D. degree in 1970 from the University of Iowa. After completing an internship in child clinical psychology at Emma Bradley Hospital, he joined the Scott County Mental Center, while continuing his graduate work. In 1969 he joined the faculty of the University of Illinois at Chicago Circle, where he is currently an associate professor on leave. In 1976 he became a Visiting Senior Lecturer in Abnormal Psychology at the University of Western Australia. His research to date has been in the areas of aggression, personality assessment, schizophrenia, and reinforcement therapy.

Leonard D. Eron is professor and former chairperson of the Department of Psychology of the University of Illinois at Chicago Circle. He received his Ph.D. in psychology from the University of Wisconsin in 1949 and has subsequently been assistant professor of psychology and chief psychologist at the Yale Psychiatric Institute, director of research and chief psychologist at the Rip Van Winkle Clinic in Hudson, New York, and director of graduate training in clinical psychology at the University of Iowa. He is the current editor of the *Journal of Abnormal Psychology.* He is the author of more than seventy articles and ten books and monographs in the areas of child psychopathology, projective techniques, and personality development. His books include *Learning of Aggression in Children* and *An Experimental Approach to Projective Technique.*

Maggi Musico Reiss received her A.B. degree in 1971 from Smith College. She was an NSF summer fellow at Yale University and later at Brown University and has conducted research on mental retardation and parental behavior toward aggressive and nonaggressive children. She is expected to receive her M.A. degree shortly from the University of Illinois at Chicago Circle, where she is successfully completing the graduate program in school psychology.

"I should not like my writing to spare other people the trouble of thinking. But, if possible, to stimulate someone to thoughts of his own."

Ludwig Wittgenstein

Contents

Part One

What Is Abnormality?

Chapter 1

The Classification of Abnormal Behavior Patterns

The validity of the conventional diagnostic system is least ambiguous and most free from potential criticism as a descriptive schema, a taxonomy of mental disorders analogous to the work of Ray and Linnaeus in biology.

ZIGLER and PHILLIPS (1961)

This chapter provides an overview of the various types of abnormal behavior patterns that will be discussed in Part III of this book. The overview is presented in the form of an introduction to classification. The classification system of the American Psychiatric Association is presented and is critically evaluated in terms of its reliability, validity, and actual use by practitioners. Several alternative classification systems are also discussed and evaluated.

THE PURPOSES OF CLASSIFICATION

A classification system consists of a series of categories or groupings that summarize important similarities among abnormal behaviors (Eron, 1966, p. 18). To appreciate the potential value of classification, consider the following four cases:

Case 1. Mr. Bem believes that he is George Washington, and it is impossible to convince him otherwise.
Case 2. Ms. Simpson believes that the Communists have issued a "contract" for her murder. So far as can be determined, she has never met any Communists, and she cannot produce any evidence that they have decreed her death. It is, nevertheless, impossible to convince her that she is mistaken. She spends much of her time avoiding "Communists," who include about half the people she sees.
Case 3. While driving his car home from work, Mr. Dean suddenly becomes afraid that something terrible is about to happen although he does not know what terrible event might occur. His fear reaches a point of panic, and he begins to think that he is having a heart attack.
Case 4. Ms. Radley refuses to leave her home for fear that she might see a spider. The mere thought of a spider makes her tremble. She knows she is afraid of spiders, and she knows that spiders are supposed to be harmless. Nevertheless, her fear is so great that she does not venture outdoors.

In the absence of any classification system, each of these cases would be considered a unique disorder. There exist, however, important similarities and differences among them. For example, both Mr. Bem and Ms. Simpson have firmly held beliefs that almost any observer would recognize as obviously false. Mr. Bem's belief that he is George Washington and Ms. Simpson's belief that the Communists are out to get her are irrational. The basic problem in these cases is an impairment in thought processes. In contrast, the important similarity in Mr. Dean's and Ms. Radley's case is the presence of fear and anxiety.

A relatively simple classification system could be constructed to summarize the behaviors in the preceding four cases. First, we can classify all four cases as examples of abnormal behavior. Second, we can subclassify two of the cases (Mr. Bem and Ms. Simpson) as psychotic because the primary problem is the presence of disordered thought, and we can subclassify the other two cases (Mr. Dean and Ms. Radley) as neurotic because the primary problem is the presence of anxiety and fear. Unfortunately, classification is often much more complicated than is suggested by these textbook cases.

Because the purpose of classification is to group abnormal behaviors in accordance with their important similarities, the question arises as to which similarities are to be considered important. A classification system, for example, could define any or all of the following as important similarities:

1. *Similarity of behaviors.* A classification category may define behavioral similarities as important. For example, the category called *neurosis* consists of disorders in which a prominent sign is the presence of nervousness or tension or fear.
2. *Similarity of etiology.* A classification category may group behaviors on the basis of similar causal origins. For example, the category called *organic brain damage* applies to abnormal behaviors that are believed to be caused by damage to the brain and/or spinal cord.
3. *Similarity of prognosis.* Another basis for classifying abnormal behaviors is in accordance with their typical future course. For example, the categories of manic depression and schizophrenia were originally distinguished from one another by the hypothesis that people suffering from manic depression are more likely to recover than those suffering from schizophenia.

There are many other ways in which one might attempt to classify abnormal behaviors. In the United States the conventional classification system is called DSM-II.

THE DIAGNOSTIC AND STATISTICAL MANUAL

A *psychologist* is a behavioral scientist who has earned either a Ph.D. or M.S. degree in psychology; a *clinical psychologist* is someone who has received advanced training in the treatment of abnormal behavior in addition to having earned a Ph.D. degree in psychology; a *psychiatrist* is a physician who has received advanced training in the treatment of abnormal behavior. Thus, both the clinical psychologist and the psychiatrist are qualified to treat abnormal behavior because each has received advanced training to do so; according to a consumer research report by Ralph Nader, moreover, the psychologist may often be able to provide the same treatment as the psychiatrist and do so at less cost to the consumer. The American Psychological Association is the professional organization of psychologists; the American Psychiatric Association is the professional organization of psychiatrists.

The *Diagnostic and Statistical Manual* (*DSM*) is the official classification system of the American Psychiatric Association (American Psychiatric Association, 1968). Classification of an individual's problems into a DSM category is sometimes called *diagnosis.* DSM has been revised; the current revision is DSM-II, and a third revision called DSM-III should appear before 1980.

DSM-II is based on a medical model of abnormality. As shown in Figure 1-1, this means that the classification of two abnormal behaviors into the same DSM-II category would ideally imply that (1) the behaviors have a similar cause, (2) specific prognostic statements are possible based on scientific knowledge of the category, and (3) specific treatment methods are suggested. These properties are characteristic of classification systems of many physical diseases. For example, the diagnosis of two illnesses as pneumonia implies a similar bacterial cause, permits predictions about the future course of the illness, and suggests the use of antibiotic drug treatment. Unfortunately, however, only a few DSM-II categories have these properties. As we shall see, classification of abnormal behavior rarely implies detailed and valid information about causal origins, is often an unreliable basis for precise predictions, and only sometimes suggests a particular treatment. Despite its many inadequacies, however, DSM-II is far from useless. Classification *sometimes* provides important information. Moreover, classification is useful for describing the range of abnormal behaviors under study.

DSM-II provides ten major categories (or types) of abnormal behavior, each of which has various subcategories (subtypes). The following discussion is intended to show the complexity of this system as well as the ambiguous and overlapping nature of many of the subcategories.

Mental Retardation

Mental retardation refers to subnormal intellectual functioning. DSM-II defines several levels of severity of retardation in terms of IQ on the Stanford-Binet intelligence test:

Borderline (IQ range: 83 to 68).
Mild (IQ range: 67 to 52).
Moderate (IQ range: 51 to 36).
Severe (IQ range: 35 to 20).
Unspecified.

Figure 1-1
Etiology, prognosis, and treatment information that would ideally be available for each disorder.

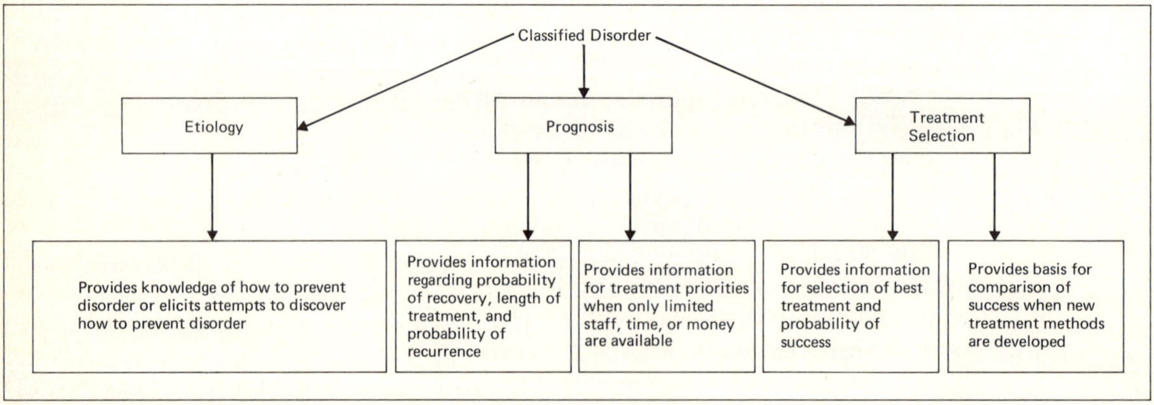

BOX 1-1
DSM-II Categories of Mental Disorders

I. Mental Retardation: A category of mental disorder diagnosed on the basis of deficits in intellectual ability. DSM-II defines mental retardation as a Stanford-Binet IQ below 84.

II. Organic Brain Syndromes: A category of mental disorders diagnosed primarily on the basis of etiology. Specifically, DSM-II defines organic brain syndromes as physical diseases of the central nervous system. In many instances the etiology is suspected rather than known.

III. Psychoses Not Attributable to Physical Conditions Listed Previously: A category of mental disorder diagnosed on the basis of symptomatology; that is, on the basis of the presence or absence of particular abnormal behaviors. The signs of psychoses include thought disorder, delusion, hallucination, social withdrawal, and profound disturbances of mood.

IV. Neurosis: A category of mental disorder diagnosed on the basis of symptomatology. Specifically, neurosis is indicated by the presence of inappropriate anxiety, tension, and depression.

V. Personality Disorders and Certain Other Nonpsychotic Mental Disorders: An exceptionally heterogeneous grouping of abnormal behavior patterns diagnosed on various grounds. Personality disorders are diagnosed partially on the basis of duration of abnormal behavior patterns; specifically, a personality disorder is a life-long pattern of inappropriate adjustment. The "Other Nonpsychotic Mental Disorders" include sexually variant behaviors and drug abuse.

VI. Psychophysiologic Disorders: A category of mental disorder diagnosed on the basis of hypothesized etiology. Specifically, psychophysiologic disorders are disturbances or damages in organ systems that are associated with anxiety, tension, and/or exposure to stressful experiences.

VII. Special Symptoms: A category of mental disorder indicated by the presence of a single prominent abnormal behavior.

VIII. Transient Situational Disturbance: A category of mental disorder diagnosed on the basis of its transitory nature.

IX. Behavioral Disorders of Childhood and Adolescence: A category of mental disorder diagnosed primarily on the basis of the age of the person.

X. Conditions Without Manifest Psychiatric Disorder and Nonspecific Conditions: A category of mental disorder diagnosed on the basis of maladjustment to a particular situation.

Adapted from *Diagnostic and Statistical Manual of Mental Disorders*, 2nd ed. Copyright, 1968, American Psychiatric Association. The names and order of categories are cited by permission of the American Psychiatric Association. The descriptions of the categories are original summaries prepared by the authors of this text.

An alternative method of defining mental retardation is provided by the American Association for Mental Deficiency (Heber, 1961). This definition requires subnormal functioning in both intellectual and adaptive skills for a diagnosis of mental retardation. Depending on a person's age, subnormal adaptive skills may refer to an inability to dress oneself, cook meals, or hold down a job. In contrast, DSM-II's definition of mental retardation does not require evidence of subnormal adaptive skills.

Mental retardation should be thought of as a grouping of many different disorders rather than as a single unitary disorder. The largest subtype is called cultural-familial mental retardation, and it is indicated by (1) an IQ in the mild or high range of retardation, (2) the absence of known central nervous system damage that could account for the subnormality, and (3) the presence of mental retardation in a parent or a sibling. The overwhelming majority of cultural-familial retardates are from the lowest socioeconomic classes.

Other types of mental retardation include *Down's syndrome* (*mongolism*) and *phenylketonuria* (*PKU*). Mongolism is associated with a number of physical anomalies, including delicate skin, a protruding belly, and eyes that slant upward and outward. Although the IQ of a mongoloid may be anywhere within the subnormal range, most mongoloids have an IQ of less than 50. The disorder is relatively rare and is caused by a chromosomal abnormality. PKU is a rare metabolic disorder that is transmitted by a single recessive gene.

Organic Brain Syndromes

Some instances of abnormal psychological functioning result from physical damage to the central nervous system. There are many ways in which such damage may occur. For example, a severe blow to the head (trauma) may rupture blood vessels (stroke) or may temporarily dislocate brain cells (concussion). An excessive intake of alcohol during a period of many years is associated with physical deterioration of brain cells (alcohol psychosis). Epilepsy is a genetic disorder in which abnormal electrical discharges occur in the brain (convulsions).

There are two basic ways in which abnormal behavior is attributed to organic (biological) factors. In some cases direct evidence of neurological impairment is available, and in other cases such impairment is inferred on the basis of theoretical convictions. Thus a diagnosis of organic brain damage sometimes means that abnormal functioning is *known* to be caused by organic factors and sometimes means that abnormal functioning is only *believed* to be caused by organic factors.

DSM-II specifies five signs for classifying abnormal behavior as caused by, or associated with, impairment of brain tissue: (1) impairment of orientation in space or time; (2) impairment of memory; (3) impairment of intellectual functions such as comprehension, calculation, knowledge, or learning; (4) impairment of judgment; and (5) lability and shallowness of emotion.

Functional Psychosis

A *functional psychosis* is a psychosis not attributable to demonstrable organic brain damage or to demonstrable central nervous system disease. DSM-II stipulates that psychoses believed to be caused by physical damage or physical disease should be classified as organic brain syndromes. All other psychoses are classified as functional psychoses.

The prominent signs of psychoses are hallucinations, delusions, thought disorder, inappropriate mood, social withdrawal, and bizarre behavior. Any particular case of psychosis, however, usually shows only some of these signs.

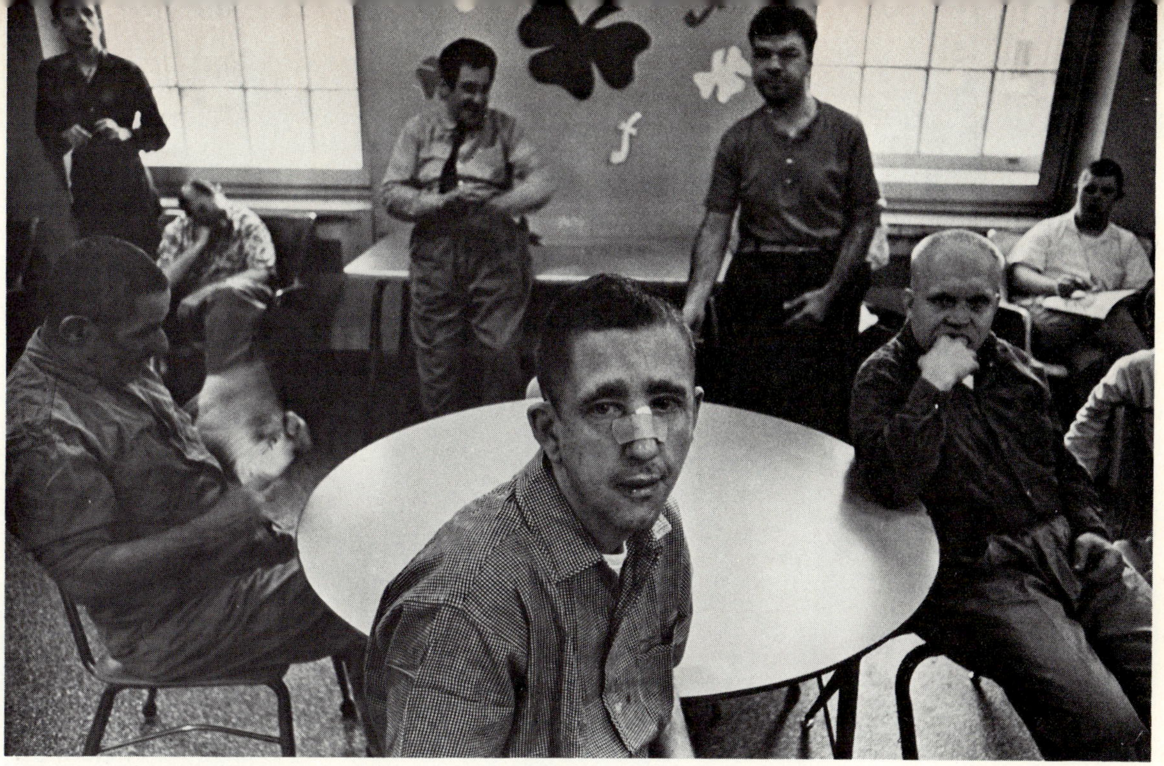

A mental retardation ward at a state mental hospital. (Photo by Bill Stanton; Magnum Photos, Inc.)

1. *Hallucinations* are sensory perceptions of stimuli that do not exist. Auditory hallucinations consist of hearing nonexistent sounds, visual hallucinations consist of seeing things that are not there, and tactile hallucinations consist of sensations of nonexistent stimuli. Auditory hallucinations are more common than visual or tactile hallucinations.

2. *Delusions* are false, irrational beliefs that are firmly held despite abundant evidence that the beliefs are false.

3. *Thought disorder* refers to disorganized thoughts and speech. This disorganization is often bizarre and obvious to observers. The following responses are examples of disordered thought:

"How old are you?"
"I am 16—a magic number. And here we are on WBZ radio—oh please, can I have another hamburger? The mustard is yellow, and the sun rises at night. Oddlepuck."

"What is a tree?"
"Chop, chop, chop—timber."

4. *Inappropriate mood* refers to feelings of depression or elation that do not appear to be justified by the person's life circumstances. In psychotic depression, for example, a person can cry for hours for no apparent reason, over some minor annoyance, or because of irrational beliefs that one is hated by others.

BOX 1-2
Some DSM-II Subcategories for Psychoses Not Attributable to Physical Conditions

A. Schizophrenia: A psychotic disorder indicated by the presence of thought disorder, delusions, hallucinations, and withdrawal from social contacts. All of these signs are not necessarily present in each case; moreover, the severity of signs that are present may vary considerably from one case to the next.
   1. Simple Schizophrenia: A subtype of schizophrenia in which the prominent sign is a gradual withdrawal from social contacts accompanied by increasing apathy.
   2. Hebephrenic Schizophrenia: A subtype of schizophrenia in which the prominent signs are thought disorder and inappropriate emotionality such as insensitive laughing at matters that are depressing to others.
   3. Catatonic Schizophrenia: A subtype of schizophrenia in which a prominent sign is abnormal motor activity. The catatonic person may show either excessive or retarded motor activity; periods of stupor may occur.
   4. Paranoid Schizophrenia: A subtype of schizophrenia in which a prominent sign is the presence of delusions, particularly delusions of persecution and of omnipotence.
   5. Acute Schizophrenic Episode: Schizophrenic behaviors occur suddenly and remit within a few weeks or months.
   6. Schizo-Affective Type: Schizophrenic behaviors accompanied by a pro-

5. *Social withdrawal* refers both to an avoidance of interpersonal contacts and to an apathy toward one's environment.

The major subcategories of functional psychoses are schizophrenia and affective psychosis. Schizophrenia is a profound disturbance of thought usually indicated by hallucinations and delusions. Excessive shyness, speech disorder, emotional unresponsiveness, a rich fantasy life, and motor disturbances are also associated with various forms of schizophrenia. The prevalence of schizophrenia in the United States is estimated at 3 per cent of the population.

The term *affect* refers to the subjective aspects of an emotion considered apart from its physiological aspects. Affective disorders are either depressive or manic in character. Depression is associated with feelings of worthlessness, guilt, apathy, and, of course, dejection. Mania, which is in many ways the behavioral opposite of depression, is indicated by euphoria, flight of ideas, and behavioral overactivity. In both depression and mania, the mood is inappropriate to the person's life circumstances. Some persons show episodes of only depression or only mania, whereas others show a pattern of mood swings between episodes of depression and normal mood or between mania and normal mood or between depression and mania. Manic-depressive psychosis may be diagnosed when any of these mood swings are present.

DSM-II defines depression as a neurotic disorder, a psychotic disorder, and a personality disorder. The distinction between neurotic and psychotic depression is based on whether or not the depressive episode appears to be a reaction to some loss (for example, death of a loved one); this distinction, however, rests largely on subjective judgment. (See Chapter 14.) Psychotic depression

found disturbance of mood indicated by either the presence of mania or depression. The mood disturbance usually remits within a few months, although episodes of mood disturbance may recur during stressful life periods.
7. Childhood Schizophrenia: Schizophrenic-like behaviors in children include thought disorder, extreme social withdrawal and self-preoccupation, hallucination, and self-stimulatory behaviors such as repetitive wiggling of one's fingers in front of one's face.
8. Undifferentiated Schizophrenia: A mixture of schizophrenic signs is present so that diagnosis into one of the preceding types of schizophrenia is difficult. It is often difficult to differentiate among the types of schizophrenia because many cases show signs indicative of more than one type.

B. Major Affective Disorders: Psychotic disorders in which the prominent signs are the presence of either mania (inappropriate elation and hyperactivity) or depression that do not seem to be in reaction to any particular event.
1. Involutional Melancholia: Depression associated with the "change of life" of either female menopause or male climacteric.
2. Manic-Depressive Psychosis: A mood disorder in which the prominent signs are mood swings or cycles. These swings may be from depression to normal mood, from mania to normal mood, or from mania to depression.

Adapted from *Diagnostic and Statistical Manual of Mental Disorders*, 2nd ed. Copyright, 1968, American Psychiatric Association. The name and order of categories are cited by permission of the American Psychiatric Association.

is more severe than neurotic depression and is most clearly indicated when depression occurs in the context of psychotic behaviors such as delusion and extreme social withdrawal. Depression is diagnosed as a personality disorder when it is associated with a life-long pattern of listlessness and poor self-esteem.

Neurotic Disorders

The central problem in neurosis is anxiety (nervousness, tension, fear, and fatigue).

Anxiety Neurosis

As its name implies, the anxiety neurosis is indicated by the direct expression of anxiety. The individual suffers episodes of visible nervousness and is typically unable to give a reason for the anxiety. For example, the person may report being terrified of some impending event without being able to report what that event may be. In many cases, moreover, episodes of nervousness alternate with episodes of fatigue and depression. (See Chapter 10 for documentation of these statements.)

Phobic Neurosis

Phobias are characterized by an intense, irrational fear of a particular object or situation. The irrational basis of the fear is often obvious; for example, the person cannot go to a ball game for fear of crowds. Phobias are subclassified in terms of the object feared; because a phobic reaction can occur in response to almost any situation or object, the list of phobias is seemingly endless. For example, *acrophobia* refers to fear of being in high places, *claustrophobia* refers to fear of being in confined areas, and *mysophobia* refers to fear of dirt or contamination.

Obsessive-Compulsive Neurosis

The obsessive-compulsive neurosis is identified by the individual's report that upsetting urges, thoughts, or actions frequently occur and cannot be prevented. The recurring thoughts or actions may be brief and nonsensical (e.g., repeatedly having the word *help* pop into thought, or repeatedly having an urge to touch one's feet); they may be complex chains of thoughts (e.g., recitations of "Mary Had a Little Lamb"); or they may be part of ritualistic behavior (e.g., cleaning ash trays whenever one cigarette ash is placed in any ash tray). In general, interference with the completion of the obsessive-compulsive behavior pattern produces discomfort.

Hysteria

Hysteria refers to the loss of a body or thought function in the absence of any physiological damage that could account for the loss. Two types of hysteria are defined by DSM-II: conversion hysteria and dissociative hysteria. Conversion hysteria refers to the loss of a body function as in hysterical blindness, deafness, and paralysis; dissociative hysteria refers to the loss of a thought function as in amnesia, fugue, and multiple personalities.

A noteworthy aspect of conversion hysteria is the manner in which the troubled person responds to his or her loss. Although the majority of persons suffering from hysteria show an appropriate concern over the loss of a body function, a large minority do not. For example, suppose that you awoke one morning and found that you were unable to move your legs. A normal reaction to this sudden disability would be one of anger and depression; moreover, when extensive medical examinations reveal no disease or damage in your body that could account for the disability, you might react with relief and confusion. In contrast to these appropriate reactions, a large minority of persons suffering hysteria show more interest in using their disability to gain attention than concern over the possibility of going through life disabled. This dramatic lack of appropriate concern has been called *la belle indifférence.*

Personality Disorders and Other Deviant Behavior Patterns

DSM-II groups together, as a major category of abnormality, general personality disorders and a series of particular deviant behavior patterns. The various syndromes lumped together are very dissimilar from one another.

Personality disorders are thought of as deeply ingrained, characteristic styles of inappropriate behavior. They are distinguished from neuroses in that

BOX 1-3
Some DSM-II Subcategories for Neurosis

A. Anxiety Neurosis: Presence of manifest anxiety usually accompanied by an impending sense of danger and a variety of physical complaints. Episodes of anxiety, depression, and neurotic fatigue often occur in the same people; whether anxiety neurosis, depressive neurosis, or neurasthenic neurosis is diagnosed may depend on whether anxiety, depression, or neurotic fatigue is most prominent at the time of diagnosis.
B. Hysteria: A loss of functioning not attributable to any physiological damage that could explain the loss.
   1. Conversion Hysteria: A loss of some bodily function in the absence of any physiological damage that could account for the loss. Examples include hysterical blindness and paralysis.
   2. Dissociative Hysteria: A loss of some intellectual function in the absence of any physiological damage that could account for the loss. Examples include amnesia (loss of memory), fugue, and multiple personality.
C. Phobia: Fear of some particular stimulus object or situation. It is often difficult to differentiate between anxiety neurosis and phobic neurosis; which diagnosis is made may depend on subjective evaluations of the extent to which anxiety is focused on a particular stimulus object.
D. Obsessive-Compulsive Neurosis: An anxiety disorder in which a prominent sign is the repetitive occurrence of a thought, impulse, or behavior.
E. Depression: Feelings of sadness often accompanied by insecurity, low self-esteem, anxiety, guilt, and fatigue.
F. Neurasthenic Neurosis: Excessive fatigue.
G. Hypochondriasis: Excessive and inappropriate preoccupation with possible illnesses. Hypochondriacal complaints almost always occur in the context of other abnormal behaviors, particularly depression.

personality disorders indicate a life pattern of maladaptive behavior, whereas neurosis is conceptualized as a reaction to stress occurring during a particular life period. Thus neurosis can occur in previously well-adjusted persons exposed to prolonged stress or emotional trauma. Personality disorders are distinguished from psychoses in that they are less maladaptive and occur in the absence of hallucinations, delusions, extreme withdrawal, and thought disorder.

One of the more widely studied personality disorders is the *antisocial personality* or *psychopath. Psychopathy* is associated with a life pattern of aggression, taking advantage of others, a low tolerance for boredom, and an impairment in the ability to feel concern and affection for others. Interestingly, many psychopaths can be charming and are often liked by others. (See Chapter 13.)

Sexual deviation refers to unusual sexual behavior such as homosexuality, fetishism, transvestitism, and sadism; *sexual dysfunction* refers to an inability to perform adequately, as in impotence and premature ejaculation. The distinc-

Antisocial behavior, as indicated by membership in a "rogue" motorcycle gang. It is important to appreciate that antisocial behavior per se is insufficient evidence to diagnose psychopathy. Members of motorcycle gangs, for example, are not necessarily psychopaths. In fact, many members show antisocial behavior as a result of peer influences rather than the personality deficiencies that define psychopathy. (Photo by Lyon; Magnum Photos, Inc.)

tion is important: Sexual dysfunctions are often caused by anxiety and can usually be treated successfully. (See Chapters 7 and 12.) In contrast, the causes of sexual deviations are less clear, and they are more difficult to treat. It is also unclear whether or not sexual deviations should even be considered abnormal. Although virtually no one is satisfied with being impotent (sexual dysfunction), many are satisfied with being lesbians or homosexuals.

There seems to be no adequate reason for considering homosexuality per se as abnormal behavior. The governing board of the American Psychiatric Association recently declassified homosexuality, but an angry response from psychiatrists who consider homosexuality a serious psychiatric condition forced a vote of the full membership. In March 1974, the full membership voted to approve the board's decision—homosexuality per se is no longer defined as a mental illness.

Psychophysiologic Disorders

Psychophysiologic disorders are emotional disorders that produce pathology in a particular organ system. Examples of psychophysiologic disorders include peptic ulcers, hypertension (high blood pressure), and frequent headaches. Although each of these disorders can be caused solely by biological factors, the available evidence suggests that tension, fear, and conflict can also lead to physical pathology.

It is important to recognize that, in psychophysiologic disorders, the physical pathology is real—physical pain and/or damage actually exist—even though emotional factors are assumed either to cause or to intensify the problem.

Special Symptoms

This category is for cases in which a single problem is presented. DSM-II classifies these problems primarily on the basis of the behavior exhibited and without reference to causal origin. Two examples of special symptoms that have received attention from research investigators are tics (nervous twitches) and enuresis (bed wetting).

Transient Situational Disturbance

This category applies to problems in adjusting to a particular situation. For example, a child who just moved into town is depressed because he has no friends. Although the child's difficulties are real, the diagnosis of "Transient Situational Disturbance" implies that the problems will disappear soon when the child makes new friends and becomes accustomed to his new environment.

The "Transient Situational Disturbance" category further complicates diagnosis under DSM-II because it adds yet another set of criteria for diagnosing abnormal behavior. We have seen that some categories are based on an assessment of abilities (mental retardation), that some are based on either the identification or the hypothesis of biological causes (organic brain damage), and that several are based on the type of behavior exhibited (e.g., psychoses and

BOX 1-4
Outline of Some DSM-II Categories

VI. Psychophysiologic Disorders.
- A. Skin disorders.
- B. Musculoskeletal disorders.
- C. Respiratory disorders.
- D. Cardiovascular disorders.
- E. Hemic and lymphatic disorders.
- F. Gastrointestinal disorders.
- G. Genitourinary disorders.
- H. Endocrine disorders.
- I. Organ of special sense.
- J. Special type.

VII. Special Symptoms.
- A. Speech disturbance.
- B. Specific learning disturbance.
- C. Tic.
- D. Other psychomotor disorder.
- E. Disorders of sleep.
- F. Feeding disturbance.
- G. Enuresis.
- H. Encopresis.
- I. Cephalalgia.

neuroses). Transient Situational Disturbance is based on the type of situation that presumably elicits the abnormal behavior.

Behavior Disorders of Childhood and Adolescence

Glidewell (1967) estimated that 9 per cent of children in the middle years of childhood are maladjusted and that in 1960 there were 2.7 million children between the ages of five and 12 in need of psychological treatment. The National Institute of Mental Health (NIMH, 1970) estimated that between 10 and 12 per cent of children in school suffer from moderate to severe emotional problems. The NIMH report further noted that the number of child admissions to mental hospitals is increasing and that many adult patients were admitted or seen during childhood or adolescence. These frightening statistics attest to the need for an appropriate classification system for studying, treating, and preventing the high frequencies of childhood disorders.

Disorders diagnosed as Behavior Disorders of Childhood and Adolescence include hyperactive behavior not due to demonstrable organic brain damage, childhood fears, high levels of aggression, and "other reactions." The categories are vague, incomplete, and unsystematic (Shaw & Lucas, 1970). For these reasons, the Committee on Child Psychiatry (1966) has proposed an alternative system.

J. Other special symptom.

IX. Behavior Disorders of Childhood and Adolescence.
   A. Hyperkinetic reaction.
   B. Withdrawing reaction.
   C. Overanxious reaction.
   D. Runaway reaction.
   E. Unsocialized aggressive reaction.
   F. Group delinquent reaction.
   G. Other reaction.

X. Conditions Without Manifest Psychiatric Disorder and Nonspecific Conditions.
   A. Social maladjustment without manifest psychiatric conditions.
      1. Marital maladjustment.
      2. Social maladjustment.
      3. Occupational maladjustment.
      4. Dyssocial behavior.
      5. Other social maladjustment.
   B. Nonspecific conditions.
   C. No mental disorder.

Conditions Without Manifest Psychiatric Disorder and Nonspecific Conditions

This category is a grouping of special problem situations rather than a definition of disorders. The special problem subcategories are listed in Box 1-4.

EVALUATION OF DSM–II

The two basic requirements of a classification system are reliability and validity.

Reliability of DSM-II Categories

The *interrater reliability* of a classification category is a measure of the extent to which independent clinicians agree on the diagnoses of the same people. A category is completely unreliable if it is used in an arbitrary manner. For example, suppose two clinicians are asked to diagnose 100 people and subsequently disagree on the diagnosis in all 100 cases. If this were to occur, it would suggest that each clinician had diagnosed in accordance with his own idiosyncratic definition of the diagnostic categories. If, however, the clinicians had agreed in a significant per cent of the cases, this would suggest that, at least to some extent, the diagnostic categories were used objectively.

The reliability of many DSM-II categories is low. Generally, however, the interrater reliability for major categories (e.g., functional psychosis) is greater than that associated with subcategories (e.g., schizophrenia, hebephrenic type). Zubin (1967) has provided a comprehensive summary of reliability of agreement on diagnosis among psychiatrists. As Table 1-1 shows, reliability for the following categories and subcategories is at an acceptable level of 70 per cent or more agreement: organic, functional psychosis, antisocial personality (psychopathy), dyssocial behavior, sexual deviation, alcoholism, drug addiction, and psychoneurosis.[1] In contrast, agreement is unacceptably low for many other categories, including psychotic depression, which is difficult to distinguish from neurotic depression (22 per cent agreement); paranoid reaction, which is difficult to distinguish from paranoid schizophrenia (13 per cent agreement); and anxiety state, which is difficult to distinguish from other types of neuroses and from neurotic personality disorders (varying estimates of 27 to 55 per cent agreement).

A more recent review of the studies on the interrater reliability of psychiatric diagnosis is provided by Spitzer and Fleiss (1974). This review concluded that interrater reliability is satisfactory for only three categories: mental retardation, organic brain syndromes, and alcoholism. The reliability for psychosis and schizophrenia was found to be fair. The reliability for the remaining DSM categories was found to be poor.

Generally, reliability of DSM-II categories is high for categories that are broadly defined (e.g., psychoneurosis), that are defined in terms of specific behaviors (e.g., alcoholism), and that are defined in terms of very strange or unusual behaviors (e.g., functional psychosis). Broad categories permit high reliability because they include so many different types of behaviors that it is likely that any given behavior is one of the many subsumed by the category. Specific behavior categories permit high reliability because they are relatively unambiguous. Extreme or unusual behavior categories permit high reliability because it is easy to detect the presence of such behavior. The difficulties that confront any classification system are to provide reliable diagnostic categories for the less extreme cases and to provide a precise and reliable system of subcategories. For example, how much anxiety must be present to justify a diagnosis of anxiety neurosis? In regard to questions such as this, DSM-II is a disappointment.

Validity of DSM-II Categories

The validity of a DSM-II classification category is the extent to which that category permits statements concerning etiology, prognosis, and treatment. Suppose someone were to suggest that abnormal behavior be classified on the basis of height. This system would have such categories as "abnormality in people five feet tall" and "abnormality in people five feet, one inch tall." Although

[1] The studies reviewed by Zubin are based on the DSM-I system, but because few important differences exist between DSM-I and DSM-II, no improvement in agreement of diagnosis should be expected.

these categories would be reliable, they would also be useless and hence would lack validity.

Classification of abnormal behavior into a DSM-II category does not usually permit valid statements concerning etiology because the cause of most disorders is unknown. The important exceptions to this general rule include some subtypes of mental retardation (e.g., Down's syndrome and PKU) and some subtypes of organic brain syndromes. Classification, however, often provides information concerning correlates of the disorder. For example, schizophrenics tend to come from families in which communication disorders exist (see Chapters 15 and 16); schizophrenia almost certainly has a genetic component; psychopaths tend to come from broken homes (see Chapter 13); and hypertensive patients (people with high blood pressure) tend to show labile blood pressure as young adults. We know that sexual dysfunctions are usually caused by inappropriate anxiety (see Chapter 11), but we do not know how such anxiety responses were originally learned. We know that neurotic depression is preceded by some type of loss. Generally, then, classification does not permit valid statements of etiology, although it sometimes permits valid statements that may prove relevant to etiology.

Classification of abnormal behavior into a DSM-II category permits only vague expectations regarding the future course of the disorder. However, exceptions exist. We now know that many sexual dysfunctions can be treated within a few weeks. We know that no more than a third of all alcoholics are likely to stop drinking for two years or more. We know that the IQ of a mentally retarded child may rise as much as 10 to 15 points as he grows older, but that it rarely recovers to a normal range and often does not recover at all. We know that neurotic and depressive episodes tend to remit; that spontaneous remission (recovery without formal treatment) is common for neurotic episodes within three years of their appearance; and that some people tend to recover from psychotic episodes in a matter of months, whereas others tend to become progressively more disturbed (Woodruff, Goodwin, & Guze, 1974). However, precise statistics, or anything approaching precise statistics, are generally unavailable.

Classification of abnormal behavior into a DSM-II category can have implications for treatment, but there are many individual exceptions to these general guidelines. Major tranquilizers are useful in the treatment of schizophrenia. Systematic desensitization and other behavior therapy techniques seem especially useful in the treatment of sexual dysfunctions, phobias, and perhaps other anxiety disorders. Electroconvulsive shock therapy is considered by many psychiatrists to be the treatment of choice for psychotic depression, although the evidence for its value is not yet compelling. Insight-oriented therapy is the treatment of choice for many personality disorders, although the evidence for its effectiveness is not solid. Operant behavior modification has been shown to be effective in the treatment of many types of special problem behaviors, but more research is still needed regarding its long-term effectiveness. Surgery is indicated for some specific subtypes of organic brain syndromes. In the past twenty-five years extraordinary progress in clinical psychology has been witnessed and, for the first time in four thousand years, treatment tech-

TABLE 1-1
Percentage Agreement on Diagnosis by Observers

	Ash 1949	Seeman 1953	Schmidt 1956	Kreitman 1961	Beck 1962	Sandifer 1964
Description						
Location of study	U.S.	U.S.	U.S.	G.B.	U.S.	U.S.
Medical facility[a]	1	1	2	3	3	2
N of patients	52	6	426	90	153	91
Sex	M	–	MF	MF	MF	MF
Sampling	Sel.	Sel.	Succ.	Succ.	Ran.	Sel.
Classification type[b]	X(1, 2)	–	X(1)	Y	X	X(1)
Interval[c]	0	0	2	1	0	0
Agreement[d]	B	A	A	A	B	B
General categories						
Organic			92	85		
Functional psychosis			80	71		71
Characterological			71			74*
Psychoneurosis				52		
Average agreement, general category	64†#		84	78	70	
Organic psychoses						
Acute brain syndrome			68			46
Chronic brain syndrome			80			66
Mental deficiency			(42)			73
Psychosis of old age				78		
Paresis		49†				
Other				62†		
Functional psychoses						
Schizophrenia		80†	75†‡	(0)	53	74
Affective			(35)	65†		
Involutional			57		40	26
Manic depressive (depressive)		82†				36
Psychotic depressive						22
Hypomanic		29†				
Paranoid reaction						13
Other reaction						(17)

Neurosis and personality disorders						
Psychoneurosis			(16)			56
Reactive depressive				18†	63	
Anxiety state				27†	55	
Psychophysiological reaction						40
Personality pattern disturbance			(8)			
Personality disorder						66
Personality trait disturbance			(6)		38	
Sociopath			58		54	
Average agreement on specific category	38†#	66†	55	63	54	57

[a] Type of medical facility:
1 = Clinic
2 = Psychiatric hospital
3 = Psychiatric unit of general hospital
[b] Type of Classification:
X = *APA Diagnostic & Statistical Manual*, 1952
(1) abbreviated
(2) with additions
Y = Special
[c] Interval between interview:
0 = Simultaneous (or within a few minutes)
1 = 1 week
2 = 2 weeks
3 = 1–2 months
[d] Kinds of agreement:
A = Criterion
B = Average group
Symbols:
– = Unspecified
(/) = N < 8
† = Calculated on data reported in another form
# = 3 psychiatrists, 2 at a time
* = The combined average of character disorders and psychoneuroses
‡ = Criterion agreement, reworked Zubin (1967). Schmidt and Fonda's 51 percent agreement refers to specific subtypes of schizophrenia

From J. Zubin, "Classification of the Behavior Disorders," *Annual Review of Psychology* (Palo Alto, Calif.: Annual Reviews Inc., 1967), p. 382. Reprinted with permission of author and publisher.

niques with demonstrable effectiveness have begun to emerge. Even though the evidence for such effectiveness is often less than compelling, and even though the treatments typically only ameliorate problems rather than eliminate them completely, progress is clearly evident. (See Chapters 5 through 9 for documentation of these statements.)

In summary, the validity of the DSM-II system is low in the sense that classification only rarely permits demonstrably valid and precise statements concerning etiology, prognosis, and treatment. The system, however, is far from useless.

USES OF DSM-II

A distinction can be drawn between the manner in which a classification system should be employed and the manner in which it is actually used. For example, psychiatric diagnosis is supposed to be based on evidence of psychopathology rather than on the information that some third party considers the client to be psychotic. In recent years, however, a number of studies have found that psychiatric diagnoses are influenced by false suggestions of illness and by other theoretically irrelevant factors.

Bias Toward False Positives

Two types of possible errors in diagnosis are *false positives* and *false negatives.* A false positive is labeling a person as mentally ill when in fact the person is normal. A false negative is labeling a person as normal when in fact the person is mentally ill. Medical diagnoses are generally biased toward false positives rather than false negatives, and psychiatric diagnoses are no exception to this rule (Garland, 1960; Feinstein, 1967).

A bias toward false positives is especially evident in mental hospital admission decisions where the general rule seems to be "when in doubt, hospitalize" (Ullmann & Krasner, 1969). This bias in part reflects diagnosticians' estimates of the relative consequences of false positives and false negatives. Rarely are psychiatrists criticized publicly for hospitalizing people who in fact are normal; such criticisms, when they are raised, are usually raised in scientific journals. In contrast, if a psychiatrist errs by diagnosing as normal someone who in fact is mentally ill, the psychiatrist may come under public criticism in those rare cases in which the individual is dangerous to others in addition to being psychologically disturbed. For example, we occasionally read in the newspapers about a disturbed person who is released from a mental hospital and who later commits murder.

The notion that most mentally ill people are dangerous is a myth. Nevertheless, many people would probably support the policy of hospitalization in instances in which there is some doubt as to whether or not an individual is dangerous. One line of argument is that the harm of hospitalizing a normal person is minimal compared with the harm of not hospitalizing a psychopath or a dangerous paranoid. This argument is, however, a bit simplistic. Hospitalization results in a loss of liberty to the individual and, once an individual is hospitalized, the length of hospitalization may be prolonged.

Susceptibility to Label Bias

Another area of research concerns the effects on diagnostic outcome of false labels and of judgments made by practitioners with "prestigious" credentials. (See Chapter 19 for a more complete review of the literature on stereotyping.) For example, Temerlin (1968) had psychiatrists, clinical psychologists, and graduate students in clinical psychology listen to a tape-recorded interview of an actor who had been instructed to portray a mentally healthy man. Shortly before listening to the interview, half of the subjects were told that a prestigious person in their field had said that the man was psychotic. The control group of subjects heard the tape-recorded interview without first hearing any suggested diagnosis. None of the control subjects thought the man was psychotic. However, 60 per cent of the psychiatrists, 28 per cent of the clinical psychologists, and 11 per cent of the graduate students to whom the diagnosis of psychosis was suggested diagnosed the man as psychotic. The study thus yielded two findings: (1) the suggestion by a prestigious individual that the man was psychotic increased the likelihood of a diagnosis of psychosis, and (2) the susceptibility to prestigious suggestion was greatest among psychiatrists and least among the graduate students in clinical psychology.

In a related study, Langer and Abelson (1974) had clinical psychologists of different theoretical persuasions view a videotape of a man being interviewed. Half of the psychologists were professionally oriented in favor of interview therapies similar to Freud's psychoanalysis, whereas the remaining half were professionally oriented in favor of the behavior therapies. Half of the psychologists within each professional orientation were told that the man being interviewed was a job applicant, and the other half were told that he was a patient. The results indicated that the insight-oriented therapists reported the man to be more disturbed if they had been told that he was a patient than if they had been told that he was a job applicant. Similar diagnostic differences, however, were not found for the behavior therapists.

Sushinsky and Wener (1975) reported a series of experiments that confirmed the existence of label bias but questioned previous findings that professional groups are more susceptible to such bias than are nonprofessional groups. These studies found that a nonprofessional group of college students is susceptible to diagnostic bias if the source of such bias is a person prestigious among college students. The results of these studies support Langer and Abelson's (1974) speculation that all groups may be subject to diagnostic bias but that some groups are more susceptible to bias from certain types of labels or from certain types of prestigious figures.

In conclusion, psychiatric diagnosis is in part a social act that can sometimes be influenced by irrevelant factors such as false suggestions of illness from a prestigious figure. It is also clear, however, that a powerful determinant of psychiatric diagnosis is the actual behavior a client exhibits or reports he has exhibited (see Sushinsky & Wener, 1975, Experiment 1). That is, given a large variety of patients with a wide range of abnormal behaviors, the behaviors exhibited will be a powerful predictor of diagnosis. However, given a normal individual who presents no obvious symptoms of abnormality, label bias and other social influence variables seem to have some predictive validity on diagnostic outcome.

On Being Sane in Insane Places

Rosenhan (1973) had eight normal people attempt to gain admittance to 12 mental hospitals. This group of pseudopatients included a graduate student, three psychologists, a pediatrician, a psychiatrist, a painter, and a housewife. Each individual contacted a hospital and complained of hearing unfamiliar voices that seemed to say "empty," "hollow," and "thud." During the initial diagnostic interviews, all other information provided except for name and vocation was reported to have been factually accurate accounts of the pseudopatients' real lives. As a group, the pseudopatients sought admission to both private and public mental hospitals across the United States.

The diagnostic results were that 11 of the 12 diagnoses on admission were schizophrenia and one was manic-depressive psychosis. All 12 were thus diagnosed as psychotic on the bases of the report of auditory hallucinations, the pseudopatients' nervousness during the interview, and possibly other information in the diagnostic interview. The mean length of hospitalization was 19 days, with a range of 7 to 52 days. Excluding the 52-day case, the mean was 16 days. Rosenhan reports that the pseudopatients received more than 2,100 pills. In all cases, the diagnosis at discharge was schizophrenia in remission.

The attention paid to Rosenhan's study has been extraordinary. The original publication appeared in the prestigious journal *Science,* which is read by a broad group of research scientists from different fields. Needless to say, the article seemed to be embarrassing to psychiatrists. Numerous letters and articles have appeared in criticism of the Rosenhan study, and the criticisms have ranged from questions of the completeness of Rosenhan's report of his procedures to compelling criticisms of the logic of the study.

The following issues may be identified in the debate on the Rosenhan study.

1. *Validity of the distinction between abnormal and normal behavior.* Rosenhan concluded that: "It is clear that we cannot distinguish the sane from the insane in psychiatric hospitals" [1973, p. 237]. Although few thoughtful scientists would argue that psychiatric judgments of mental illness are always or even usually valid, few would argue that they are useless or are impossible to render accurately. The validity of judgments of mental illness may be low; Rosenhan, however, adopted the more extreme position that the validity of judgments of mental illness is zero. Moreover, it was the very extremeness of his conclusion that, in retrospect, seems most responsible for the attention paid to his article (Crown, 1975; Farber, 1975).

A compelling criticism of Rosenhan's original conclusion that abnormal and normal behavior cannot be distinguished in mental hospitals is that a pseudopatient demonstration study does not provide a valid basis of support for such a conclusion. At most, a pseudopatient study could show that it is sometimes possible to feign mental illness, a fact known to scientists for at least several centuries. Judgments of abnormality are based on the patient's behavior and on the patient's self-report of behavior; if the information supplied is inaccurate, it should not be surprising that the diagnosis is also likely to be inaccurate. In Rosenhan's study, the diagnosticians had little reason to suspect that the pseudopatients were falsely reporting auditory hallucinations in order to conduct psychological research; hence they understandably accepted the pseudopatients' complaints at face value. The issue of whether we can tell the difference between normal and abnormal behavior is whether we can do so when the information concerning symptoms is accurate and when the diagnosticians are highly trained and competent. Because the information supplied to the diagnosticians in Rosenhan's study was in part fabricated, the study is largely irrelevant to the validity of the distinction between abnormal and normal behavior.

In support of the irrelevance of Rosenhan's study to the original conclusion drawn, suppose some pseudopatients were to present themselves at hospitals feigning every classic symptom of an impending heart attack. Suppose also that the pseudopatients took a drug that caused irregularity in their heart beats. If such patients were admitted and given a diagnosis of heart disease, this would indicate that it is possible to fake heart disease. We should not conclude from such a study that physicians can never tell the difference between normal and abnormal heart functioning.

Rosenhan's thesis is that we cannot tell the difference between normal and abnormal behavior in mental hospitals, but it is unclear what the phrase "in mental hospitals" means. Does Rosenhan mean to suggest that we can tell the difference between normal and abnormal behavior outside of, but not in, mental hospitals? If so, Rosenhan's study does not support such a conclusion in part because it did not include a group of patients and pseudopatients who were seen for diagnostic interviews in a nonhospital setting.

Spitzer (1975) has suggested that Rosenhan's data actually indicate that the pseudopatients were distinguished from real patients. Although admitted to the hospital, the pseudopatients were released after a little more than two weeks' time. This is a short period of hospitalization for psychosis, and the brevity of this period suggests that at some level there was recognition of the pseudopatients as something less than true psychotics.

There is little question that normal and abnormal behavior can be distinguished. In fact, abnormal behavior is sometimes so bizarre that it can be recognized by people with no formal training (e.g., Crocetti, Spiro, Lemkau, & Siassi, 1972; Sushinsky & Wener, 1975). Most people can detect the difference between "Goodbye—Chop, chop; I want a hamburger" and "What is the weather like today? Too bad, I had hoped it would be sunnier." The former suggests thought disorder (unless it is feigned), whereas the latter suggests normal integration of thoughts.

In a reply to his critics, Rosenhan (1975) has fallen back to a less extreme and more defensible position. Specifically, he no longer states that we cannot tell the difference between abnormal and normal behavior. Instead, he now claims that the pseudopatients should have been admitted to the hospital without having been diagnosed as schizophrenic.

2. *Validity of psychiatric diagnosis.* In his revised position, Rosenhan (1975) admits that the diagnosticians had no reasonable evidence that the pseudopatients were fabricating symptoms. He also states that the hospital acted properly in admitting the pseudopatients because to do so was a humane course of action appropriate when a person freely requests such admission. The hospital's significant error, according to Rosenhan's revised account, was in

diagnosing the pseudopatients as schizophrenic when they did not present sufficient evidence to justify the diagnosis.

The heart of the matter concerns possible differences between the ways in which schizophrenia should be and is diagnosed in mental hospitals. DSM-II (as well as every other influential definition proposed in this century) defines schizophrenia as including several symptoms other than hallucinations. The major symptom is the presence of thought disorder (a serious defect of reason; delusions; or disorganization of thought processes). Withdrawal and a rich fantasy life are other prominent symptoms. There may be a fear of experiencing intense emotions. Hallucinations alone do not, and never did, serve as the only symptom defining schizophrenia. Rosenhan argues that the pseudopatients' complaints of auditory hallucinations should have led to a diagnosis of hallucination or to a deferred diagnosis.

It is difficult to evaluate Rosenhan's position that the diagnosis of schizophrenia was not indicated because the diagnostic interviews are not a matter of public record (Spitzer, 1975). Rosenhan has understandably refused to release the transcripts in order to protect the pseudopatients from public discussion of their personalities; it is somewhat less understandable why trustworthy and distinguished colleagues could not have been called on to verify Rosenhan's own assessment that symptoms of thought disorder were not presented during the interviews. We do not know, for example, what the pseudopatients said when asked what they did when they had hallucinations. In any event, the only symptoms we know for sure were the following: auditory hallucination, the fact that the person came to the hospital to request admission (a strange behavior for a normal person), and anxiety during the intake interview itself.

Spitzer (1975) claims that these symptoms justify schizophrenia as the most likely diagnosis. In this view, hallucinations may indicate a variety of disorders (e.g., organic brain syndromes, drug abuse, affective psychosis, or physical illness) all of which are less likely than schizophrenia, given the absence of other symptoms. In other words, Spitzer maintains that the DSM-II category of schizophrenia best fits the symptoms and, hence, that the diagnosis was not unreasonable.

Despite Spitzer's conclusion that schizophrenia was a reasonable diagnosis given the symptoms, two problems remain unsolved. First, it is unclear why more extensive testing for neurological impairment (including tumors) was not conducted. Second, if evidence of thought disorder, excessive shyness, rich fantasy, and delusions was not presented during the intake interviews, one could have ruled out schizophrenia as justifiably as one could have ruled out organic brain syndrome. The truth of the matter is that the symptoms described by Rosenhan do not fit any DSM-II category well (Rosenhan, 1975). If a diagnosis of schizophrenia had to be given to justify the admission, then there should have been a more careful follow-up to confirm the diagnosis.

3. *Careless diagnostic practices.* A truly disturbing question raised by Rosenhan's study is why the diagnosticians failed to follow up their diagnoses to confirm them (Farber, 1975). How can the administration of 2,100 pills be justified in the absence of confirmed diagnoses? For reasons that are unclear, Ro-

senhan considers the diagnosticians blameless; rather, he insists that the problem rests with DSM-II and not with the carelessness of the diagnosticians.

4. *Contribution of context to diagnoses.* Rosenhan has placed considerable emphasis on the mental hospital environment as the primary villain responsible both for diagnostic errors and for perceptions of the pseudopatients' normal behavior as abnormal. Each of these points should be considered separately.

Although Rosenhan (1975) has questioned the reliability of psychiatric diagnosis, his study actually suggests that such reliability can be very high—all pseudopatients were diagnosed as psychotic, and 11 of 12 were diagnosed as schizophrenic. Moreover, the basis for the diagnoses was unquestionably the complaint of an auditory hallucination in the absence of other symptoms that would have indicated a DSM-II disorder other than schizophrenia. Thus, the diagnoses were based on self-reports of behavior and were highly reliable. If anything, the data suggest that the role of the hospital environment in distorting the diagnostic process was negligible.

Another issue is whether the hospital environment and/or diagnoses created expectations of abnormality that led to perceptions of normal behavior on a mental hospital ward as indicative of mental illness. For example, if a college student stated in class that he is normal, this behavior per se would not suggest mental illness. However, if a mental patient labeled schizophrenic argues that he is normal, Rosenhan (1975) claims that we would tend to perceive this behavior as a sign of abnormality (irrational denial of the reality of the disturbance). Rosenhan claims that the influences of the hospital environment and of diagnostic labels are such that we tend to perceive otherwise normal behavior as abnormal.

A question arises, however, regarding the evidence Rosenhan presented to support his conclusion that mental hospital environments actually color perceptions of normal behavior as abnormal. Unfortunately, Rosenhan's study did not present any solid evidence as to how the staff actually perceived any particular pseudopatient behavior. For example, the staff was never asked whether the behavior of a pseudopatient at a particular moment was normal or abnormal. The major reason Rosenhan thinks that pseudopatient behavior was perceived as abnormal is that the pseudopatients remained hospitalized for an average of 19 days following admission and following the cessation of additional reports of hallucinations. Nineteen days, however, is not an excessive length of time to hospitalize a person who voluntarily requests admission in order to seek relief from hallucinations. The fact that the pseudopatients were not discharged sooner does not mean that their behavior on the ward was seen as abnormal.

In conclusion, the thesis that an environment can lead to perceptions of normal behavior as abnormal is a reasonable one that merits study. Unfortunately, however, Rosenhan's data neither support nor disconfirm this thesis.

5. *Exclusion criteria.* An important issue raised by Farber's (1975) critique of the Rosenhan study is the criteria by which recovery from abnormality can be judged. In the initial account of his study, Rosenhan expressed surprise that the pseudopatients were not discharged sooner. His argument was that the pseudopatients had ceased feigning abnormality, behaved normally on the

wards, and therefore should have been diagnosed as having recovered and should have been released soon after their admission.

If a schizophrenic patient hallucinates on Monday, is there anything that person can do on Tuesday to convince us that he or she will not hallucinate again in the near future? Rosenhan implicitly claims that the person need only behave normally on Tuesday to convince us that recovery has occurred. Farber, however, disagrees, and he notes that the mere absence of an abnormal behavior for a short period of time is usually an insufficient basis for diagnosing recovery. According to Farber, the only thing the pseudopatients could have done to convince the clinicians that they should have been discharged immediately after admission was to report that they had feigned hallucinations in order to conduct a psychological study.

An important point in Farber's critique, then, is that DSM-II does not provide either an empirical or conventional basis for judging when a person has recovered from a mental illness. The key issues here are the need to specify the abnormal behaviors that must be absent, as well as the need to specify the length of time these behaviors must be absent, so that clinicians can objectively diagnose a recovery.

6. *Stickiness of psychiatric diagnosis.* At discharge, the pseudopatients were diagnosed as having "schizophrenia in remission." Spitzer (1975) argues that the diagnosis of schizophrenia in remission is rarely used by psychiatrists which suggests that the pseudopatients had been detected as less than truly psychotic. In reply, Rosenhan agrues that *in remission* does not mean "normal" and that *schizophrenia in remission* is a stigmatizing label. Rosenhan's reply seems convincing—even though the technical meaning of the phrase *in remission* is "without symptoms," the diagnosis *schizophrenia in remission* does not have the same connotations as does the diagnosis *normal.*

In summary, Rosenhan's demonstration that pseudopatients can feign mental illness raises some interesting issues. One issue is the extent to which psychiatric diagnosticians are careless. Another is the extent to which mental hospital environments and psychiatric diagnoses may color our perceptions of perfectly normal behavior as abnormal. Perhaps the most important issue for classification, however, is the need to formulate criteria for identifying recovery from mental disorders. Unfortunately, Rosenhan's study does not illuminate our understanding of these issues (Farber, 1975; Millon, 1975; Spitzer, 1975; Weiner, 1975).

OTHER CLASSIFICATION SYSTEMS

In order to acquaint the reader with alternatives to DSM-II, or to parts of DSM-II, several classification systems will be discussed briefly in this section.

World Health Organization (WHO)

Although DSM-II serves as the conventional system in the United States, the World Health Organization (1968) has constructed a system intended to serve as the international standard. The WHO system is similar to DSM-II. WHO is based on a medical model of abnormality, and it defines many categories in a manner similar to DSM-II. Two major differences between WHO and DSM are (1) WHO's classification of functional psychoses (e.g., schizophrenia) and psychoses attributable to organic factors as subcategories of a major category called Psychosis and (2) WHO's classification of neuroses, personality disorders, sexual deviations, alcoholism, drug dependence, psychophysiologic disorders, and special symptoms as subcategories of a major category called Neurosis, Personality Disorders, and Other Nonpsychotic Mental Disorders.

Millon's System

Millon (1969) has proposed a comprehensive alternative to DSM-II. This system is based on four types of pathology (pathological personality patterns, symptom disorders, pathological behavior reactions, and biophysical defects) and on three levels of severity (mild, moderate, and marked). Although this work is highly creative, sufficient data do not yet exist to assess the reliability and the validity of Millon's categories.

Biometric Approach

The DSM-II system defines its categories in terms of paradigm instances of a disorder. The task of the diagnostician is to select the DSM-II category that best fits the particular person being diagnosed. Zubin, Salzinger, Fleiss, Gurland, Spitzer, Endicott, and Sutton (1975) are developing an alternative method of diagnosis based on specific criteria. This system provides a list of specific symptoms and a set of rules as to exactly which symptoms and how many must be present in order for a diagnosis to apply. Table 1-2 presents some interrater reliability data that compare the Zubin et al. specific criteria method of classification and DSM-II. The measure of interrater reliability is expressed in terms of a Kappa statistic; the higher the number, the greater the reliability. As Table 1-2 shows, the specific criteria classification system was found to be more reliable than DSM-II for comparable categories.

Systems Proposed by Experimentalists

Experimental psychologists have been very critical of the value of traditional classification systems both because of the medical model on which they are based and because of the poor reliability and validity of many of their categories Ferster, 1967; Peterson, 1968; Ullmann & Krasner, 1965). Some experimental theorists have proposed classification systems based on a stimulus-response-reinforcement model (Ferster, 1967), whereas others have proposed classification systems based on highly sophisticated mathematical studies of abnormal behaviors (Baker & Dreger, 1973; & Eysenck, 1961).

Several behavior theorists have proposed conceptual models that could be developed into comprehensive classification systems (see Kanfer & Saslow, 1969; Suinn, 1970). Kanfer and Saslow (1969) have proposed a particularly interesting model in which all behavior is conceptualized as a behavior excess, as a behavior deficit, or as a behavior asset, such that only the excess and deficit groups are viewed as problems. The behavior is next analyzed in terms of the problem situation, motivation, development, self-control, social relation-

TABLE 1-2
Kappa Coefficients of Agreement for Major Diagnosis on 120 Case Records

Diagnostic Category	Kappa Using Specified Criteria	Kappa Using DSM-II Criteria
Major Groupings		
Affective	.70	.48
Schizophrenia	.84	.48
Other	.74	.61
Specific categories		
Nonaffective schizophrenia	.70	.49
Schizoaffective schizophrenia	.24	.37
Manic illness	.76	.37
Major depressive illness[a]	.66	.25
Minor depressive illness[b]	.56	.07
Alcoholism	.66	—[c]
Drug dependence	1.00	—[c]
Obsessive-compulsive	.65	.42
Anxiety neurosis	.52	.06
Phobic neurosis	.66	.32
Borderline psychosis	.20	
Undiagnosed	.59	

[a] Considered equivalent to any psychotic affective illness in DSM-II.
[b] Considered equivalent to Neurotic Depression in DSM-II.
[c] Neither of the raters used this category.
From J. Zubin, J. L. Fleiss, B. J. Garland, K. Salzinger, R. L. Spitzer, J. Endicott and S. Sutton, "Abnormal and Clinical Psychology: Statistical, Epidemiological and Diagnostic Approaches," *Annual Review of Psychology* (Palo Alto, Calif.: Annual Reviews Inc., 1975), p. 647. Reprinted with permission of authors and publisher.

ships, and an analysis of the social-cultural-physical environment. Commenting on the purposes of this system, Kanfer and Saslow wrote:

> This approach is not a substitute for assignment of the patient to traditional diagnostic categories: such labeling may be desirable for statistical, administrative or research purposes. But the current analysis is intended to replace other diagnostic formulations purporting to serve as a basis for making decisions about specific therapeutic interventions [1969, p. 437].

OBJECTIONS TO CLASSIFICATION

Many psychologists are dissatisfied with the current state of classification in abnormal psychology (see Zigler & Phillips, 1961). Some have criticized classification per se, whereas others have criticized classification in accordance with the medical model.

The position that classification per se is an inappropriate goal has been expressed most frequently by phenomenologically oriented theorists who believe that the uniqueness of each individual renders classification misleading, if not invalid (e.g., Allport, 1937). For example, by classifying two beliefs as delusions, we tend to overlook the unique individualistic qualities characteristic of each delusion. The merit to this position, discussed in greater detail in Chapter 8, seems to be an affirmation of the worth of each individual. But without denying that each person is unique and is worthy of respect for his individuality, it is nevertheless true that we can identify important similarities among behaviors. The identification of such similarities, as formalized in a classification system, is intended to summarize information and to permit a science of abnormal psychology. It is difficult to understand how the identification of true behavioral similarities necessarily detracts from human dignity.

Another objection to classification concerns the undesirable consequences of labeling (e.g., Maslow, 1948; Menninger, 1959; Rogers, 1951). By virtue of their diagnostic nature, classification systems permit the labeling of people with designations such as *retarded, psychotic,* and *neurotic.* Sometimes the effects of these labels may be undesirable. For example, a schoolchild may be diagnosed as a "slow learner" in order to identify him as a child needing extra help. As a consequence of having been labeled a slow learner, however, the child may actually receive less help if the teacher assumes that the child has been proven to be incapable of learning (see Grossman, 1971). Another possible adverse effect of labeling is on the person's self-image. For example, a child diagnosed as a slow learner may come to think of himself as stupid.

Sometimes labels may have beneficial effects. For example, people who fear that they are sinners often seem to benefit from being told that their behavior is an expression of mental illness rather than of sin.

Although psychologists have been critical of the adverse effects of labels, few believe that classification itself is an undesirable goal (Zigler & Phillips, 1961). The usual reasons for criticizing classification have been to call attention to the need for a better classification system and to the need for responsible uses of diagnoses that may stigmatize the very people they are intended to help.

SUMMARY

Classification systems are constructed to summarize important similarities among abnormal behavior. These systems are intended in part as aids in scientific communication.

A major portion of this chapter presented and critically evaluated the *Diagnostic and Statistical Manual of Mental Disorders,* Second Edition (DSM-II). DSM-II has served as the conventional system in the United States. This system is based on a medical model of abnormality and provides 10 major categories, each category having several subcategories, with some subcategories having their own subcategories. Depending on the category, the criteria of classification may be the uniqueness of the behavior (e.g., mental retardation), the hypothesized or identified causal origins of the behavior (e.g., organic brain damage), the descriptive features of the behavior (e.g., psychoneurosis), the precipitating condition (e.g., transient situational disorders), the age of the individual (e.g., behavior disorders of childhood), or even the apparent absence of mental illness (e.g., nonspecific conditions).

There is considerable opposition to DSM-II. Many (although not all) of the categories have low reliability; that is, the same behavior is often classified into different categories or subcategories by different diagnosticians. Moreover, the validity of many of the categories is undemonstrated; that is, classification rarely implies precise information about the behavior classified. Nevertheless, DSM-II is far from useless. The system remains useful for communication and for descriptive purposes, and it is unlikely that it will be abandoned before an alternative is demonstrated to be superior.

In recent years an upsurge of interest in the manner in which DSM-II is actually employed has been witnessed. Diagnostic processes at hospitals seem biased toward the tendency to admit questionable cases. The diagnostic process seems to be affected at least partially by social influence variables that are theoretically irrelevant to the true diagnosis. A study that has received extraordinary attention is Rosenhan's (1973) *On Being Sane in Insane Places.* Rosenhan's original conclusion, that we cannot tell the difference between abnormal and normal behavior in mental hospitals, is not supported by his data. His study, however, does raise some important questions about the possible carelessness of diagnosticians and about the absence of exclusion tests by which we can determine when a person has recovered from a mental illness.

Several other classification systems were discussed. The classification system of the World Health Organization is similar to that of DSM-II. Millon's (1969) system classifies behavior in terms of type and severity of abnormality, but this system has yet to be tested for reliability and validity. The biometric approach is currently generating a system based on specific behaviors. Kanfer and Saslow (1969) have proposed an interesting system designed to be valid for clinical decisions.

Several objections to classification per se have been raised. It has been argued that classification results in a loss of information regarding individual uniqueness. It has also been argued that diagnostic labels can have undesirable effects. Although these criticisms are well taken, they do not justify the abandonment of attempts to identify true similarities among abnormal behaviors.

People have been attempting to develop a valid classification system for four thousand years. The complexity and heterogeneity of abnormal behavior is such that a comprehensive and valid classification system has yet to be constructed. Some progress, however, has been made, and additional progress may occur within the next few decades. In the meantime, DSM-II will be employed because it is better than no classification system at all and because no alternative system is both comprehensive and clearly superior.

Chapter 2

Historical Perspectives and Legal Issues[1]

Medical history as it has been written during the past 100 years suffers from two corrupting biases, progressivism and hero worship.

GALDSTON (1967, p. 2)

Henry Ford once declared, "History is a pack of lies." The element of truth to this declaration is that history is a summary of the significant events of the past and what a historian considers significant depends on his biased and unique perspective. An example of bias has been the exclusion of important black people from American histories written by white Americans. Women, too, have been largely ignored by those who write political and social histories. Bias also is evident in many histories of psychology in which the historian's primary focus has been to create the impression of progress or to glorify the accomplishments of a few reformers. Thus to understand the manner in which a historical account may be biased, it is necessary to understand the viewpoint of the historian.

Most histories of abnormal psychology are written from the perspective of the scientist and/or clinician. The former reports the intellectual progress in the field from the early acceptance of demonology to the naturalistic explanations of modern science. The latter notes the significant events in treatment and care. The impression conveyed by these histories is one of progress. In reality, however, there has been little progress in the identification of the actual causes of abnormal behavior and, although scientists have been noticeably more successful in the development of clinical treatments, we still need to improve the quality of care in many large state mental hospitals. Indeed, a history of abnormal psychology written from the perspective of the person committed to a mental hospital would need to summarize only a few significant events. From the perspective of hospitalized persons, progress has been uneven and often elusive.

What follows is a brief history of abnormal psychology from the perspective of the scientist. After this history is presented, the history of the care received by patients in mental hospitals is discussed.

BASIC VIEWS OF CAUSATION

Abnormal behavior always has been studied by people with very different beliefs concerning its nature and causes. This book presents five approaches to the study and treatment of abnormality. The historical roots of this theoretical diversity are in three points of view concerning the nature of abnormality:

1. The *moral-religious position* is that abnormality is the result of an evil force. Some societies believed that people become mad as punishment for their sins, whereas others believed that the insane are innocent victims of an evil force.

2. The *somatogenic hypothesis* maintains that psychological abnormality is

[1] Based on Alexander and Selesnick (1966), Bockoven (1963), Boring (1957), Dewhurst (1966), Galdston (1967), Henderson and Gillespie (1946), Hunter and Macalpine (1968), Murphy (1929), Rosen (1968), Schneck (1960), and Veith (1957).

often caused by physical diseases. This hypothesis provides a basis for referring to psychological problems as *mental illnesses.*

3. The *psychogenic hypothesis* maintains that psychological abnormality is often caused by environmental stress and by inappropriate learning.

Although each of these above views has been expressed since antiquity, different views were dominant during various historical periods. For example, the moral-religious position was dominant in most ancient societies and in medieval Europe.

The Moral-Religious Position

The earliest expressions of the moral-religious viewpoint were notions that insanity results from possession by demons and evil spirits. Selling (1943) has suggested that such views were prevalent in Stone Age societies. The evidence for this hypothesis consists of the discovery of skulls with holes bored into their sides, the presumption being that these holes were the result of *trephining* operations designed to let out evil spirits.

The view of madness as punishment for sin is expressed in the Bible. For example, in Deuteronomy 6:5 it is written, "The Lord will smite thee with madness." King Saul's madness was widely believed to have been punishment sent by God for Saul's well-publicized moral failings.

The moral view was dominant in medieval Europe during which time the power of the Roman Catholic church was at its peak. Even though the church's authority was not seriously challenged until the Protestant Reformation of the sixteenth century, the fifteenth century witnessed the beginning of a desperate attempt by the church to seek out and to destroy "witchcraft." Thousands accused and convicted of being witches were "legally murdered" in what was known as the Inquisition. Many of those accused were women who showed signs of hysterical neurosis.

Although several causes for the Inquisition can be identified, three are of particular interest to students of abnormal psychology. The most obvious reason for the Inquisition was ideological—most people really believed that witchcraft existed. Because a witch was someone who sold her soul to the devil, it made sense to believe that the problems of the church as well as those of society were caused by evil witches. Eliminating the witches would help the cause of God and would hurt the cause of the devil. During an era when people held such beliefs, it is not difficult to understand how the publication of Sprenger and Kraemer's (1487) *Malleus Maleficarum* (*The Witches' Hammer*) could have precipitated an Inquisition.

The Inquisition was directed primarily against women, particularly women who suffered from hysterical neurosis. The church had experienced repeated scandals exposing its difficulty in keeping its priests celibate. It was natural for the male-dominated church hierarchy to place full blame for the transgressions of its priests on women. It was women who placed temptation before men; therefore, it was women who most often carried out the work of the devil. Sexism was thus a major cause of the Inquisition.

Still another contributory cause of the Inquisition was a fear that madness

The notion that illness is caused by evil forces has been expressed throughout history. In some accounts of this moral-religious position, afflicted persons are seen as innocent victims of an evil force, whereas in other accounts afflicted persons are seen as sinners receiving their just punishment. The print shows an incantation over a sick man by a Hottentot medicine man who is attempting to drive away evil spirits. Modern expressions of the moral-religious position include theories that abnormal behavior is an escape from an unjust world, that the psychologically troubled are victims of stigmatizing diagnostic labels, and that the psychologically troubled are sinners. (Drawn by Riou from a description. Reprinted by permission of Historical Pictures Services; Chicago, Illinois.)

constituted a threat to the established order. Prior to the Inquisition, Europe had witnessed several outbursts in which extremist groups, professing to be inspired by God, conducted mass orgies in public streets in the name of religious inspiration. Although the church at first sanctioned these orgies, it later came to fear that these fanatics could not be trusted despite their claims of loyalty to the church. The Inquisition was initially sanctioned by the church in part to control these groups.

As noted, publication of the *Malleus Maleficarum* precipitated the Inquisition. Sanctioned by both church and secular authorities, this book became the official statement on witchcraft. The *Malleus* is divided into three sections. The first section is a treatise designed to prove the existence of witchcraft. The second and third sections concern the identification and punishment of witches. A witch was defined as someone who voluntarily agreed to possession by the devil. The *Malleus* notes many ways for identifying witches: Women suffering from diseases of unknown origin (unfortunately, little was known about diseases at the time), "lustful" women, insane women, and women who dissented from the church—all provided abundant "evidence" of being witches. Once accused, the woman was brought before a court for inspection; lest the devil hide in the accused's pubic hair, the *Malleus* recommended that the accused be presented to the judges with her pubic hair shaved. Virtually everyone accused was convicted. The recommended and most popular method of treatment was to scare off the devil by burning the body alive. Szasz (1970) has noted that in burning witches the Inquisitors believed that they were helping the victim by increasing her chances of eventual admittance to heaven. Although the Inquisition was directed primarily against women, the *Malleus* claimed that men too could be inhabited by the devil.

The Inquisition seems so transparently inhumane and the *Malleus* so transparently pornographic in its detail that it is important to appreciate that most Inquisitors believed in witchcraft in much the same way as we believe in democracy.

The moral-religious view of abnormality declined in popularity during the latter half of the nineteenth century. Even though beliefs in demons, devils, and exorcism persist among laymen, the moral-religious view today is more typically expressed by laymen who view abnormal behavior as an expression of moral degeneracy. For example, alcoholics are often viewed as degenerates by the public. This view contrasts sharply with that of scientists and professionals, the overwhelming majority of whom have adopted a biological and/or psychological view. However, both Mowrer (1960) and Szasz (1961) are members of a small group of scientists who have recently advocated a moral view of abnormality. Szasz's view represents a modern version of the moral victim theory; Szasz believes that the mentally ill, like the witches before them, are victims of concepts such as mental illness and witchcraft. Mowrer's view maintains that abnormality can be regarded as sin on the part of the psychologically troubled.

Somatogenic View

The idea that abnormality is a mental illness caused by physical disease (somatogenic hypothesis) was expressed clearly by the ancient Greek physician Hippocrates (440 B.C.): "I do not believe that the 'Sacred Disease' [epilepsy] is any more divine or sacred than any other disease but, on the contrary, has specific characteristics and a specific cause. If you cut open the head you will find the brain humid, full of sweat and smelling badly. And in this way you may see it as not a god which injures the body, but disease."

Following the philosopher Empedocles, Hippocrates proposed that health requires a proper balance among four bodily elements called humors: blood, phlegm, yellow bile, and black bile. The Hippocratic physicians attributed melancholia to black bile and cholera (quick-tempered personalities) to yellow bile. Although both of these terms denoted states of humoral imbalance, melancholia alone was considered a type of insanity and was often equated with mania (mania is characterized by elation and hyperactivity).

Hippocrates's theory had profound consequences on the development of abnormal psychology: (1) It stressed the central role of observation in science; (2) it began the tradition of classifying personalities into types; (3) it implied that personality distortions and emotional disorders were quantitative exaggerations of normality; and (4) it tied abnormalities to an anatomical and physiological basis. The manner in which it provided for mechanistic explanations of abnormalities is exemplified by early theories of hysteria and hypochondriasis. Following ancient Egyptian thought, hysteria was attributed to a wandering uterus and was therefore believed to occur only in women. Hypochondriasis was attributed to an organ in the abdomen called the hypochondia; we now know, however, that the hypochondia does not exist.

Various formulations of the humoral imbalance theory influenced medicine through the Middle Ages and provided impetus to the development of an adequate system of classifying abnormalities. Soranus (A.D. 200) modified Hippocrates's theory by proposing an elaborate system of pathology that resulted from minute, solid particles called atoms. He also distinguished between two types of insanity, chronic (gradual onset) and acute (sudden onset). Jean Fernal (1497–1558) of France proposed a classification system in which various disorders were associated with particular organs. The Swiss physician Felix Platter (1536–1614) lived in dungeons with mental patients in order to understand them better and proposed an elaborate system based on symptomatology, the most important symptoms being pain, headache, tremors, and auditory disturbances.

Thomas Sydenham (1624–1689), a contemporary of the influential British philosopher John Locke, is credited by Veith (1957) for having shown that psychological abnormalities are related to life histories. Among Sydenham's important contributions was the conclusion that hypochondriasis in men and hysteria in women are as "one egg as to another" (see Dewhurst, 1966, pp. 46–47). Having drawn this conclusion from case histories and observations, Sydenham contradicted the notion of hysteria as a consequence of a wandering uterus. But Sydenham's theoretical writings (see Dewhurst, 1966) show that, for most disorders, he continued the Hippocratic tradition of viewing disease in terms of bodily humors.

François Boissier de Sauvages (1716–1769) grouped diseases into classes, orders, and genera in the same way that his contemporary natural scientists constructed classification systems of plants and animals. The result was an impressive but unnecessarily complex system. Sauvages considered as a different disease each group of symptoms he observed. His classification system had 10 classes, 40 orders, 78 genera, and 2,400 different diseases.

Wilhelm Wundt (1832–1920) is considered the father of modern psychology not because he was the first to study psychological problems, but because he was the first to do so as his life's work. Wundt's important contributions were in the field of experimental psychology. However, one of Wundt's several famous students, Emil Kraepelin (1856–1926), had a profound influence on abnormal psychology.

Similar to Soranus's early distinction between chronic and acute insanity, Kraepelin classified psychosis into exogenous (originating from outside the body) and endogenous (originating from the body; biological) diseases. He held that people suffering from exogenous diseases would recover without treatment, whereas those suffering from internally caused diseases were incurable. By establishing the exogenous-curable, endogenous-incurable principle, Kraepelin set prognosis (prediction) as the primary basis of classification.

Prior to Kraepelin, Kahlbausm had described a syndrome called *catatonia,* Hecker had described a disorder called *hebephrenia,* and Morel had described a disorder called *démence précoce.* Kraepelin perceived the similarities among these syndromes and classified them into a single category that he called *dementia praecox.* Dementia praecox was diagnosed by Kraepelin when an adolescent suffered from hallucinations, delusions, and/or bizarre behavior. He subdivided dementia praecox into catatonia (indicated by the symptoms of singular muscular spasms, stuporous states, and occasional violence) and hebephrenia (a puberty psychosis that rapidly deteriorates into silly, grossly inappropriate behavior). Paranoia (indicated by delusions of persecution) was originally considered a separate psychosis but was later classified as a subtype of dementia praecox.

Kraepelin's classification of psychotic disorders provides the framework for today's conventional system. His system proposed dementia praecox and manic-depressive insanity as two major types of psychosis; DSM-II provides schizophrenia and affective disorders as two major types of psychosis. Moreover, Kraepelin's dementia praecox category is similar to DSM-II's categories for hebephrenic and catatonic schizophrenia.

Belief in the biological origins of psychological abnormalities received considerable impetus when it was conclusively established that general paresis is caused by the same infectious agent that causes syphilis. General paresis was first described in 1798 by Haslam who, in published case reports, described the symptoms as restricted movement of the arms and legs, defective speech, changes in character, and the patient's general unawareness of these deteriorations. Esquirol in 1805 described the course of the disease, and Rayle in 1827 and Calmeil in 1826 hypothesized various organic origins. Correlations between the occurrence of general paresis and syphilis were noted in 1854 by Esmarch and Jessen. In 1897 the hypothesis of syphilitic causation received important experimental support from a daring investigation by Kraft-Ebing. In this study, nine paretic patients were innoculated with syphilis. Because none of them developed syphilis, it was concluded that the patients had already recovered from a previous syphilitic infection and thus had been immune to the experimental innoculation. Wasserman later demonstrated conclusively that antibodies existed that could account for the immunity found by Kraft-Ebing. And, finally, in 1913 Noguchi and Moore found the syphilis bacterium, *treponema pallidum,* in the brains of 14 of 70 paretic patients at the Central Islip State Hospital in New York.[2]

General paresis is one of the few so-called mental diseases for which biological causation has been conclusively established. Moreover, the systematic

[2] Today both syphilis and general paresis are treated with penicillin. However, brain damage caused by the spreading of syphilis to the nervous system, which happens in only a small percentage of the cases, is irreversible.

manner in which the causal agent was identified is a paradigm example of the scientific method. The impact of this success was to encourage beliefs that most other forms of abnormality, particularly the more severe psychotic disorders, are caused by physical disease. Such beliefs are popular among many scientists.

Psychogenic View

Succinctly stated, the psychogenic view is that many forms of abnormality are psychological in origin (caused by learning inappropriate behaviors of coping) and are precipitated by environmental stress. This view maintains that the study of abnormality is a social science and that psychology is more important for understanding abnormal behavior than is medicine.

Widespread advocacy of the psychogenic hypothesis is a relatively recent phenomenon, but there are several historical precedents for this position. Both Plato and Aristotle expressed psychogenic views. In particular, Aristotle suggested that psychological troubles are caused by pent-up emotions which can be released by watching plays. Another noteworthy advocate of the psychogenic hypothesis was the Roman Cicero; Cicero parted from the somatogenic ideas of Hippocrates when he maintained that bodily ailments could result from emotional factors. Cicero also rejected Hippocrates's notion that black bile caused melancholia, maintaining instead the importance of emotional factors such as violent rage, fear, and grief.

The great French psychiatrist Pinel (1745–1826) provides a reasonable starting point for the modern history of the psychogenic view. Pinel is best known for his humanitarian efforts—he freed the insane from their chains at Bicêtre and Salpêtrière hospitals in Paris. Pinel also proposed one of the more influential classification systems of the eighteenth century because it avoided both biological fictions and metaphysical hypotheses of demonology.[3]

Jean Etienne Dominique Esquirol (1772–1840) was a French physician who followed closely the basic teachings of Pinel. Esquirol's work was concerned primarily with classifying mental deficiency, and he stressed the importance of verbal ability in the measurement of intelligence.

The psychogenic view received important support from the nineteenth century advocates of moral treatment, from Sigmund Freud, and from early psychologists such as Watson. Today it is the most popular position among psychologists.

APPROACHES TO ABNORMALITY

Theoretical diversity in the study of abnormality has been basic and profound. Throughout history, each of the preceding three views has gained, lost, and regained popularity. Each is represented in contemporary psychology, although the moral-religious view has relatively few adherents.

With the rise of academic psychology during the early half of the twentieth

[3] The psychogenic view also received important support from Mesmer and his practice of "animal magnetism" (see Chapter 7 for details) and from Charcot's work on hysteria (discussed on pages 213–216.

century, basic theoretical differences were increasingly refined. Five basic ways of approaching and studying abnormality are presented in this book.

The Biological Approach

The historical origins of the biological approach are those of the somatogenic view. In contemporary science, psychiatry remains the bastion of biological theories of causation, but this view also is well represented in psychology. However, most advocates of the importance of biological factors no longer maintain that physical disease is the exclusive cause. Today biological factors are regarded as contributory causes to many types of abnormality. Moreover, much of the research on biological factors is intended to identify correlates rather than causes of abnormality. (See Chapter 5.)

The Psychoanalytic Approach

The present discussion of Freudian psychoanalysis is limited to the relations between psychoanalysis and the historical trends we have already discussed. (See Chapter 6 for a detailed account of psychoanalysis.)

Jean-Martin Charcot (1825–1893), often remembered as a teacher of Sigmund Freud (1856–1939), was the leading European neurologist of his day. He believed that psychological abnormalities were caused by neurological disease, humors, and the presence of morbid matter in the blood. Despite this basic somatogenic position, the practical influence of Charcot's work was to enhance support for the psychogenic hypothesis. It was Charcot who accepted hysterical symptoms as "real," maintained that the hysteric's loss of functioning was anatomical nonsense (that is, could not be explained by damage to the nervous system), and repeatedly demonstrated that similar behaviors could be induced by hypnosis. Freud, who studied under Charcot in Paris in 1886, was impressed with Charcot's work on hysteria and returned to Vienna as a strong advocate of hypnosis and of Charcot's theories.

After his return to Vienna, Freud collaborated with Breuer, who related to him the case of Anne O. In treating this patient between 1880 and 1882 for hysterical paralysis of the limbs, anesthesia, and disturbance of vision and speech, Breuer observed that under hypnosis Anne O. could be encouraged to talk about the life circumstances that surrounded the original development of each symptom. When discussion of these circumstances seemed to result in a release of pent-up emotion, the symptoms disappeared. This release of repressed emotion was called *abreaction.*

At first, Breuer did not attach any great significance to the successful treatment of Anne O., nor did Freud when he first heard of the case in 1882. It was not until he returned from Paris, impressed with Charcot's work on hypnosis, that Freud saw two theoretically significant aspects to the case: the role of emotional factors in hysteria and the importance of hypnosis as a therapeutic procedure. In 1895, Breuer and Freud published the case in *Studies in Hysteria;* this book proposed that hysteria is caused by an unconscious forgetting of traumatic events and is cured when the unconscious feelings are freely expressed. As Freud continued his study of unconscious forces, he became increasingly impressed with the importance of emotional factors but abandoned hypnosis as an appropriate method of treatment.[4] By the late 1890s, Freud had developed a new type of "talking" therapy that he called *psychoanalysis.*

It is misleading to attempt to classify the psychoanalytic view as somatogenic or as psychogenic. On the one hand, psychoanalysis is the dominant theory of American psychiatry and provides a medical model of abnormality complete with a basis for diagnosing various disease entities. On the other hand, the most important aspect of psychoanalysis has been its emphasis on the learning in early childhood of ways to defend against anxiety and socially disapproved sexuality. In essence, the psychoanalytic view is both somatogenic and psychogenic—Mind and body are so closely related in psychoanalytic theory that it sometimes seems that Freud viewed them as two aspects of the same thing. Psychoanalytic theory stressed the organism's totality, its integration of mind and body, and the many examples of each affecting the other.

Although Freud was not the first to speculate about unconscious motivation, he was the first to do so in great detail and to apply this concept to all varieties of neurotic behavior. The hypothesis of unconscious causation led to an emphasis on the continuity between abnormal and normal behavior; in the *Psychopathology of Everyday Life,* Freud postulated that many everyday behaviors, such as slips of the tongue and forgetting a name, are motivated by unconscious forces.

In addition to proposing a specific theory of abnormality, Freud also developed a psychoanalytic method of inquiry. To a large extent, psychoanalytic method is an attempt at a historical reconstruction of an individual's emotional life as revealed in psychoanalytic interviews. But the psychoanalytic method is also a unique combination of introspection, observation, and philosophical inquiry. The method defies classification as history, science, or philosophy because it combines various elements from each of these methods. If judged solely as a historical method of inquiry, psychoanalysis can be seen to have many shortcomings, for the therapist does not typically examine documents or interview relevant persons to verify the historical events of his patient's life. If judged solely as a science, the psychoanalytic method is inadequate because it does not permit extensive experimentation, because it is empirically vague, and because it is unclear which are the weaker hypotheses to be modified by problematic data.[5]

In borrowing elements from historical, scientific, philosophical, and introspective methods, and in demonstrating that his method can produce important insights into human emotionality, Freud developed a unique system of in-

[4] Freud's reason for abandoning hypnosis was that too many of his patients relapsed following such treatment. However, many present-day experimental psychologists believe that Freud abandoned the procedure on the basis of insufficient evidence.

[5] Any empirical test of a hypothesis, H_1, is really a test of several hypotheses, $H_1, \ldots, H_n$. In experimental science, the purpose of the study is to test the weakest hypothesis, H_1, such that disconfirming evidence is interpreted to modify H_1. In psychoanalysis, the prior support for hypotheses $H_1, \ldots, H_n$ is approximately equal, such that it is unclear which hypothesis should be modified if disconfirming evidence is obtained.

quiry. Some psychologists are strong adherents of this method, others are strong critics, and still others are not quite sure what to make of it.

Freud has had a profound influence on Western thought—his influence is evident in psychology, psychiatry, sociology, literature, and history. His ideas also have helped create a greater level of general awareness of the emotional and sexual dimensions in life.

Social Learning Theory

Social learning theory represents the purest example of contemporary thought concerning psychogenic causation of abnormality and, like psychoanalysis, it stresses the continuity between normal and abnormal behaviors. The essence of the social learning view of causation is that abnormality is often the result of inappropriate learning. (See Chapter 7.)

It is difficult to understand why many otherwise excellent histories of experimental psychology devote so little space to Darwin (1809–1882), the great English biologist. As Boring recognized: "The effect of this theory [Darwin's theory of natural selection] upon the development of psychology was tremendous. Not only did the theory challenge the authority of Genesis in respect to the special creation of species, suggesting that man has inherited his body from animal ancestors, but it also raised the question as to whether there is continuity in respect of mind between animals and man" [1957, p. 471]. Darwin's book *The Origin of Species,* first published in 1859, helped pave the way for the experimental study of learning in animals as a means to understand better some aspects of human behavior.

The modern historical origins of the social-learning approach are in the behaviorism of J. B. Watson (1913), the rise of experimental psychology beginning with Wundt's work in the latter half of the nineteenth century, and the philosophy of science called logical positivism. This approach began as an application of experimental principles of learning first discovered in animal research. However, this approach to abnormality has been broadened considerably in recent years.

Phenomenology

Unlike the preceding approaches, the historical origins of phenomenology are in philosophy rather than in medicine or in psychology. (See Chapter 8.)

In medieval Europe, the church's authority in intellectual matters was challenged only by relatively uninfluential heretics. In the thirteenth century, Thomas Aquinas claimed to have proven the existence of God even though no influential groups had had any doubt. The Reformation successfully challenged the church's authority but did so without ever questioning the existence of God. It was the French philosopher René Descartes (1596–1650) who is credited with the introduction of scientific doubt into Western thought.

At first, Descartes' doubt was extensive. He doubted the accuracy of his sensory experience ("How do I know I am not hallucinating?"), the existence of God, and even his own existence. Eventually, he concluded that in order to doubt his own existence he would first have to exist; that is, *cogito ergo sum,* or "I think, therefore I am." From this certain knowledge, Descartes proceeded to prove the existence of God and then the accuracy of his sensory experience.

But Descartes' new proof of established dogma was less influential than were the seeds of doubt with which he began. The British skeptics (John Locke, George Berkeley, and David Hume) systematically criticized Descartes' reconstructed proof of his existence, the eventual conclusion being one of pervasive doubt about the existence of the self and the accuracy of sensory experience. To the question "How do we know we are not always hallucinating?" the skeptics replied, "We do not have any certain knowledge so we could be hallucinating all the time, never perceiving the real world, but perceiving instead our hallucination."

It was the philosopher Immanuel Kant who provided the first truly brilliant reply to skepticism. Kant maintained that there existed *a priori* knowledge. A priori knowledge is known prior to experience and is thus not subject to possible defects in the sensory process. For example, prior to experiencing any object, we know that the object will be experienced in space and in time.

Kant's arguments were interpreted by many as demonstrating the logical priority of experience. Because all knowledge of the world is gained from experience, an understanding of experience seemed crucial for science. Phenomenology is the study of experience and consciousness.

Kant's *Critique of Pure Reason* was published in 1781. The early German psychologists of the latter half of the nineteenth century were very much concerned with the study of consciousness, as was the great American psychologist William James (1842–1910). Debates soon arose as to whether the elements of consciousness could be studied as separate entities or whether, as James and the German gestalt psychologists held, consciousness (experience) should be viewed as a whole above and beyond its separate elements. Both James and the gestalt psychologists also stressed the uniqueness of each individual's experience.

Although phenomenology had an early impact on psychology, its initial influence was greater in the field of perception than in abnormal psychology. During the 1950s, however, Carl Rogers developed a phenomenological theory of abnormality that received an extensive following. There are several reasons other than scientific merit that contributed to the success of Rogers's theory. First, Rogers's theory provided psychologists with an acceptable alternative to the psychoanalysis of psychiatry. In essence, psychology was given a major form of therapy it could call its own. Second, Rogers did not rely on the introspective method of examining conscious content, stressing instead the need for experimentation. Rogers's theory permits extensive experimentation, and his client-centered therapy was the first to be evaluated extensively by experimentation. Third, Rogers's theory integrated the science of phenomenology with the values of humanism, thereby providing a system that explicitly emphasized the dignity and worth of each individual. Finally, Rogers expressed much of his theory in the language of experience; that is, many people were able to perceive this theory as a meaningful statement of events in their own lives.

The phenomenological approach views abnormality as a failure, or a stunting, of normal emotional growth. It is misleading to describe its view of causation as somatogenic or psychogenic because it views the biological and experiential aspects of life as an integrated whole.

The Community Approach

The modern historical origins of the community approach to abnormality are in social science and in social theory. Its view of causation is more appropriately described as sociogenic rather than somatogenic or psychogenic. (See Chapter 9.)

The community approach is concerned with the effects of the larger social environment on the definition, development, and treatment of abnormality. In its broader aspects, it is concerned with sociological variables. This approach has also been concerned with various types of social organizations (e.g., family, factories, schools, and mental hospitals) and with the relative demands each places on the individual who must adapt to these organizations.

Today the growing popularity of the community approach is at least partially a result of heightened interest in the problems of delivering psychological and mental health services. An appreciation of the importance of these problems can be gained from a look at the history of abnormal psychology from the patient's viewpoint.

THE PATIENT'S PERSPECTIVE

The intellectual history of abnormal psychology is one of an ebb and flow of recurring ideas, with the eventual refinement of theoretical diversity into the several approaches we have described. But the human history of abnormal psychology, written from the patient's perspective, is one of the coming and passing of various types of torture, degradation, stigma, and abandonment. The progress that has been achieved is insufficient and elusive. Desperately needed social reforms have too often been reversed by economic adversity, and there is little reason for confidence that future economic recessions will not reverse recent reforms. If there is a basis for realistic hope of maintaining recent progress, it is through public awareness and concern for the problem. This book departs from the optimistic attitude of many textbooks on abnormal psychology in its explicit suggestion that continued progress is far from inevitable, and may be unlikely.

Our knowledge of care for the psychologically disturbed in ancient Israel, Greece, and Rome is based on legal codes, philosophical writings, plays, and fragmentary references in the Bible.[6] This information permits several generalities of interest to modern psychology. First, the disturbed individual was considered to be the responsibility of the family, not the state. Plato expressed this attitude as follows: "If a man is mad, he shall not be at large in the city but his relatives shall keep him at home in any way which they can; or if not, let them pay a penalty." Second, the disturbed individual was afforded little legal protection against abuse. Family members could hire a guardian, confine the disturbed person to the house, or restrain him or her as they saw fit. In fact, the

[6] Aesculapius and his followers built temples across Greece for the healing of the sick. These temples were privately supported and turned away many who sought admittance. A major reason for denying treatment was fear of failure in cases of severe illness. This prudent although ethically questionable procedure insured artificially high success rates—the Aesculapian cult influenced Greek medicine for centuries. Hippocrates denounced the practice of treating only the relatively easy cases (Alexander & Selesnick, 1966).

primary concern of public laws was to protect the community against offensive acts the disturbed person might commit. The disturbed person in ancient Rome could not buy property, make or witness a will, marry, or even expect repayment on loans. Roman law stipulated a means by which the children of a disturbed person could acquire their parent's property. Third, care for disturbed people differed on the basis of social class: Poor people often were condemned to the streets, whereas wealthier people were more likely to be kept at home. Fourth, public attitude toward people who exhibited unusual behavior was one of scorn, as suggested by references to children mocking madmen who walked the streets. Fifth, the medical profession was considered responsible for the diagnosis and treatment of disturbed people. However, only the well-to-do could afford medical advice. Finally, there was a shortage of physicians, and the number of people seeking help was greater than those for whom help was available.

European Mental "Hospitals"

The persecution of disturbed women (and many nondisturbed women) as witches has already been discussed. Our concern now is with another significant development that began during the Middle Ages, the emergence of mental hospitals in Europe. From the perspective of some historians, this development was progressive and humanitarian (e.g., Schneck, 1960). From the perspective of the disturbed individual, a new form of torture had emerged.

Although a mental hospital had been established in Jerusalem as early as A.D. 490, the hospitalization of disturbed people in any significant numbers began in Europe in the thirteenth and fourteenth centuries. This development is of considerable importance because it represented a change from the concept of family responsibility to that of state responsibility.

Insane and acutely disturbed, dangerous people were admitted to general hospitals in the fourteenth century. In 1326, a madhouse was erected in Germany; in 1403, the Hospital of St. Mary of Bethlehem, from whose name the word *bedlam* was derived, admitted six insane persons. A general criterion for admission was that the person constituted a danger to himself and/or to others. Moreover, each town admitted only persons who resided in that town, flogging and returning cases from other localities. Hospital records indicate that clothes and other services were provided for inmates; public funds also were used to send patients on pilgrimages to become healed. Initially the church tended to view donations to such hospitals as charity, thereby providing the donor with an improved position for gaining admittance to heaven.

From the fourteenth century to the seventeenth, the trend was increasingly toward specialized hospitals for the psychologically disturbed. This separation of the psychologically disturbed from the physically ill was supported by reformers during the Reformation. The costs of providing the additional institutions was kept down by transforming existing institutions, such as former houses for lepers, into mental hospitals.

In a penetrating and well-documented analysis, Rosen (1968) has explained the nature of the seventeenth-century European mental hospital in terms of increased unemployment and poverty. To a historically unprecedented extent, the established order was threatened by large numbers of poor vagrants who roamed the countryside begging for food and money. Many of these beggars sought admittance to hospitals where food and lodging were available, creating increased public concern for methods to distinguish between those who were truly ill and those who were malingering to obtain free food. Mental hospitals became overcrowded, and their character was transformed, combining in one institution aspects of a penal institution to punish idleness, an asylum to provide help, and a workshop to help pay for costs and to force the idle to work. With the rise of mercantilism, the church considered idleness a sin. Restraint, floggings, and beatings were common in many European mental hospitals. In 1788 Jean Columbier described Salpêtrière, the largest mental hospital in France, and possibly in all of Europe:

> Thousands of lunatics are locked up in prisons without anyone even thinking of administering the slightest remedy. The half mad are mingled with those who are totally deranged, those who rage with those who are quiet; some are in chains, while others are free in their prison. Finally, unless nature comes to their aid by curing them, the duration of their misery is life-long, for unfortunately, the illness does not improve but only grows worse [Rosen, 1968, p. 151].

Fortunately, not all psychologically troubled persons were confined in mental hospitals. The Tom O'Bedlams were discharged patients from Bethlehem Hospital who roamed the English countryside with state licenses to beg. They appear to have been tolerated by the general public.

The abuses of the mental hospital inspired several important reformers. In 1409 the humanitarian Valencia unshackled mental patients and established a model mental hospital that became famous throughout Europe. In 1563 John Weyer attacked the theory that witchcraft existed, proposing a theory of illness instead. In 1774 the monarch of Tuscany, Leopoldo, decreed a humane law for the psychologically disturbed. But reform was the exception, not the rule. The reforms rarely survived much beyond the lifetime of the reformer, so that conditions deteriorated until some new reformer appeared.

The seventeenth century is sometimes referred to as the Age of Reason. It was during this period that interest flourished in the humanities, the sciences, and the arts. This was the height of the Renaissance, a period of intellectual rebirth in Europe. In the Age of Reason, the psychologically disturbed were increasingly viewed as "madmen" who had lost their reason. This view provided yet another rationale for scorn and degradation; it is no virtue to be seen as irrational in a society that considers rationality a supreme virtue. Mental patients were admitted to hospitals by civilian authorities, chained to walls, and flogged frequently for even minor infractions of rigid hospital rules.

Moral Treatment

In addition to the use of restraints and flogging, overcrowding in mental hospitals reached extraordinary proportions by the eighteenth century. After only four years of operation, the Hospital General in Paris had 6,000 inmates. Similar conditions existed in hospitals throughout Europe. It was in reaction to such conditions that Pinel, often considered the father of moral treatment,

Throughout history there have been many reformers who tried to improve the conditions in state hospitals for the psychologically troubled. Phillipe Pinel (1745–1826), the French psychiatrist, is shown removing the chains of mental patients at the Hospital of Salpêtrière in Paris. In the United States today the quality of care given to mental patients depends in part on the willingness of citizens to pay the taxes necessary to support decent living conditions. (Lithograph by Goupil & Co. after a painting by Tony Robert-Fleury. Reprinted by permission of Historical Pictures Service; Chicago, Illinois.)

freed the patients at Bicêtre and later at Salpêtrière. William Tuke (1732–1822), an admirer of Pinel, founded a humanitarian retreat at York, England.

The latter part of the eighteenth century witnessed the beginnings of moral treatment. The underlying rationale was that the psychologically troubled suffered from mental diseases and should be regarded as sick people rather than as sinners. Moral treatment consisted of a good diet, social support, and rest in a pleasant environment. Moral treatment lasted for about fifty years.

Moral Treatment in America

The American colonists established few hospitals. Mentally ill persons who came to the attention of civil authorities were usually imprisoned. Some were kept in dungeons into which no light penetrated; most were restrained and occasionally flogged.

Dorothea L. Dix (1802–1887) conducted one of the most extensive and successful social reforms ever, creating thirty-two humane hospitals for the psychologically troubled. (Engraved by R. G. Teitze for *Century Magazine.* Reprinted by permission of Historical Pictures Services; Chicago, Illinois.)

Benjamin Rush is remembered as the father of American psychiatry, a signer of the Declaration of Independence, and as a controversial advocate of bloodletting treatment for physical diseases. In order to improve care for the mentally ill in America, Rush built a new wing to the Pennsylvania Hospital in Philadelphia. Although he believed that abnormality was caused by brain lesions produced by diseased arteries, some of his treatments were psychological in nature. Riese noted that, "There is a great need for emphasizing the obvious discrepancy between Rush's anatomic concept of mental disease and his major therapeutic actions which never denied the primarily psychologic approach and had their own perfect logic without basis in neuroanatomy" (1967, p. 111). Rush's treaments were thus a combination of physical and psychological methods even though his theory of causation was somatogenic. Although several of Rush's treatments inflicted physical pain on his patients, when viewed

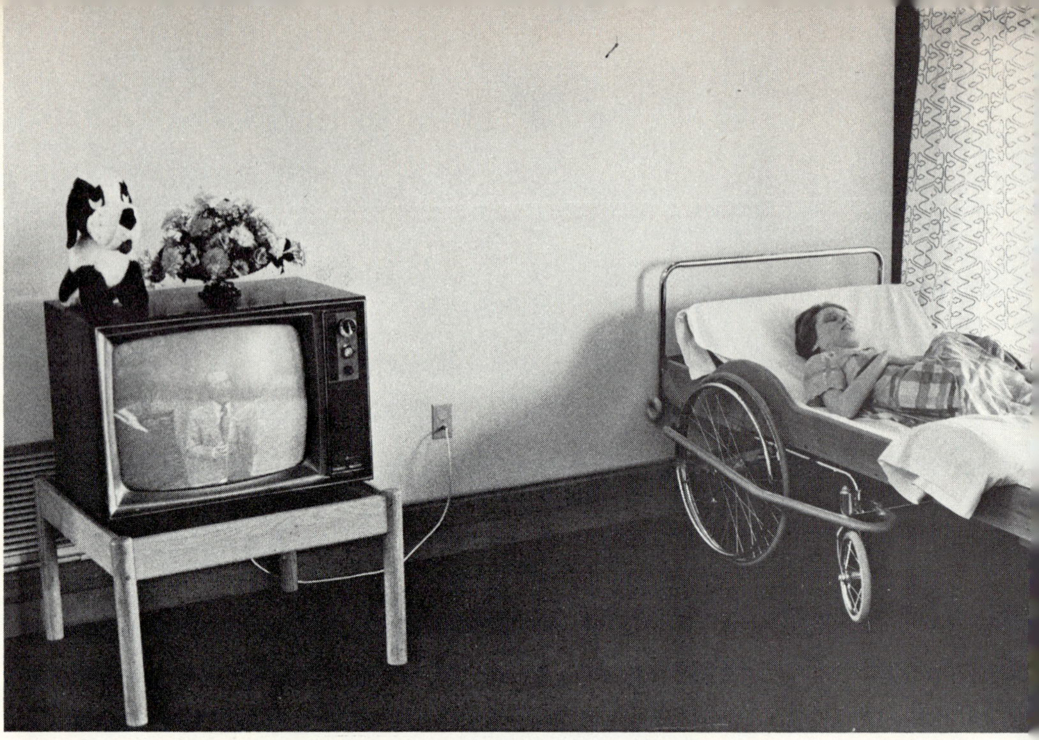

Although improvements in some physical facilities have been substantial, patient care in many mental hospitals remains custodial. (Photo by Burk Uzzle; Magnum Photos, Inc.)

in the context of his time, his overall influence was humanitarian. For example, it was Rush who installed bathrooms for patients in the Pennsylvania Hospital.

In 1841 Dorothea Lynde Dix (1802–1887) observed the inhumane suffering of insane persons in the jails and almshouses of New England. No ordinary individual, Ms. Dix conducted one of the most extensive and successful social reforms in all history. She traveled throughout the United States awakening consciences, raising money, and building 32 humane hospitals for the psychologically disabled. Her influence was such that she appeared before the Congress of the United States and the Parliament of England.

During the early nineteenth century, moral treatment became a major force in American mental hospitals. The emphasis was on a community of patients and staff within the mental hospital, on occupational therapy, on staff respect for the mental patient as a human being, and on the courtesies of civilized and social life (Bockoven, 1963). Moral treatment was successful: Between 1833 and 1852, the Worcester (Massachusetts) State Hospital reported "cures" for 60 to 70 per cent of its patients.

However, the decline of moral treatment in American hospitals was well underway by the time of the Civil War. An influx of foreign immigrants aroused the underlying racial prejudices of New Englanders, such prejudice operating in direct opposition to the goals of moral treatment. The populations of the newly created mental hospitals increased until they housed more people than their intended capacities. Conditions once again deteriorated. From the Civil War to the middle of the twentieth century, custodial care was the primary form of treatment in most large mental hospitals in the United States. In other words, mental patients lived in overcrowded hospitals in which they were fed, sometimes bathed, and often bored.

As a result of the rise of academic psychology, medical psychiatry, and social work during the twentieth century, the problems of increased numbers of mental patients were brought to the attention of energetic professionals. Reform was once again the order of the day. In 1955 the United States Congress passed the Mental Health Study Act. This act established the Joint Commission on Mental Illness and Mental Health, which undertook a five-year study of existing facilities for servicing the mentally ill. The commission's report led to the establishment of community mental health centers, thereby synthesizing the ancient doctrine of family responsibility with a modern doctrine of state responsibility. During the 1960s, community mental health centers were established across the United States. Today such centers are recognized as providing important services, although it is also recognized that they provide fewer services than current needs demand.

Large state hospitals still exist. The economic recession and high inflation of the early and middle 1970s once again threaten the quality of care that is being provided. Only the most agitated mental patients are still restrained, but custodial care is still widely prevalent throughout the United States. Although it would be misleading not to conclude that some important progress has been made, the fact is that such progress has been modest. The current status of the delivery of mental health services in the United States is discussed in detail in Chapter 9.

LEGAL ISSUES

Issues of liberty are exceedingly complex when there is a conflict of interest between the individual and the society. On the one hand, laws governing the mentally ill should protect society against insane acts; on the other hand, the mentally ill as well as those mistakenly labeled mentally ill must be protected against the abuses of society. Of course, it is the responsibility of the courts to decide the circumstances under which individual rights will prevail and those under which they will be curtailed. In making such decisions, the courts have sought opinions from psychologists and other professionals.

Several legal issues will be discussed here: involuntary hospitalization, the rights of patients in mental hospitals, competency to stand trial, and the defense of insanity. In general, laws governing these proceedings are enacted by state legislatures. However, the United States Constitution guarantees the right to due process, and this means that all legal proceedings must be conducted in accordance with nonarbitrary, nondiscriminatory, and standard procedures. For example, the individual must be notified of the proceeding and must be given a fair chance to reply to any allegations. Thus, if a state committed someone to a mental hospital without a hearing, the individual could appeal the commitment to a federal court under the due process clause.

Coercive Commitment

Coercive commitment refers to hospitalization against one's will. The period of hospitalization is often unspecified and may last as long as a lifetime. The ways in which states can abuse coercive commitment were popularized in the 1860s by Mrs. E. T. W. Packard (Schneider, 1972). Mrs. Packard claimed that she was not mentally ill but instead had been "railroaded" into commitment. She popularized her protest and, for the first time in the United States, awakened public fears of the possibility of arbitrary commitment of normal persons. Although Packard's efforts resulted in some new legislation, it was not until the 1960s that the legal profession began to take seriously the questions of who was being committed, for what reasons, and by what authority.

Every state in the country has statutes that permit the state to force an individual into a mental hospital and, thereby, deprive that person of liberty and the right to earn an income. These statutes have been justified on two grounds. First, it has been argued that the state has a parental function in which it can act to help people even if the people supposedly being helped do not want help. In this view, coercive commitment is justified on the grounds that the state can intervene to provide treatment to the mentally ill. Second, it has been argued that the state's police power entitles it to protect society from dangerous acts that are expressions of mental illness. In this view, the primary purpose of hospitalization is to confine dangerous people.

The arguments for coercive commitment based on benefit to the individual committed are unconvincing. The presumed benefit to the individual is at best intangible and vague. There is no evidence that being in a hospital is therapeutic. If anything, the available evidence suggests that hospitalization per se may be harmful because it provides prolonged exposure to a sterile environment and hence to boredom. Many mental patients receive no treatment at all except for drugs that they could easily receive on an out-patient basis. Although it sometimes may be true that hospitalization can protect a self-abusive person from himself, or that some psychotics may receive drug treatment in hospitals they would have refused as out-patients, coercive hospitalization provides no tangible benefits to most individuals who are hospitalized.

Although laws governing coercive commitment often are defended on grounds of benefit to the individual, in most cases the real basis for commitment concerns the benefit to society of confining someone who is believed to be dangerous (Brooks, 1974). In an influential article, Livermore, Malmquist, and Meehl (1968) noted two hazards to individual liberty from laws that permit the coercive commitment of persons judged to be both mentally ill and dangerous. First, the concept of mental illness is vague and, hence, can be used arbitrarily. Thus, anyone alleged to be mentally ill could reasonably argue that he was being denied due process on the grounds that the assertion of mental illness is vague and arbitrary. Second, it is difficult to determine when an individual is dangerous to others because it is difficult to predict future behavior. Most people who are mentally ill are dangerous neither to others nor to themselves.

Not only are the criteria for coercive commitment vague, but also the procedures for commitment have been criticized because they do not guarantee the proper safeguards of due process. A person charged with a crime risks a substantial loss of liberty if convicted; for this reason, our legal system attempts to provide the accused with procedural guarantees of a fair trial designed to minimize conviction on factually inaccurate information, prejudice, and misinterpretation of the laws. A person suspected of being dangerous and mentally ill also risks a substantial loss of liberty if committed and, hence, should have the same procedural protection against factually inaccurate findings, prejudice, and misinterpretation of the laws. In many instances, however, this protection has been inadequate.

The best way to ameliorate the problems of coercive commitment is unclear. Szasz has proposed the abolishment of coercive commitment, and there is some support for this view. Brooks (1974) cogently points out, however, that the public is unlikely to support the abolishment of commitment. Moreover, the abolishment of coercive commitment would probably result in the prosecution of mental patients for crimes—we might well end up renaming the Jones State Mental Hospital the Jones State Prison for Crimes Related to Mental Illness. Somehow, we need to clarify the criteria for commitment and provide better safeguards against abuse.

Rights of Mental Patients

Once committed, the mental patient loses his rights to vote, to marry, and to enter into legal contracts. In some states, the authorities are empowered to sterilize mental patients (Ennis & Siegel, 1973). In recent years many lawyers and concerned professionals have attempted to improve this situation by guaranteeing each patient a bill of rights. Two areas of particular concern in such bills are the right to receive treatment when desired and the right to refuse treatment.

As noted, one of the conventional reasons for coercive commitment is that the individual is mentally ill and needs treatment. Yet many patients committed to receive treatment in fact receive nothing beyond custodial care and drug administration. Consequently, there are an increasing number of suits in which patients demand compensation for having been hospitalized without treatment, demand to be released, or demand both damages and release. For example, in 1961 a New York patient sued that state claiming that his hospitalization would have been briefer if he had been provided proper psychiatric care (*Whitree* v. *New York,* 290 NYS). The plaintiff was awarded $300,000 in damages.

The landmark case of *Wyatt* v. *Stickney* involved a civil action in which the American Psychological Association was one of several professional groups to sponsor the suit as "friends of the court." At issue was the unsatisfactory quality of the care given to involuntarily committed mental patients at Bryce Hospital and at Searcy Hospital in Alabama. The court found that "many conditions, such as nontherapeutic, uncompensated work assignments, and the absence of any semblance of privacy, constituted dehumanizing factors contributing to the degeneration of the patients' self-esteem. The physical facilities at Bryce were overcrowded and plagued by fire and other emergency hazards. The court also found that most staff members were poorly trained and that staffing ratios were so inadequate as to render administration of effective treatment impossible" (*Wyatt* v. *Stickney,* civil action no. 3195-N). Judge Frank Johnson ruled that involuntarily committed mental patients have a constitutional right to treatment and proper care and ordered the state of Alabama to implement a highly detailed set of reforms.

Competency to Stand Trial

Competency to stand trial means that the defendant is able to understand the nature of the charges, is able to understand proceedings during a trial, and has the mental capacity to prepare an adequate defense. For example, a person who is profoundly retarded, deaf, and dumb is obviously incompetent to stand trial. The practice has been for such people to be committed to mental hospitals and for charges against them to be dropped. No trial is held. Unfortunately, some court-appointed psychiatrists have interpreted "incompetency" in a very broad manner; some intellectually capable people have been diagnosed as schizophrenic, declared incompetent to stand trial, and involuntarily committed to mental hospitals for life, when, if they had been tried and convicted, they might have gone to prison for only a few years.

On June 7, 1972, the United States Supreme Court ruled on the landmark case of *Jackson* v. *Indiana.* Jackson was a severely retarded, deaf mute who could not read, write, or effectively communicate. He was accused of having committed two robberies involving a total of about ten dollars and was found unfit to stand trial. Although the state of Indiana said it had no facilities for teaching Jackson to communicate, Jackson was committed to a mental hospital without a civil commitment hearing. Jackson's lawyer contended that the defendant was in effect given a life sentence even though he had never been convicted of any crime. Although the Indiana courts upheld the decision, the U.S. Supreme Court ruled that a defendent cannot be held for more than a reasonable period of time necessary to determine competency and that, if competency cannot be forseen in the immediate future, the defendent must be set free. Thus, it is no longer legal to incarcerate indefinitely an accused person on the basis of a mental competency examination.

Insanity Defense

Most states recognize at least two conditions that excuse individuals from the responsibility of committing a crime and one condition that justifies crime. A crime is justified when it is committed in self-defense. A crime is excusable when it is based on an innocent mistake of fact or when the individual is insane. *Insanity,* then, is a legal concept that refers to a condition that excuses people from the responsibility of a crime. In contrast, *mental illness* is a quasi-scientific concept that refers to the conditions described in DSM-II. Because the presence of mental illness is by itself often an insufficient excuse for a crime, it is inappropriate to equate mental illness and insanity.

Insanity pleas are offered when a defendent has been found competent to stand trial, admits to having committed the alleged crime, and seeks to escape responsibility on the grounds of having been insane at the time the crime was committed. If the defense is successful, the defendent is found innocent and is probably committed to a mental hospital. Livermore and Meehl (1967), for example, discussed a hypothetical case of a mentally subnormal person with an IQ in the severely deficient range. Having seen neighborhood children play cops and robbers with toy guns, the retardate plays with his father's real gun and kills another person. Given that the retardate lacks the ability to discriminate between toy and real guns and to understand what death means, many would consider it unfair to convict the retardate of manslaughter. Under such circumstances, a defense of insanity would be indicated and almost certainly would be successful.

Although we can imagine cases in which most people would consider an insanity plea justifiable, many cases are much more difficult to decide than that of a retardate who does not understand what he is doing. It is desirable, therefore, to have precise guidelines for inferring insanity. Several guidelines have been proposed. The McNaghten rule states that a person is insane if, at the time of the crime, he either did not know what he was doing or could not distinguish right from wrong. It was formulated in 1843 in a murder trial in England, and it is probably the most influential of the tests for insanity. The test is relatively precise and nonarbitrary, but it has been criticized as including too few cases (Brooks, 1974). The ALI Model Penal Code test stipulates that a person is insane if, at the time of the crime, he either could not resist commission of the crime (irresistible impulse test) or did not appreciate emotionally the immorality of the act even though he knew it was wrong. The irresistible impulse rule is vague because psychologists and psychiatrists cannot assess the irresistibility of an impulse in an objective manner (see Brooks, 1974). The Durham rule stipulates that the presence of certain mental illnesses per se is a sufficient basis for inferring insanity. It equates certain forms of mental illness with insanity and has been criticized on the grounds that it includes too many cases. Introduced in 1954, the Durham rule has been modified to include fewer mental illnesses, and it has declined in influence.

SUMMARY

The history of abnormal psychology has been considered from the perspectives of the scientist and the patient. In the former regard, the history of abnormal psychology is one of considerable theoretical diversity in the explanation of various abnormal behaviors. The common theme of *moral-religious positions* is that abnormality is the result of an evil force. The *somatogenic hypothesis* maintains that psychological abnormality is caused by physical diseases. The *psychogenic hypothesis* maintains that psychological abnormality is often caused by environmental stress and by inappropriate learning. Throughout history, each of these views has gained, lost, and regained popularity.

With the rise of academic psychology during the early half of the twentieth century, basic theoretical differences were increasingly refined. Today it is possible to distinguish five approaches, or ways of studying and thinking about abnormality. The biological approach is the purest contemporary expression of the somatogenic hypothesis. However, most present-day advocates of the importance of biological factors regard them as contributory causes to many types of abnormality and as primary causes of only a relatively few disorders. The psychoanalytic approach is neither somatogenic nor psychogenic but instead regards mind and body as an integrated whole. The social-learning approach is the clearest example of contemporary thought concerning the psychogenic causation of abnormality; this approach views most types of abnormality as caused by inappropriate learning. The origins of the phenomenological approach are in modern philosophy; like psychoanalysis, phenomenology stresses the integration of mind (experience) and body and is thus neither somatogenic nor psychogenic in its view of causation. The community approach is concerned with the effects of the large social environment on the definition, development, and treatment of abnormality.

The intellectual history of abnormal psychology is one of the ebb and flow of recurring ideas, with the eventual refinement of theoretical diversity into the several approaches described. The human history of abnormal psychology is one of the coming and passing of various types of torture, degradation, stigma, and abandonment. The rise of mental hospitals in Europe was at first humanitarian, but economic recessions quickly led to poor people seeking admittance to mental hospitals for food and shelter. This pattern of economic adversities reversing initial reforms in the treatment and care of the mentally ill is evident throughout history. It remains to be seen whether or not the recent reforms achieved by the community mental health movement will prove long-lasting.

Historically, laws concerning the mentally ill have been enacted to protect society from insane acts, with much less concern for the protection of the mentally ill from the abuses of society. However, in the last decade or so heightened interest in the rights of mental patients has appeared. In the case of *Wyatt* v. *Stickney,* Judge Frank Johnson ruled that involuntarily committed mental patients have a constitutional right to treatment and proper care.

Although often thought of as a young science, abnormal psychology is really one of the oldest of all sciences. However, the actual causes of most syndromes have yet to be identified, and there is still a need to improve the quality of care of hospitalized mental patients. The areas in which the greatest degree of progress has been made is that of the development of effective treatments.

Chapter 3

The Concept of Abnormality

And to imagine a language means to imagine a form of life.

WITTGENSTEIN (1953, remark 19)

The question "What is abnormality?" has scientific, clinical, legal, and ethical significance. A definition of abnormality has scientific significance because it provides the basis for classifying various behaviors, thoughts, and feelings into a category called abnormal. The clinical significance of a definition of abnormality concerns the criteria for initiation and termination of treatment. An adequate definition of abnormality may also have legal and ethical implications insofar as it permits clarifications of the criteria for coercive commitment.

There have been many discussions of the definition of abnormality (Adams, 1964; Ausubel, 1961; Ellis, 1967; London & Rosenhan, 1969; Mowrer, 1960; Redlich, 1952; Reiss, 1972; Szasz, 1961; Ullmann & Krasner, 1968; Wegrocki, 1939; Werry, 1965). This chapter reviews several of these previous definitions and proposes a new definition that attempts to synthesize the ideas of previous theorists.

LOGICAL PRESUPPOSITIONS

The task of defining abnormality would be pointless if any arbitrary definition were acceptable. Suppose someone were to claim that abnormality is any instance of finger waving. This would be obviously foolish, and the fact that we can recognize it as such implies that we already know many examples of behaviors that are and are not abnormal. Before we begin to try to define abnormality, we already agree on some behaviors to which the labels *abnormal* and *normal* apply. The purpose of defining abnormality is to state why we consider these behaviors abnormal or normal.

The question "What is abnormality?" presupposes that we can divide behavior into three categories: clearly abnormal, clearly normal, and neither clearly abnormal nor clearly normal. As shown in Figure 3-1, the set of behaviors and beliefs that is universally acknowledged as abnormal and must be de-

Figure 3-1
Universe of behavior. The question "What is abnormality?" presupposes that we already know paradigm examples of normal and abnormal behavior. Attempts to define abnormality are attempts to identify what is true of behaviors classified as normal that is false of behavior classified as abnormal or vice versa.

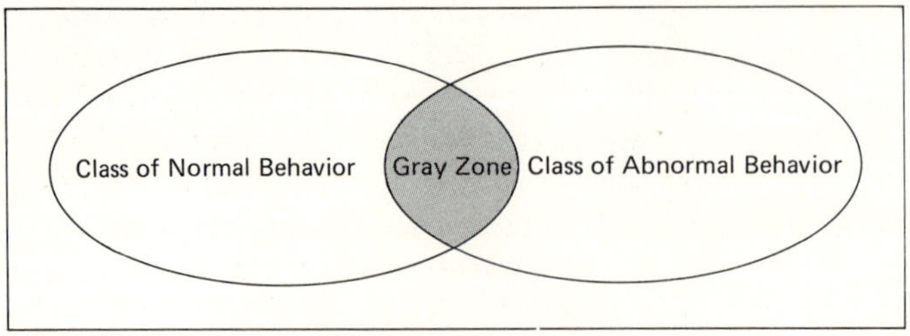

fined as such by any adequate definition will be termed the *class of abnormal behaviors.* The set of behaviors and beliefs that is universally acknowledged as normal and must be defined as such by any adequate definition will be termed the *class of normal behaviors.* The set of behaviors and beliefs about which there is debate will be termed *gray zone behaviors.* As a result of agreement on an adequate definition, we may come to consider some of the gray zone behaviors as normal and others as abnormal.

It is important to recognize that these three classes are groupings of behaviors, not people. As will be discussed in Chapter 19, some abnormal behaviors are exhibited by "normal" people, and a considerable degree of normal behavior is often exhibited by people who are labeled mentally ill.

DEFINITIONS OF ABNORMALITY

Mental Illness Definition

Many psychologists have objected to the concept of mental illness because historically it has been associated with attempts to justify medical supremacy over psychologists in the treatment of the psychologically troubled. Our concern here, however, is with the adequacy of the mental illness concept as a definition of abnormality rather than with the need for society to recognize that psychiatrists are not necessarily better qualified than psychologists to treat people who are psychologically troubled.

The concept of mental illness is vague because it has been interpreted in different ways:

1. Some theorists interpret the concept of mental illness as implying that abnormal behaviors are expressions of physical illness (see Szasz, 1961). This definition of mental illness is vague because what constitutes a physical illness is unclear. Most psychologically troubled people do not suffer from what we usually consider to be a physical illness; that is, they do not suffer from infections or broken bones or any obvious brain lesions. Moreover, a behavior cannot be assumed to be an illness merely because it is biologically caused. For example, the identification of a biological component to homosexuality would not by itself imply that homosexuality is an illness any more than would the identification of a physical basis for height imply that either tall or short people are physically diseased.

2. The concept of mental illness can be interpreted as implying that a particular type of classification system can be constructed. Diagnosis of a physical disease usually implies valid statements concerning etiology, prognosis, and treatment. For example, a diagnosis of pneumonia implies the presence of a particular bacterial infection (etiological statement), a predictable progression of the illness (prognostic statement), and the use of antibiotic drug treatment. If the classification of abnormal behaviors also permitted valid statements concerning etiology, prognosis, and treatment, it may be possible to consider the classification category a definition of a disease. However, the diagnosis of a particular kind of mental disease rarely implies any valid statements. The cause of most mental illnesses is unknown, the likely progression of the dis-

order is often unpredictable, and the appropriate treatment is only sometimes suggested by the diagnosis.

3. Another possible interpretation of the concept of mental illness is that we need to know both the nature of a behavior and the motivation for its occurrence before we can determine whether or not the behavior is abnormal (see Wegrocki, 1939; White, 1964). This mental illness definition implies that a behavior can be said to be abnormal and hence an expression of mental illness only when particular kinds of causal origins have been identified. For example, fearing that someone is about to hurt you is abnormal when it is motivated by your own unconscious hostility toward that person, but the same fear is considered normal when it results from a realistic appraisal of the other person's intentions. Thus, it is necessary to consider the motivation for a behavior in order to classify the behavior as abnormal or normal. However, this interpretation of the concept of mental illness is vague because it does not specify clearly what types of motivation or causal origins are sufficient to classify the behavior as abnormal.

The concept of mental illness is vague because it is unclear which of the preceding interpretations is to be taken as the "true" definition of mental illness. All three definitions, moreover, are problematic.

Szasz's Myth of Mental Illness

Szasz (1961, 1970) maintains that mental illness is a myth, that belief in the existence of mental illness has fostered social and ethical problems, and that the treatment of mental illness by the mental health movement is analogous to the treatment of witchcraft during the Inquisition. This view of mental illness as a myth is based on the contention that abnormal behavior is a moral and social problem rather than a medical one. According to Szasz, abnormal behavior is best viewed as a problem in living.

Szasz maintains that the concept of mental illness obscures the role of ethical values in psychotherapy. He believes that psychotherapists are in the business of changing and controlling another person's beliefs, values, and behavior. In this view, therapists must resolve the following ethical issues: (1) When is it ethical to change another person's values and beliefs? (2) Whose values and beliefs should be promoted and at whose expense; that is, should the therapist promote the values of his client or those of society? Szasz believes that the concept of mental illness obscures these ethical issues because it conceptualizes changing another person's values and behavior as healing the sick. Although we may sometimes question the ethics of changing another person's values and behavior, we rarely question the ethics of healing the sick.

Szasz maintains that the potential for abusing the patient's values is minimal in private practice but considerable in institutional practice. In private practice the client pays the therapist and has the option of discontinuing treatment at any time. These circumstances create a social situation in which the therapist is likely to be respectful of the client's values and is unlikely to experiment with possibly unethical techniques. When mental care is administered by state institutions, however, the therapist is paid by society and is thus more likely to promote societal values regardless of the individual's values and needs.

According to Szasz, a particularly objectionable consequence of the concept of mental illness is the social role it has manufactured. Much like the slave whose self-image and habits have been so affected that he rejects offers of freedom in favor of continued slavery, many people have learned to accept themselves as mentally ill. Even when hospitalization is not an issue, people labeled mentally ill may tend to fulfill society's expectations of a sick person; for example, they may act in an irresponsible manner.

Szasz maintains that the present day mental health movement is analogous to the Inquisition. [This argument is one-sided because Szasz discusses possible similarities between the two social movements but virtually ignores possible dissimilarities (Reiss, 1972).] According to Szasz, similarities between the mental health movement and the Inquisition include false beliefs (e.g., in mental illness and in witchcraft) as well as the motivation of both Inquisitors and psychiatrists to help the psychologically troubled. What is especially revealing in Szasz's book *The Manufacture of Madness* is his historical documentation that, as a result of theological beliefs in the existence of witchcraft and in the purifying of souls by burning bodies alive, Inquisitors actually believed they were helping witches to obtain a more rewarding afterlife.

Szasz has presented several reasons for rejecting the concept of mental illness and for defining abnormality instead as problems in living. However, both Ausubel (1961) and Reiss (1972) have found Szasz's position to be unconvincing. Ausubel believes that the concepts of mental illness and problems in living are compatible so that some problems in living are mental illnesses. For example, a person who rebels against all authority not only has a problem in living but also has a significant psychological problem that may be termed a mental illness.

Reiss's (1972) criticism of Szasz differs markedly from that of Ausubel. Reiss has maintained that the question of the existence of mental illness is a matter of semantics—Szasz and Ausubel agree on many substantive issues but disagree on what the concept of mental illness means. According to Reiss, Szasz has raised important issues that merit thoughtful analysis, but these issues are best discussed on their own merits and apart from the question of whether or not mental illness "exists." Moreover, Reiss maintains that Szasz's concept of problems in living is too general to serve as a definition of abnormal behavior because many problems in living are not usually associated with abnormality.

Social Definition of Abnormality

Ullmann and Krasner (1969) have advocated a social definition in which abnormal is whatever society labels as abnormal. In this view the classes *normal behavior* and *abnormal behavior* are distinguished by the fact that we label some behaviors abnormal and others normal. By implication, the relevant task for psychology is to study the labeling behavior of societies. Ullmann and Krasner expressed their position as follows:

> abnormality is the sort of deviance that calls for and sanctions the professional attention of psychiatrists, clinical psychologists, and other "mental health" professionals [1969 p. 1].

Is bizarre appearance alone sufficient to indicate mental illness?
(Photo by Bernard Pierre Wolff; Magnum Photos, Inc.)

> The act of labeling another person abnormal or mentally ill will in this book be considered a *social* behavior; that is, the act of designating a person as belonging to such a category is learned as an appropriate and reinforced behavior in certain situations. . . . The alternative to this position is that there is some group of behaviors that are abnormal in and of themselves [1969, p. 23].

The social definition may have been intended as an operational definition. The operational definition is a legitimate method of specifying an attribute for purposes of empirical investigation; however, it is usually circular to propose that an operational statement defines a concept. Compare these statements:

1. Intelligence is what an intelligence test measures.
2. Abnormality is what attracts the attention of mental health professionals.

As a definition of intelligence, the first statement is circular. How do we know which tests are tests of intelligence? As a definition of abnormality, the second statement is circular. How do we know which professionals are mental health professionals, and how do they know to what to attend? For example, suppose there existed a society in which almost everyone feared that the sun would fall and treated harshly those few who believed otherwise. In that society, how would we know if the people who dealt with ideological dissent were mental health professionals?

The social definition permits any behavior to be abnormal because any behavior can be called abnormal. The attractiveness of this definition is that it provides a basis for empirical research on how the label *abnormal* is actually used. Nevertheless, the social definition is problematic if offered as an expression of the meaning of the concept of abnormality. The substitution of studying labeling behavior for defining abnormality is as problematic as it would be to substitute the ways in which people learn mathematics for the discipline of mathematics.

Statistical Definition

Statistical abnormality refers to unusual, deviant behavior. This definition is attractive because it promises an objective basis for classifying abnormalities and because it expresses the reality that many abnormal behaviors are in fact unusual. But the statistical definition is inadequate for two reasons. One problem is that the statistical definition is incomplete because it does not specify the attributes along which deviance is to be judged. Another problem is that there exist a number of abnormal behaviors that are not necessarily unusual. Smoking, low self-esteem, aggression, mild depression, and prejudice are examples of what appear to be frequently occurring abnormal (psychopathological) behaviors.

London and Rosenhan (1968) have proposed a bidirectional definition in which abnormal behavior is simply rare behavior. The unique aspect of this definition is its explicit inclusion of positive abnormalities such as high levels of creativity and intelligence as proper subjects of abnormal psychology. The inclusion of positive abnormalities, however, is confusing because it is unclear why such a definition has been proposed. As Wittgenstein stated, "And to imagine a language means to imagine a form of life" (1953, remark 19). The task of defining abnormality is part of a meaningful human activity; we seek to define abnormality to understand better the basic difference between abnormal and normal behavior. Defining abnormality to include both extremes of the normal distribution obscures this purpose because it is unclear what important similarities might exist between positive and negative abnormalities to justify a concept that applies to them both.

Maladaptation

Coleman (1972) defined abnormality as maladaptive behavior. Behavior is maladaptive if it interferes with optimal functioning and with emotional growth. This definition is attractive because it emphasizes the individual's attempt to resolve psychological issues and to seek personal fulfillment. The concept of maladaptation, however, is vague and overinclusive. Virtually any behavior can be regarded as less than optimal functioning. A computational error, for example, is sometimes maladaptive, but only rarely would it be considered evidence of abnormality.

TOWARD AN ADEQUATE DEFINITION OF ABNORMALITY

Although each definition reviewed has some unique strengths and weaknesses, a general difficulty is the attempt to abstract common characteristics from many diverse abnormal behaviors. *Abnormal behaviors constitute a group so diverse that nothing is true of all abnormal behaviors that is false of all normal behaviors.*

There are at least two basic ways to define a concept. One method is to identify a set of uniquely common attributes. Consider this definition: Reinforcement is an event so that its presentation contingent on a response increases the subsequent probability of the response under similar stimulus conditions. This definition identifies a uniquely common property of reinforcement: All reinforcers have this property, and only reinforcers have this property. Definition in terms of uniquely common attributes is preferred in scientific work because it permits the highest degree of conceptual clarity. However, the preceding discussion suggests that the attempt to specify uniquely common attributes of abnormality is problematic. Either the attributes identified are so general as to be true of many normal behaviors, or they apply to only some examples of abnormality. Our inability to identify uniquely common attributes of abnormality may be attributable to a lack of knowledge, but it seems more likely to be attributable to an empirical reality—that is, nothing is uniquely common to all abnormalities.

A second method of defining concepts is available as a result of the revolutionary work of the philosopher Ludwig Wittgenstein. Wittgenstein, the most influential philosopher of this century in the United States and Great Britain, is generally unfamiliar to psychologists. This is unfortunate because his work is relevant to those interested in clarifying concepts of subjective states, of language, and of the relations between experience and language. Our present concern is with definition by what Wittgenstein called family resemblance. In the following passages Wittgenstein shows that the ordinary language concept of games is a family resemblance:

> Consider for example the proceedings that we call "games." I mean board-games, card-games, ball-games, Olympic games, and so on. What is common to them all?—Don't say: "There *must* be something common, or they would not be called 'games'"—but *look* and *see* whether there is anything common to all.—For if you look at them you will not see something that is common to *all,* but similarities, relationships, and a whole series of them at that. To repeat: don't think, but look!—Look for example at board-games, with their multifarious relationships. Now pass to card-games; here you may find many correspondences with the first group, but many common features drop out, and others appear. When we pass next to ball-games, much that is common is retained, but much is lost.—Are they all "amusing"? Compare chess with noughts and crosses. Or is there always winning and losing, competition between players? Think of patience. In ball games there is winning and losing; but when a child throws his ball at the wall and catches it again, this feature has disappeared. Look at the parts played by skill and luck; and at the difference between skill in chess and skill in tennis. Think now of games like ring-a-ring-a-roses; here is the element of amusement, but how many other characteristic features have disappeared! And we can go through the many, many other groups of games in the same way; can see how similarities crop up and disappear.
>
> And the result of this examination is: we see a complicated network of similarities overlapping and criss-crossing: sometimes overall similarities, sometimes similarities of detail.
>
> I can think of no better expression to characterize these similarities than "family

TABLE 3-1
Comparison of Definition by Abstraction and Definition by Family Resemblance*

	Concept A: Definition by Abstraction*	Concept B: Definition by Family Resemblance*
Example 1	*a b c d*	*a b c d*
Example 2	*a e f g*	*b c d e*
Example 3	*a h i j*	*c d e f*
Example 4	*a k l m*	*d e f g*
Example 5	*a n o p*	*e f a b*
Common elements:	*a*	none
Definition:	Concept A means that *a* is present.	Concept B refers to a pattern of elements *a,b . . . f.* Each element is present in only some of the examples to which concept B applies.

* Let each letter represent a different aspect, or element, of each concrete example of a concept.

resemblances"; for the various resemblances between members of a family: build, features, colour of eyes, gait, temperament, etc. etc. overlap and criss-cross in the same way.—And I shall say: 'games' form a family.[1] [1953; pp. 31–32].

As these passages show, there is nothing common to *all* games; instead there is a pattern of similarities Wittgenstein calls a family resemblance. (See Table 3-1.)

Like the concept of games, the concept of abnormality is a family resemblance. Specifically, it is proposed that abnormality is a family resemblance of the following attributes: (1) irrationality; (2) the presence of suffering; and (3) interpersonal maladaptation.

Irrationality

Irrationality (craziness) is the single most important attribute of the concept of abnormality. A belief is irrational if it is false, if the individual is in a position to know it is false, and if the individual nevertheless thinks the belief to be true or acts as if it is true. The criterion of *being in a position to know* (Ayer, 1959) means that the individual has access to compelling information indicating that the belief is false and is of sufficient intelligence to understand this information and to draw obvious inferences from it.

A false belief is either the result of error, ignorance, or irrationality. Suppose

[1] From L. Wittgenstein, *Philosophical Investigations* (New York: Macmillan Publishing Co., Inc., 1953), pp. 31–32. Quoted with permission of publisher.

an astronomer miscalculates that the sun will disintegrate. His belief that the sun will fall is based on an error. Suppose someone believes that the sun will soon fall because he lives in a primitive society in which everyone has been educated to believe this. This false belief is a result of ignorance. In both of these examples, neither individual is *in a position to know* that the sun will not fall because of access to inaccurate information. Suppose, however, that a layman in our society predicts that the sun will never rise again after Tuesday. This belief is irrational because the layman has been taught otherwise, has experienced the sun rising all of his life, and has no reasonable evidence on which to base his prediction. In brief, the layman has access to compelling data that the sun will rise on Wednesday as well as sufficient intelligence and education to understand these data.

A person who holds an irrational belief (for example, *the sun will fall Tuesday*) may exhibit behavior that expresses a rational inference from the irrational belief (e.g., prepares to die). Such inferences are sometimes referred to as the *internal logic* of the psychotic. It is also possible for a person to hold rational beliefs and yet exhibit behavior that expresses irrational beliefs; in other words, a person may not believe he holds a belief and yet he still might act as if he does. A phobic, for example, might intellectually believe that garden snakes are harmless and yet react to them with fear and avoidance—in this case, the behavioral reaction to snakes could be said to express the irrational belief that *garden snakes will hurt me.*

Irrationality, one of the attributes of the concept of abnormality, distinguishes relatively well, although not absolutely, between the classes of abnormal and normal behaviors. For example, playing baseball is a paradigm of normal behavior. Under most circumstances, there exists no empirical basis for assuming that this behavior expresses any irrational beliefs. In fact, no paradigm example of normality seems to be usually expressive of irrational beliefs. On the other hand, most abnormal behaviors could be said to express irrational beliefs. Delusions, for example, are irrational beliefs. Neurotic behavior is generally expressive of irrational beliefs such as *Authority is always right, I am worthless,* and *Everyone dislikes me* (Ellis, 1962). Homosexuality based on a fear of women is irrational because it is irrational to fear women; that is, the individual is in a position to know that women will not harm him. However, homosexuality based on sexual preference is not expressive of irrational beliefs.

Suffering

The presence of suffering (e.g., anxiety, discomfort, and/or depression) is an obvious characteristic of many abnormal behaviors. This attribute, however, is found in some instances of normal behavior. For example, a parent might suffer to provide a better life for his children. In fact, there is obviously nothing unusual about human suffering, especially when we consider the prevalence of poverty and war.

Interpersonal Maladaptation

The criterion of interpersonal maladaptation is intended to draw attention to the interpersonal consequences of many abnormal behaviors. The inclusion of this criterion is a recognition that humans are social beings who require both a

TABLE 3-2
Abnormality as a Family Resemblance*

Behavior	Defining Attribute		
	Irrationality	Suffering	Maladaptive
Abnormal Behaviors			
Anxiety neurosis	Usually	Always	Usually
Delusions	Always	Usually	Usually
Masochism	?	Always	Sometimes
Depression	Usually	Always	Usually
Smoking	Sometimes	Sometimes	Rarely
Hallucination	Sometimes	Sometimes	Sometimes
Impotence	Usually	Always	Sometimes
Gray Zone Behaviors			
Prejudice	Usually	Sometimes	Sometimes
Homosexuality	Sometimes	Sometimes	Sometimes
Aggression	Sometimes	Sometimes	Sometimes
Normal Behaviors			
Playing baseball	Rarely	Rarely	Never
Problem solving	Rarely	Sometimes	Rarely
Political dissent	Sometimes	Sometimes	Rarely
Eating dinner	Rarely	Never	Never
Sleeping at night	Never	Never	Never

* *Note:* The ratings are that the behavior and attribute are (almost always, usually, sometimes, rarely, and almost never) associated. Given the incomplete and controversial nature of the available data, probably few would agree with all of the ratings in this table. But it is unnecessary to agree entirely to appreciate the family resemblance nature of the concept of abnormality.

minimal level of social support and a sense of belonging to a social unit (see Sarason, 1974). More precisely, behaviors leading to the *absence* of a minimal level of social support are disadvantageous to the individual; similarly, behaviors leading to the absence of a psychological sense of belonging are disadvantageous to the individual. Depression is interpersonally maladaptive because it interferes with the person's ability to interact meaningfully with anyone and because it expresses a profound loss of a sense of purpose in life—the kind of purpose that comes from a psychological sense of belonging (Sarason, 1974). Aggression is not necessarily interpersonally maladaptive. It does not necessarily interfere with all interpersonal relations, as in the case of a Mafioso who loves and receives love from his wife. Nor does aggression necessarily express a profound loss of the psychological sense of belonging as in the example of comradeship among thieves. But aggression is *sometimes* interpersonally maladaptive.

Table 3-2 shows that no single attribute is *always* common to all abnormal behaviors under all circumstances in which they occur. Rather, there is a pattern of criss-crossing and an overlapping of the presence of various degrees of attributes as one looks at different types of abnormalities.

Implications

The proposed definition clarifies the concept of abnormality. Its implications are several. First, the proposed definition shows that abnormal behaviors are, in fact, similar to one another even though no one attribute is uniquely common. Second, the proposed definition does not prejudice future empirical research on the basis of a definitional issue; no particular model of abnormality is implied. Third, the proposed definition structures debate concerning the classification of gray zone behaviors. Finally, the proposed definition suggests that irrationality is a critical component of the concept of abnormality.

Some theorists have suggested that abnormal behaviors imply sin (e.g., Mowrer, 1960), whereas others have suggested that the judgment of a behavior as abnormal is a value judgment (e.g., Szasz, 1961, 1970). The philosopher Gert (1970) recently has maintained that the concept of irrationality is a basis on which we can justify not being immoral. Thus, it may be irrational to be immoral and irrational to engage in abnormal behavior. Irrationality seems to provide the common logical core in the concepts of abnormality and morality, but this does not imply that it is immoral to engage in abnormal behaviors.

SUMMARY

The question "What is abnormality" presupposes that we already know true examples of abnormal and normal behavior. The set of all behaviors that must be defined as abnormal has been termed the class of abnormal behaviors; the set of all behaviors that must be defined as normal has been termed the class of normal behaviors; the set of all behaviors that are neither clearly normal nor clearly abnormal has been termed the gray zone.

Several definitions of abnormality have been considered here, and each has been found to have its own unique strengths and weaknesses. The mental illness definition is vague partially because it has been interpreted in at least three different ways, all of which are problematical. The social definition emphasizes the general element of societal disapproval of many abnormal behaviors and alerts us to the potential danger inherent in political uses of the concept. This definition is problematical, however, because many abnormal behaviors are abnormal regardless of whether or not a society chooses to recognize this fact. The statistical definition focuses on the general element of unusualness that is characteristic of some but not all abnormal behaviors. The maladaptation definition expresses the general fact that many individuals who exhibit abnormal behavior are trying to cope with difficult life problems. However, the maladaptation definition is vague.

Abnormality has been defined as a family resemblance involving the attributes of irrationality, anxiety or suffering, and interpersonal maladaptation. That is, as we look at different examples of abnormal behavior, these attributes appear and disappear in varying degrees, forming a criss-crossing of overlapping patterns metaphorically referred to by the philosopher Wittgenstein as a family resemblance.

The definition of abnormality as a family resemblance has several implications. First, it shows that abnormal behaviors are similar to one another even though nothing is true of all abnormal behaviors that is false of all normal behaviors. Second, it structures debate concerning the classification of behaviors as abnormal versus normal. Third, it suggests that irrationality is a critical component of the concept of abnormality. Fourth, it suggests that the concepts of immorality and abnormality are related without also suggesting that abnormal behaviors are necessarily, or even usually, immoral.

Part Two

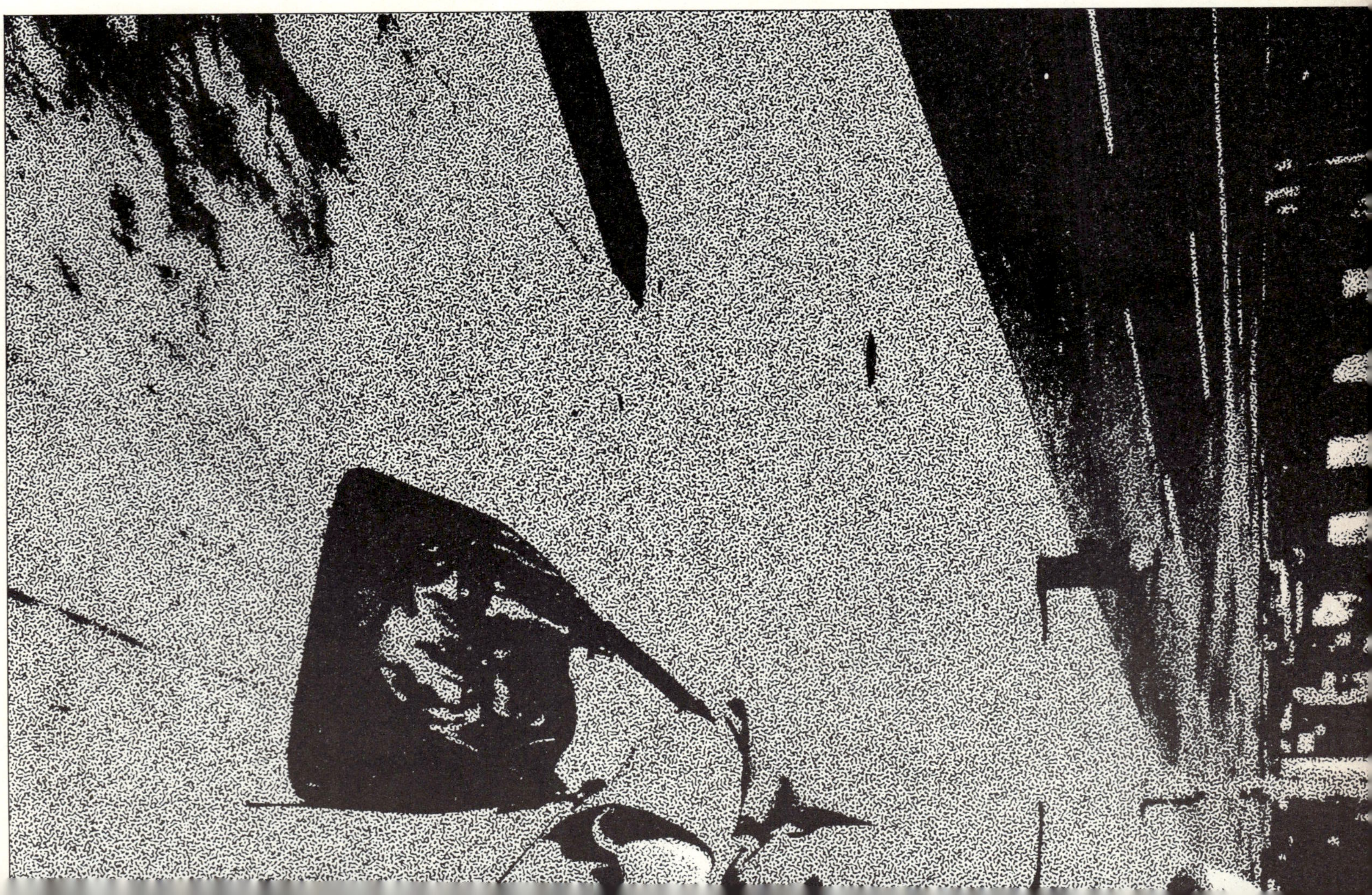

How Is Abnormality Studied and Treated?

Chapter 4

Psychological Assessment

It is clearly evident that psychological tests are currently being employed in the solution of a wide range of practical problems. One should not, however, lose sight of the fact that such tests are also serving important functions in basic research.

ANASTASI (1976)

The concept of assessment has several related meanings in psychology. On the one hand, assessment is the measurement of behavior, skills, or personality. Thus, assessment techniques (e.g., intelligence tests and projective techniques) are widely employed in basic research. On the other hand, assessment refers to the identification of patterns of abnormal behaviors. Thus, assessment techniques are used to diagnose psychological problems. When used for diagnostic purposes, assessment typically involves the administration of a battery of tests that helps the examiner to identify the presence of a particular disorder and to predict the client's suitability for therapy.

KINDS OF ASSESSMENT PROCEDURES

Observation of Behavior

One way to assess behavior is through direct observation. For example, aggressive tendencies are best assessed by observing the frequency and intensity of aggressive behavior under a variety of situations. Emotions also can be observed directly, although it sometimes takes a highly trained observer to perceive accurately someone else's feelings. Whenever it is practical to do so, direct observation of behavior is the preferred method of assessment.

Practical considerations require psychologists to be able to obtain considerable information about people in a relatively short period of time. Sometimes this can be accomplished by behavioral observations in an interview situation; for example, the client may appear depressed, express bizarre thoughts, or display inappropriate emotionality. However, when behavioral observations of a client in an office situation provide incomplete information, and when it is impractical to obtain behavioral observations of the client's behavior in natural settings, it is often necessary to rely on assessment techniques other than the direct observation of behavior.

Interview Techniques

One method for obtaining significant information about an individual in a relatively efficient manner is to ask the individual relevant questions. People, however, are often poor observers of their own behavior; they not only tend to forget or perhaps never even notice significant events, but also tend to distort information, particularly information that is emotionally charged. For these reasons, interviewers need considerable skill in order to obtain accurate information, and they must be sensitive to significant gaps and distortions in the responses of interviewees.

Interviews vary in the degree to which they are structured. An interview is highly structured when the interviewer uses the same form of questioning and collects the same type of information from each respondent. For example, an investigator interested in the manner in which parents reward and punish chil-

TABLE 4-1
Four Kinds of Psychological Tests. (Each is theoretically capable of standardization.)

	Structured Response	Unstructured Response
Structured stimulus	Minnesota Multiphasic Personality Inventory (MMPI)	Wechsler Intelligence Scale for Children (WISC)/ Wechsler Adult Intelligence Scale (WAIS) Stanford-Binet, Bender
Unstructured (ambiguous) stimulus	Multiple choice, Rorschach	Sentence completion, Thematic Apperception Test (TAT), figure drawings, Rorschach

dren's behavior might ask the same questions of each parent in the study. By contrast, unstructured interviews permit the interviewer to pursue different lines of questioning with different individuals.

A person seeking therapy at a clinic or hospital is likely to participate in an *intake interview.* The purposes of this interview are to obtain general information about the nature and seriousness of the person's problems and to obtain personal history data. If preliminary information warrants it, a *mental status* interview may be conducted. The purposes of the mental status interview are to assess the nature and extent of the abnormal behaviors that may be present; a preliminary diagnosis may be made at the conclusion of this interview.

The issues and techniques of diagnostic interviewing are beyond the scope of this book. The interested reader may consult Sullivan (1954) *The Psychiatric Interview* or Benjamin (1969) *The Helping Interview.*

Psychological Tests

Another method of assessing abnormal behavior is provided by psychological tests. A psychological test can be thought of as involving the presentation of stimuli (e.g., questions, drawings, and/or inkblots) and the elicitation of responses (e.g., answers, stories, and/or drawings). As shown in Table 4-1, both stimuli and responses vary along a structured-unstructured dimension. The question "What are the colors in the American flag?" presents a highly structured stimulus but allows for any response. The Minnesota Multiphasic Personality Inventory (MMPI), which is a personality test, presents structured stimuli (questions) and structures the response by permitting the choice of only one of three possible answers. Other psychological tests present unstructured or ambiguous stimuli. For example, the subject may be asked to react to an inkblot or to an ambiguous picture.

Psychological procedures employing unstructured (ambiguous) formats have been termed *projective techniques* because responses to unstructured stimuli have been assumed to be determined in part by personality needs,

The client reassembles blocks to match the figures. This is an example of a structured question. (Photo by Constantine Manos and Alex Webb; Magnum Photos, Inc.)

drives, and values. Because there are no right or wrong answers in reaction to an inkblot or ambiguous picture, the subject's response has been assumed to reveal his personality, needs, and emotions. As Zubin, Eron, and Schumer concluded: "Generally, then, projection, as applied to projective techniques, seems more likely to be a process by which *S*, when he is presented with a number of ambiguous or semi-ambiguous stimuli and asked to make sense, order or to give meaning to these stimuli, does so while drawing on a reservoir of his own needs, emotions, feelings, or even level of knowledge" (1965, p. 5). Examples of projective tests discussed later in this chapter are the Rotter Incomplete Sentence Test, the Rorschach, the Thematic Apperception Test (TAT), and figure drawings.

REQUIREMENTS OF A STANDARD PSYCHOLOGICAL TEST

Any psychological test is theoretically capable of standardization regardless of whether the stimuli and responses are structured or unstructured. As shown in Box 4-1, a standard psychological test includes a uniform method of test administration, an objective scoring system, norms, and demonstrated reliability and validity.

An example of a particularly good standard test is the Scholastic Aptitude Test (SAT), an intellectual aptitude test commonly referred to as the College Boards.

Administration

For a test to be standard, each subject must receive the same set of instructions and the same set of materials. If you took the SAT, you may recall that a proctor read the same set of instructions to everyone in the room.

The child is asked to tell a story using dolls and hand puppets. This is an example of an unstructured, or ambiguous, question. (Photo by Constantine Manos and Alex Webb; Magnum Photos, Inc.)

BOX 4-1
Properties of a Standard Test

1. Standard or uniform method of administration.
2. Objective system for assigning raw scores.
3. Normative sample.
4. Demonstrated reliability.
5. Demonstrated validity.

Assigning Raw Scores

To qualify as a standard test, an objective basis must be devised for assigning a numerical score. On an intelligence or aptitude test this raw score might be the number of correct responses. Often some responses are weighted more heavily than others in the assignment of raw scores.

Normative Sample

The normative sample is simply a pool of raw scores from a large group of individuals representative of the population for whom the test is designed. The normative sample provides comparative information of how frequently a given raw score occurs in a sample of individuals of a particular type. By comparing a specific raw score with scores obtained by the normative sample, it is possible to determine a percentile ranking. Raw scores on the SAT are converted into normative scores that range between 200 and 800; a percentile ranking can be obtained readily from these scores.

Reliability

Reliability refers to the extent to which a test provides consistent results for the same individual. There are several indices for assessing reliability. *Test-retest reliability* refers to the extent to which a test provides consistent results for a particular individual when the test is administered at different times. Because intelligence is considered to be a very stable attribute, an intelligence test would lack test-retest reliability if individual IQ scores varied considerably during relatively brief time periods.

A test will fail to provide consistent results for the same individual if two or more independent scorers interpret the scoring system in different ways. *Interrater* or *interscorer reliability* is an index of the degree of agreement obtained by two or more independent scorers using the same scoring rules. Interrater reliability is expected to be perfect when a test merely requires a person to answer "true" or "false" and the test score is the number of items correctly answered according to a standard key. Generally, the greater the degree of subjective judgment required to score an item, the lower is the interscorer agreement.

Another type of reliability is the internal consistency of the test, or the extent to which the items in the test all measure the same attribute. Internal consistency can be assessed by obtaining *split-half reliability* or by obtaining more general estimates of *interitem consistency.* Split-half reliability refers to the extent to which half of the items of a test provide the same score as does the other half, whereas interitem consistency refers to the extent to which each item measures the same attribute.

Each type of reliability is a measure of the degree of error, or inconsistency, in test results. If a test is readministered two weeks after initial testing, the most likely scores of error are internal inconsistency of test items, test-retest inconsistency, and interrater inconsistency. Based on the sum of these error estimates, a measure can be obtained that provides an index of the expected range of error for any given use of the test. The estimated error variance for the SAT is 30 normative points; that is, if you receive a score of 540, it is very likely that your score would fall somewhere between 510 and 570 on a subsequent retest.

Validity

Validity is the extent to which an individual's score on a test predicts some concurrent or future event. If a score of 10 or above on a particular test is highly predictive of success in therapy, the test would be considered a valid measure of success in therapy. The acceptable predictive level of an instrument depends on how well other techniques, especially simpler or more economical ones, predict the same behavior. If no other instrument is available, then an instrument is considered valid if its predictions are correct more often than would be expected by chance. Validity on the SAT refers to the extent to which a high score correlates with achievement in college.

An unreliable test cannot be valid. In other words, a test has to measure some attribute (variable) consistently before it can be said to measure that attribute at all. Moreover, a test can be reliable without also being valid for a given purpose; the test may measure some attribute consistently, but that attribute may have nothing to do with the behavior of interest.

POPULAR TESTS

To summarize, psychological tests vary along four dimensions: the nature of the stimulus (type of question asked), the structure of the stimulus, the structure of the response, and the extent to which the test has been standardized. Several popular tests are discussed here.

Wechsler Adult Intelligence Scale (WAIS) and the Wechsler Intelligence Scale for Children–Revised (WISC-R)

These tests measure cognitive abilities and meet all the requirements of a standard test. Table 4-2 shows that both tests provide an overall IQ score and scores for verbal and performance IQs (Lyman, 1972; Wechsler, 1955, 1974). Although the WAIS and WISC-R are among the best psychological tests yet developed, they are far from perfect. One problem is that they are culturally biased. Because the questions are relevant to a middle-class, academic-achievement-oriented culture, people from other cultural backgrounds tend to score lower than middle-class whites. Another problem concerns inappropriate

TABLE 4-2
WAIS and Subtest Scales*

Verbal Scale	Performance Scale
Information	Digit symbol
Comprehension	Picture completion
Arithmetic	Block design
Similarities	Picture arrangement
Digit span	Object assembly
Vocabulary	

* The WAIS test of intelligence provides a score for each of the preceding scales and subscales. A full scale IQ also is provided. The WISC scales are similar to those of the WAIS. (Verbal + performance = full scale score.)

social uses of the global IQ score (McClelland, 1973). Too many test users still act as if an overall IQ score is an absolute measure of biologically determined cognitive ability when it is only an estimate of what an individual has learned about the type of material presented, as compared to what was learned by subjects in the normative sample.

Although the WAIS and WISC-R were designed to assess intelligence, some clinicians believe that qualitative interpretation of the responses permits an assessment of the extent to which emotional problems interfere with cognitive-perceptual functioning (Matarazzo, 1972).

Stanford-Binet Scale Form L-M

The Stanford-Binet Scale Form L-M (Terman & Merrill, 1960) is based on the collaborative work of a French physician and a French psychologist, Binet and Simon (1905), and later on the work of the American psychologists Terman (1916) and Terman and Merrill (1937). Prior to the construction of the WAIS and WISC, the Stanford-Binet was the most extensively employed test of intelligence for both children and adults. Although this test is still popular for subjects from the age of two through adulthood, in recent years its primary use has been with young children, particularly those for whom mental retardation is suspected.

The Stanford-Binet consists of a series of tasks representing different age levels. The examiner first determines the age level at which the child passes all tasks and then proceeds to administer the tasks at successive age levels until an age level is reached at which the child fails all tasks. The scoring of the test provides an estimate of the child's mental age. Mental age (MA) indicates the intellectual level at which the child is functioning; thus, a mental age of six years and ten months indicates that the child is functioning at the level of an average six-year, ten-month-old child. The resulting IQ formula originally was

$$IQ = \frac{MA = \text{mental age}}{CA = \text{chronological age}} \times 100.$$

This formula, however, fails to account for differences in MA variability at different chronological ages. For example, it is more unusual for a five-year-old child to obtain a 7.0 MA score than it is for a seven-year-old child to obtain a 9.8 MA score. Thus, the five-year-old child should be considered more intelligent than the seven-year-old child; however, both children obtain an IQ of 140 when the original Stanford-Binet formula is used. To correct for this problem, IQ scores are based on a deviation IQ computation. The deviation method compares each child's performance to the performance of other children in terms of how much the score in question deviates from the average score of children in the normative sample who are approximately the same age. Unlike the original MA concept of IQ, the deviation IQ has the same meaning at all ages. That is, a five- and a seven-year-old child with deviation IQs of 140 can be assumed to be equally intelligent. Because the deviation IQ provides important information, the recently revised Stanford-Binet L-M now provides both MA and deviation IQ scores. The WAIS and WISC provide only deviation IQ scores.

Bender Visual Motor Gestalt Test

The Bender Visual Motor Gestalt Test measures perceptual-motor functioning in children and brain dysfunction in adults (Schulberg & Tolor, 1961). The Bender, as this test is commonly called, consists of nine geometric figures similar to those presented in Figure 4-1. Each design is presented to the subject with the instructions: "Here are some figures for you to copy; just copy them the way you see them" (Bender, 1938). Elaborate scoring systems, normative data, reliability of scoring, test-retest reliability, and test validity have all been obtained. Kitay concluded: "The Bender-Gestalt should be included, if possible, in every diagnostic examination of adults and of children from age five because of its unique contributions to the evaluation of perceptual-motor functioning, neurological impairment, expressive styles, and maladjustment" (1972, p. 395).

Minnesota Multiphasic Personality Inventory (MMPI)

The MMPI (Dahlstrom, Welsh, & Dahlstrom, 1972) is an objective personality test that permits the subject to answer "true," "false," and "cannot say" to 566 items. Examples of MMPI items are "Sometimes I think I may kill myself" and "I like to cook." The MMPI's original construction was relatively unique: Rather than selecting items based on theory or clinical knowledge, a large pool

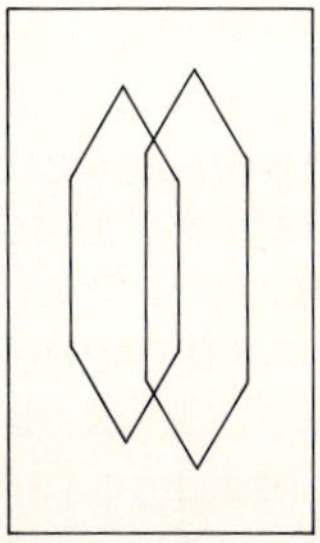

Figure 4-1
A geometric design similar to those used in the Bender Visual Motor Gestalt Test. Unusual difficulty in copying such designs is indicative of organically determined perceptual-motor difficulties, or brain dysfunction.

of questions was tested initially and analyzed for how well they discriminated between normal subjects and those diagnosed as having a particular psychopathology. An item was included in the final version of the test when it was found to discriminate between a category of psychopathology and normality. The MMPI provides scales for depression, hypochondriasis, hypomania, hysteria, masculinity-femininity, paranoia, psychasthenia, psychopathic deviate, and schizophrenia.

A potential source of error in any personality test is the tendency to present oneself in an overly positive or overly negative manner. The MMPI includes a fake good (K) and a fake bad (F) scale to assess these possibilities. The F scale consists of items that describe bizarre or unusual behaviors that very few individuals, even within psychiatric populations, rate as true of themselves. Thus, subjects who score highly on this scale are usually assumed to have been faking responses on the test by presenting themselves in an overly negative manner.

The MMPI, because of its empirical development and statistically based interpretation, has led the way in "cookbook" diagnosis and computer scoring systems. The cookbook approach (Gilberstadt & Duker, 1965; Kleinmuntz & Alexander, 1962; Marks & Seeman, 1963) allows one to administer the MMPI, count the items checked for each scale, obtain a set of scores, and then refer to a book or computer program for diagnostic statements. Even though this approach is not as exact as one would hope, the cookbooks generally do as well as, or better than, the clinician. The use of computer scoring and interpretation has flourished (Buros, 1972). In a general review of the computer approach, Eichman (1972) has suggested that computer reports are valuable to the professional tester but noted the following problems associated with this practice: (1) the validity of the reports has yet to be firmly proven, (2) the reports could be employed by unskilled examiners who might make serious errors in interpretation, and (3) the reports render personality data on individuals too readily available and therefore lend themselves too easily to unethical uses.

Despite the availability of computer scored MMPI, some clinicians still believe that clinical skill is required for valid interpretations of these data. In particular, subjective clinical judgment is believed to be useful in determining when a record is meaningful and when case history or other data should be used to qualify an MMPI result. Despite these problems, the MMPI is probably the best standard test of personality available and merits greater use in clinical settings than has heretofore been the case (Meehl, 1973).

Sentence Completion

The first published sentence completion test was Tendler's (1930) A Test for Emotional Insight. Although several forms and types of sentence completion tests have since been developed (Dole, 1958; Forer, 1950; Golde & Kogan, 1959), the Rotter Incomplete Sentence Test (Rotter & Rafferty, 1950; Rotter & Willerman, 1947) has become the most popular. The Rotter, as this test is sometimes called, consists of 40 sentence stems such as "I wish . . ." and "I failed . . . ." The subject is instructed to "Complete these sentences to express *your real feelings.* Try to do every one. Be sure to make a complete sentence" (Rotter & Rafferty, 1950, p. 5).

Interest in the Rotter and other sentence completion tests seems to be declining for no apparent reason (see Garfield & Kurtz, 1973). The *Seventh Mental Measurements Yearbook* does not even include a review of these tests. Nevertheless, Murstein concluded that, "The Sentence Completion Method is a valid test, generally speaking, and probably the most valid of all the projective techniques in the literature" (1965, p. 777). Furthermore, Goldberg stated that, "The sentence completion is a valuable instrument in the assessment of personality that compares favorably to other standard instruments. A considerable, generally favorable, research literature tends to justify its wide clinical and research use" (1965, p. 813).

The sentence completion methods are used both as subjective and as objective assessment tools. Reliable and valid scoring systems for personality interpretation, severity of psychological problems, and adjustment are available.

The Rorschach

Developed by the Swiss psychologist Hermann Rorschach (1921), the Rorschach technique consists of ten inkblot cards, some of which are black and white and some of which include color. Two sample inkblots made by the present authors are shown in Figure 4-2. In the standard procedure, the individual is shown a card and is asked to report what he sees; an inquiry phase then follows in which the subject is asked to specify the reason for the response and its location (the part of the inkblot that elicited the response). The Rorschach has been the most popular psychological test of personality (Eron & Chertkoff, 1966).

There have been many unsuccessful attempts to construct a valid scoring system for Rorschach resonses, but some evidence of validity has been obtained for the F+% scale. The F+% score refers to the accuracy of the match between the response and the physical stimulus as well as to the extent to which other people see the same response in the same location (Zubin, Eron, & Schumer, 1965). Some evidence suggests that subjects who perceive inkblots in unusual ways, and who therefore obtain very low F+% scores, tend to be disturbed (Crenshaw, Bohn, Hoffman, Matheus, & Offenbach, 1968; Stotsky & Lawrence, 1955).

Despite limited success in partially validating some scoring systems, several Rorschach authorities have concluded that the value of this test is based primarily on the clinician's ability to integrate such data with other information (e.g., Rapaport, Gill, & Schafer, 1968, p. 208). The majority of clinical psychologists appear to accept the Rorschach as a semiobjective interview procedure that requires subjective integration and interpretation with other data.

Thematic Apperception Test (TAT)

The TAT (Murray, 1943) consists of 20 pictures that depict a variety of family, social, and individual scenes. The pictures are presented one at a time with instructions to look at the picture and to tell a story with a beginning, middle, and end. In telling their stories, subjects are instructed to include how the characters feel and what they think. Murray (1965) lists the following criteria for interpreting personality themes from the TAT story content: (1) the presumed symbolic significance of the card itself—for example, one card suggests a mother-daughter relationship, whereas others suggest sexual and peer relationships; (2) repetition of a theme or event in several stories; (3) uniqueness as defined by deviation from norms of story content; (4) interrelatedness of themes, persons, and events across cards; and (5) self-involvement, or when the actions of the person taking the test, including his or her behavior while telling the story, suggest that a particular emotion has been aroused.

Although the TAT is widely employed, experimental evidence for its diagnostic and predictive validity is limited (Dana, 1972; Eron, 1972; Zubin et al., 1965). Clinicians usually interpret the TAT in a subjective manner, and many are unconcerned with its lack of experimental validation. By contrast, re-

Figure 4-2
Sample inkblots made by the authors similar to those employed in the Rorschach test.

searchers who employ the TAT to study personality have developed single-variable scoring systems that they have been trying to validate.

Two issues of projective testing are whether or not projective techniques yield information different from that easily obtained during interviews and whether the stories elicited represent actual experiences or wished-for experiences. The TAT has often been used in research designed to investigate these issues. Allport (1965) and Murstein (1965) interpret the available data as suggesting that disturbed individuals provide information in projective content they would not otherwise tell, but that normal individuals provide the same information in open questioning as in projective content. In regard to the other issue of the relation between fantasy content as represented in TAT stories and in overt behavior, both Dana (1972) and Zubin, Eron, and Schumer (1965) conclude that this relation is complex and dependent on personality, social, and situational variables.

Figure Drawings

Figure Drawings, especially the Draw-A-Person (Machover, 1949), have been a popular source of projective material. Many types of drawing tasks have been used including the Draw-A-Man, Draw-Your-Home, and most recently Loney's (1971) Draw-A-Car technique. All of the drawing techniques have been based primarily on subjective interpretation of style and content of the pictures in terms of psychodynamic principles of symbolism and projection. Figure 4-3 presents drawings of a person by three youngsters.

As is common with many clinical assessment tools, research has generally failed to support the validity of clinical interpretations based on drawings. Murstein states that, "It is true that there is some support for the notion that over-all adequacy of the figures bears some relationship to personality adjustment. The relationship, however, appears to be so slight that the Draw-A-Person test seems to be an inefficient means for measuring personality" (1965, p. 609). In his review of the Draw-A-Person test, Harris (1972) notes the failure to validate the technique but also expresses a belief in its value:

> As one who has worked a good many years with children's drawings, this reviewer must confess to his personal conviction that the individuality and uniqueness of drawings, the great variety of ways in which a subject can portray the human figure, plus the fact that many individuals adopt and follow an individual, recognizable style in their drawing, lead to the persisting belief that drawings must tell something about the person's interests, preoccupations and perhaps unconscious dynamics [1972, p. 404].

Thus, figure drawings, like the Rorschach and TAT, continue to be popular assessment tools among clinical psychologists even though solid experimental support for the validity of these tools is lacking.

USES OF PSYCHOLOGICAL TESTS

Like other assessment procedures, psychological tests are used for both clinical and research purposes. In clinical practice, a battery of psychological tests is typically administered to diagnose the client's problems. When used for this and related purposes, the examiner must rely on subjective interpretation and on previous experience in order to arrive at appropriate conclusions.

Psychological assessment is conducted in many settings, including schools, rehabilitation centers, special treatment clinics, out-patient and in-patient mental health units, and in private practice. In the majority of cases, the examiner's information is shared with other staff members via case conferences and other meetings. For example, in a school setting, the psychological ex-

Figure 4-3
Figures drawn by three youngsters. The interpretations provided are subjective impressions based on experience.

A. Drawn by a normal 10-year-old boy. Basic proportion and features are appropriate. No abnormal action or body deviation is present. The small size of the figure and the relative vagueness of the outline may suggest some insecurity.

B. This drawing was made by a 13-year-old boy who was diagnosed as brain damaged because of a head injury. The child was below normal in intelligence. The figure is poorly organized and poorly proportioned. The general smallness of the figure, the prominent head, and the general lack of development suggest immaturity, lack of body awareness, and poor self-concept.

C. This drawing was made by a 13-year-old, right-handed boy of low normal intelligence. The boy was referred because of difficulty in relating to teachers and peers, especially females. The poor development of the figure is inappropriate for age and I.Q. level. Seemingly nonuseful arms and lack of mouth suggest inability to deal with the environment, a lack of knowledge of how to deal with others, and a feeling of incompetence in social relationships. The enclosed and smaller right arm suggests a fear of, or guilt about, masturbation.

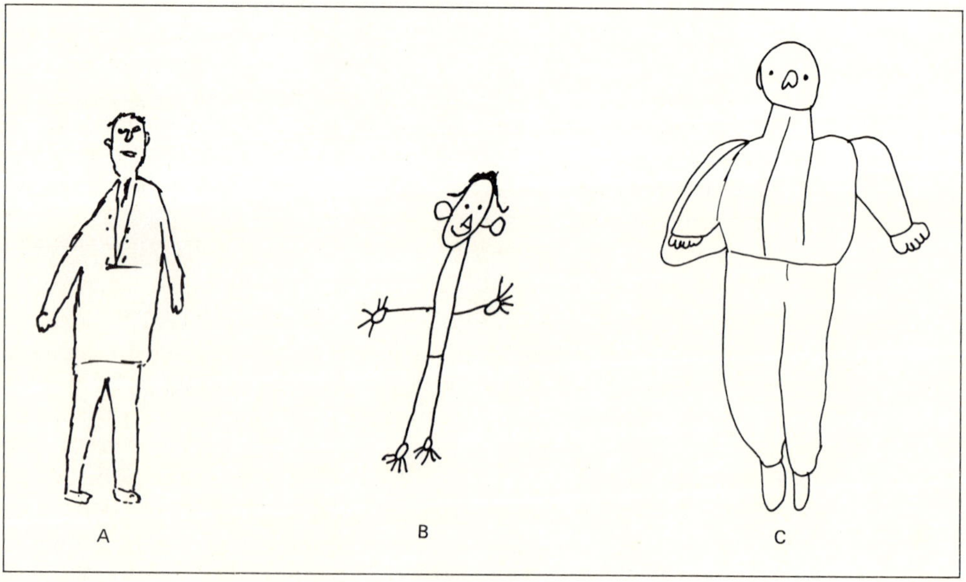

aminer usually meets with the teacher and/or parents to discuss the findings and, if warranted, to plan ways of improving the child's behavior.

By contrast, many psychiatrists seem to pay little attention to psychological reports. Adams (1972) compared initial and final diagnosis on 137 cases in which the *psychiatrist had requested testing* for diagnostic purposes. In 51 per cent of the cases, the psychologist and psychiatrist were in essential agreement on the initial diagnosis; in these cases, it was impossible to evaluate the extent to which the report affected the diagnostic decision. In 30 per cent of the cases, the psychologist's report disagreed with the psychiatrist's diagnosis, but the psychiatrist did not change his diagnosis. In only 16 per cent of the cases could it be determined that the report had any effect: In these cases, the initial diagnosis was changed to be consistent with the psychological report. These data generally support perceptions of psychological examiners as second-class citizens in settings under psychiatric control.

SUMMARY

This chapter offered a general introduction to psychological assessment. Popular psychological tests not usually associated with any particular approach to abnormality were discussed, whereas assessment procedures associated with various approaches will be discussed in subsequent chapters.

Three kinds of assessment procedures are observations of behavior, interviews, and psychological tests. Behavioral observations under a variety of situations are sometimes impractical to obtain. Interviews provide a practical method of acquiring information, but the interviewer needs considerable skill to elicit trustworthy information.

Psychological tests vary in terms of the nature of the stimulus, the degree of structure of the stimulus, the degree of structure of the response, and the extent to which the test has been standardized. By definition, a standard psychological test includes a uniform method of administration, an objective scoring system, and demonstrated reliability and validity. Any kind of psychological test is theoretically capable of standardization.

Several popular tests have been discussed. The WAIS, WISC–R, and Stanford-Binet are standard tests of intelligence. The WAIS and WISC–R provide deviation IQ scores that permit comparisons of children and adults at different chronological ages; however, the Stanford-Binet originally provided an IQ based on a mental-age concept that does not permit comparison at different chronological ages. The Stanford-Binet still furnishes IQ scores based on the mental-age concept, but it also provides an IQ score based on the deviation concept. The WISC–R is inappropriate for children under five years of age, whereas the Stanford-Binet can be used with children as young as two. Although these tests have been validated for intelligence, they are culturally biased against blacks.

The Bender Visual Motor Gestalt test has some validity as a measure of brain dysfunction, whereas the MMPI is an objective test of several personality dimensions. Although the MMPI is far from perfect, it is presently the most valid test of several personality variables.

Tests that present unstructured stimuli for the subject to interpret have been

TABLE 4-3
Frequently Used Psychological Tests

Test	Purpose (as most commonly used)	Age Range of Applicability	Experimental Evidence of Validity
Wechsler Intelligence Scale for Children (WISC)	Determines intellectual level	5–15	Good
Wechsler Adult Intelligence Scale (WAIS)	Determines intellectual level	16 and up	Good
Stanford-Binet Intelligence Scale	Determines intellectual level	2 and up	Good
Minnesota Multiphasic Personality Inventory (MMPI)	Determines diagnostic category	16 and up and 6 years education	Good
Bender Visual Motor Gestalt Test (Bender)	Determines gross perceptual-motor ability;	5 and up	Good
	determines brain dysfunction	adults	Good
Sentence completion	Determines nature of emotional disturbance	13 and up	Good (when objectively scored)
Rorschach inkblots	Determines nature of emotional disturbance	2 and up	Poor
Thematic Apperception Test (TAT)	Determines nature of emotional disturbance;	4 and up	Poor
	determines motivation-need level (many scales available)	6 and up	Fair
Figure drawings	Estimates intellectual level;	5 and up	Good
	determines nature of emotional disturbance	5 and up	Poor

called projective tests on the assumption that responses to ambiguous stimuli reflect personality needs and unconscious thoughts and emotions. The sentence completion test probably has more demonstrated validity than other projective techniques; however, the Rorschach is the most popular projective technique. Other popular projective techniques are the TAT and figure drawings. In general, projective techniques require the examiner to interpret test responses in a subjective manner. When interpreted in the context of other data, projective tests may provide important information about the person.

Chapter 5

The Biological Approach

But there are many indications that mental illness is frequently a combination of undesirable learning or ways of thinking *and* some disorder or weakness of a part of the machinery.

D. O. HEBB (1966, p. 14)

This chapter provides an introduction to biological concepts and treatment methods. The following points will be emphasized:

1. Few instances of abnormal behavior have been shown to result from biological factors alone. It seems likely, however, that many instances of abnormal behavior are the result of both biological and psychological factors.
2. The significance of the biological approach is evident from the following considerations: *Some* mental disorders have biological causes; biological factors probably contribute to many other mental disorders; some mental disorders have biological effects; and all behavior is mediated by biochemical processes.
3. Many investigators have been concerned primarily with the study of biological *correlates* of anxiety, thought disorders, intellectual deficiencies, and other forms of abnormality. Although biological correlates cannot be assumed to cause abnormality, they are, nevertheless, important for assessment (diagnosis) and for research.
4. Biological treatment procedures have frequently been criticized as unethical. Some critics have expressed concern about the potency of these procedures and about the possibility of irreversible physical damage. Historically, there are many instances of abuse of biological treatments. However, this chapter emphasizes the complexity of ethical issues. On the one hand, the patient needs to be protected against those who abuse biological treatment, even if their intentions were only to help. On the other hand, safeguards against abuse should not go so far as to deny effective treatment to suffering individuals.
5. It is suggested that biological treatment procedures may have been abused many times in the past primarily because they can be administered only under the supervision of a physician. In other words, concern should be focused on the potential for abuse inherent in unchecked power given to well-meaning individuals rather than on the potency of the treatment procedure itself.

The chapter begins with a case history of a depressed individual who was successfully treated by electroconvulsive therapy (ECT).

THE CASE OF SUSAN ANDERSON AS ADAPTED FROM A REPORT BY E. L. LYNN AND J. RACY[1]

The case of Susan Anderson (Lynn and Racy, 1969) exemplifies biological treatment of a depressive disorder. Depression is frequently preceded by the loss of a significant other and is often accompanied by feelings of grief. In fact, many

[1] Adapted from Lynn, E. L., & Racy, J. The resolution of pathological grief after electroconvulsive therapy. *The Journal of Nervous and Mental Disease,* 1969, **148,** 165–169. The adaptation is published with the permission of the authors and publisher, the Williams & Wilkins Co., Baltimore.

severely depressed patients will cry at the slightest provocation or at the remembrance of certain events. The present case is typical in that Susan's depression followed a loss, but it is atypical in that the patient was unable to experience grief.

Susan Anderson's first psychiatric hospitalization occurred in 1945 when she was 30 years old. The attending physicians described her as depressed and as markedly paranoid and chose to administer electroconvulsive therapy (ECT). ECT involves the application of electric current through the brain. The treatment produces convulsions, or states of unconsciousness characterized by violent muscular contractions and by random firing of neurons in various regions of the brain. In this instance, ECT treatment was successful, and Susan was able to return to her job teaching second grade.

When her sister Martha died in 1967, Susan reacted with depression and guilt. Significantly, she did not cry and was apparently unable to experience feelings of grief. She complained of increasing constipation, insomnia with early morning awakening, and an inability to handle simple household chores. Anorexia, a condition characterized by a refusal to eat and by a consequent loss of weight, was evident. Susan felt responsible for Martha's death—she sometimes believed that she had caused her sister's death.

Despite administration of the antidepressant drug amitriptyline, the depression deepened and Susan became more irritable, with the result that hospitalization was necessary. When asked about her sister's death, she stated that she did not feel that Martha was dead.

Drug treatment was continued during her hospitalization, and ECT was administered three times per week. After the second treatment, Susan reported a decrease in tension but noted that Martha's death was still "unreal." After the third treatment, she appeared more alert, began wearing lipstick, and ate well. After the sixth treatment, she was sleeping without sedation. She was discharged after the seventh treatment, one month following her admission.

Susan was seen at the hospital's clinic one week after discharge and shed tears for the first time since Martha's death. This expression of grief was considered significant because it represented a normal reaction. Lynn and Racy (1969), who reported Susan's case history, considered her previous inability to grieve to be evidence of pathology and had hypothesized that Susan's depressive reaction had blocked the expression of grief.

At a one-year follow-up, Susan appeared to be eating well and sleeping comfortably. She was better able to cope with the difficulties of home, including an aloof husband and an active child. The attending psychiatrists considered the ECT treatments a success.

DISTINGUISHING CHARACTERISTICS

The case of Susan Anderson exemplifies some of the distinguishing characteristics of the biological approach, particularly the tendency to rely on physical modes of treatment.

Study of Biological Factors

Bioadvocates have been concerned with three kinds of physical abnormalities as possible causes of psychological symptomatology: structural abnormalities, biochemical imbalances, and genetic abnormalities.[2] The term *structural abnormality* refers to inherited or acquired abnormalities that involve physical attributes of the nervous system. The scientific search for structural abnormalities has generated physiological studies of the nervous system and autopsies of mentally retarded, epileptic, and brain-damaged subjects. General paresis is an example of a mental disorder known to be caused by structural damage. In this disorder, viruses that cause syphilis travel through the nervous system where they cause irreversible physical damage to infected areas of the brain.

Many investigators have been concerned with the discovery of biochemical imbalances in psychotic individuals. Normal emotional behavior is known to be affected by biochemicals called neurotransmitters. Consequently, it is possible that abnormal emotionality is caused by abnormal amounts of these substances at various sites in the brain. For example, one biochemical theory postulates that schizophrenia is caused by excesses of the biochemicals serotonin and norepinephrine at various sites in the brain.

Numerous investigators have reported that some mental disorders tend to occur more often in families with at least one similarly afflicted member than in families with no prior history of the disorder. These observations have formed a basis for the nature-nurture controversy, or the issue of whether mental disorders tend to occur in the same families because of inherited or environmental factors. This controversy has been particularly evident in the disorders of schizophrenia and mental retardation. Although few mental disorders have been shown conclusively to result from genetic factors, a notable exception to this rule is PKU (a form of mental retardation).

The nature-nurture controversy has generated considerable research. Despite its historical significance, today many psychologists consider the issue of environment versus heredity an oversimplification of the facts. For most disorders, the task is not to decide on one or the other, but rather is to assess the interaction between the two sets of contributing factors. Many mental disorders probably result from a biological predisposition aggravated by environmental stress or learning. For some disorders, the inherited predisposition may be such that only an unusually favorable environment would not precipitate the condition; for other disorders only an unusually unfavorable environment would precipitate the condition.

Identification of Biological Correlates

Many bioadvocates have been primarily concerned with investigating physiological correlates of abnormal behavior. For example, considerable research activity has been concerned with the electrical measurement of neural activity in various regions of the brain. Clearly, bioadvocates do not maintain that certain brain wave patterns cause psychological symptomatology; rather, the promise is that this research will better enable us to understand neural activity and to identify biological correlates of particular emotions and disorders. Such knowledge can be useful in identifying causes even when the primary causes are psychological. For example, suppose an investigator postulated that knowl-

[2] The term *bioadvocate* is introduced as a convenient way of referring to biologically oriented investigators of abnormal behavior.

edge of possible harm from the victim inhibits aggression because it increases the subject's anxiety. One possible way to test this hypothesis is to determine whether threat of retaliation produces anxiety, as indicated by biological correlates of anxiety.

Reliance on Physical Modes of Intervention

Biological treatment of mental disorders often resembles the type of treatment medical doctors provide for physical diseases. Consequently, treatment usually requires a relatively short period of time; moreover, the nature of the intervention is active and direct. The directness of the intervention was exemplified in the case of Susan Anderson by the administration of drugs and electroconvulsive therapy.

Historically, biological treatment has included a variety of seemingly inhumane procedures (see Chapter 2). One interesting example of this is Benjamin Rush's "tranquilizer." The tranquilizer was an uncomfortable chair into which Dr. Rush strapped defiant patients for a considerable period of time. Many scientists still consider some biological treatment procedures inhumane, especially prefrontal lobotomy and other brain operations. This ethical controversy is discussed in this chapter in the section on treatment effectiveness.

The goals of the biological approach to abnormality are to understand the biological causes, correlates, and effects of abnormal behavior as well as to alleviate suffering and to modify inappropriate behavior by altering biological states. The basic concepts of this approach are discussed in the next section.

BASIC CONCEPTS

The basic concepts of the biological approach are discussed in four subsections: physiological concepts, genetic concepts, drug concepts, and drug classification.

Physiological Structures

A large cluster of neurons, the basic cells of the nervous system, form the *central nervous system* (CNS), which consists of the *brain* and the *spinal cord.* The spinal cord performs reflex functions and serves as a link in the chain of communication between various portions of the CNS and the brain; moreover, the spinal cord plays a critical role in motor activity. Perhaps the most complex and least understood part of the body is the brain. Within this structure, it is possible to distinguish three parts: the hindbrain, consisting of the medulla oblongata, pons, and cerebellum; the midbrain; and the forebrain, which includes the thalamus, hypothalamus, and the cerebral hemispheres.

The hindbrain is the most primitive part of the brain from both a functional and an evolutionary viewpoint. A simplified description of the hindbrain is that it constitutes an enlargement at the upper end of the spinal cord and includes the *reticular formation,* also called the arousal system. This system is important for the functioning of higher mental activities because it is related to wakefulness. The reticular formation affects general wakefulness and attentiveness by sending impulses throughout the higher centers of the brain.

BOX 5-1
Definitions of Terms

Addiction. See *physical dependence.*
Amnesia. The total or partial loss of memory.
Analgesia. The total or partial loss of pain; a drug that produces loss of pain is called an analgesic.
Anesthesia. The loss of sensory capacities.
Bioadvocate. A term introduced in this book as a convenient way to refer to those who adhere to the biological approach to abnormality; includes psychologists, psychiatrists, and neurologists.
Coma. A state of deep unconsciousness.
Concordance. The degree to which both members of a pair show a particular trait. If both members show the trait, they are said to be concordant for that trait; if only one member shows the trait, they are said to be discordant.
Convulsion. An uncontrollable, violent muscular contraction usually accompanied by a random firing of neurons in certain brain regions. Also called fit and seizure.
Discordance. See *concordance.*
Dizygotic twins. Fraternal twins whose genetic make-up is no more similar than that of any two siblings of the same parents.
Double-blind procedure. An experimental procedure in which neither the experimenter nor the subject knows whether drug or placebo is being administered.
Electroconvulsive therapy (ECT). The treatment of mental disorders (especially depression) by electrically inducing convulsions. This treatment also is called electroshock therapy (EST) and shock treatment.
Electrode. An end of an open electrical circuit.

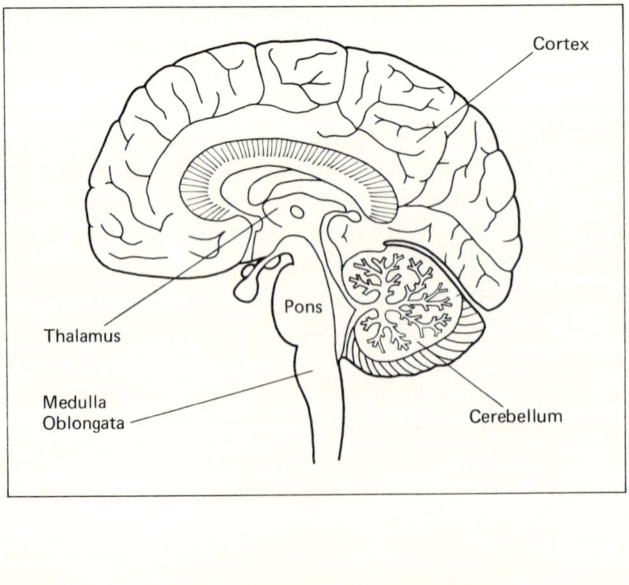

Figure 5-1
The human brain.

Electroencephalogram (EEG). A graphic display of electrical impulses from the brain.

Endogenous. Known or believed to be caused by internal factors.

Frontal lobes. A part of the cerebral cortex.

Gene. The basic unit of heredity. That part of a chromosome that determines a particular trait can be called a gene.

Hormone. A biochemical substance secreted by a ductless gland. Hormones that act on the brain are called neurohormones.

Lobotomy. A brain operation in which fibers connecting the prefrontal lobes with the thalamus are severed.

Monozygotic twins. Identical twins; twins with an identical genetic inheritance.

Neurology. A medical science concerned with diseases of the nervous system.

Neurotic anxiety. Inappropriate anxiety or inappropriate degrees of anxiety. In psychodynamic theories, anxiety caused by unconscious determinants.

Organic. This term is usually synonymous with the term *biological;* an organic disorder is one that is either known or believed to be caused by biological factors.

Physical dependence. A state of drug dependency in which abstinence produces physical disturbances.

Placebo. A chemically inert substance given as an experimental control for the chemical effects of a drug.

Psychological dependence. A state in which drugs are used on a habitual basis in order to escape psychological problems or to satisfy a psychological need.

Psychosis. Disorders marked by severe disturbances of perception and/or thinking.

Schizophrenia. Psychotic disorders marked by a severe disturbance of thinking and behavior. Several types of disorders are included.

The midbrain serves in part as a relay connection between hind and forebrain; its specific functioning is beyond the scope of this book.

The forebrain can be subdivided into the diencephalon and the telencephalon (see Deutsch & Deutsch, 1973). The diencephalon includes the thalamus, which plays a role in wakefulness, and the hypothalamus. The hypothalamus is a particularly important structure that serves as a center for certain regulatory functions. For example, the body requires a specific range of internal temperatures in order to maintain life functions. If the body becomes too warm, the hypothalamus initiates various activities such as sweating to reduce internal temperatures; if the body becomes too cold, the hypothalamus initiates a shivering reaction that produces heat via muscular contractions. The regulation of bodily activities such that a relatively constant internal environment is maintained is called homeostasis. In addition to body temperature, the hypothalamus regulates water balance and sexual activity and probably plays a critical role in determining whether or not a sensation is pleasurable.

Another major organization of neurons is the *autonomic nervous system* (ANS), which plays an important role in emotional and sexual behavior. The ANS consists of the *sympathetic nervous system,* running outside of and parallel to the spinal cord, and the *parasympathetic nervous system,* located both near the hindbrain and at the base of the spinal cord. The ANS plays a very important role in emotional behavior because it communicates with *endocrine glands* (glands with a ductless physical structure), which release chemical agents called hormones into the blood. For example, stimulation from the sympathetic nervous system to the adrenal glands releases adrenalin. This hormone not only prepares the body for a state of action but also produces emotional excitement. Specifically, adrenalin stimulates the arousal system to produce alertness. Moreover, the arousal system stimulates the sympathetic nervous system to produce more adrenalin. This loop—the sympathetic nervous system producing adrenalin, which produces arousal, which stimulates the sympathetic nervous system to produce more adrenalin—may explain biologically why it is often difficult to calm oneself after emotional excitement.

Integration of Structures

The nervous system is extremely complex, and the preceding simplified account should not be taken to imply otherwise. Complexity is particularly evident when one considers the manner in which the various parts of the brain are integrated into a functionally cohesive unit. For example, the ANS is largely under the control of the CNS and does not act as an independent nervous system. Although physiological details of the integrative aspects of the nervous system are beyond our present scope, the distinction between *neurological* and *behavioral stimulation* is important for a basic understanding of drug effects, which will be discussed later in this section.

Suppose that neural activity in a particular region of the hypothalamus (region A) produces thirst and consequent drinking behavior. As the simplified conceptual model of Figure 5-2 shows, this region is controlled by two kinds of nerves from other parts of the brain such that stimulation of one nerve stimulates region A, whereas stimulation of the other nerve inhibits neural activity in region A. That is, stimulation of the inhibitory nerve produces inhibition in

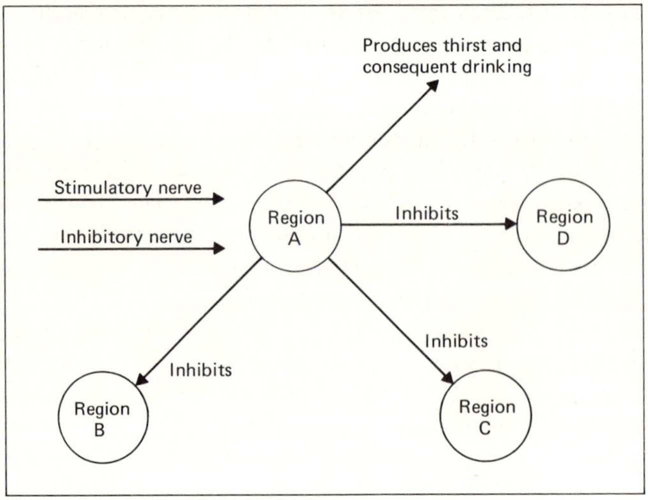

Figure 5-2
Simplified conceptual model illustrating basis for distinction between neurological and behavioral stimulation. Stimulation of region A produces behavioral activity of drinking but inhibits neurological activity in regions B, C, and D.

region A and inhibition of drinking behavior. If one considers that many more than two nerves often communicate with a brain region, and that the many regions affect one another in complex ways, it is clear *that an increase in neurological activity does not necessarily imply an increase in behavioral activity.*

Genetic Concepts

The DNA molecules in every cell nucleus, except sperms and ova, contain all the information necessary to produce a biological person. Each DNA molecule consists of four basic substances arranged in long chains that wrap around one another to form a helix. Each of these four substances is a letter in the genetic alphabet. Just as various combinations of only 26 alphabetical letters form the basis for all of the information in this text, so various combinations of only four genetic letters contain all of the information necessary to form a biological person (Lehninger, 1965). For example the four basic substances can be designated A, C, T, and G. Accordingly, the sequence of substances TTATGC represents different information than does the sequence ATATGC. The first sequence might inform biological mechanisms to create protein for building more cells, whereas the second sequence might inform biological mechanisms to create toxic substances that cause death.

A mechanism is required to read, or to use, the genetic information stored in the DNA molecule. The chemical substance RNA, located just outside the cell nucleus, is part of that mechanism. By chemical action, the DNA molecule in the cell nucleus transmits the genetic code to the RNA molecule outside the cell nucleus. The RNA molecule then travels throughout the cell initiating the chemical processes dictated by the genetic code. Thus, DNA is a chemical substance that contains the genetic information, whereas RNA is a chemical substance that transports this information throughout the cell.

Through cellular division, genetic information is transmitted from parent to daughter cell and from parent to child. The normal human cell contains 46 chromosomes except for the normal sperm and ovum, each of which contains 23. For unknown reasons, cells do not always divide evenly, and daughter cells sometimes receive fewer than or more than the normal number of 46 chromosomes. Another abnormality of cellular reproduction occurs when part of one chromosome becomes attached to part of another chromosome; this abnormality is called translocation. Down's syndrome (mongolism) is a form of mental retardation that is caused either by the presence of a 47th chromosome or by translocation of some of the 46 chromosomes. Figure 5-3 displays some of the chromosomal abnormalities that cause Down's syndrome.

A *gene* is that part of a DNA molecule that determines a specific biological capacity. For each biological capacity, a person inherits one gene from each parent. For example, for the biological capacity of how tall a child can grow if given a proper diet, a child inherits genes for tallness or genes for smallness. If the child inherits from both parents a gene for tallness, the child will be tall, but if the child inherits from both parents a gene for smallness, the child will be small. Suppose the child inherits a gene for tallness from one parent and a gene for smallness from the other parent. In this case, the child will become

BOX 5-2
Behavior Genetics

Behavior genetics is the study of genetic factors that contribute to individual differences in behavior. In order to introduce the basic concepts of behavior genetics, we shall consider various possible ways of testing the hypothesis that a predisposition to schizophrenia is inherited.

Two genes are typically present for each trait. A dominant gene usually is designated by an upper-case letter, whereas a recessive gene usually is designated by a lower-case letter. If schizophrenia were determined by a single dominant gene (*S*), most schizophrenics would have the genetic make-up of *Ss* and some would be *SS*. A normal would be *ss*. If schizophrenia were determined by a single recessive gene (*s*), a schizophrenic would be *ss*, and normals would be either *SS* or *Ss*. The symbols *SS*, *Ss*, and *ss* refer to the *genotype*, and the observable trait (presence or absence of schizophrenia) is called the phenotype.

Suppose we identify 100 schizophrenic and 100 normal people. Because this sample of 200 provides the starting point for our inquiry, we shall refer to the people in this sample as *index cases* or *probands*. If schizophrenia were determined by a single dominant gene (*S*), then a mating of two normals (*ss*) would produce only normal children (*ss*). This is because a child would inherit one gene from each parent; if the genotype of both parents is *ss*, the child must also be *ss*. If one parent is normal while the other is schizophrenic (*Ss*), the child will inherit a normal gene from the normal parent and has a 50 per cent chance of inheriting a schizophrenic gene from the schizophrenic parent. Thus, under the hypothesis that schizophrenia is determined by a single dominant gene, a mating of a normal (*ss*) and a schizophrenic (*Ss*) parent will yield 50 per cent normal children and 50 per cent schizophrenic children.

Suppose, however, that schizophrenia were caused by a single recessive gene (*s*). Marriages between two schizophrenic parents (*ss* × *ss*), would always produce schizophrenic children (*ss*). Marriages between two normal parents would be of three types. If both parents had a homogeneous genotype (*SS* × *SS*), all children should be normal (*SS*); if one parent had a homogeneous genotype and the other had a heterogeneous genotype (*SS* × *Ss*), all of the children should be normal; if both parents had a heterogeneous genotype (*Ss* × *Ss*), one fourth of the children should be schizophrenic.

The available data generally fail to support either a single dominant, or a single

just as tall as if he had inherited two genes for tallness. Accordingly, genes for tallness are said to be *dominant*, whereas genes for smallness are said to be *recessive*. Only when two recessive genes are present does the recessive trait occur. The principles of dominant and recessive genes are useful for determining the probability that a child will inherit certain tendencies for abnormal behavior (see Vandenberg, 1966). In addition to being scientifically interesting, this information can be utilized to counsel parents as to whether or not they want to have children in cases in which there is a significant probability of an abnormal child.

recessive, gene theory of schizophrenia. (See Chapter 16.) Although the parents and siblings of a schizophrenic are more likely to be schizophrenic than is someone randomly selected from the general population, the rates are not in close agreement with expectation under a single-gene theory. It is possible, however, that schizophrenia is determined by multiple genes.

One way to evaluate the general hypothesis of a genetic component to schizophrenia is provided by the *twin study. Monozygotic* (identical) twins have the same genes, whereas *dizygotic* (fraternal) twins share about half their genes. A *concordance rate* is the percentage of twin pairs who have the same phenotype (e.g., both are schizophrenic). If schizophrenia is determined solely by genetic factors, the concordance rate for schizophrenia should be 100 per cent among monozygotic twins. If schizophrenia is determined in part by genetic factors, the concordance rate for schizophrenia should be higher among monozygotic twins than among dizygotic twins. The available evidence indicates that among monozygotic twins the concordance rate for schizophrenia is less than 100 per cent but is higher than that associated with dizygotic twins. Many scientists have interpreted these data as support for the hypothesis that schizophrenia is determined by both genetic and environmental factors. The most popular theory is that a predisposition to schizophrenia can be inherited but that a predisposed person will become schizophrenic only if exposed to pathogenic psychological conditions.

It is possible to interpret the higher concordance rates for monozygotic twins as compared to dizygotic twins in terms of environmental factors alone. For example, being a monozygotic twin may be associated with special hazards in developing one's identity. The *adoption study* provides a way of testing for a genetic component to schizophrenia that rules out likely environmental explanations. The adoption study typically focuses on two groups of adopted children. One group has a biological parent who is schizophrenic and the other does not. If schizophrenia has a genetic component, then an adopted child with a biological parent who is schizophrenic should be more likely to develop schizophrenia than is an adopted child with normal biological parents. The results of the few adoption studies reported thus far generally support the hypothesis of a genetic component to schizophrenia.

Schizophrenia is caused by both genetic and environmental factors. The specific genetic and environmental factors that may engender schizophrenia are discussed in Chapter 16.

Drug Concepts[3]

A third group of concepts basic to the biological approach concerns drugs and their effects on the nervous system and on heredity. An active chemical substance that primarily affects mental experience or overt behavior is called a psychoactive drug. Aspirin, alcohol, and tranquilizers are examples of drugs

[3] Based on data summarized by Himwich, Kety, and Smythies (1967); Kalinowsky and Hippius (1969); Marks and Pare (1965); Ray (1972); Trouton and Eysenck (1961); and Goodman and Gillman (1975).

that are psychoactive. The scientific study of psychoactive drugs is called psychopharmacology.

Specific and Nonspecific Variables

When a psychoactive drug enters the nervous system, it tends to act at specific sites. That is, certain areas of the nervous system are more sensitive than others to the presence of particular psychoactive chemicals; these affected areas of the nervous system are called the sites of action for the drug in question. For example, the tranquilizer chlorpromazine (CPZ) acts in part on the reticular formation to inhibit arousal and on the hypothalamus to reduce the potential for violent behavior. Accordingly, the reticular formation and the hypothalamus constitute two sites of action for the drug chlorpromazine.

Specific variables affect the chemical interactions between a drug and its sites of action. The term *specific* refers to the interaction of a specific chemical at specific sites of the nervous system. These factors include the chemical composition of the drug, the amount of drug at the site of action, and the biochemical nature of the site of action.

The effects of psychoactive drugs are also determined by nonspecific vari-

Figure 5-3
Chromosomal abnormality in Down's Syndrome (a disorder causing mental retardation) is revealed by the additional chromosome 21-22. (Courtesy of Dr. Janette Schulz, Illinois Institute for Developmental Disabilities; Chicago, Illinois.)

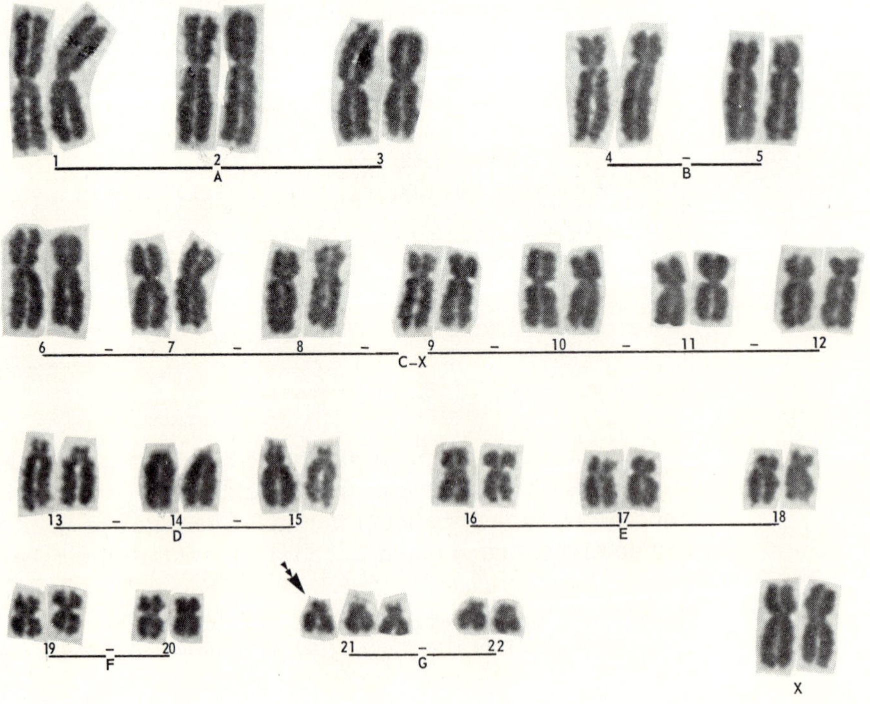

ables. Nonspecific variables include the expectations a person has concerning the effects of the drug, the social and physical environment in which the drug is administered, and both the mood and the personality of the subject receiving the drug. In general, nonspecific drug effects vary across individuals, whereas specific drug effects are relatively constant across individuals. However, some exceptions to this rule may exist. For example, some tranquilizers tend to consolidate thinking in schizophrenic subjects but tend to have little effect on the thought processes of normal subjects. Although these individual differences may appear to be the result of nonspecific factors, it may be that the brains of schizophrenics are biochemically different from those of normals, thereby implicating specific factors. Moreover, specific variables may explain the fact that an individual can react differently to the same drug at different times. For example, a person's mood is affected by the hormones secreted by endocrine glands. Accordingly, a person in a happy mood is biochemically different from the same person in a depressed mood. It is possible that these biochemical differences result in different effects of the same drug administered at different times. Thus, the fact that alcohol can have different psychological effects depending on a person's mood may be attributable to the specific factor of biochemical differences associated with different moods.

Dosage and Effective Dosage

Dosage is the amount of drug that is administered. In general, the greater the dosage, the more intense are the effects of the drug. However, additional drug effects may appear as dosage increases, especially when the dosage is extreme.

It is important to distinguish between dosage, or the amount of drug that enters the body, and *effective dosage*, or the concentration of the drug at a site of action at a specific time. The specific effects of a drug are related to the effective dosage, whereas the effective dosage of a drug depends on the method by which the drug is administered as well as on the amount ingested. If the same amount of a drug is given to the same person on two different occasions so that the drug is administered orally on one occasion and is injected directly into the bloodstream on the second occasion (intravenous administration), the effective dosage is much greater in the case of intravenous administration. Drugs administered orally must pass through the digestive system before they enter the bloodstream and are transported to the sites of action. Drugs that are injected directly into the bloodstream tend to be transported to the sites of action on a rapid basis and in concentrated form.

Therapeutic, Side, and Toxic Effects

The body reacts to a drug without knowing the purposes for which the drug was administered. Therefore, it is not surprising that only some of the body's reactions to a drug are beneficial to the patient. The term *side effects* refers to the effects of a drug that occur in addition to the therapeutic effects for which the drug was administered. Although side effects vary with different drugs and with different effective dosages, common side effects for psychoactive drugs include headaches, nausea, dryness of mouth, diarrhea, sweating, and sex disturbances. The intensity and the kind of both the therapeutic effects and the side effects associated with a particular drug depend on the effective dosage. Sometimes, side effects are dangerous to the individual, as in the case of tissue damage and death; such harmful effects are called toxic effects.

The body frequently adapts biochemically to the repeated and regular use of certain drugs. Specifically, increasing dosages often are required to continue to produce the same psychological effects. This phenomenon is called tolerance.

Another possible effect of the repeated administration of some psychoactive drugs is called drug dependency (drug addiction). Drug dependency is a scientific term that refers to the phenomenon in which the repeated use of a drug results in a need for continual use on a habitual basis. If this need is physiologically determined, the drug is said to produce *physical dependency;* if this need is psychologically determined, the drug is said to produce *psychological dependency.* In general, drugs that produce physical dependency also produce psychological dependency. However, some investigators classify certain drugs as producing psychological dependency without producing physical dependency.

The period following the termination of drug use is called the withdrawal period. A person is said to be physically dependent on a drug when physical disturbances are evident during withdrawal. By contrast, a person is said to be psychologically dependent on a drug when he uses the drug habitually to escape psychological problems.

Certain psychoactive drugs tend to produce physical dependency, whereas others do not. If a drug tends to produce physical dependency, the readiness with which it does so is dependent on the number of different occasions on which the drug is used as well as on the amount of the drug used.

Drug Classification

As in any young science, our knowledge of psychoactive drugs is contained in thousands of research studies that need synthesis and summary. For example, suppose a new drug called HYP was developed and investigated. One research study might show that HYP increases heart rate; another study might show that HYP acts on the reticular formation to increase arousal; another investigation might fail to find any clinical effects of HYP with manic-depressive patients; another might show that HYP alleviates mild depression; and still another study might show that HYP produces warts. If we added to this list several hundred studies and if we further complicated the issues by giving HYP a dozen different names, the reader could appreciate the need for a coherent summary and synthesis of the research findings. One method by which psychopharmacologists have attempted to summarize research findings is to construct classificatory systems.

A *classificatory system* is a conceptual tool created by scientists to summarize, synthesize, and simplify factual knowledge. A classificatory system involves a plan by which different elements are grouped together into the same category.

There are numerous ways to classify drugs. For example, drugs can be classified on the basis of chemical composition, clinical effects, neurological effects, sites of action, effects on simple learning processes, and even legal considerations. (The term *narcotic* is a legal classification of certain drugs.) Which classificatory system a psychologist employs depends on the purposes for which he plans to use the system. Thus, for research in animal learning it might be useful to classify drugs on the basis of their effects on simple learning processes. In the science of abnormal psychology, the most useful classificatory systems of drugs are those based on chemical composition, clinical effects, and general neurological effects.

The major categories of the chemical classification of psychoactive drugs are barbiturates, amphetamines, phenothiazines, Rauwolfia, tricyclic antidepressants, MAO inhibitors, proponediols, benzodiazepines, and opiates. The different drugs that are grouped into the same chemical category all have similar chemical compositions; for example, the drugs barbitone and phenobarbitone have very similar chemical compositions and therefore are classified as barbiturates.

The major categories of the clinical classificatory system of psychoactive drugs are as follows: major tranquilizer, minor tranquilizer, hypnotic and sedative, psychostimulant, antidepressant, hallucinogen, and analgesic. Drugs that are grouped into the same category have similar clinical uses; for example, the drugs chlorpromazine and reserpine have similar clinical effects on schizophrenic patients and thus are classified as major tranquilizers. The drug effects described subsequently are for the range of dosages usually employed in clinical practice or usually taken.

Major Tranquilizers

A drug is classified as a major tranquilizer if it can be given in a dosage that reduces agitation, produces feelings of calm, and produces either a diminution of, or an indifference to, hallucinations and delusions, without also producing considerable drowsiness. The major tranquilizers include two chemical groups of drugs, the phenothiazines and the Rauwolfia alkaloids.

The phenothiazines were first synthesized in a French laboratory as a result of a search for a more powerful drug to relieve postoperative pain (Caldwell, 1970). Chlorpromazine was the first phenothiazine to be synthesized, and its clinical use in 1952 revolutionized mental health care throughout the world. The drug is especially effective for agitated schizophrenic patients. Except for the period of initial use, chlorpromazine does not significantly affect consciousness by producing drowsiness unless a large dosage is taken. Prior to its discovery, agitated behavior in schizophrenics was controlled by physical restraints or by the administration of barbiturate drugs that produce significant drowsiness. Thus, the fact that chlorpromazine has minimal effects on consciousness has been very important to its clinical use. Additionally, the drug has antipsychotic properties in that it reduces the patient's concern with hallucinations and delusions. Chlorpromazine also has anticonvulsive effects.

In contrast to the laboratory synthesis of chlorpromazine, reserpine is a drug that was isolated from the roots of the plant *Rauwolfia Serpentine.* Indigenous to India, this plant had been used as a psychoactive agent since ancient times.

However, reserpine was not isolated from the Rauwolfia plant root until the time that chlorpromazine was introduced. The clinical effects of reserpine are similar to those of chlorpromazine, but the drug is less potent and is considered inferior to the newer phenothiazines.

Minor Tranquilizers

Minor tranquilizers are distinguished from major tranquilizers because the latter counteract psychotic thinking, whereas the former do not. In 1951, Berger and Ledwig synthesized meprobamate (Miltown and Equanil) from the muscle relaxant drug mephenesin. During the 1950s, meprobamate, as well as other minor tranquilizers, was widely prescribed for the treatment of mild anxiety in normal and neurotic individuals. Because these drugs produce tolerance as well as physical dependency, their use for normal individuals has been criticized. Furthermore, while tolerance and physical dependency are unquestionably involved in the use of many minor tranquilizers, their therapeutic effects have not been demonstrated convincingly, with the possible exception of meprobamate.

Two minor tranquilizers extensively employed to reduce agitation in psychotic individuals are chlordiazepoxide (Librium) and diazepan (Valium). These drugs are chemically different from meprobamate; their chemical classification is the benzodiazepine category, which comprises a group of drugs chemically related to the phenothiazines. These drugs are used to treat alcoholism and epilepsy, and in recent years they have been increasingly used instead of chlorpromazine in the treatment of schizophrenia. However, unlike chlorpromazine, these drugs have little effect on psychotic delusions and hallucinations.

Hypnotic and Sedative Drugs

Hypnotics are drugs that induce sleep if they are given in sufficient dosages, whereas sedatives are drugs that diminish both anxiety and alertness. Most drugs that are hypnotics are also sedatives. The barbiturates represent the major chemical group classified as hypnotics and sedatives and are frequently employed as sleeping pills and as antianxiety agents. Many physicians use barbiturates rather than minor tranquilizers to treat neurotic anxiety. However, barbiturates are not classified as minor tranquilizers because they produce a significant degree of sleepiness in dosages required to counteract anxiety.

Unlike most psychoactive drugs in clinical use today, the barbiturates have been employed extensively in medical practice since the beginning of the twentieth century. In psychiatry, barbiturates have been used to produce sleep in prolonged sleep therapy and to facilitate a reliving of repressed emotional experiences. Because these drugs have anticonvulsive properties, they are also employed extensively to treat epilepsy.

Barbiturates produce tolerance and physical dependency. A major problem associated with their use is overdosage. Each year, a large number of people die from overdosages of barbiturates. Unfortunately, these drugs have been widely abused by pleasure seekers and by others seeking to escape from psychological conflict. In slang, barbiturates are known as "downers."

Psychostimulants

Psychostimulants such as amphetamine (Benzedrine) and dextroamphetamine (Dexedrine) produce increased motor activity, elevation of mood, "jittery" feelings, transitory euphoria, and excitability. These drugs, known as "uppers," are widely abused in contemporary society. Although psychostimulants probably do not produce physical dependency, they do produce tolerance. If used for long periods, psychostimulants can produce irritability, restlessness, insomnia, and weight loss.

The clinical use of psychostimulants to counteract fatigue in normal individuals is controversial. Moreover, the use of these drugs to counteract depression is controversial because a more intense depression can follow as the drug effects diminish. Perhaps the most widely accepted clinical use of amphetamines is the treatment of hyperactivity in children with the drug Ritalin. Although Ritalin is a neurological stimulant, for hyperactive children it is a behavioral depressant. Psychostimulants are also employed to counteract narcolepsy. This is a condition in which the person falls asleep during the day. Although amphetamine treatment of narcolepsy is usually effective, undesirable side effects can occur.

Amphetamine use can be especially dangerous in suicidal and psychopathic personalities. For example, depressed patients sometimes lack the incentive necessary to commit suicide; this incentive can be provided by amphetamine drugs. Amphetamine use also can produce psychopathic symptoms in certain personalities, and such symptoms are especially evident following prolonged usage.

Antidepressants

As the term implies, antidepressants are drugs that tend to counteract depression. Two chemical groups of drugs have antidepressant properties: the tricyclic antidepressants and the MAO inhibitors. The drug imipramine is an example of the former group, and the drug iproniazid is an example of the latter group.

The synthesis of antidepressant drugs was an event in psychopharmacology the importance of which was similar to the synthesis of the phenothiazines. Prior to the synthesis of these drugs, amphetamines were used to treat depression, and barbiturates were used to counteract psychotic thought. Both amphetamines and barbiturates have general effects; amphetamines have a general stimulatory effect, whereas barbiturates have a general depressant effect. The synthesis of chlorpromazine was significant because this phenothiazine drug acts more selectively on anxiety and less generally on the nervous system than do the barbiturates. Similarly, the synthesis of antidepressants was significant because these drugs act more selectively on depression than do amphetamines.

In assessing the effects of antidepressant drugs, the standard procedure is to distinguish between psychotic and neurotic depression. There is some evidence that imipramine and other tricyclic antidepressants are primarily effective for psychotic depression and that iproniazid and other MAO inhibitors are primarily effective for neurotic depression. However, the data are not so black and white. This is not surprising if one considers that the distinction between psychotic and neurotic depression has been challenged as vague. Nevertheless, the point is clear that individual cases of depression respond differently to the different antidepressant drugs.

Hallucinogens

Hallucinogens such as peyote have been used since ancient times to facilitate religious experiences. In recent years, the hallucinogenic drugs that have received the most attention are LSD, mescaline, and psilocybin. The following remarks are restricted to LSD.

The effects of LSD are especially dependent on a variety of nonspecific factors including personality, environment, and expectation. In general, LSD's subjective effects begin approximately 20 to 30 minutes following oral ingestion of 100 micrograms and usually occur with dizziness, headaches, or nausea. Visual perception is disturbed, the sense of body and time is distorted, and delusions of persecution sometimes occur.

The subjective effects of LSD were first recognized by Hoffman in 1943 and received considerable attention from researchers who hoped to understand better the chemical basis of psychosis. However, more phenomenologically oriented individuals considered LSD an opportunity for "mind-expansion" and "increased awareness." Today the clinical use of LSD is virtually nonexistent.

Analgesics

Drugs that suppress pain are called analgesics. Opiate drugs, such as morphine and heroin, were widely used as analgesics. However, because the use of heroin was outlawed, today morphine is the opiate drug used to diminish pain. Although opium drugs diminish consciousness, relatively small dosages of these drugs do not produce a complete loss of consciousness, as is common with other powerful analgesics. Moreover, opiate drugs produce feelings of euphoria. For this reason, heroin abuse is one of the major forms of drug abuse in contemporary society. Heroin produces tolerance and physical dependency. Biological research on the treatment of heroin dependency will be discussed later in this chapter.

Neurological Classificatory System

In addition to the chemical and the clinical classificatory systems of drugs, it is useful to classify drugs according to their general effects on the central nervous system. The two major categories of this general neurological system of classification are *stimulant* and *depressant.* These terms refer to whether the general activity of the CNS is enhanced (stimulant) or retarded (depressant) by a drug. A drug can enhance general CNS activity in several ways: It can stimulate the reticular formation to increase arousal; it can enhance the transference of neural impulses across synapses; and it can affect arousal systems other than the reticular formation. The same possible sites of action exist for general depressant drugs. Although the general neurological classificatory system includes only two categories, it is possible to categorize drugs further in terms of the degree of neurological stimulation or retardation provided. By inspecting Figure 5-4, it is apparent that the general neurological classificatory system provides a useful summary and synthesis of the various kinds of drugs.

In general, drugs that produce physical dependency are depressant drugs, although not all depressant drugs produce physical dependency. Accordingly, physical dependency is associated with barbiturates, opiates, and alcohol. Most stimulant drugs do not produce physical dependency. However, even though stimulant drugs probably do not cause physical dependency, some of these drugs produce tolerance and lead to psychological dependency.

Figure 5-4
Neurological classification of drugs.

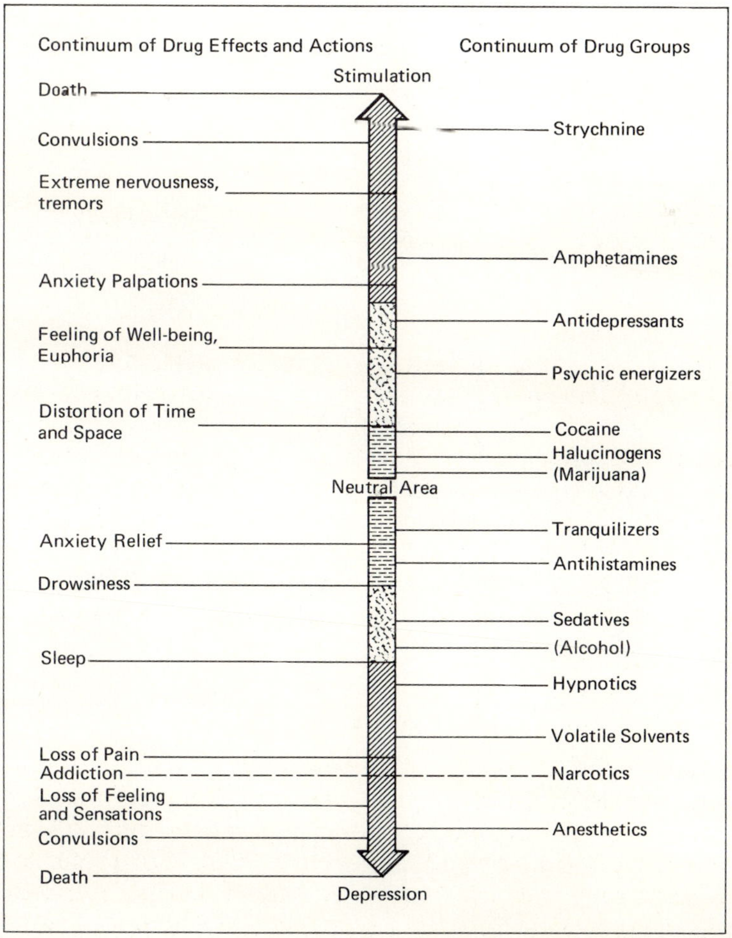

TABLE 5-1.
A Comparison of Three Systems for Classifying Psychoactive Drugs

Chemical Name (Manufacturer's Name; Trade Name)	Chemical Classification	Clinical Classification	General Neurological Classification
Chloropromazine (Thorazine; Lagactil)	Phenothiazine	Major tranquilizer	Depressant
Reserpine	Rauwolfia alkaloids	Major tranquilizer	Depressant
Amylobarbitone Sodium (Sodium Amytal)	Barbiturate	Sedative, hypnotic	Depressant
Phenobarbitone (Luminal)	Barbiturate	Sedative	Depressant
Amphetamine (Benzedrine)	Amphetamine	Psychostimulant	Stimulant
Dextroamphetamine (Dexedrine)	Amphetamine	Psychostimulant	Stimulant
Imipramine (Torfranil)	Tricyclic antidepressant	Antidepressant	Stimulant
Iproniazid (Marsilid)	MAO inhibitor	Antidepressant	Stimulant
Meprobamate (Equanil, Miltown)	Propanediols	Minor tranquilizer	Depressant
Morphine	Opiate	Analgesics	Depressant
Heroin	Opiate	Analgesics	Depressant
Methadone	Opiate	Analgesics	Depressant
LSD	Lysergic acid derivatives	Hallucinogen	Stimulant
Cannabis (marijuana)	Cannabis	Hallucinogen	Depressant

Psychological Effects	Primary Clinical Uses	Physical Dependency	Psychological Dependency
Counteracts anxiety	Schizophrenia; mania; alcoholism	No	No
Counteracts anxiety	Schizophrenia; alcoholism	No	No
Small doses relieve tension; large doses produce sleep	Neurotic anxiety; phobia; used as "truth" serum; used in narcotherapy to facilitate emotional expression	Yes	Yes
Reduces anxiety	Anxiety state	Yes	Yes
Euphoria, alertness, excitability	Fatigue, mild depression	No	Yes
Euphoria, alertness, "jitters"	Fatigue, mild depression	No	Yes
After about one week of use elevates mood and improves appetite and ability to sleep	Endogenous depression	No	No
Elevates mood	Reactive depression	No	No
Produces relaxation, relieves tension and anxiety	Neurotic conditions characterized by tension	Yes, in large dosages	Yes
Diminishes pain, produces relaxed euphoria	To relieve unbearable pain	Yes	Yes
Diminishes pain, produces relaxed euphoria	Illegal in U.S. for any purposes	Yes	Yes
Blocks euphoriant effects of heroin if taken orally; can produce euphoriant effects if injected	Heroin dependency	Yes	Yes
Unpredictable mood changes and distorted perceptions; Psychotic-like states	None; however, has been used to study psychosis	No	Maybe
Produces state of well-being, decreases social inhibitions; produces hallucinations in high doses	None	No	Maybe

Table 5-1 provides a comparison of the three systems of drug classification presently considered to be most useful in abnormal psychology. Each of these systems provides a drug with a different label. Moreover, many drugs also have numerous names given to them by manufacturing companies for marketing purposes; some of these names are shown in parentheses in Table 5-1. The student interested in reading more about drugs should see O. S. Ray (1972) *Drugs, Society, and Human Behavior.*

BIOLOGICAL ASSESSMENT PROCEDURES

Biological assessment procedures vary, depending on the particular disorder being assessed. Some procedures are employed to identify the few specific disorders known to be caused by biological factors. For example, blood tests on newborn infants are used to identify the presence of excessive concentrations of phenylalanine that cause the form of mental retardation called phenylketonuria, or PKU (Berry, 1969). Chromosome counts are used to identify Down's syndrome. Other biological procedures are employed to identify psychological disorders *believed* to be caused by biological factors. For example, the Bender Gestalt test is employed to determine perceptual difficulties in children. On the basis of this and other similar tests, some children are identified as having *minimal brain damage.* A child diagnosed with minimal brain damage is a child who is *believed* to have *some* brain damage *somewhere* in the CNS; the term is misleading if it is taken to imply that specific tissue damage is known to exist. Still other biological assessment procedures are used to study possible biological correlates of emotionality and behavior. An example of one such assessment technique is the electroencephalogram (EEG) introduced by Berger in 1929. In this section, we shall focus exclusively on the EEG as an assessment procedure.

Neural activity generates electrical impulses that can be amplified and recorded; the electronic device that records this neural activity is called an elec-

Figure 5-5
EEG recordings. Part A shows representative electrical potentials of the brain in response to auditory, somatic, and visual stimuli. Part B shows the alpha frequency of the EEG recorded from scalp electrodes on the left (LO) and right (RO) occipital areas. Part C shows the delta frequency, and part D shows the theta frequency. Part E shows contingent negative variation (CNV) which occurs between two associated stimuli, a simple flash (WS) and tone (RS) which was turned off as fast as possible by the subject. Part F shows the beta frequency. The duration of the trace shown in Part A is 0.5 second and positivity is upward. The duration of the trace shown in Parts B through F is 3 seconds. Negativity is upward in Part E. Figure and caption prepared by Dr. Rathe Karrer of the Illinois Institute for Developmental Disabilities; Chicago, Illinois.

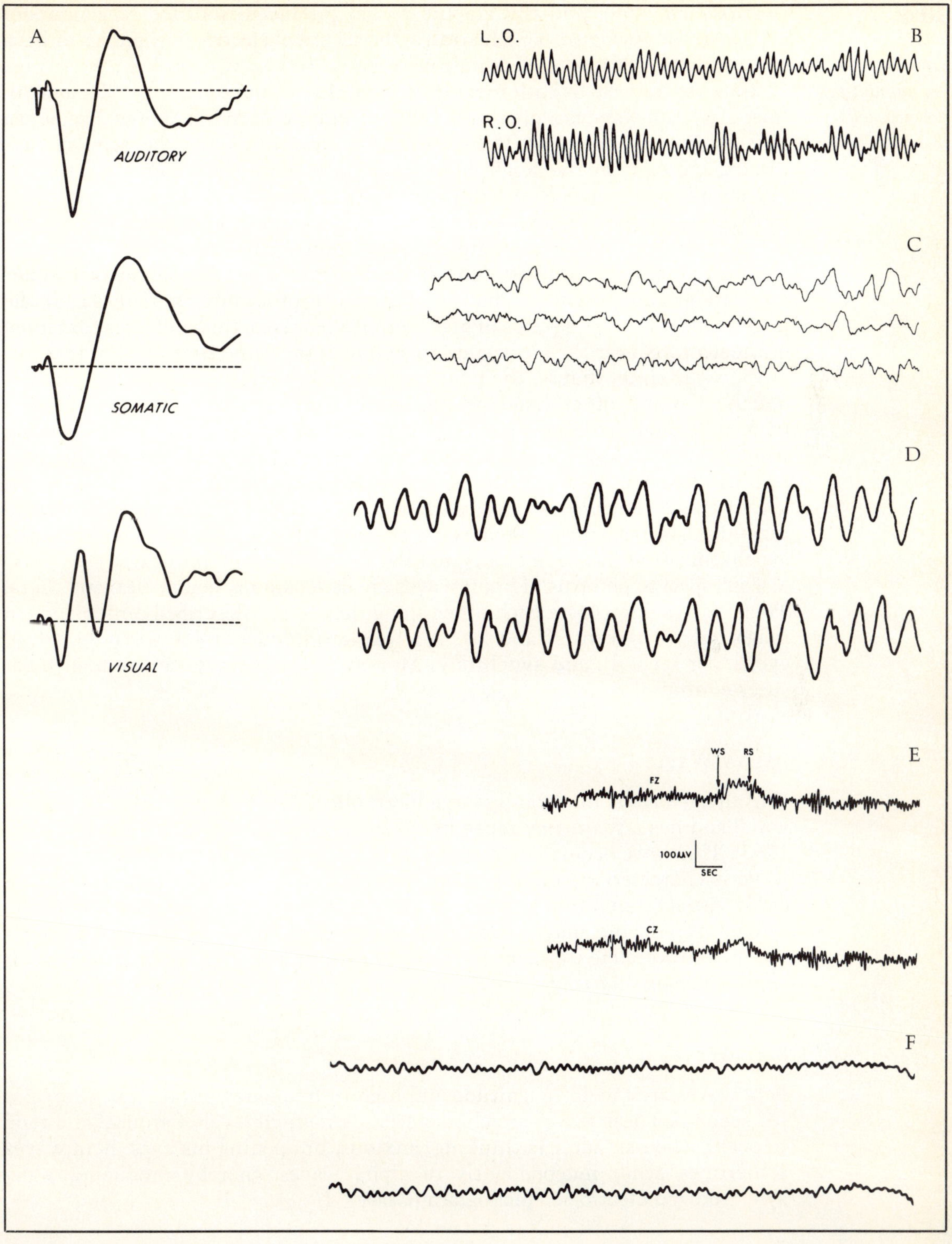
A
AUDITORY
SOMATIC
VISUAL
L.O.
B
R.O.
C
D
E
WS
RS
FZ
100µV
SEC
CZ
F

troencephalograph, and the graphic record produced is called an electroencephalogram. As Figure 5-5 illustrates, the record of electrical impulses forms a pattern of oscillations called brain waves.

Brain waves vary in both magnitude (amplitude) and frequency. The magnitude of a brain wave is a measure of the amount of electrical energy discharged at a specific point in time. In Figure 5-5, the magnitude of each wave is indicated graphically by the height of the wave at each moment. However, the frequency of a brain wave is a measure of electrical energy discharged across time. In Figure 5-5, the frequency of brain waves is indicated graphically by the number of brain waves, or complete oscillations, per unit of time.

When an EEG is administered, electrodes (the two ends of an electrical circuit) are attached to the subject's skull. (The procedure is painless.) If the graphic record shows a series of high-amplitude waves, this indicates that most of the neurons near the electrodes are active at the same time and are inactive at the same time; that is, the neurons near the electrodes are acting *synchronously.* On the other hand, if the graphic record shows a series of low-amplitude, high-frequency waves, this indicates that neighboring neurons are firing electrical discharges independently of one another; that is, the neurons near the electrodes are acting *desynchronously.* These two patterns of neural activity have been correlated with the effects of various drugs. Synchronization has been associated with several depressant drugs, whereas desynchronization has been associated with several stimulant drugs.

Four specific patterns of brain waves are called alpha, beta, delta, and theta. These waves differ from each other along the already described dimensions of magnitude (between 50 and 200 microvolts), frequency (between 1 and 50 cycles per second), and synchrony. Moreover, these waves are general measures of arousal.

Alpha Waves

The alpha wave is moderately large in amplitude (between 25 and 100 microvolts) and has a frequency range between 8 and 13 cycles per second (Glaser, 1963). This wave occurs when one is wakeful and relaxed; moreover, the alpha wave is characteristic of an intermediate level of arousal. Stimulation, especially visual stimulation as when one's eyes are open, tends to reduce both the synchrony and the magnitude of alpha waves. Some investigators have attempted to correlate those people whose EEGs exhibit high alpha activity with various personality traits.

Beta Waves

Beta waves are low in magnitude and high in frequency (more than 13 cycles per second). These waves are characteristic of a high level of arousal and tend to occur when an adult is thinking, anxious, or opening his eyes. Beta waves sometimes occur independently of alpha waves, thereby producing a desynchronized electroencephalogram (Glaser, 1963).

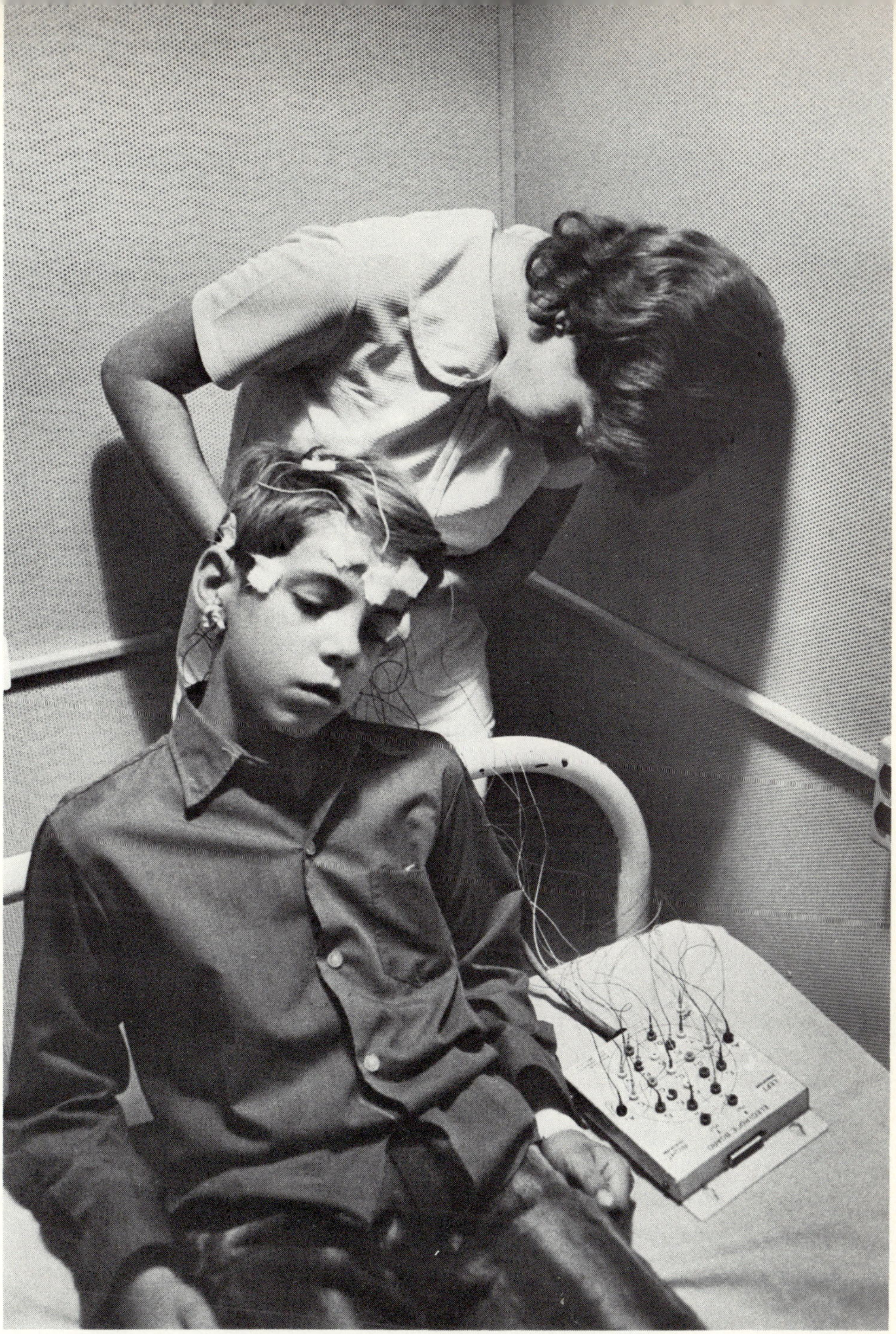

A young boy is prepared for electroencephalography (EEG). (Photo by Constantine Manos; Magnum Photos, Inc.)

Delta Waves

Delta waves are very large in magnitude and very slow in frequency (0.5 to 3.5 cycles per second). These waves are indicative of low arousal and rarely occur in adults who are awake.

Theta Waves

Theta waves have a frequency of between 4 and 7 cycles per second. Theta frequencies are the brain waves found most often in children, and they are rarely observed in adults.

Two questions can be raised regarding the use of the EEG: What is the value of the EEG for psychological research? What is the diagnostic utility of the EEG? The EEG has been employed extensively in psychological research on sleep and on the activity of the brain stem. The EEG reflects the electrical activity of regions of the cerebral cortex located just under the area of the skull on which the electrodes are placed, and electrical activity in the cerebral cortex is influenced significantly by activity in the thalamus, reticular activating system, and other areas of the brain stem. Consequently, the EEG typically is used as a measure of arousal. As such, the EEG has been especially useful in studying periods of sleep in normal and in epileptic individuals. In normal adults, a period of light sleep is characterized by low-amplitude, low-frequency waves and by the irregular occurrence of theta waves, whereas a period of deep sleep is characterized by low-frequency, desynchronous waves. However, the EEGs of some epileptics exhibit spikes in the brain waves during sleep; such spikes can be interpreted as seizure discharges.

The capacity of the EEG to assess brain activity is increased in animal subjects because it is possible to implant electrodes directly into various regions of the brain. In this manner, the EEG has been used to assess the effects on brain activity of drugs, hormones, brain lesions, and visual stimuli. However, even in studies of this kind, it is often difficult to interpret exactly what the EEG is measuring.

In contrast with its importance for some kinds of psychological research, the EEG is of limited value in the diagnosis of mental disorders. In order to use the EEG to detect abnormal neural activity, it is necessary first to define the normal EEG patterns from which the abnormal brain waves are to deviate. Unfortunately, normal people exhibit very different EEG patterns. Although it is possible to construct statistically a normal EEG profile, the large number of normal people who differ significantly from the statistical profile renders it exceedingly difficult to identify with confidence how the EEG of an abnormal personality differs from the EEG of a normal personality. Presently, the EEG alone cannot be employed to identify consistently a single category of psychological disorder. The EEG is important in the diagnosis of epilepsy and brain tumors, but this technique must be employed in conjunction with other diagnostic procedures.

Evoked Potentials

At best, the EEG is a very gross measure of brain functioning. This is not surprising because, as noted, the EEG is primarily a measure of arousal or wakefulness. Because arousal is a general characteristic of a multitude of behaviors, correlations between EEG patterns and behavior are minimal. In an effort to obtain brain wave patterns that correlate more highly with meaningful behavior, scientists have devised a variety of procedures referred to as evoked potential techniques.

Figure 5-5E shows a slow, evoked potential termed *CNV.* The recording shows normal alpha activity until a warning signal is presented to the subject; from prior experience, the subject has learned that a response signal will follow. By inspection of the figure, it can be seen that the warning signal elicits slower brain waves than the alpha activity that both preceded the warning signal and followed the response signal. These slower waves are called the evoked potential and are significant because they correlate highly with a meaningful subject behavior.

Evoked potential techniques are presently being used in many studies in an effort to differentiate between normal and abnormal subjects (Shagass, 1972). It is important to recognize that evoked potential techniques identify correlates of behavior and learning; the use of these techniques does not imply that the primary cause of the behavior under study is biological in nature. For example, Figure 5-5E probably shows a biological correlate of cognitive learning; the normal human subject whose brain activity is shown has learned to anticipate the response signal.

TREATMENT PROCEDURES

The basic treatment procedures of the biological approach are drug therapy, electroconvulsive therapy, psychosurgery, and diet therapy. By statute, these procedures are defined as medical ones and therefore can be administered legally only by a physician or under his supervision. There are several reasons for their importance to psychologists:

1. Biological treatment procedures have provided important scientific data. Regardless of professionally defined specialities, the psychologist can only gain by acquainting himself with clinical data obtained by medical doctors.

2. In mental hospitals and other settings, psychologists have contact with patients receiving drug treatment. The psychologist's treatment of a patient and his evaluation of that treatment can be accomplished more effectively if he is aware of the possible influences of a drug his patient is receiving. Furthermore, the psychologist sometimes is in a position to suggest drug treatment or drug withdrawal for a particular patient with whom the medical doctors have had less contact than has the psychologist.

3. As an outsider to the medical field, the psychologist can serve as a constructive critic of medical procedures. Historically, psychologists have been critical of the evaluation procedures used by medical doctors. This criticism has led to more rigorous evaluation studies that, in several cases, have resulted in revisions in medical treatment.

The treatment strategies of the biological approach vary with the particular treatment procedure and with the specific case under consideration. The most common treatment strategies include the prevention of mental disorders, the alleviation of anxiety for its direct benefit to the patient or for the purpose of facilitating other treatment procedures, the cure or partial cure of mental disorders, and the amelioration of the side effects of other treatment procedures. Drugs usually are prescribed for any one of these purposes except for the purpose of a cure or partial cure. Moreover, both convulsive therapy and psychosurgery usually are employed either to cure a mental disorder or to alleviate anxiety for the purpose of facilitating psychotherapy. Diet therapy usually is administered for preventive purposes. The specific manners in which these treatment strategies are implemented are discussed subsequently.

Drug Treatment

Because drug use frequently involves serious risks, the physician must subjectively weigh the potential advantages and disadvantages of drug treatment in each case. That is, the potential for therapeutic effects must be weighed against the potential for toxic effects and for possible dependency. If the decision is made to prescribe a drug, the physician should evaluate periodically the effects of the treatment to determine whether any beneficial effects are evident. These evaluations may result in a decision either to change to another drug or to modify the current dosage. However, the number of patients who seek psychiatric care is so much greater than the number of psychiatrists available that psychiatrists sometimes have only minimal contact with their patients. This is especially true in large mental hospitals where the patient-to-physician ratio is frequently as high as several hundred to one. Such case overloads often preclude a careful evaluation of drug effects, thereby forcing the physician to rely on anecdotal data. It is not uncommon in large mental hospitals for patients to receive drugs on the basis of complaints by ward attendants; nor is it uncommon in overburdened out-patient clinics for children to receive drugs solely on the basis of complaints by parents.

In drug treatment, the physician decides on the particular drug to be prescribed, the method of administration, and the dosage. The reader can consult Table 5-1 for a brief listing of the clinical effects of some widely used drugs.

Convulsive Therapy[4]

In 1933, Von Meduna observed that schizophrenia rarely occurs in people who have epilepsy. Although this observation is basically correct, the phenomenon can be easily explained: Because the probability is low that a randomly chosen person will have epilepsy or schizophrenia, the probability is significantly lower that a randomly chosen person will have both epilepsy and schizophrenia. Thus, Von Meduna's observation that schizophrenia and epilepsy rarely occur in the same person does not imply that the presence of one disorder precludes the presence of the other. Nevertheless, Von Meduna hypothe-

[4] The next two sections are based in part on data and clinical experiences summarized by Eysenck (1961), Kalinowsky and Hippius (1969), Kardener (1970), Patterson (1963), and Sargant and Slater (1963).

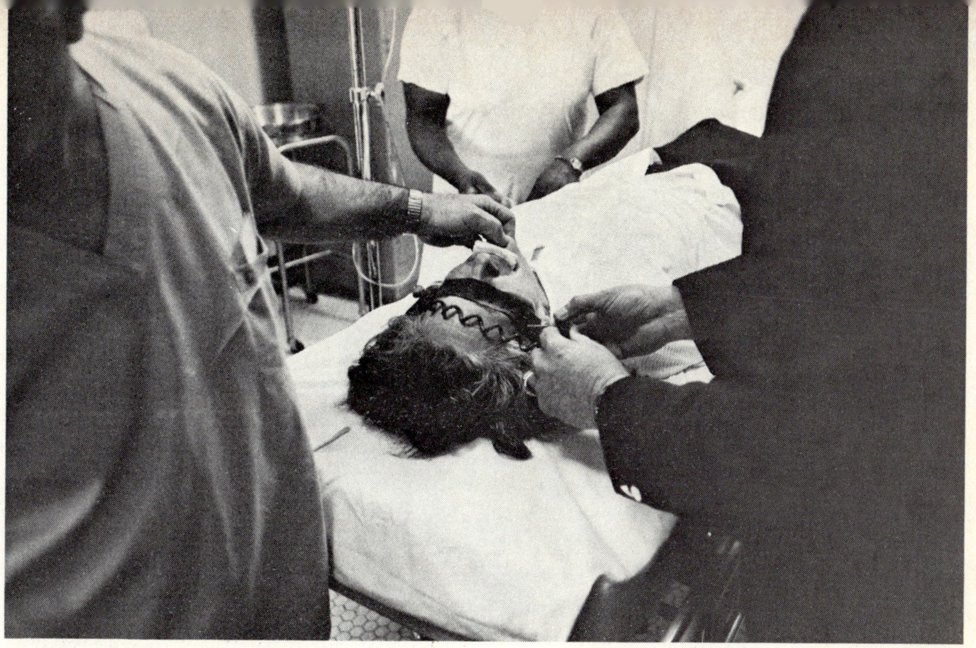

A patient being readied for electroconvulsive therapy (ECT). (Photo by Paul Fusco; Magnum Photos, Inc.)

sized that epileptic and other convulsions produce a physical state antagonistic to schizophrenia. Accordingly, he proposed that clinically induced convulsions would counteract schizophrenia and proceeded to test this hypothesis by chemically inducing convulsions in schizophrenic patients. Thus, convulsive therapy was introduced on the basis of logically fallacious reasoning concerning the incidence of epileptic schizophrenics.

It is important to distinguish between an evaluation of the theoretical rationale for a treatment procedure and an evaluation of the effectiveness of the treatment itself. Von Meduna's hypothesis has been replaced by as many as fifty alternative hypotheses, for each of which a theoretical rationale has been proposed concerning the effects of convulsive therapy (Kalinowsky and Hippius, 1969) and for each of which there are serious difficulties in explaining the available data. Nevertheless, convulsive treatment is used extensively throughout the world by psychiatrists who maintain that the treatment is effective even though the reason for its effectiveness is unknown. The logic is flawless; knowledge of the effects of a treatment procedure is sufficient to determine whether or not the procedure should be used.

As noted, Von Meduna's treatment of schizophrenia consisted of clinically induced convulsions. At first, the drug metrazol was used to induce convulsions, but in 1937 Cerletti and Bini introduced a method of inducing convulsions by the application of electric current through the brain. Today procedures that induce convulsions by electrical means are preferred because electrical methods are less elaborate and produce less discomfort for the patient.

The treatment of depression and other disorders by electrically induced convulsions is called electroconvulsive therapy (ECT). The procedure consists of placing two electrodes on the patient's skull and applying a 70- to 130-volt current for 0.1 to 0.5 second. This typically results in an immediate convulsion that usually lasts between one and two minutes, during which time the patient is unconscious. Electrically induced convulsions are very similar to convulsions in grand mal epilepsy, with one notable exception. In grand mal epilepsy, the person often is warned of an impending convulsion by preliminary symptoms called an aura; in ECT, the aura is absent.

A major problem that may occur during ECT sessions is the possibility of bone fractures. In order to reduce this possibility, many psychiatrists administer muscle relaxant drugs to diminish the intensity of muscular contractions. However, the use of muscle relaxants during ECT creates its own problems, including a slightly increased possibility of heart failure and a slightly increased possibility of suffocation due to vomiting. (The muscle relaxants depress the heart rate as well as the gag reflex that normally would clear the throat.) For these reasons, patients with cardiovascular problems receive special preparations for ECT, and all patients refrain from eating for several hours prior to treatment. Today, most psychiatrists administer ECT with muscle relaxant drugs although some do not prescribe drugs at all. Regardless of the method of administration, ECT is reported to be an exceptionally safe medical procedure, with the possibility of death being negligible and with the possibility of bone fractures being very low. Surprisingly, there are no counterindications (conditions that would preclude treatment) for ECT (Kalinowsky & Hippius, 1969; Sargant & Slater, 1963).

Another major problem associated with ECT is the patient's fear of the procedure despite its painlessness. Speculation concerning the basis of this emotional reaction has included the patient's fear of not regaining consciousness as well as the patient's interpretation of ECT as punishment. One factor that definitely contributes to the patient's fear occurs when an incomplete loss of consciousness follows the application of electric current. On such rare occasions, the psychiatrist immediately reapplies a stronger electric current, but the patient's fear of the next treatment session is often considerable. In order to reduce this fear, some physicians prescribe sedative drugs (barbiturates).

In addition to the patient's fear, it seems likely that family members undergo complex emotional reactions that may include guilt as well as fear for the patient's well-being.

As in the case of Susan Anderson, ECT usually is given two or three times per week for a total of about six sessions. Unfortunately, it has not been uncommon for physicians to experiment by giving as many as a hundred ECT sessions in a difficult case. Following each session, the patient enters a coma from which he awakens in a confused state. If approximately six evenly spaced treatment sessions are given in a two-week period, the confusional state usually dissipates in a matter of hours. However, in some cases, prolonged confusion may necessitate the termination of treatment. Long-lasting confusional states are especially evident following massive treatment involving scores of daily sessions.

Patients usually awaken from an ECT session with a loss of memory for many events that occurred prior to the treatment. This consequence has stimulated research designed to determine whether some memory loss is permanent (Campbell, 1961). There is general agreement that memory is gradually restored during a brief period of time. However, it is still a matter of controversy as to whether permanent memory loss results for some events. Even if some permanent memory loss does result, the loss is not sufficiently significant to preclude the use of ECT.

Psychosurgery

In medieval Rome, a person supposedly recovered from a psychosis after a sword wound had violated the brain region. Subsequently, some Roman physicians attempted to cure psychosis by boring holes into the skull to let out the diseased body humors. The noted physiologist Alexander Messaria maintained that body humor is too thick a fluid to evaporate, and so the method was abandoned until Burckhardt revived it in 1888. Moniz then introduced the procedure to psychiatry in 1935.

Although the term *psychosurgery* includes the removal of brain tumors, our concern here is with the surgical disruption of neural fibers connecting the prefrontal lobes of the cerebrum to the thalamus. This procedure, called a prefrontal lobotomy, was once performed by boring holes into the skull and by introducing alcohol to the exposed areas to destroy brain cells. Several refinements have since been developed. The major advance in surgical technique occurred when the use of alcohol was replaced by a physical severing of the neural fibers by fine needles called leucotomes. Today a complete prefrontal lobotomy is becoming increasingly rare; the more typical procedure is to sever only some of those fibers that are severed in a complete lobotomy. A similar operation is called leucotomy. The physical destruction of brain cells that results from these operations is irreversible.

The short-term effects of a lobotomy often differ from the long-term effects. Immediately following the operation, patients can be confused and hostile. They may exhibit crazy beliefs, agitation, or retarded activity. Although patients tend to recover gradually from these effects, counseling and/or rehabilitative psychotherapy often are recommended. If the surgical cut is made in the intended area, the long-term effects of a lobotomy usually include a reduction of psychological tension, a loss of ability to concentrate, and increased apathy.

Because the cerebral cortex is considered to be the site of symbolic activities, it was expected that severing some of the connections between the frontal lobes and the thalamus would profoundly affect intellectual ability. Surprisingly, the long-term effects of lobotomy do not usually include a loss of intellectual capacity (Willett, 1961).

Although lobotomies and leucotomies were once widely employed in the United States, only 145 operations were performed in the United States in 1972 in 1,750 hospitals surveyed.[5] However, they are given more frequently in some other countries, and there are some attempts being made to revive these operations in the United States. The decline in the use of this operation has

[5] Professional Activities Study, Commission of Professional Hospital Activities, Ann Arbor, Michigan (personal communication, 1975).

been related to the synthesis of tranquilizing drugs that produce improvement in schizophrenic individuals without also producing irreversible physical damage. Ethical opposition also has contributed to the decline in lobotomies.

Other Biological Procedures

Introduced by Sakel in 1935, insulin coma treatment constituted the first of the so-called shock therapies. The treatment consists of the injection of insulin and the consequent gradual onset of a coma. Each treatment session lasts approximately five to six hours, after which the coma is terminated by the injection of glucose (sugar). Although the procedure is usually safe, the coma sometimes fails to terminate, thereby resulting in death. In successful cases, the predominant effects of insulin coma include a reduction in psychotic thought and an increase in social responsiveness. Today most psychiatrists prefer to use convulsive therapy instead of insulin coma treatment.

In recent years, bioadvocates have paid increasing attention to the role of diet in emotional and in intellectual abnormalities (Krieger, 1966; Warren, 1973). That even minor deviations from a proper diet can produce emotional effects has long been recognized. For example, emotional irritability typically results if a meal is delayed for several hours. Moreover, diets deficient in vitamins tend to have noticeable effects on behavior. In this regard, recent psychological research has been especially concerned with the need for the vitamin B complex for the maintenance of healthy psychological functioning. In cases in which emotional or behavioral difficulties are related to an improper diet, treatment is basically a matter of providing a properly balanced diet.

Diet therapy is much more complicated when used for the prevention of PKU (e.g., Berry, 1969). Approximately one child in every ten thousand has phenylalanine concentrations in his blood sufficient to produce mental retardation. If untreated within the first three months of life, the child will be severely retarded and will probably require institutionalization. However, special diets can be prescribed that reduce the concentration of phenylalanine in the blood, thereby avoiding permanent brain damage. Nevertheless, this treatment is complicated by the body's need of phenylalanine for normal growth; that is, although excessive phenylalanine concentrations correlate highly with PKU, a low phenylalanine concentration prevents normal growth. In order to ensure that blood phenylalanine concentrations are at optimal levels, continual biochemical monitoring and dietary adjustments are required.

To summarize, biological treatment procedures tend to be very direct ones in which the physician attempts to alter the patient's biochemical and/or physiological states. Except in the case of diet therapy, the theoretical rationale for these procedures is inadequate; for example, we do not know why convulsive therapy produces the effects that it does. Moreover, the administration of several of these procedures includes a possibility of serious harmful consequences despite recent advances in techniques that have reduced significantly complications in ECT and in psychosurgery. The continued use of these procedures is predicated on the belief that, in most cases, the potential beneficial effects outweigh the potential harmful effects. This claim is evaluated in the next section.

TREATMENT EFFECTIVENESS

This section briefly reviews the effectiveness of several biological treatment procedures, primarily by reporting those conclusions on which clinical observers generally agree. The review is organized in terms of which treatments are effective for accomplishing each of the three strategies of prevention, relief, and cure.

Prevention

Two classic examples of preventive biological treatment are diet therapy for PKU and antibiotic drug treatment for syphilis infections that produce general paresis. These treatments prevent the disorder in the majority of patients, provided that treatment is administered prior to the occurrence of irreversible brain damage (e.g., Lilienfeld, 1969; Knox, 1960). However, effective preventive treatments are unavailable for most mental disorders known to be caused by biological abnormalities.

Symptomatic Relief

There is general agreement that psychoactive drugs produce symptomatic relief rather than cures. That is, a drug's effects usually last only as long as the patient continues to use the drug, and drugs usually affect behavior in a manner that is not specific to the patient's emotional problems. For example, an anxious person who is given a barbiturate as a sedative not only becomes less anxious but also becomes drowsy. The sedative does not cause the person to respond more constructively to anxiety-provoking stimuli but rather reduces the person's capacity to respond with anxiety to any stimulus.

As previously noted, both tranquilizer and antidepressant drugs tend to produce more specific behavioral effects than those produced by the barbiturates. Both experimental and clinical evidence indicate that the phenothiazines, particularly chlorpromazine, are especially useful in treating schizophrenic agitation, delusions, and hallucinations. Moreover, most clinicians consider imipramine to be an effective treatment for depression—particularly for psychotic depression—although the question is debatable as to whether imipramine is more or less effective for depression than is ECT (see Chapter 14). Antidepressant drugs are not usually considered useful for cures because the patient's symptoms usually reappear when drug treatment is discontinued. In those cases in which symptoms do not reappear following the termination of drug treatment, it is often difficult to know whether the continuance of improved behavior is attributable to the specific effects of the drug or to "spontaneous" remission.

Although the hope that psychoactive drugs would "cure" mental disorders is unfulfilled, the discovery and synthesis of drugs that relieve anxiety, depression, and other evidence of psychological suffering are nevertheless noteworthy achievements. In addition to its obvious benefit to the patient, symptomatic relief may be important to enhance interpersonal exchanges in psychotherapy. Moreover, drugs that induce relaxation have been used to facilitate desensitization in behavior therapy.

Cure or Partial Cure

For most depressive states, and particularly for psychotic depression, ECT has been reported to be effective by practitioners throughout the world. Psychiatrists have reported remission rates of between 70 and 100 per cent for psychotic depression (Kalinowsky & Hippius, 1969). However, reports on the use of ECT with nondepressive disorders have been less favorable and more ambiguous. In particular, ECT has rarely been reported to be effective for schizophrenic patients even though convulsive therapy was originally introduced for the treatment of schizophrenia (Lewis & Maher, 1966).

Some scientists would question the classification of ECT as a method that can be administered to cure depression. In this regard, some quasi-scientific data suggest that a depressed person who improves under ECT is more likely to experience a relapse than if he had improved under psychotherapy (Salzman, 1947). Even though some patients experience a relapse following ECT, it is noteworthy that many do not and that those who do can be treated again (see Sargant & Slater, 1963). ECT has also been employed to relieve depressive symptoms in order to facilitate psychotherapy.

The treatment strategy for the administration of prefrontal lobotomy is to cure partially a severely debilitating psychological disorder from which there is no realistic hope for improvement. Friedman, Moore, Ranger, and Russman (1951) reported an extensive, two-year evaluation of the effects of lobotomy. The study included 254 patients who received lobotomies and 100 patients who served as controls. All of the control subjects were recommended for lobotomies but never received them because permission for the operation was denied. The results showed that 57.8 per cent of the lobotomized patients were rated as significantly improved two years following the operation and that 37.6 per cent of these patients were released from the hospital. By comparison, 3 per cent of the control subjects were rated as significantly improved, including 2 per cent who were released from the hospital. Although lobotomy and other psychosurgical operations have been criticized as unethical, the results of this and other studies suggest that, in completely hopeless cases, there may be some justification for the operation.

Both ECT and prefrontal lobotomy are controversial procedures (see Patterson, 1963). Although both procedures have been criticized as unethical, ECT gradually is becoming accepted as an effective treatment for depressive states, whereas lobotomy has become virtually extinct in the United States.

Ethical Considerations

Ethical opposition to biological treatments has been based on: (1) the absence of an adequate theoretical rationale for the effects of some treatment procedures; (2) beliefs that certain biological treatments (particularly lobotomy) produce deleterious effects in too many patients; and (3) concerns that safeguards against abuse are inadequate because only physicians can employ these procedures. In regard to the first objection, it was previously noted that the effects of treatment procedures can be known in the absence of adequate theoretical rationales and that knowledge of effects is sufficient to justify treatment. In regard to the second objection pertaining to possible deleterious effects, it seems fair to conclude that this issue is best resolved by systematic and better-controlled research. Even though the data reviewed suggest that fears of deleterious effects have been exaggerated, particularly with ECT, the position is well taken that better evaluative studies are needed. However, ethical objections based on hypotheses suggesting that biological treatments lend themselves to abuse should be considered even when these procedures can be demonstrated to be effective.

A striking social aspect of biological treatment is the investment in the physician of enormous power that can be abused by using treatment in a punitive manner or for purposes of experimentation. Suppose that in a large mental hospital a patient dislikes a ward attendant and rebels by behaving aggressively or by refusing to cooperate with his requests. Angered by the patient's defiance, the attendant may seek to punish the patient by convincing the supervising psychiatrist, who may be too busy to have personal knowledge of the case, that the patient's behavior is a sign of worsening "illness." Consequently, the psychiatrist may drug, shock, or lobotomize the patient into submission.

Biological treatment has a long history of abuse. The predecessors of current biological treatments include procedures that clearly involved physical torture; whatever success such procedures may have achieved could have been the result of the patient's desire to improve in order to escape further treatment. The question arises as to whether this historical tendency to abuse biological treatment procedures is evident in today's practices.

Szasz (1970) has advanced the thesis that the social conditions that permitted the abuse of biological treatment in the past are still in existence. Although Szasz's thesis is complex, one specific point concerns the concentration of social and legal power in one group of individuals. The physician possesses considerable power over patients, particularly institutionalized patients; the physician sometimes has the power to decide what is best for the patient even if the patient disagrees. What protects the patient from a physician who wants to experiment by administering a new drug or hundreds of ECT sessions? If the patient cannot afford legal redress, the only safeguard against abuse is professional ethics. Unfortunately, professional ethics affords the patient less protection than he sometimes needs.

Biological treatment procedures lend themselves to abuse primarily because physicians possess too much power. Although Szasz (1970) has concluded that the solution lies in reducing the physician's power by eliminating mental institutions and by attacking as unethical many biological treatment procedures, other less drastic solutions are possible. For example, the elimination of physicians' unique access to biological treatment and the threat of effective legal action for unethical experimentation may provide a counterforce to check the power of the physician, thereby reducing the possibility of abuse.

In conclusion, whether or not the use of biological treatment procedures is ethical is a complex question. On the one hand, it is important that these procedures be evaluated experimentally so that their full effects can be understood. We would not want to deny effective treatment to suffering individuals in the name of ethics and humanitarianism. On the other hand, social sanctions are needed against the abuse of effective and therefore powerful proce-

The medical profession experimented with all sorts of techniques for treating psychologically troubled people. The print depicts suspensory treatment for nervous ataxia at the Salpêtrière Hospital in Paris and was originally published in Frank Leslie's *Illustrated Newspaper* in April, 1889. If these treatments had any beneficial effects, it may have been because the patients wanted to improve to escape therapy. The ethics of such treatments are discussed in the text. (Reprinted by permission of Historical Pictures Service; Chicago, Illinois.)

dures. This is not to imply that physicians are less moral than the rest of us; rather, it is doubtful whether any large group of individuals can be trusted with so much power.

RESEARCH METHODOLOGY

Because biological hypotheses concerning mental disorders have generated physiological and genetic studies as well as psychological studies, numerous research methodologies have been used. In this section we shall focus on drug research in order to exemplify some of the complex issues that arise in experimental studies within the biological approach. Specifically, three strategies of experimentation are discussed: *uncontrolled clinical trials* (case history), *single-blind experiments,* and *double-blind experiments.*

The simplest method of evaluating a drug's effects is to observe patients prior to, during, and following the administration of that drug. This method of uncontrolled clinical trials allows the investigator to describe the changes in behavior that correlated with the administration of the drug. However, uncontrolled clinical trial studies do not allow the investigator to determine whether or not the observed behavior changes following drug administration were causally related to the chemical properties of the drug. The observed effects could have resulted from nonspecific factors such as the patient's expectations concerning the drug's effects, the attention given to the patient during the administration of the drug, or the patient's desire to please the investigator by rendering the treatment effective. The uncontrolled clinical trials methodology is useful only for preliminary studies in which the purpose is limited to obtaining a general idea of what the specific effects of a drug might be so that a more informative study can be planned. Unfortunately, a considerable amount of research on drugs has employed the methodology of uncontrolled clinical trials.

In order to determine whether or not observed behavior changes are causally related to the specific variables of a drug, it is necessary to include at least two groups of subjects in the experiment—the drug treatment group receives the drug under investigation, while the other group receives a placebo. A placebo is a chemically inert substance, such as water or sugar, that is given as an experimental control for nonspecific drug effects. The behavior changes observed in the drug treatment group are attributed to both specific and nonspecific factors, whereas the behavior changes observed in the placebo control group are attributed only to nonspecific factors. Thus, the specific effects of the drug are the *differences* in behavior changes between drug treatment and placebo control groups. In other words, if the drug treatment group exhibits greater improvement than the placebo group, the drug is considered to be effective for behavioral improvement.

Placebo effects can be considerable in drug research. Symptoms such as anxiety, headaches, tension, pain, fever, and phobia can be significantly affected by placebos (McNair, Kahn, Droppleman, & Fisher, 1968). Moreover, placebos sometimes produce side effects that include headaches, diarrhea, and nausea. Because some people do not react to placebos, some investigators have attempted to describe possible personality differences between people who do react to placebos and those who do not. The results of this research are inconclusive although it is noteworthy that people who are highly suggestible are generally considered to be likely to react to placebos.

Two sources of possible bias in drug studies arise if subjects know whether they are receiving drug or placebo and if the observers who evaluate behavior changes—and the experimenter who administers the drug and the placebo—know which subjects are receiving the drug and which are not. In *single-blind* drug studies, the subject does not know whether he is receiving drug or placebo; in *double-blind* drug studies, neither the subject nor the observer nor the person who administers the substances knows who is receiving

Treatments can be effective merely because the troubled person expects the treatment to work. The print shows an attempt to treat a patient with electrowave therapy. The elaborate apparatus gave the impression of a credible, scientific treatment, and this placebo effect might explain whatever success this form of treatment might have had. (Reprinted by permission of Historical Pictures Service; Chicago, Illinois.)

the drug or the placebo. The best methodological procedure is the double-blind experiment because it eliminates more sources of bias than does the single-blind experiment.

In addition to placebo effects, a major methodological problem in the study of drugs concerns the selection of subjects. In human studies, experimental drugs usually are administered to people who volunteer for the experiment. However, the solicitation of volunteers raises the issue of whether or not people who volunteer for drug studies are systematically different, along some personality dimensions, from those who do not. Trouton and Eysenck (1961) have suggested that volunteers may tend to be more neurotic than nonvolunteers. If this suggestion is true, experimental results obtained on volunteer subjects may not be applicable to nonvolunteer subjects. Thus, in human research on volunteer subjects, the problem of *generalizing* the results to nonvolunteer subjects requires serious attention.

Still another methodological issue raised by drug research concerns the difference between the dosage and the effective dosage. Even though two subjects may be given the same amount of a drug, the amount of the drug at a site of action at any particular time can differ. Consequently, two people can react differently to the same dosage of the same drug because the effective dosage may vary. In drug research on a small number of subjects, it can be very difficult to assess this problem. However, with a large number of subjects, the problem is not likely to be significant. In some animal studies it is possible to avoid this problem altogether by applying the drug directly to its site of action.

In conclusion, a careful experimental evaluation of drug treatment effects must be concerned with placebo effects, the subject's knowledge of whether he is given drug or placebo, experimenter bias, possible personality characteristics of volunteer subjects, and the distinction between dosage and effective dosage. Clearly, drug studies that simply observe behavior prior to, during, and following the administration of a drug are of limited value.

EXAMPLE OF RESEARCH ISSUE: METHADONE MAINTENANCE

Heroin dependency leads to considerable suffering for the individual involved and for the community in which he resides. Once addicted, the user is likely to take heroin on a daily basis for periods totaling at least six months per year (Bowden & Maddux, 1972). During these periods of daily use, the addict is usually unable to work or to cope with family responsibilities and problems. So many addicts have been forced to resort to theft to support their habit that heroin use has become a major factor contributing to crime.

Opiate Drugs

Like morphine, heroin is a derivative of the opium poppy plant. These drugs—chemically classified as opiates and legally defined as narcotics—have powerful euphoriant effects. Opiate drugs act on the central nervous system and have been used in cases of extreme pain; the analgesic effects of opiates tend to be relatively specific in that motor activity and other CNS functions are not affected to as great an extent as that associated with other pain-killing drugs (Ray, 1972).

Opiate drugs have a long history of medical use primarily because of their analgesic properties. During the nineteenth century, morphine and codeine were used for these purposes and could be purchased easily with a prescription at local drugstores. Many physicians also prescribed opiate substances as a substitute habit for alcoholism (Ray, 1972). The addicting properties of morphine led to a search for an alternative. In the late nineteenth century, heroin was introduced as the sought-for alternative. Although chemically similar to morphine, it is more potent and was originally marketed as a nonaddicting substitute for morphine and codeine. Several early scientific reports concluded that heroin was in fact a satisfactory, nonaddicting substitute for morphine. This view, however, soon gave way to reality; heroin is more addicting than morphine. The Harrison Act of 1912 and subsequent laws and court decisions progressively restricted the legal use of heroin; today its use is illegal for any purpose.

Although the beneficial effects of completely outlawing heroin are contro-

There are more than 100,000 heroin addicts in New York City alone. (Photo by Ian Berry; Magnum Photos, Inc.)

versial, the harmful consequences are apparent. With the price of heroin relatively high, considerable profits can be made in its illicit sale. The number of heroin addicts in urban ghettos is alarming; in 1972, there were more than 100,000 addicts in New York City alone and more than 1,100 deaths as a result of heroin abuse. In 1971 it was estimated that between 10 and 15 per cent of the American force in Vietnam were users of heroin (Ray, 1972).

To support a habit that can cost up to $100 per day, many addicts resort to crime. Because stolen goods sell for far less than their retail value, the amount of crime caused by heroin addiction is considerable.

During the early 1960s, treatment for heroin addiction primarily consisted of forced abstinence in an emotionally supportive atmosphere. For about ten days following the termination of heroin use, the addict experiences unpleasant physical disturbances. Although the nature of these withdrawal symptoms varies depending on the individual, typical withdrawal symptoms include vomiting, loss of appetite, restlessness, delirium, and alternating periods of chills and excessive perspiration. However, forced abstinence programs are considered ineffective for two reasons: Few addicts voluntarily agree to participate in treatment, and among those who do volunteer for and complete treatment, many return to heroin shortly after being discharged from the hospital. Dole and Nyswander's (1965) report of successful methadone treatment has provided a controversial alternative to forced abstinence.

Methadone Blockage Effect

Methadone was synthesized as a substitute for morphine by German scientists during World War II. Although it produces physical dependency, it has recently been experimented with as a substitute habit for heroin. The presumed benefits to the client have been related to the belief that a methadone habit is less debilitating than is a heroin habit.

The methadone blockage effect refers to the fact that moderate dosages of methadone block the euphoriant effects of smaller dosages of heroin. The nature of this effect is controversial. At first, it was assumed that methadone satisfied a physical need for opiate substances without also producing debilitating psychological effects. However, most heroin addicts are accustomed to intravenous injections, while methadone usually is administered orally. Because oral administration usually leads to a lower effective dosage than does intravenous administration, methadone may have less debilitating effects primarily because it is being taken in effectively smaller dosages. If methadone is taken in higher dosages orally, or if it is administered intravenously in moderate dosages, it has euphoriant effects similar to those of heroin (Lennard, Epstein, & Rosenthal, 1972).

The Williams Study

Williams (1971) compared the effects of high- and low-dosage methadone maintenance programs at the Narcotic Addiction Foundation of British Columbia, Canada. The low-dosage program provided daily methadone doses of 40 milligrams to 101 subjects whose mean age was 44; the high-dosage program provided daily doses of 100 milligrams to 82 subjects whose mean age was 33.

The uncontrolled clinical trials methodology was employed. In order to determine whether subjects on methadone were still taking heroin, urinalysis was performed seven times per month on each subject in the high-dosage program. The investigator also interviewed each subject to assess the effects of treatment on employment and on criminal activity.

The results suggested that both programs were effective treatment for heroin addiction. Of the 101 subjects in the low-dosage program, 80 remained in treatment for two months or longer. Of these, 60 per cent had shown no evidence of heroin use. Moreover, criminal activity decreased in 66 per cent of the patients and increased in only 9 per cent; employment increased for the majority of males. Similarly, of those who received high methadone dosages and who stayed in treatment for two months or longer, 54 per cent showed no evidence of heroin use, and 70 per cent of those considered employable were employed in full- or part-time positions or were housewives. Moreover, a 70 per cent decrease in criminal activity was noted.

The Weppner, Stephens, and Conrad Study

As previously noted, relatively high dosages of methadone produce euphoriant effects. This property may allow some clients to defeat the purposes of methadone maintenance either by using the drug as a euphoriant or by selling it to other addicts and using the money to buy heroin. Weppner, Stephens, and

Conrad (1972) attempted to estimate the extent to which illicit methadone use has occurred.

The subjects were 336 patients admitted to the NIMH Clinical Research Center at Lexington, Kentucky. Following admission to the program and withdrawal from heroin, each subject was given a questionnaire to assess the nature of the subject's experience with methadone.

The results indicated that 63 per cent had prior experience with methadone—43 per cent had used methadone illegally and 33 per cent had been in methadone maintenance programs. Because these latter subjects came to the Lexington Center for treatment, they represented failures of previous methadone programs. Moreover, the data indicated that, of the 145 persons who had used methadone illegally, 44 per cent received the drug from their regular heroin pusher, whereas 37 per cent received it from a methadone maintenance patient. The average cost of an illegal methadone habit was estimated at four dollars per day, far below the cost of a heroin habit. Of particular interest were the data obtained from the 111 subjects who had previously participated in methadone maintenance programs. Of these, 78 per cent reported that they had abused at least one illegal drug during methadone treatment. (This does not mean that 78 per cent of all people who participate in methadone programs abuse another drug; rather, 78 per cent of those who participated in methadone treatment and who later returned still addicted to heroin abused another drug during the original methadone treatment.)

From these data, the investigators concluded that (1) many heroin addicts have had experience with methadone; (2) methadone is used extensively by addicts as a euphoriant; and (3) many addicts cheat by using other narcotic drugs while participating in methadone maintenance programs.

Discussion

The two studies reviewed are representative of the presently available data concerning methadone maintenance programs. The Williams study is typical of the kind of support available to methadone proponents, and the Weppner, Stephens, and Conrad study is typical of the kind of negative data cited by critics of methadone programs.

When methadone was introduced, many believed that almost *any* indication of effective change in the addict's habit was a significant step forward. The early evaluations of methadone were constructed to maximize the probability of finding beneficial treatment effects. The Williams study exemplifies this kind of bias in three ways. First, the Williams study evaluated the effects of an entire treatment program—not just the effects of methadone—on heroin use, criminal activity, and unemployment with hardened addicts. Because the figures prior to treatment indicated heavy heroin use, high criminal activity, and high unemployment, the measures could only improve. A second source of bias was the exclusion of variables that were likely to show harmful treatment effects or no treatment effects. For example, Williams did not report on the extent to which his subjects used methadone as a euphoriant. A third source of bias was the evaluation of treatment after only two months; perhaps if Williams had evaluated the treatment after six months, he might have found considerable tendencies to return to old styles of behavior.

By contrast, the Weppner, Stephens, and Conrad study was designed in a way that emphasized the negative aspects of methadone treatment. For example, this study focused on the more difficult cases for treatment—those who previously participated in a methadone program but still required additional help.

In conclusion, the use of methadone maintenance for heroin addiction has both advantages and disadvantages. As suggested by the Williams study, the advantages include a diminution of the addict's suffering, decreased criminal activity, and increased employment. On the other hand, the disadvantages include the development of methadone addiction, illicit use of methadone, and the expensive nature of the treatment. Finally, it should be noted that many have questioned the ethics of treating one drug habit by producing another.

SUMMARY

The biological approach focuses on the study of biological causes and correlates of abnormal behavior. Some disorders are caused primarily by biological factors, but many more are assumed to be caused by both biological and psychological factors. Disorders caused primarily by biological factors include the organic brain syndromes, some forms of mental retardation such as Down's syndrome and PKU, and general paresis. Perhaps the most noteworthy example of a syndrome that apparently is caused by both biological and environmental factors is schizophrenia. A considerable proportion of biological research activity, however, is concerned with identifying biological correlates of abnormal behavior rather than biological causes. The presence of excessive amounts of serotonin in the brain, for example, is a correlate of schizophrenia.

The central nervous system consists of the brain and spinal cord. The hindbrain is the most primitive part of the brain and includes a structure called the reticular formation. Stimulation of this structure increases neural activity generally and produces alertness and wakefulness; for these reasons, the reticular formation is sometimes referred to as the arousal system. The midbrain serves in part as a relay connection between the hindbrain and the forebrain. An important structure in the forebrain is the hypothalamus. This structure regulates sexual activity and has an important role in aggression.

It is important to distinguish between neurological and behavioral arousal because an increase in neurological activity does not necessarily imply an increase in behavioral activity, even though it usually does. A child with a chronically underaroused central nervous system, for example, may be overactive behaviorally in an effort to increase neurological stimulation to some optimal level. Hyperactive children usually are treated with stimulant drugs. Another reason why neural stimulation does not always translate into behavioral activity is that the stimulation of some nerves inhibits behavior.

The effects of a psychoactive drug depend on both specific and nonspecific factors. The specific effects of a drug are those attributable to the chemical interactions of a drug and its sites of action. The most important specific properties are the chemical composition of the drug and the effective dosage. The nonspecific effects of a drug are those attributable to psychological factors such as expectations of effects and the personality of the drug recipient.

The introduction of chlorpromazine (CPZ) in the early 1950s revolutionized psychiatric treatment for schizophrenic patients. Prior to CPZ, barbiturate drugs sometimes were used to calm agitated patients. The dosages required to produce calm, however, also produced considerable drowsiness and sometimes sleep. In contrast, CPZ can induce tranquility at a dosage level below that at which CPZ induces high levels of drowsiness. As a consequence, many agitated schizophrenics disturbed by frightening hallucinations and delusions can be treated on an out-patient basis.

Table 5-1 summarizes the effects of various drugs discussed in the text.

One biological assessment procedure that has received considerable attention is the EEG. EEG brain waves are primarily measures of degree of arousal near the sites under the electrodes employed to obtain the EEG recordings; because abnormal behavior usually is not correlated with degree of alertness, the EEG is of little value for diagnosis. An important exception, however, is the use of the EEG as one of several possible indicants of epilepsy. A much more promising procedure is the study of evoked potentials—that is, brain wave reactions to stimuli presented by an experimenter.

Biological therapy includes the administration of drugs, electroconvulsive therapy, psychosurgery, and diet therapy. The major tranquilizers are administered primarily for schizophrenia although they also are used to control anxiety in neurotics. The minor tranquilizers are given to control temporary nervousness. Antidepressant drugs are used primarily in cases of depression. Electroconvulsive therapy (ECT) consists of the induction of convulsions by application of electric current across the skull. ECT has been widely reported to be effective in the treatment of psychotic depression, and there are some large control group studies that lend support to these claims. ECT has been opposed, however, on the grounds that there exists no convincing rationale as to why it should work and that it is cruel and unethical. A lobotomy is a surgical disruption of the neural fibers that connect the prefrontal lobes of the cerebrum to the thalamus. The procedure has been used to treat hopeless cases of schizophrenia and cases of intractable pain. Despite the existence of some outcome data indicating possible beneficial effects and that fears of harmful effects have been exaggerated, the procedure is controversial for two reasons. First, there is no adequate treatment rationale for the procedure. Second, the biological effects of the separation are irreversible because neural fibers do not regenerate. Another concern is that the operation may not always have been employed in hopeless cases. Although the operation is rare in the United States, it is performed more frequently in other countries. The decline in the use of lobotomies in this country was caused by the introduction of tranquilizer drugs. Diet therapy is used primarily for preventive purposes. An excellent example of diet therapy is the prevention of mental retardation in PKU infants.

Biological treatments have a long history of abuse. One possible explanation for this is that physicians have not been held sufficiently accountable to their patients.

The best way to evaluate the effects of a drug is in the double-blind experiment in which one group receives the drug in question, another group receives a placebo, and neither experimenter nor subject knows whether a drug or a placebo is being administered.

The methadone blockage effect refers to the fact that moderate dosages of methadone satisfy physical cravings for heroin without producing debilitating psychological effects. If methadone is given in larger doses, however, it has euphoriant effects similar to those of heroin. In the last decade the use of methadone maintenance treatment for heroin dependency has increased. Advocates claim that methadone treatment is the only real hope addicts have to overcome their habits, whereas critics argue that methadone maintenance is undesirable because it creates an addiction to methadone.

Chapter 6

The Psychoanalytic Approach

And, therefore, it is reasonable to expect that an emotion, which is strongly felt by great numbers of people, but whose natural manifestations are constantly repressed in compliance with the usages of society, will be the ones whose morbid effects are most frequently witnessed. This anticipation is abundantly borne out by the facts; the sexual passion in women being that which most accurately fulfills the prescribed conditions, and whose injurious influence upon the organism is most common and familiar. Next after it in power may be placed those emotions of a permanent character, which are usually concealed, because disgraceful or unamiable, as hatred or envy; after them others equally permanent, such as grief or care, but which, not being discreditable, are not so liable to be repressed.

CARTER (1853, p. 21)[1]

Robert Carter's *On the Pathology and Treatment of Hysteria,* from which the preceding passage was taken, presented the first published theory of hysteria in terms of unconscious (repressed) sexual impulses. In 1853 Carter's ideas constituted a major advance, for he had clearly noted the emotional causes of a neurotic disorder as well as the appropriateness of psychotherapeutic treatments. Yet Robert Carter's theory was largely ignored. Sigmund Freud expressed similar ideas approximately 40 years after Carter and at first he too was largely ignored.

Sigmund Freud was born in Moravia in 1856. He was awarded his MD degree in 1881 from the University of Vienna, and he later studied neurology under the great French master Jean-Martin Charcot. It was through his contact with Charcot that Freud became interested in hypnosis. In collaboration with Joseph Breuer, he published "On the Psychical Mechanisms of Hysterical Phenomena" in 1883 and *Studies in Hysteria* in 1895. Although these early works reported the success of hypnosis in the treatment of hysteria, Freud gradually abandoned hypnosis in favor of a talking therapy he called psychoanalysis. The more neurotic people he interviewed using the psychoanalytic method, the more convinced Freud became that repressed sexual desires are responsible for many neuroses. He proposed a theory of sexual development, including a theory of childhood sexuality. The conservative medical establishment of Vienna, however, disagreed with Freud's focus on sex and criticized him for speculating on the basis of insufficient evidence. For almost a decade, Freud was regarded as a crackpot by his medical colleagues (Ford & Urban, 1963). His fortunes gradually improved, however, and in 1909 the American psychologist Stanley Hall invited Freud to give a series of lectures at Clark University in Worcester, Massachusetts.

Psychoanalysis became a dominant school of thought in both American psychology and psychiatry during the period 1920 to 1950. Its influence has declined considerably during the last three decades, particularly in psychology. Part of the reason for this decline has been the emergence of alternative theories, such as Carl Rogers's self-theory (see Chapter 8) and the various social-learning theories (see Chapter 7). Moreover, orthodox (Freudian) psychoanalysis is rarely practiced in its pure form because it takes too long and hence is too expensive. Today, psychoanalytically oriented therapy is much more common than is standard, orthodox psychoanalytic therapy (Luborsky &

[1] We are indebted to Veith (1965, p. 201) for bringing this remarkable passage to our attention.

Sigmund Freud, the founder of psychoanalysis, is probably the most influential psychological thinker of the century. He is shown here holding a phallic symbol, which, as he himself once stressed to some enthusiastic followers, is also a cigar. (Reprinted by permission of Historical Pictures Service; Chicago, Illinois.)

Spence, 1971). The case study that follows exemplifies the more commonly used psychoanalytically oriented approach rather than the classical Freudian approach.

THE CASE OF JOSEPH KELLY AS ADAPTED FROM A REPORT BY L. S. ROGERS[2]

Joe Kelly went to a psychiatric clinic at age 34, complaining of impluses to kill his wife, to drive into another car, and to drive off high places; he also complained of repeated attacks of panic when present in an audience, colitis, loss of appetite, and nausea. The intake interview revealed a largely unremarkable medical history, except for asthma attacks at age four when he was staying

[2] Adaptation of "An Adult Neurotic" by Lawrence S. Rogers in *Clinical Studies of Personality*, Vol. I, Edited by Arthur Burton and Robert E. Harris. Copyright 1955 by Harper & Row, Publishers, Inc. Printed by permission of author, editors and publisher.

with relatives during his mother's second pregnancy. Although Mr. Kelly requested treatment by a physician, he was assigned to a psychoanalytically oriented psychologist.

Psychoanalysis is a talking therapy in which the therapist attempts to help the client understand better his or her emotions and their relations to early childhood experiences. The therapeutic process is time-consuming, in part because it takes time for the therapist to get to know his client, in part because it takes time for a trusting relationship between therapist and client to develop, and in part because people often resist acknowledging many of their innermost feelings.

One way in which the therapist begins to learn about his client is through analysis of the manner in which the client relates to the therapist. Joe Kelly's interpersonal style revealed a difficulty in expressing anger, and this problem seemed to be caused by a fear that the expression of anger would cause the therapist to dislike him. This suggests that Mr. Kelly's need to be accepted by other people was excessive. Mr. Kelly had difficulty even recognizing his own anger, and he tended to express anger in a disguised and passive manner.

For example, Mr. Kelly was annoyed at the clinic because they assigned him to a psychoanalytically oriented psychologist rather than to a physician. He believed that his problems were caused by biological rather than by emotional factors, and he resented the psychologist's suggestions of possible emotional causes. His negativism toward the clinic was expressed indirectly, as in his failure to show for a medical examination that he had requested himself. The therapist decided to discuss those negative feelings concerning psychological treatment. Mr. Kelly first resisted the suggestion that he was angry at the clinic but later acknowledged having had such feelings. When Mr. Kelly realized that he could express anger toward the therapist without losing the therapist's acceptance, he began talking more freely about his problems and emotions.

Rejection and domination are the primary themes in the events remembered by Mr. Kelly. Mother was viewed as ruler in the home and as having rarely interacted with the patient except to issue orders or to scold him for lack of tidiness. Mr. Kelly recalled his not being allowed to have friends in the house because they might make the house dirty. Although Mr. Kelly resented this treatment, and although he blamed his mother for his lack of friends during his youth, he could neither express this resentment nor deal with its reality.

Joe Kelly's memory of his father was also one of little mutual involvement. He remembered his father as argumentative, rejecting, and severely critical toward him. His younger sisters were favored by the father, and he was jealous of their apparently happy and well-adjusted lives.

Mr. Kelly's discussion of childhood sex training provided evidence of parental domination. Sex was not mentioned in the home. When he did learn some exciting information, he related this to other boys in the neighborhood. This passing of information once provoked a complaint from a neighborhood mother, with the result that he was branded a sinner by his parents and was spanked. At the time, he was confused and frustrated because he was not told why he was being punished.

Mr. Kelly discussed in detail many of the events of his early adulthood.

After serving two years in the armed forces without apparent difficulty, he was sent overseas where, after a nine-month period, he was hospitalized for asthma. He denied that any emotional factors were involved even though the therapist suggested to him the similarity between being sent overseas and being sent away from home during his mother's pregnancy. In the service, as later in every job, Joe Kelly always felt that his co-workers looked down on him. He frequently was afraid of making mistakes and did not enjoy his work. After the service, Mr. Kelly worked as his father's assistant but quit because his father always criticized him. As therapy progressed, the patient was able to recognize that he frequently acted in a way that upset his father. Rather than express anger toward his father directly, he expressed anger by acting in a manner that was annoying to his father and that provoked his censure.

Mr. Kelly's relationship with his wife was characterized by emotional confusion. His wife was the first female with whom he had more than a casual relationship. When they first had sexual intercourse, he became so anxious that he could barely perform the act. Afterward, he suffered feelings of extreme guilt and worthlessness, went into a state of panic, and was hospitalized in a psychiatric ward for two weeks. Shortly after his release from the hospital, he insisted that she marry him and she agreed. Why did he marry her? Throughout the course of therapy, Mr. Kelly provided varying answers to this question. At first he stated that he was in love with her; later in treatment he stated that he married her because they had had sexual intercourse; finally, he explained that he feared no other woman would accept him. Mr. Kelly experienced his first impulses to stab his wife within a few weeks after their marriage.

Mr. Kelly's ambivalent feelings toward his wife suggest that she represented an unconscious symbol of his mother. He told the therapist that he wanted his wife to assume all aspects of their household, and that he felt that his wife did not love him. These feelings seem to express his dependency needs and his feelings of rejection by his mother. His anger toward his wife, including his impulses to kill her, seems to express his anger toward his mother for having rejected him, as well as his anger toward those who frustrate his desire for autonomy by gratifying his excessive needs to be taken of. The self-induced nature of his feelings toward his wife was suggested in part by Mr. Kelly's feeling that his wife did not love him. If she complained about his hobbies, he interpreted this as a lack of love, but if she failed to complain, he interpreted this as indicating a lack of interest in him.

After 52 sessions, Joe Kelly was transferred to another city by his company. At the time of transfer he believed that he no longer required professional help. Accordingly, he did not plan to seek treatment at his new location, at least not until he had a chance to see if he could make it on his own. Some improvement had occurred. He was considerably more relaxed, felt better about himself, and his colitis had disappeared. He reported more involvement in family activities and better relationships with friends and co-workers. Panic attacks were still experienced but were less frequent: He was able to tolerate longer automobile drives and experienced panic only in heavy traffic or in mountain driving. He could attend outdoor movies and some public meetings, but he could not attend an indoor movie.

DISTINGUISHING CHARACTERISTICS

The case of Mr. Kelly provides a basis for discussion of several characteristics that set psychoanalysis apart from the other approaches to abnormality.

Symptoms as Disguised Manifestations of Psychic Conflicts

Mr. Kelly's presenting symptoms included the following:

1. Conscious impulses to kill his wife.
2. Colitis.
3. Asthma.
4. Passive (or indirect) expressions of aggression. For example, instead of informing the therapist that he did not want to be tested, Mr. Kelly failed to keep scheduled appointments.

Under psychoanalytic theory, these symptoms are regarded as disguised manifestations of excessive dependency needs that conflict with a natural desire to be independent and self-determining (Freud, 1924). The evidence for this hypothesis consists of the following:

1. The symptoms of colitis and asthma typically elicit maternal caring from others. These symptoms thus place one in a dependent state of receiving help from others, and at the same time they disguise one's need to be dependent.
2. Mr. Kelly's desire for his wife to assume command of all aspects of the household may be considered a direct expression of dependency needs.
3. Mr. Kelly's apparent fear of therapist rejection suggests a fear of losing a relationship in which he plays a dependent role. Similarly, Mr. Kelly's passive style of interacting with others, as exemplified by the way in which he backed into marriage, suggests a fear of asserting himself and of being rejected.
4. The intensification of Mr. Kelly's symptoms when he was sent overseas (away from home) supports the hypothesis that his symptoms are disguised manifestations of dependency needs.

In summary, under psychoanalytic theory Mr. Kelly's symptoms are regarded as a disguised manifestation of a conflict between excessive dependency needs and a natural desire to be independent. The symptoms are regarded as surface phenomena; the fundamental problem is assumed to be the unconscious conflict manifested by the symptoms.

Developmental Theory of Personality

Psychoanalytic theory maintains that many adult personality traits are the result of childhood experiences. Each child is seen as progressing through five stages of development, and either excessive or insufficient gratification of the child's needs during any of the first four stages is postulated to cause a partial arrest of psychological development. These partial arrests of development are called fixations, and they determine adult personality needs and areas of psychological vulnerability. For example, under psychoanalytic theory, the parental rejection Mr. Kelly experienced as a young child resulted in a lifelong need for dependent relationships, an excessive sensitivity to rejection and criticism (these stimuli arouse fear of abandonment), and a reluctance to express anger that might cause rejection by others.

Study of Symbolic Functions

Another characteristic of the psychoanalytic approach is the study of the symbolic functions of behavior and objects. Freud hypothesized symbolic meaning for a wide range of behavior: ". . . I have shown you that neurotic symptoms have meaning, like errors and like dreams, and that they are closely connected with the events of the patient's life" (1924, p. 280). The psychological meaning of a particular symbol is determined by its universal (cultural) meaning and/or by its meaning for a particular individual. For example, shoes and slippers universally symbolize female genital organs, and a deep hole caused by the removal of a tree might symbolize castration for a particular individual, even though it has no universal symbolic significance (Freud, 1924; Monroe, 1955).

Symbols have a defensive function because they disguise the true psychological meaning of an object. For example, Joe Kelly was angry toward his mother, but he was so fearful of expressing this anger as a child that, even as an adult, he still could not acknowledge his anger. Instead the anger was transferred from mother to wife; his wife was thus an unconscious symbol for his mother. In this way Mr. Kelly could release pent-up anger toward his mother, but only in the disguised form of impulses to kill his wife.

Principle of Psychic Determinism

Another distinguishing characteristic of psychoanalysis is the principle of psychic determinism. This principle states that all behavior is caused and thus has meaning. A slip of the tongue, for example, is regarded as nonaccidental and as caused by the interplay of conscious and unconscious forces. Although psychoanalysis is not unique in its hypothesis of a cause for all behaviors, advocates of other approaches are less inclined to find behaviors like slips of the tongue to be psychologically revealing.

Comment

Psychoanalysis is a complex theory that has several different conceptual levels. On the one hand, Mr. Kelly is seen as having an unconscious conflict over unacceptable dependency needs. On a deeper level, the conflict is explained as a consequence of early childhood experiences. It is important to recognize that different types of evidence are offered for the various levels of the theory. The evidence concerning the existence of Mr. Kelly's unconscious conflicts was provided by Mr. Kelly himself in his interactions with the therapist and in his report of significant life events. On the other hand, the belief that Mr. Kelly's dependency conflicts are related to early development is supported primarily by Mr. Kelly's recall of his childhood experiences. Thus, the evidence for the hypothesis of an unconscious conflict is stronger and of a different nature than is the evidence that this conflict is related to childhood experiences.

HYPOTHESES AND BASIC CONCEPTS

Psychoanalysis is one of the more comprehensive and sophisticated theories of human behavior ever proposed. Although it is subject to criticism on the grounds that many of its specific hypotheses are not supported by the available evidence (see Chapters 10 through 20), psychoanalysis provides many insights into the human condition. The following is a detailed overview of the psychoanalytic theory of personality. The psychoanalytic theory of neurosis is discussed in Chapter 10, and other psychoanalytic hypotheses are discussed in Chapters 11 through 20.

Psychic Energy

Freud hypothesized that psychic energy is the motivational source of both behavior and mental life. In his earlier theories, he postulated only one drive, which he called *eros.* Eros is the life instinct that is the source of a sexual energy called *libido.* In the atmosphere of post-World War I, Freud postulated a second drive, *thanatos.* Thanatos is a death instinct that is the source of aggressive energy.

The important theoretical attributes of instincts are these:

1. Instincts are sources of continual psychic energy that are always seeking discharge and thus affecting mental life.
2. Instincts have a source, an object, and an aim. The source is the body, the aim is to remove bodily excitation, and the object is the means by which bodily excitation is removed. For example, the source of sexual instincts is a physiological need, the aim is to reduce this need, and the objects may include a spouse or a parent.
3. There is a fixed amount of instinctual energy for each individual at any given point in time. The energy system is closed, so that the expenditure of energy to keep threatening thoughts out of consciousness reduces the amount of energy left to pursue other life activities. When little energy is available for normal life activities, the individual experiences neurotic fatigue.

Psychic Structure

Psychic energy operates within a personality system composed of the id, ego, and superego. Each of these concepts refers to a kind of psychic functioning.

Id

The id, which is present at birth, is the reservoir of all instinctual energy. It operates in accordance with both the *pleasure principle* and the *primary process.* The pleasure principle is a principle of immediate gratification of all instinctual impulses (e.g., sex, thirst, hunger, and aggression). The primary process is a means of gratifying impulses through the creation of wish-fulfilling fantasies (e.g., a hungry person has a fantasy of eating a gourmet meal). Two important examples of the primary process are dreams and daydreams. For Freud, all dreams are wish-fulfilling. The primary process, however, is a primitive and relatively ineffective means of impulse gratification.

BOX 6-1
Psychoanalytic Terms

Abreaction. The release of energy associated with unconscious impulses.
Catharsis. A method of achieving abreaction by re-experiencing repressed feelings and gaining insight into their source.
Displacement. A defense in which unconscious impulses toward one object are released toward another object that is less threatening.
Ego. One of three parts of the psychic structure. It is the awareness of oneself as a distinct person, and its functions include discrimination and the discharge of id impulses in a realistic manner.
Fixation. The long-term attachment of libido to a particular erogenous zone and a consequent partial stunting of psychological growth.
Free association. A technique in which a subject is asked to generate associations "freely"—that is, without conscious control. The subject may be asked to free associate to concrete thoughts or to specific stimuli.
Id. One of three parts of the psychic structure. It is the origin of the sex and aggression drives.
Libido. Sexual (or pleasurable) energy.
Oedipal and Electra conflicts. The Oedipal conflict refers to the boy's wishes to marry the mother and to kill the father. The Electra conflict refers to the girl's wishes to marry the father and to kill the mother.
Projection. A defense in which one's own unacceptable impulses are attributed to someone else.
Regression. A defense indicated by a return to behavior characteristic of an earlier developmental period.
Repression. The psychic defense that creates the unconscious.
Superego. One of three parts of the psychic structure. It is the moral arm of the personality.
Transference. A phenomenon in which an adult patient feels and acts toward a therapist as he or she did toward parents or siblings during childhood.

Ego

Demands for immediate gratification and the use of wish-fulfilling fantasy to gratify needs are especially evident in young children. With increasing age, the child must learn to delay gratification and to rely on a more realistic mode of functioning. These functions are accomplished by the ego, which develops out of the id and which is the awareness of one's self as an organism.

The ego operates in accordance with the *reality principle* and the *secondary process.* The reality principle refers to the gratification of instinctual impulses based on a realistic perception of the environment and hence on a distinction between reality and fantasy. An example of behaving in accordance with the reality principle is a hungry person's eating food rather than some inappropriate object (e.g., plastic). The secondary process is the generation of reality-oriented thought in order to gratify instinctual needs.

The ego serves three masters: the id because it must gratify instinctual impulses, the external environment (reality) because it must gratify instinctual impulses in a manner that minimizes realistic danger, and the superego, to which we now turn our attention.

Superego

The superego, which develops from the ego, is the internalization of the values of one's parents and of society. Freud (1933) ascribes three functions to the superego: self-observation, conscience, and the holding up of ideals. The conscience, which is the representative of all moral restrictions, is the means by which guilt and self-punishment are induced. Freud considered the superego particularly relevant to cases of melancholia (depression). He stated, "The melancholiac during periods of health can, like anyone else, be more or less severe towards himself; but when he has a melancholic attack, his superego becomes over-severe, abuses, humiliates, and ill-treats his unfortunate ego, threatens it with the severest punishments, reproaches it for long forgotten actions . . ." (1933, p. 87). In most people, guilty feelings can be alleviated by punishment. Thus, guilty people are generally assumed by psychoanalysts to have a psychological wish to be punished and hence may act in a manner that elicits punishment from other people.

Another function of the superego is evident when one fails to live up to the expectations of one's *ego-ideal* (the standards of achievement set by the superego). Failure to live up to one's ideals may produce shame, imagined loss of parental love, and feelings of depression. On the other hand, living up to one's ideals generally produces a measure of self-love.

Psychodynamics

The interplay of forces within the psychic structure is called *psychodynamics.* Behavior is almost never the result of any one force or any one psychic structure but rather is the result of interactions among psychic structures and forces. In order to understand how the three structures interact, consider the hypothetical case of a person who is frustrated and who feels an urge to kill the frustrator. In accordance with the pleasure principle of immediate gratification, the id impulse is to aggress. In accordance with the reality principle, the ego impulse depends on how safe it is to aggress—assuming there is little realistic chance of being caught and that the frustrator is a physically weaker individual, the ego's impulse may be to aggress. In most people, however, the superego would induce fear and guilt in reaction to the ego impulse to kill. Instead of actual aggression, the result may be a fantasy of killing. In this way, the ego has served its three masters: the id is gratified by the fantasy of killing, reality is served because the fantasy is not dangerous, and the superego is served because the fantasy of killing is felt to be less morally objectionable than is the actual act. Figure 6-1 illustrates some simplified psychodynamic processes.

Anxiety

In psychoanalytic theory, anxiety is a signal to the ego of impending danger. We can distinguish between normal and pathological anxiety. Normal anxiety signals impending danger from the environment. Moreover, anxiety is considered normal when the following conditions are fulfilled: (1) the ego's perception of danger is realistic—that is, an external threat actually exists; (2) the level of anxiety is appropriate in intensity to the existing threat; and (3) the anxiety dissipates when the external danger is avoided. Such anxiety is nonpathological because the organism can make some appropriate response to avoid the danger. Pathological anxiety signals the impending danger that an unacceptable impulse is about to enter consciousness. The impulse is unacceptable only because, as a result of childhood experiences, the ego fears punishment for the expression of the impulse—this fear of punishment, however, is unrealistic and inappropriate because the individual is no longer a child. Although there is no physical escape from pathological anxiety, there is a form of psychological escape—the impulse is separated from consciousness and is kept unconscious. Unlike normal anxiety, pathological anxiety is exaggerated

Figure 6-1
Psychodynamics is the interplay of forces among the id, ego, and superego.

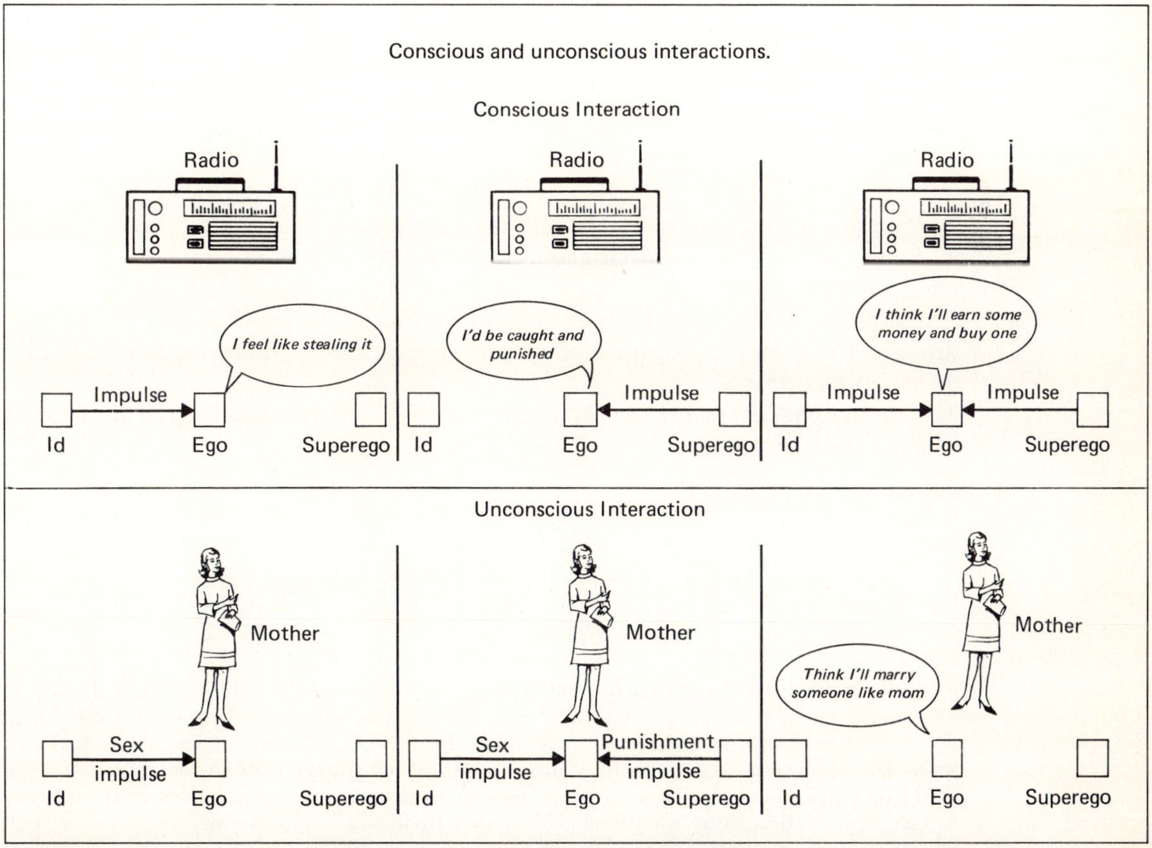

or prolonged and can interfere significantly with the individual's normal functioning.[3]

Ego Defense

The ego develops ways of preventing the expression of impulses it judges to be dangerous. This is accomplished first by converting psychic energy into anxiety and then by defending against the anxiety. All defenses are ego functions, all defenses are ways of handling anxiety, and all defenses are either unconscious or semiunconscious. Defenses rarely occur in isolation and usually occur in combination with other defenses. The principal means of defense are *repression* and *denial* (*suppression*).

It is important to appreciate that ego defenses are normal processes; under psychoanalytic theory, psychopathology results either when there is a breakdown in ego defenses or when there is an excessive commitment of libidinal energy to the defensive process.

Repression

Freud distinguished three levels of awareness: conscious, preconscious, and unconscious. The *conscious* mind consists of those experiences of which one is aware, whereas the *preconscious* mind consists of those experiences that can be brought readily into consciousness by focusing attention on them. The *unconscious* mind consists of those experiences of which one is unaware and that one resists acknowledging. More specifically, there are four related properties to unconscious experiences:

1. People are unaware of unconscious experiences.
2. People resist acknowledging unconscious experiences even when their presence is pointed out.
3. People have difficulty focusing attention on unconscious experiences when directed to do so. For example, they may try to change the topic, draw a blank, or become confused.
4. People experience anxiety or discomfort when their attention is directed to unconscious material.

It is as if there is a force that keeps the individual from attending to unconscious material. Freud postulated the existence of such a force and called it *repression.* Specifically, repression is a defense mechanism that creates the unconscious and accounts for the resistance people show in acknowledging and in attending to unconscious material.

[3] The distinction between normal and pathological anxiety is actually a simplification of the psychoanalytic position. Freud defined three types of anxiety according to the source of the threat: " . . . the three main varieties of anxiety—objective anxiety, neurotic anxiety, and moral anxiety—can easily be related to the three directions in which the ego is dependent on the external world, on the id and on the superego" (1933, p. 119). Freud's objective anxiety is normal anxiety as defined here. Both neurotic and moral anxiety are pathological: However, neurotic anxiety is induced by the ego in reaction to an id impulse, whereas moral anxiety is induced by the ego in reaction to the superego.

The concept of unconsciousness is different from that of unawareness. People are unaware of both preconscious and unconscious material. Although they readily will acknowledge preconscious experiences, they resist acknowledging unconscious experiences. Thus, unconscious implies more than unaware; namely, it implies a force (repression) that keeps the material out of consciousness. Repression is the fundamental defense mechanism because it is the force that creates the unconscious. Moreover, repression is a healthy process; Freud believed that the creation of civilization would be impossible were it not for our ability to repress sexual and aggressive impulses.

The distinction between conscious, preconscious, and unconscious cuts across the distinction between id, ego, and superego in a manner exemplified in Figure 6-2. As this figure shows, the id, the ego, and the superego each contain unconscious, preconscious, and conscious experiences. For example, there are sexual impulses of which we are aware (conscious id), of which we would readily become aware if they were pointed out (preconscious id), and that we would resist acknowledging (unconscious id).

Denial (Suppression)

Denial is the rejection of feelings, attitudes, behaviors, or events that were once conscious but now have become too painful to accept. Thus denial operates by expelling material from consciousness, whereas repression operates by keeping unconscious material from entering consciousness. Examples of normal uses of denial are the use of fantasy (Freud, 1946) and daydreams as means of denying one's present situation. Other examples of denial include the adolescent who pretends to be disinterested in members of the opposite sex and the child who refuses to admit a mistake. The underlying principle of denial is something like "if you pretend it isn't there it will go away" (Ford & Urban, 1963, p. 145).

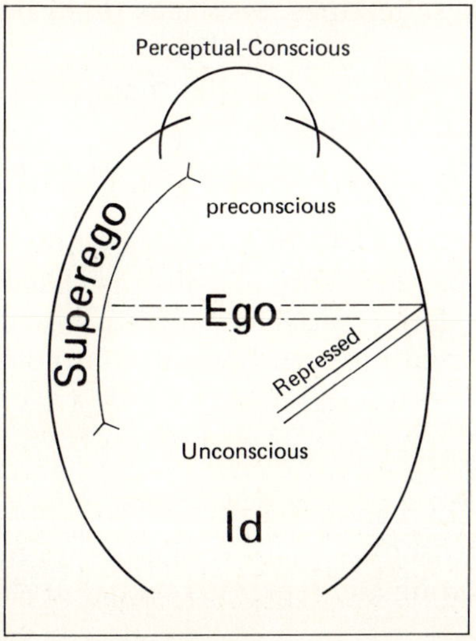

Figure 6-2
Personality Structure Under Psychoanalytic Theory. From S. Freud's *New Introductory Lectures on Psychoanalysis.* New York: W. W. Norton & Co., 1933, p. 111. Reprinted with permission of publisher.

Displacement

Displacement is the discharge of unconscious impulses by changing the object of the impulse from a dangerous or unacceptable object to a less dangerous or more acceptable object. For example, suppose a man is berated by a boss whom he regards as a father figure and later explodes over a minor annoyance by a junior employee. The excessiveness of the man's anger and the inappropriate choice of a junior employee as the object of that anger are significant. Psychoanalytic theory provides the following explanation. The man has repressed anger toward his father and is unconscious of the fact that his boss symbolizes his father. The anger toward the father has been *displaced* onto the boss. The scolding by the boss reactivates this unconscious hostility, which is later displaced onto, and expressed toward, the junior employee. The man is confused by his behavior because he does not recognize its unconscious meaning; moreover, the man would resist any suggestion that the outburst toward the junior employee was related to the scolding by the boss. It is instructive to compare this example of defense in terms of repression and displacement to an example of nondefensive displacement. Suppose another man is berated by his boss, is aware of his anger, and consciously holds back expressions of anger for fear of losing his job. When he returns to his office, the man yells at the junior employee to vent his emotion, but he quickly realizes that he was really mad at the boss. In this example, the displacement toward the junior employee is nondefensive because it occurred largely as a result of conscious processes designed to protect the man's job.

Projection

Projection is the attributing of one's faults, anger, and unacceptable id impulses to someone else. As with all defenses, some use of projection is normal and is found in most everyone. An example of a pathological use of projection would be a paranoid reaction in which Ms. Jones feels sexual attractions toward her father, represses these feelings, displaces them onto other people, and then projects the feelings so that she unrealistically believes that men are waiting around every corner to rape her. In this manner Ms. Jones remains unaware of her sexual feelings toward her father.

An example of projected anger is provided in a case reported by Lazarus. When the therapist suggested that the patient be more assertive, the patient replied, "But why give someone the satisfaction of letting him know that he can bug you or hurt you?" (1971, p. 120). This response is based on the inappropriate assumption that others derive satisfaction from hurting you and thus suggests that the patient projected his own hostility onto other people.

Reaction Formation

Reaction formations defend against anxiety through the adoption of values and behaviors opposite to the unconscious wish. A classic example of a reaction formation is the person with strong and repressed sexual urges who becomes a crusader against smut.

Undoing

Undoing defends against anxiety by engaging in an action that unconsciously disproves or undoes an imagined harm to someone else. For example, a child with hostile wishes toward a younger sibling rescues sick or injured animals in an effort to undo, and to keep unconscious, the imagined harm of his hostility toward the younger brother.

Isolation

Isolation is the process by which the knowledge of some attitudes, beliefs, or behaviors is unavailable under threatening circumstances but is present under nonthreatening circumstances. One may be aware of certain feelings while on a trip and be totally unaware of them while at home. Isolation becomes pathological when the individual totally forgets threatening experiences and cannot become aware of that aspect of his or her life, as in amnesia.

Rationalization

Rationalization is the explaining to others and to oneself the reasons for a behavior or belief on the basis of facts, feelings, or events that make the behavior appear appropriate when in fact it may have been inappropriate. A shy student may explain his lack of social activity by the need to get all As for admittance to medical school when in fact he is afraid of social interactions. All individuals use some rationalization, and it operates at both conscious and unconscious levels.

Sublimation

The transformation of sexual impulses into nonsexual activity is called sublimation. This defense results in the transfer of sexual energy into productive activity—for example, work, play, friendship, and art. Sublimation is the means by which we use the libidinal energy for all our constructive, acceptable activities.

Psychosexual Development

Psychoanalytic theory assumes the occurrence of a natural progression through five phases of psychosexual development. These phases develop as the child's natural commitment to derive pleasure progresses to different areas of the body; these areas are called erogenous zones and include the oral, anal, and genital regions. Originally Freud spoke of this development as sexual within the traditional meaning of the term *sex*. But as Fine points out, " . . . the concept of sexuality was broadened and the term *psychosexual* came to be used. The broadening involved first an extension of sexuality to all physical pleasure, and, second, its extension to affection, love, and all tender emotions" (1973, p. 14). Thus, in modern psychoanalytic theory, *sexual* often means "pleasurable."

Freud (1924) likened the progression of the libido through the psychosexual stages to that of a band of people migrating through a wilderness fraught with dangers. At each dwelling stop along the way, a small group stays behind and establishes a settlement, while the main body moves on to its new destination. If the entire group stays at a dwelling stop for an excessive period of time, a larger subgroup stays behind and hence fewer people move on. If too few people move on, subsequent dangers may be overwhelming because the group is too small to protect itself. When danger is encountered, the advancing group returns to the dwelling stop at which the largest settlement had been established.

Similarly, Freud held that the libido progresses through five stages of psychosexual development called the oral, anal, phallic, latent, and genital stages. A certain amount of libido is left behind (*fixated*) at each stage, and the rest advances to the next stage of psychosexual development. If gratification at a particular stage of development is either excessive or minimal, an excessive amount of libido is fixated at this stage, and hence there is less libido to move on to the next stage. Under psychoanalytic theory, excessive fixations of libido result in personality traits, cause areas of psychological vulnerability, and predispose one to psychopathology. For example, fixation at the oral stage may create an excessive need for dependent relations and psychological vulnerability to events that preclude gratification of dependency needs (e.g., rejection by others and/or expression of anger toward others). Moreover, when energy is fixated at the oral stage, the person has less energy to deal with life problems in general. Should frustrations occur, the libido returns (regresses) to the earlier stage at which excessive libidinal energy had been fixated. This regression is almost always partial, and it is typically manifested by an increase in immature behavior characteristic of the earlier developmental period.

Freud's theory of psychosexual development is a theory of the developmental phases of the instinctual energy of the id. Erik Erickson (1950) has elaborated a complementary series of psychosocial stages of ego development and self-identity. One important aspect of his theory is the identification of a series of nuclear conflicts that the ego must resolve for normal development. The following discussion of psychosexual development includes several of these nuclear conflicts, but for a more complete account the reader should consult Erickson (1950) *Childhood and Society.*

Oral Stage

The oral stage is that period of time (usually the first year of life) during which the primary area of libidinal gratification is the oral region. The young infant, for example, derives gratification through sucking responses. The oral stage is also a period during which the infant is highly dependent on the mother for food and protection (Cameron, 1963; Erickson, 1950). If the infant's needs are frustrated and if fixation occurs, Freud postulated that the person may be overly dependent on others in later life. For the dependent adult, stressful situations are those that preclude gratification of the dependency needs (e.g., being a boss, being in large groups in which the individual feels lost).

According to Erickson, the nuclear conflict of the oral stage is that of trust versus mistrust. If the mother fails to gratify the infant's needs, the child learns that other people can be unreliable, inconsistent, or otherwise unable to meet one's needs. Similarly, if the mother abruptly weans the infant as he develops teeth and begins to bite "the forbidden apple" (nipple), the abrupt loss of a dependable source of gratification may promote a basic sense of distrust. Thus, it is during the oral stage that the infant encounters the first of Erickson's nuclear conflicts, that of the extent to which other people can be trusted.

Anal Stage

The anal stage is that period, usually the second year of life, during which the primary area of libidinal gratification is assumed to be the anal region; this erogenous zone theoretically becomes a means for expressing both the sexual drive (pleasurable feelings associated with defecation) and the aggressive drive (causing frustration for others when feces are retained or are deposited in unapproved locations). It is during this period that toilet training is usually attempted; toilet training often constitutes the parents' first systematic attempt to teach the child to delay gratification of strong impulses. If the child reacts to toilet training by holding back and becoming constipated, fixation at this stage can lead to the development of the personality trait of obstinacy. If the child reacts aggressively by defecating in places or at times that are particularly annoying to the parents, fixation at this stage can lead to the development of an explosive personality (e.g., "hot" temper or aggressiveness). Freud also hypothesized that habits of neatness and disorderliness often originate in the extent to which the child is retentive or explosive with his or her feces.

For the child, toilet training represents an early encounter with authority; hence, it seems likely that attitudes and reaction patterns toward toilet training affect later attitudes and reaction patterns to authority (White, 1964). Moreover, Erickson (1950) has noted that implicit in the parental request to control one's urges and to eliminate in an appropriate place is whether the child learns to do this and hence behaves in a "good" or "bad" fashion. According to Erickson, normal development during this stage includes the acquisition of a sense of competence and a sense that one has performed well, particularly as these feelings pertain to a sense of autonomy. On the other hand, maladaptive development leads to shame (for one has visibly performed against parental wishes) and to doubt in oneself (for one has performed incompetently).

Phallic Stage

During the phallic stage, which usually occurs during the third and fourth years of life, the primary means of libidinal gratification is through the genitals. It is during this phase that the *Oedipal conflict* occurs in boys and the *Electra conflict* occurs in girls.

The Oedipal conflict, consisting of the boy's unrealistic wishes to marry his mother and to kill his father, is resolved by keeping these wishes unconscious and by unconsciously identifying with the father. According to Freud, the motivation for this resolution is the boy's fear that the father will retaliate by cas-

BOX 6-2
The Neo-Freudians and Ego Psychology

Some fundamental aspects of Freud's theory of personality are its postulate of infantile sexuality, its postulate of the psychosexual developmental stages of the id, and its postulate of a psychic apparatus that is largely designed to discharge the biological impulses of the id. This view of a pervasive influence of sexual motivation has been a point of contention since Freud proposed it, and we can distinguish three groups of critics. One group of theorists challenged Freud's theory of sexuality on the grounds of inadequate evidence; this position has typically been advanced by theorists who were unsympathetic to psychoanalysis or who preferred a more experimental approach to the study of personality. Another group of theorists proposed modifications in Freud's concept of sexual energy, or they proposed some other striving as having a pervasive influence on mental life. Jung and Adler were two of the major figures in this early group of critics. A third group of theorists concluded that Freud's hypothesis of id motivation needed to be complemented with a theory of ego motivation. This movement began in the late 1930s; some of its major figures were Anna Freud (1946), Hartmann (1939), Erickson (1950), Horney (1937), Kardiner (1939), Sullivan (1953), and White (1964).

CARL JUNG

Jung's *Analytical Psychology* departed from Freud's psychoanalysis in at least three important ways. First, Jung broadened the concept of libido from that of sexual energy to that of a more general life energy: "Here we see only a continuous life impulse, a will to live which will attain the creation of the whole species through the preservation of the individual" (1952, p. 145). This view of the libido supported a complex model of personality that included the *principle of equivalence* (if energy is not used for one activity, it is available for another) and the *principle of entropy* (energy will always flow to the structure of the personality that has the least energy in a never-ending attempt to reach equilibrium). A second major point of departure from Freud was Jung's incorporation of mysticism into his theory of personality:

> That is to say, that the driving strength of our own soul, which we call libido, and whose nature it is to allow the useful and injurious, the good and the bad, to proceed. That this comparison is no mere play of words is taught to us by the mystics. When by looking inward (introversion) and going into the depths of their own being they find in their heart the image of the Sun, they find their own love of libido, with which reason, I might say with physical reason, is called the Sun; for the source of energy and life is the Sun [1952, p. 128].

A third major point of departure from Freud was Jung's concept of a *collective unconscious* in which is stored the memory of past events of the race, the species, and evolutionary development.

Although Jung has had little influence on psychology, he does have a small but committed group of followers. Several analytic institutes operate in the United States, and the Analytic Society publishes a *Journal of Analytical Psychology.* A recommended overview of Jung's work is Storr (1973), *C. G. Jung.*

ALFRED ADLER

Adler postulated one overriding innate drive, the *striving for superiority* (Adler, 1927; Dreikurs, 1953). Under this view, all drives are derivatives of a striving for superiority, and this striving is a natural attempt to overcome feelings of inferiority that result from the infant's initial reliance on adults for life support and from the adult's continued reliance on the environment. Adler accepted Freud's notion of unconscious activity and maintained that all behavior is part of an unconscious life plan: " . . . we insist that, without worrying about the *tendencies, milieu,* and *experiences,* all psychical powers are under the control of a directive idea and all expressions of emotion, feeling, thinking, willing, acting, dreaming, as well as psychopathological phenomena, are permeated by one unified life plan" (1927, p. 6). A behavior disorder, according to Adler, is the result of an inability to accept one's strivings for superiority. The striving for superiority can result in extraordinary accomplishments (the overcoming of extreme handicaps) or in an inferiority complex (the denial of the desire to be superior while ruminating and overreacting to one's inferiority). The striving for superiority is a constant source of energy because perfection can never be reached. Therefore, all individuals can potentially overreact to whatever area or degree of inferiority they perceive in themselves.

Adler's movement was named *individual psychology,* and a significant number of modern-day psychologists subscribe to an Adlerian model. The reader interested in seriously pursuing individual psychology should read Dreikurs (1953), *Fundamentals of Adlerian Psychology.*

ANNA FREUD

Sigmund Freud's emphasis on sexual motivation and its repression reflected a concern for understanding the functioning of the id, most of which is unconscious. During its early development, psychoanalysts focused on the study of unconscious id impulses, and the notion arose that the goal was to understand these depth (unconscious) motives. Ego functioning was regarded as somehow less important, and those who attended primarily to the conscious aspects of the ego were regarded as superficial in their approach. The emergence of ego psychology in the late 1930s was an attempt to correct this emphasis on the id at the expense of the study of the ego and to reaffirm the importance of the ego as a central and active aspect of the personality.

Sigmund Freud's daughter, Anna, was a major figure in the movement to study ego processes. Her classic work, *The Ego and the Mechanism of Defense,* is one of the most detailed psychoanalytic accounts of the ego's active role as an integrator of personality functioning and as a force maintaining the personality.

ERIK ERICKSON

Erickson developed a theory of developmental stages of the ego to complement Freud's developmental stages of the id; he postulated an ego motive to achieve a meaningful psychological identity of oneself, and he applied psychoanalysis to the study of historical figures such as Martin Luther and Adolph Hitler. More than any other ego psychologist, his work has been influential outside of psychoanalytic circles. His theory of ego developmental stages and nuclear conflicts and his analysis of the rise of Nazism are discussed in the text. (See pages 170–172.)

HEINZ HARTMANN

Hartmann and his colleagues objected to Freud's view that the ego develops out of the id and is dependent on the id for all of its psychic energy (Hartmann, 1948; Hartmann, Kris, and Loewenstein, 1946). They maintained instead that many ego functions such as perception, memory, object discrimination, and motility exist at birth in an undifferentiated state. They also proposed that all human behavior cannot be understood in terms of biological drives and that it is therefore necessary to postulate autonomous ego drives. Although these modifications of Freud's theory were influential, unlike Erickson, Hartmann and his colleagues did not propose an elaborate theory of developmental stages of the ego (Rapaport, 1959).

HENRY STACK SULLIVAN

A unifying theme of ego psychology is the focus on interpersonal determinants of psychodynamic processes, and Sullivan went further than most in elaborating the position that the roots of neuroses are disturbed interpersonal relations. "Sullivan constructed an elaborate theory of personality, neurosis, and psychotherapy centered around the notion that personality is entirely the product of interpersonal forces" (Martin, 1971, p. 35). Under this view, the origins of intrapsychic conflicts are interpersonal conflicts. Sullivan's views were very influential and are presented in his two major works, *The Psychiatric Interview* (published posthumously in 1954) and *The Interpersonal Theory of Psychiatry* (published posthumously in 1953).

trating him. The Electra complex, consisting of the girl's unrealistic wishes to marry the father and to kill the mother, is resolved by keeping these wishes unconscious and by unconsciously identifying with the mother. The hypothesized motivation for this resolution was described by Freud: "She is wounded in her self-love by the unfavorable comparison with the boy who is so much better equipped [that is, she feels inferior to boys because she has no penis], and therefore gives up the masturbatory satisfaction which she obtained from her clitoris, repudiates her love toward her mother and at the same time often represses a good deal of her sexual impulses in general" (1924, p. 172). The girl assumes she has been castrated by the mother in retaliation for her sexual desires toward her father and interprets this as evidence of the dangerousness of her sexual impulses toward her father.[4] Thus, the hypothesized motivation for resolution of the Oedipal conflict is the fear of castration, and the hypothesized motivation for resolution of the Electra conflict is fear of future danger based on the interpretation that one has already been castrated.

Contemporary psychoanalytic theorists have questioned Freud's view of female inferiority feelings caused by penis envy and by assumptions of having been castrated (Salzman, 1971; Stroller, 1973).[5] Nevertheless, the Oedipal and Electra complexes are assumed by psychoanalysts to play a major role in children's development. The appropriate resolution of both complexes consists of a massive and permanent repression of the conflict, a resulting same-sex identification, and an opposite-sex object choice of sexual gratification. The

[4] Freud (1924) also noted that feminine development is complicated partially because the girls must switch love objects from the mother during the oral stage to the father during the phallic stage.

[5] It should be noted that Freud did not say that women are inferior. Rather, he attempted to explain feelings of inferiority in women in terms of a hypothesis of penis envy. The extent to which inferiority feelings actually exist in females is unclear. Moreover, females who feel inferior to men might do so by reason of social-cultural training rather than penis envy.

process of identifying with the same-sex parent results in the development of superego functions insofar as parental values and goals are internalized and adopted as one's own.

According to psychoanalytic theory, fixation at the phallic stage, characterized by an unresolved Oedipal or Electra complex, can lead to lifelong proclivities toward anxiety and guilt, especially in regard to sexual activities but also in regard to issues related to the expression of aggression. Proclivities toward sexual dysfunction (e.g., impotence) and toward sexually variant behaviors (e.g., homosexuality) have been hypothesized to be related to failure to resolve the Oedipal and Electra conflicts. For Erickson, the nuclear conflict during the phallic stage is whether the child learns to take initiative and to express sexual curiosity or whether the child learns to be guilty through the establishment of an oppressive superego that punishes initiative.

Latency Period

The period between resolution of the Oedipal or Electra complexes and puberty is called the latency period. During this period sexual desires are largely repressed and sublimated. For Erickson, the child who learns to create, to work with tools, and to develop his skills acquires a sense of industry, whereas the child who fails at these tasks or who unfavorably compares his products to those of other children develops a sense of inferiority.

Genital Phase

The increase in sexual drive during puberty is hypothesized to re-establish the individual's intense interest in genital sexuality. Although the genital phase is similar to the phallic phase in that the primary area of gratification is the genital region, the phases differ in terms of the object of genital gratification; during the phallic phase, the sexual object is the opposite-sex parent, but during the genital phase the sexual objects are members of the other sex. Difficulties in sexual adjustment during the genital stage can cause interpersonal anxiety and a general loss of self-esteem.

Erickson (1950) described the initial stages of adolescence as involving rapid physiological change. Additionally, the young adolescent shifts his concerns to how others perceive him and to the possibilities of a future career. An adaptive reaction to these changes results in a sense of identity that comes from joining social groups and clubs and from perceiving oneself as a member of various groups. Maladaptive reactions result in role confusion.

Postgenital Stages

Although Freud's theory of psychosexual development ends with the achievement of adult sexuality during the genital stage, Erickson's theory of ego development includes three additional stages: young adulthood, adulthood, and maturity. The nuclear conflict of the young adulthood stage is that of intimacy versus isolation. The young adult, having found his own identity, seeks to fuse

TABLE 6-1
Developmental Stages

Stage	Psychosexual Fixations of the Id	Nuclear Conflicts of the Ego
Oral	Dependency, aggression	Trust vs. mistrust
Anal	Obstinacy, neatness, explosive traits, disorderliness rebelliousness	Autonomy vs. shame and doubt
Phallic	Anxiety and guilt, sexually variant behavior	Initiative vs. guilt
Genital		Industry vs. inferiority
Young adulthood		Intimacy vs. isolation
Adulthood		Generativity vs. stagnation
Maturity		Ego integrity vs. despair

Note: Freud's account of psychosexual stages of libidinal development ends at puberty with the genital stage; because the genital stage is the last stage of libidinal development, it makes no sense to talk of a "fixation" at this stage. Erickson's developmental life cycles of the ego continue beyond libidinal development stages.

his identity with those of others. If successful, he or she learns how to be intimate with others; if unsuccessful, a tendency for social isolation develops. In Erickson's adulthood stage, the nuclear conflict is one of generativity (including procreation, the raising of children, productivity, and creativity) versus stagnation. The nuclear conflict of Erickson's maturity stage is that of ego integrity versus despair. Erickson considers ego integrity as the ultimate developmental possibility; the individual who has achieved ego integrity is not afraid of death, whereas the individual who has not achieved ego integrity observes that time is running out and eventually develops a sense of despair.

Table 6-1 provides an overview of the psychoanalytic theory of psychosexual development.

Psychopathology

Fixations at various points in the developmental process are assumed by psychoanalysts to create lifelong conflicts concerning modes of libidinal gratification. Fixation at the phallic stage, for example, can create a lifelong conflict between needs for sexual objects resembling the opposite-sex parent and a fear of sexual expression toward such objects. Under psychoanalytic theory, this conflict predisposes the individual to anxiety reactions in situations that arouse sexual impulses in a manner that threatens recognition of the unresolved Oedipal or Electra conflict. Prolonged exposure to situations that

Psychoanalytic theorists have noted that some young women turn to prostitution as a means of rebelling against their parents. (Photo by Burt Glinn; Magnum Photos, Inc.)

rearouse an unconscious conflict causes the ego to experience high levels of anxiety as a warning that the conflict is about to enter consciousness. If the ego cannot maintain control through repression alone, it regresses and calls on other defenses that permit the disguised expression of the conflict. The behavior through which the conflict is expressed in disguised form is called a *symptom.* If the regression is partial, the individual develops a neurotic symptom. If the regression is more complete and to the point where one actually begins behaving as if he were of Oedipal age, psychotic symptoms develop. Figure 6-3 summarizes the psychoanalytic theory of how symptoms develop.

As noted previously, a key aspect of the Freudian concept of a symptom is that the conflict, not the symptom itself, is the real psychological problem. Thus, the Freudian approach hypothesizes that if you merely treat and remove the symptoms without also treating the underlying conflict, a new symptom will develop. This hypothesis is called *symptom substitution.* For example, if one could remove Mr. Kelly's colitis by use of drugs, then it would be predicted

Figure 6-3
Psychoanalytic theory of symptom formation.

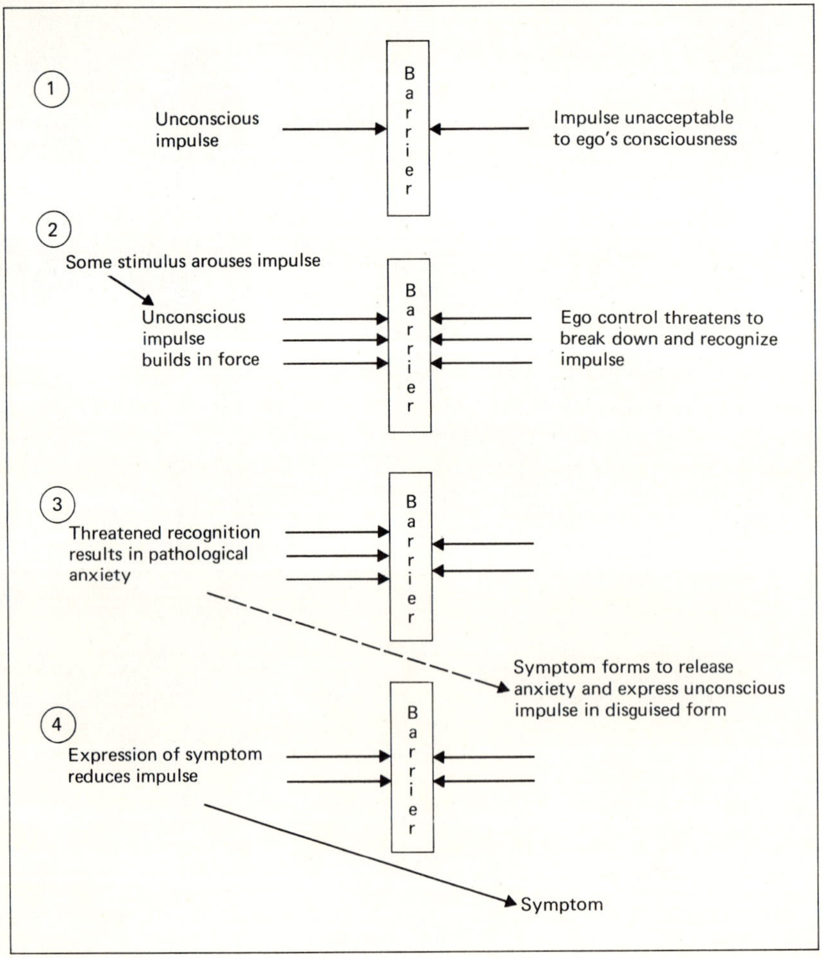

BOX 6-3
The Symptom Substitution Hypothesis

The symptom substitution hypothesis is central to the psychoanalytic model of abnormality. This hypothesis predicts that the direct removal of symptoms eventually will result in the formation of new symptoms unless the symptoms are removed as a consequence of resolutions of unconscious conflicts. Consider the example of Mr. Kelly's wish to kill his wife; this wish can be conceptualized as a symptom that expresses Mr. Kelly's unconscious anger toward his mother. Suppose treatment were provided by having Mr. Kelly self-administer some punishment every time he thought of killing his wife. This "thought-stopping" procedure would probably eliminate Mr. Kelly's conscious wish to kill his wife but, according to psychoanalytic theory, it would not affect Mr. Kelly's anger toward his mother and hence some other symptom eventually would develop. In essence, the psychoanalyst considers anger toward mother the "real" problem that should be treated.

The symptom substitution hypothesis has merit for at least two reasons. First, it clearly expresses the fact that, for any particular patient, some problems (symptoms) are related to other problems (basic conflicts). A therapist should not attempt to treat every complaint his client might have but instead must evaluate the manner in which the patient's various complaints might be related to basic needs, conflicts, and frustrations. Second, the experience of many clinicians suggests that circumstances exist under which the direct treatment of symptoms is of minimal benefit to the patient. Moreover, many clinicians would agree that the successful elimination of symptoms through the resolution of conflict is often more desirable, in the sense that it is more comprehensive, than is the removal of the symptoms alone. For example, the resolution of Mr. Kelly's dependency conflicts and a consequent removal of many of his symptoms would constitute a remarkably successful treatment.

Nevertheless, the symptom substitution hypothesis is problematic as it stands. The hypothesis is difficult to falsify because it does not predict what new symptoms will develop, nor does it predict when these symptoms will develop. Thus, if Mr. Kelly's wish to kill his wife had been removed by direct means, the symptom substitution hypothesis could be supported by any problem Mr. Kelly might later develop—including problems that might develop years following the symptom removal—provided such problems could be psychodynamically conceptualized as expressions of dependency needs. A second problem with the symptom substitution hypothesis concerns the success of recently developed symptom-oriented approaches. (See Chapters 5 and 7.)

that other problems such as low back pain or headaches might appear to serve the same function as the colitis. The available evidence does not support the symptom substitution hypothesis. (See Box 6-3.)

PSYCHOANALYTIC ASSESSMENT TECHNIQUES

The purposes of psychoanalytic assessment are to describe psychodynamic processes, to evaluate the extent to which unconscious conflicts are interfering with normal psychological functions, and to assess the strengths a person may possess to cope with his or her conflicts. In this section three assessment techniques primarily associated with psychoanalysis are discussed: *free association, dream interpretation,* and *interpretation of transference phenomena.*

Free Association

The technique of free association consists either of asking a patient to report whatever comes to mind or of asking a patient to report associations that come to mind in response to a particular stimulus. The patient is instructed to associate in as uninhibited a manner as possible and to report all associations no matter how unimportant or ridiculous they may seem. Even though the rules state otherwise, the patient typically resists allowing some associations to come to mind. Examples of such resistance include not being able to think of anything to say, guarded associations, and attempts to divert attention from the task by complaining about the ineffectiveness of therapy or the unattractive decor of the therapist's office. For example, suppose a therapist asks a patient to report whatever comes to mind to the stimulus "father," and the patient says "man" and then stops. This would be interpreted as resistance, and the therapist would restate the rules and encourage the patient to try again. Eventually the patient might produce a more revealing chain of thoughts such as "tall, handsome, husband." This would suggest that the patient's husband is an unconscious symbol for the patient's father.

Free association is employed to identify the unconscious symbolic meaning a particular stimulus may have for a particular patient. Under psychoanalytic theory, after resistance is minimized, the associations are free in the sense that they are relatively uninhibited (free of repressive action and hence determined largely by unconscious feelings).

Dream Interpretation

Freud (1924, 1933) called dreams the royal road to the unconscious because he believed that repression operated less effectively during sleep. Accordingly, analysts usually require patients to recall a recent dream hoping that an interpretation of the dream will reveal significant psychodynamic processes. The recalled (consciously experienced) dream is called the *manifest content* and the unconscious (symbolic) meaning of the dream is called the *latent content.*

The psychoanalytic interpretation of dreams is guided in part by the principle that all dreams are wish-fulfilling. A dream that one has climbed a mountain, for example, might be interpreted as a wish for sexual intercourse because Freud maintained that mountain climbing is a symbol for sexual intercourse. A dream in which one has lost a tooth might be interpreted as a wish for castration as punishment for guilt associated with unacceptable sexual impulses or with masturbation.

Interpretation of Transference Phenomena

Transference refers to a phenomenon in which a patient feels and acts toward a therapist as he or she did toward parents or siblings during childhood. For example, an adolescent boy who was treated by one of the male authors brought the therapist gifts, especially rings, and wanted to hold hands and to talk about going out together. These behaviors represented a transference of a sex dependency conflict that the boy appeared to have with his mother. When the therapist suggested to the boy that he seemed to want both a mother and a wife in one person, the boy at first violently rejected this notion and accused the therapist of disliking him. However, later in therapy the boy was able to see how he had confused the mother and wife roles, although he never was able to deal with his sexual feelings toward his mother.

The transference is primarily a function of the internal conflicts of the patient. Any feeling may be transferred, and the therapist may be perceived as any or all of the significant people in the patient's life. A male therapist may serve as a transferred mother, sister, or sex object for either sex, just as a female therapist may serve as a transferred sister, brother, mother, or father figure. *It is the transference phenomenon that most clearly indicates to the therapist the nature of the patient's unconscious conflicts.*

A phenomenon that works against the therapist's ability to interpret a patient's behavior is called the *countertransference.* This phenomenon occurs when the therapist relates to the patient, or interprets the patient's behavior, in accordance with the therapist's own unresolved conflicts. Lion and Pasternak (1973) define countertransference very broadly as any emotional reaction the therapist has toward the patient, and they report that such reactions are particularly prevalent toward patients with a history of violence. In order to correct for countertransference bias in the assessment of a patient's psychodynamic processes, psychoanalysts (1) undergo an analysis as part of their training and (2) may have another analyst available to discuss a case.

PSYCHOANALYTIC THERAPY

The goal of psychoanalytic treatment is to free psychic energy associated with conflicted unconscious feelings.

Context of Treatment

Psychoanalysis involves the creation of a relationship between two people, the therapist and the patient. Both of these people usually enter this relationship from different backgrounds and expectations. Generally, the therapist expects that the patient will unconsciously resist treatment and that he may even terminate therapy if he feels threatened too quickly. Moreover, the therapist expects that treatment will require several years of two to four weekly meetings, each meeting involving 50 minutes, and for each meeting the therapist expects to be paid. On the other hand, the patient expects to get better. Many patients may expect to get better within a few months' time; such a patient may think that the therapist will quickly come to understand his problem, will tell it to him, and that consequent improvement will be evident within a matter of months. Other patients may imagine that therapy sessions will provide an opportunity for self-exploration and, believing themselves to be exceptionally complicated people, they may expect therapy to last a very long time. Very often, the patient's expectations prove incorrect; in these cases, the patient either revises his thinking or terminates therapy after only a few sessions.

Psychoanalytic interviews are usually conducted in the therapist's office. In classical psychoanalysis, the patient lay on a couch in such a way that he could be seen by the therapist but could not see the therapist. Some psychoanalysts still use the couch, whereas others do not.

Interpretation

As the therapy process begins, the therapist occasionally suggests the presence of feelings or conflicts in the patient, or he may suggest that the patient is defending against these conflicts in particular ways.[6] Interpretations vary considerably in terms of their depth, ranging from interpretations of thoughts and feelings at a preconscious level to interpretations of thoughts and feelings at deep, unconscious levels (Colby, 1951). When the therapist suggested to Mr. Kelly that he was angry with him for not being a medical doctor, the therapist was interpreting anger at a slightly unconscious level. This interpretation was important because it appeared that Mr. Kelly was unaware of why he was uncomfortable with the therapist. A deeper-level interpretation that may have occurred in Mr. Kelly's case is the suggestion that whatever his wife did would make him feel rejected. This interpretation is anxiety-laden because to recognize this thought is to recognize that the feeling of rejection is self-produced rather than the fault of someone else. Two additional examples of the use of interpretation follow.

EXAMPLE 1

THERAPIST: You don't seem to have anything to say today.
PATIENT: No, I can't think of anything. (*Resistance.*)
THERAPIST: What do you suppose that means?
PATIENT: Oh, I don't know.
THERAPIST: Maybe you are thinking about something you are afraid to tell me about. (*Interpretation of resistance.*)
PATIENT: Could be.

EXAMPLE 2

The following exchange might occur in the case of an overly protective wife who the therapist feels is unconsciously displacing hostility toward her father onto her husband.

THERAPIST: Are you too protective?
PATIENT: Sometimes, sometimes I worry about silly things.
THERAPIST: Does he get upset with your concern?
PATIENT: Yes, he says I mother him too much but I just love him.
THERAPIST: But sometimes your worries are over silly things. It seems as if you feel he is in danger or something. (*Interpretation.*)
PATIENT: (*40-second pause.*) Oh, next week is a holiday so I guess we will skip next week. (*Resistance to interpretation.*)

[6] The term *interpretation* has two meanings: (1) It refers to the analyst's judgment of the unconscious meaning of behavior, and (2) it refers to a clinical technique in which the presence of particular unconscious processes is suggested to the patient.

The preceding interchanges exemplify the importance of gradually introducing interpretations of unconscious material lest the patient become too threatened and reject the interpretation entirely. When interpretations of unconscious feelings are introduced gradually, the patient can deal with the material as he or she is capable. Even with interpretations of a fairly surface type (e.g., anger at the therapist), however, the patient may reject the interpretation several times before finally accepting it. Thus, interpretation is a slow process that frequently requires many repetitions in a variety of forms.

Catharsis

Abreaction is the release of energy associated with unconscious thoughts or feelings. The freeing up of such energy is the goal of psychoanalytic therapy. *Catharsis* is a method by which abreaction can be achieved. Specifically, catharsis is hypothesized to occur when the patient re-experiences actual childhood feelings and recognizes that the expression of these feelings need no longer be feared because the patient is no longer a child subject to parental punishment. The recognition of the current inappropriateness of formerly repressed feelings produces abreaction. Thus, psychoanalytic therapy is designed to help patients work toward re-experiencing repressed feelings so that insight into their inappropriate nature can be obtained.

The concepts of abreaction and catharsis explain why intellectual insight alone is insufficient to produce genuine therapeutic progress. An intellectual understanding of one's problems is helpful only when it gradually leads to the conscious experience of formerly repressed emotion. Intellectual understanding in the absence of conscious experience of the unacceptable impulse does not lead to abreaction.

EFFECTIVENESS OF PSYCHOANALYTIC THERAPY

In 1952 Eysenck published his now famous review of psychotherapy based on interview techniques. This review was based on therapists' subjective judgments of improvement and counted as failures of treatment patients who prematurely self-terminated treatment. Eysenck calculated outcome rates for various types of interview psychotherapy and compared these rates to a presumably untreated group of patients who had been committed to state hospitals. Eysenck's data failed to produce evidence that interview psychotherapy was effective—the data suggested that "roughly two-thirds of a group of neurotic patients will recover or improve to a marked extent within about two years of the onset of their illness, whether they are treated by means of psychotherapy or not" (Eysenck, 1952). Eysenck's overall improvement rate for psychoanalytic therapy was 44 per cent, a figure lower than the two-thirds figure for other treatments and for no formal treatment at all.

Eysenck's conclusion that the effectiveness of psychotherapy, including psychoanalytic therapy, has yet to be proven or disproven has been accepted by the large majority of the scientific community. Bergin (1967, 1971), however, has questioned the utility of global conclusions about the effectiveness of psychotherapy. Bergin suggested that psychotherapy is effective for some therapist-patient combinations and that it is harmful for others. Several writers and researchers have acknowledged that a therapist's personality and training are relevant factors in treatment success (Meltzoff & Kornreich, 1970; Luborsky & Spence, 1971). Bergin's hypothesis that some people actually get worse from psychotherapy, however, requires more study before it can be accepted or rejected.

Patient Variables Affecting Success

In his book *A Primer for Psychotherapists,* Colby (1951) suggested that the following patient variables affect successful outcome in psychoanalytically oriented therapy.

Age

Traditional analysis is generally considered appropriate for individuals between the ages of 16 and 50. Children and adolescents under 16 usually lack the motivation or the verbal skills necessary to explore unconscious material in an interview situation. Accordingly, play therapy and adolescent group analytic therapy have been developed to treat these individuals. On the other hand, adults over 50 are generally considered too old for psychoanalysis. In Freudian analysis, the patient should have referred himself for treatment, thereby showing a personal commitment to solve his problems. Individuals beyond the age of 50 are considered unlikely to benefit from psychoanalysis.

Intelligence

The client should possess at least average intelligence. Intelligence, a high level of verbal skill, and imagination are necessary to ensure that the patient can communicate accurately and can understand what the therapist relates to him. In this regard, psychoanalysis might be called a thinking man's therapy.

History of Success

The clients most likely to profit from psychoanalytic treatment are those who have been successful in a competitive vocation or in social pursuits. This requirement suggests difficulties in treating people with histories of arrest for criminal behavior as well as people with immature personalities who have never functioned independently from their parents.

Observation Ability

The suitable client has both ego strength and objectivity sufficient to evaluate himself. He is also able to see aspects of his behavior as self-induced rather than as mainly controlled by other people or situations. Accordingly, the client should have psychological strengths sufficient to be able to reveal and to face negative aspects of his or her personality.

Neurotic Benefit

Environmental benefits, called *secondary gains,* that result from the neurosis should be minimal. For example, if an obsessive-compulsive neurosis leads to the writing of great books, social and monetary benefits may outweigh the neurotic pain. Thus, if one can lose love, sympathy, money, or dependency by solving the neurotic conflict, it is unlikely that the solution will be sought once the person realizes (or imagines) the consequent losses.

Psychological Basis of Behavior

It is generally recognized by psychoanalysts that several types of abnormal behavior may, in fact, have biological causes. The psychoanalytic approach is considered inappropriate for disorders caused primarily by biological factors.

Standard psychoanalytic treatment requires a considerable length of time and, hence, is an expensive form of treatment. In part to counteract this difficulty, many psychologists, psychiatrists, and social workers have adopted modified versions of traditional psychoanalytic treatment. These professionals are not trained as traditional psychoanalysts, nor do they claim to be, but they subscribe to the general psychoanalytic approach and generally are considered to be practicing psychoanalytic therapy even though their methods differ somewhat from Freud's. Unfortunately, there is little evidence bearing on the question of which variations in psychoanalytic therapy are most effective.

PSYCHOANALYTIC RESEARCH METHODOLOGY

Two research methodologies that have been employed to test psychoanalytic hypotheses will be discussed here: the case history and the cross-cultural correlational study.

The psychoanalytic case history is a historical reconstruction of the important psychological events in a person's life. In constructing a case history, the analyst is concerned more with discovering a person's feelings concerning childhood events than with identifying events. The formulation of this position on the importance of feelings rather than actual events is considered by some to be one of Freud's most important contributions (Brenner, 1955). At first, Freud believed many of his patients' stories of sexual seduction in childhood, but later he was forced to recognize that in many instances the stories were fantasies rather than memories of actual events. "This discovery was at first an overwhelming blow to Freud, who castigated himself as the credulous dupe of neuropathic patients and who, in his despair and shame, was nearly ready to return to the respectable fold of the local medical society from which those researchers had ostracized him" (Brenner, 1955, p. 197). Instead, Freud reformulated his theory, hypothesizing that what was significant was his patients' *feelings* and fantasies of having been seduced, for these feelings were psychologically real even though the reported seductions never occurred.

The use of psychoanalytic case histories as the primary source of support for psychoanalytic theory has been objected to on the following grounds:

1. The therapist is a biased observer who is aware of the hypotheses being investigated and is in a position to create a demand for certain types of information from the patient. Grinker, a proponent of psychoanalytic theory, has expressed these problems as follows:

> Using the tools of psychoanalysis, [psychoanalysts] find what they search for and little else. . . . The patient is the psychoanalyst's biased collaborator. Each interpretation may be a hypothesis . . . but there are no alternatives and little possibility that the patient-collaborator will refute it, although theoretically much is made of the patient's behavior as an index of correctness or of refutation of interpretation. . . . The patient is not an unbiased scientific colleague [1958, p. 137].

2. Case histories cannot be replicated because every psychoanalytic case involves a unique history of unconscious dynamics and interpretations.

3. At best, case history data can permit inferences of correlations between two variables; such data do not permit inferences of causality. When a patient recalls a threat by the father and also recalls developing a fear of horses, these recollections are only correlated. It is possible that threat by the father caused a fear of horses, it is possible that a fear of horses led the patient to provoke a threat from the father, and it is possible that some third event caused both the threat and the fear. Correlational data do not permit inferences of causality.

The case study research methodology is empirical (pertaining to factual matters), but it is not experimental because the methodology does not include the use of control groups and control procedures. To their experimentally oriented critics, many Freudians reply that the nature of the psyche (mind), with its conscious and unconscious forces, is too complex to understand by investigating only those variables that can be studied in an experimental fashion. Accordingly, many Freudians emphasize what can be learned by skilled observation and by interview techniques. Other psychoanalytically oriented investigators, however, have attempted to test psychoanalytic hypotheses by employing research methodologies less controversial than the case history. An example of such research is provided by the cross-cultural correlational study.

Cross-cultural studies have been employed to test psychoanalytic hypotheses on the relation between childhood rearing practices and adult personality traits (e.g., Whiting & Child, 1966). The unique feature of this type of research is that the unit of study is a particular culture or society rather than a particular individual. In essence, the method consists of the following procedures. The investigator rates ethnographic or anthropologic descriptions of each culture under investigation for the presence or absence of particular childhood training practices (e.g., a negative and restrictive attitude toward homosexuality). The cultures are also rated for the prevalence of various personality traits or specific behaviors (e.g., homosexuality). The investigator then evaluates statistically the degree of association between the childhood training practice and the particular adult behavior under study. This method does not permit inferences that the childhood training practice caused the adult behavior because it is possible that the adult behavior caused the childhood training practice or that some third variable caused the observed correlation. Nevertheless, the cross-cultural study can provide important information.

BOX 6-4
Marry One's Sister and Kill One's Maternal Uncle?

In *Sex and Repression in Savage Society,* the anthropologist Malinowski (1927) examined the universality of the Oedipus complex. Specifically, he questioned whether the Oedipus complex is primarily the result of biological factors and hence is likely to be found in all societies, or is it instead the result of the Western civilization's definition of family roles and hence likely to differ across societies.

Malinowski studied the Trobriand Islanders of northeastern New Guinea. In this primitive society, kinship was reckoned through the mother only, the natives believing the father to have no role in the conception of the child. The authority figure for the child was the mother's brother (maternal uncle)—the children were heirs to the maternal uncle's possessions, the maternal uncle was responsible for producing enough food for them and for their mother, and the maternal uncle was responsible for disciplining the children. By contrast, the father's role was that of protecting and cherishing his wife's children.

Another important difference between the Tribriand society and our own was a strong taboo against brother-sister incest. To discourage tender relations between brothers and sisters, they were separated in the family at an early age.

Malinowski (1927) hypothesized that the psychosexual development of the Trobriand Islanders differs markedly from that of Western children. One specific difference is the composition of the Oedipus complex. According to Malinowski, the strong sister-brother taboo leads to repression of these incestuous impulses, while the authority role of the maternal uncle leads to the repression of hostile feelings toward this figure. Thus, rather than the Oedipal wishes to marry one's mother and to kill one's father, Malinowski hypothesized wishes to marry one's sister and to kill the maternal uncle.

Jones (1925) challenged Malinowski's interpretation of his data, hypothesizing that the Oedipal complex is universal and can be found in the Trobriand Islanders. According to Jones, savages must, "in order to make social life possible at all, maintain much more elaborate and formidable devices of control over their cruel and sadistic impulses" (1925, p. 110). In the Trobriand society this additional form of control is a displacement to the sister of the wish to marry the mother and a displacement to the maternal uncle of the wish to kill the father. Moreover, Jones hypothesized that the Trobriand Islanders' denial of the father's role in procreation was a consequence of the repressed hostility toward the father.

The central difference between the hypotheses advanced by Malinowski and Jones concerns the direction of the cause-and-effect relations between psychological forces and culture. Jones assumes that the Oedipal complex is universal and explains Trobriand society as a primitive attempt to deal with the powerful Oedipal urges. Malinowski, on the other hand, explains the Oedipal complex largely in terms of cultural forces operating in Western societies and hence hypothesizes a different complex when other cultural forces are operative.

EXAMPLES OF PSYCHOANALYTIC RESEARCH

Psychoanalysis is at its very core a historical science that relates childhood experiences and (more recently) cultural forces to adult personality. In this section two outstanding examples of psychoanalytically oriented research will be reviewed. The first example is Erik Erickson's case history analysis of how Germany's culture and history combined with a genius of propaganda to create "a hell on earth which seems impossible even to those who know it has been fact" (Erickson, 1950, p. 237). Although Erickson's analysis of the rise of Nazi Germany is admittedly impressionistic and is largely unsupported by hard evidence, it is, nevertheless, offered here for the insights it contains. The other research example presented is Whiting and Child's (1953) cross-cultural study of child training and personality.

The Legend of Hitler's Youth

Erickson's (1950) analysis of the rise of Nazi Germany is concerned primarily with the question of how the histrionics of one master orator could lead a civilized nation to mass murder and totalitarianism. Erickson notes that Hitler was born in the Austrian town of Braunau, which Hitler described in *Mein Kampf* as "Bavarian by blood and Austrian by nationality." Hitler also tells us in *Mein Kampf* that he loved his mother and that she devoted herself "to the cares of the household and looking after her children with eternally the same loving care." Hitler reported that he respected his father who had once run away from home to become something "better" only to return to live the mundane life of a minor official. His father drank heavily and beat his wife, who was 23 years his junior. Psychoanalytically, this equation suggests "that in Hitler's case the love for his young mother and the hate for his old father assumed morbid proportions, and that it was this conflict which drove him to love and to hate and compelled him to save or destroy peoples who really 'stand for' his mother and his father" (Erickson, 1950, p. 329). Although Hitler's love for the eternal mother (Germany) and his adolescent rebellion against his tyrannical father suggest an Oedipal complex, Erickson cautions us against so narrow an explanation of the Nazi movement. If Hitler were either neurotic or psychotic to an extreme degree, his disturbance would have immobilized him and interfered with his plan to rule Germany. Hitler was a highly skilled orator and politician who planned and brought to temporary fruition the political and social restructuring of a nation. According to Erickson, what is important is not that Hitler's Oedipal conflict assumed morbid proportions, but that it represented in exaggerated form themes with which millions of Germans could identify. Moreover, Hitler was sufficiently aware of the nature of the German neurosis to manipulate his oratory for his maximal personal advantage. The success of Hitler tells us as much about Germany as it does about Hitler.

Historically, Germany had been a loose collection of provinces located at the center of Europe. It lacked a self-identity, and its location at the center of Europe and its encirclement by great powers implanted fears of foreign encroachment. Not only did many Germans fear military invasion, but also they feared cultural invasion, or the introduction of foreign values. Fears that social or political walls would divide Germany date back to the walls actually built by the ancient Romans across Germany's southern frontier. Two issues before the collective German ego have been that of encirclement versus *Lebensraum* (living space) and that of disunity versus unity.

Erickson suggested that the Nazi movement unleashed the fury of adolescence and directed it against those who represented symbols of dismemberment. (Photo by Shalmon Bernstein; Magnum Photos, Inc.)

In addition to these historical factors, Erickson suggests that German culture engendered rebellion in its youth. The German father was aloof, dominant, harsh, and lacking in tenderness. In contrast, the German mother was playful, warm, and generous until the father came home; the father would not tolerate any "nonsense" and when he was home the mother attended to his needs. This family constellation engendered the seeds of rebellion against the aloof father for interfering with the child's warm relations with his mother.

Hitler presented himself to the masses as the rebellious adolescent who successfully opposed his father's plans for him. He was the adolescent who never gave in and who told the Germans that "no old man, be he father, emperor, or god, need stand in the way of [a German's] love for his mother Germany" (Erickson, 1950, p. 336). He offered Germany the identity of himself, the German army, and the purity of the Ayrian race. He promised to defend Germany against the invasion of foreign values. He promised unity through obedience.

Erickson explains Hitler's campaign against the Jews in terms of the Jews' symbolic meaning to non-Jewish Germans. The Jew is a member of the most dispersed nation in history and yet somehow Jews manage to retain their identity. The Jew thus aroused in Germans fears of dismemberment (castration) of Germany as well as envy of a national identity. As members of a dispersed nation, moreover, Jews became a mediator of cultural change and thus aroused the German adolescent fear of contamination. Symbolically, then, Erickson sees the Jew as having unleashed in part the fury of the rebellious adolescent mentality of Nazi Germany.

In summary, Erickson's analysis of the rise of Nazi Germany stresses a rebellious adolescent spirit against the aloof German father, the absence of a unifying German identity, and German fears of dismemberment and encirclement. Hitler's propaganda played to these themes partly because Hitler was an excellent propagandist and partly because Hitler's own Oedipal conflict was an exaggerated form of the national neurosis. This psychological climate, Hitler's political and oratory skills, and the economic desperation of post-World War I Germany are seen by Erickson as the factors that combined to produce Nazi Germany.

The Whiting and Child Study

The psychoanalytic theory of fixation proposes that events occurring in childhood with respect to a particular system of behavior (oral, anal, or sexual) may increase for life the importance of that system of behavior, in comparison to the importance that system would have had in the absence of those childhood events (Whiting & Child, 1966, p. 130). Following Freud, Fenichel (1945) proposed two basic factors that evoke fixations: fixations are evoked (1) when a system of behavior is associated with excessive frustration, and (2) when a system of behavior is associated with excessive satisfactions. In a study first reported in 1953, Whiting and Child (1966) modified the psychoanalytic hypothesis of fixation in two important ways. First, they abandoned the psychoanalytic hypothesis that fixations are related to universal phases of libidinal development and instead focused on the general notion of childhood events that increase for life the importance of a system of behavior. Second, they distinguished between negative fixations that are caused by excessive frustration and positive fixations that are caused by excessive satisfactions. The study was designed in part to test hypotheses that negative and positive fixations are real phenomena.

The method consisted of rating anthropological reports on 75 different cultures of nonindustrialized societies. Two types of global measures of child training customs were obtained from unbiased judges who read the anthropological accounts. One type of global rating concerned the extent to which the customs of the society engendered what was called *socialization anxiety.* Separate ratings were obtained for the extent to which the society's child rearing customs aroused anxiety in the oral behavior system (e.g., practices concerning weaning), in the anal behavior system (e.g., customs concerning defecation control training), in the sexual system, in regard to learning to be independent, and in regard to learning to control aggression. In rating socialization anxiety, the judges were instructed to take into account the following types of evidence so that the greater the presence of each, the greater should be the level of socialization anxiety: (1) the brevity of the period of transition from freedom in initial habit control to the requirement of acceptance of adult or childhood inhibitions; (2) the severity of the punishment used in imposing inhibitory control; (3) the frequency of the punishment used in imposing inhibitory control; and (4) evidence of emotional conflict. The other type of global measure of child training practices was the extent to which the customs of the society engendered initial satisfaction with the behavior system. An initial satisfaction measure was obtained for each of the five behavior systems, and in making these ratings the judges were instructed that the greater the presence of each of the following the higher the level of initial satisfaction: (1) the length of time the child is permitted to perform initial habits; (2) the amount of freedom the child has to perform the initial habits; (3) the amount of encouragement the child receives to perform the initial habits; and (4) the extent to which the performance of the initial habits may be anxiety-reducing.

The global measures of socialization anxiety and initial satisfaction were conceptualized as antecedent measures of childhood rearing customs. As mentioned previously, the purpose of the study was to evaluate the extent to which childhood rearing customs predicted to cause fixations are actually associated with increased importance of that behavior system for the adult. The measure of how important a behavior system is for an adult was obtained by rating the extent to which that behavior system was involved in cultural explanations of sickness or death, or treatments for illnesses. Explanations of sickness, death, and therapy were selected as the measure of adult concern with a behavior system because sickness and death are universal phenomena about which all of the cultures under investigation held beliefs.

The hypothesis of *negative fixation* was that the greater the extent to which the child rearing customs of a society engendered socialization anxiety in a particular behavior system, the more likely it would be that the culture invokes that system of behavior as an explanation of sickness. For example, a culture that weaned abruptly and at a young age would be expected to be more likely to attribute sickness to eating, drinking, verbal spells, or incantations. The results support the hypothesis by showing that "the custom potential of the anxiety developed in any of five systems of behavior . . . is related to the tendency for adults in that society to show continued concern about that system of behavior . . ." (Whiting & Child, 1966, p. 213). The hypothesis was strongly confirmed for the oral, dependent, and aggressive behavior systems; only weak support was found for the anal and sexual behavior systems.

The hypothesis of *positive fixation* was that the greater the extent to which the child rearing customs of a society engendered initial satisfaction in any system of behavior, the more likely it would be that the culture invokes that system of behavior in therapeutic practices. The results provided "no consistent evidence that high initial satisfaction potential of a given system of behavior in infancy and early childhood would lead to a lasting reliance on that system as a source of security, as in the selection of therapeutic practices (Whiting & Child, 1966, p. 215). Some evidence was found, however, that high levels of satisfaction in a behavior system at some point after childhood was related to a lasting reliance on that behavior system as a source of security.

Discussion

The two investigations reviewed exemplify different types of research on psychoanalytic theory. The Erickson case study of the rise of Nazi Germany rests largely on Erickson's impressions of German culture. Note that Erickson did not provide us with any precise statistics on the harshness of the German father and that he did not refer to any solid empirical studies that German culture was in fact as he presented it. As a consequence of these methodological inadequacies, the Erickson study is best interpreted as a series of suggestive insights on which future research may be conducted. In contrast, the Whiting and Child study represents an attempt to introduce some methodological rigor into research on psychoanalytically oriented hypotheses. Unfortunately, this impressive study did not generate a sustained series of follow-up studies. We can only conclude, therefore, that psychoanalysis is an insightful theory that has broadened our understanding of human behavior and that stands in desperate need of more rigorous investigation.

Although it is true that other theories of abnormality also stand in need of more rigorous analysis, what is presently most disappointing about psychoanalysis is the absence of any visible and sustained attempt at rigorous study. All things considered, however, it is important to recognize that psychoanalysis has contributed substantially to our understanding of human behavior.

SUMMARY

The psychoanalytic approach views abnormal behavior as a product of predisposing personality traits and real or imagined precipitating environmental events.

Predisposing Personality Traits

Psychoanalytic theory postulates that early psychological development can be viewed as a natural progression through five psychosexual stages: oral, anal, phallic, latency, and genital. Both excessive and insufficient gratification of needs at any stage is postulated to lead to a fixation, or partial arrest of development, at that stage. Fixations create lifelong areas of psychological vulnerability and determine maladaptive personality traits. For example, fixation at the oral stage of development is seen as creating a lifelong need for dependent relations. This excessive need frustrates the person's natural desire for independence so that conflict may arise between a need for dependency and hostility toward those who gratify these needs. Fixations at the phallic stage are postulated to lead to conflicts concerning sex. (See Table 6-1.)

Under psychoanalytic theory, excessive fixations limit the range of life circumstances to which an individual can adapt. For example, if fixation at the anal stage of development leads to compulsive personality traits, the individual has difficulty handling ambiguity. If fixations at the oral stage lead to dependent personality traits, the individual may be overly sensitive to rejection and criticism and tasks that demand independence.

Anxiety and Defense

It is sometimes the case that fears that were realistic in childhood are no longer appropriate for the adult. For example, an infant who experiences diffuse anxiety when paid insufficient attention can be viewed as responding to the objective reality of dependence on the parents for survival. The young child who fears parental punishment for urinating in his pants, the child who fears punishment for overt sexual interest in the opposite-sex parent, and the child who fears parental displeasure for his or her masturbation are all to some extent expressing a realistic fear. These same fears, however, are inappropriate for the adult, who no longer needs to be concerned about parental punishment. For example, it is inappropriate for an adult to fear parental abandonment because of the loss of a job or to fear parental punishment for sexual intercourse with a spouse. Psychoanalytic theory proposes that neurotic and psychotic behavior in an adult often can be understood as related to childhood fears and conflicts, the adult not having insight into the fact that these childhood fears are still motivating behavior and are no longer appropriate.

Psychoanalytic theory accounts for the persistence of childhood conflicts into later life partially in terms of the processes of anxiety and defense. The ego (self; the conscious awareness of oneself as a distinct entity) has the function of protecting the individual from realistic dangers so that in childhood the ego resists the expression of ideas and behaviors that may lead to parental punishment. This resistance is postulated to create an unconscious mind. For example, the ego may defend against any of the following: fears of parental abandonment associated with excessive dependency needs, fears of parental retaliation for being messy associated with compulsive personality traits, and fears of parental castration associated with a boy's sexual interests in his mother.

All defenses are ego functions, all are unconscious or semiunconscious, and all are directed against anxiety. Under psychoanalytic theory, anxiety is a signal to the ego that some unacceptable impulse is about to enter consciousness.

The primary ego defense is repression; repression is the psychological force that accounts for resistance in acknowledging and thinking about unacceptable ideas and impulses. Repression is the force that creates the unconscious. Other defenses include denial (unconscious rejection of feelings, attitudes, or behaviors), displacement (discharge of unconscious impulses by changing the object of the impulse from an unacceptable object to a less unacceptable object), projection (attribution of one's feelings to someone else), reaction formation, isolation, rationalization, and sublimation.

Because unacceptable childhood conflicts are repressed (unconscious), the adult does not realize that current behavior is being motivated by irrational childhood fears. For example, people who are sensitive to rejection react to rejection with anxiety and depression rather than calmly realizing and acting on the need to find other people with whom they can relate in a meaningful manner.

Symptom Formation

As mentioned previously, predisposing personality traits are seen as limiting the range of life circumstances to which the person can adapt. A person who unconsciously hates his or her parents experiences authority situations as stressful; a young male who is fearful of sex experiences social pressures to date women as stressful. Under psychoanalytic theory, any life circumstance that rearouses unconscious childhood conflicts and threatens their recognition is experienced as stressful. When the stress becomes too great for the ego to contain the hostility through repression and denial alone, psychopathological symptoms are postulated to develop. Consider the case of an adult who has excessive unconscious hostility toward his parents and who has just been drafted into the army. The army provides many authority figures that unconsciously symbolize parents, unconscious hostility toward the patents is rearoused, and the ego commits more psychic energy to the defensive process in an effort to keep the man from recognizing his unacceptable feelings toward his parents. With so much energy committed to the defensive process, the ego undergoes a partial regression to earlier periods of psychosexual functioning. This regression is manifested as an increase in childish behavior. With continued exposure to the stressful environment, neurotic symptoms such as anxiety and interpersonal (displaced) hostility toward peers may occur. The interpersonal hostility is seen as a disguised expression of parental hatred that releases pent-up aggression in a manner that precludes conscious recognition of the true object of hatred.

Assessment Techniques

The purposes of psychoanalytic assessments are to describe psychodynamic processes, to evaluate the extent to which unconscious conflicts are interfering with normal psychological functions, and to assess the strengths a person may possess to cope with the conflicts. The technique of free association consists of asking a client to report whatever comes to mind or of asking a client to report associations that come to mind in response to a particular stimulus. The associations then are analyzed for unconscious symbolic content. Another psychoanalytic assessment technique is dream interpretation. The primary psychoanalytic assessment technique, however, is interpretation of the transference. Transference refers to a phenomenon in which a patient feels and acts toward a therapist as he or she did toward parents or siblings during childhood.

Psychoanalytic Therapy and Effectiveness

As a talking therapy, the purpose of psychoanalytic treatment is to improve psychological functioning by encouraging the client to develop insight into the inappropriate relations between childhood experiences and current behavior. The therapist attempts to accomplish this goal by interpreting the unconscious meaning of the client's behavior. There exists no solid evidence that psychoanalytic therapy is effective. Patient variables hypothesized to be associated with a successful outcome for psychoanalytic therapy include the following: patients between the ages of 16 and 50, average or above-average intelligence, adequate to good adjustment prior to neurotic or psychotic episode, ego strength, minimal benefit to having psychological problems, and psychologically caused problems.

Research Methodologies

Two methodologies employed to test psychoanalytic hypotheses are the case history and the cross-cultural correlational study. The psychoanalytic case history is a historical reconstruction of the important events in a person's life. Erickson's (1950) analysis of Hitler's life and the rise of Nazi Germany was presented as an example of psychoanalytic research based on the case history format. The unique feature of the cross-cultural study is that the unit of analysis is a particular culture or society rather than a particular person. The Whiting and Child (1966) study exemplifies this type of research methodology. It found some support for the hypothesis that childhood training methods are associated with adult personality traits.

Chapter 7

Social Learning Theory

First they tell you you're wrong, and they can prove it. Then they tell you you're right, but it's not important. Then they tell you it's important, but they've known it for years.

CHARLES F. KETTERING (Ayllon & Azrin, 1968)

Behavioral psychology suffers from a poor public image (Oelsner, 1974; Trotter & Warren, 1974). The behaviorist is often perceived as a mechanistic, cold person who stands ready to condition people to think the "right" thoughts and to conform to society's rules. In the public's mind, moreover, behaviorism is often associated with brainwashing and with psychosurgery. The public image of the behaviorist is unjustified: One purpose of this chapter is to dispel this and other myths about social learning theory (also called the behavioral approach).

An important aspect of the behavioral approach is the application of two areas of substantive knowledge, operant and Pavlovian conditioning, to the understanding and treatment of abnormal behavior. To some extent, operant and Pavlovian conditioning have been applied by different groups of investigators. Skinner's theoretical application of operant conditioning language to human behavior appeared in *Walden Two* in 1948 and in *Science and Human Behavior* in 1953. Although some experimental tests of Skinner's theories were conducted during the 1950s (e.g., Azrin & Lindsley, 1956), it was not until late in that decade that Lindsley established behavior laboratories at the Metropolitan State Hospital near Boston. Psychologists such as Ayllon (1963), Bijou and Baer (1961), Ferster and DeMyer (1962), Goldiamond (1962), Lovaas, Berberich, Perloff, and Schaeffer (1966), Staats (1965), Wolf, Risley, and Mees (1964) and Yates (1958) were among the early pioneers whose work consistently demonstrated the importance of this approach. The publication of Ullmann and Krasner's *Case Studies in Behavior Modification* in 1965 marked the beginning of a period during which many psychologists were to take a serious look at the practical importance of reinforcement procedures.

The early pioneers in applying Pavlovian conditioning principles to abnormal behavior were Watson and Raynor (1920) and Jones (1924). The Watson and Raynor study, known as the case of Little Albert, demonstrated that Pavlovian conditioning procedures can induce phobic reactions in young children. The case study is of questionable ethics, however, because it intentionally induced a fear in a child; as we shall see, this study is atypical of behavioral research insofar as ethics is concerned. Far more typical was Jones's (1924) demonstration that gradual exposure to feared stimuli is an effective procedure for reducing fear. After Jones's work, there was relatively little interest in the application of Pavlovian conditioning until Eysenck (1952, 1955, 1961) and Wolpe (1958) appeared. Eysenck's (1952) conclusion that the effectiveness of insight psychotherapy had yet to be demonstrated against appropriate control groups helped to increase receptivity to a new behavioral approach. But it was the development of effective treatment procedures that generated the greatest interest in social learning theory. Specifically, Wolpe's publication of *Psychotherapy by Reciprocal Inhibition* in 1958 reported a remarkably effective treatment procedure called systematic desensitization. Wolpe's work was followed by other important investigations of systematic desensitization, including those by Paul (1966) and by Lang and Lazouik (1963).

The young history of the behavioral approach has been one of broadening the range of phenomena studied. In this effort, important work was conducted by Bandura and Walters (1963), who extended the behavioral approach to modeling and observational learning. Other efforts to broaden the behavioral approach are Ellis's (1962) theory of rational-emotive processes, Lazarus's (1967) technical eclecticism, Kanfer's (e.g., Kanfer & Marston, 1963) studies on self-control, and O'Leary's (Drabman, Spitalnik, & O'Leary, 1973; O'Leary, Poulos, & Devine, 1972) theoretical discussions of reinforcement therapy.

The behavioral approach also has been broadened by applications of modern animal learning phenomena. Seligman and his colleagues have been pioneers in these efforts (Seligman, 1970; Seligman, Maier, & Geer, 1968). Seligman's concept of preparedness, which is based on research by Garcia and others, is discussed in this chapter. Seligman's theory of learned helplessness, however, is presented in Chapter 14. Another leading theorist who has systematically applied learning theory to social phenomena is Staats (1975).

This chapter begins with a case history of a retarded, emotionally disturbed, institutionalized child whose screaming behavior resulted in a referral for reinforcement therapy.

THE CASE OF ANNETTE

Ten-year-old Annette was referred for psychiatric treatment because her persistent and furious screaming disturbed the entire ward of the state hospital in which she resided. After observing Annette's bizarre behavior, the psychiatrist was unable to devise a program of treatment. Instead, he referred Annette to a psychologist who specialized in reinforcement therapy.

Annette, the sixth in a family of nine children, was severely retarded. By the time she was six years old, she still was not toilet trained, she could not dress herself, she could not feed herself, and she could not use language to communicate with others. The burdens of caring for Annette were so great that her parents requested institutional placement. Thus, at age six, Annette was admitted to a large state hospital for the mentally retarded. The child's diagnosis on admission to the institution was severe mental retardation with organic brain disorder of natal or prenatal etiology.

During Annette's initial two years in the institution, she was described as a happy and cooperative child by attendants on her ward. At this point, a member of the institution's professional staff began to see Annette on a regular basis. In the opinion of this professional, Annette possessed greater intellectual potential than had been recognized previously. The professional's interest in Annette intensified, and the child became emotionally dependent on her visits. These visits terminated abruptly when the professional left the institution. Following this loss, Annette began to display outbursts of the screaming behavior that led to her referral for psychiatric treatment four years after she had been admitted to the institution.

Description of Problematic Behavior

When the psychologist first met Annette, the child's hands were tied behind her back with a small cloth towel. The ward attendants explained that this restraining of Annette's hands was necessary to prevent her from screaming. When her hands were freed at the psychologist's request, the child immediately displayed a sequence of behavior that the therapist was to observe again on many occasions. Specifically, the child first raised her hands to cover her ears, lowered her head, and assumed a squatting position. In this position, Annette screamed, loudly and incessantly, while hopping about the ward. Without interrupting her screaming, Annette occasionally looked up to observe nearby adults. Moreover, when the psychologist moved away from Annette, the child stood up, walked over to the psychologist, and resumed her squatting position without any interruption in the screaming. As soon as Annette's hands were again restrained behind her back with the cloth towel, she stopped screaming.

Annette's screaming was accompanied by self-abusive behavior. Her neck, underarms, and knees were abraded. In the opinion of an examining physician, these abrasions were so deep that serious infection, and even death, could result if the self-abusive behavior continued. The abrasions on the child's neck resulted from scratching that occurred when Annette placed her hands over her ears. The underarm and knee abrasions resulted from the friction generated from hopping up and down while screaming in a squatting position.

During a period of several weeks, the psychologist assessed Annette's psychological problems by systematically observing her behavior, by identifying the stimulus conditions that elicited or suppressed her problematic behavior, and by identifying the environmental consequences of her behavior. In order to describe Annette's behavior in greater detail, the child's hands were untied for 90 consecutive minutes. Although Annette began to scream immediately, she would stop briefly on command by the psychologist. When the psychologist offered to restrain her hands, Annette stopped screaming, stood up, and voluntarily placed her hands behind her back to have them tied. The speed with which she could calm herself to have her hands tied was remarkable. However, if the restraint was not secure, Annette would free herself, raise her hands to cover her ears, and scream.

At the beginning of the 90-minute session, self-abusive scratching and rubbing were minimal. As time progressed, however, the child became increasingly agitated: Whining and crying began to interrupt screaming, self-abusive behavior increased in both intensity and frequency, urination and defecation occurred, and the child removed her clothes. In this state, the psychologist could not stop the tantrum for even brief periods. When the 90-minute session was over and the child's hands were again restrained, she did not become calm for about 20 minutes. Subsequent observations revealed that when screaming was not accompanied by crying, Annette could calm herself, but when screaming was accompanied by crying, Annette could not control her own screaming behavior.

Annette's speech was echolalic. That is, she repeated what was said to her, or she said nothing at all. Nevertheless, Annette understood and could follow simple commands such as "Come here," "Walk around the table," and "Sit down."

In addition to descriptions of inappropriate behavior, the assessment of Annette's psychological problems included descriptions of Annette's appropriate behavior. Unlike many severely retarded children, Annette was very much aware of her social environment. The more the psychologist observed Annette, the more convinced he became that she was socially alert in that she noticed many details about the people in her environment. Her keen interest in people was illustrated by the fact that when she imitated a word, she not only imitated the sound but also imitated the entire facial expression of the person who had spoken the word.

Assessment of Screaming Behavior

After Annette's behavior had been described, the reinforcement therapist observed the stimulus conditions that elicited or suppressed important behavior patterns. This assessment of stimulus conditions began with an effort to determine why the restraining of Annette's hands behind her back suppressed screaming. Two hypotheses were entertained. The aversion hypothesis maintained that hearing herself scream was so repugnant that Annette screamed only when she could muffle the sound; the symbolic hypothesis maintained that the restraint served as a "security blanket," and thus its presence alone suppressed screaming. To test these hypotheses, the psychologist tied Annette's hands in front of her with the towel so that she could raise her hands to cover her ears. Annette covered her ears and screamed. The aversion hypothesis was confirmed: The restraint was important because when her hands were tied behind her back, Annette could not mitigate the punishing consequences of hearing the full intensity of her own screams.

Behavioral assessment of psychological problems also includes the identification of rewards and punishers that can be employed to modify the child's behavior. Adult attention (especially adult affection such as hugging and kissing), ice cream, and candy were identified as rewards for Annette; social isolation (being placed alone in a small area from which other people could not be seen) was identified as punishment.

Treatment Using Reward and Punishment

The psychologist attempted to understand Annette's behavior in terms of its consequences on her environment. One obvious consequence of Annette's screaming and self-abusive behavior was the adult attention it received. Screaming often elicited attempts by the staff to tie Annette's hands more securely, whereas self-abusive behavior resulted in daily trips to the nurse's office for medical attention. Thus, Annette's problematic behavior often resulted in rewarding adult attention. Moreover, the fact that Annette looked at nearby adults and followed them around while screaming supports the hypothesis that screaming and self-abusive behavior were maintained in part by the consequent rewards of adult attention.

The treatment strategy was to rearrange the environmental consequences of Annette's behavior so that appropriate behavior had rewarding consequences and inappropriate behavior had punishing consequences. Specifically, appropriate behavior was rewarded with affection and candy, and inappropriate behavior was punished with social isolation. This strategy was implemented during 20-minute sessions in a large treatment room in the training and evaluation center of the institution. Immediately prior to her entrance into the treatment room, the restraint was removed. Whenever Annette raised her hands to cover her ears, she was punished by being placed immediately in social isolation in a small hallway adjacent to the treatment room. After Annette was in social isolation for 20 seconds, the psychologist returned her to the treatment room and demanded that she lower her hands and stop screaming. If screaming continued, the child was again punished with social isolation for 20 seconds; however, if Annette stopped screaming when she was removed from the social isolation area, the psychologist immediately rewarded her by embracing her and by giving her candy. If Annette remained quiet, she was seated and shown pictures of animals. About once every minute, the psychologist embraced Annette and dispensed a candy reward unless, of course, Annette screamed and had to be removed to the social isolation area.

After only a few treatment sessions, Annette occasionally exhibited appropriate speech. Consequently, the treatment program was modified so that Annette could earn affection and candy only by correctly identifying pictures of animals and letters of the alphabet. Whenever she made a mistake, the psychologist ignored her for ten seconds. This procedure of ignoring Annette consisted of the therapist's turning his back to her so that he would not inadvertently reward her with attention by glancing in her direction. If Annette screamed at any point, the social isolation procedure was followed.

Some reinforcement therapists may question the wisdom of the social isolation procedure because, by removing Annette from the social isolation area while she was still screaming, the therapist may have unwittingly rewarded the child's persistent screaming; that is, the child could have learned that continuing to scream would be rewarded with adult attention and with the termination of social isolation. A more standard procedure is to isolate a child for a longer period, such as two minutes, during which time there is nothing the child can do to escape social isolation. However, once the two-minute period elapses, social isolation is terminated as soon as the tantrum stops. This more typical procedure was not followed in Annette's case, however, because she would have screamed continuously in social isolation and reopened her self-inflicted wounds. Accordingly, it was considered more desirable to limit the social isolation period to twenty seconds and to remove Annette from social isolation regardless of her behavior at the time of removal.

Following ten treatment sessions, Annette stopped screaming in the presence of the psychologist. In other words, wherever she went, Annette would not scream when unrestrained, provided that she could see the psychologist. However, if she could not see the psychologist, Annette screamed continuously unless her hands were restrained behind her back.

Programming Generalization

Five adult female volunteers were recruited to employ the reinforcement therapy program with Annette in the same room in which the psychologist had treated her. This treatment was conducted under experimental conditions. The psychologist sat behind a one-way mirror and timed, with a stopwatch, the interscream intervals. An interscream interval began with the onset of the treatment session or with Annette's return from the social isolation area and terminated with the onset of Annette's screaming. For example, an interscream interval of 5 seconds means that Annette was quiet for 5 seconds immediately following her return from the social isolation area. An interscream interval of 20 minutes means that Annette did not scream at all during an entire treatment session.

Figure 7-1 displays the results of treatment with the five volunteer therapists. The data show that the first volunteer worked 22 sessions before Annette stopped screaming in her presence. The next volunteer to treat Annette worked for 14 sessions before Annette stopped screaming, and the third volunteer worked for only six sessions. Subsequently, there was no screaming at all for the fourth and fifth volunteers.

In order to demonstrate that Annette's behavioral improvement resulted

Figure 7-1
Mean interscream interval for an emotionally disturbed, retarded child across sessions with different adult female reinforcing agents. The lower the interscream interval, the greater was the observed screaming. The data show that the first adult required 22 sessions for screaming to be eliminated during an entire 20-minute treatment session. Successive adults required 14, 6, 1, and 1 session(s), respectively, before screaming was completely suppressed. (Adapted from Reiss and Redd [1970].)

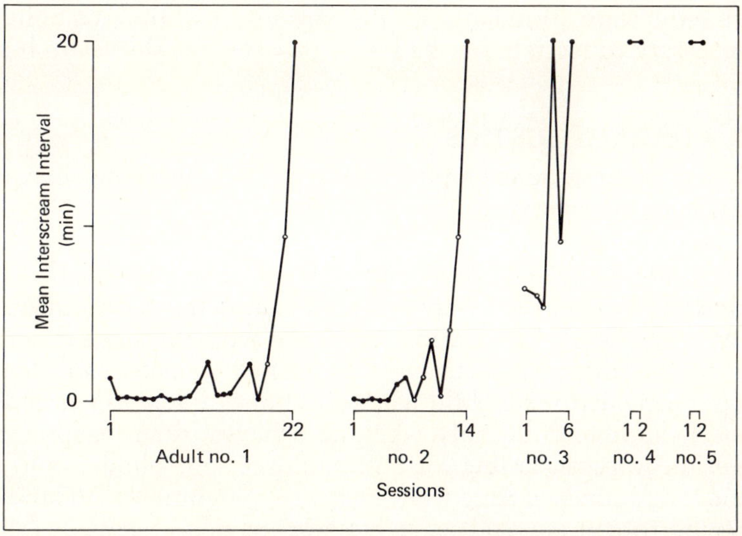

from the treatment program, a sixth female adult volunteer treated Annette by dispensing candy and affection on a predetermined time interval basis without regard to the child's behavior. The number of rewards this adult dispensed matched the total number of rewards plus punishments dispensed by the third volunteer. The rewards-only volunteer treated Annette for six sessions that were alternated with the treatment sessions of the third volunteer. The results showed that although Annette quickly learned to stop screaming for the volunteer who employed the reinforcement therapy program, the child screamed almost continuously for more than 80 per cent of the sessions with the volunteer who rewarded her regardless of her behavior (Reiss & Redd, 1970). This comparison supports the hypothesis that the behavioral treatment program constituted an effective means of suppressing Annette's screaming.

Annette's verbal behavior exhibited steady progress during the course of treatment. Two months after treatment began, she could use several hundred words appropriately; for example, she could ask for food, ice cream, a doll, a coat, and for particular individuals. During this period, Annette smiled and laughed much more frequently than she had prior to treatment. The physicians reported substantial healing of the abraded skin.

Plans were made to transfer Annette to another ward in which the attendants had been trained in reinforcement therapy techniques. Unfortunately, the initial attempt to transfer Annette failed. Because treatment could not be implemented on Annette's original ward (the patient to staff ratio was about 20 to 1), treatment was discontinued, and Annette's condition rapidly deteriorated. After six months had elapsed, Annette was transferred on a gradual basis to the reinforcement therapy unit. When the transfer was finally completed, the treatment plan was again implemented but this time by the staff of Annette's new ward. Although Annette again exhibited behavioral improvement—her wounds healed, screaming was not as continuous as it had been, her speech included several hundred words, and she smiled and laughed more often—the ward attendants, against the advice of the psychologist, considered it necessary to restrain her hands by pinning her sleeves to her pants.

DISTINGUISHING CHARACTERISTICS

The case of Annette exemplifies several distinguishing characteristics of the social learning approach.

Conceptualization of Abnormality as Learned Behavior

A characteristic of the behavioral approach is the conceptualization of abnormality as behavior learned in accordance with the same experimental principles by which normal behavior is learned. Suppose an elementary school teacher attends to one child whenever he completes an assigned task and attends to another child only when he behaves in an inappropriate manner. If attention were rewarding for both children, one child would be expected to spend long periods of time working on his assignments, and the other would be expected to call out and leave his seat on many occasions. In one case the behavior is considered appropriate, but in the other case the behavior is considered inappropriate. Nevertheless, both children are engaging in the behavior that consistently attracts teacher attention. According to many behavior therapists, what makes one behavior normal and another abnormal are value judgments people make about the behavior. In other words, these theorists consider abnormality a social judgment made concerning behavior rather than a property of the behavior itself (e.g., Bandura, 1969; Ullmann & Krasner, 1969).

This view of abnormality as behavior learned in accordance with experimental principles applies to emotional behavior. Suppose that one shopper witnesses a terrible accident in a store he is visiting for the first time and a second shopper, visiting the same store at a different time, observes many attractive members of the opposite sex. The first shopper would be expected to associate the store with feelings of anxiety (fear); in extreme cases, the shopper might become phobic and avoid shopping altogether. The second shopper, however, would be expected to associate pleasant feelings with the store. In both cases, the same principles of associative learning account for the shopper's emotional reaction to the store.

Extensive Use of Experimental Methodology

An unusual aspect of the behavioral approach is the *degree* to which behavior theorists have insisted on experimentation as the foundation of abnormal psychology. This concern for experimentation is expressed eloquently by Kanfer and Phillips: "What is novel in the behavior therapies is their adoption of methods that shift from laboratory to clinic and back to laboratory in a self-conscious testing of the utility and validity of their operations, and with a data-oriented, hypothesis-testing frame of reference within the treatment setting itself" (1970, p. 1).

Distinction Between Original and Current Causes

Behavior theorists distinguish between the conditions that led to the original development of abnormal behavior and the conditions that are currently maintaining abnormal behavior. In some cases, the original and current causes are the same, but in other cases they are different. For example, Annette may have begun crying and screaming as a natural reaction to the loss of the staff member to whom she was emotionally attached. However, Annette may have continued to scream long after this staff member resigned from the institution because screaming behavior consistently elicited rewarding attention from the ward attendants who remained. Thus, the condition that originally produced screaming (loss of a significant other) may have differed from the condition that maintained screaming (reward of screaming behavior). The behavioral treatment program concentrated on altering the maintaining conditions of screaming behavior rather than on obviating the original cause.

Direct Treatment of Symptomatology

In general, behavior therapists are willing to treat "symptoms," or behaviors that psychodynamic theorists conceptualize as indicative of deeper conflicts. For example, in the case of Annette, the treatment program was a direct attempt to improve the child's overt behavior rather than an indirect attempt to improve overt behavior by attacking the child's underlying feelings of guilt and abandonment.

Some critics of behavior therapy have mistakenly interpreted the concern for symptomatology as implying that behavior therapists always and only treat the client's presenting problems. Consider the following hypothetical case. Suppose a client unconsciously fears that he will kill somebody by driving a car. To defend against this unconscious hostility, the client avoids driving and eventually seeks therapy with the complaint of an inability to drive. If the behavior therapist were to ignore the unconscious determinants of the client's inability to drive and were to treat this symptom, some critics would argue that the client might learn to drive and then kill somebody or that he might develop an even more debilitating defense against driving. This criticism is based on a misconception of behavior therapy. In actual practice, the behavior therapist always assesses the full range of the client's problems prior to treatment and, thus, would most likely become aware of the client's hostility. The behavior therapist would then try to identify the current causes of the excessive hostility. Rather than view the hostility as an outcome of unresolved psychodynamic conflicts, the behavior therapist would treat the hostility by direct means; for example, cognitive restructuring and/or assertive training might be used. (See the section on behavioral treatment later in this chapter.)

It is important to recognize that even in cases in which the goal of behavioral treatment is to modify overt behavior, the effects of successful treatment can include beneficial emotional and cognitive changes. For example, a side effect of the reduction of screaming in the case of Annette was improved emotionality—the child appeared much happier. It should not be surprising that the improvement of a significant problem in an individual's life can have generalized behavioral effects.

SOCIAL LEARNING THEORY

A fundamental assumption of the behavioral approach is that many abnormal behaviors are learned and thus can be understood in terms of the principles of learning. We begin our discussion by defining *learning* as any relatively enduring change in behavior that results from experience. Examples of learned behaviors include fear of driving a car, compulsive cleanliness, delusions, and tantrums. In contrast, changes in behavior resulting from fatigue, mood changes, or drugs are not considered examples of learning because they are temporary or, in the case of drugs, because they are not attributable to experience.

Operant (Instrumental) Conditioning

As exemplified in the case of Annette, operant conditioning is a procedure in which behaviors are learned by the contingent application of rewards or punishments. This type of learning most readily occurs for voluntary behavior and is difficult, if not impossible, to produce by rewarding or punishing involuntary behaviors such as heart rate, salivation, and emotional reaction. There is some evidence, however, that special *biofeedback* techniques may produce operant conditioning of involuntary behaviors, but this evidence is controversial. (See Box 7-2, on p. 200.)

Scientific interest in the effects of rewards and punishments dates back to Thorndike's (1898) early studies of trial-and-error learning in cats. In these studies, hungry cats were placed in puzzle boxes, which were so constructed that the cat could open a door and escape by performing some simple response such as pulling a string or depressing a pedal. Food was placed outside the cage in full view of the hungry animal. At first, the cats tried to escape by clawing their way through the cage, ramming the cage wall, or squeezing the cage bars together. Eventually, however, they stumbled on the correct response that opened the cage door and permitted access to the food. Across subsequent trials, the cats required increasingly less time to perform the correct escape response.

Thorndike proposed the *law of effect* to explain how animals learn escape responses. This law states that the association between a stimulus and a response is strengthened when a response leads to success or reward or satisfaction and is weakened when a response leads to punishment or dissatisfaction. The law has been criticized on a number of grounds, one of which is that success often weakens the tendency to perform the response that led to success. For example, once an adult succeeds at solving a puzzle, he is less likely to play with the puzzle again than he would be if he did not solve it (see Rosenzweig, 1933). Similarly, a college student who obtains a grade of A in some course is not more likely to take that course again (Allport, 1946). In these examples success actually seems to weaken the response. How can the law of effect account for such findings? One way is to reinterpret the law of effect so that the reponse is any behavior that is actually strengthened and that is more likely to occur again as a consequence of reward or success. Under this view, success at solving some puzzle may strengthen the tendency to solve puzzles in general even though it weakens the tendency to re-solve the original puzzle. Similarly, a college student who receives a grade of A in a course may be more likely to take similar courses even though he is not more likely to take the same course again. Thus, whether or not the law of effect is viable depends on how one defines the response that is actually supposed to be strengthened by reward.

The modern law of effect stipulates precise definitions of stimulus, response, reinforcement, punishment, and operant conditioning. This law states: If a response is reinforced on a contingent basis in the presence of a stimulus, the probability is increased that the response will occur again in the presence of that stimulus, and the resultant behavior change is termed *operant conditioning.* Thus:

1. A *stimulus* is any event whose presence and absence differentially affect the probability of a learned response.
2. A *response* is any behavior whose probability of occurrence can be modified by the contingent application of reinforcement.
3. A *reinforcer* is any event that can increase through learning the probability that a response will occur under particular stimulus conditions.

Similarly, if a response is punished in the presence of a stimulus, the probability that the response will occur again in the presence of that stimulus is decreased, and the resultant behavior change is termed *punishment*. By definition, reinforcement always increases the probability of a response, whereas punishment always decreases the probability of a response.

Like Newton's basic laws of motion, the modern law of effect is true by definition. It constitutes a functional equation of stimulus-response-reinforcement in which the empirical task is to identify events that actually function as stimuli, responses, and reinforcers. Scientific interest rests with identifying the range of phenomena to which the law applies. At first it may seem implausible that a conceptual schema that originated in Thorndike's research on cats escaping from a puzzle box could have broad applicability to human behavior. Nevertheless, the results of many studies indicate conclusively that a wide range of human behavior can be modified by operant conditioning. Of special interest in this chapter is the applicability of the principles of operant conditioning to abnormal behaviors. For example, it has been suggested that tantrums are often maintained by rewarding environmental consequences, that alcoholism is a well-learned habit in which drinking is rewarded by alcohol-induced anxiety-reduction, that aggression in delinquents is often maintained by rewarding peer group approval, that compulsive habits are maintained by a rewarding reduction in anxiety, and that husbands and wives in disturbed marriages unwittingly reward one another for the very behavior they find annoying. Moreover, operant principles of reward and punishment have implications for the treatment of tantrums, aggression, and some psychotic behaviors.

There are many events that can function as stimuli. In the case of Annette, the psychologist was a stimulus that suppressed screaming—that is, the probability that the child would scream was much less when the psychologist was present than when he was absent. Emotional responses can also function as stimuli. For example, anxiety sometimes serves as a stimulus for increased cigarette smoking. Even rewards have stimulus properties than can exert control over voluntary behavior. For example, some people with very low self-esteem

Figure 7-2
Schematic outline of the law of effect.

$S^D \longrightarrow R \longrightarrow S^R$	Increases probability of future occurrence of R in presence of S^D
$S^D \longrightarrow R \longrightarrow P$	Decreases probability of future occurrence of R in presence of S^D

S^D = symbol for a discriminative stimulus—that is, a stimulus that signals the availability of reinforcement (or punishment) for a response that is (or is not) performed
R = symbol for response
S^R = symbol for a reinforcing stimulus (reinforcer)
P = symbol for punishment

BOX 7-1
Some Behavioral Terms

Analogue study. A laboratory experiment. The term is associated with experimental studies of fear reduction and serves to emphasize the fact that a subclinical fear is under study.

Avoidance conditioning. One paradigm for studying avoidance learning presents a stimulus (CS) that is followed by an aversive stimulus (US) unless a specific coping response is performed. By performing the coping response, the subject avoids the aversive stimulus.

Behaviorism. (1) A philosophy of psychology maintaining that the subject matter of psychology is behavior rather than mental events. (2) The study of conditioning processes.

Behavior therapy. The clinical techniques based on the behavioral approach.

Noncontingent reinforcement. A procedure in which reinforcement is dispensed regardless of the subject's behavior. This procedure serves as a control for the effects of response-contingent reinforcement.

Operant conditioning. A form of learning in which response patterns are altered by their environmental consequences.

Pavlovian excitatory conditioning. A form of learning that results from the pairing of two stimulus events, the CS and US. The US reliably elicits a reflexive response called the UR, and, as a consequence of CS-US pairings, the CS comes to elicit a response (CR) that resembles the UR.

Pavlovian inhibitory conditioning. A form of learning that results when one stimulus event (CS) predicts the absence of another stimulus event (US). The US reliably elicits a response called the UR, and, as a consequence of training, the CS acquires the capacity to inhibit CRs.

Semantic generalization. (1) An ordering of stimuli based on the similarity of the labels applied to those stimuli. (2) The spread of excitation to stimuli labeled in a manner similar to the label applied to the CS.

Vicarious extinction. A form of learning in which emotional responses to a stimulus are extinguished (unlearned) as a consequence of repeated observations that the stimulus does not lead to feared consequences in others.

behave in a manner that avoids success (Mettee, 1971; Musico, 1971); for these people, reward functions as a stimulus for behaviors that will lead to failure.

There are many events that can function as reinforcers. Some theorists categorize these events into tangible, social, and behavioral reinforcers. Examples of typical tangible reinforcers include food, money, tokens (objects used to "purchase" other rewards), and toys. Examples of typical social reinforcers include praise, affection, attention, and certificates of achievement. Examples of typical behavioral reinforcers include preferred activities such as the opportunity to play ball (see Premack, 1956). Similarly, there are many events that can function as punishers; typical examples include response cost (reward penalties such as loss of money or tokens), noxious odors, and social isolation. It is important to recognize that what is reinforcing (or punishing) for one person may not be reinforcing (or punishing) for another.

Social reinforcers such as friendship are influential in shaping individual behavior. (Photo by Burt Glinn; Magnum Photos, Inc.)

Types of Reward Procedures

The effects of reward depend considerably on the specific manner in which the reward is dispensed. Thus, we should be concerned with the effects of reward *procedures* rather than with the effects of reward per se. One of the more important contributions to psychology was made by Skinner and his colleagues who found that different types of reward procedures are associated with characteristically different response patterns (see Ferster & Skinner, 1957).

We distinguish between contingent and noncontingent reinforcement procedures. Contingent reinforcement procedures provide rewards only after a particular response has occurred, whereas noncontingent reinforcement procedures provide reward regardless of the subject's behavior (e.g., reward is provided once every minute). The law of effect applies only to contingent reinforcement procedures and, with these procedures, a critical determinant of the effect of the reward is the aspect of the response on which the reward is contingent. Consider, for example, a procedure in which children receive a reward for drawing with crayons. If reward is contingent on how fast the children draw, the children will learn to draw fast and will probably produce inferior drawings (Reiss & Sushinsky, 1975, 1976). If, however, reward is contingent on the quality of the drawing, the children will learn to draw carefully. With contingent reinforcement procedures, then, one gets what one rewards. Similarly, the effects of noncontingent reinforcement procedures are critically dependent on the manner in which the reward is dispensed. Seligman (1975) recently predicted that some noncontingent reinforcement procedures produce a "learned laziness" syndrome in which subjects show a general suppression of behavior. It is as if they say to themselves: "Why should I bother to do anything when I

Slot machines pay on a partial reinforcement schedule. These schedules can maintain high rates of behavior even when they provide a low level of reinforcement. (Photo by Abigail Heyman; Magnum Photos, Inc.)

get rewarded no matter what I do?" Seligman has also suggested that some noncontingent reinforcement procedures are associated with mild depressive moods. (See Chapter 14.)

Another important distinction is between continuous and partial reinforcement procedures. In continuous reinforcement procedures, contingent reinforcement is presented for each occurrence of a criterion response; in partial reinforcement procedures, contingent reinforcement is dispensed for only some occurrences of a criterion response. Learning is more rapid under continuous schedules, but once an equal degree of learning has occurred, withdrawal of a continuous reinforcement schedule leads to more rapid extinction of learned behavior than does withdrawal of a partial reinforcement schedule.

Extinction and Persistence

An issue of both practical and theoretical importance is what happens to reinforced behavior after the reinforcement procedure is withdrawn. In animal laboratory situations, the most typical result is that the animal eventually stops performing the response. Suppose, for example, that a hungry rat has learned to bar-press in order to obtain food. When food is no longer available for bar-pressing, the rat eventually stops pressing the bar, although he may at first press the bar more often in a frustrative reaction to his inability to obtain food. The eventual unlearning of a previously learned response is called extinction.

In instances in which human behavior is modified by reinforcement, the effects of terminating a reinforcement procedure are less clear-cut. The conventional wisdom is that, as with animals in laboratory situations, the withdrawal of reinforcement programs leads to an eventual extinction of the learned behavior. Although it is true that the cessation of reinforcement programs often leads to extinction, it is also true that the learned behavior often persists even though it is no longer being explicitly reinforced. Annette's speech, for example, remained considerably improved despite termination of the reinforcement program. The fact is that little solid research has been conducted on the effects of withdrawing applied reinforcement procedures with human subjects and, hence, very little is actually known (Kazdin & Bootzin, 1972).

As mentioned previously, one factor that has a powerful effect on persistence is the extent to which the training procedure provides reinforcement continuously or intermittently. Partial (intermittent) reinforcement procedures lead to much greater persistence than do continuous procedures. That is, the fewer the number of rewards needed to maintain a learned response, the more the response will persist after the reinforcement procedure has been withdrawn.

Reiss and Sushinsky (1975, 1976) have proposed that one factor that affects persistence in a rewarded activity is the degree to which the reward procedure is enjoyed. Although we may tend to think of rewards as enjoyable, there are many ways in which a reward procedure can be unpleasant. For example, a reward can be dispensed in a manner that insults people, as in the example of offering someone money to tell a lie. A reward procedure, moreover, can arouse performance anxiety. (*Will I perform well enough to earn the reward?*) Reward procedures can also be distracting, and it is possible that distractions sometimes interfere with the enjoyment of an activity (e.g., thinking about a reward at the expense of enjoying an activity.) Reiss and Sushinsky's competing response hypothesis proposes that the greater the extent to which a reward procedure is enjoyed, the greater the degree of persistence following withdrawal of the procedure.

Punishment

There has been considerable speculation concerning the effects of parental punishment on the emotional development of children. Some popular myths maintain that "If you spare the rod, you spoil the child," whereas other myths maintain that punishment is usually experienced as a traumatic event.

In animals, the effects of punishment depend on many variables (see Church, 1963; Solomon, 1964): (1) The more intense the punishment, the less likely is the punished behavior to recur; (2) when a sequence of behavior is punished, punishment is most effective if it occurs at the beginning of the sequence; (3) the effects of punishment depend on the type of behavior punished (e.g., reflexive, consummatory, or instrumental); (4) the effects of punishment vary with the individual's prior experiences with punishment; and (5) the effects of punishment depend on the strength of the response punished. Before it is possible to provide educated guesses on the emotional and behavioral effects of punishing children, it is important to know the following: (1) Is the child being punished for a consummatory behavior (e.g., eating cookies before meals), partially reflexive behavior (e.g., premature excretion in his pants), or an instrumental behavior (e.g., calling his teacher a dirty name)? (2) How intense is the punishment and what is its nature (e.g., physical beatings, not being allowed to play ball after school)? (3) To what extent has the child had previous experience with the punishing event? (4) How old is the child? In other words, the effects of punishment on behavior are very complex and are not amenable to simple statements such as "Punishment is bad and leads to abnormality" or "Punishment is good and teaches self-discipline."

Parental punishment of children may be less likely to produce feelings of resentment and alienation when alternative responses leading to positive reinforcement are specified. For example, a child is permitted a cookie after a dinner (alternative response) but is punished for taking a cookie before dinner.

Self-reinforcement

An important issue in social learning theory concerns the manner in which people learn to reward and to punish themselves. In some instances, self-reward and self-punishment may involve tangible rewards and punishers (e.g., allowing or denying oneself a new suit or dress); in other instances, only cognitions (thoughts) such as *I did well* or *I did rotten* may be involved. Some people are very hard on themselves—if they do not achieve at very high levels, they will not engage in self-reinforcement. Other people, however, tend to reward themselves for mediocre or even poor performances. Self-reinforcement provides a mechanism by which people control their own behavior; for this reason, self-reinforcement has often been viewed as a means of self-control (Skinner, 1953).

Research on self-reinforcement has focused on experimental situations in which rewards are freely available but the individual does not self-administer as many rewards as he could. In general, people tend to self-administer rewards on performance tasks in accordance with standards previously established by experimenter instructions, by observations of models, or by direct experience in the experimental situation (Bandura, 1969; Kanfer & Phillips, 1970). For example, Kanfer and Marston (1963) rewarded the performance of one group of adults in a lenient manner and rewarded the performance of a second group in a strict, miserly manner. When the subjects were permitted to reward themselves on a different, more difficult task, the subjects who had received lenient training rewarded themselves much more frequently than those who had received strict training, even though both groups had objectively performed equally well on the difficult task.

Research on self-reinforcement is potentially relevant to etiological theories of some abnormal behaviors in which inappropriate self-control mechanisms are involved. For example, some problem behaviors can be understood in part as resulting from overly lenient self-reinforcement patterns (e.g., obesity and tantrums), whereas other problem behaviors may result in part from overly strict self-reinforcement patterns (e.g., depression).

Symbolic Processes

One of the more consistent findings on the effects of reinforcement therapy is that the successful modification of problem behavior often occurs in the context of general psychological and behavioral improvement. These beneficial side effects may include a positive evaluation of oneself (enhanced self-esteem), improved self-control, feelings of well-being and happiness, greater acceptance of responsibility for one's behavior, and improved appearance. In the case of Annette, for example, the suppression of screaming was accompanied by a remarkably rapid improvement in appropriate speech, noticeably elevated mood, a greater tendency to be playful, a decrease in her overall anxiety level, and greater cooperation in dressing and eating. One reason generalized improvement may accompany successfully modified problem behavior is that reinforcement programs are typically fun—in particular, children typically enjoy receiving rewards. Another related reason is that rewards are often perceived as symbols of success that suggest that one is capable of meeting the demands of life and of overcoming one's previously debilitating problems.

A question that merits greater research attention, therefore, is the manner in which people interpret behavior changes resulting from reinforcement procedures. In all probability, there are wide individual differences in such interpretations. Consider, for example, the following two children. Before receiving reinforcement therapy, one child rarely studied and always obtained poor grades because he felt he was incapable of performing successfully, whereas the other child thought that adults did not like him and rebelled in his classroom by behaving disruptively. In the former case, rewards may be perceived as symbols of success so that the child's self-image changes from *I never do anything well and always get into trouble* to *I can do well in school.* In the latter case, rewards may be perceived as symbols of adult affection and concern so that the child's self-image changes from *Adults do not like me* to *Some adults like me and others do not.*

Pavlovian Conditioning

As mentioned previously, operant conditioning is only one of two types of conditioning, and it applies primarily (if not exclusively) to voluntary behaviors—that is, to behaviors controlled by the central nervous system. The other type of conditioning is called *Pavlovian,* or *classical, conditioning.* This type of conditioning most readily occurs for involuntary behavior such as anxiety and salivation—that is, behaviors controlled by the autonomic nervous system.

Pavlovian conditioning is a procedure in which the occurrence of one stimulus event (called the CS) signals the immediate future occurrence, or nonoccurrence, of some other stimulus event (called the US). Prior to training, the US reliably elicits an unlearned, unconditioned response called the UR. For example, food (US) elicits salivation (UR) and electric shock (US) elicits fear (UR). Prior to training, the CS is said to be neutral with respect to the UR because it does not elicit this or any similar response. There are two types of Pavlovian conditioning: excitatory conditioning, in which the CS and US are paired (positively correlated), and inhibitory conditioning, in which the CS and US are unpaired (negatively correlated).

Excitatory Conditioning

In Pavlovian excitatory conditioning, the CS predicts the immediate future occurrence of the US. As a result of repeated CS-US pairings, the CS comes to elicit a conditioned response (CR) that resembles the unconditioned response (UR). An example of Pavlovian conditioning in humans is provided in a study by Ohman, Erixon, and Lofberg (1975). In this study, college students were shown pictures of houses and immediately after were presented with a mild electric shock. Following repeated CS (house)-US (shock) pairings, the house elicited conditioned anxiety so that the presentation of the house produced anxiety in anticipation of shock. Figure 7-3 presents a symbolic representation of this kind of learning.

An important feature of the conditioned response is that it is involuntary. In the preceding study, the students *reflexively* responded to pictures of houses with anxiety; they did not consciously decide to become anxious. Another feature of the conditioned response is that it is *anticipatory;* for example, conditioned anxiety occurs in anticipation of an aversive event.

Pavlovian conditioning has considerable importance for abnormal psychology because it provides possible explanations of how previously neutral stimuli can come to elicit anxiety and fear. Thus, Pavlovian conditioning has been invoked to explain phobias, sexual dysfunctions caused by anxiety, and neurotic anxiety in general.

Pavlovian Conditioned Inhibition

Suppose that instead of a CS (e.g., bell) predicting the immediate future occurrence of a US (e.g., food), events were arranged so that the CS predicted the immediate future *non*occurrence of a US (e.g., no food). For example, on some training trials an animal experiences pairings between a light stimulus and

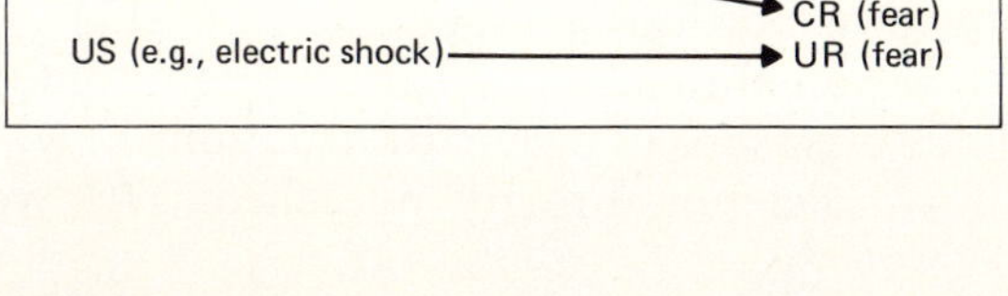

Figure 7-3
Schematic paradigm of Pavlovian excitatory conditioning.

food, whereas on other training trials the animal experiences a light stimulus and a bell stimulus presented together:

some trials: light ⟶ food
other trials: light + bell ⟶ no food

Under these conditions, the bell (CS) signals the immediate future nonoccurrence of food and acquires the capacity to inhibit the occurrence of conditioned salivation responses to the light. Thus the bell is termed a conditioned inhibitor. In Table 7-1 Pavlovian excitatory and inhibitory conditioning are compared.

If the US is an aversive event (e.g., shock, a loud noise, or a picture of a disfigured person), a conditioned inhibitor can be thought of as a "safety" signal: Its occurrence means that the aversive event is unlikely to occur in the immediate future. Under such circumstances, presentation of the CS should diminish anxiety.

In contrast to Pavlovian excitatory conditioning, which has been studied extensively during the last five decades, interest in Pavlovian inhibitory conditioning is relatively recent (e.g., Rescorla & Wagner, 1972). Unfortunately, the promising work on conditioned inhibition that has been conducted by investigators of animal behavior has received relatively little attention from investigators of human behavior. The eventual application of this knowledge to human emotionality promises to increase greatly our understanding of the manner in which abnormal behavior is learned and unlearned.

Active Avoidance Learning

In active avoidance learning, the individual must perform a particular response in order to avoid an aversive event. In the paradigm avoidance learning experiment, subjects are presented with a CS that remains present for a fixed time interval. If the subject performs the response, the CS is terminated, and the aversive event (US) is not presented; if the subject does not perform the response, the US is presented.

Mowrer (1939) proposed an influential two-process theory of avoidance learning. Under this theory, the first process is that of Pavlovian excitatory conditioning of fear to the CS; the second process is operant conditioning of the avoidance response, which is reinforced by fear reduction.

Principles of avoidance learning are especially relevant to theories of abnormal behavior. In particular, many neurotic behaviors can be conceptualized as learned avoidance responses. For example, the performance of a compulsive ritual can be viewed as a means of avoiding high levels of anxiety. The conceptualization of neurotic behaviors as avoidance responses is discussed in greater detail in Chapter 10.

Observational Learning

In operant and Pavlovian conditioning procedures, the subject directly experiences the US, reward, or punishment. A considerable amount of learning, however, occurs through observations of others in situations in which the observer is neither directly rewarded nor directly punished. The work of Bandura,

TABLE 7-1
Comparison of Pavlovian Excitatory and Inhibitory Conditioning

	Procedure	Symbols	What Is Learned	CS = Bell US = Shock
Excitatory	CS predicts immediate future occurrence of US.	CS → US	CS comes to elicit CRs.	Bell means shock will be presented. Animal is fearful (CR) in anticipation of shock.
Inhibitory	CS predicts immediate future nonoccurrence of US.	CS → $\overline{\text{US}}$	CS comes to inhibit CRs.	Bell means shock will not be presented immediately. Bell is thus a safety signal. Animal relaxes in anticipation of safety from shock.

Walters, and their colleagues has contributed substantially to our scientific understanding of observational learning (Bandura, 1969; Bandura & Walters, 1963).

Bandura's research has demonstrated that entire patterns of overt behavior can be learned by observing a model. Whether or not the learned behavior patterns are subsequently performed by the observer is a function of the observed consequences of the model's behavior. If the model is observed to experience rewarding consequences, individuals tend to perform the modeled behavior. If the model is observed to experience aversive consequences, individuals tend not to perform the modeled behavior. This phenomenon in which the frequency of a behavior pattern is increased or decreased by observation of rewards and punishments for a model's behavior is called *vicarious conditioning.*

Bandura (1969) has distinguished three effects of modeling. First, new response patterns can be acquired. For example, an individual learns the combination to a safe through observation of a model. Second, response patterns that were previously punished or rewarded can be inhibited or disinhibited by observations of the consequences of the model's behavior. For example, a child takes a cookie after watching a film in which a boy steals a cookie and gets away with it. Third, the model facilitates a response pattern that was not previously rewarded or punished. For example, a pedestrian observes someone gazing at a store window and takes a look for himself. These three effects of modeling are controlled by different sets of variables.

Of particular interest for abnormal psychology is Bandura's research on vicarious conditioning of emotional behavior. As Bandura observed:

> It is generally assumed that persons develop emotional responses on the basis of direct painful or pleasurable stimulation experienced in association with certain places, peo-

BOX 7-2
Operant Conditioning of Involuntary Behavior (Biofeedback)

Although operant and Pavlovian conditioning are procedurally different in the sense that an investigator must wait for a response to occur before presenting the reward in operant conditioning but not in Pavlovian conditioning, a number of important similarities have been noted. Perhaps the most important similarity is the sequence of events. In operant conditioning, a stimulus (S) signals that reinforcement can be obtained; the subject then performs a learned response (R), the response is followed by reinforcement (US), and the subject shows a reflexive reaction to the reinforcement (UR). In Pavlovian conditioning, a stimulus (CS) that signals the future occurrence of reinforcement is presented; the subject then performs a learned response (CR), the learned response is followed by reinforcement (US), and the subject shows a reflexive response to the reinforcement (UR). Thus, despite some differences in terminology, the sequence of events is the same (stimulus, learned response, reinforcement, and unlearned response). Another important similarity between operant and Pavlovian conditioning is that the same rewards (or aversive events) that can serve as reinforcers (or punishers) in operant conditioning also can serve as USs in Pavlovian conditioning (Staats, 1975). These similarities have led some theoreticians to postulate that operant and Pavlovian conditioning may be the same form of learning.

There are, however, a number of differences between operant and Pavlovian conditioning. Perhaps the most significant difference is that in operant conditioning the learned response is typically a voluntary behavior, whereas in Pavlovian conditioning the learned response is typically a reflexive, involuntary behavior (Miller & Konorski, 1928). Voluntary behaviors are controlled primarily by the central nervous system even though they can be influenced by activity in the autonomic nervous system. Involuntary behaviors are typically controlled by the autonomic nervous system even though they can be influenced by activity in the central nervous system.

A critical question in resolving the issue of whether operant and Pavlovian conditioning are basically the same or different types of learning is whether or not it is possible to establish operant (voluntary) control over autonomic behaviors such as heart rate, salivation, blood pressure, and dilation of blood pressure. As Black (1973) noted, a few failures to establish such control in the 1920s and 1930s

ple, or events. Although many emotional responses are undoubtedly acquired by means of direct classical conditioning, affective learning in humans frequently occurs through vicariously aroused emotions. Many phobic behaviors, for example, arise not from actual injurious experiences with the phobic objects, but rather from witnessing others either respond fearfully toward, or be hurt by, certain things [Bandura, Blanchard, & Ritter, 1968; Bandura & Menlove, 1968]. Similarly, persons often acquire, on the basis of exposure to modeled stimulus correlations, intense emotional attitudes toward members of unpopular minority groups or nationalities with whom they have had little or no personal contact [1969, p. 167].

Stimulus Generalization of Behavior Changes

Stimulus generalization refers to instances in which behavior changes learned under one stimulus condition also occur under some other stimulus condition. Examples of stimulus generalization issues include (1) the manner in which prematurely led to the belief that the enterprise was fruitless. In 1960, Kimmel and Hill reported a successful attempt at operant conditioning of the galvanic skin response (GSR), a response consisting of changes in electrical potential on skin as a result of sweating. Because sweating is controlled by the autonomic nervous system and is a consequence of heightened anxiety, this study encouraged other attempts to demonstrate operant conditioning of involuntary activity. Along this line, a number of preliminary studies demonstrated operant conditioning of heart rate (Banuazizi, 1967; Bleecker & Engel, 1973; DiCara, 1970; Engel & Melmon, 1968; Miller & DiCara, 1967; Trowill, 1967; Weiss & Engel, 1971). At first, these and other studies seemed to constitute a successful challenge to the belief that it is impossible to establish operant control over autonomic activity, but two important problems have since emerged. One problem is that the early studies have yet to be replicated in a convincing fashion. Another problem is that it is possible that in these studies operant control was established by the conditioning of voluntary behaviors that had autonomic consequences. For example, if the subject learned to control heart rate by positioning his body in a particular way or by thinking particular thoughts, it would seem that a voluntary behavior had been conditioned and that no direct control over the involuntary behavior had been acquired. Kimmel (1974) has discussed this issue and has cited evidence suggesting that direct control can be established over autonomic activity. Nevertheless, the issue of whether or not involuntary behavior can be brought under direct voluntary control remains unresolved.

A potentially important consequence of the preceding theoretical issue has been the development of some treatment procedures. The term *biofeedback* refers to procedures in which subjects are informed of their own internal physiological processes; for example, the subject may be shown an electrocardiagram display of heart rate activity or an amplified polygraph of tension in a particular muscle. Using such procedures, one set of investigators brought tension headaches under control (Budzynski, Stoyva, Adler, & Mullaney, 1973). Other investigators have attempted to treat heart problems by conditioning heart rates, hypertension by conditioning blood pressure (e.g., Lisina, 1960), epilepsy by conditioning brain wave activity, and ulcers by conditioning stomach motility, but the effectiveness of these procedures is presently unclear (see Blanchard & Young, 1974). Thus, with the exception of biofeedback training for tension headaches, the clinical potential of biofeedback techniques has yet to be realized (Bootzin, 1975).

learning a behavior in the presence of one reinforcing agent (e.g., a mother) affects behavior to other reinforcing agents (e.g., a father); (2) the manner in which a frightening experience in the presence of one stimulus (e.g., being hit on the head by a falling light while in an office on the sixteenth floor of the Time-Life Building) affects fear to other stimuli (e.g., does the acquired fear of the sixteenth floor of the Time-Life Building generalize to a fear of all heights?); and (3) the manner in which learning behavior in a therapist's office or some other treatment situation affects behavior outside the therapist's office.

Learned behavior generalizes from a stimulus A that has acquired the capacity to control the behavior to some stimulus B in direct proportion to the similarity between stimuli A and B. This similarity may be along physical or semantic dimensions. (See Table 7-2.) The principle of *primary stimulus gen-*

TABLE 7-2
A Comparison of Physical Versus Semantic Similarity

1. Consider the Following Cues

   A C △

2. Arranged on Basis of Physical Similarity

   A △ C

3. Arranged on Basis of Semantic Similarity

   A C △

   "Letters of alphabet" "Triangle"

eralization states that behavior learned under some stimulus S_1 generalizes to some other stimulus S_2 in direct proportion to the physical similarity between S_1 and S_2; the principle of *semantic generalization* states that behavior learned under some stimulus S_1 generalizes to some other stimulus S_2 in direct proportion to the conceptual or semantic similarity between S_1 and S_2. For example, suppose a child learns to hate her cold and rejecting father, and further suppose that the father happens to have a noticeably large nose. Under the principle of primary stimulus generalization, feelings of hostility will generalize more to adults whose physical appearance is similar to the father—for example, to adults with a large nose. Under the principle of semantic generalization, feelings of hostility will generalize more to authority figures than to nonauthority figures. Both primary and semantic generalization occur; however, in humans, semantic generalization is probably the more significant process (Reiss, 1973).

Dollard and Miller have discussed semantic generalization as follows:

> Five dimes and a fifty cents piece present cues that are innately quite different. Since they both elicit the same label . . . , "fifty cents," they have a certain amount of

Figure 7-4
Primary stimulus generalization around a training stimulus, CS_1.

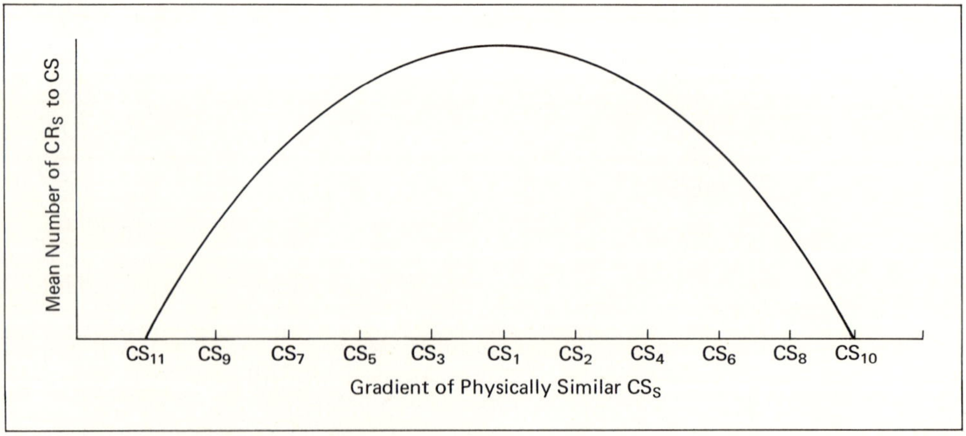

learned equivalence for adults in our culture. Similarly, the label of "Doctor" tends to mediate the transfer of confidence and respect to any one to whom it is attached [1950, p. 101].

In therapy the issue of generalization concerns the manner in which behavior changes in one situation (treatment situation) affect behavior in another situation (nontreatment situation). Generalization is an issue relevant to all forms of treatment in which behavior is improved in a defined situation. Even though generalization may fail to occur with other therapies, failure of behavior changes to generalize from treatment to appropriate nontreatment situations has been a matter of special concern in treatments based on operant conditioning (e.g., Kazdin & Bootzin, 1972; O'Leary & Drabman, 1971). The case of Annette exemplifies the failure of generalization; after treatment with the psychologist, the elimination of Annette's screaming was evident only when she could see the psychologist. After training with several volunteers, however, the suppression of screaming generalized to additional adults. Thus, this case not only exemplifies the problem of generalization but also suggests that generalization can be facilitated by training with a variety of reinforcing agents.

Most behavior theorists stress the importance of programming generalization by teaching self-control techniques and/or by administering treatment under a variety of situations (e.g., Drabman, Spitalnik, & O'Leary, 1973). Although some studies suggest that various techniques for programming generalization are in fact more likely to produce appropriate generalization, the available literature contains many studies that found generalization effects in the absence of any explicit attempts to teach self-control strategies (e.g., Altman, 1971; Horton, 1972; Lovaas, Koegel, Simmons, & Long, 1973).

In a controlled study conducted in an experimental class, Reiss (1973) found that success training produced generalization of behavior changes in the absence of any modification of the reinforcement schedule in the nontreatment situation, whereas failure training did not produce appropriate generalization. In this study, children with poor attention spans earned reinforcement by solving simple arithmetic problems during two separate class sessions. The two sessions were defined on the basis of which one of two teachers (A and B) was present to distribute the math problems and to dispense reinforcement. When teacher A was present, some children were given success training (reinforced for solving only a few problems), while other children were given failure training (an impossibly long task to complete in order to obtain reinforcement). When teacher A was present, the results of success training were to increase the amount of work the children did, while the results of failure training were to decrease the amount of work the children did. Of primary interest was the manner in which behavior changes to teacher A affected behavior to teacher B. For the group that received success training, increased work to teacher A generalized to teacher B; however, for the group that received failure training, decreased work to teacher A did not affect behavior to teacher B. Reiss (1973) suggested that these results can be understood in terms of semantic generalization: Specifically, the children who received success training from teacher A attributed success to their ability to solve the problems. Thus, when teacher B gave them similar problems, these children assumed that they could do the work and hence solved more problems to earn more reinforcement. However, the children who received failure training from teacher A attributed failure to teacher A's unfairness at having given them so many problems to solve for a single reinforcement; consequently, the failure training given by teacher A did not affect the amount of work these children did for teacher B. To summarize, this study found that success training produced generalization, whereas failure training did not.

BEHAVIORAL ASSESSMENT

Behavioral assessment includes direct observation of behavior, questionnaires, and interview techniques.

Direct Observation of Overt Behavior

Ullmann and Krasner (1965) have identified three basic questions involved in the behavioral assessment of overt behavior:

1. How can the individual's behavior be described in an objective manner so that responses can be identified?
2. What stimulus events control these responses?
3. What are the environmental consequences of the individual's behavior?

Identifying Responses

As exemplified in the case of Annette, the first task of behavioral assessment is an objective description of the individual's behavior. Suppose one child hits another in a schoolyard. The reinforcement therapist would describe this behavior as "one child hitting another." This simple description contrasts markedly with descriptions such as "The child is expressing aggressive tendencies," "The child is displacing unconscious hostility," or "The child is expressing anger." The term *hitting* describes the behavior observed, whereas the terms *aggressive tendencies, displacement of unconscious hostility,* and *anger* are based on inferences from the hitting behavior.

Identifying Effective Stimuli

An event is identified as a stimulus when its presence and absence are associated with different frequencies (or intensities) of behavior. Sometimes, skilled reinforcement therapists become sufficiently confident that an event is a stimulus simply by observing behavior under naturalistic conditions: If it were observed that structured activities were consistently associated with a higher level of hitting than were unstructured activities, it might reasonably be assumed that structured activities were stimuli for hitting. In this example, both the presence and the absence of stimuli occurred as part of the subject's everyday experience. However, it is usually necessary to experiment to deter-

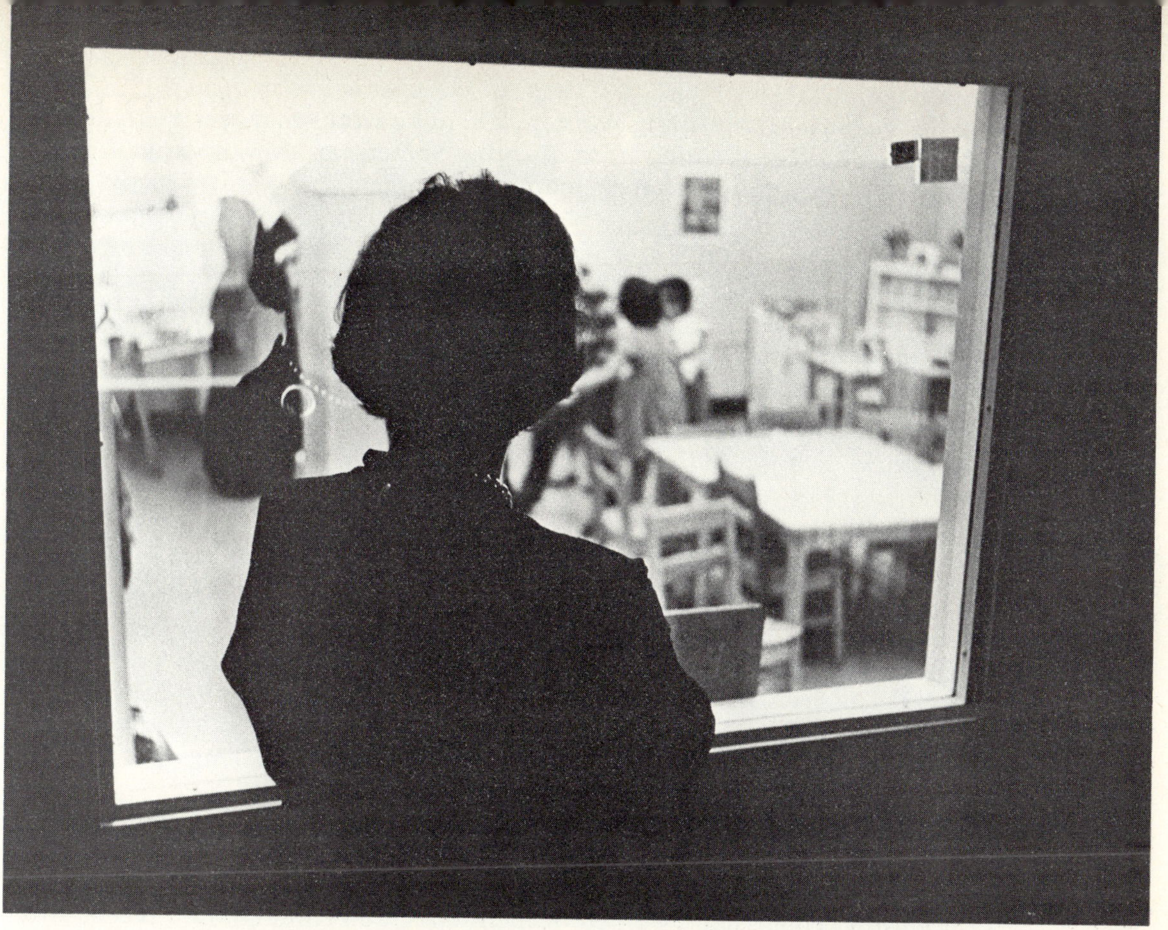

Observations of behavior are more accurate when they are unobtrusive. The use of a one-way mirror, for example, minimizes the degree to which observation affects the behavior being observed. (Photo by Charles Harbutt; Magnum Photos, Inc.)

mine whether or not an event is a stimulus. In the case of Annette, the psychologist experimented to determine whether the restraining of Annette's hands behind her back was a discriminative stimulus that directly suppressed screaming or an event that prevented Annette from muffling the aversive quality of her own screams.

Identifying Reinforcers

The reinforcement therapist also assesses the environmental consequences of behavior: How does the teacher react when one pupil hits another? How do other pupils react? Do some laugh or get excited? Of particular concern are those environmental events that regularly and immediately follow the behavior of interest.

In addition to obvious reinforcers such as tangible rewards, attention often serves as social reinforcement for deviant behavior. For example, the husband who is always complaining about how hard he works may receive reinforcing attention for complaining from his wife. Sometimes even negative forms of attention (e.g., criticism) are reinforcing.

Direct Observation of Emotions

Like any other behavior, emotionality can often be directly observed. For example, by direct observation it is possible to assess the extent to which a man is anxious or depressed in a variety of situations. Whenever possible, behavior theorists assess emotional behavior by direct observation. Nevertheless, it is sometimes more practical to assess emotionality through questionnnaire and interview techniques that rely on the client's self-reports.

Fear Survey and Other Questionnaires

The Fear Survey Schedule (FSS) (Lang & Lazouik, 1963) is administered for the purposes of obtaining the individual's self-reports of specific anxiety-eliciting stimuli and of assessing whether or not general themes are evident (Adams, 1972; see Yates, 1970). Although this test has four forms, FSS-I through IV, FSS-II has been standardized to the greatest extent and is therefore the preferred form. The FSS tests require the individual to rate on a scale of one to seven the amount of fear he has to various stimuli. Some examples of the items on FSS-II are sharp objects, worms, and driving a car.

Cautela and Kastenbaum (1967) have developed the Reinforcement Survey Schedule (RSS) for identifying possible reinforcing stimuli. This test requires the client to rate the degree to which he or she likes stimuli such as beautiful people, nude women or men, dogs, and children. In a recent study that exemplifies the research uses of the RSS, Cautela, Kastenbaum, and Wincze (1972) found that juvenile delinquents preferred items associated with loved ones, whereas nonoffenders preferred items associated with being correct or being praised.

Although subjects' self-reports on questionnaires may be helpful in structuring the search for potentially anxiety-provoking and reinforcing stimuli, many behavior therapists attempt to confirm self-reports by direct observation of behavior. For example, a client who reports a fear of snakes may be shown pictures of snakes or may be asked to handle a real snake so that the therapist can observe directly the nature and the extent of the client's fear. A client who reports a fear of airplanes may be asked to visualize flying while the behavior therapist observes him or her for indications of anxiety. Of course, the extent to which a behavior therapist seeks confirmation of self-report data varies, depending on practical considerations and on the therapist.

BEHAVIOR THERAPY

Behavior therapists employ many treatment techniques and emphasize the importance of selecting an appropriate technique for the particular problem at hand.

The guiding principle of operant conditioning is that behavior can be modified by altering its environmental consequences. Accordingly, the most frequent use of operant procedures has been in situations in which the therapist can obtain significant control over the individual's environment. For example, these procedures have been employed extensively with children and with adults in state hospitals, laboratories, and schools. Operant procedures have also been employed in counseling situations to alleviate marital problems (e.g., Stuart, 1969) and to reduce smoking behavior (e.g., Bernstein, 1969; Lichtenstein, Harns, Birchler, Wahl, & Schmahl, 1973; Sushinsky, 1972). In the counseling format, the therapist must rely on the client's cooperation in order to modify the consequences of the client's behavior in a natural environment.

Operant treatment strategies are remarkable for their simplicity. The strategy for increasing appropriate behavior frequencies is to arrange environmental conditions so that appropriate responses are consistently followed by reinforcement; the strategy for decreasing inappropriate behavior frequencies is to arrange environmental conditions so that inappropriate responses have no reinforcing consequences or are consistently followed by punishment. In some cases, the strategy for decreasing the frequency of inappropriate behavior is to reinforce appropriate behavior that is incompatible with the inappropriate behavior. Thus one strategy for decreasing a high frequency of a child's not being in his seat in a classroom is to reinforce the child for sitting in his seat.

Positive Reinforcement

The technique of positive reinforcement consists of providing reinforcement contingent on the occurrence of appropriate behavior. It is generally recommended that reinforcement be dispensed in a contingent, systematic, and immediate manner. *Contingent* means that reinforcement is dispensed only when the appropriate behavior is performed; *systematic* means that reinforcement is dispensed in a relatively consistent manner for a sustained period of time; and *immediate* means that the delay between the completion of the response and the receipt of reinforcement should be as brief as possible.[1]

There are effective and ineffective ways to dispense positive reinforcement. Consider the case of a retarded adolescent whose parents must dress and undress the child every day. In this case, a behavioral consultant might advise the parents to (1) tell the child that, from now on, he must put on his own pants; and (2) praise the child whenever he does so. The parents' use of praise (positive reinforcement) is likely to be ineffective if they do any of the following: (1) praise the child very frequently for many other behaviors; (2) praise the child in an unconvincing manner; or (3) praise the child after considerable time has elapsed since his completion of the task.

[1] However, it is not *always* necessary to follow these guidelines to produce behavior change. For example, it is sometimes possible to change behavior with reinforcement delays as long as several hours (e.g., Schwartz & Hawkins, 1970).

Extinction

Extinction is a procedure in which contingent reinforcement is discontinued in order to decrease the frequency of a previously reinforced response. With tangible reinforcers, extinction is relatively simple to implement, for it is easy to stop dispensing concrete, reinforcing objects. When social reinforcers are involved, extinction consists of ignoring inappropriate behavior. For example, to extinguish a child's tantrums, a parent should ignore the tantrum completely and should not say "Stop it" or even look at the child to indicate disapproval.

Extinction of inappropriate behavior is frequently used in conjunction with positive reinforcement for appropriate behavior.

Shaping

Shaping is a procedure in which the behavioral requirements for reinforcement are gradually made more similar to some ultimately desired (goal) behavior. Lovaas's research on teaching language to nonverbal, autistic children (Lovaas et al., 1973; Lovaas et al., 1966) provides an excellent example of shaping procedures. The therapist in these experiments did not wait for the nonverbal children to emit appropriate speech before dispensing reinforcement; if he had, the children would have never emitted the response, and learning would not have occurred. Lovaas and his colleagues analyzed the learning of language into a series of steps, each of which constituted a successive approximation to the normal use of language. Before a child was required to use sentences, he was required to use each word individually; before this was required, the child learned to imitate sounds.

Punishment

Behavior can be punished by the presentation of an aversive stimulus, by the reclamation of a tangible reinforcer, and by the withdrawal of the opportunity to earn positive reinforcement. The presentation of an aversive stimulus is the method least frequently chosen by behavior modifiers. The reclamation of a reinforcer, termed *response cost* (Weiner, 1962), has been used extensively in training situations in which tangible reinforcers are dispensed (see Kazdin, 1972). The withdrawal of the opportunity to earn positive reinforcement, termed *time-out from positive reinforcement,* also has been used extensively, as in the example of removing a child from a classroom in which positive social reinforcement has been systematically programmed. In actual practice, it is sometimes difficult to distinguish between time-out and presentation of an aversive stimulus because removing a person from a reinforcing environment may involve placing him in an aversive situation. For example, when Annette was placed in the social isolation area, she not only lost the opportunity to earn positive reinforcement in the treatment room (time-out) but also was placed in the aversive situation of social isolation.

Like positive reinforcement, punishment is usually most effective when it is immediate and systematic. If a sequence of behavior is to be punished, punishment should follow the very first segment of the sequence rather than the

To extinguish the child's reluctance to work cooperatively with the other children, the teacher looks away from the child and does not respond to the child's attempt to gain his attention. (Photo by Burt Blinn and Sepp Seitz; Magnum Photos, Inc.)

completion of the sequence (Bandura, 1969). It is recalled that Annette was punished when she began to raise her hands to cover her ears even though she may not yet have begun screaming. In addition to punishing immediately and systematically, the behavior modifier should reinforce an alternative behavior (Solomon, 1964). Accordingly, in addition to receiving social isolation for screaming, Annette earned affection and candy by correctly identifying pictures of animals.

Contingency Contracting

The unique characteristic of contingency contracting is that the therapist and the client discuss and then contract behavioral requirements for reinforcement (e.g., Homme, Csanyi, Gonzales, & Rechs, 1969). Consequently, contracting provides a means by which a therapist can obtain a measure of control over the consequences of an adult's behavior in natural environments. For example, in an attempt to reduce the weight of eight obese adults, Mann (1972) had each person surrender valuable property prior to treatment. These people then signed a legal contract that specified how much weight had to be lost for a valuable to be returned. The results indicated that contingency contracting was effective for producing weight losses of more than 2 pounds per week.

Token Economy

The token economy is a system of reinforcement in which objects called tokens are dispensed contingent on the occurrence of specified behavior (see

Kazdin & Bootzin, 1972; O'Leary & Drabman, 1971). When a predetermined number of tokens is earned, the individual can "buy" any one of a variety of reinforcers. The reinforcers exchangeable for tokens can include tangible rewards, privileges, or activities.

Token reinforcement sometimes allows the therapist to maintain behavior changes for long periods of time. If praise or any other single reinforcer were employed, the client might become temporarily satiated and hence uninterested in obtaining additional reinforcements. This possible loss of interest in reinforcement is relatively unlikely to occur with tokens that can be exchanged for a variety of rewards.

The token economy is a motivational system within which it is possible to employ all of the operant techniques described thus far. Within a token economy, positive reinforcement consists of dispensing tokens contingent on appropriate behavior; extinction consists of no longer dispensing tokens for previously reinforced behavior; punishment (response cost) usually consists of reclamation of a previously earned token; and contingency contracting involves the therapist and the client contracting on the behavioral requirements for tokens.

Token economies have been implemented in a variety of settings (e.g., classrooms, state hospitals, prisons, and sheltered workshops) and with a variety of populations (e.g., normal and disturbed children, schizophrenic adults, and the mentally retarded). For additional reading on token economies, the student might consult Ayllon and Azrin's 1968 book, *The Token Economy.*

Systematic Desensitization

Systematic desensitization is a graded presentation of phobic stimuli while the client is in a state of relaxation. Treatment usually progresses in accordance with the following steps:

1. The therapist assesses the nature of the client's problem. In a case of a 22-year-old man complaining of impotence, the therapist begins by assessing the full range of the client's problems and psychological strengths.

2. Having decided to desensitize the phobic stimuli, the therapist and client construct an ordered list of stimuli beginning with those that elicit minimal anxiety and proceeding to those that elicit considerable anxiety. A graded list of phobic stimuli is called a *stimulus hierarchy.* In a case of impotence resulting from fear of inadequate performance, a portion of the stimulus hierarchy might include entering the bedroom with one's wife, hugging and kissing, breast and genital touching, stimulation of the penis in a teasing manner, and penile insertion.

3. After the stimulus hierarchy is constructed, the client is taught to relax. Wolpe (1958) provides training in Jacobson's (1938) deep-muscle relaxation techniques, but other procedures such as hypnosis and drugs are available.

4. The therapist chooses between *imaginal* and *in vivo* desensitization. The major difference between these procedures is whether the stimulus items are imagined or actually presented in their naturalistic context. In imaginal desensitization, the subject is relaxed and is then instructed to visualize a stimulus

item that elicits minimal anxiety. For example, the impotent man might imagine entering the bedroom with his wife. If anxiety from this scene interrupts the state of relaxation, the subject is instructed to stop imagining the scene and to relax once again. When relaxation is achieved, the client imagines the scene again. This procedure is repeated until the client can imagine the scene of entering the bedroom without experiencing any anxiety. Once this stimulus has been desensitized, the procedure is repeated for the next item on the stimulus hierarchy, then the item after that, and so on, until the client is no longer impotent. In *in vivo* desensitization, the client is given homework assignments that require contact with items on the stimulus hierarchy. For example, the impotent man might be instructed to enter the bedroom with his wife, to kiss and hug, but not to go any farther. Relieved of the fear of inadequate performance, the client learns to engage in these preliminary behaviors without appreciable anxiety. The homework assignments gradually require the client to approximate more closely sexual intercourse until the client reports successful performance.

Several theoretical rationales have been proposed to explain the effectiveness of desensitization techniques. Wolpe (1958), who developed desensitization techniques through modification of earlier procedures (Jones, 1924), conceptualized desensitization in terms of reciprocal inhibition and counterconditioning. In this view, anxiety and deep-muscle relaxation are hypothesized to be competing responses so that elicitation of one inhibits the other. Through Pavlovian conditioning, items on the stimulus hierarchy become associated with relaxation, and through reciprocal inhibition, relaxation inhibits anxiety. This explanation of desensitization is often referred to as counterconditioning, which Davison and Neale define as "relearning achieved by eliciting a new response in the presence of a particular stimulus" (1974).

Despite the popularity of the counterconditioning model of desensitization, other equally attractive models have been proposed. The habituation model (see Lader & Mathews, 1968; Wilson & Davison, 1971) proposes that desensitization occurs simply as a result of the repeated presentation of hierarchical stimulus items. Still another model, that of Pavlovian conditioned inhibition, was recently proposed by Rizley and Reppucci (in press). While most explanations of desensitization focus on the relearning that occurs to the CS (anxiety-eliciting stimulus), the conditioned inhibition explanation focuses on the learning that may occur to incidental stimuli that occur in compound with the CS. For example, an airplane phobic asked to visualize buying a ticket will imagine some stimuli that elicit anxiety (e.g., the ticket and the airline employee) as well as many that do not (e.g., a clock on the wall and cars going by the airport). These stimuli that do not elicit anxiety are "incidental" in the sense that the therapist had not explicitly intended that they be imagined. According to the conditioned inhibition model, imagining a scene consisting of both anxiety-eliciting stimuli (CSs) and incidental stimuli results in the acquisition of Pavlovian conditioned inhibition to the incidental stimuli. In other words, it is these incidental stimuli that inhibit anxiety. At present, this theory is supported by data obtained in animal laboratories but has yet to be tested in humans.

Implosion

Stampfl and his colleagues have developed a technique called implosion (e.g., Stampfl, 1967; Stampfl & Levis, 1967a, 1967b). This procedure also involves a hierarchy of graded stimuli, but the client progresses to high-anxiety-provoking stimuli relatively rapidly and may be asked to imagine items with psychodynamic content. The client is instructed to lose himself in the scenes described by the therapist. Implosion therapy provides vivid accounts of dire consequences that the client is unlikely to experience. For example, in a case of a rat phobia, the client might be instructed to imagine the rat biting him, running over his body, devouring his eyes, jumping inside his mouth, and devouring his organs. The therapist verbalizes such scenes to the client in great detail while encouraging the client to achieve a maximal level of anxiety until a spontaneous reduction of fear occurs. This procedure is based on extinction principles. In this instance, the feared object and the resulting high anxiety occur without any real danger or negative outcome. After several trials of the stimuli and the nonoccurrence of the feared event, the stimuli no longer elicit anxiety.

Assertive Training

A considerable amount of human suffering results from an inability to stand up effectively for one's rights, to express one's feelings, and to avoid interpersonal domination by others. Believing that their opinions and desires are unimportant, some people are overly submissive. The indicated behavioral treatment for such problems is called *assertive training.*

The goal of assertive training is to enhance the client's interpersonal skills by teaching more direct ways of handling hostility and other emotions (Salter, 1949). This is accomplished by discussing alternative ways of interacting in specific situations, followed by *behavioral rehearsal* in which the client practices assertive behavior while the therapist offers encouragement and constructive criticism (see Serber, 1972; Wolpe, 1970).

It is important to recognize that assertive responses are different from aggressive responses (Lazarus, 1971). For example, the following compares an assertive and an aggressive reply to someone who is always interrupting you:

A: Shut up and let me finish! (*Aggressive response.*)

B: I know you sometimes have an urge to make a comment, but I would appreciate your letting me finish first and then I'll be pleased to listen to what you have to say. (*Assertive response.*)

Modeling

Studies by Bandura and his co-workers (Bandura, Grusec, & Menlove, 1967; Bandura, Blanchard, & Ritter, 1968; Bandura & Menlove, 1968) suggest that modeling procedures can effectively alleviate anxiety reactions through *vicarious extinction.* Vicarious extinction of anxiety is a procedure in which models are exposed to a stimulus that elicits anxiety in the observer; by observing nonharmful consequences to the model, the observer's fear is gradually extinguished.

Bandura, Blanchard, and Ritter (1968) compared the efficacy of modeling and of desensitization techniques in the treatment of adolescents and adults who suffered from severe snake phobias. Prior to treatment, all subjects were administered a behavioral test of snake avoidance as well as attitudinal and fear surveys. The subjects were then assigned to one of four treatment groups. The "symbolic modeling" group observed a film depicting young children, adolescents, and adults engaging in progressively more threatening interactions with a large snake. Moreover, these subjects had been trained to relax while viewing the film and were able to regulate the rate of presentation of the film by means of remote control devices. The "live modeling with participation" group observed a fearless model and then received *in vivo* desensitization in which the model guided their approach to, and handling of, the feared snakes. The "desensitization" group received imaginal desensitization in accordance with procedures discussed previously, whereas control subjects received no treatment other than pre- and postadministration of the behavioral test of avoidance and of the fear and attitudinal surveys.

As shown in Figure 7-5, the live modeling with participation was highly successful in eliminating snake phobia, whereas symbolic modeling and desensitization were less successful treatment procedures. The modeling procedure not only produced significant behavioral improvement but also led to significantly less subjective fear as reported by subjects. By comparison, the control subjects exhibited no improvement.

Hypnosis

Anton Mesmer received his doctorate from the University of Vienna in 1776 for his thesis on a subtle fluid called *animal magnetism.* The heavenly bodies were presumed to act on people through this fluid, causing them to behave as if in a state of stupor. A period of emotional frenzy, called a crisis, sometimes developed in magnetized patients, and when it did the patient would typically emerge cured of previous aches, pains, and other hysterical conversion symptoms.

Invited to Paris by the king, Mesmer enjoyed greater success with the ladies of Paris than with the established medical community. Distrust of Mesmer and his methods grew to the point where a commission was established to investigate the validity of animal magnetism. This commission found that the crisis occurred only when the subject was aware he was being magnetized. The majority of the commission's members concluded that animal magnetism did not exist and was a "mere" phenomenon of the "imagination." Mesmerism, which was later renamed hypnosis, remained in disrepute until it was utilized by Charcot in 1878 in his famous studies on hysteria.

The history of hypnosis is instructive because it exemplifies a refusal to accept basic facts for which there is no adequate explanation. Although the theory of a subtle magnetic fluid is puzzling, the fact was that mesmerism actually produced successful cures of hysterical conversion symptoms (i.e., mysterious aches, pains, blindness, and paralyses). Rather than abandon mesmerism, the scientific community should have accepted the facts and sought a more plausible theory to explain those facts.

The credulous-skeptical controversy concerns the issue of whether or not a special state of consciousness, called the hypnotic trance, actually exists and accounts for hypnotic behaviors such as hallucinations, relative unresponsiveness to pain (analgesia), selective loss of memory (amnesia), and age regression. The existence of a special state of consciousness is accepted by the credulous position but is rejected by the skeptical position. A major obstacle in resolving this dispute is the lack of clarity concerning the empirical meaning of the phrase *hypnotic trance.*

Barber (1969), Sarbin (1964, 1965), and Sarbin and Coe (1972) have proposed that hypnosis can be best understood by detailed descriptions of hypnotic behavior, by a search for antecedent variables that produce hypnotic behavior, and by the objective measurement of individual differences in susceptibility to

Figure 7-5
Reduction of fear as a function of treatment method. (Adapted from A. Bandura, E. B. Blanchard, and B. Ritter. The relative efficacy of desensitization and modeling approaches for inducing behavioral, affective, and attitudinal changes. Unpublished manuscript, Stanford University, 1968. Adapted with permission of authors.)

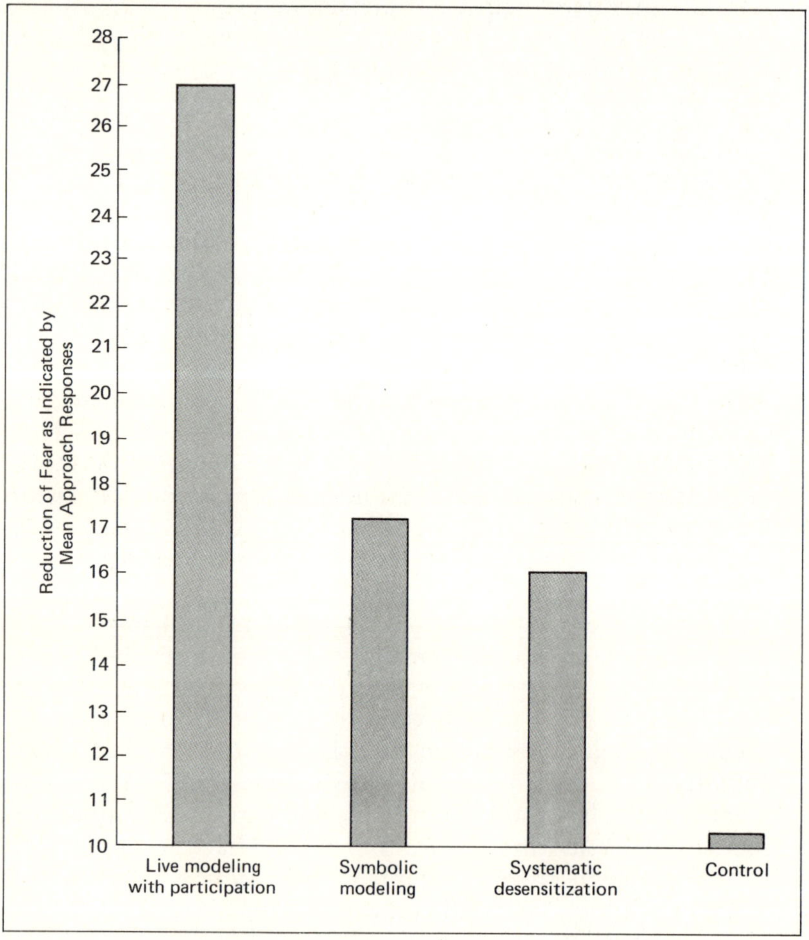

Anton Mesmer (1734–1815), the founder of animal magnetism (hypnosis). (Reprinted by permission of Historical Pictures Service; Chicago, Illinois.)

hypnosis. The importance of describing hypnotic behavior in considerable detail has been emphasized by Barber (1969). For example, it is possible to induce analgesia by hypnotic suggestion and by drugs; in either case, the individual shows relatively few overt signs of pain. However, when greater detail is considered, it is found that only drug-induced analgesia suppresses physiological correlates of pain.

Hypnosis did not gain respectability among scientists until Charcot endorsed the procedure as legitimate. The print shows the great French master demonstrating hypnosis at Salpêtrière. The physician holding the subject is Babinsky, the neurologist who discovered the Babinsky reflex. (Reprinted by permission of Historical Pictures Service; Chicago, Illinois.)

Sarbin (1964) has conceptualized hypnosis as a social role. This implies that hypnotic subjects behave in accordance with their understanding of how other people behave under hypnosis; in other words, hypnotic behavior is seen as a type of conformity. For example, after informing a group of students that "catalepsy" was common during hypnosis, Orne (1959) found that these students later exhibited such behavior when they were hypnotized. By comparison, a control group of subjects who had not been given this false information did not show cataleptic-like behavior.

The most prevalent use of hypnosis in behavior therapy is to relax clients and to facilitate imagery in desensitization (Weitzenhoffer, 1972). A recent study by Lazarus (1973) found that clients who entered therapy believing in hypnosis progressed faster when hypnosis was given than did clients who received standard relaxation training. The point Lazarus emphasized was that hypnosis can serve as a self-fulfilling prophecy for clients who believe in its therapeutic power.

Covert Sensitization

Covert sensitization is employed to condition aversive properties to previously pleasurable but undesirable acts (Cautela, 1966). The procedure involves relaxing the client and instructing him to visualize the commission of the undesirable act. After visualizing the act, the client is then instructed to imagine an aversive event such as feelings of nausea. Thus the procedure is cognitive visualization of the act followed by cognitive visualization of an aversive consequence. Training is also provided in imagining the avoidance of the act followed by imagining a pleasurable consequence of the avoidance. For example, covert sensitization with an alcoholic might consist of having the alcoholic imagine taking a drink and then feeling nauseous and of having him imagine refusing a drink and then feeling the experience of breathing fresh air.

Rational-Emotive Therapy

The basic premise of Ellis's (1962) rational-emotive therapy is that neurotic anxiety is often maintained by irrational thoughts. This position suggests a close relation between thought and emotion such that unadaptive anxiety often results from an illogical interpretation of events. The purpose of rational-emotive therapy is to identify the irrational sentences (e.g., *"I am worthless"*) of the client and to point out to him that these sentences are irrational and are not supported by available evidence. An excellent example of this form of therapy is provided by Lazarus:[2]

PATIENT: So I became so upset when my father disagreed with me and I found myself doubting.

THERAPIST: What were you really telling yourself?

PATIENT: I'm not sure.

THERAPIST: Let me guess. I would guess that your internal sentence went something like this: "Authority is always right and should never be challenged."

PATIENT: That could be it. My dad always said that he knows best and that we should not question his opinion or judgments.

THERAPIST: Okay, fine. Now, think over the argument again, only this time remember that we never bow to authority but we always examine the evidence, no matter how dependable and knowledgeable the source of the evidence may be. What conclusions do you arrive at?

PATIENT: That I was right and he was wrong. But he has a way of throwing his weight around that undermines my confidence. There's another irrational sentence in there somewhere, and I haven't been able to find it. I wish I could identify it. What do you think?

THERAPIST: Well, tell me what else went on during the discussion.

[2] Reprinted from Lazarus, A. A. *Behavior therapy and beyond.* New York: McGraw-Hill Publishing Co., 1971, pp. 183–184, with permission of author and publisher.

PATIENT: I began to buckle, you know. I mean, I just felt like a kid again. Is that what you mean?

THERAPIST: What else did he do or say?

PATIENT: I don't remember. I mean he got nasty all right and that's maybe when I kind of gave in.

THERAPIST: What do you mean when you say "he got nasty"?

PATIENT: He started cursing at me. Like, I mean, you know, putting me down.

THERAPIST: Maybe that's the missing sentence.

PATIENT: What?

THERAPIST: Words can hurt me.

PATIENT: Words can hurt me. Yeah! I think that's it. Of course, I said to myself that being cursed was like being whipped. I let them hurt . . . no, I *made* them hurt me. Yeah! I'll watch out for that from now on. He sure as hell didn't use sticks and stones to break my bones.

Cognitive therapy need not always require extensive challenging of what the client is telling himself. Indeed, in some cases, the client's troubles are directly related to misinformation. For example, a male client may feel sexually inadequate because he thinks his penis is too small, or a young couple may look for depth causes to explain why they have intercourse "only" five times per week. In such cases, the primary therapeutic technique is to correct misconceptions by explaining the facts. Although it is relatively rare that a client's problems can be solved simply by providing accurate information, it is nevertheless true that this is all the treatment that is needed for some clients.

TREATMENT EFFECTIVENESS

Behavior therapy has been employed successfully for a remarkably broad range of problems; moreover, success has often been achieved in relatively brief time periods such as a few months. The following is a brief review of the outcome literature on most of the techniques discussed in the previous section.

Problem Behavior Suitable for Operant Treatment

The effectiveness of operant procedures for a particular case seems to be determined more by the ingenuity of the therapist than by properties inherent in the behavior being treated. Indeed, the range of behaviors that can be treated by operant procedures is remarkable (see Bijou & Redd, 1974). Specifically, operant procedures can be employed in accordance with three strategies: to establish behavior not in the person's repertoire, to elicit a higher frequency of appropriate behavior, and to eliminate inappropriate behavior.

Operant procedures can be used to teach new adaptive skills and behaviors (e.g., Ferster, 1961). Typically, the use of behavior modification for these purposes involves extensive shaping. Operant procedures have been successfully employed to establish speech in nonverbal autistic children (e.g., Lovaas et al., 1973; Lovaas et al., 1966), self-help skills in mentally retarded children (e.g., Barton, Guess, Garcia, & Baer, 1970; Peterson & McIntosh, 1973; Watson, 1967), academic skills (e.g., Corey & Shamow, 1972; Lovitt & Esveldt, 1970;

Staats, 1965), and even appropriate sex identity (Barlow, Reynolds, & Agras, 1973).

Operant techniques have also been employed successfully to increase the frequency of appropriate behaviors already in the individual's repertoire. In these cases, extensive shaping may be unnecessary; sometimes it is sufficient simply to motivate the individual to perform the behavior. Examples of successful attempts to increase the frequency of appropriate behavior include increased cooperative play (e.g., Altman, 1971; Azrin & Lindsley, 1956), increases in appropriate social behavior (e.g., Ayllon & Azrin, 1968; McReynolds & Coleman, 1972), and improved classroom behavior (e.g., Cossairt, Hall, & Hopkins, 1973; Hall, Lund, & Jackson, 1968; Reppucci & Reiss, 1970).

Operant procedures have been extensively employed to decrease inappropriate behavior frequencies. For example, Goldiamond (1965) has developed effective treatment for correcting stuttering. Other successful treatments include elimination of tantrums (e.g., Corte, Wolf, & Locke, 1971; Reiss & Redd, 1970; Williams, 1959), reductions in aggressive behavior (e.g., Bostow & Bailey, 1969; Foxx & Azrin, 1972; Vukelich & Hake, 1971), elimination of enuretic behavior (e.g., Peterson, 1971), suppression of inappropriate behavior in hospitals (e.g., Ayllon & Azrin, 1968; McReynolds & Coleman, 1972), treatment of alcoholism (see Bandura, 1969), weight reduction (e.g., Stuart, 1971; Wollersheim, 1970), alleviation of sexual problems (e.g., Wagner, 1968), and smoking behavior (see Bernstein, 1969).

Azrin and his colleagues have developed several creative treatment procedures, including treatment for eliminating tics (Azrin & Nunn, 1973) and procedures for toilet training within approximately 24 hours (Foxx & Azrin, 1973).

Systematic Desensitization

Systematic desensitization is particularly effective in cases of monosymptomatic phobia (e.g., Bernstein & Beaty, 1971; Paul, 1966; Wolpe, 1958). Moreover, desensitization is often effective in cases that can be reconceptualized as involving fear responses. For example, some instances of compulsive behaviors can be treated by this method (e.g., Rackensperger & Feinberg, 1972; Wolpe & Lazarus, 1966); sexual dysfunctions that involve fear of inadequate performances such as premature ejaculation and frigidity (e.g., LoPiccolo, Stewart, & Watkins, 1972; Wincze, 1971) and fears of asserting oneself (e.g., Weinman, Gelbart, Wallace, & Post, 1972) can also be treated by this method. However, systematic desensitization is not indicated in cases in which the fear avoidance produces environmental rewards or "secondary gains." In conclusion, systematic desensitization is often successful in eliminating fears and is one of the most effective treatment procedures yet to be developed.

Implosion

The experimental and clinical literature on implosion was recently reviewed by Morganstern (1973), who concluded that implosive therapy is probably less effective than desensitization and that, in successful cases, its effectiveness is probably due to extraneous factors such as demand characteristics and the client's expectancy of change. Levis (1974) has taken strong exception to Morganstern's conclusion, suggesting instead that the technique does seem to be effective when used properly, even though future research is needed to isolate the reasons for its effectiveness. Wolpe and Lazarus (1966) have observed that some clients seem to get worse, whereas others improve under implosive therapy. Although the effectiveness of implosive therapy is still controversial, future research may identify the kinds of people and/or problems for which this therapy is indicated.

Modeling

Modeling techniques are only first beginning to be employed in clinical practice. The promise of these techniques is suggested by a spate of studies. Eisler, Hersen, and Miller (1973) and Goldstein, Martens, Hubben, Van Bella, Schaaf, Wiersma, & Goedhart (1973) found that a modeling procedure produced more assertive and more independent behavior than did appropriate control procedures. Jaffe and Carlson (1972) vicariously extinguished test anxiety in a group of college students using modeling procedures, and modeling has been found effective in cases of extreme social withdrawal (O'Connor, 1972; Ross, Ross, & Evans, 1972). Thus, modeling seems to be an effective treatment technique, but its full potentiality has not yet been explored.

Cognitive Treatments

The most extensively studied cognitive treatment is covert sensitization (e.g., Ascher & Cautela, 1972; Cautela, 1966; Manno & Marston, 1972; Wisocki, 1973). In a particularly interesting study, Callahan and Leitenberg (1973) found some evidence that covert sensitization treatment for sexual deviations is more effective for long-term improvements than is shock punishment.

Meichenbaum (1972) investigated the effects of a cognitive treatment in which test anxious college students were trained in coping imagery (visualizing becoming anxious and then visualizing coping by breathing slowly and attending to the task). This study found cognitive modification effective for reducing test anxiety in college students.

There have been only a few experimental evaluations of rational-emotive therapy. In one recent study, Trexler and Karst (1972) found that rational-emotive therapy was more effective than control procedures for eliminating public-speaking anxiety.

Comment

The behavioral model of abnormality has been frequently criticized (e.g., Breger & McGaugh, 1965). Although some of these criticisms have been constructive (e.g., London, 1972), many others have been based on an inaccurate understanding of contemporary behaviorism. Coleman (1972, p. 64) identified five frequent criticisms of behaviorism; these criticisms and our comments follow.

CRITICISM 1: The behavioristic model ignores subjective experience.

REPLY: Animal learning theorists have long studied the role of expectation (r_g), and Skinner (1966) has stipulated that behaviorists must come to grips with conscious experience. In this chapter, we have already seen that behaviorists have studied the emotional and the cognitive aspects of abnormality.

CRITICISM 2: Behavior theory relies too heavily on animal research.

REPLY: As the present chapter shows, the focus of the behavioral approach has been on the study of human behavior. Nevertheless, animal research should not be criticized simply because it studies animals. Medicine and biology have profited considerably by the study of animals, and so have patients suffering from a long list of physical diseases. This chapter documents the fact that psychology has also profited from the study of animals.

CRITICISM 3: Behavior therapy is concerned with the simpler phenomena of human life and ignores complex phenomena such as love and courage.

REPLY: Behavior therapy has been applied to many cases involving complex phenomena, examples of which are lack of assertion, compulsive behavior, sexual problems, marital problems, and depression. It is difficult to find a case that a behavior therapist could not attempt to treat with as much or more hope for success as any other psychotherapist might legitimately claim.

CRITICISMS 4 AND 5: Behavior theorists have ignored the importance of values and employ mechanistic techniques.

REPLY: It is difficult to find an influential book in behavioral psychology that has not included a detailed discussion of ethics (see Bandura, 1969). In general, behaviorists believe that effective treatment should not be withheld, in the name of ethics, from patients who voluntarily request alleviation of their suffering. It would seem ungrateful to damn a physician for removing a cancerous tumor on the grounds that he is being mechanistic, and the same applies to the behavior therapist whose primary goal is successful treatment.

One force behind objections to behavioral psychology is a desire to affirm the value of each individual. People are not machines; they are important and are capable of transcending their environments through love and self-awareness. It is important to understand that the behavioral psychologist affirms these values; he, too, considers each person a subject of worth and dignity. His compassion for humanity is expressed on two levels: on the interpersonal level through his interactions with others and through his concern for the welfare of his clients, and on the scientific level in his attempt to develop a factual basis from which humanistic concerns can be translated into effective help.

RESEARCH METHODOLOGY

Behavior theorists stress the importance of controlled, experimental research. Because there are many ways to control experiments, no single research methodology characterizes the behavioral approach. However, two popular methodologies associated with the behavioral approach are *individual analysis* and *analogue* studies.

Individual Analysis

This kind of experimentation differs in two respects from that employed in most other psychological studies. That is, the individual analysis design does not include experimental and control groups, and it does not require statistical analysis to interpret the results.

Most experimental studies in psychology employ a *group design* in which experimental and control conditions are presented to different groups. By contrast, individual analysis experiments present both experimental and control conditions to the same subjects but at different times. Consequently, the individual analysis experiment requires at least three experimental phases. The first phase is termed *baseline,* the second phase is termed *treatment,* and the third phase is termed *return to baseline.*

During the baseline phase of the experiment, the investigator determines for each subject the frequency of a specified behavior prior to the introduction of treatment procedures. For example, in the case of Annette, baseline observations provided an estimate of the frequency of screaming prior to treatment.

Following assessment of baseline frequencies, each subject receives the behavioral treatment. For example, when treatment was introduced, the frequency of Annette's screaming was less than that during baseline.

The third phase of the individual analysis experiment is a return to baseline. The purpose of this phase is to determine the frequency of the specified behavior following discontinuance of treatment. For example, when the behavioral treatment program was discontinued, the frequency of Annette's screaming increased.

Considered together, information from the three phases can provide convincing evidence of the effects of the behavioral treatment procedure. That is, if the presence of the treatment procedure is reliably associated with one rate of behavior and if its absence is reliably associated with another rate of behavior, then the causal effects of the treatment procedure can be determined by comparing these two rates (Sidman, 1961).

It is critical that observed behavior occur at a steady frequency within each experimental phase. Figure 7-6 displays hypothetical results from two experiments employing individual analysis designs. The results displayed in the left-hand section of the figure are clearly interpretable. Within all three phases, responding occurs at a stable rate. In technical language, the behavior within each experimental phase reaches a *steady state.* These data support the conclusion that treatment produced an increase in the rate of responding exhibited by the subject. On the other hand, the results displayed in the right-hand section of the figure are difficult to interpret.

Analogue Study

In order to conduct an experiment, the investigator must have a high degree of control over experimental variables. For this reason, it is often impractical to conduct experimental research in clinical settings. Instead, many investigators have created laboratory analogues of clinical situations. For example, an investigator may study a monosymptomatic phobia such as fear of snakes rather than a more debilitating phobia. Although research on monosymptomatic phobias is not a substitute for research on clinical phobias, such research can provide information relevant to our understanding of clinical phobias. Moreover, some monosymptomatic phobias, such as fear of flying, afflict many people and thus are sometimes important to treat.

Several behavior theorists have discussed the concept of the analogue study in great detail (e.g., Bernstein & Paul, 1971; Kanfer & Phillips, 1970). The value of these discussions is their elucidation of sound methodology for experimental research in clinical psychology. However, the concept of an analogue study is potentially more confusing than clarifying if it is interpreted as suggesting anything more than a laboratory study. All laboratory experiments are intended as analogues of nonlaboratory conditions in the sense that their purpose is to discover cause-effect relations in the laboratory that apply to the real world.

Figure 7-6
Hypothetical results from two experiments using the individual analysis design. Results of Experiment I reveal that the treatment decreased the target behavior. Results of Experiment II are uninterpretable because of the instability of the target behavior within experimental phases.

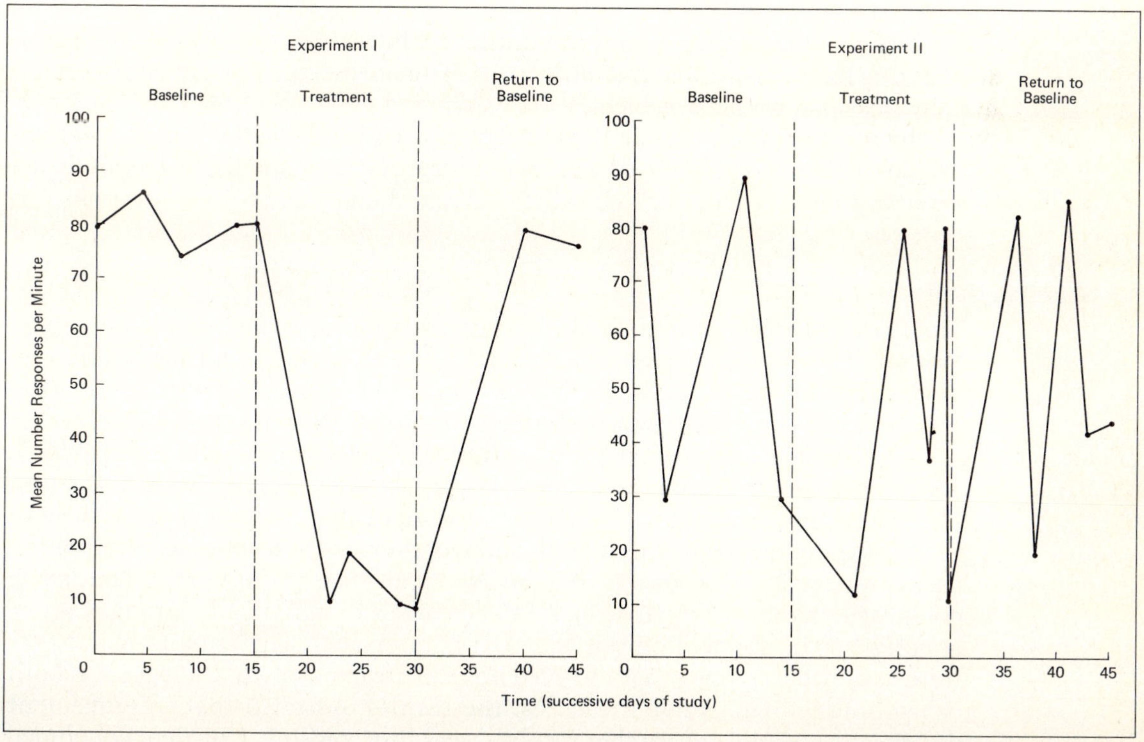

EXAMPLE OF RESEARCH ISSUE: EFFECTIVE METHODS OF FEAR REDUCTION

In recent years, we have witnessed an increased interest in analogue studies of fear reduction. The attempt has been to assess the relative effectiveness of various behavioral techniques and to identify the effective components of these techniques.

The Paul Study

Paul's (1966) doctoral dissertation compared the effects of insight therapy with the effects of systematic desensitization in the treatment of fear of public speaking. Ninety-six subjects were selected from 710 college students enrolled in public speaking courses at the University of Illinois at Urbana-Champaign. The subjects were selected on the basis of a battery of measures that indicated fear of public speaking and were randomly assigned to one of five groups. The insight-oriented group received psychodynamically oriented therapy designed to give the student insight into his or her fear, whereas the systematic desensitization group received "a slightly modified and formalized form of the treatment advanced by Wolpe (1958) and Lazarus and Rachman (1960)" (Paul, 1966, p. 18). The remaining three groups served as controls. Of special interest was the inclusion of an attention-placebo control group, the purpose of which was to assess the effects of factors such as expectation of improvement, suggestion, and the relationship between therapist and client. This group received a discussion of the prior history of their problem, a detailed explanation of the treatment rationale, and encouragement for expectations of improvement from a pill described as a "fast-acting tranquilizer." In reality, the pill was a placebo and thus had no psychoactive properties. The entire study involved five treatment sessions for each subject.

The results indicated that 100 per cent of the students who received systematic desensitization exhibited significant improvement and that systematic desensitization was superior to insight-oriented therapy and to attention-placebo controls.

The Sherman Study

The Paul study provided evidence that five sessions of systematic desensitization are superior to five sessions of insight-oriented therapy for fear reduction. More recent studies on desensitization have been concerned with identifying the most effective ways in which desensitization can be accomplished.

Sherman (1972) evaluated the importance of real-life exposure to the phobic object in desensitization treatment. Using the Fear Survey Schedule and a behavioral avoidance test, 54 coeds were identified as having some fear of being in water (e.g., entering a pool) and were termed aqua phobics. Half of the coeds were assigned to groups that received real-life exposure to the swimming pool; these subjects were instructed to perform a hierarchically arranged series of activities in the pool only if they felt comfortable. The remaining subjects were assigned to groups that received no real-life exposure to the pool. On both behavioral and subjective measures, the results indicated that improvement was greatest for the groups that received real-life exposure. Sherman concluded that real-life exposure may be an important, if not critical factor, in the desensitization of fear.

Discussion

The two studies reviewed above exemplify the kind of analogue research currently being reported. The Paul study is appropriately regarded as an excellent example of sound methodological research. The Sherman study is suggestive of the importance of real-life exposures in desensitization, but additional research is needed to clarify many other questions concerning the effective components of desensitization procedures.

Many analogue studies on fear reduction are currently being conducted. The treatment effectiveness section briefly reviewed some of these studies under the subheadings of systematic desensitization and of modeling. For a more detailed understanding, the student should consult excellent reviews by Wilson and Davison (1971) and by Rizley and Reppucci (in press).

SUMMARY

Social learning theory (behavioral approach) is based in part on a conceptualization of abnormal behavior as behavior learned in accordance with the same experimental principles by which normal behavior is learned. A distinction is often drawn between the conditions that led to the original development of abnormal behavior and the conditions that are currently maintaining it. For example, a child may begin crying and screaming as part of a natural reaction to the loss of a close relationship, but prolonged continuance of the screaming could be maintained by the adult attention it may receive.

There are many ways in which abnormal behaviors can be learned and maintained. Operant (or instrumental) conditioning is a form of learning in which response patterns are altered by their rewarding or punishing environmental consequences. Thorndike's law of effect is an attempt to explain operant conditioning by postulating that stimulus-response bonds are strengthened by success or satisfaction or reward and are weakened by failure or dissatisfaction or punishment. This law is in no obvious way valid, in part because rewards do not always strengthen the tendency to repeat the exact response that led to reward and in part because the effects of rewards and punishments do not necessarily cancel one another in the specified manner. Revisions in the law of effect have resulted in a functional law that is tautological. The modern law of effect stipulates: If a response is reinforced (or punished) on a contingent basis in the presence of a stimulus, the probability is increased (or decreased if punished) that the response will occur again in the presence of that stimulus. The resultant behavior change is termed operant conditioning. Operant conditioning most readily occurs for voluntary behaviors.

The effects of rewards (or punishments) depend considerably on the specific manner in which the reward (or punishment) is dispensed.

An issue of both practical and theoretical importance is what happens to reinforced behavior after the reinforcement procedure is withdrawn. In animal laboratory situations, the most typical result is an eventual extinction of the learned response. In reinforcement therapy situations with humans, the learned behavior may extinguish or persist after the reinforcement procedure is withdrawn. One factor that has a powerful effect on persistence is the extent to which the training procedure provides reinforcement continuously or intermittently—the more intermittent the reinforcement training procedure, the more persistent is the learned response after the reinforcement is withdrawn.

Self-reinforcement refers to the manner in which people reward themselves. Generally, the available research suggests that people tend to self-administer rewards on performance tasks in accordance with standards previously established by experimenter instructions, by observations of models, or by direct learning in the experimental situation.

Another important aspect of rewards is their symbolic nature. Rewards are often perceived as symbols of success, and successful reinforcement therapy for problem behavior is often accompanied by generalized behavioral and psychological improvement.

Pavlovian (or classical) conditioning is a form of learning in which reflexive behaviors are conditioned to a previously neutral cue. The training procedure may be one of two basic types—either the onset of the CS predicts the onset of the US or the onset of the CS predicts the absence of the US. The former procedure is called excitatory conditioning because the CS acquires the capacity to elicit CRs, and the latter procedure is called inhibitory conditioning because the CS acquires the capacity to suppress CRs that otherwise would have occurred. Pavlovian conditioning applies to involuntary responses such as emotional reactions.

Many learning situations involve a combination of Pavlovian and operant conditioning. The manner in which such combinations may sometimes occur is suggested by the two-process theory of avoidance learning. In avoidance learning, a CS is presented and is followed by an aversive US after a fixed time interval. During the CS-US interval, the subject can perform a specific response that will prevent the US from coming on. Under the two-process theory of avoidance learning, fear is conditioned to the CS via Pavlovian conditioning, and the avoidance response is learned through operant conditioning because it is reinforced by fear reduction.

In operant and Pavlovian conditioning procedures, the subject directly experiences the US, reward, or punishment. In observational learning, however, the subject learns by observing the consequences of someone else's behavior or simply by imitating a model. Bandura's (1969) research has demonstrated that emotional responses to stimuli can be acquired and extinguished by observation of CS-US associations.

Behavior learned under one stimulus condition often generalizes to some other stimulus conditions. The principle of *primary stimulus generalization* states that behavior generalizes from stimulus condition S_1 to stimulus condition S_2 in direct proportion to the physical similarity between S_1 and S_2; the principle of *semantic generalization* states that behavior generalizes from stimulus condition S_1 to stimulus condition S_2 in direct proportion to the conceptual or semantic similarity between stimulus conditions S_1 and S_2. Both types of generalization occur.

A number of important treatment procedures have been based on the principles of learning. Operant therapy procedures include the techniques of positive reinforcement, extinction, shaping, response cost, time-out from positive reinforcement, and contingency contracting. The guiding principle of these techniques is that abnormal behavior can be treated by altering its environmental consequences. A token economy is a motivational system within which these various techniques can be used. Operant techniques have been utilized in treating a wide range of inappropriate behaviors including tantrums, speech problems, disruptive classroom behavior, marital problems, and smoking.

Systematic desensitization is a therapy procedure that provides a graded presentation of phobic stimuli while the client is in a relaxed state. This treatment is particularly effective for instances in which the problem behavior can be conceptualized as a fear of some specific stimuli. Other behavior therapy techniques discussed in this chapter include implosion, assertive training, modeling, hypnosis, covert sensitization, and rational-emotive therapy.

Two research paradigms associated with the behavioral approach are called individual analysis and analogue studies. The individual analysis design presents both experimental and control conditions to the same subjects but at different times and usually includes baseline, treatment, and return-to-baseline experimental phases. The analogue study is a laboratory experiment in which a subclinical problem such as snake phobia is treated.

Chapter 8

Phenomenology and Mental Health

I have described the human dilemma as the capacity of man to view himself as object and as subject. My point is that both are necessary—necessary for psychological science, for effective therapy, and for meaningful living.

ROLLO MAY (1967, p. 20)

Phenomenology is an attitude, a philosophy, and a science. The phenomenological attitude is one of dignity and respect for people as human beings. The individual is seen as an object of worth and importance who is capable of love, beauty, happiness, and despair. Consistent with this attitude, phenomenologists have objected to scientific languages that convey impressions of people as objects of study rather than as objects of worth. As a philosophy, phenomenology is associated with doctrines of indeterminism (free will), philosophies on the essential (logical) priority of experience as the basis of all knowledge, and a unique philosophy of human nature that recognizes the human being as both immanent in and transcendent of the physical and cultural orders. As a science, phenomenology is concerned with understanding the individual's unique perceptions of stimuli and how these perceptions mediate experience and overt behavior. In this chapter all three aspects of phenomenology (attitude, philosophy, and science) will be discussed.

To emphasize the importance phenomenologists place on the study of psychological growth, we begin with Ricks and Wessman's (1966) case history of a happy man. Although happiness is generally desirable and indicative of psychological health, there are circumstances under which it is abnormal to be happy (e.g., after the loss of a loved one). Moreover, as the investigators noted, happiness per se cannot be equated with self-actualization. Indeed, complete happiness suggests a kind of psychological contentment that is incompatible with the strivings of continued emotional growth. Under normal circumstances, however, happiness is a major component of psychological health and, therefore, a proper subject for psychological research.

The case history that follows consists of passages from the Ricks and Wessman (1966) article. The present writers merely deleted portions of the article for the purposes of this text. Because the case history is lengthy, we decided not to extract the material with smaller print as we did with other, much shorter passages that consist of direct quotations.

WHY IS THIS MAN HAPPY?[1]

Conditions favorable to happiness and the characteristics of the happy man have always interested thoughtful people. But happiness is not a favored topic in psychology, nor are case studies of even moderately happy men frequent in our literature. Most psychologists with whom we have discussed Winn have been skeptical, cautious, or even pessimistic and cynical about the possibility that we have been able to study a really happy man. But is this pessimism justified? With Aristotle, we might ask if we have to wait until an exemplary man is

[1] Adapted from D. F. Ricks and A. E. Wessman, Winn: A case study of a happy man. *Journal of Humanistic Psychology,* 1966, 2–16. The case also appeared in *Mood and Personality,* by A. E. Wessman and D. F. Ricks; New York: Holt, Rinehart & Winston, Inc., 1966. Printed by permission of authors and publisher.

dead before we can say that he was happy, and whether, while he is still alive, we cannot try to speak the truth about him.

"Winn" was studied for three of his undergraduate years by a team of psychologists directed by Henry A. Murray. Consistent with Murray's belief in consensual validation, Winn was studied by many people using their own special methods, all ultimately related into a consistent case formulation. Winn wrote an autobiography, took over a dozen tests, confronted himself on film, and opened his memory, moods, and fantasies to psychological scrutiny. This report draws on everything we know of Winn, with particular emphasis on a six-week study into the variations and levels of his moods.

Winn was originally picked for study after his self-report indicated a higher general level of happiness than other students. His happiness was confirmed by an exceptionally low score on the MMPI Depression scale and by consistently high hedonic levels during the intensive study of moods. Independent observers of his behavior ranked him at the top of the group on current happiness, while those who studied his life history considered it the happiest of the twenty we investigated. It might be possible to find more happy men, but these data seem sufficient to show that Winn can serve as a model of happiness until they are discovered.

Winn's Beliefs and Character

The language of psychology, like the language of everyday discourse, provides many words for misery and few for happiness. Our description of Winn suffers from this poverty, and we will have to resort too often to words that common use has so weakened and vulgarized that we distrust their communicative power. When we say that Winn had always had the admiration and love of a fine family; that he was satisfied with his background and his accomplishments; that he enjoyed life and expected to go to Heaven, we know that these words fail to convey the full meaning they had for Winn. Some readers will ask themselves, "What was he trying to hide?" We believe that he hid very little, and that what he did hide from himself was partly revealed in our tests and observations.

When we first met him in the fall of his sophomore year, Winn impressed us as tall, lean, handsome, and a good natural athlete. Busy with his own activities, he was cooperative with our research project but not overly involved with it. Although he was always friendly, an intrusive question could bring a quick flush of anger to his face and a good-natured but sharp retort. He had the manly ability to know his ground and stand on it.

If Winn created any negative reaction, it was a feeling that he was too good to be true, too assured of his own superiority, or too limited in his perspectives. He was generally tolerant and he detested dogmatism, but he had apparently not given much consideration to ways of others or seriously doubted that his current track in life was the best possible.

Winn had noticed his impact on girls and female teachers since early adolescence, and he was equally confident about his other qualities:

> I would regard my customary attitude as genial and confident. I am sure most people like and respect me. I am likewise sure some people feel me conceited and self-centered,

especially if they know me only slightly. My good friends find me understanding and interested in them. Many people have me marked for success.

Well aware of his own good fortune, he felt that "fortunate people should use some energy in making others happy," and hoped to help solve some of the world's problems of hunger, despotism, and poverty. "I would like to make some truly great contribution in the field of science, believing that this will, in the long run, help almost everyone." He esteemed "people engaged in the search for truth and also people who make life happy and good for others." He had tasted strong draughts of success but felt that American society overstressed competition, since "some people cannot stand the strain." For himself, though, competition was a stimulus: "I have always found that as soon as I attained something I had hoped for something else always attracted my ambition. . . . I have the potentialities to do something really worthwhile." His anticipated future included raising a good family, contributing to knowledge, helping people, and a substantial income.

Success was important to Winn, as was the innate satisfaction of work, but these were not exclusive goals. Although he occasionally felt that he should be more conscientious, he contented himself with a high but not spectacular grade record and reserved time for music, talk with friends, dating, and social life.

Winn had thus far been able to get and to do almost everything he wanted. Like most of the other happy people, he had a strong bent toward sociability, enjoyed his work but was not immersed in it, and was able to relax and enjoy both active play and the passive pleasures of food and rest.

Personal Philosophy

Winn's beliefs, although apparently strongly felt products of personal experience, sounded closer to the well-trodden utilitarian ways of J. S. Mill than to contemporary philosophies of anxiety and despair:

Central to my philosophy of life is happiness. I think I have the right to be happy and I want to make other people happy. . . . Often the two aspects are concomitant—I am happy when I have made someone else happy. . . . To be fully happy, I need to be loved, and thus I feel marriage is essential to my complete happiness. I want to be loved for what I do, to be sure, but mostly I want to be loved for what I am.

Gratification of the senses, when not immoderate, brings happiness. I do not mean only sexual gratification; pleasant and beautiful sights and sounds are included. My religion is essentially personal; I need not be a devout member of any religious sect to live a good life. . . . My concept of the after-life does not include a hell . . . because I feel everyone has the same right to heaven. . . . If one has lived a bad, unhappy life on earth, there are too many contributing factors to say he is bad and should be punished. In my after-life I will be happy and I will be with all those I loved while alive. Also in my after-life, infinite wisdom and knowledge will be available. I love knowledge, or truth; I find it beautiful.

I think the criterion for action is this: do what you will, just so long as you retain your self-respect. . . . This self-respect ties in with my happiness and with the happiness of loved ones, for to respect myself I cannot make them unhappy.

I have the right to my own philosophy and every person has the right to live his own life according to his own philosophy, so long as he does not interfere with my happiness. . . . My philosophy is not one that everyone can live by; it is not a universal one, it is mine. This is important; some people would not live good lives according to my philosophy, I imagine.

Winn was deeply aware that he was "society's child." Since "society has laid down some good rules for the protection of the human race," he did not care to oppose society. The tinge of rebellion in his philosophy, and his assertion of individuality, were mild compared to the philosophies of his peers. Winn was essentially in harmony with his family, his community, and his religion.

The only *passion* Winn strongly expressed was a "thirst" for knowledge. Pure thought provided some of his most intense experiences. He compared mathematics to music, in that each time he worked with a familiar set of equations it was like listening to a symphony that he knew well but in which new things appeared on each new hearing.

Winn's philosophical emphasis on happiness, the possibility that any admission of unhappiness would be an admission of shortcoming, raises a question as to the validity of his conscious descriptions. We believe that his desire to be good may have slightly biased the report of his moods, but careful examination of his life history, and of the deeper levels of his personality, show that Winn's happiness had a solid foundation.

Life History

Until he came to Harvard, Winn lived in "the middle of a middle class area" in a small Middle Western city. According to his autobiography, both of his parents were white, Protestant, and valedictorians. Winn's father worked his way through college during the depression, then taught school, served as Sunday School Superintendent, and took an active part in community affairs. When Winn was about ten years old his father, with a growing family, left teaching for more lucrative work in industry, and the family moved into an upper middle class social position. Winn's early life was bounded by his neighborhood and the farm of his mother's parents, but in this little territory Winn was top dog: the boss of younger brothers at home, the most talented student in schools, a leader in every activity. At college he continued near the top, no longer the most brilliant student, but still bright enough to major in physics, graduate with honors, compete for major fellowships, and enjoy college social life and the Harvard band. He might have realized that there were larger worlds to conquer—but except for science, in which he knew he was a novice, he was not troubled by ambitions beyond his present reach. Like his father, he had "done excellent jobs on all projects he entered," and that was enough.

Winn's family life was conventional—the middle class home, summer trips to Grandpa's farm, and the relatives' pride in his accomplishments could come out of stock fiction—but it was unusual in its happiness. His parents' harmony and affection reflected their continuing affectionate ties with their own families. Both were highly respected in their community. Neither parent had disappointed Winn and both had been "wonderful, kind, and understanding."

"Perhaps they do a little too much to see that I have the best in life, but they are firm with me when needs be." In Winn's training, "all of the vices and virtues were stressed, truth perhaps more than the others." Winn was punished by a spanking, by either parent, if he "got too far out of line." He attended Sunday School regularly.

Winn began his own life story with his uneventful birth, bottle feeding, and the foods he liked as a child. He was not an exceptionally happy baby—"I did cry a great deal, or so I am told"—but he was soon a self-confident child, "I was not retarded in learning to walk, and I was in general confident on my feet." A dislike for being alone began early and persisted, "solitariness was my one important fear." He did not want to "leave my Mommy" in the first two grades and frequently missed school. He still felt that he was not so adventurous as Billy, his next younger brother, nor so independent as Carl, the youngest. The combination of an exceptional interest in food and a marked dependence on adults, particularly his mother, indicated a lasting theme in Winn's life. Winn was still his family's and his society's child, with a philosophy of life that was "pretty much of a family philosophy" and "not independent of the way my society looks at things." Luckily for Winn's oral optimism, the world was still his oyster, and, as we will see when we reach his Rorschach, his breast of chicken, ice cream, and lemon meringue pie as well.

Another theme began with his first memory, the birth of his brother Billy when he was two and a half years old:

> I was playing outside with a ball and a stick. It was a rather dark, cloudy, November day, and my father came out of the house (Billy was born at home) and told me I had a little brother. This did not "shake me up" at all, and I went inside to see my new brother. I was not impressed and went back outside to play ball.

Given Winn's close tie to his mother, it is likely that he was impressed by this intruder. In Winn's loving but controlled family it is probable that open anger about Billy and his claims on their mother was not encouraged. Minor "accidental" injuries to Billy punctuated the next several years of Winn's history and continued to find reflections in Winn's projective tests.

Winn's tie with his mother might have made trouble later, but the birth of Billy, and later of Carl, seemed to shake him up, in spite of his negation, and to force him to work free. His dependency was overcome and his self-control established early in life. He became quite adept in dealing comfortably with peers and potential rivals. This pattern was long established and by the time he was in high school "I quarreled seldom (usually my word was *law!*) and was not too moody."

An element of over-control, however, ran through Winn's history. His steady girl, for example, accused him of never acting on impulse. His brother, Billy, unlike Winn, was a "wild" boy, often hurt in accidents, and his example may have pushed Winn to caution. Also, Winn recalled that he had acted on impulse and hurt himself. Once he fell down stairs and bent his nose. Once he ran into a fence and cut his jaw. Neither of these defects was apparent to the observer, but to Winn, who had few, any defect made a difference.

From childhood on Winn had a varied but not exceptionally intense fantasy life. He was troubled by the quick vividness of his fantasies, so unlike the restrained quality of his everyday thought. For a while he played with a fantasy of being a kind of turtle, possibly in reponse to feelings of holding himself in check. Until the age of sixteen he occasionally had a dream of being carried off his feet by a tornado, probably a fear of what would happen if his impulses were allowed expression. This dream was always the same, and eventually he feared it enough to permanently refuse sulfa drugs, which seemed to cause it.

Winn's school history was filled with steady achievement, prizes, adulation, and affection from teachers. He was "president of everything," and his best friend was a boy who "usually ran against me for office, and was always very gracious when he lost." Winn had many playmates when he was little. When he entered high school he limited himself to a few intimate friendships, though his activities produced many casual ones. An early admiration for athletes had given way, by junior high school, to a desire to be a professional musician. Although Winn was regarded as a "near-prodigy," he disliked his music teacher and decided by ninth grade to be a scientist, a career that embodied the qualities he most admired—beauty, truth, dignity, and intelligence. A theme in his fantasies became, and continued to be throughout college, somehow combining these goals with making money. At the end of high school these fantasies reached preliminary fruition when Winn won a large Harvard scholarship.

Winn's sexual activities were not unusual—some mutual fondling in preadolescence, a bit of sexual display with other boys, spin-the-bottle and post-office in early adolescence, quickly settling to steady dates with a girl whose background was like his own. He received sex instruction from his parents, beginning with his mother's explanation of pregnancy when he was eight and ending with his father's discussion of masturbation when he was thirteen. His sexual fantasies were about girls he knew and involved ordinary sexual play. He had not engaged in intercourse at the time we knew him, and he had never picked up girls. It would be hard to regard either Winn's behavior or his fantasies as wild, yet he reported:

> I've got a pretty good imagination and will run hog-wild and crazy sometimes so that what I do isn't—never is it—well, almost never—a reflection of some of the wild things that go on within.

In his behavior, on the other hand, he felt:

> I have been pretty conventional. The first son . . . always make your parents proud of you. . . . Very little rebellion at all really.

His sexual fantasies from thirteen to sixteen concerned romantic conquests and erotic adventures. But from sixteen on he had even stronger, more frequent fantasies of a satisfying, harmonious, and enduring marriage that would produce a large, happy family. His fantasies were almost as monogamous, faithful, and mature as his behavior.

The marriage Winn fantasied for himself was very close to the one that nurtured him. Winn's innocent narcissism might have played some part in this —he was not critical of the family that produced his own character—but more important was love for his parents and identification with his admired father. Winn, as a little boy, listened in wonder to his father's series of bedtime stories about an original mock-heroic character. Later, he watched his father become a community leader while remaining a loving parent. In school he was given special attention by teachers who liked his father. The fact that his college age fantasies had already moved beyond adolescent identity turmoil and on to intimacy and family life was probably due to the model provided by his father's exemplary role in his family and community.

Case Summary

Every source of data seems to confirm Winn's happiness and to show consistent themes in his character. Other men we studied surpassed Winn in depth and extent of social awareness, in richness of personality, in dedication to particular goals, or in other valued characteristics. But none equalled him in genuine, consistent zest and happiness.

What generated and sustained Winn's happiness? Part of the explanation seems rooted in his background and his gifts. Favored with a loving family that was respected in its community, fostered growth, and provided worthy and approachable models; possessed of sufficient means and opportunities; and gifted in face, form, intellect, health, and talent, Winn was consistently successful in his enterprises and his relationships. To the degree that the future is his responsibility this success seems likely to continue.

But Winn can also be seen as more than the sum of his background and his talents. His current personality showed a steadfast optimism, supported by a lively, active orientation toward the world, love of human contact, and balanced, mature judgment. We found only minor flaws in his general well-being, the main ones being an overly strong barrier between rationality and impulse and too much fear of community disapproval. But Winn's successes were not crass or calculating, and one of the sources of his happiness was reasonable willingness to accept limitations, to curb any inclinations toward narcissistic insatiability he may have had, and to tread the middle road between excess and deprivation with caution, intelligence, and due regard for his fellow man.

General Characteristics of Happy and Unhappy Men

We noted that Winn was studied as part of a general investigation of mood and personality. The contrasts between the happy and unhappy men suggest some general characteristics of happiness. The happy men possessed self-esteem and confidence. They were successful and satisfied in interpersonal relations. They showed ego-strength and a gratifying sense of identity. Their lives had organization, purpose, and the necessary mastery of themselves to attain their goals. The less happy men were pessimistic in their expectations and lower in self-esteem and self-confidence. More unsuccessful with their interpersonal relations, with evidence of isolation, anxiety, and guilt, they showed little sense of satisfying ego-identity. They felt inferior in their academic performance and their lives lacked continuity and purpose.

No single developmental success or trauma seems to account for happiness or unhappiness. Rather, multiple sources are found in the cumulative series of an individual's long-term life experiences. Important bases for self-esteem had been impaired in the lives of the unhappy men. Their damaged identities hampered their potential for intimacy and satisfying commitment. Unfavorable outcomes of several developmental crises had left the unhappy men prone to self-limitation, frustration, and disappointment. Nor could one source account for the success of the well-adjusted, social extroverts such as Winn. These men were not of a single pattern, but did generally come from warm, supportive home environments that were conducive to growth and responsibility. Though there were exceptions, developmental transitions were generally smooth and residual conflicts subdued. Important needs had not become overly checked by disturbing affect. They were able to make positive identifications with respected, approachable role models and these had in turn favored the establishment of a worthwhile sense of self.

Lest our readers conclude that this is a simple and unqualified paean to happiness, let us make our position clear. We hold that it is desirable that people be happy—it is generally superior to misery. But happiness can also be constricting. There was much to admire and respect in the lives of some of the more complicated and less happy men.

This marks the end of the material that is directly quoted from the Ricks and Wessman article.

DISTINGUISHING CHARACTERISTICS

The case of Winn exemplifies one of the distinguishing characteristics of phenomenology, namely, the study of mental health and psychological growth. The discussion here focuses on this and several other characteristics that set phenomenology apart from the other approaches to abnormality. The discussion is intended to answer the question "What is phenomenology?"

Focus on Experience and Perception

Phenomenology is based on a distinction between appearance and reality—between subjective experience and objective reality—and this distinction dates back to Plato. In his allegory of the cave, Plato suggested that we perceive sensory images of the world rather than the world itself. He likened our perception of the world through sense organs to that of a man who is bound in a cave so that he sees only the shadows of people who walk by and never sees the people themselves. In this manner, the distinction between appearance (the shadow on the cave wall, sensory images, subjective experience) and reality (things apart from their appearance) was introduced into Western thought.

One of the more influential statements on the distinction between appearance and reality was provided by the late eighteenth century philosopher Immanuel Kant. Kant called the world of appearance *phenomena,* and he called things as they are apart from appearance *noumena.* The term *phenomenology* refers to the study of phenomena, that is, to the study of appearances, subjective perceptions, and experience.

Phenomenology rejects the position that behavior can be understood as a consequence of objectively defined, environmental stimuli. Instead, phenomenology proposes as its basic tenet a model in which meaningful behaviors are consequences of a person's unique perception of environmental and internal stimuli. For example, suppose that two men walking along a street encounter a woman. One man perceives the woman to be attractive and hence observes her closely as she walks by; the other man perceives the woman as unattractive and hence is less observant of her. The same stimulus (e.g., the woman) can thus evoke different behaviors, depending on individual perceptions and experiences of that stimulus.

Phenomenology is the study of individual differences in the perception of other people and environmental stimuli as well as the study of conscious experience. Research topics include issues such as the role of self-perception (self-concept) in mental health and in psychological disturbance, perceptions of each other in disturbed and in nondisturbed marriages, and the role of conscious experience in abnormal behavior.

The manner in which phenomenologists focus on perceptions and experience is exemplified in Carl Rogers's client-centered therapy. Rogers distinguished between an internal and an external frame of reference. Attending to the internal frame of reference means that the therapist is trying to understand the world as the client perceives it; attending to the external frame of reference means that the therapist is trying to help the client perceive the world in a more objective manner. For example, suppose an individual were to declare in therapy: "I am useless because everything I do is a failure." Albert Ellis, who is not a phenomenologist, would adopt an external frame of reference to show the client that his feelings of worthlessness are irrational; that is, the fact that a person may lack certain skills does not mean that he is worthless but may mean that he should practice those skills to improve them. In contrast, Rogers would adopt an internal frame of reference and hence would react to the client's declaration by expressing the client's feelings more clearly. For example, Rogers might say, "It bothers you that you see yourself as unable to do certain things." Precisely because phenomenology focuses on experiences as they are perceived and understood by clients, people tend to find phenomenology meaningful to their own lives. *To adopt an internal frame of reference is to use the language of experience.*

To summarize, one characteristic that sets phenomenology apart from the other approaches to abnormality is its focus on the world as it appears to individuals. This means that phenomenologists study perceptions of environmental stimuli and that they study conscious experience. It also means that phenomenologists adopt an internal frame of reference and that they use the language of experience.

Emphasis on the Here and Now

Phenomenology is similar to psychoanalysis in that both approaches study the interplay of mental forces (psychodynamics) that contribute to personality and to abnormal behavior. There exists, however, an important difference in the extent to which the two approaches focus on conscious versus unconscious experiences. In contrast to the psychoanalytic focus on childhood experiences as unconscious determinants of adult behavior, phenomenologists focus much more on the study of current interpersonal behavior and the "here and now" of conscious experience. For example, an adult who has the annoying habit of interrupting others' speech may do so as a defense against an unconscious fear of rejection. The phenomenologist would study the adult's behavior, its interpersonal consequences, and its defensive characteristics, but compared to the psychoanalyst, the phenomenologist is less likely to study childhood experiences that may have produced the adult's sensitivity to rejection. Thus, phenomenology is unique in the extent to which it focuses on the study of current ("here and now") experiences.

Adoption of Naturalism and the Motive of Higher Striving

People are willing to endure considerable discomfort in their strivings for love, success, and knowledge. Freud held that these higher strivings should be understood in terms of a drive to release libidinal (sexual) energy. (See Chapter 6.) Learning theories generally maintain that these higher strivings are learned, or secondary, drives in contrast to the innate drives of hunger, thirst, sex, and the motive to avoid pain and anxiety. (See Chapter 7.) In contrast to these views, phenomenology posits a basic drive for human growth and psychological development. Rogers (1951), for example, calls this drive for human growth *self-actualization.* Thus, phenomenology differs from psychoanalysis and most learning theories in its postulate of a self-actualization motive to account for higher strivings.

Phenomenology's postulate of a self-actualization drive is associated with a naturalistic philosophy of human nature (see, e.g., Maslow, 1959; May, 1967). Under naturalism, there are two basic aspects of human nature, called *immanence* and *transcendence.* There is evidence that people are immanent in (part of) a natural and social order, and there is evidence that people can transcend both the natural and the social order. Evidence of immanence in the biophysical world includes one's own biological composition and the consequent need for inorganic substances such as water, oxygen, and food. The body obeys the laws of biology, chemistry, and physics. Evidence of immanence in the social order includes the facts that one's behavior, thinking, self-concept, and experiences are influenced considerably by one's culture, learning experiences, and significant others. People usually behave in accordance with the principles of psychology. Immanence, however, is only one of the two aspects of human nature, the other being transcendence. Evidence that people can transcend the biophysical order includes the human ability to become conscious of that world, to develop symbols to describe it, and to think about past and future biophysical events. Consciousness of the biophysical world serves as evidence of transcendence of that world in the sense that in memory and in awareness we can transcend our biophysical existence at a particular place at a particular time. Moreover, evidence that people can transcend the social order includes self-consciousness of oneself as a unique entity—the awareness that one is different from others and that one's behavior is affected by others. In this awareness, we can set ourselves apart from the social-cultural order and hence "transcend" it. (See Figure 8-1.)

Some phenomenologists maintain that this dual nature of immanence and transcendence is an ontological conflict that creates ontological anxiety (anxiety related to the nature of the human condition). This anxiety motivates the individual to solve the ontological conflict (human dilemma) by becoming either more immanent or more transcendent—the individual either strives for greater self-awareness or attempts to unite with the biophysical and cultural order. Not all phenomenologists, however, posit the existence of ontological anxiety. Instead, many simply posit a drive for psychological growth.

As a philosophy of human nature, naturalism is distinguished from dualism and from materialism. *Dualism* is a philosophical doctrine that posits a physical substance to account for immanence and a spiritual substance to account for transcendence. The philosophical concept of substance precludes causality across substances; under dualism, then, the mind and body are held to function independently of one another. *Materialism* is a philosophical doctrine that attempts to explain both the biological and psychological aspects of human nature in terms of a single substance. In contrast to these two philosophies, *naturalism* posits no substance at all but instead adopts the position that there is evidence that people are both immanent in, and transcendent of, the natural order.

May (1967), Rogers (1951), and Maslow (1954) are three influential phenomenologists whose theories suggest a naturalistic philosophy of human nature. May (1967) describes our dual nature as subject and object, rather than as transcendent and immanent, and he refers to the ontological conflict as the human dilemma. Rogers's (1951) concept of self-actualization through self-awareness is

Figure 8-1
The philosophy of naturalism maintains that there are two aspects to human nature, called immanence and transcendence.

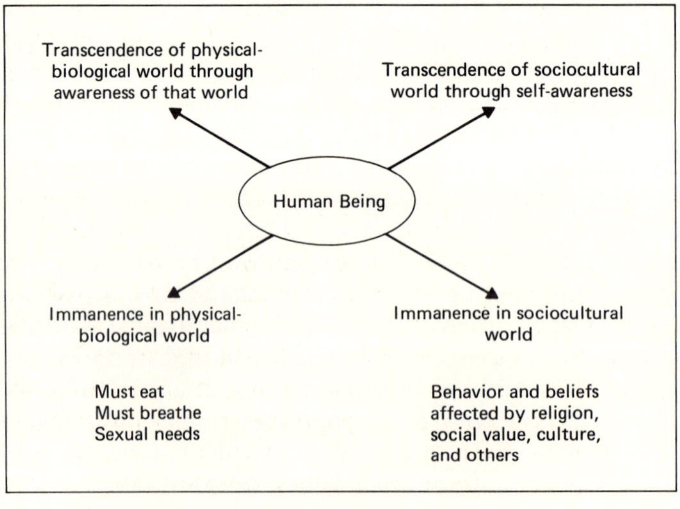

essentially the concept of transcendence. Moreover, naturalistic philosophy is implicit in Maslow's (1954) theory of human strivings.

In summary, one way in which phenomenology differs from the other approaches in this book is that it postulates a motive of higher strivings, or self-actualization. Moreover, the postulate of a motive of higher strivings usually has been made within the framework of a naturalistic philosophy of human nature. This means that a motive of higher striving is maintained to be as fundamental to human nature as are the biological motives of thirst, hunger, and sex.

Abnormality as the Absence of Mental Health

Phenomenologists typically consider abnormality to be the absence of psychological growth. In fact, some phenomenologists regard anything less than full self-actualization of one's potential as cause for psychological concern. For example, the husband and wife who get along sufficiently well to raise a family, but whose relationship is characterized by a lack of communication, have not fully self-actualized even though they are not usually anxious or otherwise exhibiting so-called abnormal behaviors. Thus, in many phenomenological theories, the criterion for judging abnormality is a comparision between what an individual is and what that individual can become.

Affirmation of Humanistic Values

Phenomenology is also an attitude toward people, toward the activity of studying people, and toward the activity of psychotherapy (May, 1967). This attitude has been called *humanistic* because it encompasses a sense of respect and dignity for each individual as a unique person. Although phenomenologists are not the only group of behavioral scientists who endorse humanistic attitudes toward other people, no other group has expended as much energy elucidating and reaffirming the need to remember that psychologists study people and not chemicals or cells.

Unfortunately, statements of phenomenological attitudes have sometimes been confused as statements of possible fact, and this confusion has led to some fruitless debates. For example, many phenomenologists maintain that each individual is unique and, based on this view, some have objected to the classification of abnormal behavior as "pigeon-holing" people rather than dealing with each individual's uniqueness. As a statement of possible fact, it is unclear what the expression "Each individual is unique" means. People obviously behave in different ways, and no competent scientist contests this fact. Rather, the experimental scientist maintains that individual differences in behavior are lawful so that through experimental research we can discover general laws of behavior to explain why people behave in different ways. The phenomenologist does not contest that behavior is lawful (he does not maintain, for example, that behavior is random). Thus, there is agreement on the basic issues that people differ in their behavior and these differences are not random and hence are lawful. What, then, really is being contested by phenomenologists when they state that each individual is unique? In our view, what is often at issue is the attitude we adopt toward the basic facts rather than the facts themselves. The phenomenologist senses that classifying or labeling people is often accompanied by an attitude that the person is some type of object or thing, and he says things like "Each individual is unique" in order to replace the objective attitude with one that reaffirms the essential worth of each individual.

Summary

In summary, phenomenology is an attitude, a philosophy, and a science. The phenomenological attitude is that of respect and dignity for the individual person. As a philosophy, phenomenology is associated with the view that we perceive sensory impressions of stimuli rather than stimuli themselves. Phenomenology is also associated with a naturalistic philosophy of human nature. As a science, phenomenology is concerned with the study of perceptions and conscious content. A basic tenet of phenomenological psychology is that behavior is a function of individual perceptions and experiences of stimuli—that is, to understand the effects of a stimulus on behavior, it is first necessary to understand how the individual perceives the stimulus.

PHENOMENOLOGICAL THEORIES

Carl Rogers's Self-actualization Theory

Few theorists have had as much impact on contemporary views of human development as has Carl Rogers. Rogers's (1947, 1959, 1961) self-actualization theory is discussed here. The therapy based on his theory, termed *client-centered therapy,* will be discussed later in this chapter.

Rogers's theory of emotional growth and psychological development hypothesizes that "the organism has one basic tendency and striving—to actualize, maintain, and enhance the experiencing organism" (1951, p. 487). This actualizing tendency includes a tendency to maintain oneself—to assimilate food, to behave defensively in the face of threat—and a tendency to enhance oneself—to move in the direction of gradual psychological growth. Another basic proposition is that "as experiences occur in the life of the individual, they are either (a) symbolized, perceived, and organized into some relationship to the self; (b) ignored because there is no perceived relationship to self-structure; (c) denied symbolization, or given a distorted symbolization, because the experience is inconsistent with the structure of the self" (1951, p. 503). Psychological growth occurs when experience is symbolized, perceived, and organized into the self-structure. Psychological growth is stunted, and abnormality may result, when experience is denied symbolization or is given a distorted symbolization.

The Rogerian theory of emotional growth postulates that experiences are likely to be integrated into self-concept only if they fulfill what Rogers calls "the conditions of worth"—that is, only if they can be positively regarded by the individual. Every individual is assumed to have a need for positive regard of the self. In other words, there are certain experiences that an individual considers worthy of becoming part of his self-concept (e.g., *I am in love; I am a good athlete*), and other experiences that cannot be positively regarded (e.g., *I always fail at academic tasks; Everybody seems to dislike me*). As the individual comes to value certain experiences more than others, experiences perceived as threatening to the self are denied or are symbolized in a distorted fashion. Threat occurs when experiences are perceived as incongruent with the self-structure. "Defense" in the form of denial or distortion is the response to threat, the goal of defense being the maintenance of the self-structure by reducing the awareness of the threat, but not the threat itself. By denial, Rogers means that experiences inconsistent with the self-concept are ignored; for example, the child whose concept of self is that of one who is grateful to his parents may organically experience the physiological changes that accompany anger toward his parents, but his conscious self will likely prevent these experiences from being symbolized and hence perceived; consequently, the child's self-concept is maintained and is *not* changed from *I am grateful to my parents* to *I am resentful of my parents' interference.* By distortion, Rogers means that experiences inconsistent with the self-concept are inaccurately symbolized so that they are no longer contradictory to the self-structure; for example, a child might symbolize the physiological accompaniments of anger toward his parents as a bad headache. Excessive denial or distortion of experiences precludes emotional growth (self-actualization) because it is an effort to maintain one's current self-structure at the expense of becoming self-aware of one's true experiences.

For Rogers, the defenses of denial and distortion are the defining attributes of maladjustment. Conscious control becomes more difficult as the individual strives to satisfy needs that are not consciously admitted and to react to experiences that are denied by the conscious self. Anxiety occurs under these circumstances, and the individual is characterized as in a state of disharmony between self-structure and actual experiences. By *disharmony* Rogers means that the individual's experience is not organized into a consistent, compatible gestalt but, instead, is denied or distorted. These feelings were denied only because they were threatening to the self; thus the critical task for a Rogerian therapist is to create a climate of unconditional positive regard for the client in which denied feelings will no longer be perceived as threatening. The goal is for the client to achieve a reorganization of self that allows for continued self-actualization; that is, the goal is to help the client become himself.

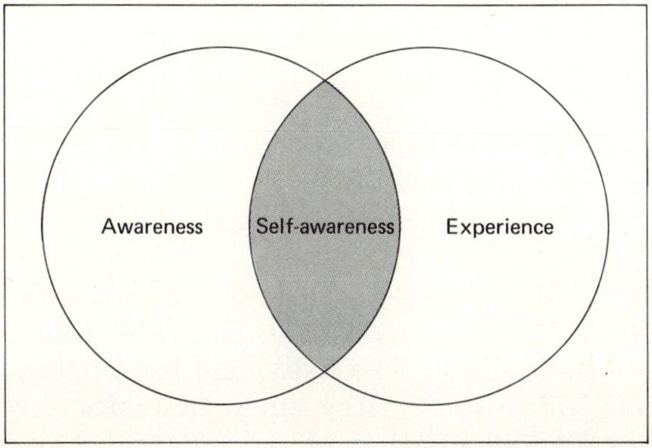

Figure 8-2
Rogers's self theory maintains that psychological abnormality results from a disharmony between experience and one's awareness of one's experience. The less the overlap between awareness and experience, the greater is the degree of maladjustment, and the less is the degree of self-actualization.

Figure 8-2 provides a brief summary of Rogers's theory of abnormality. The smaller the overlap between awareness and experience, the lesser is the degree of self-actualization and psychological health.

R. D. Laing: Alienation and Human Potential

According to Laing (1967), behavior is a function of experience, and the purpose of psychology is to understand the relations between experience and behavior. But instead of providing this understanding, Laing believes that psychologists have depersonalized the individual by treating him as an *object* of study, as something to be labeled and pigeonholed, rather than as a *subject* of experience. "But just as Kierkegaard remarked that one will never find consciousness by looking down a microscope at brain cells or anything else, so one will never find persons by studying persons as though they were only objects" (Laing, 1967, p. 8). This depersonalization of man by science is seen as part of a more general depersonalization imposed by contemporary society. Our social lives are frauds. We never *meet* one another but keep masks and games between us. We always pretend. And this pretending, this shell of humanity, is what we call *normal.*

Laing is bitter toward society's concept of normality: "What we call 'normal' is a product of repression, denial, splitting, projection, introjection, and other forms of destructive action on experience" (1967, p. 11), and "Normal men have killed perhaps 100,000,000 of their fellow normal men in the last fifty years" (1967, p.12). In this view, what we call normal are acceptable forms of alienation and what we call abnormal are statistically unusual forms of alienation. Laing dares us to compare modern man who plays games, denies his own experience, and destroys others, to man's potential as an experiencing, loving being. Viewed in terms of human potential, man is an echo of himself.

Laing's major contribution to abnormal psychology is his description of the schizophrenic experience. He regards the superficially "crazy" behavior of the schizophrenic as " . . . a special strategy adopted by the individual in order to live in an unlivable situation" (1967, p. 79). Seen as an object, the schizophrenic has an illness and this illness is the root of his problem. Seen as an experiencing subject by Laing, the individual labeled schizophrenic has had his humanity violated by family and society and has found it necessary to defend himself by playing the game of craziness. The schizophrenic has rejected the outer world of ordinary relations because it is too terrifying and has entered instead the "inner" world of experience. The inner and outer worlds are parts of us all, but we "normals" have been conditioned to regard the outer world as healthy and the inner world as deviant. We have denied the inner world of seeing and hearing; we are alienated from it; however, the schizophrenic has escaped to explore it. He may have lost his way in exploring this inner world, but he has also learned something about human experience.

Abraham Maslow: The Hierarchy of Human Needs

Abraham Maslow's (1954, 1962) theory of human motivation postulates a hierarchical ordering of basic needs. The individual has important physiological needs such as eating, homeostasis, sleep, and sexual release. When these needs are unfulfilled, they tend to be prepotent and affect much of our behavior and thought. For example, a sleepless soldier is likely to fantasize about sleep and be concerned with thoughts about when sleep may be possible. When the physiological needs are fulfilled, the safety needs emerge. These needs include security, stability, dependency, and freedom from fear and anxiety. Frustration of these needs is likely to be perceived as a threat to survival. Maslow has hypothesized that many (but by no means all) neurotic individuals have not satisfied their need for safety:

> Some neurotic adults in our society are, in many ways, like the unsafe child in their desire for safety, although in the former it takes on a somewhat special appearance. Their reaction is often to unknown, psychological dangers in a world that is perceived to be hostile, overwhelming, and threatening. Such a person behaves as if a great catastrophe were almost always impending, i.e., he is usually responding as if to an emergency. His safety needs often find specific expression in a search for a protector, or a stronger person on whom he may depend, perhaps a Fuehrer. [1954, p. 42]

PHENOMENOLOGICAL ASSESSMENT

Phenomenological assessment techniques measure a subject's perception of his own interpersonal behavior and experience. The Q-sort technique, developed by Hartley (1951) and Stephenson (1953), is probably the most widely used phenomenological technique. This technique requires the subject to sort statements into piles from those that are least like oneself to those that are most like oneself (Butler & Haigh, 1954). The subject then repeats the sorting procedure for piles that range from least to most like the person he would like to be. Examples of the items to be sorted are: "I am a submissive person"; "I am likable"; and "I am afraid of a full-fledged disagreement with a person." This procedure has been used to assess the effectiveness of therapy based on Carl Rogers's theory and to assess self-concept in research studies. A variety of scoring techniques are available (see Rogers & Dymond, 1954).

Another phenomenological assessment technique is the Interpersonal Perception Method (IPM). As developed by Laing, Phillipson, and Lee (1966), this technique assesses the quality of dyadic relationships. Let Peter and Paul be two friends—the IPM would provide an assessment of Peter's view of himself, Peter's view of Paul, Paul's view of himself, and Paul's view of Peter. Dyadic relationships are assessed in terms of six categories: (1) interdependence and autonomy; (2) warm concern and support; (3) disparagement and disappointment; (4) flight/fight; (5) contradiction and confusion; and (6) extreme denial or confusion. An example of a research use of this technique is provided on page 255.

PHENOMENOLOGICAL TREATMENTS

In general, phenomenological treatments focus on the client's current feelings and dilemmas, with emphasis on self-concept and interpersonal behavior. This focus contrasts sharply with verbal insight therapies that explore childhood experiences and involve deep-level interpretations.

Client-Centered Therapy

Carl Rogers has pioneered a system of psychological counseling that has been variously termed *nondirective, client-centered,* and *Rogerian.* As noted, Rogers conceptualizes maladjustment as an incongruence between the individual's conditions (standards) of self-worth and his experience. Accordingly, the goals of client-centered therapy are to increase the client's unconditional acceptance of himself and to help the client become himself by integrating experiences with self-concept.

If the client's unconditional self-regard is to be enhanced, the therapist must unconditionally accept the client and treat him with respect and warmth. By "unconditional positive regard," Rogers means that therapist approval of the client as a person does not depend on the client's morality, feelings, or behavior. Only in a context of unconditional acceptance is the client likely to feel sufficiently comfortable to express denied feelings. Thus Rogers considers therapist attitudes toward the client critical for a successful outcome:

> The primary point of importance here is the attitude held by the counselor toward the worth and the significance of the individual. How do we look upon others? Do we see each person as having worth and dignity in his own right? If we do hold this point of view at the verbal level, to what extent is it operationally evident at the behavioral level? [Rogers, 1965, p. 20]

Client-centered therapists are nondirective in that they allow the client to explore his feelings as he desires and do not provide "deep"-level interpretations of unconscious content. The therapist's role is that of clarifying the client's expressed feelings, thereby allowing the client to understand better his own dilemmas and to work toward his own resolution. In clarifying the client's feelings, the therapist attempts to provide interpretations that are neither so obvious to the client that they appear uninformative nor so "deep" that they appear confusing. Rather, the therapist interprets at the "edge" of the client's awareness; this means that the therapist describes the client's expressed feelings in a manner that will be perceived as meaningful by the client.

The process of client-centered therapy has been captured well by Snyder's (1947) transcribed interviews with Robert Winslow Smith. Winslow had sought help because he felt he worried too often about insignificant matters. In the following interview, the first part of Winslow's fourteenth interview with Snyder, the therapist tries to help the client clarify his feelings concerning sex and his perceptions of how others view his attitudes toward sex.[2,3]

(The client started with a discussion of the date he had had the previous Friday. On the whole, it went off rather well and he was quite satisfied; except for the dancing, it had been pleasant. He felt that the dancing was different from the type he had been used to at home. He then began discussion of the second of the three phases of his treatment, the matter of sexual adjustment.)

[2] The responses of the counselor and the subject are designated C and S, respectively.

[3] From W. U. Snyder, The case of Robert Winslow Smith. In W. U. Snyder, Editor, *Casebook of Nondirective Counseling,* pp. 129–203. Boston: Houghton Mifflin Co., 1947. Printed by permission of author and publisher.

S201. Just one other thing. I don't know what. If I had a measuring stick that I could compare my actions to, I'd get along a lot better. I haven't any.

C201. M-hm. You want to carry that a little farther?

S202. Well, if I could tell how many friends I should have and what type of friends. What type of friendships? How should I act under certain conditions? That's the principal thing.

C202. You feel you're looking for some sort of standard.

S203. Yes, I'm trying to set up my own standards by watching other people who I believe are correct.

C203. You're more or less unsure about what's the best form of behavior.

S204. Yes, just where and when certain things would apply or were correct and when they were not.

C204. M-hm. You feel that there are specific problems which worry you in this sense.

S205. Yes, not anything concerned with the table but with general conduct at social functions and just to find out. You hear so much about sex life, to put it bluntly. What is a normal sex life? In the first place I don't *understand* the whole thing.

C205.* M-hm. You want to carry that farther?

S206. I don't know what a normal sex life would be. Of course, it's plainly because I never had any contact at home with kids, either boys or girls, in my class. I drew behind my wall of superiority and sat at home. The last year I went to dances. But I never knew what to do. I used several petting techniques. Sometimes I kissed. But I never knew what to do after I kissed her.

C206. M-hm.

S207. That's as far as I ever got.

C207. You feel possibly it wasn't as far as some people would go.

S208. It was as far as I wanted to go. It seems when I went with a girl she considered me a safe date. Girls went with me with their parents' fullest consent. "Winslow is a good boy. You needn't worry," or "Bring her home any time." I had heard a lot of dirty anecdotes about things that happened but I could never picture any of our group being as low and as smutty as that. But the girls didn't say anything about it. The other kids just considered me slightly a drip because I never went any farther than just kissing a girl.

C208. You were somewhat looked down upon because of your standards.

S209. Yes, I had my own ideas of social conduct and how I should behave. I used to take pride in thinking that I didn't do anything untoward. I wasn't ashamed of anything I had done. Yet everyone else in the school seemed, to be very blunt, always "on the make." Maybe I'm wrong. Maybe I *am* a drip. But I'm happy that way.

C209. You feel there's a marked difference between your own standards and those of the rest of the people. Some of the things they suggested as having happened were disgusting or smutty.

S210. Disgusting isn't the word for it. Spending three hours on a country road with a girl would be more than my gullet could stand. There'd be a distinct aversion to it. I could never look anyone in the eye again. Furthermore, I could never look any girl in the eye again. I believe you know what I mean. I'm no 'goody-goody.' Maybe I'm just undersexed.

C210. You feel it's disgusting or unclean to have sex relations of any kind.

S211. Yes. It seems to lower oneself. It lowers one practically down to the level of an animal.

* This is a good nondirective lead. The client has not expressed much regarding his feelings about sex, although he has indicated that he is puzzled.

C211. M-hm.

S212. To go as far as that!

C212. People have to be pretty cheap to go that far.

S213. *Very* cheap! People thought I was very much of a droop because I wouldn't come along.

C213. M-hm. You feel sex behavior is strictly an animal performance.

S214. Yes, plainly. It might be all right if found in its proper place—in the home.

Family Therapy

Family therapy refers to many different treatment approaches, the only common element being the concurrent treatment of two or more family members. Psychoanalytic, behavioral, and phenomenologically oriented family therapists may focus on family members as individuals, as when the therapist meets separately with each family member, or they may focus on the family as a social unit, as when the therapist meets with several family members at the same time. Phenomenological treatment of the family as a unit is called *conjoint family therapy.* In this form of treatment, the family is viewed as a social system in which one component of the system cannot be damaged without affecting other components (Napier, 1972). Jackson's (1957) concept of family homeostasis exemplifies one specific way in which the family has been conceptualized as a gestalt. This concept implies that each family strives to achieve a complex balance of relationships that satisfies the needs of individual members (see Jackson, 1957; Satir, 1967). An imbalance in part of the system will affect the system as a whole and cause efforts to restore balance. Moreover, considerable psychological energy may be expended by members to restore a precarious balance. For example, Mary is an insecure person who feels worthless and fears that others will reject her. She defends against these feelings through overindulging those she loves. Her husband Joe is afraid to be tender, considering displays of affection unmasculine and a sign of weakness. Joe's fear only exacerbates Mary's insecurity and she reacts by desiring a child to cement their marriage. As Johnny grows up, Mary indulges in his every whim out of fear that her own child will reject her if she behaves otherwise. In this example, Johnny's immature behavior comes to serve a family function—he satisfies Mary's need to be overindulgent and Joe's need not to display affection. A functional balance is achieved, but later when Johnny's immaturity comes to the attention of school authorities, Mary and Joe are confronted by the fact that Johnny's behavior is not functional outside the family. Another possible threat to family balance would occur if Joe required hospitalization for an operation. Under these circumstances, Mary's fear of losing Joe would probably become stronger and result in even greater overindulgence of Johnny's demands. Of course, this example illustrates only one of many ways in which complex family relationships achieve balance and function as a gestalt.

Family therapists believe that psychological problems in children are often related to family problems. Support for this hypothesis is found in the many cases of children referred for therapy after a parent's absence or illness. In such cases it seems reasonable for the therapist to meet with one or both parents rather than meet only with the child. Phenomenologically oriented family therapists focus on the interpersonal behavior of the husband and wife: their inability to communicate deep fears about themselves, the manner in which their behavior toward one another creates undue stress, their unadaptive reactions to problems, and so on.

Although children's problems are often related to family problems, an inflexible reliance on family therapy is not recommended by the present authors. Children can incur psychological problems even in the "healthiest" of families, as in cases in which a child has difficulty finding acceptance from peers. Moreover, changing the behavior of a family is sometimes impractical and exceedingly difficult to accomplish. The father or mother may refuse to cooperate, and either parent may have problems that are much more serious and difficult to change than the unadaptive behavior observed in the child. When a child's problem seems related to family problems, but family therapy is impractical, some behaviorally oriented therapists attempt to teach the child a discrimination between home and nonhome situations. For example, a teacher might be trained to reinforce (reward) Johnny when he engages in specified "mature" behaviors and to ignore or punish him when he engages in specified immature behavior. Johnny would be explicitly told on many occasions that his teacher treats him differently than do his parents, and that school is different from home. The underlying rationale is that the child's family problems are unresolvable, but that the child can be taught to learn to adapt to school, in the hope that at least one source of satisfaction for the child can be created.

To conclude, we advocate a flexible approach to family therapy that involves assessing both the extent to which the child's problems reflect family problems and the practicality of family treatment for each particular case. The student interested in reading further on family therapy can consult Virginia Satir's (1967) book entitled *Conjoint Family Therapy.*

Encounter Groups

Educational and therapeutic groups have become increasingly popular during the last decade. Chapter 9 provides a discussion of T-groups, which are educationally oriented and intended for normal individuals who want to learn more about themselves, how others perceive them, and how to relate to others in a more meaningful manner. On the other hand, encounter groups vary considerably in format and philosophy—the range is from T-groups to nude encounter groups. Marathon groups involve two co-leaders and the group runs for 24 to 72 continuous hours.

Unfortunately, groups have attracted what May (1960) calls the "lunatic fringe," and as a result of incompetent, emotionally destructive leadership, some participants in some groups have been unable to cope with the experience. Yalom and Lieberman (1971) have reported a suicide that apparently resulted from an encounter group experience. If conducted by a professionally competent leader who does not allow group pressure to focus unmercifully on particular individuals, encounter groups can be rewarding. But one must be careful to determine the credentials of the group leader(s) and to check with previous participants before joining an encounter group.

A group meeting at a residential drug treatment center in New York City. (Photo by Rene Burri; Magnum Photos, Inc.)

Logotherapy

Although Rogers and Maslow have conceptualized man as striving toward self-actualization, this striving is not phenomenologically present in many individuals. One need look no further than our own violent society to observe people who do not appear to strive for self-actualization; perhaps this is why self-actualization has been variously thought of as an ideal and as an unconscious striving. By contrast, many seem to be consciously concerned with the meaning (logos) or meaninglessness of their lives. Frankl (1963, 1967), the creator of logotherapy, has termed feelings of meaninglessness the "existential void" and has developed techniques to treat these feelings.

Frankl stressed that life can be made meaningful in many ways. His own tragic experiences in Nazi concentration camps show that life can be made meaningful even in situations of unavoidable suffering. The person can give meaning to suffering by making it heroic, as in the case of helping other prisoners rather than focusing on self-preservation (see Patterson, 1973). The Nazis had imposed physical imprisonment, but the prisoners were still free to give meaning to their lives.

Frankl's existential philosophy is a very pragmatic approach to life. In particular, he has developed the techniques of *paradoxical intention* and *dereflection.* Paradoxical intention is a procedure in which the patient is encouraged to do, or to wish to happen, the very thing he fears. Such encouragement is generally given in a relaxed, humorous manner and Frankl and others have reported that it is sometimes effective for cases of obsessive compulsive neurosis (Frankl, 1963). Dereflection is a technique for treating patients who are excessively concerned with their problems. This technique consists of instructions to ignore one's problems and to concentrate instead on positive alternatives.

An encounter group meeting at a divorce clinic. (Photo by Wayne Miller; Magnum Photos, Inc.)

Although logotherapy was derived from an existential philosophy, logotherapeutic techniques are very similar to some techniques of behavior therapy. (See Chapter 7.)

TREATMENT EFFECTIVENESS

Many phenomenologists have shown little interest in experimentally evaluating the effectiveness of their counseling procedures, but Carl Rogers and his colleagues are important exceptions to this rule. For example, Rogerian therapists typically report transcribed interview data so that therapist-client interactions can be studied more objectively. Moreover, Rogers and Dymond's (1954) *Psychotherapy and Personality Change* constituted one of the first systematic, long-term experimental evaluations of a psychotherapy based on verbal interviews. That work is discussed briefly in this section.

To evaluate client-centered therapy with adult clients exhibiting a range of problems, Rogers and his colleagues (Rogers & Dymond, 1954) utilized a research design that included one experimental and two control conditions. In the therapy condition, clients received client-centered therapy from expert practitioners at the University of Chicago. In order to assess the possibility that expectation of therapy is itself beneficial, a second group of clients were assigned to a 60 day wait control condition; tests were administered to these individuals, but therapy was not received for 60 days. A third group of clients were assigned to a no-treatment control condition. Accordingly, the possible effects of client-centered therapy would be suggested by greater changes in the therapy condition as compared to the two control conditions.

The results provided little support for the effectiveness of client-centered therapy. For example, behavior ratings made by the clients' friends did not indicate a greater overall improvement for the clients who had received therapy. Moreover, although a greater number of therapy clients exhibited gains as measured by the Thematic Apperception Test, these test data also suggested that only 20 to 25 per cent of the therapy group showed moderate improvement.

As noted, the research reported by Rogers and Dymond (1954) constituted a significant methodological advance at the time it was conducted. When judged by today's standards, however, the basic research design employed by these investigators was methodologically problematic in two important respects. First, the control procedures were inadequate because the control group received no treatment. A better design would have been to compare changes in a therapy group to changes in an attention-placebo control group; for example, the effects of client-centered therapy could have been compared with the effects of administering a psychologically inactive drug under circumstances that encouraged the client to believe that the drug would help. Placebo control groups often show measurable improvement. A second methodological problem with the Rogers and Dymond study concerns their finding that, prior to the study, the therapy group was significantly more disturbed than was the control group. Consequently, some of the findings might have been attributable to preexisting subject differences rather than to differences in treatment procedures.

RESEARCH METHODOLOGY

Research methodologies employed by phenomenologists vary considerably. Phenomenologists engaged in empirical research have employed structured and unstructured interviews designed to encourage a subject to talk freely (e.g., Cherniss, 1972) and experimental methodologies (e.g., Rogers & Dymond, 1954). Although no particular research methodology characterizes this approach, one method that has been used by several phenomenologists concerns an analysis of intra- and interpersonal data. This kind of analysis has been seen as particularly relevant to the study of marital problems and other issues of dyadic relationships.

In a marriage, intrapersonal perception concerns one's own behavior and feelings, whereas interpersonal perception concerns the behavior and feelings of one's spouse. An assessment can be made of each individual's actual and ideal intra- and interpersonal perceptions, thus generating eight basic percepts:

1. Wife's perception of actual self.
2. Husband's perception of actual self.
3. Wife's perception of ideal self.
4. Husband's perception of ideal self.
5. Wife's perception of actual husband.
6. Husband's perception of actual wife.

7. Wife's perception of ideal husband.
8. Husband's perception of ideal wife.

Having obtained these data, it is then possible to test hypotheses concerning perceptual congruence (agreement); for example, is there more agreement between the wife's perception of her actual and ideal husband in nondisturbed or in disturbed marriages?

Laing, Phillipson, and Lee (1966) have extended this basic research strategy to second- and third-order interpersonal perceptions. The basic percepts in this system, as provided by the IPM Questionnaire, are as follows:

He says: he loves her (first order)
he thinks she thinks he loves her (second order)
he thinks she thinks he thinks he loves her (third order)

These data also may be used to study the perceptual congruence of relationships; for example, does agreement between the husband's and wife's first-, second-, and/or third-order percepts of each other distinguish between nondisturbed and disturbed marriages? Moreover, second- and third-order perceptual data have been employed as measures of the degree to which partners understand one another. Of course, these data can be obtained for any interpersonal relationship and employed to test many hypotheses. However, the discussion in the next section of this chapter concerns the use of interpersonal perception data to describe differences between nondisturbed and disturbed marriages.

EXAMPLE OF RESEARCH STUDIES EMPLOYING PHENOMENOLOGICAL DATA: DISTURBED AND NONDISTURBED MARRIAGES

Psychoanalysts have speculated that people select marital partners on the basis of their unconscious needs (e.g., Kubie, 1956). Giovacchini expressed this view as follows:

> One soon learns that there are many variables that determine the choice of one's spouse. The psychoanalysis of a married person reveals that unconscious determinants are highly significant in determining such a choice. Data from the psychoanalytic frame of reference cause us to emphasize that there is much more than mere contemporary significance in the attraction between two persons and that marital interaction is founded largely on infantile attitudes. I do not intend that this conclusion become the basis of a generalization for all marriages [1965, pp. 43–44].

According to this unromantic view, many people select partners who symbolize a parent or otherwise allow for the fulfillment of neurotic needs. In "pathological" marriages, the neurosis of husband and wife are complementary, as would be the case if the husband had a neurotic need to protect and the wife had a neurotic need to be taken care of.

Phenomenological theories of marriage differ significantly from psychoanalytic ones because they place a greater emphasis on current problems; for example, they emphasize poor congruence between a husband's and a wife's perceptions of their marriage. Each partner is seen as striving for a meaningful (genuine) relationship, but each sometimes comes to believe that this is impossible and settles for less (Satir, 1965). Phenomenologists conceptualize marital problems in terms of interpersonal perceptions and modes of communication.

Recently, several investigators have used phenomenological data in an effort to describe differences between disturbed and nondisturbed marriages. Two investigators who have been prominent in this area are Bernard I. Murstein and R. D. Laing. Although Murstein has proposed a theory of marriage that could not properly be termed phenomenological, several studies designed to test this theory have utilized phenomenological data.

The Murstein Study

Murstein (1970) has proposed a stimulus-role-value theory of marriage. His theory postulates that culturally defined characteristics largely determine an individual's "value" in the marriage market. Thus, "too-good-to-be-true" Winn has a high value as a prospective husband by virtue of his good looks, emotional health, athletic prowess, intelligence, and comfortable family status. One fully expects that a follow-up of Winn's case would reveal that he married the most attractive, emotionally stable, and intelligent woman in Boston. The rest of us are less fortunate than these two and thus have less value on the market. When we select a partner less desirable than Winn or his presumed partner, it is not because we are fulfilling neurotic needs, but rather because we must "settle" for the best we can get.

In a study of 99 couples who were engaged or "going steady," Murstein (1973) tested two hypotheses, one of which was derived from his theory of marriage. Hypothesis I was that, compared with nonneurotics, neurotics perceive their partners as less desirable. Murstein proposed this hypothesis because his theory assumes that neurotics are in fact socially defined as relatively undesirable marriage partners; they marry because they cannot do better. However, Murstein reasoned that psychoanalytic theory predicts the opposite—that is, that neurotics do not perceive their partners as less desirable because they come together to fulfill one another's unconscious needs.[4] Thus Hypothesis I was designed to provide a test between Murstein's theory and a psychoanalytic theory of marriage. Hypothesis II was that neurotics show less congruence in their perception of their partners than do nonneurotics. This hypothesis was derived from a characterization of neurosis as interfering with accurate interpersonal perception.

Using the MMPI to measure degree of neurosis and the Edwards Personal Preference Schedule to measure intra- and interpersonal perception, Murstein (1973) found inconsistent support for Hypothesis I. On the one hand, those individuals who scored high in neuroticism did not denigrate their partners any

[4] Murstein (1973, p. 23) is properly cautious in deriving this prediction from psychoanalytic theory. The present authors believe that many psychoanalysts would maintain that complementary neurotic attraction does not preclude negative feelings. In support of this belief, we note that psychoanalytic theory allows a person to both love and hate a parent.

more than did those who scored low on neuroticism. On the other hand, a reanalysis of his data using all couples, rather than just couples who scored high or low on the neuroticism scale, found a correlation supporting Hypothesis I. However, further research is needed to determine whether or not neurotics, compared to nonneurotics, perceive their partners as less desirable.

Hypothesis II was confirmed; that is, there was greater disagreement in the perception of each other when both subjects had high neuroticism scores than when both subjects had low neuroticism scores.

The Laing, Phillipson, and Lee Study

Laing, Phillipson, and Lee (1966) administered the IPM (see assessment section) to 12 couples who requested counseling (disturbed marriages) and to 10 couples who were judged by physicians to be satisfied with their marriages (nondisturbed marriages). The results were in general agreement with Murstein's data in that the disturbed couples exhibited less perceptual congruence of each other than did the nondisturbed couples. However, Laing, Phillipson and Lee are careful to note that some couples desire agreement with their partners, but others find "seeing eye to eye" on issues regarding each other boring and undesirable. These investigators have stressed the complexity of marital relationships.

Discussion

To conclude, objective studies on the phenomenology of marriage promise to contribute significantly to our understanding of this and other close relationships between two people. Although the studies reviewed represent advances on important issues, few reliable facts have been established. Marriage remains poorly understood (Greene, 1965), but it is to be hoped that this will not always be true.

SUMMARY

Phenomenology is an attitude of respect for the individual; a philosophy of human nature in which people are seen as both immanent in and transcendent of the biophysical and sociocultural orders; and a psychological science concerned with the study of conscious content and with the study of individual differences in the perception of meaningful experiences. Many phenomenologists posit a drive toward higher strivings and psychological growth and define abnormality as an absence of mental health or as a stunting of psychological growth.

Rogers's self-actualization theory is one of the more influential of the phenomenological theories of personality development. Under this view, psychological growth consists of symbolizing one's meaningful experiences accurately and in a manner that organizes experiences into one's self-concept. Psychological growth is stunted, and abnormality may result, when one's experience is denied symbolization or is given distorted symbolization. The greater the degree of overlap between one's experience and the awareness of that experience, the greater is the degree of psychological growth.

To a significant degree, Laing's influential writings are concerned with alienation from one's own experiences and with the discrepancy between human potential and our actual current state of existence. Laing has suggested that schizophrenics withdraw from reality and show an excessive fantasy life because they are escaping from an unbearable environment in order to explore a potentially more rewarding inner life.

Maslow's theory of personality development posits a hierarchy of human needs. The lowest needs concern physiological functioning and the highest needs concern self-actualization. Under this view, the individual will not be motivated to fulfill a higher-level need unless the lower-level needs are fulfilled.

Phenomenologically oriented therapies include Rogers's client-centered therapy, family therapy, encounter groups, and Frankl's logotherapy. The goals of client-centered therapy are to increase the client's unconditional acceptance of himself and his symbolization of his experience. In an effort to accomplish these goals, the therapist clarifies the client's experiences in as nondirective a manner as possible. Family therapy refers to a number of different treatment approaches in which two or more members of the same family receive help. This format is used most often in treating children and disturbed marriages. Encounter groups of many types also have been developed.

Client-centered therapy and T-groups (see Chapter 9) are the only phenomenologically oriented techniques that have been evaluated to any significant degree. Although the outcome research on client-centered therapy failed to find convincing evidence of effectiveness, some evidence does suggest possible benefits.

An example of a phenomenological research issue discussed in this chapter is the factors that contribute to disturbed marriages. Generally, phenomenological theories of disturbed marriages focus on the discrepancies between the perceptions that a husband and wife have of each other. Murstein (1973) found that such discrepancies are higher when both partners of an engaged couple have high MMPI neuroticism scores. Laing, Phillipson, and Lee (1966) found greater discrepancies in the perceptions of one another in couples requesting counseling than in nondisturbed marriages.

Chapter 9

Community Psychology and Community Mental Health

Traditionally, the human professions have responded to the countless "others" by placing them in large institutions, out of the public eye, where everyone could assume that something positive was happening. Occasionally, when an expose appears, people are shocked to hear that not only is there little therapy but it is also common for the inmates' condition to deteriorate over time.

DENNER and PRICE (1973, p. 1)

The community approach is concerned with the study of social systems such as hospitals, communities, schools, and mental health agencies, and with the manner in which these social systems affect the development, definition, and treatment of abnormal behavior. The focus is on issues such as these: How can mental health services be delivered more effectively and to a greater number of people? What can schools do to prevent abnormal behavior? What are the effects on mental health of working on an assembly line in a factory? We begin our discussion of these and related issues by examining some of the reasons for the emergence of the community approach.

FACTORS LEADING TO THE EMERGENCE OF COMMUNITY PSYCHOLOGY

The community approach developed as an attempt to meet at least five needs that arose from the study and treatment of abnormal behavior. In each instance, the attempt to solve the problem led either to the study of community settings or to the actual implementation of services in community settings.

Need for Community Mental Health Centers

Perhaps the most important impetus to the development of community psychology was the need for a viable alternative to mental hospitals. For the last eight centuries, it has been obvious to anyone who bothered to investigate that many mental hospitals are overcrowded custodial institutions in which patients are maintained in sterile environments that provide little if any treatment. Not surprisingly, many patients seem more likely to deteriorate in these environments than to improve (Goffman, 1959; Goldman, Bohr, & Steinberg, 1970; Rosenhan, 1973; Szasz, 1970). After centuries of attempts to reform mental hospitals, the United States finally decided that perhaps the best solution to the problem was to rely more on out-patient care and to utilize the mental hospital only when a person cannot function in his or her community. This decision led to the creation of community mental health centers across the United States.

Need to Increase Manpower

Another impetus to the community movement was the need to increase the supply of mental health practitioners (Cherniss, 1972; Zax & Cowen, 1972). Nichols (1963) has estimated that at least 3 million people annually seek some kind of psychological service. Moreover, additional millions are believed to be in need of help. Despite a 500 per cent increase in the number of psychologists between 1950 and 1966 (Arnhoff, Rubenstein, Shriver, & Jones, 1969), the supply is hopelessly inadequate to meet the need. Cowen recently summarized the situation as follows:

> All this adds up to an ever-growing demand for mental health services—a demand that exceeds available resources now or in the forseeable future. With a spate of epidemiological-demographic studies suggesting that the need far exceeds evident demand (Albee, 1959; Arnhoff, Rubenstein, & Speisman, 1969; Joint Commission on Mental Illness, 1961; Leighton, 1956; Ryan, 1969; Srole, Langner, Michael, Opler, & Rennie, 1962), it is fair to say that one significant problem facing MH fields today is that they cannot meet pressures, expressed and latent, for help. Our most recent refresher course (Joint Commission on Mental Health of Children, 1970) tells us the same thing in slightly different form: i.e. nearly 1½ million children under 18 are estimated to need immediate professional assistance; less than 30% of them are getting such help [1973, p. 427].

It is important to distinguish between demand and need for mental health services. Unfortunately, the need is even greater than the demand, in part because many people cannot afford mental health services.

Paraprofessionalism is an attempt to increase the supply of mental health services by redefining who is, and who is not, qualified to provide mental health services.

> Our inability to provide services will derive largely from the defects in the conceptual model that dictate the kinds of manpower required. Much useful and effective intervention with emotionally disturbed children and adults could be done by people with bachelor degrees (or even less education), who are in potentially large supply. But exploration of these routes is blocked by our present model [Albee, 1967, p. 64].

Residing in most communities are many people with time, motivation, and interpersonal skills. By effectively employing these human resources, the available supply of mental health services can be significantly increased.

Need to Prevent Abnormality

A cornerstone of the community mental health movement is the creation of programs designed to prevent mental disorders (Cowen, 1973; Denner & Price, 1973). Three types of prevention are distinguished:

1. *Primary* prevention is designed to prevent the occurrence of abnormal behavior before it begins. This includes educational programs that promote psychological health in young children and programs that improve the diet of disadvantaged children.

2. *Secondary* prevention is designed to prevent mild problems from becoming more severe. This includes the use of screening tests to detect children who are high risks for emotional and educational problems.

3. *Tertiary* prevention is intended to minimize the consequences of abnormal behavior in persons who are already profoundly affected. In essence, tertiary prevention is just another name for therapy and, hence, is not really a form of prevention at all.

Existence of Services for the Community

An important stimulus to the community mental health movement was the existence of psychological services that can be implemented in community agencies such as schools, factories, and management firms. These services include reinforcement therapy, organization development, and drug abuse programs. In each of these examples, the development of the service led to a large group of mental health persons working in the community; this, in turn, led to an inevitable concern for understanding community settings (see Reppucci & Saunders, 1974).

Need for a Broader Conception of Abnormality

Another impetus for the emergence of a community psychology has been the modern tendency to understand abnormal behavior as a failure to adapt to significant social systems (Zax & Cowen, 1972). For example, there are many children who are diagnosed as having borderline or mild mental retardation and who come from a poverty background. These children are sometimes said to be culturally deprived. Community psychologists, however, have suggested that the problem is less one of cultural deprivation and more one of cultural conflict. The child from a poverty background, for example, may learn that the word *draw* refers to drawing a welfare check, whereas the school culture teaches that the word *draw* means to create pictures with crayons or paint. (See Chapter 18 for documentation of these statements.) The result is that the child from a poverty background has learned a language that is adaptive in the home but not in the school.

MODELS OF COMMUNITY PSYCHOLOGY

Having examined some of the factors that led to the emergence of the community approach, we now turn our attention to some of the theoretical models of this approach. This section presents four models of community psychology.

Creation of Mental Health Settings and Reasons New Settings Often Fail

One of the purposes of the community mental health movement is the development of innovative, community-based services designed either to prevent or to treat abnormal behavior. In recent years there have been numerous attempts to develop such innovative programs, but unfortunately many of these programs seem to have had only limited success, having at most only a temporary impact on the problem under attack. In fact, a large majority of mental health programs last for only a few years. In recent years a number of community psychologists have attempted to identify the reasons why so many new, innovative mental health programs seem to fail.

One of the reasons innovative programs are usually short-lived is that they have difficulty renewing the grants that provide their funding. Innovative programs are typically funded by either the federal government, a state government, or a private foundation. These grants usually last only one, two, or three years, after which application must be made for a renewal. The difficulty of obtaining a renewal, however, is greater for an innovative program than for a traditional program because of what we shall call the *evaluation paradox.*

This paradox arises because the people who are called upon to evaluate grant renewals are often people who distinguished themselves by gaining expertise in the old, traditional methods of providing services. The evaluation paradox may be stated as follows:

1. If the innovative program is truly innovative and different from traditional programs, it is unlikely to be evaluated favorably by people whose reputations are based on their expertise in traditional methods.
2. If the innovative program is innovative in name only and is really a traditional program, it is likely to be evaluated favorably by people who are traditionalists.

Thus innovative programs either tend to receive unfavorable evaluations and, hence, have their funds discontinued or tend to receive favorable evaluations because they are not really innovative (e.g., Graziano, 1969). No wonder it is difficult to create lasting innovations!

It is presently impossible to disassociate the study of the creation of mental health settings from the work of Seymour Sarason and his colleagues at the Yale Psycho-Educational Clinic. The central concept of Sarason's model is that of a *setting,* which Sarason has defined "as any instance in which two or more people come together in new relationships over a sustained period of time to achieve certain goals" (1972, p. 1). The term *setting* is similar in meaning to the terms *social system* and *social organization;* it does not imply a particular place or physical building. Examples of settings include marriages, schools, prisons, governments, and revolutions.

Although he does not deny that social change occurs, Sarason focuses on the tendency of social systems to resist change. This attitude is summarized by the French saying "The more things change, the more they remain the same." In fact, Sarason's experiences have led him to conclude that most attempts to create new settings fail. This conclusion is supported by the numbers of new innovative mental health programs supplanting a previous administration's new innovative programs. In his book *The Creation of Settings and the Future Societies,* Sarason (1972) discussed the following interrelated reasons for the failure of many new settings.

Failure to Confront History

One reason for the failure of many new settings is that creators sometimes act as if they are the first ones to try something new, or as if their experiences are bound to be different from those who have preceded them. The past, however, is often the best predictor of the future. It is important to ask what has happened to those who have made similar attempts at social change in the past and what contributed to the success or failure of their efforts.

One of the most significant of Sarason's ideas is his thesis that the manner in which a setting is created often affects the development of the setting, if not its very survival. Sarason has observed that new settings created from an existing complex of settings tend to inherit the conflicts of the already existing settings. Consider: (1) a parent setting perceives a problem (e.g., an agency of the federal government is concerned that the supply of existing mental health services is less than the demand); (2) the parent setting decides that it is ill-equipped to solve this problem itself (e.g., the federal agency decides that it is too bureaucratic to attempt to operate mental health facilities); (3) the parent agency thus decides to create a new setting (e.g., the federal agency awards a grant for the development of innovative mental health facilities); (4) the new setting inherits the conflicts of the parent setting (e.g., the federal agency must account for its expenditure of funds and thus requires the new setting to perform a seemingly endless list of bureaucratic chores in order to keep its funding); and (5) the new setting fails for the very reasons the parent setting decided it would fail if it attempted to solve the problem itself (e.g., the bureaucratic chores and deadlines take too much time and energy away from the task of creating this setting properly).

Myth of Unlimited Resources

Another reason for the failure of many new settings is the unrealistic estimates of available resources. The number of otherwise practical people who overestimate available resources is surprisingly large.

Unrealistic Time Perspective

New settings sometimes fail because they are based on an unrealistic time perspective.

The creation of settings model is important because of the extraordinary generality of the concept of setting and because of the contemporary need for effective social change, including improvement in mental health delivery systems.

Organization Development

One approach to the prevention of abnormality is to change existing social systems so that people can work and live in more fulfilling environments. This implies that clinical psychologists have a legitimate role in consulting to corporations because such institutions have important influences on the emotional well-being of their employees. It also implies that we should concern ourselves with the well-being of the staff of human service settings. For example, if teachers were more satisfied and stimulated in their jobs, schools might educate better and allow students to develop more positive self-images (Silberman, 1970).

Hornstein, Bunker, Burke, Gindes, and Lewicki define *organization development* (OD) "as the creation of a culture which institutionalizes the use of various social technologies to regulate the diagnosis and change of interpersonal, group, and intergroup behaviors, especially those behaviors related to organizational decision making, communicating, and planning" (1971, p. 343). The targets of OD interventions are groups and subsystems rather than individuals. Typical goals of OD consultants include democraticizing decision making and authority (Bennis, 1966; Hornstein et al., 1971) and widening the responsibilities of various roles (Hornstein et al., 1971).

The *Handbook of Organization Development in Schools*, by Schmuck, Runkel, Saturen, Martell, and Derr (1972), provides an excellent discussion of OD applied to schools. These authors identified the target of school consultation as subsystems (classrooms, departmental groups, special committees, and administrative groups). Of particular concern is the manner in which various subsystems communicate with one another. The greater the degree to which communication channels allow for misunderstanding, the greater is the potential for organizational conflict. Thus one task of the OD consultant is to identify and, if necessary, to restructure communication channels.

Three types of communication channels were identified by Schmuck and his colleagues: *one-way, directive,* and *transactional.* A one-way channel involves a source of communication (speaker) and a receiver who cannot communicate back to the source. When a president can send a message to an aide who cannot directly return a message, the channel of communication is one-way. If the aide were to misinterpret the directive, the president would be unable to clarify its meaning. By virtue of inherent structure, one-way channels have a high potential for communication errors. A directive channel involves a speaker who can send any message he desires, but the receiver's reply to the source is limited to requests for clarification of the message. For example, the aide can report back to the president that the message was received and understood and that the directive will be carried out. Transactional communication channels allow each participant to initiate and to receive messages. These channels provide the least potential for misunderstanding and conflict. Thus one specific purpose of OD consultation is to restructure communication channels toward the transactional model.

Ecological Models

Sometimes behavioral scientists become so engrossed with measuring changes of target populations that they overlook the effects of psychological interventions on larger systems. Biologists have learned that when one aspect of a total environment changes, individuals as well as whole species must learn new ways of adapting to the altered environment. This concern has been extended to human behavior; for example, changes in a client's behavior through psychotherapy mean that significant others must find new ways of interacting with the client. Changes in one component of an organization mean that other components must adapt to these changes. Kelly has summarized the basic assumptions of an ecological model as follows:

> The major premise is that as an environment varies in function, such functions will affect the generation and control of normative values, requirements for adaptation, and the expression of relevant coping styles by members. Adaptation is viewed as specific to a particular social setting, and as dependent upon the congruence between the particular coping styles—that is, individual preferences for mastering the environment—and the normative requirements of the environment. Thus, a particular set of coping styles will be relevant to adaptation in one environment but not in another. The research task is to specify the environmental conditions for adaptive and maladaptive behavior in different settings [1969, p. 184].

Kelly (1966) has identified three areas of ecological concern: (1) the effects of changes in one social system on another; (2) the effects of changes in the physical environment on individuals; and (3) the study of how individuals adapt to different social environments. His own research in high schools provides an interesting example of different individuals' adaptation patterns to relatively fluid and to relatively constant social environments. One of the high schools studied had a high rate (42 per cent) of student turnover, or a "fluid" environment, whereas the other had a low rate (10 per cent), or a "constant" environment (Kelly, 1968). Kelly predicted that students in the fluid environment would be more concerned with personal development and would display greater variability in behavior across time and across settings, whereas students in the constant environment would be more concerned with occupying their niche in a monolithic, unchanging status hierarchy. Of particular interest is Kelly's hypothesis concerning expressions of abnormality; specifically, expressions of isolation and identity confusion were predicted to characterize maladaptive behavior in the fluid environment, whereas acts that go against normative roles and structures were predicted to characterize maladaptive behavior in the constant environment. Although Kelly (1968) noted possible confounding variables between the two high schools studied, the results provided partial and encouraging support for his ecological approach.

Another example of an ecological approach to understanding problems in adjustment is provided by a series of studies on open-space classroom environments (Reiss, 1974). The term *open space* refers to an architectural concept in which several teachers and classes meet in a large area without walls; the concept of *open education* refers to a variety of practices that include self-directed learning and a humanistic attitude toward the student (Walberg & Thomas, 1972). In a series of evaluative studies on open-space programs with varying degrees of open-education practices, a team of investigators found evidence that some types of children fared better in open classes and that others fared better in traditional classes. For example, creative children had healthier self-images in open-classes than in traditional classes (O'Neill, 1974), whereas nonpersistent children had lower achievement in open classes than in traditional classes (Reiss & Dyhdalo, 1975). Thus the ideal educational format would seem to be one that provides different types of environments for different types of children.

Community Planning and Experimental Social Innovation

George W. Fairweather (1967) has defined a strategy for social change that focuses on experimental evaluation of community interventions. These evaluations are concerned with identifying the critical aspects of the program that account for its overall results. For example, if an open classroom produces positive attitudes toward learning, the experimentalist might determine whether this effect was produced by team teaching, by the more interesting educational materials in the open classroom, or by some other aspect of the open format. From a practical, decision-making perspective, however, society's immediate concern is how the innovative program compares with what is already being done. Until the innovator can provide this information, there is little hope for accomplishing social change. For this reason Fairweather has recommended that the effects of innovative programs first be compared with the effects of usual methods.

Fairweather's (1964) study of a psychiatric ward exemplifies his strategy of experimental social innovation. The significant social problem studied was defined as a low rate of discharge of chronic mental patients. Based on observations of the ward environment, an innovative plan for a small-group ward was formulated. Patients in the small-group ward proceeded in a stepwise fashion through a treatment program that provided monetary reward and special privileges for improved behavior. Another important feature of the small-group ward was increased decision-making responsibilities. When the effects of the small-group regime were compared with those of a traditional regime, the results indicated that the patients in the small-group ward averaged 41 fewer hospitalized days than did patients in the traditional ward. Thus, although this study did not identify the effective components of the small-group ward, it did suggest the superiority of this environment.

PREVENTION AND TREATMENT

In addition to the development of models for understanding social change and community organizations, the community approach also is associated with a number of techniques and strategies designed either to treat abnormal behavior, to prevent it, or to promote mental health.

Consultation with Community Agencies

This discussion is limited to consultation between a human service agency (e.g., school or hospital) and a psychologist who is not a formal member of the agency.

The first issue of consultation is whether a request for services should be accepted or rejected. In making this decision the consultant needs to evaluate the reasons for the request in terms of the contribution, if any, his services might be able to make. In many instances the consultant will want to reject the request because the conditions are unfavorable for any meaningful change. For example, an organization might seek a consultant's advice in order to obtain support for a decision already made. Organizations also seek consultation services to resolve "crises," particularly crises that result from the public exposure of everyday practices. In such situations, the consultant's presence tends to give a misleading impression to the public that something is about to be done in regard to the underlying causes of the crises. On the other hand, if an agency is genuinely concerned with attacking a particular problem or with obtaining expert information, a consultant can provide an important service.

The issue of port of entry into an organization concerns the subgroup with which the consultant initiates contact (Schein, 1969). For example, a consultant might gain access to a school system through the board of education, the superintendent, the principals, or the teachers. Organizational consultants differ on the relative merits of entering from the top of the hierarchy (thus having to win the support of the staff while in a position of perceived authority) versus entering from the lower levels (thus having to win the support of the administrators while in a position of little authority).

The student interested in learning more about consultation can read Caplan (1964), *Principles of Preventive Psychiatry.*

T-Groups

The T-group has been defined as a small group of normal individuals who hold meetings over an extended period of time. A leader is present but refrains from setting rules or defining topics; the leader may, however, define the group's goals as a commitment to personal growth in interpersonal situations, and he may define his own role as that of another group member (Argyris, 1964; Golembiewski, 1972). The role of each member is one of an observer-participant who both discloses information about his own experiences and provides positive feedback to others. T-groups are distinguished from traditional therapy groups because they are based on the assumption that group members are healthy rather than sick, because they are concerned with the here and now rather than with past experiences, and because they focus on conscious and preconscious feelings rather than on unconscious feelings.

Argyris (1964) has discussed the use of group experiences to augment what he calls "pyramidal values." Pyramidal values, prevalent in many organizations, are logical outcomes of task-oriented systems designed almost exclusively for success. These values include the following beliefs: (1) the purpose of human relations in a task-oriented organization is to get a job done; (2) this purpose is best facilitated by emphasizing logical-cognitive interactions and by de-emphasizing emotions; and (3) human interactions are best motivated by authoritative means complemented by a system of reward and punishment. Argyris has attempted to employ T-groups to augment pyramidal values with ones that (1) stress the importance of members' adaptation to the organization's internal system; (2) recognize emotional as well as cognitive aspects of human relations; and (3) recognize as a source of interpersonal motivation the importance of authentic relationships based on mutual respect and self-awareness.

The manner in which T-groups can be utilized to augment pyramidal values was discussed by Golembiewski (1972) in terms of the processes of unfreezing (unlearning old values), changing (learning new values), and refreezing (integrating new values with personality). The lack of structure in T-groups as well as the ethos of the equality of all members is hypothesized to create a "fundamental feeling" of the inadequacy of old values. In other words, authoritative and nongenuine styles of interacting are inappropriate in T-groups, and the experience of this inappropriateness by group members is postulated to produce an unfreezing process that motivates change. The change process is supported by a psychological feeling of safety within the group and is postulated to occur as a result of both feedback from others and vicarious learning.

Advocacy

Frustrated by the slow pace of social progress, inconsistent financial support from governmental agencies, and bureaucratic red tape, mental health professionals have shown increasing interest in political efforts to force improvement in the delivery of mental health services (e.g., Denner & Price, 1973; Hornstein et al., 1971; see O'Neill, 1973). These efforts vary from legal redress to political activism. In state hospitals advocates are concerned with securing patients' rights and privileges by working against arbitrary punishment, by requiring researchers to obtain patients' permission, and by demanding proper health standards. In urban communities advocates may help troubled people establish self-help corporations, resolve disputes between clients and social welfare agencies, or find employment. A particularly interesting aspect of advocacy is the attempt to ensure the legal rights of the mentally ill.

The purpose of pretrial mental competency hearings is to determine whether an accused person is mentally competent to stand trial (see Chapter 2); for example, does the defendant understand the charges against him? Defendants found to be incompetent do not stand trial but instead are committed to mental hospitals. The vague criteria by which some psychiatrists have judged competency are scandalous. Szasz (1965) documents the case of Mr. Perroni, which exemplifies this abuse of psychiatric authority. Mr. Perroni's "crime" stemmed from his efforts to resist harassment from a real estate agency that planned a new shopping center on the grounds of his gas station. When men came to erect a sign on the station, Mr. Perroni fired warning bullets into the air. Mr. Perroni was arraigned but not indicted; instead he was given a pretrial examination by two court-appointed psychiatrists. One psychiatrist, who was unaware of the charges against Mr. Perroni, nevertheless found him incompetent to understand those charges. On cross examination, this psychiatrist cited as evidence of Mr. Perroni's incompetency his having the top button on his shirt open (evidence of untidiness) and his refusal to answer a few questions. (The psychiatrist could not recall any specific questions Mr. Perroni refused to answer.) The evidence presented for mental incompetency was extraordinarily vague. Nevertheless, Mr. Perroni was confined to a state institution for more than seven years until an appeals decision finally ordered that he stand trial. The charges were dismissed and Mr. Perroni was finally set free.

Commitment procedures also leave much to be desired. Miller and Schwartz's (1966) observational study of 58 county lunacy hearings documents the mockery of justice that sometimes occurs. The examining physicians not only recommended in all 58 cases some form of treatment for emotional disorders but also recommended the overwhelming majority for commitment. Some fortunate defendants who understood English (many defendants only spoke Spanish) and who had an opportunity to speak at the hearing complained that the interview with the doctors had lasted only a few minutes. The median duration of the hearing in which a commitment decision was reached was 3 minutes. (The average was 3.8 minutes.) The investigators found that 68 per cent of those who came before the commission were committed, 10 per cent were held over for further examination, and only 22 per cent were released. A finding of particular interest is that those who understood what was going on and who resisted had a 50 per cent chance of release; however, resisters who became angry and who objected to medical recommendations were more likely to be committed than those who could elicit the judge's sympathy. In another study, Wenger and Fletcher (1969) found a high correlation (.94) between the presence of legal counsel and a decision not to commit; however, in 81.5 per cent of the 81 cases in this sample, no defense counsel was present. Lower-class people, who have minimal access to counsel and who may not understand the potential consequences of the hearings because they either do not speak English or were never properly informed, have a much higher probability of being committed as compared to middle- and upper-class people.

The work of Mendel and Rapport (1969) and of Scheff (1963, 1964) suggests that organizational factors motivate examiners to bias decisions in favor of commitment. Interviews conducted by Scheff (1963) indicate that once commitment proceedings had begun, the examiner needed to spend more time building a case justifying termination of the proceedings than building one recommending continuance. Apparently commitment served as bureaucratic justification for the professional time and expense expended to initiate hearings. Moreover, the judge who fails to commit someone who later engages in criminal activity must explain his decision to angry voters, whereas a judge who guards against this possibility by overcommitting is almost never asked to explain his behavior. (See Chapter 1.)

The role of the mental health advocate regarding commitment includes exposing the activities described here, educating professionals and enlisting their support for change, and ensuring that the defendant in a commitment hearing has legal counsel and understands the nature of the proceedings. In brief, the advocate plays a role of "social counsel." In so doing, however, the advocate risks embarrassing the established powers, who may perceive his role as one of a nuisance or troublemaker (see Wineman & James, 1969).

Crisis Intervention

Crisis intervention is brief, emergency psychotherapy or emotional support given to a person experiencing an acute problem. Bellak and Small (1965) have defined *brief* as one to six interviews of 45 to 50 minutes each. The goal of this intervention is limited to ameliorating the symptoms causing the intense emotional stress or to modifying the maladaptive behavior that is intensifying the situation; no attempt is made to change personality or to deal with "deeper" issues. Some of the techniques used are psychoanalytic interpretation, reassurance, attempts to enlist family support for the client, placebo "drugs," and advice (the most commonly used technique). As formulated by Bellak and Small (1965), crisis intervention is for use by the experienced therapist who has the skill to assess problems quickly and who can provide immediate support. Several centers that rely largely on paraprofessional manpower, however, have been created across the country; the best known of these are called *hot lines,* in which people with problems can call for help at any time. Young adults on a bad trip and lonely people considering suicide are among those who might be helped by talking on a hot line with a supportive peer.

Community Mental Health Centers

The Congressional Mental Health Act of 1955 established a Joint Commission on Mental Illness and Health that for five years investigated national methods for delivering mental health services. The commission recommended an end to the construction of large mental hospitals and proposed instead the creation of mental health centers that would provide a flexible array of services. The guiding principle was that mental health care should not disrupt the client's normal life pattern. In 1963 President Kennedy called for a "bold new approach" and Congress responded by appropriating funds to create community mental health centers within the framework of state mental health departments.[1,2] Several hundred community mental health centers have been created across the country.

As formulated by Smith and Hobbs (1966), a basic principle of the community mental health center is community involvement in, and control of, the activities of the center. This means that the professionals of such centers should be agents of the community. Other basic principles of the Smith and Hobbs model are extensive use of community resources (particularly nonprofessional manpower) and the conception of the center as an organization of services rather than as a particular place. The services that ideally would be provided are (1) in-patient care; (2) out-patient care; (3) crisis intervention; (4) diagnosis; (5) consultation to schools, hospitals, and community planning groups; (6) professional and paraprofessional training; and (7) research and evaluation facilities to gather information that could be used to improve such centers.

It is best to consider the Smith and Hobbs model as an ideal rather than as a description of existing mental health centers. This gap between ideal and real programs is the result of several factors. In particular, few centers have the resources for all of the services provided in the ideal model. One service area that usually is not included in most real world centers is that of research and evaluation. This is especially unfortunate because evaluation can lead to the improvement of other services and can serve as a source of intellectual stimulation for the center's staff. Other factors limiting the effectiveness of community mental health centers are community resistance to certain programs and a general suspicion of professionals by community members (Freed, Schroder, and Baker, 1970). Although these problems seem surmountable (Goldenberg, 1971), they nevertheless must be regarded as sobering influences on the enthusiasm generated by the relatively new ideas of community mental health.

[1] Congressional laws do not necessarily imply federal expenditure of the full amount authorized. In 1971 Congress appropriated $63 million for a learning disability program; however, only 3.25 million was actually provided (Senf, 1973). This was before former President Nixon publicly announced his intentions of impounding funds.

[2] The nature of the funding mechanism is worthy of detailed study by community psychologists. (This idea was suggested to the authors by Seymour Sarason.) Typically, the appropriation of federal funds results in a call for proposals from the states. The proposal is often formulated by individuals working in state government; the people who will actually implement the program may be contacted at a later time, after the proposal has been written and accepted. Thus, the program director is sometimes hired to implement a program developed by someone else. The potential for stifling creativity and for misunderstanding is maximal from such a system. An alternative funding mechanism would be direct grants to people who are qualified, motivated, and creative. Thus $1 million given to a responsible social worker or agent of the community may be more likely to produce effective service centers than would $1 million given to a state department of mental health.

TREATMENT EFFECTIVENESS

The major accomplishments of community psychology to date appear to be the formulation of concepts for describing organizational development and the delineation of a set of issues concerning the delivery of mental health services. However, there is a considerable need for empirical assessments of the effectiveness of community treatment and prevention procedures. In regard to prevention programs, these writers could find no empirical evidence that any community mental health program prevents abnormal behavior; rather, the only evidence for this claim is a blend of common sense and theoretical considerations. It is perhaps unfair to expect that evidence for prevention be presented so shortly following the emergence of community psychology; moreover, the practical exigencies of an empirical study demonstrating preventive effects on a community population would seem to render such studies beyond the resources of the overwhelming majority of investigators. Nevertheless, the problems of evaluating preventive programs demand the attention of future investigators.

Although consultation is used widely by community psychologists, Cowen's (1973) recent review of the literature found only a few isolated studies on its effectiveness. Cowen attributed this lack of evaluative research to the enormous diversity of consultative strategies. Their theoretical diversity renders an evaluation of any one strategy less important to the field as a whole. However, several case histories do provide some empirical evidence supporting potential effectiveness (e.g., Huessy, 1966; Spielberger, 1967).

In recent years we have witnessed phenomenal growth in the training and use of nonprofessionals. The largest single group of nonprofessionals are college student volunteers in mental institutions, community projects, schools, prisons, and other settings. Gruver's (1971) review of college students as therapeutic agents noted a wide range of participation but is critical of the lack of proper methodological evaluations concerning their effectiveness. Housewives, grandparents, teachers, police, ex-convicts, ex-patients, and retired individuals also have served as nonprofessionals in mental health projects (Cowen, 1973). Nonprofessionals have served as therapists (Rioch, 1966), as companions (Goodman, 1967), and as reinforcement therapists (see Guerney, 1969). It seems plausible to expect that the effectiveness of nonprofessionals will vary with different roles. For example, convincing evidence exists that nonprofessionals can learn to implement relatively simple operant procedures with children and institutionalized adults. (See Chapter 7.) Training on a professional level, however, is necessary for T-group leaders.

One theme of this chapter has been the importance of anticipating problems. Professional resistance to nonprofessional manpower has been anticipated and directly confronted by community psychologists (Cowen, Gardner, & Zax, 1967). Little attention, however, has been given to the possible development of professional nonprofessionals. This possibility was suggested to us by the emergence of union-type organizations of paraprofessional lawyers in the Chicago area and by similar developments in school districts we have known. Originally recruited on the assumption that many nonprofessionals have skills that can be put to use, the tendency may be for on-the-job experience to produce feelings of greater know-how and superiority as compared to inexperienced nonprofessionals. The human desire to protect one's own financial interests might further reinforce this possible trend toward exclusion. Although the problem would not be expected to arise in college student programs with high rates of volunteer turnover, it might emerge as a force with older, paid nonprofessionals in community projects.

In an excellent review on the T-group literature, Campbell and Dunnette (1971) identified the following as the problems present in an evaluation of the effects of T-groups: (1) the lack of clarity concerning the learning processes that are hypothesized to occur complicates the problem of determining whether the desired learning actually occurred; (2) the issue of transfer of learning to situations outside the T-group raises fundamental problems of measurement of change; and (3) the construct of interpersonal sensitivity is difficult to measure. Many research studies on T-group effectiveness have used questionnaire ratings by co-workers or perceived changes in both behavior and sensitivity. Several such studies (e.g., Bunker, 1965; Miles, 1965; and Valiquet, 1964) provided important evidence that Campbell and Dunnette have summarized:

> The evidence, though limited, is reasonably convincing that T-group training does induce behavioral changes in the "back home" setting. This statement is based primarily on results from the first five studies reviewed. However, the subjective probability estimate of the truth of this generalization is not 1.00 because of the confounding elements already discussed, namely, the manner of choosing control groups, and the fact that most observers probably knew who had or had not received T-group experience [1971].

In addition to the need for research clarifying the nature of behavioral changes resulting from T-group experience, it is important to note that group leadership is a difficult task that should not be undertaken by unqualified people (Benne, 1964). Group participation can be a very intense emotional experience for some individuals; the potential for harm from inexperienced leaders who are unqualified to screen out poor risks and who are unqualified to handle difficult situations is considerable (Zax & Cowen, 1972).

EXAMPLE OF A RESEARCH ISSUE IN COMMUNITY PSYCHOLOGY: THE MENTAL HOSPITAL

Table 9-1 indicates that 1,721,389 people were hospitalized for psychiatric care in 1971, 745,259 of them in state and county mental hospitals. Since 1955 the number of people in state and county mental hospitals has declined slightly, while this number as a percentage of all people receiving mental health services has declined sharply from 48.9 to 18.5. These figures reflect a modern trend toward increasing reliance on care provided by out-patient community mental health centers and toward a decreasing reliance on state and county

TABLE 9-1
Number and Per Cent Distribution and Rate Per 100,000 Population of Patient Care Episodes, by Type of Facility, All Psychiatric Facilities, United States, 1955, 1965, 1967, 1969, and 1971 *

		In-Patient Services of						Out-Patient Psychiatric Services of		
Year	Total, All Facilities	All In-patient Services	State and County Mental Hospitals	Private Mental Hospitals†	General Hospitals/ Psychiatric Service	VA Hospitals	Community Mental Health Clinic	All Out-patient Services	Community Mental Health Clinic	Other
Number of Patient Care Episodes										
1971	4,038,143	1,721,389	745,259	126,600	542,642	176,800	130,088	2,316,754	622,906	1,693,848
1969	3,572,822	1,678,371	767,115	123,850	535,493	186,913	65,000	1,894,451	291,148	1,603,303
1967	3,139,742	1,659,391	801,354	124,258	578,513	128,196	27,070.	1,480,351	97,351	1,383,000
1965	2,636,525	1,565,525	804,926	125,428	519,328	115,843	–	1,071,000	–	1,071,000
1955	1,675,352	1,296,352	818,832	123,231	265,934	88,355	–	379,000	–	379,000
Per Cent Distribution										
1971	100.0	42.6	18.5	3.1	13.4	4.4	3.2	57.4	15.4	42.0
1969	100.0	47.0	21.5	3.5	15.0	5.2	1.8	53.0	8.1	44.9
1967	100.0	52.9	25.5	4.0	18.4	4.1	0.9	47.1	3.1	44.0
1965	100.0	59.4	30.5	4.8	19.7	4.4	–	40.6	–	40.6
1955	100.0	77.4	48.9	7.3	15.9	5.3	–	22.6	–	22.6
Rate per 100,000 Population										
1971	1981.5	847.2	364.9	66.1	265.7	86.9	63.7	1134.3	305.0	829.3
1969	1797.7	849.6	384.2	62.0	268.2	93.6	41.7	948.1	145.2	802.9
1967	1604.3	847.9	409.5	63.5	295.6	65.5	13.8	756.4	49.7	706.7
1965	1374.0	815.9	419.5	65.4	270.6	60.4	–	558.1	–	558.1
1955	1032.2	798.6	504.5	75.9	163.8	54.4	–	233.5	–	233.5

* Reprinted from *Utilization of mental health facilities: Mental health statistics, 1973,* Series B, no. 5 (Bethesda, Md.: National Institute of Mental Health, 1973), p. 43.

† Includes estimates of episodes of care in residential treatment centers for emotionally disturbed children.

hospitals. The apparent desirability of this trend is indicated by repeated observations that many mental hospitals do little for their patients.[3]

The Goldman, Bohr, and Steinberg (1970) Study

A social psychologist and a clinical psychologist feigned illness in order to gain admittance to a large metropolitan state mental hospital. The facility served more than 6,000 patients but was designed for only 3,000; more than 80 per cent of the population had been in residence for longer than two years.

Once in the hospital the normality of the pseudopatients went undetected. The pseudopatients have described some aspects of their experience of becoming mental patients.

1. Immediately following admission the pseudopatients felt betrayed and became concerned that they might be left and forgotten in the hospital. They even went so far as to plan an escape.
2. The sterile hospital environment produced an overwhelming reaction of boredom. Minor events, such as having ice cream for dessert, became the major novel events in their lives. They began to lose track of time.
3. The pseudopatients observed and began to accept as natural a humiliating system of rewards. Attendants met their needs for more labor in the understaffed hospital by promising a minor reward (e.g., a cup of coffee) for work (e.g., cleaning a floor).

The investigators concluded that some of the behaviors (e.g., loss of time perspective) interpreted as expressions of mental illness are really reactions to the hospital environment.

Description of Institutional Life

The case of Annette was presented in Chapter 7 without a description of the institutional life to which this child had been subjected. The following is a brief description of the Jones School for the mentally retarded in which Annette resided.[4]

As a state institution for the mentally retarded, the Jones School housed approximately 2,000 patients in a score of buildings. In general, the staff of each building included one ward attendant for approximately every 20 or 30 patients. Some ward attendants were licensed practicing nurses while others held no degree. Each building was also staffed by a registered nurse and by a doctor (usually a neurologist) who visited on several occasions each week to prescribe drugs and to treat other medical problems that might arise. For psychological services, each building had to call on a central staff whose offices were situated in an evaluation center. This staff of approximately six full-time psychologists,

[3] Some attempts to make people appear dangerous in order to hospitalize them can be amusing. One of these writers had the experience of sitting in on an admission committee meeting for problem children. A social worker reported the parents' description of the child's long history of abnormality beginning with the child's crawling away from home at age two, stopping traffic at a busy intersection while playing policeman at age five, and stealing cars at age seven. The child supposedly came to the attention of authorities when he was arrested for driving without a license.
[4] The *Jones School* is a fictitious name.

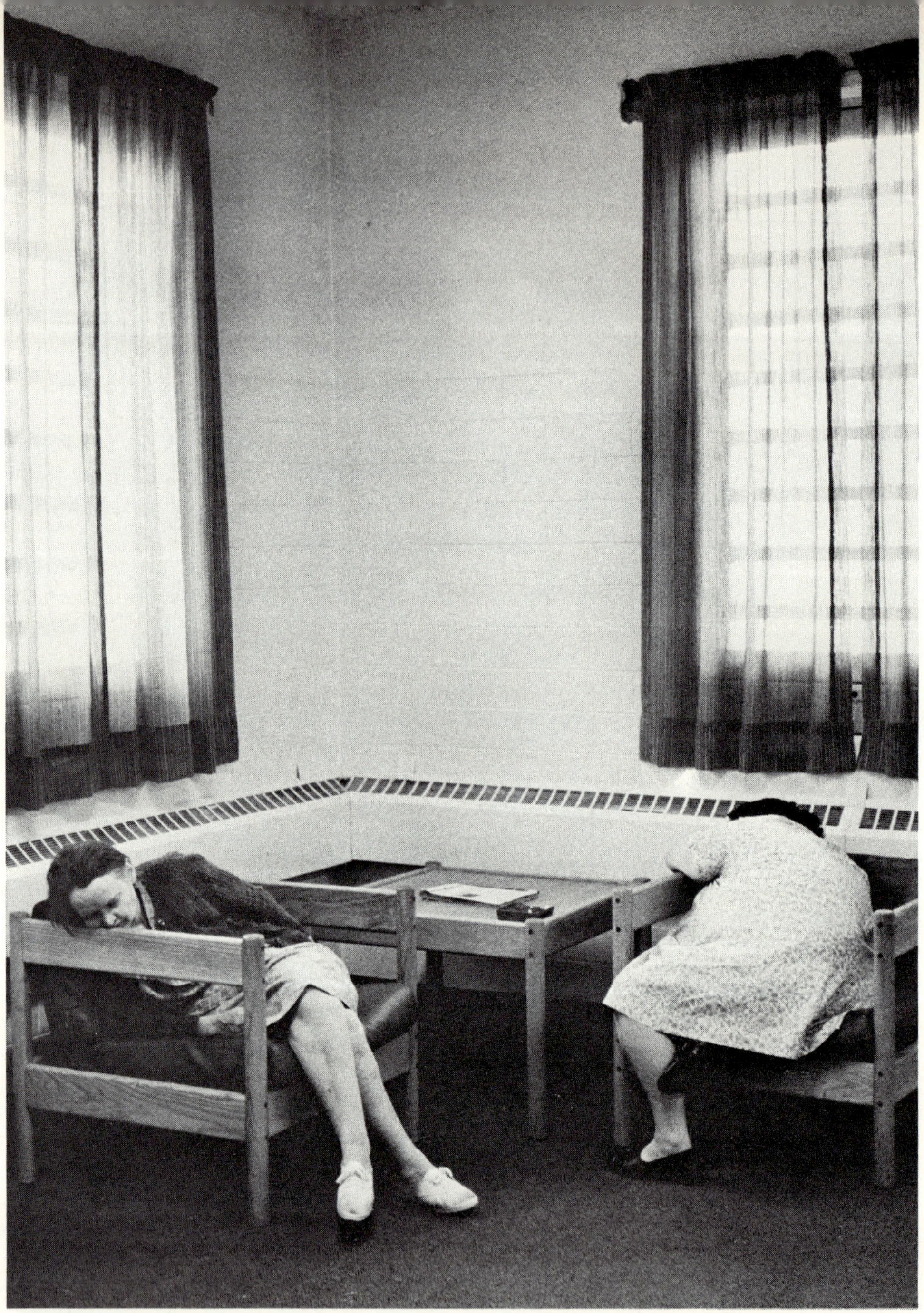

A major problem with institutional life is that there is little for the patients to do. (Photo by Burk Uzzle; Magnum Photos, Inc.)

A noteworthy aspect of mental hospitals throughout history is the discrepancy between their outer and inner appearances. The print shows Bethlehem hospital as it appeared to a passer-by in about 1740. This picture of serenity and cleanliness is deceptive; the word *bedlam* was coined to describe the conditions inside this hospital. (Reprinted by permission of Historical Pictures Service; Chicago, Illinois.)

an equal number of part-time psychiatrists and neurologists, and about six full-time social workers was responsible for serving the entire institution, for evaluating admission and transfer applications, and for providing community services, such as consultation to local associations for the mentally retarded.

The living conditions on some wards were abominable. Feces remained smeared on walls for hours. Patients slept in rows of single beds with as many as 40 beds in one room. The professional staff suspected certain attendants of physical brutality; in such instances, the staff patiently collected evidence of brutality because state civil service employees cannot be dismissed with anything less than semilegal proof of charges. Periodically, the Jones School would be exposed by local newspapers. On such occasions angry letters and editorials would be written, some politicians would appear horrified, and high state officials would make rare visits for firsthand accounts of the situation. Remarkably enough, public anger sometimes was directed toward the professional staff for tolerating the existing conditions. The solution invariably was the same: Some professional staff members would leave, a new administrative head would be appointed, and totally impractical, idealistic goals would be set. For example, the new staff of six psychologists might be charged with diagnosing and treating each of the 2,000 patients at least once per year. Unfortunately, living conditions for the patients were no better after the crises had subsided.

Annette's ward was neither one of the best nor one of the worst. A typical day for Annette was to be awakened at 7, to be bathed, to eat breakfast, and

Retarded young people at work in a community-based occupational training program. (Photo by Hiroji Kubota; Magnum Photos, Inc.)

then to be locked in a large, sterile playroom with 20 other children. A slight variation in this routine occurred in the summer when the children were locked in a large, fenced-in yard adjacent to the building. Except for lunch at noon, dinner at 5, bed at 8, and a trip to the nurse's office for medication, there was little that occurred in Annette's daily life. Occasionally a student volunteer would take Annette for a walk and would buy her some candy.

Discussion

The two descriptive studies of mental hospitals reviewed here speak for themselves and explain in some detail why psychologists have been concerned about developing community mental health alternatives to hospitalization. Although these descriptions are obviously not representative of all state and county mental hospitals, they are unfortunately not atypical insofar as they describe many (if not most) such facilities.

SUMMARY

Community psychology is concerned with the study of social systems such as hospitals, communities, schools, prisons, and mental health agencies. Its emergence as a subdiscipline of psychology was stimulated by five issues: (1) the failure of mental hospitals to provide adequate treatment for the mentally ill; (2) projected manpower shortages in the mental health professions; (3) the need for programs of prevention and early intervention; (4) the development of services that could be administered within the context of community agencies; and (5) a modern tendency toward a broader conception of abnormal behavior.

Many attempts to create innovative mental health programs have failed for reasons apart from the effectiveness or ineffectiveness of the programs. Sarason has attempted to understand these failures in terms of his theory on the creation of settings. According to Sarason's theory, innovative mental health problems and other settings often fail for the following reasons: (1) they represent an implicit threat to existing, more established settings; (2) the leaders fail to anticipate problems; (3) the new setting inherits the conflict and problems of parent settings and/or funding agencies; (4) the leaders overestimate what can be accomplished given limited resources; and (5) the leaders have an unrealistically optimistic and brief time perspective.

Organization development (OD) is an attempt to promote mental health in organizational settings by creating a climate in which people better understand one another and communicate effectively. One way in which these goals may be partially accomplished is through the educational format of a T-group, in which members of an organization discuss interpersonal issues along with a group leader.

Ecological models of abnormality focus on the different types of adjustment problems created by different environments. For example, Kelly (1968) reported some evidence that social isolation and identity confusion were maladaptive in fluid high school environments with a high rate of student influx, whereas nonconformity behaviors were maladaptive in constant high school environments. Reiss and Dyhdalo (1975) and O'Neill (1974) found that some types of children adapt better to open-space classes, whereas other types adapt better to traditional classroom environments.

Fairweather (1967) has defined a strategy for social change that focuses on an experimental evaluation of community interventions. One tenet of this strategy is that the effectiveness of innovative programs should be compared with typical programs in order to establish first their practical benefits.

The treatment and prevention techniques and formats discussed in this chapter include consultation, T-groups, advocacy, crisis intervention, and community mental health centers. The T-group has been defined as a small group of normal people who hold meetings during an extended period of time; there exists some tentative evidence that T-groups can have lasting, beneficial effects in developing work environments that are more rewarding. Community mental health centers ideally provide an array of services that include in-patient and out-patient care, crisis intervention, diagnostic services, professional and paraprofessional training, consultation to schools and other community agencies, and research and evaluation services. Unfortunately, few if any mental health centers have the funding and qualified personnel necessary to permit the full range of ideal services.

An example of a research issue in community psychology is the study of mental hospitals and their effects on patients. Unfortunately, there is little to do in many mental hospitals, and becoming a mental patient is too often a dehumanizing experience.

Part Three

What Has Been Learned About Abnormality?

Chapter 10

The Neurotic Syndromes

The neurotic is mysterious because he is *capable* of acting and yet is *unable* to act and enjoy. Though physically capable of aggression, he is meek; though capable of affection, he is cold and unresponsive. As seen by the outside witness, the neurotic does not make use of the obvious opportunities which life offers him.

DOLLARD AND MILLER (1950, p. 12)

The central issue in neurosis is anxiety and how it is managed. Examples of neurotic syndromes discussed in this chapter include anxiety neurosis, phobia, amnesia, sleepwalking, and multiple personalities. Neurotic depression is discussed in Chapter 14.

The term *neurosis* was introduced in 1781 by William Cullen in an effort to explain emotional disturbances as generalized weaknesses in the nervous system. Because Cullen also proposed that physical diseases are caused by weaknesses in the nervous system, his identification of the nervous system as having explanatory relevance for emotional disturbance appears to have been little more than a lucky guess (see Riese, 1958). In fact, medical history is replete with wild hypotheses attributing emotional disturbance to deficiencies of particular organs. Prior to Cullen, for example, hypochondriasis (a neurotic syndrome characterized by a morbid concern over the possibility of becoming ill) was attributed to the hypochondria—the hypochondria is a nonexistent organ once believed to exist in the upper abdomen (Chrzanowski, 1959; Kenyon, 1965). Thus, in proposing that emotional disturbances are caused by deficiencies of the nervous system, Cullen was merely continuing the historical practice of guessing which bodily organ is the site of emotional disturbance. In this instance Cullen's guess earned him everlasting fame—the nervous system not only exists but also plays an important role in emotional disturbances, even though that role is much different from what Cullen proposed. In any event, the term *neurosis* has survived as a way of referring to emotional disorders in which the chief symptom is anxiety.

EMOTIONAL REACTIONS

The neurotic syndromes are sometimes referred to as emotional disturbances in recognition of the debilitating presence of anxiety, grief, guilt, or anger. Compared to normal emotional reactions, neurotic emotional reactions are inappropriate and are of longer duration. This section is an introduction to the nature of anxiety and grief reactions and to the manner in which they can be identified.

Measures of Emotional Reactions

Research on emotional states requires reliable and valid measures of the presence of the particular emotion under investigation. Three kinds of measures of emotional states are self-reports, behavioral measures, and physiological measures.

Self-report Measures

An example of a simple self-report measure of anxiety is the subject's rating of the extent to which he feels anxious. For example:

I usually feel

Anxious____:____:____:____:____:____:____Relaxed

Another example of a self-report measure of anxiety is the Taylor Manifest Anxiety Scale (Taylor, 1953). This questionnaire provides 50 items, similar to the following examples:

1. I have difficulty sleeping.	<u>True</u>	False
2. I sweat easily.	<u>True</u>	False
3. I usually have enough energy.	True	<u>False</u>

The underlined responses are those of an anxious subject. The total number of anxious responses made by the subject is considered an index of his or her general level of anxiety. Similar self-report measures and questionnaires can be administered to assess the presence of grief.

Behavioral Measures

Behavioral measures of emotional states can be obtained by objective observation of the subject's behavior, as discussed in Chapters 4 and 7. For example, fear can be inferred from observations of trembling, sweating, and flight, whereas grief can be inferred from observations of whining, crying, and apathy. Grief is also manifested in terms of retarded movements and a loss of interest in, or minimal response to, the environment. Shame is usually revealed by blushing, hanging the head low, and averting one's gaze (Martin, 1971). Anger is usually displayed by aggressive behavior, verbal abuse, and actions that have the consequence of hurting others.

Physiological Measures

The autonomic nervous system plays a central role in the mediation of emotional responses. As noted in Chapter 5, this system is under the control of the central nervous system and comprises the sympathetic nervous system and the parasympathetic nervous system. Arousal of the sympathetic nervous system prepares the organism for emergencies requiring "fight or flight" (Cannon, 1929); specifically, arousal increases heart rate, constricts blood flow to the digestive system and skin, and increases the blood flow to the muscles and brain. On the other hand, arousal of the parasympathetic nervous system conserves bodily energy; specifically, arousal decreases heart rate and reduces blood pressure. Arousal of the parasympathetic division also increases digestive and eliminative activity.

The presence of anxiety is correlated with strong sympathetic arousal, although parasympathetic involvement is not uncommon (Martin, 1971). The physiological correlates of anxiety attributable to sympathetic arousal include rapid and irregular heart rates and breathing, increased systolic blood pressure, dryness in the mouth, sweating on the palmar surfaces of the hands and feet, coldness in the extremities, shivering, and muscular tremors; the physiological correlates of anxiety attributable to parasympathetic arousal include stomach distress and diarrhea. Different levels of anxiety, however, are associated with varying levels and kinds of physiological responses; for example, intense anxiety (panic) is associated with very strong parasympathetic arousal and with fainting because the blood supply to the brain is reduced drastically.

The presence of grief is correlated with a reduction in parasympathetic activity, producing a large decrease in the activity of the digestive organs.

Agreement Across Measures

Different measures of the same emotional state do not always lead to the same conclusion in regard to the presence or absence of that emotional state, thereby creating a major problem for researchers. In particular, self-reports do not necessarily correlate highly with behavioral and physiological measures. For example, a person may say he feels fine even though the behavioral evidence indicates the presence of grief. Similarly, a subject may report being relaxed even though other evidence suggests he is anxious. In an effort to minimize these problems in identifying emotional states, sophisticated researchers rarely rely on self-report measures alone.

The various measures permit different distinctions among emotional states. For example, anxiety and fear can be distinguished on the basis of behavioral and self-report measures, but not on the basis of physiological measures. It is possible to differentiate anxiety and fear by considering the source of the threat. In anxiety reactions the threat is from within the individual, and the individual is often confused as to exactly what it is that frightens him. In fear reactions the threat is external to the individual, the danger coming from an external source known to the individual. Thus self-reports of "I feel apprehensive about something—I feel like something terrible is about to happen" suggest anxiety, whereas self-reports of "I am petrified of driving" suggest fear. By observing whether the anxiety response is relatively ubiquitous and seemingly elicited by internal rather than external (environmental) stimuli, behavioral measures also can be utilized to distinguish between anxiety and fear. Physiological measures, however, suggest that the emotional response of anxiety and fear are actually quite similar; in fact, it is impossible to differentiate the two on the basis of physiological measures alone.

Similarly, self-report and behavioral measures can be used to differentiate between guilt and shame, but physiological measures do not permit this distinction. Thus, the bases for distinguishing between guilt and shame are in the eliciting stimulus conditions and in the cognitive component of the reaction. In general the eliciting conditions of guilt reactions are transgressions one disapproves of, whereas the eliciting conditions of shame are transgressions disapproved of by others.

CLASSIFICATION OF NEUROTIC BEHAVIOR

The question "What is a neurosis?" cannot be answered in a simple, straightforward manner. There are different types of neurosis, and it is misleading to consider all types as having something in common. Statements such as "Discomfort characterizes the neuroses" are true only in a general sense because, as we study the different types of neuroses, we find both qualitative and quantitative differences in discomfort. For example, in anxiety neurosis discomfort is in the direct experience of anxiety; in depressive neurosis discomfort is in the direct experience of grief; in the obsessive-compulsive neurosis, discomfort is indirect, caused by the interference of compulsive behavior with the performance of everyday activities. We must recognize, therefore, the general nature of definitions of neuroses, and we must complement this general understanding with a more specific understanding of the details of each type of neurotic syndrome.

General Characteristics of Neurotic Behavior

In general, neurotic behavior is characterized by discomfort, distorted perceptions of inner feelings and of interpersonal events, and self-defeating (irrational) behavior.

Discomfort

The chief characteristic of neurotic behavior is anxiety. In other words, neurosis is characterized by suffering. Perhaps because there is nothing unusual about human suffering, there is a tendency among lay people to belittle neurotic problems and to regard neurotics as malingerers (Dollard & Miller, 1950). Neurotic suffering, however, is real and is not to be equated with the conscious chicanery of the malingerer.

Distortion of Interpersonal Events and Inner Feelings

A remarkable characteristic of neurosis is that it appears to be unnecessary. No obvious external pressure forces the neurotic to respond in inappropriate and unsatisfying ways. The neurotic does not suffer because he lost a loved one in a senseless accident; he does not suffer because his crops were devastated by adverse weather; nor does he suffer because the stock market crashed and he lost all of his money. Because there are typically no obvious external causes of the suffering, the neurotic himself is often confused as to the nature of his problems. It is the neurotic's distorted interpretation of reality, not the reality per se, that causes the suffering. The neurotic may suffer because he interprets the slightest criticism as a rejection, because he interprets his performances as failures when objectively they are average or above average in quality, or because he interprets anger toward an overbearing parent as sin.

The neurotic interprets inner feelings in a distorted manner. Inner feelings often are interpreted to be something other than what they really are; this distortion is a defensive reaction that has the consequence of protecting the neurotic from recognizing unacceptable impulses. For example, rather than recognize sexual or aggressive feelings, the neurotic may experience anxiety or guilt.

The neurotic's distortion of feelings often seems immature and childish. Preoccupied with his own problems, the neurotic does not accurately perceive the feelings and needs of others. This lack of sensitivity often leads to ineffective attempts at meaningful relationships.

Self-defeating Behavior and the Neurotic Paradox

The neurotic paradox refers to the perpetuation of self-defeating behavior, as exemplified in the following anecdotes:

1. A young man wants very much to be a success in his chosen profession but behaves in a manner that ensures failure. This pattern repeats itself as the man goes from one job to the next.
2. A young woman wants to be loved by her parents but is angry because she feels rejected. She spites her parents by becoming pregnant. She has an abortion and later spites her parents by getting arrested on a drug charge. The charges are dropped, and she later spites her parents by marrying someone of whom they strongly disapprove. These behaviors not only have punishing consequences but also are self-defeating because they increase parental rejection, thereby creating even greater anger in the child.
3. A college student wants to be attractive to women but repeatedly behaves in an awkward manner when in their presence.
4. A father wants to be loved by his daughter but fears rejection. The father is authoritarian in an effort to compel love, confusing obedience for genuine love. The daughter rebels. At each sign of rebellion, the father's insecurity is heightened, and authoritarian attempts at control are increased.

As these examples suggest, neurotic behavior is *rigid* in the sense that alternative ways of satisfying basic needs are not explored; it is *repetitive* in the sense that it typically recurs throughout life; and it is *self-defeating* in the sense that it frequently precludes satisfaction of the very need it expresses.

Normal, Neurotic, and Psychotic Behavior

A basic distinction in abnormal psychology is that between normal, neurotic, and psychotic behaviors. Continuity theorists propose that the distinction is primarily one of degree (Buss, 1966).

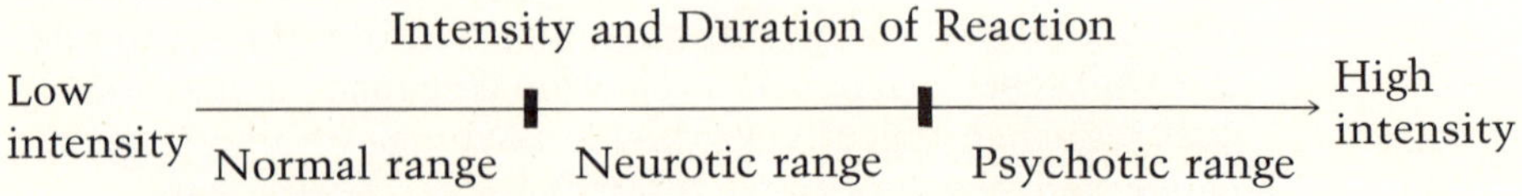

Discontinuity theory, however, proposes that neurotic and psychotic behaviors are qualitatively different. The controversy between continuity and discontinuity theory is a bit vague because it is unclear precisely what is meant by a qualitative versus a quantitative difference. In any event, Eysenck (1961)

and his co-workers found that neurotic and psychotic disorders do not fall on a single continuum as suggested by continuity theory but instead form different continua as suggested by discontinuity theory. This work, however, is inconclusive, and the continuity-discontinuity controversy is unlikely to be resolved for quite some time, if ever.

PREVALENCE OF NEUROSIS

Estimates of the prevalence of neurosis have ranged between 10 and 75 per cent of the general population (Redlich & Freedman, 1966). The discrepancy among these estimates is largely attributable to the following two problems:

1. There is no objective, conventional basis for distinguishing between mild neurotic episodes and episodes of normal tension and anxiety. On the one hand, a clinician can estimate the prevalence of neurosis to be as high as 50 per cent or more of the population by diagnosing as neurotic minor fears and episodes of nervousness. On the other hand, a clinician can estimate the prevalence of neurosis to be about 15 per cent of the population by diagnosing as neurotic only relatively severe or prolonged episodes of anxiety and fear. Thus, one reason for the wide discrepancy among clinicians in their estimates of the prevalence of neurosis is that some clinicians are estimating the prevalence of severe neurotic disorders while others are including less severe problems.
2. Clinicians differ on the meaning of basic diagnostic terms. What is a neurosis to one clinician might be a personality disorder to another and a psychophysiologic disorder to a third.

For the preceding reasons we should consider statistics on the prevalence of neurosis as rough estimates. This is especially true of estimates of the prevalence of particular neurotic syndromes such as phobia and compulsive neurosis. It also is true of estimates of the prevalence of mild neurosis, although it is less true of estimates of the prevalence of severe neurosis. For severe neurosis, several studies suggest a prevalence rate of approximately 15 per cent of the population (Srole et al., 1962; Phillips, 1966; Pasamanick, 1961).

THE NEUROTIC SYNDROMES

A syndrome is a clustering of "symptoms"—that is, a group of behaviors, feelings, and/or beliefs that tend to occur together. Hypochondriasis, for example, is a neurotic syndrome characterized by the following symptoms:

1. A habitual overconcern about one's health.
2. Chronic feelings of weakness and fatigue.
3. Various aches and pains.
4. Strange physical sensations.

Additionally, melancholy is frequently observed in hypochondriacal persons.

An important empirical question concerns the extent to which symptoms of a particular syndrome actually occur together. For example, some people are excessively concerned about health but do not have aches, pains, or strange physical sensations, whereas other people are weak and depressed, have aches and pains, but are not excessively concerned about their health. In such cases the diagnosis may be unclear under the definition given here of hypochondriasis.

The extent to which the symptoms of a syndrome actually intercorrelate is a major research question facing clinical researchers. One approach to the question has been to analyze mathematically descriptions of large numbers of neurotics (e.g., Cattell & Scheier, 1961; Eysenck, 1957; O'Connor, 1953; Wittenborn, 1951). Although this approach has shown promise, its highly detailed and complex mathematical nature seems to have precluded its widespread acceptance.

The definitions of the clinical syndromes presented in this chapter are based primarily on observations by clinical observers. The definitions provided are the classical descriptions of the neurotic syndromes. It is often necessary to appreciate that these are textbook descriptions and that in real life many neurotics show a mixture of symptoms from several of the syndromes listed here. In such cases the diagnosis is often the DSM-II syndrome that best matches the client's problems.

Anxiety Neurosis

The prominent features of an anxiety neurosis are discussed here.

1. *A history of periodic attacks of nervousness or panic; in these attacks, anxiety is directly expressed under conditions that pose no realistic danger.* The defining symptom of anxiety neurosis is the direct expression of anxiety under conditions that pose no realistic danger. The level of anxiety expressed and the frequency of anxiety attacks vary considerably, depending on the individual. In mild cases the person experiences episodes of nervousness, whereas in more severe cases the person experiences episodes of intense apprehension or even panic. Usually there are recurring life periods during which there are relatively frequent episodes of nervousness, apprehension, or possibly panic. Occasionally, however, no such history of an anxiety attack is evident.

The anxiety neurosis is distinguished from a normal anxiety reaction and from phobia. Normal anxiety attacks are temporary reactions to objective dangers, whereas neurotic anxiety reactions occur in the absence of any objective threat sufficient to justify the level of apprehension. The basis for distinguishing between phobia and anxiety neurosis is the extent to which the fear is localized to a consciously recognized stimulus. In phobia the person is aware of the object of his or her fear, and the fear is localized to some specific stimuli; in anxiety neurosis the person is confused by the anxiety because he is unaware of the object of his or her fear. For example, some anxiety neurotics have a sense of impending disaster but have no conscious idea what this disaster may be. Moreover, the anxiety neurotic is apprehensive under a much wider range of situations than is the phobic; in fact, anxiety in the anxiety neurosis is sometimes so pervasive that it has been referred to as "free-floating" anxiety.

In many instances, however, a clinical observer can identify stimuli that arouse anxiety in anxiety neurosis—thus the anxiety is free-floating in the sense that the controlling stimuli either are not obvious or are pervasive in the person's environment; the anxiety is not free-floating in the sense that there are no controlling stimuli.

Anxiety reactions may have an acute (sudden) or chronic (gradual) onset (Cameron, 1963), although acute onsets are more common. Occasional attacks of anxiety occur in all types of neurosis (Portnoy, 1959), but anxiety neurosis is not diagnosed unless the direct expression of anxiety is the prominent symptom. Some clinicians are reluctant to diagnose anxiety neurosis unless there is a history of anxiety attacks (Woodruff, Goodwin, & Guze, 1974).

2. *Somatic complaints and the development of secondary fears of serious illness.* The experience of frequent episodes of nervousness is often accompanied by somatic complaints, but the nature of these complaints can vary considerably, depending on the individual case. The most frequent complaints in anxiety neurosis are rapid and irregular heart beats, chest pains, and difficulty in breathing (see Woodruff et al., 1974). These symptoms are usually pronounced during anxiety attacks and often lead to a secondary fear that one is having a heart attack. The physiological symptoms of anxiety attacks are in fact similar to those of heart attacks, and physicians often confuse the two; if a physician expresses concern that a heart condition may exist, the patient's fear is usually enhanced and the symptoms intensify. In some instances the only sure way to diagnose the absence of a heart condition is by a blood test. Physicians also confuse anxiety attacks with ulcers because severe stomach pains and abdominal cramps sometimes accompany anxiety attacks.

Other somatic complaints that may accompany anxiety neurosis are trembling and shaking, as well as the so-called irritable colon syndrome of cramping, diarrhea, nausea, belching, and flatus (Woodruff et al., 1974). The presence of these symptoms for a period of several weeks leads to fears of serious illness and to fears of death.

Despite exposure to periods of nervousness, the life expectancy of anxiety neurotics is the same as that of normals; moreover, the anxiety neurotic is not more prone than is the normal individual to physical disease (see Woodruff et al., 1974).

3. *The presence of selective fatigue during periods between anxiety attacks.* In many (although by no means all) cases of anxiety neurosis, the person is mentally and physically tired between episodes of nervousness. The person may be too tired to perform minor tasks such as shopping and may spend a considerable amount of time sleeping. An interesting aspect of the fatigue reaction is that it is often specific to everyday situations insofar as opportunities to do something one really enjoys or is interested in can arouse a temporary resurgence of energy. This fatigue reaction is referred to as *neurasthenia.*

Laughlin has reported several cases of anxiety neurosis. In a case of an acute reaction, a 46-year-old businessman was having difficulties with his wife and his boss. While driving to work one morning, he suddenly began to shake all over, felt pains in his chest, and thought he was dying. He felt something awful was about to happen, but he did not know what it was. In another case a 34-

year-old housewife was continually tense and fearful following a visit to her parents' home. She told her physician: "I feel like something bad is about to happen. I don't know what it is, and I feel afraid" (1967, p. 112).

Anxiety neurosis usually occurs in mild forms that are not debilitating in the sense that the person can perform life chores even though he is often more nervous or tired than most people. The syndrome is one of the more frequently diagnosed forms of neurosis; including mild forms of the disorder, the prevalence of anxiety neurosis has been estimated at about 5 per cent of the population (Woodruff et al., 1974).

Phobia

The prominent features of the phobic neurosis (Westphal, 1872; Freud, 1895) are discussed here.

1. *Apprehension about a particular object or situation.* Unlike anxiety reaction, phobias consist of fears of specific stimuli. The fear, however, is irrational in the sense that the phobic stimulus does not constitute a realistic threat sufficient to justify the level of fear.

2. *Avoidance of the feared object.* Presumably, this behavioral avoidance is reinforced by fear reduction.

3. *The fear is unusually highly resistant to extinction.* Providing objective information on the harmlessness of the phobic object is insufficient to alter significantly the level of fear. Typically, the individual is aware of the irrationality of his fear and frequently is confused as to why he is fearful of the phobic object.

Phobias occur in varying degrees. In mild cases the individual avoids the phobic object without any serious alteration in his life-style. For example, a factory worker who is afraid of flying simply drives wherever he wants to go. In more extreme cases the individual's entire life is organized to avoid the phobic object. For example, a man afraid of driving refuses to leave his house for fear of seeing cars or the many objects that remind him of cars.

The number of objects and situations that can become phobic is seemingly unlimited. Examples of phobic objects include snakes (zoophobia), bugs (zoophobia), heights (acrophobia), open space (agoraphobia), and confined places (claustrophobia). Dixon, deMoncheau, and Sandler (1957) factor analyzed 26 phobic stimuli and found that they clustered along two factors, fear of separation (e.g., being left alone, open spaces) and fear of harm. Similar results have been reported by Lader (1967).

Freud (1895) distinguished between common and specific phobias. Common phobias are those shared by large numbers of persons and include fear of snakes and death. On the other hand, specific phobias are those that occur less frequently, such as a fear of horses.

Phobias occur in both children and adults. The incidence of mild phobias is quite high, but meaningful statistics are complicated by vagueness about the level of fear necessary for a state to be considered a phobia. The incidence of debilitating phobic neuroses, however, is much lower.

One specific phobic pattern in children that has received some attention is the school phobia (Jenkins, 1968; Johnson, Falstein, Szurek, & Svendson, 1941; Waldfogel, 1959). However, the term *school phobia* is misleading because often the child fears separation from home rather than going to school (Johnson et al., 1941). Kennedy (1965) estimated the frequency of school phobia to be 17 per 1,000 per year and found them to be more prevalent in girls.

Obsessive-Compulsive Neurosis

Obsessions are recurring ideas that a person cannot stop thinking even though he knows they are absurd. Compulsions are repeated impulses to carry out certain acts; if the person does not carry out these acts, he becomes anxious. Both obsessions and compulsions tend to occur in the same individuals, and there exists little reason not to consider the obsessive-compulsive neurosis as a single syndrome. The semantic suggestion of two syndromes—obsessive neurosis and compulsive neurosis—is a result of a historical oddity. Freud and Kraepelin called this syndrome *Zwangsneurose.* In London this was translated into obsession and in New York into compulsion (Rado, 1959). Hence the semantic suggestion of two syndromes resulted when in reality there appears to be only one.[1]

The prominent features of the obsessive-compulsive neurosis are:

1. A sense of compulsion, of being impelled to think certain ideas and/or perform certain behaviors. The individual is usually aware of this loss of control and is sometimes frightened by it.
2. The frequent recurrence of these obsessions and compulsions.
3. A desire to resist the obsessions and compulsions, often associated with fears of losing control.
4. The obsessions and compulsions usually occur in a context of high levels of anxiety and are usually followed by a reduction in anxiety (Carr, 1974).

Cameron (1963) reports the case history of a 12-year-old boy who had recurring impulses to call his parents obscene names. The child maintained control by saying out loud to himself "Stop it! Stop it!" In another case reported by Cameron, a middle-aged lady had repeated impulses to choke her husband while he slept but controlled them by going to the bathroom. Laughlin (1967) has reported a case of a 28-year-old man with an obsessive preoccupation with cleanliness, accompanied by a hand-washing compulsion. This man cleaned the keys of his business machines with a strong disinfectant before and after each use, handled his undergarments with sterile tissues, dry-cleaned his clothes if he brushed against another person, and washed his hands to reduce tension.

A seemingly unlimited number of ideas and behaviors can become obsessions and compulsions. Common symptoms include spells of brooding and doubting, indecisiveness, impulses to use obscenities, impulses to check and not rely on memory (e.g., returning to the kitchen to see if you really turned off the stove), rituals such as hand washing and wearing particular apparel or

[1] Although our consideration of the obsessive-compulsive neurosis as a single syndrome is in agreement with data summarized by Carr (1974) and represents the opinion of most current workers, others disagree and continue to distinguish two syndromes.

lucky objects, and exaggerated attention to details. Like most neurotic symptoms, these symptoms occasionally occur in normal people, but they occur with much greater frequency and intensity in the neurotic.

The incidence of obsessive-compulsive neurosis is generally reported to be low, although accurate statistics are unavailable.

Clinical observers have reported that obsessive-compulsive neurotic symptoms usually develop in a certain personality type, called the *obsessive-compulsive* personality. The obsessive-compulsive personality has been described as thorough, punctual, and orderly. A factor-analytic study by Sandler and Hazari (1960), however, found no relation between obsessive-compulsive personality traits and the occurrence of obsessive-compulsive neurotic symptoms.

Conversion Hysteria

The prominent diagnostic feature of hysteria is the loss of some bodily or psychological function in the absence of any neurological damage sufficient to account for this loss. Two types of hysteria are sometimes distinguished: *conversion hysteria* in which a bodily function is lost, and *dissociative hysteria* in which a psychological function is lost. Classic examples of conversion symptoms include fits, blindness, deafness, tics, paralysis, and anesthesias (loss of sensation at various parts of the body); more common, however, are complaints of burning pains or sores (e.g., painful throbbing of blood in one's legs), fainting, and menstrual bleeding. In many cases the hysteric complains of a large number of aches, pains, and other physical problems that suggest difficulties with nearly all organ systems (Woodruff et al., 1974). The most common conversion symptom is pain (Chodoff & Lyons, 1958; Purtell, Robins, & Cohen, 1951). A particularly dramatic conversion symptom is pseudocyesis, or false pregnancy.

Although hysteria has been considered a female syndrome, conversion symptoms do occur in men. During World War I, and perhaps to a lesser extent during World War II, many cases were reported of conversion symptoms in combat soldiers. Studies conducted since World War II, however, have generally found that the incidence of conversion symptoms in women is indeed much greater than the incidence of these symptoms in men (Purtell, Robins, & Cohen, 1951; Stephens & Kamp, 1962).

Laughlin (1967) has reported several case histories of conversion hysteria. In a case of a hysterical fit, a 16-year-old boy was referred for behavior resembling an epileptic convulsion. Medical examination, however, revealed no organic disability; moreover, the adolescent's "convulsion" occurred without the loss of consciousness characteristic of epileptic convulsions. In another case, during basic training a 17-year-old army recruit suddenly was unable to use one leg while standing or walking. Neurological examination revealed normal physiological functions and the ability to move the leg while prone or sitting; the patient was unable to explain this disability. Brady and Lind (1961) reported a case of a 40-year-old man who suddenly became blind in both eyes even though there was no apparent physiological problem. This patient was not alarmed by his loss of sight, but instead had an attitude of forebearance.

There was also some biological evidence that the patient could see despite his report of total blindness. Walters reported a case of a 36-year-old man who suffered left facial pain for more than a year: "His psychological sore was that he drank, had lost his first wife because of this, remarried, and then had his second wife upset by drinking. One night she slapped his left cheek as she threatened to leave. For the next year he remained sober but the left face pain set in at the site where he had been slapped" (1961, p. 8).

Clinical observers have reported that hysteria tends to occur in people with a hysterical personality disorder (e.g., McNeil, 1970). The hysterical personality style includes an unrealistic, romantic, and idealized manner of relating to other people. This proclivity toward exaggerated emotionality is expressed by the term *histrionics;* that is, a play-acting unreality characterizes the hysteric's behavior (McNeil, 1970). When exposed to excessive stress, the hysterical personality is hypothesized as likely to develop conversion symptoms. The actual extent to which conversion symptoms are associated with hysterical personality disorder, however, remains to be determined by future research.

Many hysterics love to talk about their physical complaints, and they often do so in an attention-seeking, exaggerated manner. One patient, for example, reported the following: "I can lose weight just walking down the street. I can hold my breath and lose weight. I was down to 65 pounds at one time" (Woodruff et al., 1974, p. 63). In some cases what is particularly striking in the hysteric's reaction to conversion symptoms is the absence of alarm or depression or what would normally be considered appropriate concern. For example, in the case of hysterical blindness we reported previously, it was noted that the patient's attitude about his mysterious blindness was one of forebearance rather than alarm. This complacent attitude toward conversion symptoms has been called *la belle indifférence* and is found in about one third of all patients with conversion symptoms (Abse, 1959; Buss, 1966).

History

Hysteria, which is the Greek word for *womb,* has a rich and fascinating history. Two thousand years before the birth of Christ, Egyptian physicians attributed emotional instability in women to a "wandering" uterus. Hippocrates was able to distinguish hysterical convulsions (hysterical fits) from true epileptic fits and followed the Egyptians in attributing the disorder to the uterus. Charles Lepuis (1563–1633) attributed the disorder to the brain, and in so doing appears to have been the first to have clearly disavowed the theory of a mispositioned uterus.

The great nineteenth-century French neurologist Charcot demonstrated that many hysterical symptoms are "anatomical nonsense." For example, the conversion symptom of glove anesthesia consists of a loss of sensation in the hand up to the wrist. Charcot noted that this was anatomical nonsense because no nerve controlled sensation only in the hand; thus, neurological damage resulting in a loss of sensation in the hand would also cause a loss of sensation above the wrist.

In addition to his theory that neurological damage cannot explain hysterical conversion symptoms, Charcot popularized his students' findings that hysterical symptoms could be induced by hypnotic suggestion and, as Mesmer had claimed, also could be removed by hypnotic suggestion (Veith, 1965). In one famous account of this discovery, Charcot's students presented him with a "true" hysteric and one that had hysterical symptoms hypnotically induced. The great master could not tell them apart.

Two of Charcot's disciples, Janet and Freud, made important contributions to the study of hysteria. Janet conducted observational studies of hysteric patients and found them to be neither more nor less erotic than normals, a finding Freud considered simplistic. Freud conducted in-depth interviews with hysteric patients and proposed that their symptoms represented a conversion of repressed sexual energy into sensory organs in a way that blocked sensory functioning. Robert Carter, however, had proposed a similar theory of hysteria more than forty years prior to Freud, but Carter's work was ignored by Freud as well as by others (Veith, 1965).

A recent issue concerns the possible disappearance of hysteria, at least in its classic form (Veith, 1965). Coleman reported a decline in conversion symptoms and explained it as follows: "Interestingly enough, their decreasing incidence seems to be closely related to our growing sophistication about medical and psychological disorders; an hysterical disorder apparently loses its defensive function if it can be readily shown to lack an organic basis" (1972, p. 235). Veith (1965) explains the disappearing nature of hysteria in terms of the individual's no longer being able to receive as much attention for hysterical symptoms.

Theoretical debate on the disappearing nature of hysteria is, however, premature because it has yet to be established that the disorder has in fact been declining in incidence. In one of the few empirical studies relevant to this question, Stephens and Kamp (1962) found that the prevalence of hysteria was about 2 per cent of all patients seen at an out-patient clinic during each of two eras, 1913–1919 and 1945–1960.

Historically, there has been ample skepticism about the "reality" of conversion symptoms, with many suspecting fakery (Szasz, 1961; Veith, 1965). Such concerns are based partially on the fantastic nature of the more flamboyant hysterical symptoms, and partially on the so-called secondary gains, or reinforcement, for hysterical behavior. For example, hysterical conversion symptoms often elicit sympathy and attention, and in the case of the combat soldier may lead to hospitalization instead of battle assignment. Today, theorists are in general agreement that hysterical symptoms are not conscious attempts at fakery. Redlich and Freedman, however, have noted that ". . . differences between malingerers and hysterics are not absolute, and we often find many hysterical traits in malingerers and some near-conscious dramatic play-acting in the hysterical patient" (1966, p. 371). Thus excessive feigning of abnormal behavior is itself an abnormal behavior—if a person is always pretending to be sick, he or she is in fact "sick," for a considerable amount of energy has been devoted to an inappropriate and unsatisfying life of pretention.

Dissociative reactions refer to a splitting off of psychological functions (Cameron, 1963). Nonneurotics sometimes experience mild dissociative episodes such as transient estrangement and "wanderings of thought" when they first learn of tragic news. Neurotic estrangement, however, refers to relatively severe and long-lasting losses of psychological functioning not attributable to any physiological damage. Most neurotic dissociative states seem to represent an attempt to escape from stressful and anxiety-arousing stimuli.

Dissociative states are common, but they rarely occur with sufficient intensity to warrant a diagnosis of dissociative neurosis.

Amnesia

Amnesia refers to the loss of memory. Total amnesia, in which the patient forgets his own identity (e.g., name, occupation, and where he lives), is very rare (Redlich & Freedman, 1966). The more typical case is partial amnesia in which there is a forgetting of a traumatic event.

Fugue

Fugue is a state of flight, or wandering away, which Laughlin (1967) defines in terms of three criteria: (1) the person has wandered away from his usual environment; (2) the person is partially amnesic for events leading up to and including the wandering; and (3) the person seems to be suffering from intolerable psychological conflicts.

Janet (1924) reported a case of a 17-year-old boy who worked in Paris, seemed generally nervous, and was described as passive, unambitious, and mild-mannered. One day the boy inexplicably found himself in a suburb of Paris. He did not know how he got there, so he returned to Paris and resumed his routine existence. This pattern of suddenly discovering his whereabouts in some place other than Paris continued for a number of years with the boy returning to Paris whenever he realized he had somehow wandered away.

Somnambulism

Somnambulism refers to sleepwalking, or the performance of some act while asleep. The sleepwalker either returns to bed while asleep or awakens and then returns to bed. The sleepwalker is usually unable to report his experience even if awakened in the middle of a sleepwalk. The incidence of somnambulism is relatively high, particularly in children.

Sleepwalking can be dangerous, as in isolated examples of people walking out of windows. It is generally believed to be accompanied by dream activity, and Cameron (1963) has reported several cases in which the sleepwalker seemed to be trying to escape from a terrible dream.

Depersonalization

Depersonalization is a sense of estrangement from one's self—the patient may report subjective feelings that seem strange or peculiar, or he may sense that he has somehow become different (Fisher, 1959; Jacobson, 1959). An example of depersonalization that occasionally occurs in normal people is the feeling of *déjà vu,* which means "already seen"—an experience one senses as having had before.

Dissociative Personality States

Perhaps the most interesting cases of dissociative reactions are those involving dissociated personalities, or states in which two or more personalities co-exist. Although no more than a dozen cases of dissociated personality have been reported, theorists usually distinguish between *alternating personality* and *multiple personality.* Robert Louis Stevenson's *Dr. Jekyll and Mr. Hyde* is a fictional account of alternating personality. In this syndrome, two or more personality organizations alternate dominating roles as often as several times a day. Cameron has noted that the alternating personality may be an exaggeration of normal differences in everyday behavior: "There is, for example, the hard-boiled businessman driving a bargain, who shows little or no consideration for the feelings of others and the same man at home an easy mark for everyone in the family" (1963, p. 359).

In the multiple personality there is no real alternation in dominance: One of the personalities is usually dominant and more completely developed. The concept of multiple personality was introduced by Morton Prince, an 1879 graduate of Harvard Medical School and the founder in 1906 of the *Journal of Abnormal Psychology.*

Prince (1905) reported the case of Miss Beauchamp, a Radcliffe coed who exhibited two separate personalities: The dominant personality was self-righteous and moralistic, whereas a second personality was strongly ambitious and aggressive. Under the influence of hypnosis, a third personality called Sally emerged. After six years of therapy, Miss Beauchamp finally functioned as a single, integrated personality.

A more recent case of multiple personality was reported in Thigpen and Cleckley (1954) *The Three Faces of Eve.* In this case, there were three personalities called Eve White, Eve Black, and Jane. Eve White was described as colorless, demure, and utterly self-controlled and calm. She would suddenly change into Eve Black, a more adventurous and lively personality. A third personality, Jane, emerged after eight months in therapy. The therapist achieved a successful integration of Eve's personalities by employing psychodynamic interview therapy.

Hypochondriasis

Hypochondriasis is an irrational and habitual overconcern about one's health often accompanied by unrealistic assumptions of illness. Chrzanowski (1959) summarized the usual presenting symptoms as including some, but not necessarily all, of the following:

1. Chronic feelings of weakness and fatigue.
2. Various aches and pains. Any part of the body may be affected, and the pains

BOX 10-1
Behavior Genetics

Rosenthal (1970) has summarized the data relevant to the question of whether or not behavioral predispositions to neurosis are inherited. In general, the available literature suggests the involvement of genetic factors, although the data are open to alternative explanations and are thus far from conclusive.

An early study by Brown (1942) compared the incidence of psychoneurosis in the parents and siblings of psychoneurotic and normal individuals. For the psychoneurotics, 16.4 per cent of the parents and siblings were judged to be psychoneurotic; for the normal controls, the corresponding incidence figure was 1.1 per cent.

Eysenck and Prell (1951) reported a particularly interesting study on the heritability of *neuroticism,* a trait considered by these investigators to be crucial for the development of psychoneurosis. The investigators studied 25 monozygotic (identical) and 25 dizygotic (fraternal) twin pairs, all of whom were schoolchildren. The neuroticism score for each subject was obtained from a battery of psychological tests. The results revealed a 0.85 correlation for monozygotic twins, compared to a 0.22 correlation for dizygotic twins. These data thus support the hypothesis that neuroticism is inherited.

may be general or localized. The most frequent type of pains is gastrointestinal.

2. A morbid preoccupation with illness, a desire to talk about one's complaints and, in severe cases, delusions of injury and delusions of the absence of an internal organ (Redlich & Freedman, 1966).

According to Kenyon, in 1651 Burton described hypochondriacal melancholy as "besides fear and sorrow, sharp belchings, fulsome crudities, heat in the bowels, wind and rumblings in the guts, vehement gripings, pain in the belly and stomach . . . cold sweat . . . cold joints, indigestion, they cannot endure their own fulsome belchings . . . midriff and bowels are pulled up, the veins about their eyes look red, and swell from vapours and wind" (1965, pp. 308–309). More recently, Laughlin (1967) reported several case histories of hypochondriasis. In one case a seven-year-old boy became uneasy and frightened when he noticed heart palpitations. The boy restricted his exercise, but his concerns rapidly dissipated when his parents provided a simple explanation and reassurance. In another case a 38-year-old electronics engineer complained of frequent headaches, nausea, abdominal cramps, leg pains, frequency of urination, nervousness, and lack of energy. He was absorbed in his complaints, which lacked any organic basis, and he was eager to discuss them.

Historically, hypochondriasis has been considered a male syndrome (Kenyon, 1965) and was originally distinguished from fatigue. One basis for the distinction between hypochondriasis and fatigue was that hypochondriasis was considered a localized problem attributable to the malfunctioning of an organ called the hypochondria, which was believed to exist in the soft part of the abdomen below the ribs and above the navel. On the other hand, fatigue was attributed to a general weakening of the nervous system; in fact, the clinical term for fatigue is neurasthenia, a combination of *neuro,* meaning "nervous system," and *asthenic,* meaning "weak." Today, some clinicians consider hypochondriasis and neurasthenia a single syndrome (Buss, 1966; Cameron, 1963; Pronko, 1963), but others do not (Laughlin, 1967).

Kenyon's (1965) review of the literature on hypochondriasis is a model of excellent scholarship and should be read by anyone with a serious interest in this syndrome. He identified as one historical and current issue the classification of hypochondriasis as a syndrome. The difficulties of identifying this disorder are considerable. Because hypochondriasis is often accompanied by delusions about illness and organ damage—in one case reported by Redlich and Freedman (1966) a man thought his abdominal pains indicated pregnancy—some theorists have classified hypochondriasis as a psychosis (e.g., Kraepelin, 1919, 1921). Most theorists, however, have classified the syndrome as neurotic (e.g., Freud, 1895; Eysenck, 1961). Another classificatory issue concerns the wisdom of considering hypochondriasis a separate syndrome (see Gillespie, 1928; Roth, 1959). In fact, hypochondriacal symptoms usually occur in context with other symptoms, particularly depression, but they also occur as accompaniments to delusions and hysterical symptoms. Although there is no *la belle indifférence*—the attitude toward imagined illness is one of overconcern, not indifference—the hypochondriac resembles the hysteric in the attention-seeking quality of his desire to talk incessantly about his symptoms. Hypochondriasis also resembles hysteria in that the usual presenting complaints of both syndromes include somatic pains and disabilities in the absence of any physiological bases for these complaints.

One of the best objective techniques for identifying hypochondriasis is the MMPI (see Chapter 4), which includes a 33-item scale mainly concerned with pains (see McKinley & Hathaway, 1940, 1944). Projective techniques such as the Rorschach also have been used, particularly with the intention of exploring the patient's body image.

Like hysteria, the incidence and nature of hypochondriacal reactions seem particularly sensitive to cultural influence (see Chrzanowski, 1959). As early as 1733, Cheyne entitled a treatise on hypochondriasis as "The English Malady," suggesting that hypochondriasis was peculiarly British. Chrzanowski (1959) noted the cultural tendencies for housewives to be exhausted by dinner's end, and for professionals to be preoccupied with fatigue at the end of a day's work. That such reactions are not entirely physiological is suggested by the ease with which good news or free tickets to the theatre can interrupt the pattern. The current preoccupation with health foods is often cited as an example of a cultural influence on hypochondriacal concerns.

A remarkable feature of mild cases of hypochondriasis is the ease with which people can be talked out of their complaints. For example, in the case of the boy concerned about heart palpitations, information and reassurance were sufficient to reduce the child's concern. Cases of this type are very common at all age levels (Redlich & Freedman, 1966; Laughlin, 1967). In the more severe cases, however, the exact opposite is true: It is extremely difficult to convince the patient that he does not suffer from an organic problem.

One perplexing complaint physicians frequently encounter is that of a pain for which no organic basis can be found. Such complaints sometimes involve car accident victims who claim they are hurt even though no hard evidence supporting this claim can be found. The extent to which future research is likely to show that such pains have physiological versus psychological determinants is unclear.

The incidence of hypochondriacal complaints is very high, but the incidence of hypochondriasis as a neurosis depends largely on how one defines the disorder. Different incidence figures for hypochondriasis, ranging from 3 to 14 per cent of all neurotic cases, have been reported in various studies (Shirvaikar, 1957).

Existential Neurosis

Based on the observations of social theorists and on his own clinical experience, Maddi (1967) has defined a syndrome called existential neurosis. The salient features of this syndrome are:

1. A sense of meaninglessness, or chronic inability to believe in truth, importance, usefulness, or the interest value of anything one is engaged in or can imagine doing.
2. Apathy, punctuated by occasional depression.
3. The individual considers what he does to be unimportant. There is a tendency to engage in activities that minimize activity.

Maddi's definition of existential neurosis, a syndrome that does not appear in DSM-II, is remarkable for its clarity. He has attempted to differentiate existential neurosis from other syndromes, particularly depression. According to Maddi, depression usually is characterized by sadness, whereas existential neurosis is characterized by apathy. Moreover, depressives have not necessarily concluded that *anything* they might do is meaningless, whereas existential neurotics have.

Accurate statistics on the incidence of existential neurosis are unavailable, but the disorder is believed to be prevalent. In this regard it is noted that many social observers have commented on the prevalence of alienation in our times.

Traumatic Neurosis of War

Military combat exposes soldiers to extreme degrees of stress. There is the possibility of death and/or mutilation, the excessive noise, the necessity to kill others, and the observation of death and injury to others. Not only does the soldier's own life depend on his combat performance, but also the lives of others. The level of stress is so high that the fact "That so relatively few become psychologically incapacitated under these conditions is remarkable in itself" (Merbaum & Hefez, 1976, p. 1). The incidence of neurotic breakdown for combat soldiers, however, is much higher than that for the general population. The longer the length of time exposed to combat, the greater is the probability of neurotic breakdown. Moreover, few soldiers, if any, are totally immune to the psychological effects of war (Grinker & Spiegel, 1944).

Combat neurosis was called *shell shock* during World War I; during the Vietnam War the same syndrome was called combat fatigue. (Reprinted by permission of Historical Pictures Services; Chicago, Illinois.)

Combat neurosis has been given several labels. During World War I this syndrome was called *shell shock.* During World War II and the Vietnam War it was called *combat fatigue.* Kardiner (1959) called this syndrome *traumatic neurosis of war.*

The initial signs of combat neurosis are largely the behavioral indicants of anxiety states: poor appetite, carelessness, jumpiness, fear of noise, inability to relax, and inability to sleep (Kardiner, 1959). States of hypersensitivity to environmental stimuli may be followed by virtually any of the neurotic behaviors already described in this chapter, including fatigue, conversion symptoms, compulsive rituals, fainting, tremors, depressive reactions, amnesia, and fugue. Particularly common signs include a recurring catastrophic dream, hypersensitivity, being startled by noises, and, at least among American soldiers, a proclivity to aggression (Kardiner, 1959).

Merbaum and Hefez (1976) administered the MMPI to 24 Israeli soldiers who were psychiatric casualties of the Yom Kippur War and to 12 Israeli soldiers who were wounded in the Yom Kippur combat. The results revealed that, as a group, the psychiatric casualties showed more evidence of psychopathology on the MMPI than did the medical casualties. At least 25 per cent of the psychiatric sample, moreover, had had some form of psychological treatment prior to their combat experience. These findings suggest the existence of a predisposition to neurotic breakdown resulting from combat experience. Despite the overall group differences, however, the majority of the psychiatric casualties provided "little evidence about their premorbid background that might have predicted that these individuals would experience psychological breakdown" (p. 5). The findings, then, are consistent with Swank's (1949) observation that psychological background is less important than duration of exposure to combat in predicting whether or not psychological disability will occur.

THE PSYCHOANALYTIC THEORY OF NEUROTIC ETIOLOGY

The basic elements of psychoanalytic theories of neurosis are those of anxiety and defense. The ego defends against anxiety because, as a result of childhood experiences, it unconsciously fears punishment for the expression of forbidden impulses. Specifically, the expression of sexual and aggressive impulses in children is punished, resulting in the association of these impulses with anxiety. When the impulses are subsequently experienced, the ego interprets the associated anxiety as a signal that expression of these impulses will result in punishment. The ego attempts to prevent the expression of anxiety in both action and consciousness. (See Chapter 6.)

Psychoanalytic theory assumes a conflict between anxiety-associated impulses and the defensive action of the ego. The impulses are forces seeking expression; defensive actions are counterforces designed to keep anxiety-associated impulses unconscious:

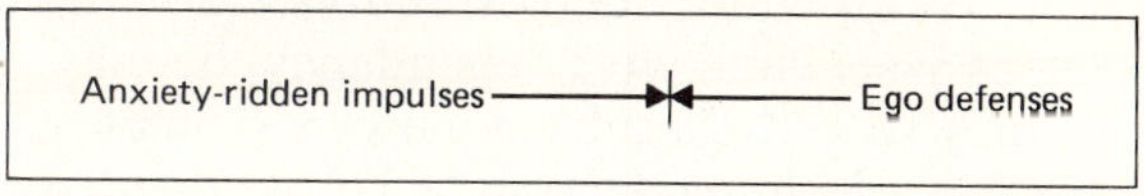

The interplay of these forces is called the dynamics of the neurosis. Within this basic schema, neurosis can develop when the forces behind the anxiety-ridden impulses become too great, the ego weakens, and anxiety is expressed either directly or in the form of a neurotic symptom:

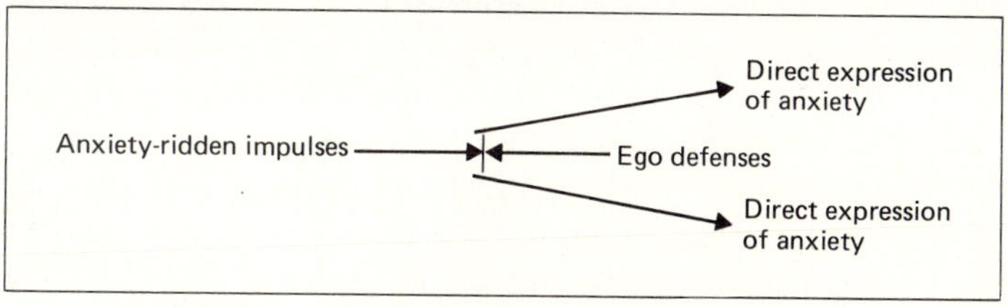

or

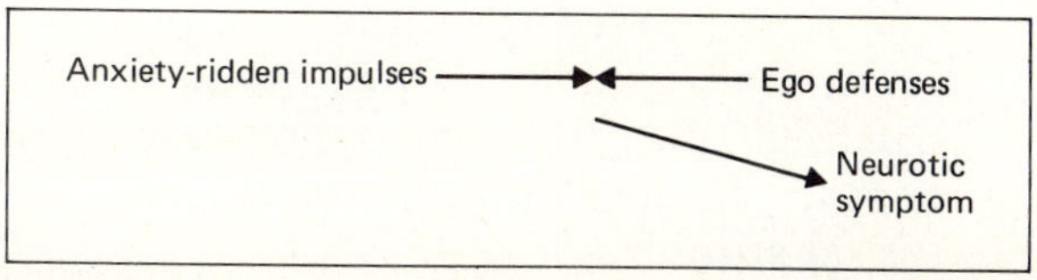

If the individual experiences trauma and the ego defenses break down completely, anxiety floods consciousness and a state of panic results:

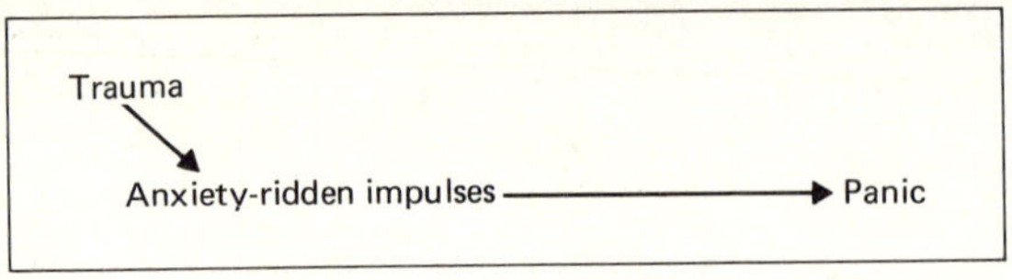

If the ego must call on vast amounts of psychological energy to defend against anxiety, the individual experiences neurotic fatigue and has little energy left for normal functioning. In this state a relatively minor stimulus exciting the anxiety-ridden impulses may be sufficient to cause a breakdown in the ego defenses.

Cameron's (1963) theory of neurotic etiology follows closely the account offered by Freud. Cameron's theory explains neurotic etiology in terms of six basic ingredients: predisposition, stress, conflict, regression, anxiety, and defense.

Predisposition

Cameron assumes that life experiences in general, and interpersonal childhood experiences in particular, create predispositions to neurotic behavior. For example, frustration of dependency needs of the infant can result in the association of these needs with anxiety, and the consequent life-long need to defend against impulses toward dependency in order to ward off the anxiety associated with their expression. As an adult, such an individual is likely to be particularly sensitive to issues associated with dependency; he may overract to rejection from others, he may tend to form friendships too quickly, or he may avoid close friendships for fear of later rejection. In interpersonal relationships he may be excessively demanding in an unconscious effort to obtain reassurance that the significant other will not leave or reject him. But even though this person, like all of us, shows areas of particular sensitivity and vulnerability, he does not necessarily have a neurosis and may be capable of functioning in a relatively normal way if stress and conflict do not interfere.

Consider the following hypothetical examples of predisposition to neurotic behavior. The parents of a young girl indicate their displeasure virtually every time the girl expresses sexual feelings, asks questions on the topic, walks around the house naked, and so on. The child is taught that sexuality is "dirty" and "wrong." Normal sexual desires thus become associated with anxiety; sexual impulses are repressed and denied. As an adult this woman is overly sensitive to sexual stimuli. She considers men in bathing suits disgusting; that is, psychodynamically, semiexposed men arouse sexual impulses and associated feelings of guilt and anxiety. Thus ego defenses (e.g., reaction-formation—"it's disgusting") are called on to repress the anxiety. Accordingly, this woman is predisposed to develop a neurosis, for she is vulnerable and overly sensitive to sexual stimuli.

Another common area of vulnerability concerns issues associated with authority. Consider a father who insists that his son obey him, demanding conformity in both thought and action. The boy's own desires are frustrated, causing anger and resentment toward the father. But the young child fears the father's punishment and thus represses his hostility. In later life, he will be overly sensitive to stimuli associated with authority, anger, and rebellion.

Stress

In Cameron's theory, neurosis develops either when a traumatic experience is encountered, or when an individual predisposed to neurotic behavior experiences stress. For example, if a person with strong dependency needs were to be rejected by his wife, the ensuing divorce proceedings would create prolonged stress and possibly precipitate a neurosis. If a woman with repressed guilt about normal sexual desires were to have an affair, the intensification of her guilt could precipitate a neurosis. If a young man with ambivalent feelings toward authority were to join the army, repressed feelings of hostility would be rearoused and could precipitate a neurosis.

Stress has two simultaneous effects in Cameron's theory. First, it causes a regression to a more immature level of functioning. Second, it rearouses unconscious conflicts.

Conflict, Anxiety, and Defense

The basic conflict consists of anxiety-associated impulses (e.g., dependency, sexuality, and hostility) and ego defenses against anxiety. If the ego cannot contain the anxiety, a neurotic symptom emerges.

Neurotic Symptoms

Cameron discusses three functions of the neurotic symptom:

1. It is a sign that the balance of force within the personality system is disturbed.
2. It is a sign that infantile conflicts have been reactivated.
3. It is itself an attempt at spontaneous cure, that is, an attempt at adaptation [1963, p. 451].

It is this latter function, that of an attempt at adaptation, to which we now turn our attention. When the ego is threatened with disintegration by the reactivation of infantile conflicts, it calls on auxiliary defenses to maintain itself. These defenses transform the infantile, unconscious impulses so that a compromise, called the neurotic symptom, is formed. Because the auxiliary defenses succeed in repressing the fundamental nature of the infantile conflict and thereby prevent a state of panic, the individual often is confused by the occurrence of the neurotic symptom and its meaning. The neurotic symptom is a compromise between the defensive functions of the ego and the unconscious forces seeking expression: The neurotic symptom permits the release of anxiety-ridden impulses, but only in a disguised form.

Psychoanalysts distinguish between the *primary* and *secondary* gains of neurotic symptoms. The primary gain relates to the adaptative (or defensive) functions of the symptoms and consists of the avoidance of overwhelming tensions and anxiety (Cameron, 1963). The secondary gain relates to the advantages of being sick and usually consists of sympathy from others, escape from the necessity of going to work, and so on.

The Psychodynamics of Neurotic Syndromes

In psychoanalytic theory the primary defense mechanism is repression. When anxiety and tension have reached intolerable levels, auxiliary defenses such as regression, displacement, projection, denial, and reaction-formation are used to control the release of anxiety. Compared to psychosis, regression in neurosis is partial and incomplete.

Cameron (1963) explains anxiety neurosis as a weakening of the ego's ability to repress anxiety. Stressful life circumstances reactivate infantile emotional conflicts causing intolerable levels of anxiety and tension. Repression continues to operate by keeping the source of anxiety unconscious so that the person is anxious but does not know what he or she is afraid of. Regression occurs, permitting the discharge of anxiety in infantile outbursts of emotion. Projection is to a diffuse source; that is, the person attributes anxiety to some unknown danger. In conclusion, Cameron explains anxiety neurosis in terms of defective repression and the consequent diffuse expression of anxiety, with defensive regression and projection operating in a desperate effort to avoid a state of panic.

Cameron has noted that parents sometimes directly train children to be anxious. This occurs when the parents themselves model anxiety, and the child learns to imitate the parental model. An overprotective mother, for example, frequently is training her child to fear many activities. Thus several studies have found positive correlations between overprotective parents and generally anxious children (e.g., Eisenberg, 1958; Jenkins, 1968).

Psychoanalytic theorists have explained phobia in terms of a projection or displacement of anxiety from its original source to a symbolic source. In the famous case of Little Hans, Freud treated a five-year-old boy who was afraid of horses and thus was reluctant to leave his home. Based primarily on the father's reports of Hans's behavior—Freud saw Hans only once—Freud hypothesized that the boy suffered from an unresolved Oedipal complex; that is, he unconsciously feared castration by his father in retaliation for his unconscious sexual attraction toward his mother. Unable to cope with his fear of castration, the boy displaced his fear onto horses, horses functioning as unconscious symbols for his father. Although some hailed this analysis of Little Hans as providing a major contribution to our scientific understanding of phobia (e.g., Glover, 1956), others have criticized it as being far-fetched (e.g., Wolpe & Rachman, 1960). The critics have noted that Freud's interpretation of Little Hans was based on questionable, second-hand accounts of Hans's behavior.

The obsessive-compulsive syndrome is associated with repression and with several auxiliary defenses including undoing, reaction formation, isolation, and displacement (Straus, 1948; Cameron, 1963). In Shakespeare's *Macbeth,*

TABLE 10-1
Defense Mechanisms and Symptoms for Some Neurotic Disorders

Disorder	Defenses	Examples of Symptoms
Anxiety neurosis	Physical release of tension; regression; repression	Fears, general overactivity, sweating, crying
Conversion symptoms	Displacement, projection, repression, regression	Improper functioning of some body part without a medical reason
Obsessive-compulsive neurosis	Reaction-formation, isolation, displacement, regression, repression	Repetitions, rituals, overconcern with cleanliness, health, sin, etc.

Lady Macbeth developed compulsive hand-washing behavior following the murder of a king. Psychodynamically, this compulsion was an unconscious attempt to reduce guilt by undoing the murder—that is, removing the imagined blood from her hand symbolized the undoing of the murder.

Table 10-1 provides a summary of the psychoanalytic interpretation of some neurotic syndromes. The reader should note the simplified nature of this table—rarely is any particular neurosis characterized by only one or two defense mechanisms, and there are many exceptions to the general rule concerning the type of defenses usually found in a particular neurotic syndrome.

Experimental tests of the psychoanalytic theory of general neurotic etiology are virtually nonexistent. The theory is based almost exclusively on clinical case histories. Many psychologists consider this support inadequate and have criticized the theory as being vague and highly speculative. Another difficulty concerns the unexplained problem of choice of symptoms; that is, when a breakdown occurs, why does one type of neurosis develop rather than another. But in recognizing the limitations of psychoanalytic theories, we should not deny its several strengths. In particular, it seems difficult to deny the essential validity of the psychoanalytic concepts of anxiety and defense.

LEARNING THEORY EXPLANATIONS OF NEUROTIC BEHAVIORS

Many learning theorists conceptualize psychoneurotic symptoms (e.g., phobia, conversion symptoms, compulsive symptoms) as behaviors that avoid or escape high levels of anxiety. In this general view, the acquisition of neurotic symptoms can be understood as involving two learning processes (see Mowrer, 1939):

1. Through Pavlovian conditioning, vicarious emotional conditioning, imitation of anxious parents, or covert sensitization (see Chapter 7), the neurotic learns to fear environmental and covert stimuli; that is, environmental and covert cues become conditioned stimuli (CSs) for an anxiety and/or guilt response. The behaviorist thus rejects the notion of free-floating anxiety—all anxiety is elicited by stimuli, although sometimes these stimuli are covert (thoughts and response feedback cues), whereas at other times these stimuli are environmental.

2. By means of operant conditioning (escape and avoidance learning), the individual learns behaviors (psychoneurotic symptoms) that mitigate the level of anxiety actually experienced. The performance of neurotic symptoms other than the direct expression of anxiety, depression, or fatigue is reinforced by anxiety reduction or avoidance.

The paradigm applications of this two-process model are phobias. Through Pavlovian conditioning, the individual learns to fear the phobic object, and through operant conditioning the individual learns to avoid the phobic object. Similarly, the model can be applied to other psychoneurotic symptoms; for example, through Pavlovian and covert conditioning, Lady Macbeth became extremely guilty over her role in the murder, and through operant conditioning she learned to mitigate the guilt by compulsive hand-washing.

Conditioned Emotional Responses

The first process in the two-process theory of neurosis is the acquisition of anxiety or fear to environmental or covert stimuli. There are many ways in which this type of learning might occur:

1. Environmental and covert cues can become CSs for anxiety as a result of Pavlovian excitatory conditioning in which the unconditioned stimulus (US) is a traumatic or frightening event. Consider the case of a man who is afraid of driving following a car accident:

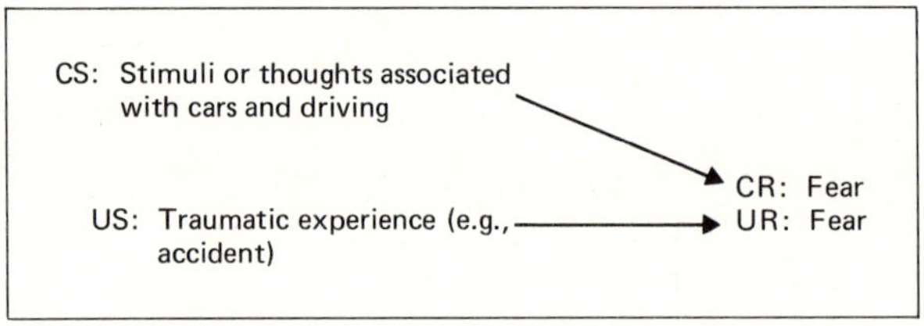

2. Environmental and covert cues can become conditioned stimuli for anxiety as a result of Pavlovian excitatory conditioning in which the US is a psychological conflict (Dollard & Miller, 1950; Wolpe, 1958). Wolpe (1958) discussed a hypothetical case of a woman who was engaged to a man she later decided she did not want to marry. This woman experienced an intense conflict between wanting to breaking the engagement but not wanting to be embarrassed about changing her mind. This conflict lasted for several months, becoming increasingly intense as the wedding day neared. Thus many environmental stimuli associated with the conflict could have become CSs for anxiety.

3. Environmental and covert cues could become, or be maintained as, CSs for anxiety as a result of covert sensitization (see Chapter 7; also see Ellis, 1962;

Rizley & Reppucci, 1975) in which the US is a frightening thought or image. For example, a young executive is afraid of promotion because he tells himself repeatedly that promotion will lead to failure.

4. Environmental cues could become CSs for anxiety as a result of observational learning in which the cue is seen to frighten others.

A major problem with behavioral explanations of neuroses is that, if neurotic emotionality functions as conditioned responses, treatment should be a relatively straightforward matter of extinction; that is, nonreinforced exposures to the anxiety-eliciting stimuli should readily lead to marked improvement and eventual cure. Neurotic anxiety is, however, highly resistant to extinction. There are several possible explanations for the persistence of neurotic anxiety. One explanation concerns the complexity of the stimulus configuration that must be extinguished or desensitized (Wolpe, 1958). In this view the typical neurotic has learned to respond with anxiety to so many stimuli, or to so many aspects of a particular stimulus, that extinction is a potentially long and arduous undertaking. A second explanation concerns covert reconditioning trials. As both Ellis (1962) and Rizley and Reppucci (1975) suggest, conditioned fear could be maintained by thinking about the US. For example, a person sees a snake and thinks "a snake could bite me." Because the sight of the snake (CS) is associated with an anxiety-eliciting thought (US), the process is really one of continued conditioning (CS-US pairings) rather than extinction (CS alone).

Preparedness

Seligman's (1970, 1971) concept of preparedness provides another possible explanation of the persistence of neurotic anxiety. This concept suggests that, depending on the species, some CS-US associations are biologically prepared; prepared associations are readily acquired and are relatively persistent under conditions of extinction. For example, rats learn very quickly to avoid the taste of a food that once made them feel nauseated but have difficulty learning to avoid visual stimuli that predict nausea. It is as if the rats are biologically prepared to learn some associations (e.g., taste-nausea) and biologically unprepared to learn other associations (e.g., light-nausea).

Seligman's concept of preparedness provides a theoretical explanation of common phobias in humans. Across the world many people are afraid of snakes, bugs, heights, cats, and dogs, whereas relatively few people are afraid of lambs, houses, and trees. According to Seligman (1971), a possible explanation is that, in humans, Pavlovian conditioned associations between snakes and anxiety are prepared, whereas associations between lambs and anxiety are unprepared. Seligman (1970) has also proposed that humans are prepared to acquire language.

Seligman's concept of preparedness does not deny the role of experience in the acquisition of fear. Rather, it postulates a biological predisposition to learn to associate certain stimuli. The assumption that certain associations are biologically prepared is theoretical and has yet to be subjected to systematic testing.

BOX 10-2
Experimental Neurosis?

The hypothesis that conflict plays a central role in the development of neurotic behavior once seemed to derive important support from animal studies on "experimental neurosis." The classical experiment is by Shenger-Krestonvnikova and was reported by Pavlov (1928). In this study dogs provided with Pavlovian discrimination training learned to salivate when shown a circle but not when shown an ellipse. The experimenter then made the discrimination increasingly difficult by making the ellipse stimulus increasingly circular. Eventually the dogs began to howl, showed evidence of emotionality, and lost the capacity to salivate discriminatively when the CSs were again a circle and a clearly different ellipse. This study has been interpreted as showing that conflict produces an "emotional breakdown" or "experimental neurosis" in dogs and has been cited as support for psychodynamic theories that posit the importance of conflict in human neuroses.

In a series of poorly controlled studies, Masserman (1943) extended Shenger-Krestonvnikova's findings. Hungry cats were trained to perform a simple response on signal to obtain food from a box. An aversive stimulus (e.g., an air blast or an electric foot shock) then was delivered, and the animals subsequently developed a number of "neurotic" behaviors including a rapid heart beat, catchy breathing, raised blood pressure, sweating, erection of hair, extreme startle to minor stimuli, "irrational" fears of physically harmless lights or sounds, gastrointestinal disorders, recurrent asthma, sexual impotence, peculiar "compulsions," and helplessness. Masserman considered these behaviors to be expressions of an experimental neurosis, and he regarded experimental neurosis in animals as a valid model of neurosis in people.

Two important problems in the experimental neurosis literature have been identified and, unfortunately, these problems greatly limit the significance of the animal research. One problem is whether or not animals can exhibit a neurosis. In this regard, it has been noted that neurosis in humans has an important cognitive component (see, e.g., Ellis, 1962). Because it is difficult, if not impossible, to evaluate the presence or absence of cognitions in animals, it is possible that qualitative differences exist between neurosis in animals and in humans. The other problem with the experimental neurosis model is that the animal studies do not demonstrate that conflict causes emotional disorders because the findings can be interpreted in other ways. The Masserman studies, for example, confounded exposures to conflict with exposures to an aversive stimulus, and there is evidence that it was exposure to the aversive stimulus that produced the effects (Smart, 1965; Wolpe, 1958). Other potentially important factors Masserman did not control are the presentation of an uncontrollable versus a controllable aversive stimulus and the length of time in the experimental apparatus. Dmitruk (1974), for example, found that mere confinement in an experimental apparatus is sufficient to produce experimental neurosis in cats.

In conclusion, it has yet to be demonstrated that conflict causes experimental neurosis.

TREATMENT

Although progress in identifying the actual causes of neurotic disorders has consisted largely of the formulation of theories rather than factual demonstrations of etiology, considerable progress has occurred in the area of treatment. (See Chapters 5, 6, 7, 8, and 9.) Psychoanalysis and the subsequent development of psychodynamic therapy are regarded by many as important advances in the treatment of neurotic disorders. Drug treatment is also a recent development; various tranquilizers and antidepressants are now available. The development of systematic desensitization and of other behavior therapy techniques unquestionably constitutes a major advance in the treatment of neurotic disorders; the available evidence strongly suggests that the proper implementation of systematic desensitization is partially effective in the treatment of a wide range of disorders in which the patient's problem can be conceptualized in terms of fear (see Chapter 6).

SUMMARY

The neurotic syndromes sometimes are referred to as emotional disturbances in recognition of the debilitating presence of anxiety, fear, grief, or anger. The extent to which these emotional states are present has been assessed by self-report, behavioral, and physiological measures. In some cases it is possible to distinguish among emotions in terms of behavioral measures but not in terms of physiological measures. For example, the physiologic responses of anxiety and fear are indistinguishable; however, psychoanalytically oriented psychologists usually distinguish anxiety from fear on the basis of the source of the threat. Anxiety is indicated when the threat is from within, whereas fear is indicated when the threat is external.

Neurotic behavior is characterized by discomfort, distortion of interpersonal events and inner feelings, and self-defeating behavior. The neurotic paradox is that neurotic behavior is both self-defeating and self-perpetuating. Neurotic behavior is rigid in the sense that alternative ways of satisfying basic needs are not explored, it is repetitive in the sense that it typically recurs throughout life, and it is self-defeating in the sense that it frequently precludes satisfaction of the very need it expresses.

The prevalence of severe neurosis has been estimated to be about 15 per cent of the population. Anxiety neurosis and phobia appear to be among the most prevalent types of neurosis, whereas classical hysterical reactions and hypochondriasis are less prevalent.

Several neurotic syndromes were discussed. The prominent signs of anxiety neurosis are episodes of anxiety (nervousness, tension, apprehension), somatic complaints suggesting the presence of anxiety (e.g., constipation, chest pains, irritable colon), and the subject's confusion as to why he is nervous and tense. Episodes of anxiety, depression, and fatigue often alternate; whether anxiety neurosis, depression, or neurasthenia is diagnosed can depend on which episode is most prominent at the time the diagnosis is made. Often there is a history of life periods during which the individual frequently experiences episodes of anxiety; sometimes, however, no such history is evident. The onset of anxiety attacks can be acute (sudden) or chronic (gradual).

Phobia is diagnosed when the person fears some object or situation that does not pose any realistic threat. The person avoids the phobic object. In minor cases, avoidance of the phobic object does not interfere significantly with the person's ability to lead a normal life (e.g., a snake phobic avoids looking at pictures of snakes or going to places where snakes happen to be). In more significant cases, the phobic organizes a significant portion of his daily life with the goal of avoiding the feared object (e.g., not marrying for fear of sex).

The defining diagnostic feature of hysteria is the loss or impairment of a body or psychological function in the absence of any tissue damage or disease that could account for the loss. Conversion hysteria is indicated when there is a loss of a body function, and dissociative hysteria is indicated when there is a loss of a psychological function. Examples of conversion symptoms are unexplained pains, paralyses, and fits resembling epileptic seizures. Examples of dissociative reactions are amnesia, fugue (a wandering away), and multiple personality. A significant minority of persons with conversion symptoms have an attitude of dramatic forebearance toward their disability. This attitude, called *la belle indifférence,* is striking because the normal reaction to disability is depression and/or anger rather than an attention-seeking, dramatic forebearance. Many dissociative reactions appear to be attempts to escape psychologically from stressful situations.

Hypochondriasis is characterized by a habitual overconcern about one's health. This syndrome is similar to hysteria, is more prevalent in men, and almost always occurs in the context of other neurotic symptoms. Compulsive neurosis is characterized by recurring thoughts or impulses toward some act, a fear of losing control, and a measure of anxiety-relief following performance of the compulsive behavior. The prominent signs of existential neurosis are apathy and a belief that life is meaningless. The defining diagnostic feature of traumatic neurosis is the occurrence of neurotic symptoms in the context of very stressful situations, such as war. Neurotic breakdowns during wars are related more to the degree of stress to which the soldier is exposed than to the soldier's maladjustment prior to his entering the army.

Cameron's psychoanalytic theory explains neurosis in terms of predisposing personality traits acquired in childhood, stress, anxiety and defense, regression, and symptom formation. More specifically, personality traits acquired in childhood are postulated to create areas of psychological vulnerability. For example, a dependent person is vulnerable to rejection, a controlling person is vulnerable to ambiguous situations, and a person who believes that sex is disgusting is vulnerable to marriage. It is assumed that psychological forces operate to keep a person from consciously recognizing certain vulnerabilities. Stress occurs when a person is exposed to the life situations that threaten recognition of unconscious vulnerabilities. Under stress the ego calls on defenses to contain the anxiety associated with the threat of recognizing unacceptable impulses. One of these defenses is a partial regression (immature behavior) to an earlier and more manageable developmental period. Other defenses result in the development of neurotic symptoms.

Social learning theory postulates that neurosis results from the classical conditioning of anxiety to neutral cues, and the subsequent learning of behaviors (neurotic symptoms) that reduce anxiety. Several ways in which these conditioning processes might occur were discussed.

The many different treatment approaches to neurosis were discussed in Chapters 5 through 8 and briefly summarized in this chapter on page 309.

Chapter 11

Psychophysiologic Disorders and Sexual Dysfunctions

STEVEN REISS, LEONARD W. SUSHINSKY, and ALFRED W. KASZNIAK[1]

. . . these physicians possess no clear conception of the ways the body tends to be influenced by the state of the mind. Perhaps it is because they do not even know that the pulse becomes turbulent because of strife and fears which suddenly disturb the mind.

GALEN (2nd century A.D.)

The disorders discussed in this chapter include essential hypertension, peptic ulcer, bronchial asthma, migraine headache, and a variety of sexual dysfunctions. Essential hypertension, which is indicated by high blood pressure, constitutes one of the nation's most serious health problems. Peptic ulcer is a lesion or hole in the stomach or duodenum caused by hypersecretion of gastric juices. Migraine headaches result from the dilation of blood vessels in the brain, and bronchial asthma is a respiratory disorder. These syndromes are classified as psychophysiologic disorders because (1) they all involve either a lesion in, or a dysfunction of, particular organ systems in the body, and (2) psychological factors such as frustration, conflict, and excessive emotionality are believed to play an especially important causal role in the development of the syndromes.

The historical origins of the concept of a psychophysiologic disorder are in the ancient philosophical debates on the "mind-body" problem. It seemed obvious to many ancient thinkers that there exist both psychological and biological aspects to human nature. Some philosophers postulated a mental substance ("mind") to account for the psychological aspects of human nature and a material substance ("body") to account for the biological aspects. Within this framework a major issue was the manner in which the mind and the body could affect one another: How is it possible, for example, that the mind can will the body to move, as in the example of deciding to sit down. Although the mind-body issue was debated by philosophers and theologians for centuries, some of the greatest physicians throughout history resisted the notion that emotional factors can cause breakdowns in organ systems. In fact, it was not until the Psychosomatic Society was founded in 1939 that the medical establishment formally recognized the legitimacy of the scientific study of the role of psychological factors in physical diseases (Wittkower & Dudek, 1973). The critical achievement that seemed to pave the way for this acceptance was the development of a behavioral, objective language for describing psychological states (Stainbrook, 1952).

In recent decades psychological factors such as frustration, conflict, and excessive emotionality have been implicated in the etiology or exacerbation of many physical diseases. Thus it is misleading to distinguish absolutely between psychophysiologic and nonpsychophysiologic diseases on the grounds that the former are believed to be caused by emotional factors and the latter are not. *The emotional causation of physical diseases is a matter of degree rather than an either-or proposition; the disorders considered psychophysiologic are those in which psychological factors are believed to play an especially important causal role.*

---

[1] Steven Reiss and Alfred W. Kaszniak wrote the section of this chapter on psychophysiologic disorders. Leonard W. Sushinsky wrote the section of this chapter on sexual dysfunctions.

DSM-II distinguishes among nine types of psychophysiologic reactions on the basis of the part of the body that is affected. These are:

1. Psychophysiologic skin reactions: various inflammations and itchings of the skin, eczema, and hyperhydrosis (dry skin).
2. Psychophysiologic musculoskeletal reactions: various backaches, tension headaches, and muscle cramps.
3. Psychophysiologic respiratory reactions: bronchial asthma, hyperventilation (rapid breathing), and hiccoughs.
4. Psychophysiologic cardiovascular reactions: essential hypertension, congestive heart failure, and migraine headaches.
5. Psychophysiologic hemic and lymphatic reactions: psychologically induced disturbances of the blood and lymphatic system.
6. Psychophysiologic gastrointestinal reactions: peptic ulcer, spastic colitis, and mucous colitis.
7. Psychophysiologic genitourinary reactions: various menstrual disorders, and dyspareunia (pains in sexual organs during sexual activity).
8. Psychophysiologic endocrine reactions: psychologically induced glandular disturbances.
9. Psychophysiologic reactions of organs of special sense: any psychologically induced disturbance of the sense organs.

Psychophysiologic disorders are often confused with hysterical conversion reactions. The important differences between these two categories of disorders are that (1) psychophysiologic patients usually suffer real tissue damage, whereas hysterical conversion patients do not, and (2) psychophysiologic reactions usually affect internal organs controlled primarily by the autonomic nervous system, whereas hysterical reactions usually affect behavior controlled primarily by the central nervous system. Exceptions exist to these general rules; for example, migraine headaches are considered psychophysiologic disorders even though they do not seem to involve tissue damage.

GENERAL THEORIES OF PSYCHOPHYSIOLOGIC DISORDERS

Role of stress

Stress has been implicated in the etiology of several psychophysiologic disorders. In order to understand how stress might cause a breakdown in an organ system, it is necessary to recall that psychophysiologic disorders generally involve breakdowns in organ systems controlled by the autonomic nervous system (see Figure 11-1) and that this system consists of two major divisions called the sympathetic and the parasympathetic nervous systems (see Chapter 5). Cannon (1927) proposed that these two components of the autonomic nervous system act to maintain a constant internal environment called *homeostasis.* Selye (1946), using Cannon's notion of homeostasis in his theory of stress, proposed (1) that stress stimuli disrupt the constant internal environ-

Figure 11-1
A simplified and schematic representation of the autonomic nervous system. (From S. J. Lachman, *Psychosomatic disorders: A behavioristic interpretation.* New York: John Wiley & Sons, Inc., 1972, p. 18. Reprinted by permission of author and publisher.)

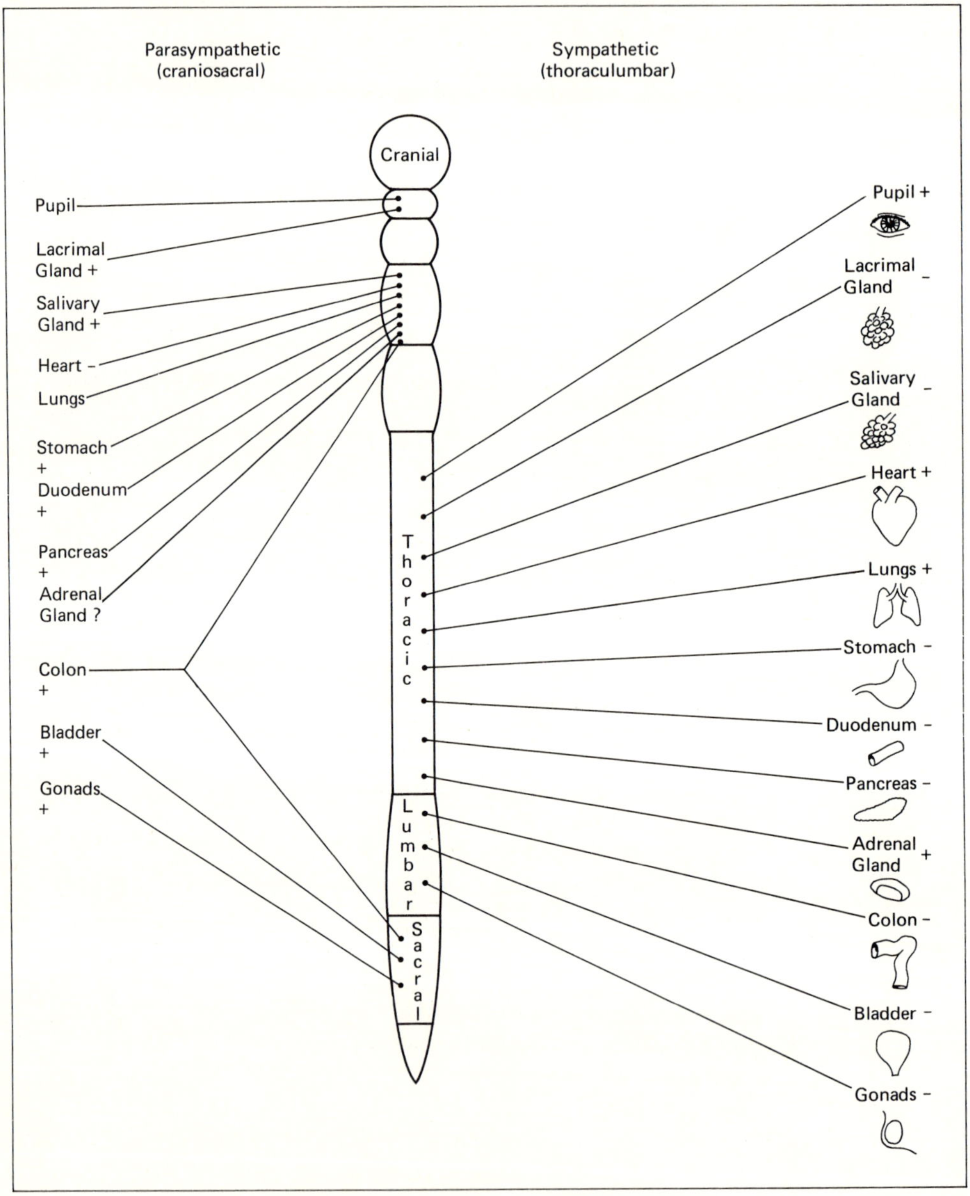

ment, and (2) that the autonomic nervous system reacts by attempting to reinstate the constant environment. If stress is prolonged, the autonomic system must be persistently active in its attempt to reinstate homeostasis, and organs controlled by this system may become overworked and eventually suffer a breakdown. Specifically, Selye proposed that stress (infections, toxic substances, or emotionally arousing stimuli) elicits a general adaptation syndrome consisting of three stages:

1. *The alarm stage.* The stressor stimuli alter the physiological balance causing an immediate coping reaction consisting of ACTH secretion from the pituitary gland and of activity in the autonomic nervous system.
2. *The resistance stage.* The organism defends against the stressor and thus restores physiological balance (homeostasis).
3. *The exhaustion stage.* Prolonged exposure to the stressor depletes physiological resources and decreases the organism's capacity to resist. Eventually a breakdown in one of the organ systems may occur.

Although Selye's theory of stress and psychophysiologic disorders is generally accepted, there remains the question of why different organs become diseased in different individuals—for example, why does exposure to prolonged stress produce gastrointestinal ulcer in some people and high blood pressure in others. Three general theories have been proposed to explain individual differences in specific psychophysiologic reactions: personality theories, emotional reaction theories, and genetically determined organ vulnerability theories.

Personality Theories

Personality theories posit particular personality traits as characteristic of patients suffering psychophysiologic disorders. Perhaps the best known of these personality theories is the nuclear conflict approach of Alexander (1950) that posits a particular psychodynamic conflict as characteristic of each particular disorder. For example, Alexander hypothesized that the nuclear conflict associated with asthma concerns repressed dependency needs, whereas the nuclear conflict associated with hypertension concerns repressed anger. The available data, however, do not seem to provide much support for Alexander's notions. As Wittkower and Dudek (1973) noted, psychodynamic conflicts of dependency and hostility are themes common to psychophysiologic disorders so that it is not really possible to associate a particular disorder with a particular psychodynamic conflict, with the possible exception of migraine headaches.

Specific Emotional Reaction Theories

Specific emotional reaction theories explain individual differences in psychophysiologic reactions in terms of both the individual's emotional response to stress and the hypothesis that specific emotional responses have a unique pattern of physiological correlates. For example, suppose that one individual is under stress because of the persistent experience of anger, whereas another individual is under stress because of the persistent experience of fear. If the experience of anger were associated with a primary increase in heart output, whereas the experience of fear were associated with the hypersecretion of gastric juices, the former individual might be predisposed to develop hypertension, whereas the latter individual might be predisposed to develop ulcers. A critical issue raised by this theory is whether different emotions are, in fact, related to different patterns of physiological activity. Ax (1953), for example, has demonstrated that fear elicits autonomic nervous system responses different from those elicited by anger. In general, however, it seems that different emotions are *not* associated with specific patterns of physiological activity.

Genetically Determined Organ Vulnerability

The basic notion expressed by organ vulnerability theories is that when a system is placed under stress, the weakest part of that system is the first point of breakdown. These theories further propose that different individuals inherit different organ vulnerabilities. For example, suppose that for a particular individual the hypersecretion of gastric juices is a relatively frequent response to many emotionally arousing (stressful) stimuli, whereas muscular contraction is a relatively high threshold response that occurs in reaction to only a narrow range of stimuli. When placed under stress, this individual would be more likely to develop stomach ulcers than muscle tension headaches.

Support for the hypothesis of genetically determined vulnerability in specific organ systems comes from several sources. In addition to the fact that individuals appear to have characteristic physiological reaction patterns to all emotionally arousing stimuli (Lacey, Bateman, & VanLehn, 1953), it seems that individuals with psychophysiologic disorders tend to respond most in those organs in which symptoms appear. For example, it has been demonstrated by Malmo and Shagass (1949) that patients with cardiovascular symptoms are more likely to react to stress with increased cardiovascular activity than with increased muscle tension, whereas headache patients are more inclined to react with increased muscle tension than with cardiovascular symptoms. This consistent tendency for a person to react more with one organ system than another (e.g., skeletal muscle rather than the intestinal tract), and the specific association of symptoms with particular physiological mechanisms, have been termed *symptom specificity* (Malmo, Shagass, & Davis, 1950).

The characteristic physiological reaction patterns of individuals appear to be present from infancy. Grossman and Greenberg (1957) have found that in using any single index of autonomic nervous system function (e.g., heart rate), a given group of newborn infants will show a normal distribution with gradations from rigidity (very little response to stimulation) to lability (extreme response to stimulation). The same individuals may show reversed degrees of responsivity when some other autonomic response is measured. Although such findings in newborns are consistent with a genetically determined organ vulnerability theory, it is also possible that environmental influences contribute to symptom specificity. It has long been known that various autonomically mediated responses (e.g., constriction of blood vessels) can be classically conditioned (Menzies, 1937; Roessler & Brogden, 1943). Thus, although the available data support the notion of individual differences in organ vulnerability, it is possible that such vulnerabilities are learned rather than inherited.

ESSENTIAL HYPERTENSION

Hypertension, the medical term for high blood pressure, is one of the most serious health problems facing our nation. It is a major cause of heart failure, cerebral ischemia (stroke), and kidney disease (Keith, Wagener, & Barker, 1939; Smith, Odel, & Kernohan, 1950). People with high blood pressure are much more likely to die at early ages (Society of Actuaries, 1959); in fact, blood pressure is used by most life insurance companies as the major predictor of life expectancy. The seriousness of this disease is further suggested by its high prevalence and by the fact that many cases of hypertension go undiagnosed. The United States National Center for Health Statistics (1964) has estimated that approximately 20 per cent of the adult population has high blood pressure, and it has been estimated that as many as 75 per cent of these people may not be receiving treatment. For example, of 22,929 male and female industrial workers in a Chicago survey by Schoenberger, Stamler, and Shekelle (1972), 59 per cent of the hypertensives had not been diagnosed previously and only 25 per cent of the hypertensives were receiving medical treatment.

Some hypertensive patients may show behavior indicative of mild anxiety or tension, including insomnia, fatigue, dizziness, sweating, and headaches. In general, however, hypertensive patients show no particular symptoms other than the high blood pressure that defines the condition.

In approximately 10 per cent of all patients with hypertension, elevated blood pressure is a result of some demonstrable disease. Because in medicine the term *essential* means "of unknown etiology," the remaining 90 per cent of all patients with high blood pressure are said to suffer from *essential hypertension.* There are two physiological ways in which essential hypertension occurs. One way is through a primary increase in heart output in which elevated pressure results from the pumping of blood through the arteries at a faster rate. This type of hypertension generally is found in younger patients, who also show greater than usual variations in blood pressure. A second way in which essential hypertension occurs is through constriction of the peripheral arteries through which the blood must travel. Such occurrences of essential hypertension are found primarily in middle-aged patients (Finkielman, Warcel, & Agrest, 1965). It has been hypothesized that the condition of unusual variations in blood pressure found in young hypertensives is the precursor of the condition of constricted peripheral arteries found in older hypertensives. Support for this hypothesis is provided by Eich, Cuddy, and Smulyan (1966), who found that there is a tendency for heart output to fall, and for peripheral resistance of blood flow to rise, with advancing age in young hypertensives. The exact nature of this relation is, however, unclear. Specifically, it is not yet known whether large variations in blood pressure are causally related to constricted arteries or whether this relation is only correlational. Nevertheless, the information is useful because it aids in the early identification and treatment of hypertensive patients.

Although the etiology of essential hypertension is unknown, a number of variables have been shown to be related to high blood pressure. Three such variables are sodium (salt) intake, weight, and stress. Small increases in sodium intake can cause significant increases in blood pressure. Hypertensive patients are thus placed on low sodium diets in an effort to reduce blood pressure. Although the relation between salt intake and blood pressure has been suspected since antiquity, the physiological mechanisms through which salt intake affects blood pressure are not yet known.

Weight is another factor related to blood pressure, with obese people tending to show blood pressure in higher than normal ranges. With each extra pound of fat, the heart must pump harder to supply the fatty cells, thereby increasing blood pressure. In some cases even an extra two pounds can cause a measurable increase in blood pressure.

A third factor implicated in the etiology of hypertension is exposure to psychological stress. Exactly what constitutes "stress" is, however, vague. In general, scientists have used a commonsense notion in which stress refers to anything that is emotionally arousing, including frustration, exposure to catastrophe or conflict, and having to make difficult decisions.

The Role of Stress

In one of the best known field studies on the role of stress in hypertension, Ruskin, Beard, and Schaffer (1948) found that 56 per cent of the people exposed to a 1947 explosion in Texas City had blood pressure in the hypertensive range one to two weeks following the catastrophe. Other field studies suggest that essential hypertension can be caused by prolonged exposure to modern urban life. For example, Miall and Lovell (1967) found that in modern society blood pressure is higher for older people. In contrast, Cruz-Coke, Etchenerry, and Nagel (1964) found that native Easter Islanders, who live traditional lives in isolation from modern culture, show no tendency for blood pressure to rise with age. This study did find age-related increases in blood pressure for Easter Islanders who migrated to urban areas. Thus, there seems to be something about modern life that increases blood pressure. One possibility is that modern life involves a high diet of sodium. Another possible explanation is that the greater psychological stress of modern life causes elevated blood pressure. Support for this latter hypothesis was provided by Reiser, Brust, and Ferris (1951), who found that stressful psychological events preceded the onset of hypertension in 41 of 80 patients for whom the time of onset was known. Moreover, Harris and Forsyth, in their review of a number of life history studies, concluded:

> At several ages and in both sexes persons with the higher pressures seem to experience many kinds of personal interactions as stressful and as the occasion for emotional arousal. Thus it seems likely that they experience emotional upsets more often, more intensely and for longer times than other persons, and that these upsets are accompanied by vasopressor episodes and possibly other neurogenic-humoral influences on peripheral vascular processes [1973, p. 132].

Experimental research on essential hypertension has focused primarily on the short-term effects of psychological stress. For example, Wolf, Cardon, Shepard, and Wolff (1955) observed the reactions of 216 hypertensives to an interview situation that provided discussions pertaining to both stressful and relaxing topics. Blood pressure was found to rise during the periods of increased stress; moreover, this elevation of blood pressure was particularly high during discussions of frustrating and threatening life experiences. Hardyck, Singer, and Harris (1962) found similar increments in blood pressure in a group of hypertensive women during interviews concerning personal history and current life situations. Moreover, moment-to-moment variation in blood pressure of each subject appeared to be related to the degree to which the subject became emotionally involved with the interviewer and with the topics under discussion. In another study, Forsyth (1971) found that rhesus monkeys showed significant increases in mean arterial blood pressure on a continuous 72-hour schedule requiring shock-avoidance. At 20 minutes into the stressful shock-avoidance period, cardiac output was found to rise, whereas peripheral resistance decreased. Progressively at 4, 24, and 72 hours, cardiac output decreased and peripheral resistance increased. These results support the notion that chronic, high levels of stress may be the mediating factor leading from the condition of unusual variations in blood pressure found in younger hypertensives to the condition of constricted arteries found in older hypertensives.

Specific Organ Vulnerability Hypothesis

Although exposure to stress is an important variable in the etiology of hypertension, individual differences in reaction to stress also must be considered. It has been suggested, for example, that in different people different organ systems are vulnerable to stress. Exposure to stress might lead to hypertension in some individuals but, in other individuals who have different organ vulnerabilities, stress might lead to ulcer rather than to high blood pressure. Some support for the hypothesis that hypertensives are especially likely to react to stress and to other stimuli primarily in terms of increased resistance to blood flow has been found. For example, Engel and Bickford (1961) reported that patients with essential hypertension react to many different types of stimuli primarily in terms of systolic blood pressure rather than in terms of other modalities such as heart rate, skin temperature, or galvanic skin response. Similarly, Moos and Engel (1962) found that, compared to patients with rheumatoid arthritis, hypertensive patients tend to show blood pressure changes to a wider range of stimuli.

Repressed Anger Hypothesis

Alexander has hypothesized that essential hypertension is caused by repressed anger and hostility (Alexander, 1950; Alexander, French, & Pollock, 1968). Kaplan, Gottschalk, Magliocco, Rohovit, and Ross (1961) tested this hypothesis by eliciting from subjects five minutes of uninterrupted speech about any personal experience. Reliable and blind scoring of these verbal samples revealed significantly greater hostility in the speech of hypertensives. Moreover, the blood pressure of hypertensive subjects was found to rise during periods of talking. In another study, Matarazzo (1954) found that, compared to normals, hypertensive patients expressed less direct hostility when harshly criticized by an experimenter. Studies with normal subjects also offer some support for the repressed anger hypothesis. For example, Hokanson and Shetter (1961) found that blood pressure increased in situations in which an experimenter instigated anger by insulting the subjects and that it returned to normal when the subjects were permitted to behave with hostility to the perceived source of anger. In subjects not given the opportunity to aggress against the experimenter, blood pressure remained high.

Although there is some evidence suggesting an association between unexpressed anger and hypertension, the hypothesis that chronic hypertension is usually caused by such anger remains largely unproven. It is unclear how many of the millions of people suffering from essential hypertension can be considered as having difficulty expressing anger. It also is unclear whether anger is associated with psychophysiologic problems in general or with hypertension in particular.

Treatment

Several approaches exist to the treatment of essential hypertension, including medical management, behavior therapy, and psychotherapy. Medical treatment generally consists of dietary control, such as reduction of sodium intake, and may also include the administration of drugs to reduce blood pressure. Because excess weight of even a few pounds can cause an elevation of blood pressure, dietary control may include an attempt to have the patient lose weight. Behavior therapists also have developed various procedures for weight control.

Recent developments in biofeedback appear especially promising. As noted in Chapter 7, biofeedback is an attempt to bring involuntary behavior under voluntary control. Learned control of blood pressure, produced by feedback contingent on blood pressure changes, has been demonstrated in animals (DiCara & Miller, 1968) and recently has been applied to the treatment of essential hypertension in humans. Presently, however, the small number of hypertensives treated, and questions concerning the replicability of the early studies, suggest caution in drawing any firm conclusions as to the ultimate clinical relevance of biofeedback in the treatment of essential hypertension.

Although psychotherapy has been used to treat essential hypertension, the effectiveness of this procedure has yet to be demonstrated convincingly.

GASTROINTESTINAL ULCER

Gastrointestinal ulcer is an erosion of the mucous membrane either of the duodenum (upper portion of the small intestine) or of the stomach (Bogoch, Wilson, Fishman, Kliman, Trueman, & Norton, 1973; Lachman, 1972). It is believed that the immediate physiological cause of an ulcer is a corrosive effect of hypersecretion of gastric juices, particularly pepsin, on the gastrointestinal lining. Correlational data suggesting that this is the case have been obtained in a series of studies by Mirsky and his colleagues. In one study, Weiner, Thaler, Reiser, and Mirsky (1957) tested 2,073 newly inducted draftees to determine the level of pepsinogen in the blood, resulting in the identification of 63 individuals who had high levels of pepsinogen and 57 who had low levels. (Pepsinogen is a progenitor of pepsin; that is, it is secreted into the stomach where it is converted by chemical action into pepsin.) At the time of induction, gastrointestinal X rays revealed only one active and three healed ulcers in the high-pepsinogen group and no active or healed ulcers in the low-pepsinogen group. After 16 weeks of exposure to the stress of basic training, however, X rays revealed that nine cases of ulcers had developed in the high-pepsinogen group, while no cases had developed in the low-pepsinogen group. Moreover, personality tests revealed that those inductees who had developed ulcers tended to have "oral dependent" personality traits in addition to high levels of pepsinogen. In a subsequent study, Mirsky (1958) identified groups of adults and children with high and low pepsinogen levels from a sample of 4,460 adults and 1,600 children. During the course of several years of study, a number of cases of ulcers developed, all in the high-pepsinogen group. Other relevant findings were that: (1) high pepsinogen levels are three times more likely in men than in women, a figure in noticeable agreement with reports that ulcers are three times more likely to develop in men than in women, and (2) neonates show marked individual differences in level of pepsinogen, a finding consistent with the notion that a predisposition toward hypersecretion of pepsinogen is determined genetically. In sum, Mirsky and his colleagues have shown that the hypersecretion of pepsinogen is related to ulcer development. Although it is reasonable to suspect that excessive pepsinogen secretion causes ulcers, the correlational nature of the data does not permit the inference of a causal relation. Nevertheless, the possibility of a causal relation between pepsinogen level and ulcer development has seemed so plausible that gastrointestinal ulcer has also been termed peptic ulcer.

Although ulcer of the stomach and ulcer of the duodenum have many aspects in common, several significant differences can be noted (Yager & Weiner, 1971):

1. Duodenal ulcer is prevalent in men (particularly in younger men), whereas gastric (stomach) ulcer occurs with equal frequency in both sexes.
2. Gastric ulcer patients have a high incidence of stomach cancer that is associated with, or occurs after, the onset of the disease; this is not true for patients suffering from duodenal ulcer.
3. Both hydrochloric acid and pepsin are gastric juices that are secreted by the stomach, particularly during the digestion of food. The secretion of hydrochloric acid and of pepsin is markedly increased with the duodenal ulcer, whereas the gastric ulcer is characterized by normal or subnormal levels of gastric secretion. Compared to normals, duodenal ulcer patients have been found to secrete 4 to 20 times more hydrochloric acid during the night (Dragstedt, 1956).
4. Emotional factors are believed to play a more important role in duodenal ulcer than in gastric ulcer.

Because duodenal ulcer is far more prevalent than gastric ulcer, the remaining discussion will focus primarily on this particular disease. Duodenal ulcer is an extremely painful disease and, if the ulcer becomes perforated (that is, if a hole develops through the intestinal wall), death may result.

Incidence

Several methodological difficulties have been encountered in assessing the incidence of gastrointestinal ulcers. One problem is that higher socioeconomic groups, who have greater access to physicians, have been found to have a higher incidence (Buchan, 1973). Thus, it is difficult to assess the extent to which findings of greater incidence in individuals in positions of responsibility, such as physicians, managers, and foremen, are attributable to the greater availability of diagnostic procedures for these individuals, or to the greater stress experienced by these individuals in their occupations. Another problem in assessing the incidence of gastrointestinal ulcer is the difficulty of obtaining accurate diagnoses. The criterion of symptomatic complaint is problematic because X ray examinations of persons free of complaints demonstrate that between 1 and 2 per cent of such persons have duodenal ulcer. Furthermore, the criterion of X ray examination is problematic because radiologists presented with the same X rays agree on a diagnosis in only 60 per cent of the cases (Etter, Dunn, Kammer, Osmond, & Reese, 1960). Estimates of the incidence of ulcer based on hospital records are subject to sampling bias because these estimates reflect only those cases thought to require hospitalization. Even the criterion of postmortem examination is questionable because pathologists do not always agree on the interpretation of postmortem findings (Pflanz, 1971).

With these reservations in mind, the following statistics are reported. Hospital records indicate that duodenal ulcer occurs in people throughout the world. In general, the incidence of duodenal ulcer seems to be greater in the industrialized nations. Approximately 10 per cent of the American population are expected to develop ulcers at some time in their lives (Necheles, 1970). Duodenal ulcers are more prevalent in men—depending on the method of detection, the ratio of prevalence for men to women varies between three to one and six to one (Pflanz, 1971). Although duodenal ulcer was once a disease especially prevalent in young men, today this illness occurs with equal frequency among all men beyond the age of 20.

The incidence of peptic ulcer is particularly great among physicians (especially surgeons), business executives, officers in the armed services, naval pilots, and foremen in industry. Pflanz (1971), among others, has suggested that it is not the profession per se that predisposes one to develop ulcers, but rather it is the stress imposed by the profession that predisposes the individual to develop ulcers.

Personality Theories

A number of psychoanalytic theorists have hypothesized that the major personality traits of ulcer patients are repressed dependency wishes and repressed aggression. As expressed by Alexander (1950), this view maintains that early frustration of dependency needs leads to repressed anger and to a life-long attempt to gratify dependency needs through overcompensation in the form of high achievement striving. The stress produced by these neurotic conflicts is postulated to produce ulcers.

It is unclear how some personality hypotheses about ulcer patients can ever be tested. For example, Garma (1958) has proposed that a predisposition to ulcer occurs in the early months of life and that when the ulcer patient is faced with conflict later in life, he undergoes an "oral digestive regression" in which the "internalized bad mother aggressively acts in his digestive tract in the form of biting." Many psychologists are puzzled by such remarks and have no idea how to test them.

The Role of Stress

The physiological effects of stress have been studied by observing stomach activity. In one of the best known of these studies, Wolf and Wolff (1947) reported their observations of a patient named Tom who had a gastric fistula (a hole in the stomach enabling observation of its activity) caused by a childhood accident. The motility, acid secretion, and blood flow in Tom's stomach were found to change dramatically in response to conversations that disturbed him. It was also found that these functions increased when he felt angry, resentful, or anxious and decreased when he was sad or frightened.

Other experimental studies have had subjects swallow recording instruments in order to monitor stomach activity. In one such study, Mittelman, Wolff, and Scharf (1942) recorded the stomach activity of normal subjects and of ulcer patients under various emotion-arousing situations. They found that, compared to most normals, ulcer patients exhibited greater motility and acidity of the stomach under conditions of emotional arousal. It was also found that ulcer patients showed a greater reduction in stomach acidity and motility under conditions of emotional contentment. These results support the specific organ vulnerability hypothesis of ulcer development because they suggest that stomach motility and acidity are aroused more easily in ulcer patients than in nonulcer patients.

Experimental investigations using animals sometimes can be more informative than human studies because they permit a higher degree of experimental control over both relevant and extraneous variables. In one important study, Sawrey and Weiss (1956) administered shock to a group of hooded rats whenever they approached food or water. Following two weeks of such training, several rats were found to have ulcers, and a few had died from gastrointestinal hemorrhages supposedly caused by bleeding from perforated ulcers. This study, however, did not permit a determination of the extent to which ulcer formation was caused by a conflict between the tendencies to approach food and water and to avoid shock versus the extent to which ulcer formation was caused simply by constant exposure to threat.

Another early investigation of the role of stress in ulcer formation was the so-called executive monkey study by Brady, Porter, Conrad, and Mason (1958). The general notion underlying this study is that an organism who has to worry about when to emit a coping (avoidance or escape) response is under greater psychological stress than is an organism who cannot emit effective coping responses and hence need not worry about doing so. More specifically, this study tested the hypothesis that a monkey who can make effective coping responses is more likely to develop ulcers than is a monkey who cannot emit effective coping responses. Four pairs of monkeys were placed in yoked restraining chairs. In each pair, one monkey could prevent shock both to himself and to his partner by pressing a lever at least once every 20 seconds. The monkeys who could prevent shock both to themselves and to their partners were called "executive monkeys" because they were charged with the "responsibility" of performing coping responses. The other monkeys, called yoked monkeys, were subject to the same number of shocks as were their partners, but they could not perform any behaviors that avoided shock. Thus only the executive monkeys were under the "psychological stress" of having to press the lever once every 20 seconds. The monkeys were placed on a continuous schedule of six hours of shock avoidance followed by six hours of rest; for the executive monkeys, a red light signaled when the avoidance period was in effect. Following prolonged training, three of the four executive monkeys died, but none of the yoked monkeys died. Autopsies on the executive monkeys revealed large perforations in the walls of the duodenum. The control monkeys, sacrificed in good health, showed no gastrointestinal abnormalities. Another important finding was that, for the executive monkeys, stomach acidity rose during the period when the animal was resting; that is, the poststress periods were characterized by higher stomach acidity levels than were the stress periods.

Even though the executive monkey study has been widely cited as evidence for the hypothesis that the demands of making coping responses lead to ulceration, it has been shown that this study is not methologically sound. Specifically, at first the investigators placed all eight monkeys on an executive-training schedule and then designated the first four who learned to make avoidance responses as the executive monkeys. It has since been shown that the monkeys who learn avoidance responses quickly are those who are most anxious (Sines, Cleeland, & Adkins, 1963). Thus the executive monkeys may have developed ulcers because they were highly anxious rather than because they made coping responses.

In a series of highly impressive studies, Weiss (1971a, 1971b, and 1971c) identified important conditions under which the availability of coping responses *decreases* the probability of ulceration and other behavioral signs of stress. Specifically, Weiss's data indicate that being able to make a controlling response reduces the probability of ulceration, provided *feedback* is available concerning the effectiveness of that response in escaping or avoiding shock. In other words, if an animal performs a coping response but receives no feedback as to whether the response was successful, he is a prime candidate for ulcer formation. If, however, the animal performs a coping response and is informed that shock was avoided, he is unlikely to develop an ulcer—it is as if such an animal could relax knowing that he can successfully avoid shock. Weiss's data show that the greater the amount of feedback, the less likely are ulceration, weight loss, and increased emotionality. Unlike the data obtained from the executive monkey study, Weiss's data cannot be explained in terms of a nonrandom assignment of subjects to experimental and control groups.

Treatment

Medical treatment of ulcers primarily consists of diet management and drug administration (Müller-Wieland & Ossenberg, 1971). Specifically, patients are typically instructed to restrict their intake of high protein foods that stimulate the secretion of hydrochloric acid. Such foods include fish, chicken, meat, cheese, and milk. Patients also are instructed to decrease any heavy use of alcohol, coffee, and tea as well as cigarette smoking. Antacid drugs such as magnesium bicarbonate often are administered in an attempt to lower the acidity level of the stomach. In general a duodenal ulcer responds to such treatment and, even if untreated, the lesion usually heals in from six to eight weeks. Relapses, however, are very common (Nemiah, 1971).

Orgel (1958) reported favorable results of psychoanalytic therapy with ten ulcer patients, five of whom had stomach ulcer and five of whom had duodenal ulcer. All ten patients who completed analysis were completely free of symptoms when followed up for ten to 22 years. By contrast, five other ulcer patients, who started analysis without completing treatment, continued to have ulcer symptoms. As impressive as these results are, however, it is difficult to assess the extent to which the therapy itself was responsible for the curative effect because the study included no control for the non-specific (placebo) effects of treatment. Controlling for such effects is especially important in treatment studies of ulcer because a number of studies have found that ulcer patients respond well to placebo treatment. For example, Backman, Kalliola, and Ostling (1960) found that 71 per cent of 97 peptic ulcer patients reported symptomatic relief after being given an antacid drug, whereas 73 per cent of 97 other peptic ulcer patients reported similar relief after being given a placebo. Gill (1947) followed 20 patients with chronic gastric ulcers, each of whom was allowed to smoke and to eat as he pleased. The only "medication" was a daily injection of a placebo consisting of one milliliter of distilled water. Of the 20 patients, 19 lost their symptoms as rapidly as those treated by an orthodox medical regimen. Thus a valid evaluation of the specific benefit of psychotherapy in the treatment of ulcers requires the use of a placebo control group. Such research has yet to be done.

An interesting biofeedback method with potential clinical applications was reported by Welgan (1974). In this study, ten patients swallowed tubes that measured the acidity level (pH) of gastric secretions. By observing the measurement instrument, the subject received feedback as to when the gastric acidity level was high and low. All ten subjects learned to control voluntarily the acidity level of their stomachs. In a second study, five subjects were given baseline acidity recordings and subsequent feedback, whereas another five were given only baseline recordings. The results demonstrated that learned control over gastric acidity level is attributable to specific feedback rather than to nonspecific (placebo) factors. Additional research, however, is needed to assess whether these studies have any significant implications for therapy.

BRONCHIAL ASTHMA

Bronchial asthma is a respiratory disorder characterized by symptoms of shortness of breath, gasping, coughing, wheezing, and reports of thoracic constriction. During an asthma attack the mucous linings of the bronchi thicken, and the epithelial cells of this region become enlarged. This results in a narrowing of the air passages, which are obstructed further by an excessive secretion of thick mucus. Subsequently, the narrowing of the air passages interferes with both inspiration and expiration although more so with expiration. Estimates of the prevalence of asthma in the population range between 2 and 5 per cent (Graham, Rutter, Yule, & Pless, 1967).

Psychological Factors Versus Allergy

There has been energetic debate as to whether asthma should be considered an allergy or a psychophysiologic disorder. The position that bronchial asthma is an allergy is supported by many clinical cases in which specific allergins (for example, animal hair, feathers, and drugs) have been identified as triggering asthmatic attacks (Lyght, 1966). The position that bronchial asthma is a psychophysiologic disorder is supported by evidence that psychological factors can precipitate acute asthmatic attacks. Such evidence is generally related either to personality theories of asthma or to hypotheses positing an etiological role of stress.

Alexander (1950) hypothesized that asthma is partially a consequence of neurotic dependency strivings in which the individual wants to be protected by his mother. These dependency strivings are believed to be heightened in situations involving or suggesting a threat of separation from the mother, and increased strivings of this sort are hypothesized to precipitate an asthmatic attack (Alexander, 1950). Consistent with this general theme of dependency, some psychoanalysts have posited that the asthmatic attack itself is a substitute response for crying, in that wheezing resembles sobbing without tears (Weiss & English, 1957). Although the validity of these hypotheses is unclear, it is recalled that, in the case of Joseph Kelly (see Chapter 6), asthmatic attacks in fact followed events that psychologically suggested separation from the mother (e.g., being sent overseas while in the army). More extensive case history data were reported by Metcalfe (1956), who instructed a young female asthmatic patient to keep a diary of her daily activities and of the occurrence of asthmatic attacks. The diary revealed that asthmatic attacks occurred during nine of 23 days following visits with her mother but on only six of 62 days when she had not been with her mother. Although this report suggests that psychological factors play an important role in the occurrence of asthmatic attacks, it is possible that the patient was a biased observer who inaccurately reported events in her diary.

Other attempts to identify psychological factors in asthma concern the extent to which these patients show evidence of psychopathology. For example, Knapp and Nemetz (1957) found a correlation of .81 between independent ratings assessing the severity of respiratory disability and the severity of personality disturbance in 40 asthmatic patients. There are, however, problems in interpreting this correlation. One problem is that the criteria for judging psychopathology were not clearly reported. The other problem is that psychological adjustment problems could be a result, rather than a cause, of asthma.

The strongest evidence that psychological factors have an important etiological role in asthma comes from experimental studies of patients' reactions to induced stress. Masuda, Notske, and Holmes (1966), for example, observed the reactions of 17 asthmatic patients to a stressful interview. The study demonstrated that the psychological stress of the interview induced wheezing in seven of the 17 patients, thereby supporting the hypothesis that psychological stress elicits asthmatic attack. Psychological stress, however, was insufficient to induce asthmatic attack in ten of the 17 patients, raising the possibility that there might be more than one type of asthmatic condition.

Finally, it should be noted that scientific inquiry into the relative importance of allergenic and psychological factors in asthma has been complicated by the possibility that asthma is not a single disorder. Some evidence suggests that there exist at least two different types of asthmatic children, with psychological factors having a more important etiological role in one of these types. Purcell, Bernstein, and Bukantz (1961) divided asthmatic children into one of two categories on the basis of their response to a special residential unit designed for their care. Those who recovered rapidly without much need for medication were termed rapidly remitting, whereas those who needed steroid medication to remain symptom-free were termed *steroid dependent.* For rapidly remitting children, but not for steroid dependent children, autocratic and restrictive attitudes of the mother were found to be associated with the late age of asthmatic onset (Purcell & Metz, 1962). Moreover, Baraff and Cunningham (1965) found differences between these two groups of asthmatic children on semantic differential ratings of the concepts *me, mother, father,* and *asthmatic.*

Treatment

Treatment of an acute asthmatic attack typically consists of the administration of epinephrine or related compounds and of the removal from the patient's environment of any allergens known to trigger attacks. Psychotherapy also appears to have been successful in at least some cases (see Graham, 1972).

MIGRAINE HEADACHES

The migraine syndrome has been defined as a periodic headache usually beginning on one side of the head and sometimes generalizing to both sides (Wolff, 1946). These headaches are often accompanied by nausea, sensitivity to light, vomiting, and constipation or diarrhea. The headaches are frequently preceded by scotomata (a blind spot in the visual field), unilateral paresthesia (changes in sensation on one side of the body), and speech disorders. Very often other members of the patient's family develop similar headaches.

The classical migraine headache is a type of vascular headache in which pain results from the dilation and distension of the arteries in the head (Graham, 1972). Muscle-contraction headaches can be differentiated from migraine by the following symptoms:

1. Unlike migraine, muscle-contraction headaches are not preceded by a prodome (symptomatology) of scotomata, unilateral paresthesia, and speech disorders.
2. Unlike migraine, the pain in the muscle-contraction headache is usually bilateral and "hatband" in distribution.
3. Unlike migraine, muscle-contraction headaches have a gradual onset and may be accompanied by a variety of complaints including anxiety and dizziness.
4. Muscle-contraction headaches may last for hours or days and are nonpulsatible, whereas migraine headaches are throbbing and are usually shorter in duration (Friedman, 1973).

Friedman (1973) has estimated the relative incidence of various types of headaches from a sample of all patients admitted to New York's Montefiore Hospital Headache Unit during the last 25 years. Approximately 90 per cent of this sample was diagnosed as having a vascular headache of the migraine type, muscle-contraction headache, or a combination of these. Approximately 7 per cent of the general population seems to suffer from such headaches. Severe headaches also can be caused by intracranial disorders such as brain tumors or brain abscesses—these causes account for approximately 10 per cent of all cases of severe headache.

Wolff (1963) has noted that an episode of migraine often occurs at the end of a period of striving as the individual begins to relax. Almost unanimous agreement exists among investigators that migraine sufferers tend to be people who are ambitious, striving, perfectionistic, efficient, orderly, inflexible, cautious, and compulsive (Wolff, 1963). It also has been reported that migraine attacks can terminate abruptly if the patient becomes conscious of his anger and expresses it via abusive language (Alexander & Flagg, 1965). However, in part because dilation and pulsation of the arteries are very difficult to measure, very little research has been conducted relating specific psychological factors to specific physiological indicators of migraine. Some evidence suggests that a predisposition to migraine attack is inherited through a recessive gene.

Treatment

Medical treatment for acute migraine attacks usually consists of the administration of the drug ergot or one of its derivatives; ergot drugs produce dramatic relief from migraine because of their vasoconstrictive effects (Alexander & Flagg, 1965). Psychological treatment for migraine headaches sometimes consists of psychotherapy; in recent years, however, psychologists have experimented with new treatments based on biofeedback techniques. The initial reports indicate that these biofeedback techniques are promising (Budzynski, Stoyva, & Adler, 1970; Sargent, Green, & Walters, 1973; Schultz & Luthe, 1969). (See Chapter 7 for a discussion of biofeedback.)

TYPES OF SEXUAL DYSFUNCTIONS

Sexual dysfunctions resemble psychophysiologic reactions because in sexual dysfunctions psychological factors lead to the dysfunction of an organ system. Perhaps the most important difference between sexual dysfunctions and psychophysiologic disorders is that the former typically do not involve any actual tissue damage, whereas the latter usually do.

Erectile Impotence

Impotence refers either to a man's inability to initiate or to sustain a penile erection sufficient to penetrate a sexually well-functioning woman or to cases in which penetration occurs but erection rapidly dissipates without ejaculation. Males suffering from *primary impotence* are those who have never been able to perform successfully heterosexual or homosexual intercourse. Males suffering from *secondary impotence* are those who have had at least one successful experience of sexual intercourse but who currently are impotent at least 25 per cent of the time. Another type of impotence is *situational impotence;* in these cases, the male is potent only with certain partners (e.g., prostitutes but not his wife) or only under specific circumstances (e.g., only if the partner is absolutely passive).

Ejaculatory Dysfunction

This category includes *ejaculatory incompetence* and *premature ejaculation.* Ejaculatory incompetence is the male's inability to ejaculate even though there is a desire to do so and even though a successful erection and sustained penetration have been achieved. Premature ejaculation refers to ejaculation before or shortly after penetration. In the case of heterosexual intercourse, "shortly after " or "premature" has been defined operationally as the failure to inhibit ejaculation long enough for the woman to experience orgasm at least 50 per cent of the time (Masters and Johnson, 1970). This definition, however, is problematic because it depends on the woman's sexual functioning, the male's erotic style, and other psychological factors. Another definition of prematurity is based on Kaplan's hypothesis that "the crucial aspect of prematurity is *the absence of voluntary control* over the ejaculatory reflex, regardless of whether this occurs after two thrusts or five, whether it occurs before the female reaches orgasm or not" (1974, p. 290). Kaplan defined prematurity as the inability to tolerate high levels of sexual arousal without "reflexive" ejaculation. Although this definition is not without its own difficulties, it does have the advantage of defining premature ejaculation in terms of the male alone and hence without reference to the behavior of the partner or to a hypothetical normative standard.

Male Dyspareunia

Male dyspareunia refers to the experience of severe pain in the genital region. The physical distress usually occurs during orgasm but may also occur during intromission or after ejaculation and orgasm. This type of reaction, of course, usually interferes with both the desire and the ability to engage in sexual behavior.

Incidence of Male Disorders

Although detailed and accurate data are not available for each of the male sexual dysfunctions, the prevalence of male sexual inadequacy is generally assumed to be significant. For example, the Kinsey et al. (1948) data indicate that after the age of 35 approximately 6 per cent of the male white population are sexually impotent, with as many as 25 per cent impotent by the age of 65 and 75 per cent impotent by the age of 80. Data based on hospital and clinic records reveal that secondary impotence (including situational impotence) comprises about 50 per cent of all referrals for male sexual dysfunction. Premature ejaculation accounts for the majority of the remaining problems (Masters & Johnson, 1970; Johnson, 1968). Although these data may not represent the actual incidence of male sexual dysfunctions in the total population, they probably indicate accurately that primary impotence, ejaculatory incompetence, and male dyspareunia occur much less frequently than premature ejaculation and secondary impotence.

Orgasmic Dysfunction in Females

In *primary orgasmic dysfunction* the woman reports no history of orgasmic experience whether through intercourse, noncoital stimulation by a partner, or masturbation. This phenomenon is not a simple analogue of male primary impotence because, in the case of primary impotence, the male almost always has had orgasmic experience through partner stimulation or through masturbation. In *situational orgasmic dysfunction* the woman is able to achieve orgasm in some ways but not in others; for example, orgasm may be achieved through masturbation but not through intercourse. Another example of situational orgasmic dysfunction is the ability to achieve orgasm only occasionally and unpredictably.

General Sexual Dysfunction in Females

This syndrome is connoted by a lack of erotic feeling and by an absence of vasocongestive response that typically prepares a woman for intercourse (Kaplan, 1974). Women having general sexual dysfunction are not necessarily inorgasmic.

Vaginismus

The involuntary spasm of the muscles surrounding the vaginal entrance whenever vaginal penetration is attempted is termed vaginismus. Women exhibiting vaginismus do not necessarily lack general sexual responsiveness or the ability to achieve orgasm through stimulation by oneself or one's partner.

Female Dyspareunia

This term is applied to the experience of extreme pain during or after sexual intercourse.

Incidence of Sexual Dysfunctions in Females

Kinsey's survey data on female sexual inadequacy can be interpreted as indicating that about one in every four women demonstrates consistent if not complete failure to experience orgasm during the early years of marriage (Kinsey et al., 1953). These data further indicate that approximately one half of all married women have not experienced orgasm by the time of their first anniversary. This figure decreases somewhat as marriage progresses—by the twentieth year of marriage, approximately 65 per cent report regular orgasms, and more than 90 per cent report at least some orgasmic experiences.

Using referrals to Masters and Johnson's clinic as an indicator of the incidence of various female sexual problems, primary orgasmic dysfunction accounts for more than half of all female sexual difficulties. Situational orgasmic dysfunction accounts for another 40 per cent, and vaginismus comprises about 7 per cent of female sexual inadequacies.

EXPLANATIONS OF SEXUAL DYSFUNCTION

Virtually every major writer on sexual functioning supports the view that most cases of sexual dysfunction are due to psychological factors (Allen, 1969; Ellis, 1960; Kaplan, 1974; Masters & Johnson, 1970; Menninger, 1937). In fact, with the possible exception of dyspareunia, it is generally assumed that only 5 to 15 per cent of all cases of sexual dysfunction are attributable to known organic and physiological causes (Ellis, 1960; Kleegman, 1959; Masters & Johnson, 1970). This 5 to 15 per cent figure includes cases in which sexual inadequacy is attributable to deformities, obesity, rheumatic fever, hepatic cirrhosis, urethritis, pernicious anemia, mumps, spinal cord lesions, diabetes mellitus, alcohol, and drugs.

Psychological explanations of sexual dysfunction recently have shifted from an emphasis on intrapsychic causation to an emphasis on the variables that currently affect sexual behavior regardless of the individual's idiosyncratic developmental history (Ellis, 1960; Kaplan, 1974; Masters & Johnson, 1970; Wolpe, 1958). This interest in the current causal factors, however, does not deny that intrapsychic, developmental events may have contributed to the initial occurrence of sexual inadequacy.

The following five factors are commonly hypothesized as the causal conditions that maintain sexual dysfunctions: conditioned anxiety, performance anxiety, critical self-monitoring, an inadequate partner, and ignorance. Conditioned anxiety is particularly useful in conceptualizing the maintenance of sexual dysfunction, especially in cases of vaginismus in which conditioned spasmodic contractions of the outer third of the vaginal barrel occur. Performance anxiety and critically observing one's own behavior seem to be especially relevant to understanding male impotence and female orgasmic dysfunction. A man's apprehension about his ability to produce or to sustain an erection interferes with the natural course of sexual arousal and contributes to erectile failure. Similarly, a woman's anxious concern about achieving orgasm interferes with the natural process of sexual responding. Ignorance of sexual anatomy and activities can militate against successful sexual interaction and may even lead to insufficient stimulation of one's partner and to the development of a related sexual inadequacy in the partner.

Although these five factors probably account for many cases of sexual inadequacy, other psychological factors are frequently important in understanding the maintenance of sexual inadequacy. For example, sexual dysfunction can be a secondary consequence of anxiety or mood disorders (Johnson, 1968). Moreover, sexual dysfunctions are sometimes a reaction to broader difficulties in one's relationship with a partner. In this regard, lack of communication and of sensitivity are often postulated as primary causes of sexual problems (Masters & Johnson, 1970; Kaplan, 1974). Wolpe, for example, presents the hypothetical scenario of the husband who "does not show his wife reasonable consideration. Perhaps he comes home from work at irregular hours without ever telling her in advance or phoning her. Such behavior can be extremely disturbing and, if persistent, may transform a woman's attitude from affection to aversion, and her sexual pattern from passion to frigidity" (1973, p. 178).

The principal evidence for psychological explanations of sexual dysfunctions comes from clinical case studies, interview surveys, and questionnaire studies (Fisher, 1973; Kinsey et al., 1953; Masters & Johnson, 1970). Although these data suffer from serious methodological weaknesses (see Faulk, 1973), they constitute the best information available. The case histories provided by Masters and Johnson (1970) are particularly important in implicating psychological factors as causes of human sexual inadequacy.

The relation between general maladjustment and sexual dysfunction is unclear (Faulk, 1973; Lidberg, 1972). From case histories such as those provided by Masters and Johnson (1970), there is reason to suspect that many individuals exhibiting sexually dysfunctional behavior are otherwise normal or are at least not severely psychologically disturbed. Of course, the frustration and distress caused by sexual problems can lead to marital and emotional difficulties.

TREATMENT OF SEXUAL DYSFUNCTIONS

Therapy Techniques

Significant advances have been made in the treatment of sexual dysfunctions. The publication of Masters and Johnson's *Human Sexual Inadequacy* (1970) represented, as one observer has noted, a major revitalization, if not revolution, in the treatment of sexual inadequacy (Dengrove, 1971). Nevertheless, many behavior therapists antedating Masters and Johnson had developed similar and apparently equally successful techniques (Ellis, 1960; Hastings, 1963; Lazarus, 1963; Semans, 1956; Wolpe, 1958).

Modern treatments of sexual dysfunctions have in common techniques that reassure, persuade, and educate patients, desensitize debilitating fears, and gradually shape successful sexual behavior. The following are some examples of successful treatments of sexual dysfunctions.

Fear of Sexual Intercourse

Lazarus (1971) reported the case of a nineteen-year-old male psychiatric patient who had been diagnosed as having deep-seated castration anxieties, with only a fair prognosis of recovery even if given long-term psychoanalysis. This man had come to believe, probably from the descriptions offered by friends, that during sexual intercourse the vagina may sometimes produce such violent spasms and contractions that the penis could be seriously injured. This fear apparently dissipated when the man was provided with appropriate information by one of his doctors.

Erectile Impotence

Wolpe (1958) treated a man who had engaged in successful heterosexual relationships but who failed to maintain penile erection during his first attempt at sexual intercourse with a woman to whom he was strongly attracted. Analysis of the case suggested that the protestations of his girl friend had elicited strong anxiety, perhaps conditioned in part by an earlier experience in which he had heard his mother protest and weep during intercourse with his father. In any event, dysfunction during intercourse was related to the patient's current fear of pain and injury. The therapist therefore used systematic desensitization to desensitize the patient to "vocal violence" (e.g., a quarrel in his family), "vocalization of suffering" (e.g., an unseen hospital patient groaning), and "injury and suffering" (e.g., the idea of the uterus being scraped). Within twenty sessions, the patient was reporting successful and regular sexual intercourse with a new girl friend.

Premature Ejaculation

In treating sexual dysfunction, Masters and Johnson define the problem as one of the marital unit, not of the individual. Accordingly, they attempt to remove either partner's feelings of being the "culprit" or "victim." Treatment begins with a detailed history taking; a male therapist and a female therapist conduct separate interviews with each spouse. A round-table discussion between both therapists and both marital partners follows. Myths, misconceptions, and factual information concerning the sexual difficulty are discussed. In the specific case of premature ejaculation, the couple is "assured unequivocally that [this problem] can be reversed successfully" [1970, p. 101].

One treatment procedure for premature ejaculation involves gradual approximations of sexual intercourse utilizing what is termed the "squeeze technique." Specifically, the woman manually stimulates her partner until he signals that ejaculation is imminent. She then ceases stimulation and applies pressure to the glans (head) of the penis, which when performed properly causes a decrease in erection and a diminution in the urge to ejaculate. Altering periods of stimulating and depressing sexual arousal are repeated for four or five trials. After several days of similar sessions, penile intromission is permitted in the female superior position, thus allowing the woman to aid her partner in withdrawing his penis when he senses impending ejaculation. At this point the squeeze technique is applied; coital stimulation and destimulation are then repeated. Eventually the male partner practices intromission under more demanding conditions; for example, he practices penile thrusting as the couple continues to use the squeeze technique. In this manner ejaculatory control during intercourse is gradually learned.

Orgasmic Dysfunction

Anon (1971) has developed an approach to female orgasmic dysfunction that involves directed use of masturbatory behavior, or what he terms "self-exploration." The client is requested to explore her body in order to learn what elicits pleasurable sensations. Once orgasm is attained, the client gradually modifies her stimulatory techniques to approximate more nearly heterosexual intercourse; that is, at the point of orgasm, masturbatory movement is shifted to condition high levels of sexual arousal to vaginal stimulation.

Vaginismus

A case reported by Fuchs, Hoch, Paldi, Abramovici, Brandes, Timor-Tritsch, and Kleinhaus (1973) is representative of the type of modern approach used to treat vaginismus. The patient was a nineteen year-old woman who had been married for two and a half years to a man nine years her senior. In the early days of their marriage, attempts at intercourse were unsuccessful due to the wife's reports of pain. The couple had not attempted intercourse since those early days. Treatment involved training the wife to relax and, while relaxed, to insert progressively larger vaginal dilators. Eventually penile intromission was successfully attempted in the female superior position and under the wife's control. Follow-up sessions indicated regular and orgasmic sexual intercourse.

Effectiveness of Therapy

The evidence for the efficacy of these approaches to the treatment of sexual dysfunction comes primarily from therapists' reports of their patients (Fuchs et al., 1973; Hartman & Fithian, 1972; Kaplan, 1974; Lobitz & LoPiccolo, 1972; Masters & Johnson, 1970; Wolpe, 1973). Problems in determining the representativeness of the samples, problems in assessing actual change, and variations in defining success notwithstanding (Kaplan, 1974; LoPiccolo, 1972), the clear impression is that, compared to traditional forms of therapy (see Johnson, 1968), modern sex therapy is highly effective. Masters and Johnson (1970), for example, reported initial failure rates of about 26 per cent for secondary erectile impotence, 20 per cent for some types of situational orgasmic dysfunction, 18 per cent for ejaculatory incompetence, 17 per cent for primary orgasmic dysfunction, 2 per cent for premature ejaculation, and 0 per cent for vaginismus.

William Masters and Virginia Johnson, pioneers in the scientific study of human sexual behavior and in the treatment of sexual dysfunctions. (Photo by Magnum Photos, Inc.)

Recently, Obler (1973) has provided data based on a controlled investigation of behavioral treatment of male premature ejaculation and ejaculatory incompetence and of female primary and situational orgasmic dysfunction. The 64 subjects included 37 females and 27 males, all clinically evaluated as having no related psychological or physiological disorders. Subjects received behavior therapy (systematic desensitization and assertive therapy), traditional group therapy, or no treatment at all. Self-report, psychological test, and in-session physiological measures indicated that behavioral therapy was more effective than group therapy, with the latter no more effective than no treatment.

SUMMARY

A psychophysiologic condition is diagnosed when there is a breakdown in an organ system that cannot be explained in terms of infectious agents or physical trauma. These breakdowns may be indicated by actual lesions in, or by dysfunctions of, the affected organ system. It is assumed that emotional factors have an important role in the development of psychophysiologic disorders; the original notion of a *psycho-* ("mind") *physiologic* ("body") disorder was that of a bodily disease caused by disturbances of the mind. This terminology can be misleading, however, because the precise role of emotional factors in causing physical disorders has yet to be discovered. There is evidence, moreover, that emotional factors may have an etiological role in physical diseases that are not usually considered to be psychophysiologic.

Four psychophysiologic disorders were discussed. Essential hypertension is chronically high blood pressure not attributable to demonstrable physical causes. Ulcers are actual lesions in the gastrointestinal wall. Bronchial asthma is a respiratory disorder characterized by shortness of breath, gasping, coughing, wheezing, and reports of thoracic constriction. Migraine headaches are headaches that result from the dilation of blood vessels in the brain.

Selye's adaptation theory of psychophysiologic disorders postulates that the body acts to maintain a constant internal environment (homeostasis). Any stimulus that disrupts this environment is called a stressful stimulus. A three-stage model was proposed: (1) the stressor stimulus alters the internal physiological balances, causing an immediate coping response; (2) the coping response restores important internal conditions that had been disrupted by stress; and (3) physiological exhaustion occurs, resulting in a breakdown in an organ system active in maintaining homeostasis under conditions of stress. Selye suggested that sometimes the stressor stimuli are infectious agents and that sometimes they are psychologically disturbing situations.

Although Seyle's theory is generally accepted, there remains the question of why different organs break down in different people. For example, why does stress cause ulcers in some people and hypertension in others? Three influential theories have addressed this question.

1. Personality theories postulate an association between organ vulnerability and personality traits. The available evidence supports the hypothesis that people who have problems expressing anger and asserting themselves tend to develop psychophysiologic problems in general. More specifically, anger, de-

pendency, achievement striving, and depression all seem to be associated with an increased risk of psychophysiologic disorder. The problem with personality theories, however, is that different personality traits do not seem to be associated with different psychophysiologic disorders. One likely exception to this rule is that migraine sufferers tend to be compulsive, ambitious, and perfectionistic.

2. Specific emotional reaction hypotheses posit that each psychophysiologic condition is associated with the chronic arousal of a particular emotion. If anger produces higher blood pressure than fear, people who experience a great deal of anger should be more likely to become hypertensive than people who experience a great deal of fear. The available evidence does not support these hypotheses because different emotions are, in general, not associated with unique patterns of physiological activity.

3. Genetically determined organ vulnerability hypotheses propose that people differ in terms of which organs in their body will react most to a wide range of stressful stimuli; that these individual differences in organ reactivity are inherited; and that the more reactive an organ system, the more likely it is to become "overworked" and eventually break down or function improperly. There is some evidence to support this view. For example, compared to non-hypertensive people, hypertensive patients show increased blood pressure to a wide range of emotionally arousing stimuli.

Approximately 20 per cent of the American population suffers from hypertension. Three factors that increase blood pressure are salt intake, excessive weight, and exposure to trauma and stress. Blood pressure tends to increase with age for people living in urban societies but not for people living in primitive societies. It is unclear whether this is due to the greater stress of urban living or to dietary factors.

The immediate cause of duodenal ulcers is the hypersecretion of gastric juices, particularly pepsinogen, a progenitor of pepsin. Brady and his colleagues reported that monkeys subjected to painful electric shock are more likely to develop ulcers when they can emit responses that avoid the shock than when they can do nothing to affect their plight. These findings were explained in terms of the greater stress experienced by an "executive" monkey who is charged with the responsibility of coping with a difficult situation. The Weiss studies, however, substantially modified the conclusions Brady offered. These studies suggest that being able to perform coping responses *decreases* the probability of ulcer formation when feedback is provided regarding the success of the coping response.

Research on bronchial asthma has focused on the issue of whether asthma is an allergy or a psychological disorder. In many cases asthmatic attacks can be precipitated by exposure to specific allergens. It also has been shown, however, that emotionally arousing conversations can produce asthmatic attacks, particularly in dependent people. Perhaps there are two types of asthma, with psychological factors having a more critical role in one of these types. Some evidence was reviewed that supports this view.

Tension headaches result from prolonged contractions of muscles in the neck and in the head, whereas migraine headaches result from dilation of blood vessels in the brain. The treatment for migraine includes the administration of drugs with vasoconstrictive effects, psychotherapy, and biofeedback techniques.

Sexual dysfunctions resemble psychophysiologic reactions in that psychological factors lead to the dysfunction of an organ system. Clinical and operational definitions of a number of sexual dysfunctions were presented. Based primarily on clinical case studies and on interview and questionnaire data, the following five factors have been implicated as the most frequent causal conditions maintaining sexual dysfunction: (1) conditioned anxiety that interferes with sexual performance, (2) performance anxiety (e.g., fear of inadequacy), (3) critical self-monitoring during sexual acts, (4) an inadequate partner, and (5) ignorance.

In recent years we have witnessed extraordinary progress in the treatment of sexual dysfunction. The work of Masters and Johnson is especially significant here, although it should be noted that in essence these investigators developed techniques similar to those that already had been developed by behavior therapists. For many cases of sexual inadequacy, these methods of treatment are effective.

Chapter 12

Sexual Variance

LEONARD W. SUSHINSKY
and STEVEN REISS

The histories which have been available in the present study make it apparent that the heterosexuality of many individuals is not an all-or-none proposition. . . . Males do not represent two discrete populations, heterosexual and homosexual. The world is not divided into sheep and goats. Not all things are black nor all things white.

KINSEY, POMEROY, AND MARTIN (1948, p. 638)

Sexually variant behaviors have atypical sexual activity as their salient diagnostic feature. Examples of sexually variant behaviors are homosexuality, lesbianism, transsexualism, and sadism. Although these behaviors traditionally have been regarded as psychopathological perversions of normal sexual development, many authorities now regard several types of sexually variant behaviors, particularly homosexuality, as psychologically healthy except when the individual is dissatisfied with his or her sexual preference.

The scientific study of human sexual behavior is a relatively recent development. From a historical perspective, the emergence of a science of human sexuality has been possible because our society's attitude toward sexuality has become much less restrictive. An early impetus to this change was Freud's theory of the pervasive importance of sexual motivation in everyday life. But if people came to think of human nature as more sexual, it was the kind of sexuality that resulted in dyadic heterosexual coitus. Although Freud shocked Western society with his ideas of childhood sexuality, he also reassured his contemporaries by maintaining that sexually variant behaviors are perversions that express mental illnesses.

As the shock waves of Freud's revolutionary ideas began to settle, society's image of human sexual behavior was dealt a second blow by Kinsey and his coworkers. The Kinsey studies of the late 1940s, based on personal interviews with more than 5,000 men, reported that 37 per cent of their sample had experienced homosexual orgasm at some time since the onset of adolescence and that an additional 13 per cent had felt homosexual urges. Homosexuality was reported prevalent at all socioeconomic levels, and the groundwork had been laid for a broader conception of normal sexual behavior.

A third major development in our society's redefinition of normal sexual behavior is the growing recognition of female sexuality. Increased public consciousness of female sexuality, particularly the female orgasm, is partially a consequence of the research conducted by Masters and Johnson (1966, 1970). Masters and Johnson were the first influential investigators to study human sexual behavior under laboratory conditions.

CLASSIFICATION OF SEXUAL VARIANCE

The distinction between sexual dysfunction and sexual variance is crucial for a proper understanding of the material in this chapter. Sexual dysfunction implies problems in the actual performance of sexual behavior. Because such problems involve difficulties in the functioning of the genitourinary system, sexual dysfunctions can be considered psychophysiologic disorders and were discussed as such in the preceding chapter. By contrast, sexual variance refers to unusual or socially disapproved modes of sexual gratification or to unusual or socially disapproved choices of sexual objects.

DSM-II classifies the following as Sexual Deviations: homosexuality (sexual attraction to members of one's own sex); pedophilia (sexual attraction to children); fetishism (the habitual use of a part of the body or an inanimate object to produce sexual gratification); transvestism (cross-dressing; the act of dressing in the clothes of the opposite sex); exhibitionism ("indecent exposure"; the attainment of sexual gratification by exposing sex organs to the opposite sex); voyeurism (observing nudes or the sexual behavior of others as the primary mode of sexual gratification); sadism (obtaining sexual gratification through inflicting pain); and masochism (obtaining sexual gratification through receiving pain). In this chapter, we shall refer to these behaviors as *sexual variance* to avoid the implication that they are necessarily psychopathological.

It should be noted that sexually variant behaviors are either illegal or related to behaviors that are illegal. For example, exhibitionism is illegal because it involves public exposure; homosexuality itself is not illegal, but anal intercourse, fellatio, and cunnilingus violate the sodomy laws of most states.[1] By contrast, sexual dysfunctions are not illegal; you cannot go to jail for being impotent or for having an orgasmic dysfunction.

TYPES OF SEXUAL VARIANCE

Male Homosexuality

Homosexuality refers to sexual attraction to a member of one's own sex, with the individual manifesting this attraction through fantasy or through overt sexual activity with same-sex partners. Homosexual activity thus refers to sexual activity (e.g., kissing, fellatio, and anal intercourse) among same-sex partners.

For more than sixty years, theorists have attempted to delineate different types of homosexuality (see Allen, 1969). One popular distinction is between active and passive homosexuals (e.g., Ferenczi, 1914; Socarides, 1968). Active male homosexuals are those who assume the "masculine" or dominant role in the relationship and who deviate from the norm only in the choice of sexual partners—that is, they prefer men rather than women. For example, in anal intercourse, the active male is the inserter; fellatio is performed on the active male. Passive male homosexuals are those who "play the woman's role"—that is, their deviation from the norm is not only in the choice of a same-sex partner but also in the desired form of sexual activity. Thus the passive male homosexual fellates and has anal intercourse performed on him.

The available literature indicates that the active-passive dichotomy is an invalid basis for distinguishing among male homosexuals in terms of their overt behavior. The majority of male homosexuals engage in both active and

[1] Homosexuals are usually prosecuted under criminal statutes prohibiting "lewd and lascivious" behavior, "outrageous" behavior, or "vagrancy." The few states that have explicitly legalized homosexuality between consenting adults have not revoked the criminal laws under which homosexuals are actually harassed and prosecuted (see Hoffman, 1968; Weinberg & Williams, 1974). Oral-genital and anal-genital conduct is illegal whether practiced by homosexual or heterosexual partners. The law is thus nondiscriminatory. In practice, however, sodomy laws are applied almost exclusively to homosexuals.

A gay liberation demonstration and march. DSM-II no longer defines homosexuality per se as a mental illness. (Photo by Leonard Freed; Magnum Photos, Inc.)

passive sexual behavior (Hooker, 1969; Saghir, Robins, & Walbran, 1969). However, there is some evidence that homosexuals differ in terms of *preferences* for active or passive roles (Haist & Hewitt, 1974; Hoffman, 1968). Heterosexuals also differ in terms of preferences for active or passive roles.

A more recent attempt to identify types of homosexuality was made by Feldman and MacCulloch (1971). These investigators distinguish between primary and secondary homosexuality. Primary homosexuals are those who report never having experienced interest in the opposite sex, whereas secondary homosexuals are those with a history of at least one pleasurable heterosexual experience. Feldman and MacCulloch suggest that primary homosexuality is biologically determined and that secondary homosexuality is determined by social learning. This hypothesized learning consists of an acquired aversion to females that is a result of anxiety-provoking experiences with females. Furthermore, it is proposed that the same biological variables causing primary homosexuality preclude successful treatment.

To their credit, Feldman and MacCulloch noted that they were engaging in "speculative theorizing," proposing ideas that lack solid support. Nevertheless, as Barlow (1972) has noted, their reasoning is circular. When homosexuality is profound and untreatable, they assume biological causation and then use biological causation to explain why homosexuality is profound and untreatable. Despite 60 years of theorizing, no one has yet to develop a valid system for distinguishing different types of homosexuality. (See Box 12-1.)

The available data indicate the following about male homosexuals:

1. They engage in sexual activities with a much larger number of persons

and in a more impersonal manner than do heterosexuals. Nevertheless, the majority of adult male homosexuals, particularly older homosexuals, become emotionally involved in serious dyadic relationships. Fidelity is relatively unusual during extended emotional relationships between two homosexual partners (Loney, 1972; Saghir, Robins, & Walbran, 1969).

2. The most prevalent homosexual activities are fellatio and, to a lesser extent, anal intercourse, with the majority of homosexuals interchanging active and passive roles (e.g., Saghir, Robins, & Walbran, 1969).

3. There are different degrees of involvement in homosexual activities. The majority of adult homosexual men neither engage in heterosexual activities nor experience heterosexual arousal (Loney, 1972; Saghir, Robins, & Walbran, 1969; Evans, 1969; Bieber et al., 1962), but a large minority engage in both homosexual and heterosexual activities. Kinsey, Pomeroy, and Martin (1948) constructed a scale for distinguishing among seven levels of homosexual involvement.

4. Contrary to popular myths, the vast majority of homosexuals are not effeminate, nor are they likely to be found in "effeminate" occupations such as hairdressing. Most homosexuals perceive themselves as masculine.

Saghir and Robins (1973) asked male homosexuals to describe themselves as appropriately masculine, inappropriately feminine, or as "neuter." Compared to 97 per cent of heterosexuals, 60 per cent of the homosexuals perceived themselves as masculine. Only 20 per cent of the homosexuals described themselves as feminine. Furthermore, in an independent assessment based on overt behavior and demeanor, the interviewer rated only 16 per cent as feminine in appearance. These findings are consistent with Evans's (1969) study in which 95 per cent of a homosexual sample rated themselves as "moderately or strongly masculine" and with Bieber et al.'s (1962) study in which a group of psychoanalysts rated only 2 per cent of their homosexual patients as effeminate.

In conclusion, most experts agree that the blatantly effeminate homosexual is rare (Pomeroy, 1966; Ketterer, 1971). This does not mean, however, that effeminate behavior never occurs in homosexuals. In fact, Gagnon and Simon (1973) suggest that feminine behavior is particularly likely when the young homosexual is confirming his homosexual identity. In such cases, feminine behavior may function as a defensive proclamation of the homosexual role. According to this view, feminine behavior usually is abandoned when the individual no longer feels a need to publicize his homosexual proclivities.

5. Homosexuality is more prevalent in some societies than in others, although sometimes these differences may have been exaggerated. Ancient Greece, for example, is often cited as a society in which homosexuality flourished. Although Greek plays and philosophy contain several endorsements of homosexuality, the extent to which Greek audiences shared these feelings is unknown. Karlen (1971) and Lacey (1968) have suggested that Greek society was not as homosexually oriented as is generally supposed. Whatever the prevalence of homosexuality in ancient Greece may have been, however, it is clear that homosexual activity is more prevalent in some societies than in others.

BOX 12-1
Some Classificatory Systems of Homosexuality

As noted in the text, many investigators have theoretically suggested the existence of various types of homosexuality. Keeping in mind the highly speculative nature of such suggestions, the following are a few of the classificatory systems that have been suggested.

HENRY AND GROSS (1938)

The respectable homosexual: The secret homosexual whose only deviation from the norm is his sexual orientation.

The prostitute: The individual who uses his homosexuality for profit.

The hoodlum: The homosexual who blackmails other homosexuals.

HUMPHREYS (1970)

Trade: The individual, usually married, lonely, and unsuccessful in work or marriage, who slips away for brief, impersonal homosexual encounters in public restrooms or steam baths.

Ambisexual: Similar to trades, but more open with friends and more knowledgeable about his homosexuality.

Gay homosexual: Usually young, single, educated, effeminate, and part of a homosexual subculture.

Closet queen: Usually a lonely individual, less educated than gays, who cruises the streets in search of teenage boys, who are preferred as sex partners.

COLEMAN (1976)

The blatant homosexual: The male homosexual who caricaturizes femininity or the female homosexual who flaunts her masculinity.

The "desperate" homosexual: The individual who compulsively seeks out brief homosexual encounters.

The secret homosexual: The individual who lives an overt heterosexual or "straight" life, camouflaging his homosexual activities and living in fear of being discovered or disgraced.

The bisexual: The individual who engages in both homosexual and heterosexual behavior. Persons falling into other categories (e.g., "desperate" homosexual) may also fall into this category.

The situational homosexual: The person who engages in homosexual activity when a heterosexual partner is unavailable and who typically does not consider himself homosexual, but, rather, considers himself dominant, assertive, and masculine.

Lesbianism

The overt sexual activity of the female homosexual is most remarkable for its similarity to female heterosexuality (Kinsey, Pomeroy, Martin, & Gebhard, 1953; Saghir & Robins, 1969; Wolff, 1971). Based on data obtained by Saghir and Robins (1973, 1969), Hedblom (1973), Loney (1972, 1973), Wolff (1971), and Kinsey, Pomeroy, Martin, and Gebhard (1953), the following statements about lesbianism can be made. Lesbians tend to engage most frequently in manual-genital stimulation and somewhat less frequently in cunnilingus. Although apparently having preferences for specific sexual activities, the majority of fe-

The adjusted homosexual: The individual who adjusts well to a homosexually oriented social life and who, particularly if female, may establish relatively stable homosexual relationships.

Allen (1969)

Shy male: One who "drifts into" homosexuality by default.

Homosexuality associated with neurosis: This usually is hysterical or anxiety neurosis.

Compulsive homosexuality: The homosexuality is the neurosis.

Deprivation homosexuality: This occurs when heterosexual partners are unavailable, as in prisons.

Bisexual: The individual is basically heterosexual but engages in some homosexual interactions.

Normal homosexual: The choice of same-sex partners is the individual's only deviation from the norm.

Homosexual with ancillary endocrine deficiency: This deficiency usually is associated with testicular failure.

Blatant homosexual: The homosexual who talks in falsetto voice, dyes his hair, wears extravagant clothes, and so on.

Homosexual psychopath: This individual is essentially like other psychopathic personalities, except he is homosexually oriented and his antisocial conduct involves other homosexuals.

The drinking homosexual: Alcohol coexists with the homosexuality and may or may not play a maintaining role in the sexual behavior.

Homosexuality associated with psychosis: The psychosis may or may not play a causal role in the homosexuality.

Homosexuality released by cerebral damage.

As Coleman specifically notes, such categorization "is crude and stereotyped at best and misleading at worst, but it nevertheless does give some idea of the range of homosexual patterns and life styles, . . ." (1976, p. 590).

The Henry and Gross categories are based on Allen's (1969) descriptions of their work.

male homosexuals report ease in assuming both the "masculine" (aggressive) and "feminine" (passive) roles. Compared to male homosexuals, lesbians have fewer sexual partners, engage in fewer short-term sexual contacts, and more frequently enter into lasting relationships characterized by fidelity and by strong emotional attachments. Compared to heterosexual women, lesbians report experiencing orgasm more frequently as well as earlier in their sexual lives.

The vast majority of homosexual women report having had heterosexual experience, with more than 75 per cent of all lesbians having engaged in het-

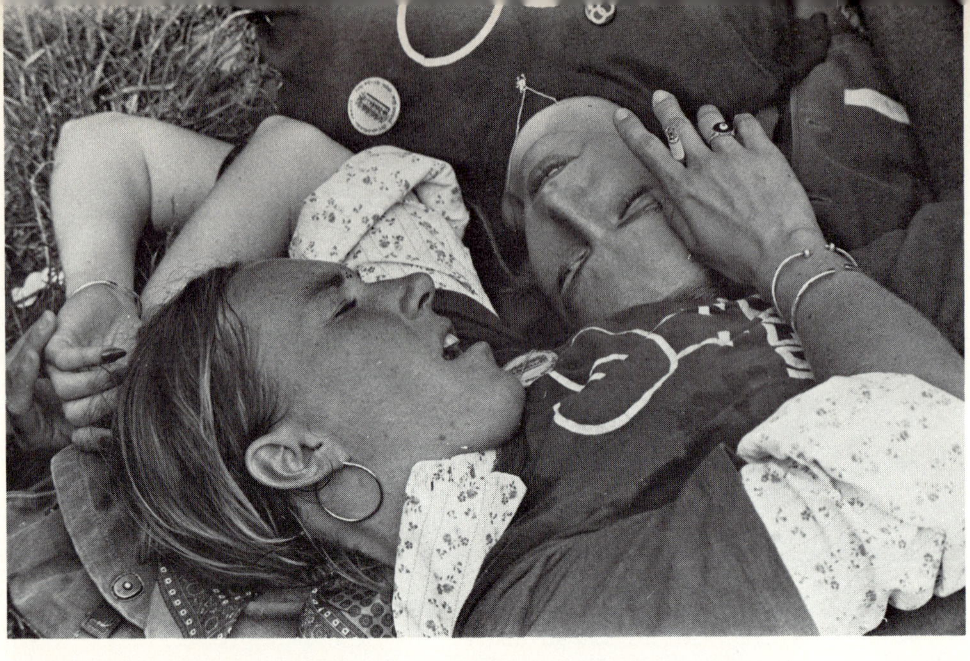

Lesbian relationships are often characterized by fidelity and strong emotional attachments. (Photo by Sepp Seitz/Magnum Photos, Inc.)

erosexual intercourse. Although the ability to become aroused with a male declines significantly after adolescence, as young adults many have had sexual experiences with more males than females. Approximately one third of those who engage in heterosexual intercourse report having experienced orgasm.

Interviews with lesbians (e.g., Gagnon & Simon, 1973; Wolff, 1971) have provided evidence of important nonsexual aspects of lesbian relationships. To a large extent, the bond between lesbians is emotional. In fact, Wolff (1971) has suggested that a more appropriate term for lesbians would be *homoemotional women.*

An emphasis on the sexual life of lesbians should not obscure the reality of a "whole person" who has to deal with the specific problems of being a woman as well as with general problems in living (Gagnon & Simon, 1973). For example, because many lesbians are single, they must learn to cope with the usual problems of a single woman, including that of finding a satisfying job in a male-dominated society.

Transsexualism

Scientific interest in transsexualism is relatively recent. Transsexualism is indicated by an intense denial of one's biological sex and usually occurs in individuals with a history of cross-dressing. The transsexual has a sense of having been born the wrong sex—of being "a man in a woman's body" or "a woman in a man's body."

Because the male transsexual thinks of himself as a woman, he desires sexual relations with men. But this similarity between homosexuals and transsexuals is superficial (e.g., Money & Brennan, 1968). The male homosexual perceives himself to be masculine, does not want to become a female, and never believes that he is really a woman. In contrast, the male transsexual perceives himself as a female, views sexual relationships with men as *hetero*sexual, and seeks to become a female via surgical operation. Phallometric tests—that is, measures of changes in penile volume to films of nude females and males—have found that transsexuals are more aroused to males than to females (Barr, 1973). These differences, moreover, are even greater than that found for male homosexuals. Also, male transsexuals display a greater interest in women than do male homosexuals, but this interest is as a woman (e.g., interest in female fashions).

Although both male transsexuals and male transvestites cross-dress, male transsexuals do not obtain sexual gratification from the act of cross-dressing (Freund, Langevin, Zajac, Steiner, & Zajac, 1974a). Instead, they experience a psychological uneasiness when they wear clothes appropriate to their biological sex.

The prevalence of transsexualism is unclear. Within three years of its becoming known to the public, the Johns Hopkins Gender Identity Clinic received 1,500 transsexual inquiries. Walinder (1968) has estimated the prevalence in Sweden to be one in 37,000 for males and one in 103,000 for females. Recently, Hoenig and Kenna (1973) reported similar estimates for England and Wales. The lower estimated rates for females may be attributable in part to the awareness that surgical procedures are less satisfactory for transforming a biological woman into a "man" than for altering the appearance of a male to approximate that of a female (Steiner, Zajac, & Mohr, 1974).

Transvestism

Transvestism is the act of dressing in the clothes of the opposite sex to obtain emotional and/or sexual gratification (Hirschfield, 1948; Prince, 1967). Hirschfield (1948), who introduced the term, categorized transvestism into four types: heterosexual, homosexual, narcissistic, and asexual. Today, some researchers limit the term to individuals who are principally heterosexual but who cross-dress, usually for the purpose of achieving sexual arousal but sometimes as a prerequisite for heterosexual intercourse (e.g., Prince & Bentler, 1972).

Generally, the transvestite is not considered to have a fetish for opposite-sex dressing. A fetish would imply only fondling and observing opposite-sex clothes. By contrast, the transvestite fondles, observes, and wears opposite-sex apparel and, to some degree, enters the social role of the opposite sex. Prince (1967) has suggested that the term *femmiphilia* (loving the feminine) is descriptive of the male transvestite, and Prince and Bentler (1972) have reported that the majority of male transvestites feel they have a feminine side seeking expression and consider themselves to be a "different personality" when cross-dressing.

The overwhelming majority of transvestites are male (Stoller, 1968; Randall, 1969). In questionnaire mailings to 1,300 readers of *Transvestia,* a magazine published for heterosexual cross-dressers, the 504 respondents were all males (Prince & Bentler, 1972). Although the incidence of transvestism is very low—Brown (1973) reports estimates from less than 1 to 3 per cent of the

Transvestites in their dressing room backstage at a musical review. (Photo by Leonard Freed; Magnum Photos, Inc.)

population—throughout history there have been many eminent transvestites. Religious, social, and legal prohibitions notwithstanding, Roman emperors (Elagbalus), European kings (Henry III of France), clergymen, diplomats, and writers have been identified as transvestites (Brown, 1973; Allen, 1969).

The Prince and Bentler (1972) survey noted here provides the most important data on male transvestites currently available. These data indicate that an appreciable number of transvestites perceive themselves as independent and ambitious and have a history of participation in high school or collegiate sports. Eighty-six per cent of the respondents indicated average or above average interest in women, 28 per cent reported having had some homosexual experience, and 78 per cent were or had been married. More than one-third of the divorced transvestites indicated that their cross-dressing had been a cause of their divorce.

Fetishism

The habitual use of a part of the body or of an inanimate object to produce sexual arousal is termed *fetishism.* However, the woman who is attracted to muscular men and the man who is attracted to women with large breasts are generally not considered as having a fetish. A "true" fetish is defined by one or more of the following characteristics: (1) sexual arousal only when the fetishistic object is present, (2) involuntary and irresistible sexual arousal whenever the object is observed, (3) interest in the fetishistic object as the primary means of sexual gratification rather than as a prelude to coitus, and (4) a compulsive seeking of the fetishistic object. The individual may forego a promising career in favor of a job that permits access to the fetish, and he may commit crimes in order to obtain the object.

Virtually all of our knowledge of fetishism is based on clinical case studies, the majority of which were male patients (e.g., Krafft-Ebing, 1886; London & Caprio, 1951; Junke, Hahn, Lindbergh, & Brasseur, 1967). Perhaps the most interesting aspect of fetishism is the wide range of objects that become fetishes. Krafft-Ebing (1886) collected reports on patients having fetishes involving animals, clothing, shoes, ears, eyes, mouths, noses, feet, hair, hands, skin, voices, odors, gloves, flowers, jewelry, and physical disabilities. More recently, Allen (1969) has offered an additional range of cases including those of a woman who achieved orgasm from the sight of light reflecting off eye glasses and of a man who was sexually aroused by women smoking cigarettes. The act of illegally entering a home can serve as a fetish (Coleman, 1976; Caprio, 1973). More typically, however, the fetish is an object that the individual can fondle and kiss while masturbating, into which he can masturbate (e.g., underwear fetish), or that he may request his partner to wear during lovemaking (e.g., shoe fetish).

Pedophilia

Pedophilia refers to the use of children by an adult for sexual gratification. Important research on pedophilia has been reported by Cohen and Seghorn (1969), Fisher (1969), Gebhard, Gagnon, Pomeroy, and Christenson (1965), and Revitch and Weiss (1962). The data from these investigations indicate that the pedophile, who is usually a male, may be either heterosexual or homosexual.

Heterosexual pedophiles tend to be devoutly religious, moralistic, and Victorian in their attitudes toward sex. Although often uncomfortable with adult females, most male pedophiles marry. As a group, pedophiles are older than other sex offenders, with 35 as the average age at first conviction.

The older pedophile tends to find physically immature children most desirable, whereas the younger pedophile often is more interested in children over 12. In either case, the offender may expose his genitals to the child, stroke or fondle the child, and manipulate the child's genitals. Only very infrequently, however, is there any attempt at coitus. Contrary to popular belief, the child molester is not a stranger who attacks young children as they travel to and from school, the store, or a friend's home. More than half of the victims are known to the pedophile, and almost four of every five instances occur in either the child's or the offender's home. Also contrary to popular belief, most pedophiliac acts do not involve force or violence, and the child rarely is physically traumatized. It is the potential psychological effects for the victim that are of most concern to parents and professionals. And here it may be crucial that the child not be exposed to the hysterical reactions of others. Such reactions may serve only to define as disastrous and shameful an otherwise unfortunate and undesirable experience (SIECUS, 1970).

Like the heterosexual pedophile, the homosexual pedophile is invariably male, is usually older than other sex offenders (the average age at conviction is over 30), feels uncomfortable around adults, and tends to approach children already known to him. Sexual activity with the child may include fondling and stimulating the boy's genitals, requesting or demanding the child to perform fellatio on him, and anal intercourse. Contrary to public opinion, however, homosexual pedophiles comprise only a small percentage of the overall population of homosexuals.

Voyeurism

Voyeurism originally referred to the act of observing nudes for sexual gratification, but it has come to include scoptophilia, the act of observing the genitals and the sexual behavior of others in order to obtain erotic pleasure. During these activities, in which the "victim" is usually a stranger and is unaware of being observed, the voyeur will often masturbate.

The term *voyeurism* is not used to refer to the behavior of men who engage in "girl watching" on the beach or who attend burlesque shows, erotic movies, or read pornographic literature. As a clinical syndrome, voyeurism is distinguished from culturally acceptable interest in observing nudity and coitus by its exclusiveness as a means of achieving sexual gratification even when heterosexual coitus is available, by its surreptitiousness, by its offensiveness to the victim (the involuntary participant), and by its compulsiveness even in the face of serious risk (i.e., voyeurs have been known to fall off roofs, to be shot at as burglars, and, of course, to be arrested and imprisoned). Most voyeurs are younger than 24 at first conviction, male, and unmarried (Gebhard, Gagnon, Pomeroy, & Christenson, 1965).

Exhibitionism

"Indecent exposure," or exhibitionism, involves an individual's obtaining sexual gratification by exhibiting one's genitals to members of the opposite sex. Most exhibitionists are males. As in voyeurism, the victim ordinarily is unknown to the exhibitionist and is typically a young or middle-aged woman (Mohr, Turner, & Jerry, 1964).

The exhibitionist may expose himself in any of a variety of places, for example, parks, stores, movie theaters, subways, or from his car. There is often a compulsive quality to the behavior; the offender may feel "driven" to exhibit himself, may repeatedly select the same place and time of day to expose himself, and even after a number of convictions may resume his deviant behavior. The exhibitionist usually remains at a "safe" distance from his victim (6 to 60 feet away), often has an erection upon exposure, and usually achieves emotional, if not sexual, gratification at the sight of the shocked victim. Some men ejaculate upon exposure, others masturbate afterward, and still others merely enjoy the feeling of high arousal and excitement. The actual act of exposure may last only seconds, with the offender fleeing as soon as he has seen the fear or shock reaction elicited by his act (Gebhard, Gagnon, Pomeroy, & Christenson, 1965).

Voyeurs and exhibitionists comprise the largest percentage of all sex offenders reported to the police.[2] Despite public concern, however, these individuals are usually not dangerous or "oversexed psychopaths"; if anything, they tend to be undersexed and unassertive (McCary, 1973).

[2] A survey of mental health professionals in Hawaii, Jamaica, Mauritus, and nine Far East, four African, four Middle East, and four South American countries indicates that exhibitionism is extremely rare outside the United Kingdom and mainland United States (Rooth, 1972).

Sadism

As a sexual variance, sadism refers to the achievement of sexual arousal through inflicting either excessive physical pain (e.g., by whipping, biting, choking, and cutting) or psychological suffering (e.g., by threatening, teasing, and bullying) on others. The term derives from the name of the late eighteenth and early nineteenth-century French author, the Marquis de Sade, who was notorious for his writings depicting his adventures in using cruelty to obtain sexual gratification. The majority of individuals with strong sadistic proclivities seem to restrict their behavior to reading literature in which protagonists engage in violent and sometimes exotic sadistic activities (Katchadourian and Lunde, 1972). Usually, sadistic fantasies or behavior culminate in masturbatory or coital orgasm. In extreme cases the sadistic act itself leads to orgasm, the most socially heinous case being that of the sexual murderer for whom torture and killing provoke sexual gratification (Hirschfield, 1948).

Masochism

The exploits of the nineteenth-century novelist Leopold von Sacher-Masoch, as well as those of his fictional characters, involved the enjoyment of sexual pleasure through receiving pain, punishment, or psychological humiliation. The term *masochist* has come to refer to an individual who habitually achieves sexual gratification from suffering physical or mental pain. Like sadists, most masochists employ fantasy and literature to achieve arousal. Nevertheless, masochists sometimes pay prostitutes to inflict pain on them (e.g., by whipping or cutting them). Both sadism and masochism can be conceptualized as special instances of fetishism.

Rape

There are a variety of other activities that may be considered sexual variances, particularly if engaged in exclusively or compulsively. Some of these are described in Box 12-2. The most socially significant, sexually related behavior is forcible, heterosexual rape. Although legal definitions differ across jurisdictions, rape commonly refers to sexual intercourse without the partner's consent and usually with force or deception. Probably more than 100,000 forcible rapes occur annually (FBI, 1971; President's Commission, 1967). The offender is typically a married male less than 30 years of age. The victim is generally in her twenties although women as old as 70 have been victims of rape (Gebhard, Gagnon, Pomeroy, & Christenson, 1965). The relations among sadism, aggression, and sexual gratification in acts of rape are complex. In any event, the act itself is often profoundly disturbing to the victim and her family. In recent years organizations have been formed to counsel rape victims, to train women in protective techniques, to educate the public, and to lobby for more sensitive police and medical attention to rape victims.

BIOLOGICAL THEORIES OF SEXUAL VARIANCE

Many of the early investigators of sexual variance assumed that biological factors cause at least some forms of sexually variant behaviors. For example, Forel (1907), Krafft-Ebing (1886), and Hirschfield (1944) were among those who

BOX 12-2
Rare Types of Sexual Variance

Bestiality: Engaging in sexual activities with animals. Such behavior is not considered highly unusual when it is occasional or can be regarded as youthful experimentation.

Compulsive masturbation: Engaging in self-stimulatory behavior to obtain sexual pleasure, either compulsively or to the exclusion of available heterosexual activities.

Frottage: Obtaining sexual pleasure from rubbing or pressing against someone else. This behavior usually occurs in crowded public places and may go unnoticed. When a frotteur does come to the attention of the professional, it is usually found that the person has engaged in other sexually aberrant behavior (e.g., exhibitionism).

Incest: Sexual relations between individuals who, in a given jurisdiction, cannot be legally married. Brother-sister and father-daughter relations are the most common forms of incest.

Mysophilia, coprophilia, urophilia: Obsessive interest in filth, feces, or urine, respectively. Such behavior is assumed to involve sexual pleasure. Urophilia appears to be more common in women than men.

Necrophilia: The use of a dead body as a sexual object. This rare phenomenon is usually associated with psychosis, especially when mutilation or cannibalism occurs.

Nymphomania, satyriasis: Excessive and compulsive sexual behavior in a woman and man, respectively. The term *nymphomaniac* is sometimes too readily applied to women who are merely honest in admitting that they enjoy sex. True nymphomania and satyriasis are extremely rare and are characterized by the individual's inability to become satiated.

Saliromania: Obsessive desire to damage or soil the body or clothes of a woman or a representation of a woman (e.g., a picture or statue).

Troilism: Sexual activity among more than two persons and involving both sexes. Troilism has been theoretically associated with voyeurism, exhibitionism, and homosexuality.

These definitions are based partly on material presented by Allen (1969) and McCary (1973).

presupposed that sexually variant behavior is caused by an innate predisposition. Whereas the early theorists were often unclear about what they meant by terms such as *heredity* and *innate,* modern investigators have defined their research as focusing primarily on genetic determinants and on sex hormonal imbalance. Furthermore, unlike their theoretical predecessors, modern biological investigators have thus far focused on the biogenesis of homosexuality, transsexualism, and transvestism.

Genetic Studies

The evidence for genetic determinants of sexual variance is inconclusive and is generally subject to alternative explanations. The early investigators reported that male homosexuals are more likely to have brothers than sisters; in other words, the parents of male homosexuals were originally reported to be more likely to have male children (Kallmann, 1952; Lang, 1940).[3] Because sex is genetically determined, this finding was at first interpreted as suggesting that homosexuality also is genetically determined. Later investigators, however, have failed to replicate the earlier findings, and it now appears that male homosexuals are not more likely to have brothers than sisters. Even if the original findings had replicated, moreover, this would not necessarily suggest genetic causation. As Money noted: "The findings may signify not a genetic predisposition to homosexuality, but a tendency for an effeminate gender identity to develop more easily in boys whose families have a shortage of sisters and daughters" (1970, p. 27). Money also noted that Slater's (1958) findings that male exhibitionists are more likely to have sisters than brothers is explicable in terms of the male's having "an excess of female sibs to form an audience for their show-off brother" (1970, p. 427).

Many biological investigators of homosexuality have focused on the study of twins. A genetic theory predicts that if one member of a twin pair is homosexual, a co-twin is more likely to be homosexual if he has an identical genetic constitution (identical twin) than if he does not have an identical genetic constitution (fraternal twin). The term *concordance* refers to the extent to which the same attribute (e.g., homosexuality) is exhibited by both members of a twin pair. Thus a genetic theory of homosexuality predicts a higher concordance rate for identical twins.

The best-known twin study is that reported by Kallmann (1952) in which a 100 per cent concordance rate for homosexuality was found for 37 pairs of identical twins and a 12 per cent concordance rate was found for 26 pairs of fraternal twins. Kallmann himself, however, expressed caution in interpreting these findings, and others have readily concurred with him on their problematic nature. Kallmann's findings are difficult to interpret as support for a genetic hypothesis because the co-twins were reared in the same households; therefore, the greater tendency for identical twins to be concordant for homosexuality could be attributed to the potentially more similar social learning histories for the identical than for the fraternal twins. Moreover, Allen (1969) has argued that at least some of Kallmann's data are hearsay, and Heston and Shields (1968) have questioned the appropriateness of Kallmann's sampling techniques.

Although other investigators also have reported higher concordance rates for identical twins than for fraternal twins, nobody has been able to replicate Kallmann's 100 per cent figure. Heston and Shields (1968) found that of five identical twins who were homosexuals, two had a co-twin who was also homosexual, and one had a co-twin who desired to change his sex. By contrast, of seven fraternal twins who were homosexuals, only one had a homosexual co-

[3] See Karlen (1971, Ch. 20), Money (1970), and Rosen, Fox, and Gregory (1972, Ch. 15) for an explanation of the theoretical rationale of sex-ratio studies as well as for the literature citations of studies that failed to replicate the earlier findings.

A display of sadomasochistic sexual devices offered for sale in a specialty shop. (Photo by Magnum Photos, Inc.)

twin. Like Kallmann's data, these findings are subject to alternative explanation.[4]

Another approach to evaluating the possible genetic bases of sexual variance is to investigate the correlation between known sex-chromosomal defects and sexual variance. Researchers have studied both the prevalence of chromosome anomalies in individuals who engage in unconventional sexual activity and the prevalence of sexually aberrant behavior in individuals who have known chromosomal abnormalities.

Correlational studies of known chromosomal disorders and sexual variance have provided only suggestive evidence of a possible relationship (Money & Pollitt, 1964; Pritchard, 1962; Raboch & Nedoma, 1958). Specifically, chromosomal abnormality is neither a necessary nor a sufficient cause of sexual variance, but there may be a small number of cases in which chromosomal irregularities increased vulnerability to personality disorder in general and to inadequate psychosexual differentiation in particular (Money, 1972).

Hormonal Studies

Knowledge concerning the possible role of hormonal factors in sexual variance comes from three sources: animal research, human clinical cases, and research studies comparing the levels of sex hormones in adults who do and do not show sexually variant behavior. The general purpose of this research has been to understand better the effects of sex hormones on sexual behavior as well as on nonsexual behaviors that are characteristically masculine or feminine (see Reinisch, 1974).

In research on animal subjects, the classic experimental studies have focused on a male sex hormone called *androgen.* Although the effects of androgen are not completely understood, in the fetal and neonatal animal the presence of androgen leads to the development of male characteristics. If androgen is not present in sufficient amounts, female characteristics develop. Experimental studies have altered the level of androgen in animals by surgical

[4] Rimland (1969) noted that even when identical twins are not concordant for some trait, thereby ruling out genetic causation, it still can be possible to explain the discordance (e.g., why one twin is a homosexual and his co-twin is not) in terms of biological factors. For example, homosexuality may sometimes be a result of biochemical changes induced by particular types of prenatal injuries, birth difficulties, or postnatal infections. Unfortunately, however, many behavior theorists have been inclined to dismiss all possible biological explanations when evidence exists against a genetic explanation.

Rimland is correct in noting an antibiological bias among behavior theorists. Too many psychologists have dismissed biological explanations with summary statements of "unproven," "unimpressive," or "unlikely" and then have proposed equally inconclusive social learning or psychodynamic hypotheses.

Part of the reason for an antibiological bias among psychologists who have discussed sexual variance is a desire to avoid any implication that sexually variant behavior is a mental disease. Demonstrations of a biological determinant of homosexuality, however, would not establish that homosexuality is a mental disease, nor would it in any way provide support for those who seek to outlaw homosexual activity. Skin pigmentation is a genetic trait, yet no reasonable person would argue that having white skin is a disease or that it justifies racial discrimination against whites. Homosexuals are entitled to basic human rights because they are people; their claim to human rights is not contingent on the validity of any particular theory of causation.

castration of the neonate (Grady, Phoenix, & Young, 1965; Jost, 1961) or by administration of sex hormones to the fetus via injection in the pregnant mother (Neumann & Elger, 1966).

A review of the literature indicates that decreases in effective androgen levels in males increase feminine behaviors and that increases in effective androgen levels in females increase male behaviors. In many of these studies, masculine behaviors are those that involve a relatively high level of energy expenditure, whereas feminine behaviors are those that involve a relatively low level of energy expenditure. The finding that the presence of androgen affects the level of energy expenditure, as well as other findings indicating a critical period for the effects of androgen on sex-related behaviors, suggest the following possibilities:

1. Even without directly affecting sexual behavior, hormones may influence the proclivity toward masculine or feminine activities, thereby affecting psychosexual development. For example, in the developing human female fetus, relatively high levels of androgen may lead to relatively high levels of energy expenditure as a child and, hence, to a consequent proclivity toward activities such as sports. Even though it may be unfair to associate sports with men, the fact that people generally do so can affect the psychological development of the girl who likes to engage in physical activities.

2. Some investigators have proposed that the presence of androgen during critical prenatal periods may create a sensitivity in the central nervous system to male sex hormones, whereas the absence of androgen during critical prenatal periods may permit the development of sensitivity to female sex hormones. The emphasis here is on action during critical prenatal periods—the injection of androgen after the critical period has passed is not postulated to have the same sensitizing effects.

Clinical data on humans provide further evidence of critical prenatal periods during which the presence of androgen affects proclivities toward masculine and feminine behavior. Ehrhardt, Epstein, and Money (1968) and Ehrhardt and Money (1967) have investigated several samples of girls exposed to excessive androgen prior to birth. Because corrective therapy had been instituted in all cases, the investigators were able to study the behavioral consequences of prenatal masculinization. Self-reports obtained from these girls, as well as reports given by their mothers, consistently indicated both an unusually high interest in tomboy activities and a correspondingly low interest in female activities. Compared to only a single matched control subject, more than half of the girls with this adrenogenital syndrome expressed ambivalence over the advantages and disadvantages of being female. In brief, these studies provide some empirical support for a correlation between the presence of high levels of androgen in prenatal human females and subsequent preferences for masculine activities.

In addition to experimental studies on animals and investigations of clinical syndromes in humans, a third line of evidence on hormonal factors comes from studies that compared the relative levels of male and female sex hormones in homosexual and heterosexual adults (Kolodny, Masters, Hendryx, & Toro, 1971; Margolese, 1970). The data obtained from these studies are generally consistent with hormonal theories of homosexuality.[5] Compared to heterosexual men, homosexual men were found to have (1) lower levels of the male sex hormone testosterone; (2) lower ratios of the male sex hormone (testosterone) to the female sex hormone (estrogen); (3) lower sperm counts; and (4) a greater percentage of structurally abnormal sperm. Although these findings support hormonal theories of homosexuality, the correlational nature of the data permits alternative explanations. That is, we do not know whether hormonal differences cause homosexuality or whether homosexual activities cause hormonal differences (Loraine et al., 1971; Kolodny et al., 1971).

Conclusion

The research studies reviewed here have not established any conclusive evidence that biological factors cause homosexuality or any other unconventional sexual behavior. The available data are generally consistent with biological hypotheses, but they are also subject to explanation in terms of psychological hypotheses.

PSYCHOLOGICAL THEORIES OF SEXUAL VARIANCE

Psychological theories of sexual variance include psychoanalytic hypotheses of irrational motivation (e.g., Bieber et al., 1962) and hypotheses of sexual variance as learned behavior affected by cultural factors (e.g., Gagnon & Simon, 1973; Ullmann & Krasner, 1969). What these hypotheses have in common is an explanation of sexual variance in terms of socioenvironmental, rather than biological, factors. The following has been cited as evidence for socioenvironmental factors:

1. Sexual orientation often varies during the course of the individual's life. For example, Kinsey, Pomeroy, and Martin's (1948) classic survey found many males who were exclusively homosexual for extended periods of their lives but who subsequently engaged principally in heterosexual activity. Such variations in sexual orientation are usually explained in terms of social learning experiences. It should be noted, however, that it is theoretically possible to explain these variations in sexual orientation in terms of biological factors.

2. The incidence of homosexuality and of other forms of sexually variant behaviors differs across cultures, thereby suggesting that cultural factors influence the development of sexually variant behaviors (e.g., Edwardes & Masters, 1963; Ford & Beach, 1951; Marshall & Suggs, 1971). One specific hypothesis is that cultural-social sanctions against homosexuality lead to a relatively low incidence of homosexual behavior. Data presented by Ford and Beach (1951) are relevant to this hypothesis. These investigators reviewed 76 primitive societies for which information on sexual behavior was available. In 49 of these societies some form of homosexual activity was considered socially acceptable, whereas in 26 other societies there were explicit social sanctions against

[5] Similar data supporting a hormonal theory of transsexualism is available, indicating that female transsexuals have higher levels of male hormones than do typical females (Fulmer, 1973). However, other data dispute this (Jones & Saminy, 1973).

adult homosexual activity. In general, homosexual behavior was less frequent in those societies in which it was socially unacceptable to engage in homosexual activities. In one society, male homosexuality was condemned and occurred infrequently, while female homosexuality was tolerated and occurred more frequently than did male homosexuality. These data are thus consistent with the hypothesis that social prohibitions affect the incidence of homosexuality. It is interesting to note, nevertheless, that in the Siriono of Eastern Bolivia homosexual behavior was rare even though there were no apparent social sanctions against homosexual activity.

3. The viewpoint that socioenvironmental factors influence sexually variant behavior receives its strongest support from therapy studies. It is clear that psychological intervention has successfully altered sexually variant behavior (e.g., Bieber et al., 1962; Davison, 1968; Evans, 1967; Feldman & MacCulloch, 1971). The fact that psychological therapies alter sexually variant behavior implies that psychological factors *can* cause sexual variance; it does not imply that psychological factors in fact cause sexual variance.

Theories of Male Homosexuality

Fear of Women

Many psychoanalytic and other theorists have hypothesized that homosexual males have learned to fear women (Ellis, 1956; Freud, 1924; Ovessey, Gaylin, & Hendin, 1963; Socarides, 1968; Stevenson & Wolpe, 1960). Support for this hypothesis consists largely of psychodynamic case histories and of evidence suggesting that effective psychological treatment of homosexuality usually requires procedures that decrease heterosexual anxiety (see Feldman & MacCulloch, 1971). These data, however, are inconclusive. Homosexuals who have undergone treatment may not be representative of those who have not sought treatment. In fact, it would not be surprising if there are two groups of homosexuals, those who are fearful of women and are dissatisfied with their homosexuality, and those who are not fearful of women and are satisfied with their homosexuality. The former group may be more likely to seek therapy. Moreover, even in homosexuals who are afraid of women, it is unclear if this fear is a cause or a result of homosexual behavior: Did these men become homosexuals because they feared women, or did they have anxiety-provoking experiences with women because they were homosexuals?

Psychoneurotic Disorder

Another psychoanalytic hypothesis is that homosexuality is an expression of overall psychological maladjustment (e.g., Bieber et al., 1962). This hypothesis is supported by studies of psychoanalytic patients (Bieber et al., 1962), air force disciplinary cases (Doidge & Holtzman, 1960), and psychotherapy patients

(Bergler, 1957). The value of these data, however, has been challenged on the grounds that they are based on unrepresentative samples of homosexuals.[6]

There are a number of other studies relevant to the hypothesis that homosexuality is an expression of general psychoneurotic disturbance. Many of these studies involved surveys of homosexual or lesbian organizations or of subjects recruited through friends of the investigators (Evans, 1969; Hooker, 1957; Loney, 1972; Myrick, 1974; Saghir & Robins, 1973; Thompson, McCandless, & Strickland, 1971). These studies generally show that homosexuals are no more psychologically maladjusted than are heterosexuals. The value of these findings, however, is questionable: Some studies utilized questionable measures of psychological maladjustment (see Hooker, 1957), and in some studies the samples may have been unrepresentative of homosexuals in general.

Curran and Parr (1957) evaluated more than 100 cases of homosexuals who had come to their private psychiatric clinic for reasons varying from difficulty with the law to unhappiness with their sexual orientation. These investigators found no evidence of psychological abnormality in approximately half of these cases and only minimal evidence of psychiatric disturbance in the remaining cases. Comparing this study to that of Bieber et al. (1962), Hoffman (1968) concluded that a major determinant of a diagnosis of psychological "sickness" may be the investigator's theoretical orientation.

Childhood Experiences

Although social learning theories of homosexuality generally stress the importance of early sex role modeling (e.g., Bandura & Walters, 1963; Bandura, 1969; Mischel, 1966), the hypothesis that homosexuality is the result of childhood experiences is most closely associated with psychoanalysis. The fundamental empirical question raised by this hypothesis is whether early childhood experiences of homosexuals are different in any theoretically important ways from those of heterosexuals.

A number of studies suggest that many male homosexuals tend to have backgrounds that differ from those of heterosexual controls. For example, a growing body of research supports Bieber et al.'s (1962) finding that homosexuals often report having had overprotective or possessive mothers, who presumably impaired their sons' developing maleness, as well as fathers who discouraged identification with them (e.g., Evans, 1969; Stephan, 1973; Thompson, Schwartz, McCandless, & Edwards, 1973). Other data also suggest that homosexuals may differ from heterosexuals on specific sociodevelopmental factors (e.g., Apperson & McAdoo, 1968; Siegelman, 1974a).

[6] All possible positions seem to have been taken on the question of whether homosexual therapy patients are more disturbed than homosexuals in general. Hoffman (1968) suggests that homosexual therapy patients are more disturbed. Socarides (1972) suggests that homosexual therapy patients are the better adjusted members of a large class of psychoneurotics because they at least have enough insight to perceive their need for help. Loney (1972) has postulated that homosexuals in therapy are either unusually healthy or unusually defensive.

All findings that homosexuals have a particular pattern of childhood experiences have been challenged. Briefly, it has been noted that the samples of homosexuals studied may have been unrepresentative of homosexuals in general, that the studies relied on adult memories of childhood experiences rather than on direct observations of children, and that subjective judgment is often necessary to provide a theoretically relevant interpretation of these data (e.g., Hooker, 1969; Davison & Neale, 1974; Rosen, Fox & Gregory, 1972).

There may well be some truth to the hypothesis that childhood experiences affect sexual orientation, but the present data are inconclusive. It is clear that psychoanalytic insights will continue to be regarded as little more than insights as long as psychoanalytic investigators continue to rely almost exclusively on clinical case material. Psychoanalytic hypotheses of chilhood experiences are best tested by observing children; adult memories of childhood can only provide indirect and unconvincing tests of such hypotheses. It is unfortunate that the outstanding ideas and insights of psychoanalytic theorists do not usually receive the opportunity for the kind of widespread acceptance that comes from *direct* empirical tests.

Theories of Lesbianism

Psychological theories of lesbianism are generally similar to those of homosexuality. Even though investigators have shown only a limited interest in testing hypotheses about lesbianism, there is some evidence that this interest is currently increasing (see Saghir & Robins, 1973).

Thompson, McCandless, and Strickland (1971) found no differences between young, well-educated lesbians and female heterosexuals on measures of defensiveness, personal adjustment, and self-confidence. Similarly, Hedblom (1972) found no evidence that lesbians are emotionally disturbed individuals. Saghir and Robins (1973) found that homosexual women, as compared to heterosexual controls, tended to identify themselves as masculine, to drop out of college, and to abuse alcohol. The alcohol abuse constituted the principal indicant of psychopathology but characterized only about 35 per cent of the homosexual sample. Furthermore, the degree of impairment in the psychological functioning of this subsample was minimal and was no greater than in the heterosexual sample. Thus the evidence generally supports the view that lesbians are no more psychologically maladjusted than are heterosexuals.

Several studies have suggested that lesbians may have a particular pattern of childhood experiences. Thompson, Schwartz, McCandless, and Edwards (1973) found that lesbians had a more "masculine" childhood and tended to remember feeling more distant from both parents than did controls. Saghir and Robins (1973) found that the vast majority of homosexual women in their study tended to report either identifying with their fathers or with neither parent. These investigators noted that the general failure to identify with the mother may have been a consequence of the prehomosexual girl's greater interest in activities of less interest to mothers. Siegelman (1974b) found a tendency for lesbians to report having had less loving and more demanding mothers as well as rejecting and distant fathers, as compared to reports from heterosexual controls. In all of these studies, it is unclear whether the childhood experiences were causes or effects of lesbian tendencies.

Theories of Transsexualism

Psychological explanations of transsexualism range from underlying personality disturbance (Allen, 1969; see Freund, Langevin, Zajac, Steiner & Zajac, 1974a) to unique family role constellations that reinforce transsexual behavior (Stoller, 1968, 1972). Apart from isolated clinical cases, there is no consistent evidence that transsexualism is associated with underlying personality disturbance. For example, Freund et al. (1974a) found no pathological narcissism, masochism, or aversion to the penis in a sample of 52 male transsexuals. Except for a desperate desire to change their biological sex and the possibility of conceptualizing as psychotic the belief that one's real sex is other than it is, the transsexual often shows no evidence of psychopathology.

There is some evidence that transsexuals often exhibit profoundly unusual gender behavior at very early ages (Green, 1968; Money & Primrose, 1968). For example, Stoller's (1968) observational data of young transsexual boys and their mothers indicate an unusually deep physical and emotional intimacy.[7]

Theories of Other Forms of Sexual Variance

Psychological explanations of transvestism, exhibitionism, voyeurism, sadism, masochism, and pedophilia generally have followed psychoanalytic models (see Kolb, 1973; Salzman, 1962; London & Caprio, 1951; Fenichel, 1934), but recent theorists have begun to derive elaborate formulations based on principles of conditioning (e.g., Kanfer & Phillips, 1970; Yates, 1970; Millon, 1969; McGuire, Carlisle, & Young, 1965). The available scientific evidence, however, is minimal. In general, our knowledge of these forms of sexual variance is based largely on clinical case histories.

The most informative studies on transvestism were conducted by Bentler and his colleagues (Bentler & Prince, 1969, 1970; Bentler, Sherman, & Prince, 1970). The transvestites studied by these investigators were all readers of *Transvestia* magazine and were thus potentially a biased sample. One noteworthy finding from these surveys was that transvestites were no more psychologically disturbed than were matched controls. Moreover, a more recent study by these investigators (Prince & Bentler, 1972) revealed no support for popular psychological explanations of transvestism based on broken homes, poor father image, and dominant mothers (e.g., Stoller, 1968).

There is some evidence that voyeurs, exhibitionists, and especially pedophiles are psychologically immature and interpersonally inadequate (Fisher, 1969; Cohen & Seghorn, 1969; Witzig, 1968; Gebhard, Gagnon, Pomeroy, & Christenson, 1965; Mohr, Turner, & Jerry, 1964). We do not know, however, whether these psychological correlates are effects or causes of sexual variance.

Rachman's (1966) demonstration that a mild "fetish" can be conditioned

[7] Although Freund, Langevin, Zajac, Steiner, and Zajac (1974b) found no evidence of unique mother-child relationships in transsexuals, the subjects in the study were recalling parent-child interactions past the age of five. By contrast, Stoller's (1968) data were based on observations of behavior and on reports of behavior current at the time the study was being conducted.

provided important data for a conditioning explanation of sexual variance. In this study, the Pavlovian conditioning procedures consisted of pairings of slides of women's boots with slides of nude and attractive women. The subjects were three adult males, and arousal to the women's boots was measured by change in penile volume. In addition to the finding that sexual arousal was conditioned to women's boots, there was some generalization of the conditioned arousal to objects resembling boots. Rachman and Hodgon (1968) replicated these findings with five additional subjects.

TREATMENT OF SEXUAL VARIANCE

Treatment of Homosexuality

Effective treatment of homosexuality is available for those who desire it. The treatment of homosexuals may involve either helping the individual to adjust to a society that still generally disapproves of homosexuality (Wilson & Davison, 1974) or aiding the homosexual in altering his or her sexual orientation and in developing gender-consistent behavior, attitudes, and feelings. With respect to this latter and more typical goal, orthodox psychoanalysts, psychodynamically oriented therapists, and behavior therapists have reported success in 25 to 65 per cent of their cases (e.g., Bieber et al., 1962; Feldman & MacCulloch, 1971; Hatterer, 1970). Success in reorienting sexual interest is more likely to occur with the younger, shorter-term, more motivated homosexual who already engages in some heterosexual behavior (Miller, Bradley, Gross, & Wood, 1968). Successful therapy also may be related to the extent to which the treatment trains heterosexual skills as well as heterosexual arousal (Bancroft, 1970; Barlow, 1973).

An interesting approach to helping a homosexual pedophile live with his homosexuality is illustrated in a recent report by Kohlenberg (1974). The patient was a 34-year-old male who was twice arrested for molesting young boys. An important characteristic of this case was the client's fear of contact with adult homosexuals. Although therapy involved several phases, the effective feature of the treatment apparently was an *in vivo* desensitization procedure (Masters & Johnson, 1970; Wolpe, 1958). The goal of this procedure was to train the patient to be attracted to adult males, and the procedure involved a graded series of sexual interactions between the patient and a 30-year-old male volunteer. These interactions included lying together while engaging in nongenital touching and caressing without demand for sexual arousal, exploratory touching of the genital area, simultaneous genital touching with orgasm not permitted, genital contact with orgasm not permitted, and, finally, unrestricted sexual activity. Gradually the patient became more comfortable with his adult partner and was able to achieve orgasm. A six-month follow-up reported less preoccupation with children and more adult homosexual fantasies and activities.

Treatment of Transsexualism

Unlike the other forms of sexual variance discussed in this chapter, transsexualism resembles a thought disorder insofar as the individual believes he is other than his biological sex. For example, the male transsexual usually believes he is a woman trapped in a male body. In contrast, the male homosexual knows he is a man; in fact, evidence indicating that male homosexuals perceive themselves as masculine was summarized earlier in this chapter.

Psychological and surgical treatments are available for transsexualism. The goal of psychological treatment is to alter gender identity; if successful, the biological male becomes satisfied with being a male. The goal of surgical treatment is to alter the individual's physical features so that his appearance is congruent with his feelings.

Psychotherapeutic attempts at altering the gender identity of adult transsexuals have met with minimal success (Gelder & Marks, 1969; Green & Money, 1969; Pauly, 1965). One major problem is that few transsexuals want their gender identity changed (Hoenig, 1974). Some successful cases, however, have been reported (see Barlow, Reynolds, & Agras, 1973; Green, Newman, & Stoller, 1972; Rekers & Lovaas, 1974).

The popular treatment of adult transsexuals has been through hormone and surgical intervention to actually change the individual's sexual appearance (see Money, 1972). The outcome data available (e.g., Benjamin, 1966; Money, 1971; Pauly, 1968; Randall, 1969) suggest that it is the exception for the patient to be dissatisfied with treatment. Nevertheless, there are profound legal, religious, moral, and ethical considerations (see Green, 1969; Money, 1972; Smith, 1971), as well as unknown medical and psychological ramifications (Stoller, 1973). Although some gender identity clinics are extremely cautious in selecting patients for treatment, Stoller has voiced particular concern about the indiscriminate use of surgical intervention by many of his colleagues. More broadly, Stoller has strongly criticized the medical profession for undertaking "sex change" treatment in an uncharacteristically uninformed manner:

> Any other new and potentially dangerous surgical procedure would have been tested more thoroughly. But there is something about the person who requests sex reassignment that brings out or attracts a lower level of medical performance in all areas of evaluation and treatment (1973, p. 539).

That "something about the person" may well be the profound sense of desperation that the transsexual presents to the professional. For instance, Benjamin, a cautious and competent professional and a celebrated pioneer in this area, has remarked that transsexuals are the unhappiest people he has ever met (see Karlen, 1971).

Treatment of Other Forms of Sexual Variance

Although there is a dearth of controlled therapy research on fetishism, transvestism, voyeurism, exhibitionism, sadism, and masochism, the increasing number of reports of successful treatment by behavior therapy is impressive. In general, behavior therapists have employed aversive conditioning procedures in which the sex object is repeatedly paired with a noxious stimulus (e.g., Evans, 1967; Marks & Gelder, 1967). In more recent reports, investigators have claimed successful treatment using desensitization and positive reinforcement procedures (Wickramasekera, 1968) and classical conditioning of appropriate fantasies with masturbatory orgasm (Davison, 1968; Marquis, 1970).

IS SEXUALLY VARIANT BEHAVIOR PSYCHOPATHOLOGICAL?

There is energetic debate as to whether sexually variant behavior is psychopathological. In general, psychoanalysts maintain that sexually variant behavior is a symptomatic expression of neurosis. Redlich and Freedman expressed this view as follows:

> Sexual deviations of adults, also called perversions, are patterns of sexual behavior that predominantly and habitually satisfy other sexual needs than those gratified by natural coitus. Sexual deviations are impulsive and inflexible acts, the individual feels he is under pressure to commit the act and does not have the ordinary capacity to resist or to change his behavior [1966, p.384].

In contrast to the view expressed by Redlich and Freedman, some theorists maintain that sexual variance per se is not psychopathological. In this view, sexual variance simply represents a socially disapproved or unusual choice of sexual expression.

Homosexuality is a noteworthy example of the present debate on the psychopathology of sexual variance. In early 1974 the American Psychiatric Association voted to discard homosexuality as a distinct category in DSM-II and to substitute a category called Sexual Orientation Disturbance. The new category is intended to include only those homosexuals unhappy with their sexual orientation. The meaning of this vote is unclear. As Spitzer has emphasized:

> In removing homosexuality per se from the nomenclature we are only recognizing that by itself homosexuality does not meet the criteria for being considered a psychiatric disorder. We will in no way be aligning ourselves with any particular viewpoint regarding the etiology or desirability of homosexual behavior [1973, p. 1216].

Whether sexual variance is psychopathological seems to depend on the type of variance and on the individual under consideration. Many homosexuals seem to be as psychologically healthy as is the general population. On the other hand, transsexualism could be regarded as psychopathological because it is associated with profound desperation and, to some extent, with psychotic-like denials of reality. Voyeurism can be regarded as psychopathological because it is often conducted under unnecessarily dangerous circumstances. The compulsive quality of exhibitionism also suggests psychopathology.

SUMMARY

Sexually variant behaviors have atypical sexual activity as their salient diagnostic feature. They are distinguished from sexual dysfunctions because they are characterized by unusual or socially disapproved choices of sexual objects, or by unconventional modes of sexual gratification, rather than by an impairment in the functioning of the genitourinary system.

The most extensively investigated form of sexually variant behavior is male homosexuality. The most prevalent homosexual activities are fellatio and anal intercourse, with the majority of homosexuals interchanging active and passive roles. The majority of homosexual men neither engage in heterosexual activities nor experience heterosexual arousal, but a large minority engage in both homosexual and heterosexual activities. Contrary to popular myths, the vast majority of homosexuals are not effeminate, nor are they likely to be found in "effeminate" occupations such as hairdressing. The overwhelming majority perceive themselves as masculine.

The overt sexual activity of female homosexuality is most remarkable for its similarities to female heterosexuality. Compared to male homosexuals, lesbians have fewer sexual partners, engage in fewer short-term sexual contacts, and more frequently enter into lasting relationships characterized by fidelity and by strong emotional attachments. To a large extent, the bond between lesbians is emotional.

Transsexualism is indicated by an intense denial of one's biological sex and usually occurs in individuals with a history of cross-dressing. Because the male transsexual thinks of himself as a woman, he desires sexual relations with men. But this similarity between transsexualism and homosexuality is superficial because male homosexuals perceive themselves as masculine, whereas male transsexuals perceive themselves as women trapped in a male body.

Transvestism is the act of dressing in the clothes of the opposite sex to obtain emotional and/or sexual gratification. The overwhelming majority of transvestites are male.

Fetishism is the habitual use of a part of the body or of an inanimate object to produce sexual arousal. The objects that can become fetishes are seemingly countless.

Pedophilia refers to the use of children by an adult for sexual gratification. Contrary to popular belief, the child molester is not usually a stranger who attacks children as they travel to and from school, a store, or a friend's home. More than half of the victims are known to the pedophile, and almost four of every five instances occur in the child's, or in the offender's, home.

Voyeurism originally referred to the act of observing nudes for sexual gratification, but it has come to include scoptophilia, the act of observing the genitals and the sexual behaviors of others in order to obtain erotic pleasure. As a diagnostic entity, voyeurism is distinguished from culturally acceptable interest in observing nudity by its exclusiveness as a means of achieving sexual gratification, by its surreptitiousness, by its offensiveness to the involuntary participant, and by its compulsiveness even in the face of serious risk.

Exhibitionism refers to the obtainment of sexual gratification by exhibiting one's genitals to members of the opposite sex. Sadism refers to the achievement of sexual arousal by causing either excessive physical pain or psychological suffering in others. Masochism refers to the obtainment of sexual gratification from suffering physical or mental pain. Forcible rape is also considered a form of sexual variance.

Although virtually all of the available evidence is consistent with biological theories of homosexuality, these theories are far from proven. There is replicated evidence that the concordance rate for homosexuality is higher for identical than for fraternal twins. Several lines of evidence, moreover, implicate the sex hormones *androgen* and *testosterone* as possibly having an etiological role in sexually variant behavior.

Virtually all of the available evidence is consistent with psychological theories of causation of sexually variant behavior. The evidence usually cited as implicating socioenvironmental causal factors includes the following: Sexual orientation often varies during the course of an individual's life; the incidence of homosexuality and other forms of sexually variant behaviors differs across cultures; sexually variant behaviors can be induced experimentally via learning experiences and can be treated by psychological techniques.

Specific psychological hypotheses of male homosexuality include the notions that homosexuals fear women, that homosexuality is an expression of overall psychological maladjustment, and that homosexuality in adults is a result of childhood experiences. There is evidence consistent with each of these hypotheses but, overall, the evidence is inconclusive for two reasons. First, much of the available data is based on clinical case studies, and these cases may provide a biased sample of the overall population of homosexuals. Second, the available data are correlational in nature. For example, even in homosexuals who in fact fear women, it is unclear if this fear is a cause or a result of homosexual behavior. Did these men become homosexuals because they feared women, or did they have anxiety-provoking experiences with women because they were homosexuals?

Many behavior theorists who have reviewed the evidence pertaining to the causes of homosexuality have done so in accordance with a double standard biased against biological causation. Part of the reason for this antibiological bias is a desire to avoid any implication that homosexuality is a mental disease. The identification of biological causation, however, does not permit inferences of a mental disease. If homosexuality is biologically determined, then so is heterosexuality, and hence there would be no more reason, from this consideration alone, to consider homosexuality a disease than there would be to consider heterosexuality a disease. Because they are people, homosexuals are entitled to basic human rights, including freedom from harassment. Their claim to human rights is not contingent on the validity of any particular theory of causation.

Chapter 13

Personality Disorders, Psychopathy, and Alcoholism

pathological personalities are distinguished from normal personality patterns by their adaptive inflexibility, their tendency to foster vicious circles, and their tenuous stability under stress.

MILLON (1969, pp. 222–223)

For decades the term *psychopathic personality* was officially used to refer to criminals, liars, sexual deviates, alcoholics, socially withdrawn people, very suspicious people, people subject to mild, recurring mood alternations, compulsive people, and emotionally unstable people. With the introduction of DSM-II in 1952 the term *personality disorder* replaced that of *psychopathic personality,* and the following classification system was created:

I. Personality Disorders

1. Personality pattern disturbance.
   a. Inadequate personality.
   b. Schizoid personality.
   c. Cyclothymic personality.
   d. Paranoid personality.
2. Personality trait disturbance.
   a. Emotionally unstable personality.
   b. Passive-aggressive personality.
   c. Compulsive personality.
   d. Personality trait disturbance, other.
3. Sociopathic personality disturbance.
   a. Antisocial reaction.
   b. Dyssocial reaction.
   c. Sexual deviation.
   d. Addiction: alcoholism and drug addiction.
4. Special symptom reaction.
   a. Learning disturbance.
   b. Speech disturbance.
   c. Enuresis.
   d. Somnambulism.
   e. Other.

Despite the revised terminology, the preceding syndromes are very dissimilar. In this chapter we shall restrict the concept of personality disorder to the syndromes defined in Box 13-1. Thus, alcoholism will not be considered a personality disorder even though it is discussed later in this chapter.

THE CONCEPT OF PERSONALITY DISORDERS

Personality disorders are thought of as deeply ingrained, characteristic styles of inappropriate behavior. They are distinguished from neuroses in that personality disorders describe life-long patterns of maladaptive behavior, whereas neuroses are conceptualized as a reaction to stress occurring during a particular life period. Thus neuroses can occur in previously well adjusted persons exposed to prolonged stress or emotional trauma. Personality disorders are distin-

BOX 13-1
Personality Disorders

Paranoid personality: A life-long pattern of excessive and inappropriate suspicion and lack of trust of others. Jealousy, envy, and the habitual perception of one's problems as someone else's fault are common attributes of the paranoid personality.

Cyclothymic personality: The pervasive alternation of depressed and elated mood states. The alternating moods may be of any length; the usual intensity of the moods varies from one individual to another.

Schizoid personality: A life-long pattern of avoidance of social relations. Shyness, frequent daydreaming, and a tendency not to express anger directly are frequently considered part of the cluster of behavior describing the schizoid personality.

Explosive personality: A life-long pattern of behavior characterized by frequent outbursts of verbal or physical aggression. Although the intense episodes are out of character in regard to everyday behavior, impulsiveness and overreactiveness to stress are characteristic of average functioning.

Obsessive-compulsive personality: A life-long pattern of excessive concern with conformity to a set of rules concerning right and wrong. These individuals frequently are described as rigid, uncomfortable, and overconscientious.

Hysterical personality: A life-long pattern of inappropriate attention-seeking behavior. The attention seeking is often of a seductive nature and is part of a general overreactiveness and lack of emotional consistency. The individual denies attention-seeking motivation if confronted. Generally, these individuals are viewed as self-oriented and immature.

Asthenic personality: The persistent lack of energy and enthusiasm as a long-standing trait. These individuals usually consider most types of entertainment and activities as too tiring to be enjoyed.

Antisocial personality: A life-long pattern of antisocial behavior accompanied by a lack of normal guilt. These individuals are frequently and repeatedly in trouble with the law.

Passive-aggressive personality: A life-long pattern of passive behaviors as a means of expressing anger and frustrating other persons. These people habitually cause problems for others in apparently accidental and unintended ways.

Inadequate personality: Generally inept and unable to deal with the stress of everyday life although intellectually and physically capable of doing so. Generally, this type of person is very dependent on others and relies on others to solve his problems.

guished from psychoses in that they are less maladaptive and occur in the absence of hallucinations, delusions, and thought disorders.

Because personality disorders describe a life-long pattern of maladaptive behavior, they have no definite onset, course of development, or point of termination. For example, a person with a paranoid personality is unusually suspicious of others and, although the degree of suspicion varies depending on life circumstances and on situational factors, there is usually no clear point at which one can say that the tendency to be excessively suspicious either began or terminated. A schizoid personality is someone who is socially withdrawn to the point of organizing his life to avoid interpersonal contacts. Although this

Antisocial or aggressive behavior also occurs in many nonpsychopathic persons. (Photo by Burk Uzzle; Magnum Photos, Inc.)

pattern of behavior often begins during adolescence, its onset is gradual and it is generally evident throughout the person's life. In contrast, the onset, process, and/or termination of neurotic and psychotic episodes of behavior are much more definable even though there exist considerable individual differences in such behaviors.

Another characteristic of personality disorders is that they represent a borderline adjustment. Persons exhibiting personality disorders have generally managed to adjust sufficiently well to meet the minimal demands of life (e.g., work, marry, raise a family), but the adjustment is precarious because it is predicated on an inflexible adherence to certain inappropriate and often highly defensive patterns of behavior. A person with a schizoid personality, for example, manages to adjust because he is generally capable of minimizing interpersonal contact. The withdrawal is relatively severe as compared to normal behavior, but it is often not so severe as to preclude marriage or employment. However, if such an individual is exposed to close interpersonal contact for sustained periods, a psychotic episode may occur consisting of symptoms such as delusions, hallucinations, thought disorder, paranoia, and/or extreme withdrawal. Thus the notion of a borderline adjustment implies in part a heightened vulnerability to stress. As Millon noted: "Given the ease with which past sensitivities can be reactivated, and the inflexibility and relative paucity of the coping strategies they have at their command, these individuals are extremely susceptible to disruptions or breakdowns in their established patterns" (1969, p. 223).

PSYCHOPATHY (ANTISOCIAL PERSONALITY)

The personality disorder that has received the most research attention is variously called *psychopathy, sociopathy,* or *antisocial personality.* Because psychopaths are capable of brutal acts of aggression and ruthless acts of criminality, psychopathy has been called the most destructive and costly form of psychopathology. All criminals, however, are not psychopaths; rather, aggression and other antisocial behaviors occur for many reasons other than true psychopathy:

1. Many so-called normal people engage in aggressive and/or criminal acts. The psychology of aggression is discussed in detail in Chapter 20.
2. Aggression sometimes occurs as an expression of a neurotic disorder. Such behavior, variously called *neurotic* or *secondary psychopathy,* differs markedly from *true* or *primary psychopathy.* Specifically, neurotic psychopathy is accompanied by guilt, anxiety, and depression, whereas primary psychopathy is indicated in part by a relative absence of these emotions.
3. Aggression sometimes occurs in the context of a social group that reinforces and values such behavior. Aggression occurring under these circumstances is called *dyssocial* or *subcultural psychopathy.* For example, members of street gangs are frequently described as dyssocial psychopaths.

McCord and McCord have defined primary psychopathy as follows: "The psychopath is an asocial, aggressive, highly impulsive person who feels little or no guilt and is unable to form lasting bonds of affection with other human beings" (1964, p. 3). A more detailed definition of primary psychopathy was provided by Cleckley (1964), who noted 16 clinical characteristics.

1. *"Superficial charm and good 'intelligence'."*[1] The psychopath is of at least average intelligence and generally is well liked by casual acquaintances. He may be an expert at small talk, and his behavior often has the initially convincing sincerity and likability of the "con man." Psychopaths often know just what to say to make someone like them, to relieve others' anxieties, or to get themselves out of trouble. Generally, it is not until one knows the psychopath for a long period of time that the manipulative nature and superficiality of the charming personality become evident. For example, McNeil's (1967) case description of Don F., a psychopathic personality, includes the following: "Don F. had charm plus. He always seemed to know when to say the right thing with exactly the proper degree of concern, seriousness, and understanding for the benighted victim of a harsh world" (1967, p. 86). The manipulative nature of Don's charm, however, is clearly seen in the following passage, in which he tells how he dealt with the police in his many encounters with them as an adolescent:

I could con them the same as I fooled my own folks. When I got caught by the cops I always blamed the other guy. I would admit to just enough to make me appear to be a

[1] The 16 characteristics that appear in direct quotation marks, as well as their order, is printed with permission of both author and publisher from the following source. From H. Cleckley, *The mask of sanity* (5th ed.). St. Louis: The C. V. Mosby Co., 1976. The descriptions of the characteristics are the responsibility of the present writers.

slightly imperfect but honest guy who deserved another chance. They went for it time and time again, not because they believed it, but because they couldn't stand the idea that I was really a rotten kid [1967, p. 88].

2. *"Absence of delusions and other signs of irrational thinking."* Psychopaths are of at least average intelligence, and they do not display psychotic symptoms such as delusions and thought disorder. Nevertheless, psychopaths seem insane because they repeatedly engage in unrewarding and self-damaging behavior. For example, many psychopaths engage in senseless crimes over and over again even though they are repeatedly caught and punished. This pattern of unrewarding and self-damaging behavior led Pritchard (1835) to coin the phrase *moral insanity* as a reference to psychopathy.

3. *"Absence of 'nervousness' or psychoneurotic manifestations."* The psychopath is unusual in the extent to which he remains calm and poised and does not become anxious and depressed.

4. *"Unreliability."* Psychopaths are unfaithful friends and unfaithful spouses. There is no "honor among thieves" among psychopathic criminals.

5. *"Untruthfulness and insincerity."* Psychopaths are "pathological liars." Yet they are very convincing liars, so convincing that it seems as if they really believe what they are saying at the time they say it. In describing the case of a psychopathic criminal, Cleckley noted:

Like many psychopaths, he is quite familiar with the correct ethical criteria. He claims allegiance to such criteria and can in words formulate excellent rules and plans for himself to follow. One could scarcely imagine that, in the full sense of the word, he is sincere in all this. Yet, like many psychopaths, he does not seem to be simply lying, or at any rate to be quite aware that he is lying, or even to grasp emotionally the essence of what is falsehood. Perhaps such people mean for the moment to do what they promise so convincingly, but the resolution passes almost as the words are spoken [1959, p. 572].

Psychopaths not only exhibit a remarkable capacity for solemn falsehoods but also lie even when it is unnecessary and seemingly without purpose. For example, a psychopathic man, writing a letter to a woman from whom he was divorced, described an insurance policy he was sending to provide for her and the children. There never was such a policy, the man never intended to buy such a policy, and his wife had not expected that he would buy her any policy; hence, he lied even though he would be caught and had nothing to gain.

6. *"Lack of remorse or shame."* The psychopath shows a relative impairment in the ability to experience guilt.

7. *"Inadequately motivated antisocial behavior."* Psychopaths steal, swindle, and murder, and they usually do so to gratify immediate impulses and whims. For example, a psychopath may rob a store and then squander or give away the money; he may murder because of a minor annoyance or for kicks. Often psychopathic antisocial acts are ruthless and are conducted with minimal regard for others.

8. *"Poor judgment and failure to learn from experience."* No matter how many times he is caught and punished, the psychopath generally continues his basic pattern of antisocial behavior.

9. *"Pathologic egocentricity and incapacity for love."* Psychopaths are self-centered, immature, and selfish.

10. *"General poverty in major affective reactions."* Although the psychopath may know all the right things to say to others, he does not experience normal human affection and hence has difficulty in forming lasting relationships with other people. As Johns and Quay (1962) have noted, the psychopath knows the words of human emotions but not the music. This emotional poverty is revealed clearly in the following passage from McNeil's case of Don F.:

> I can remember the first time in my life when I began to suspect I was a little different from most people. When I was in high school my best friend got leukemia and died and I went to his funeral. Everybody else was crying and feeling sorry for themselves and as they were praying to get him into heaven I suddenly realized that I wasn't feeling anything at all. He was a nice guy but what the hell. That night I thought about it some more and found out that I wouldn't miss my mother and father if they died and that I wasn't too nuts about my brothers and sisters, for that matter. I figured there wasn't anybody I really cared for but, then, I didn't need any of them anyway so I rolled over and went to sleep [1967, p. 87].

11. *"Specific loss of insight."* The psychopath lacks insight into the nature of his problems.

12. *"Unresponsiveness in general interpersonal relations."*

13. *"Fantastic and uninviting behavior with drink and sometimes without."* An unusual proportion of psychopaths seem to become heavy drinkers even though most heavy drinkers are not psychopaths.

14. *"Suicide rarely carried out."* Because suicide is associated with depression, and because psychopaths show a relative lack of manifest depression, it is not surprising that as a group they rarely commit suicide.

15. *"Sex life impersonal, trivial, and poorly integrated."*

16. *"Failure to follow any life plan."* The psychopath seeks excitement, usually has no stable life goals, and has a low tolerance for boredom. His crimes frequently are engaged in at the spur of the moment rather than after careful planning and preparation. The psychopath's impulsive proclivities have been demonstrated empirically in a number of delay of gratification studies. In many of these studies subjects are provided with a choice between an immediate, smaller reward and a delayed, larger reward (e.g., "Would you like $1 now or $10 next week?"). Compared to other groups, Mischel (1961) found that juvenile delinquents preferred the immediate reward. Similarly, Rosenquist and Megaree (1969) found that, compared to nondelinquents, delinquents were more likely to report that if given money by an experimenter, they would spend it immediately on pleasurable items rather than save it.

Prevalence

Most clinicians agree that psychopathy can be diagnosed by late adolescence although some believe that the disorder may be evident by the age of eight (Gray & Hutchison, 1964). Accurate statistics on the incidence and prevalence of psychopathy are unavailable, in part because there is so much confusion among primary psychopathy, criminal behavior, and alcoholism. Page (1971) has estimated the prevalence of psychopathy to be about 1 per cent of the male population and about 0.50 per cent of the female population.

Theories of Etiology

Research on the causes of primary psychopathy has focused on correlations between psychopathy and extreme forms of parental rejection, on impaired moral development, on a chronically underaroused central nervous system, on correlations between abnormal EEG brain waves and psychopathy, and on deficits in learning to fear and avoid punishment.

Parental Rejection

The male psychopath's brutal anger, his relative inability to experience guilt, and his lack of internalized values suggest the incomplete formation of a conscience and an incomplete identification with the father. Such development might be expected when a child is severely rejected or when one of the parents is absent from the home. Some evidence supports this view that parental rejection and parental loss increase the likelihood of psychopathic development (e.g., Bandura & Walters, 1959; Greer, 1964; Gregory, 1958; Jenkins & Hewitt, 1944). For example, Partridge (1928) conducted extensive interviews with 12 psychopathic male delinquents and found that all hated their parents and that all had been rejected as young children. More recently, Greer (1964) found that, compared to 28 per cent of 387 neurotics and 27 per cent of 691 normals, 60 per cent of 79 psychopaths had experienced parental loss. In a large scale survey, Eron, Walder, and Lefkowitz (1971) reported that rejection by parents was significantly related to aggressive behavior in school as reported by peers. (See Chapter 20.) Moreover, some evidence suggests that the type and severity of parental rejection and loss are related to psychopathy. For example, Baldwin, Kalhorn, and Breese (1945) found that psychopathic development is associated with the more severe forms of parental rejection, and Oltman and Friedman (1967) found that psychopathy is related more to parental loss due to separation than to parental loss due to death or to severe illness requiring hospitalization. These findings suggest that marital discord preceding parental separation may be a crucial factor associated with psychopathic development. In this regard, a review of the relevant literature by Peterson and Becker (1965) suggests that parents of psychopaths tend to be discontented and short-tempered and that they often provide models of antisocial behavior for their children to emulate.

There is, then, support for the hypothesis that early emotional deprivation and parental rejection are related to psychopathy. Several investigators, however, have encouraged caution in interpretation of these data (e.g., Hare, 1970; McCord & McCord, 1964). It has been noted, for example, that much of the available data are correlational and hence do not permit inferences of causality. Moreover, many studies relied on retrospective accounts of family interactions or on other subjective methods of data collection. Perhaps the most important basis for caution is that, although psychopaths tend to come from broken or rejecting homes, most people who come from such homes are not psychopaths.

Research on the causes of psychopathy has implicated parental rejection, impaired moral development, and certain brain as well as learning deficiencies as possible factors in the development of this behavior. (Photo by Wayne Miller; Magnum Photos, Inc.)

Thus parental rejection is at most only one of several possible factors that lead to psychopathy.

Moral Development

Kohlberg (1964, 1969) has developed a six-stage scale of moral reasoning; the normal individual progresses from one stage to the next as he matures. Although the Kohlberg scales may be of limited value because they lack demonstrated validity (Kurtines & Greif, 1974), studies using these scales have found that the moral reasoning of aggressive children is less mature than that of normal children (Campagna & Harter, 1975; Jurkovic & Prentice, 1974).

Cortical Immaturity Hypothesis

EEG brain wave abnormalities have been found in 31 to 58 per cent of the samples of aggressive psychopaths studied (see Hare, 1970). This abnormality consists of the presence of slow wave activity in many parts of the brain (Hare, 1970; Hill & Watterson, 1942). These data, however, are difficult to interpret because it is unclear what the EEG measures. It has been suggested that because the brain wave abnormality (theta waves) found in many psychopaths resembles normal brain wave activity in children, psychopathy is related to an inadequate physical maturation of the central nervous system (see Hare, 1970). Presently, however, there exists little support for this hypothesis other than the EEG findings.

Cortical Underarousal

The concept of an optimal level of cortical arousal implies that people are motivated to obtain a particular level of sensory stimulation. When the level of sensory input is above the optimal level, there is motivation to reduce stimulation; when this level is below the optimal level, there is motivation to seek out stimulation. The concept of arousal is important here because there is evidence that psychopathy is associated with a chronic condition of cortical underarousal.

1. If psychopaths are underaroused, they should seek out sensory stimulation. The available evidence supports this prediction. Wiesen (1965), for example, found that college students who scored high on scales indicating psychopathy pressed a lever more often when it was reinforced by the onset of stimulation than when it was reinforced by the offset of stimulation. Skrzypek (1969) also found that psychopaths seek higher levels of sensory stimulation than do nonpsychopaths. Clinical observations, moreover, suggest that psychopaths seek out excitement much more than do nonpsychopaths.

2. Psychopathy seems to be associated with an attenuation of sensory input that may produce cortical underarousal; that is, the sensory nervous system of psychopaths appears to be less excitable than that of nonpsychopaths (e.g., Shagass & Schwartz, 1962).

3. Psychopaths commit antisocial acts repeatedly despite the fact that they are often caught and punished. This behavior pattern, characterized by a failure

to learn from previous experiences that result in punishment, could be a consequence of cortical underarousal. Specifically, psychopaths may not learn how to avoid punishment because aversive stimulation is reinforcing insofar as it raises arousal levels from a low to an optimal level. Empirical support for this hypothesis has been obtained in several studies that compared the performance of psychopaths and nonpsychopaths on an avoidance learning task. In the most influential of these studies, Lykken (1957) found that psychopathic criminals were deficient in learning not to press a lever that produced electric shock, as compared to the performances of nonpsychopathic criminals and of college students. If this deficiency in learning how to avoid electric shock is caused by cortical underarousal, then it should not occur under conditions that increase cortical arousal. This prediction has been confirmed. Schachter and Latane (1964), for example, found that psychopaths were deficient in learning how to avoid a shock-lever under conditions of placebo injection but not under conditions of adrenalin injection. Chesno and Kilmann (1975) had psychopathic and neurotic criminals perform a shock-avoidance task under conditions of low, medium, and high background stimulation. As predicted by the cortical underarousal hypothesis, primary psychopaths learned how to avoid shock more effectively under conditions of higher auditory stimulation, whereas the avoidance behavior of control subjects was not affected by changes in the level of auditory stimulation.

In conclusion, there is evidence that cortical underarousal is associated with primary psychopathy. This underaroused state may be responsible for the psychopath's failure to learn to avoid punishment because, for the psychopath, aversive stimuli may have the reinforcing consequence of enhancing arousal toward an optimal level. The psychopath's deficiency in learning how to avoid punishment, moreover, may explain why psychopaths show a life pattern of antisocial actions. It is emphasized, however, that the hypothesis of cortical underarousal is far from proven and that much more research is needed to test its implications.

SELECTED PERSONALITY DISORDERS

As already noted, primary psychopathy is only one of a number of life patterns of maladaptive behavior that have been described by clinical investigators. Descriptions of some other personality disorders appear here.

Schizoid Personality

A schizoid personality is indicated by a life pattern of detachment from, and avoidance of, close interpersonal relations (Cameron, 1963; Millon, 1969). This includes extreme shyness, mild social withdrawal (the hermit type), and an overly intellectual style of interaction (e.g., an individual who discusses philosophy-of-life issues while avoiding situations or topics that elicit interpersonal feelings.) Some schizoids live alone and rarely venture out when other people are around, whereas others work continually in order to avoid interpersonal contact.

The schizoid personality (schizoidia) is considered by many to be a mild form, or possibly even a precursor, of schizophrenia. The major similarity between these two syndromes is that both involve an apparent fear of interpersonal feelings and interactions. Also, a rich fantasy life is often seen in both syndromes. The major dissimilarity is the absence of psychotic behaviors (delusions, hallucinations, and thought disorders) in schizoidia and the presence of such symptoms in schizophrenia. If schizoidia is a mild form of schizophrenia, a schizoid person exposed to significant stress should experience a schizophrenic episode. Although this sometimes occurs (Cameron, 1963), the extent to which a schizoid personality is a precursor of schizophrenia has yet to be established.

The antecedent conditions that lead to schizoid development are unknown. However, Millon (1969) has hypothesized that interpersonal experiences are aversive for schizoids because of previous rejection by significant others, especially parents. Cameron (1963) has suggested that schizoid personality development is a result of a lack of basic trust similar to that seen in schizophrenia; unlike the schizophrenic, however, the schizoid has developed sufficient ego strength and self-identity to preclude the loss of reality contact.

Passive-Aggressive Personality

A passive-aggressive personality is indicated by a life pattern of aggression expressed in passive and often unrecognizable forms as well as by an accompanying reluctance to express anger directly. The passive aggression may take many forms and serves to frustrate, distress, or pain others. For example, a man's tardiness in picking up his date may prevent them from attending an event of special interest to her. Typically, the man would have a good excuse for being late, but such behavior would not be an isolated instance in the case of a passive-aggressive personality.

The passive-aggressive person is hostile toward others but is afraid to express this anger and hostility. Psychodynamic theory suggests that these individuals experienced inadequate gratification of dependency needs as children (Cameron, 1963), are angered by the restrictions on their freedom that their need for dependency creates, and yet are so in need of acceptance from others that they dare not risk its loss by expressing aggressive feelings directly. Thus they express their aggression in a disguised, passive form.

Obsessive-Compulsive Personality

An obsessive-compulsive personality is indicated by a pervasive, life pattern of ritualistic behavior and by an extreme concern with morality and rightness. A certain degree of compulsiveness is appropriate and is expressed by normal concerns with neatness, cleanliness, and conformity. Such behaviors are abnormal only when they are extreme, consume a major portion of the person's time, and limit significantly the individual's ability to solve life problems and to enjoy himself. For example, excessive compulsiveness may take the form of a need for neatness and accuracy that results in the repeated redoing of written papers or in continual house cleaning. As host or hostess of a party, the individual may continually clean ash trays, refill snack trays, and prepare food.

An especially important indication that a person is compulsive is when any interference with the behavior pattern or compulsive thought results in anxiety and discomfort. The compulsive person has difficulty relaxing by temporarily forgetting his concerns. Nevertheless, most individuals suffering from a compulsive personality do not become neurotic or psychotic (Cameron, 1963); they maintain normal vocational and social interests even though their lives tend to be excessively rigid, orderly, and ritualistic.

Psychodynamic theory suggests that compulsive behavior is a defense against recognizing hostility and places the origin of this unacceptable hostility in childhood experiences during toilet training.

ALCOHOLISM

Alcohol is the most abused drug in the United States, and its cost to our society is considerable:

1. Alcohol-related automobile accidents are responsible for approximately 28,000 deaths each year. Approximately 60 per cent of those killed in such accidents are between the ages of 16 and 24. Additionally, approximately 500,000 alcohol-related automobile accidents occur each year, and many of these result in some type of injury (NIMH, 1972).
2. The life expectancy of alcoholics is ten to 12 years shorter than that of nonalcoholics. Each year approximately 13,000 Americans die from alcohol-related diseases (NIMH, 1972).
3. The families of alcoholics, especially children, may suffer considerably. Alcoholism is associated with unhappy homes, divorces, and parental mistreatment of children.
4. Alcohol-related crimes account for half of all homicides or approximately 11,700 deaths each year (NIMH, 1972).
5. The prevalence of alcoholism in American Indian reservations is very high, with as many as 25 to 50 per cent of the population of some reservations being alcoholic.

Definition of Alcoholism

Approximately 80 to 100 million Americans drink alcoholic beverages, but the extent and frequency to which they do so varies from the social drinker who consumes alcohol primarily at parties to the alcoholic who regularly drinks in excessive amounts. The many individual patterns of drinking habits, as well as the fact that moderate drinking does not seem to be associated with any lasting harm, make it difficult to define alcoholism in a precise manner. The various definitions of alcoholism usually emphasize at least one of the following: (1) the consumption of alcohol to the extent that it causes a problem, such as difficulty at work or at home; (2) a loss of control over the drinking habit; and (3) the consumption of alcohol to the point that it causes physiological damage. Keller has defined alcoholism as follows:

> Alcoholism is a chronic disease or disorder of behavior, characterized by the repeated drinking of alcoholic beverages to an extent that exceeds customary dietary use for ordinary compliance with the social drinking customs of the community, and which interferes with the drinker's health, interpersonal relations or economic functioning [1962].

The FAIREST
The FUNNIEST
WALT DISNEY'S
MARY POPPINS
David Tomlinson
Glynis Johns
TECHNICOLOR
COMING SOON
LOEW'S
MID-CITY

Prevalence

The prevalence of alcoholism in the United States has been estimated to be between 5 and 9 million people (Chafetz, 1967; NIMH, 1972; Wanberg & Horn, 1970). Including the family and employers of alcoholics, NIMH (1972) estimates that alcoholism is directly affecting 27 million Americans. Approximately four times as many males as females are alcoholics.

The prevalence of alcoholism varies considerably across religious groups, cultures, and nations. The French seem to be the greatest per capita consumers of alcohol in the world; the French government has estimated that 15 per cent of the male population are alcoholics and that 30 per cent consume alcohol in amounts dangerous to their health (Ray, 1972). These data suggest that alcoholism is approximately seven times more prevalent in France than in the United States. Alcoholism is relatively rare in southern Italy but is prevalent in the industrialized north. In the United States alcoholism is prevalent among Irish Americans and is relatively rare among Italians and Jews.

The Drug Alcohol

There are many types of alcohol, all of which have toxic effects if taken in sufficient dosages. The type of alcohol that is found in all alcoholic beverages is ethyl alcohol (C_2H_6O).

Ethyl alcohol is produced naturally by yeast fermentation. The process requires yeast, sugar, and water. Because yeast are pervasive in the air around plants and because fruits contain sugar, fermentation occurs naturally when yeast and rain fall on crushed fruits from plants. This natural occurrence of fermentation accounts for the discovery of alcohol by primitive man.

Because yeast cannot survive in solutions greater than 15 per cent alcohol, fermentation cannot produce beverages with an alcoholic content greater than 15 per cent. *Distillation*, introduced in Europe during the fifteenth century, but probably discovered by the Arabs in the ninth century, is a method of increasing the alcoholic content of beverages. Alcoholic solutions produced by fermentation are heated and then the vapors that form are condensed; because alcohol has a lower boiling point than does water, the vapors that are condensed into liquid form have a much higher alcoholic content than did the original solution.

The alcoholic content of a beverage is expressed in terms of its proof, which is twice the actual percentage of alcohol. Thus, a 100-proof bottle of whiskey is 50 per cent alcohol. Generally, American beers are about 4 per cent alcohol, table wines are between 17 and 20 per cent alcohol, liquors are between 22 and 50 per cent alcohol, and distilled spirits (e.g., whiskey) are between 40 and 50 per cent alcohol.

Alcohol is a central nervous system depressant. As noted in Chapter 5, however, it is important to distinguish between physiologic and behavioral drug

The prevalence of alcoholism in the United States has been estimated to be between 5 and 9 million people. (Photo by Bob Adelman; Magnum Photos, Inc.)

depressants. For example, if stimulation of a nerve inhibits a certain behavior (e.g., aggression), then a drug that depresses this neural activity can have the effect of stimulating that behavior (e.g., increases aggression). Although alcohol is a central nervous system depressant, in a certain range of effective dosages it stimulates behavioral activity.

Alcohol is not digested but instead is absorbed directly into the blood stream through the walls of the stomach and the small intestine. Although some alcohol is excreted by the lungs, kidneys, and skin, between 90 and 98 per cent of the alcohol ingested is metabolized in the liver (Ray, 1972). The rate at which the liver metabolizes alcohol is independent of the concentration of alcohol in the blood. Hence the rate of becoming sober cannot be hastened or slowed; the individual must simply wait for the liver to do its job. Black coffee and activity cannot hasten sobriety (NIMH, 1972; Ray, 1972). The metabolism of alcohol produces approximately 200 calories per ounce; the metabolic products are nonnutritional and cannot be stored.

Short-Term Effects

The short-term effects of alcohol depend considerably on the level of alcohol in the blood. In addition to the amount of alcohol consumed, the blood level of alcohol depends on the following factors:

1. *Speed of drinking.* The faster a given amount of alcohol is consumed, the greater is the concentration of alcohol in the intestinal tracts and in the stomach. Because the rate at which alcohol is absorbed into the blood stream is greater for higher concentrations of alcohol in the stomach and intestines, the faster a given amount of alcohol is consumed, the greater is its peak concentration in the blood.

2. *Body weight.* The greater the weight of a person's muscles and the more body fluid a person has, the lower is the peak concentration of alcohol in the blood.

3. *Presence of food in stomach.* Food in the stomach can retard the rate of alcohol absorption by as much as 50 per cent. Thus drinking a given amount while eating affects a person much less than does drinking the same amount on an empty stomach.

4. *Drinking history.* Alcohol produces tolerance with prolonged use. A given amount of alcohol will have less effect on a person with a history of alcohol use than on an individual with no such history. Goldberg (1943), for example, found that impaired performance on a variety of simple visual motor tasks occurred at an average blood alcohol level of 0.05 per cent in abstainers, 0.07 per cent in moderate drinkers, and 0.10 per cent in heavy drinkers.

5. *Body chemistry.* Individual differences in physiologic functioning and in psychological constitution affect reactions to alcohol. Thus, all other things being equal, a given amount of alcohol may still have different effects on different people.

Because of significant individual differences in reactions to alcohol, only approximate relations between blood alcohol levels and psychological effects can be stated. On the average, blood alcohol levels of 0.05 per cent are associated with relaxation and feelings of well-being. At about this level, reflexes tend to be more rapid and perceptual judgment is impaired. As blood alcohol levels rise to about 0.10 per cent, muscular coordination, perceptual judgment, and reaction time become progressively impaired. At this level the drinker may stagger and have difficulty walking. The drinker is obviously intoxicated when blood alcohol levels rise to between 0.15 and 0.20 per cent, and he experiences severe perceptual-motor disturbances at blood alcohol levels of 0.25 per cent. Death occurs when the level of alcohol in the blood reaches 0.5 to 0.6 per cent.

Bogen (1932) described the relation between blood alcohol levels and behavior a bit less objectively: at 0.03 per cent one is still dull and dignified, at 0.05 per cent one is dashing and debonair, at 0.10 per cent one may become devilish and dangerous, at 0.20 per cent one is dizzy and disturbing, at 0.25 per cent one is disgusting and disheveled, at 0.30 per cent one is delirious and disoriented, at 0.35 per cent one is dead drunk, and at 0.6 per cent one is dead.

The individual who drinks in moderation does not risk any serious harm unless he drives. In a study summarized in a government publication (NIMH, 1972), experienced bus drivers were asked to estimate the distance between two poles, to state whether they could drive through the poles, and to estimate their degree of confidence in their ability to do so. The researchers found that as the amount of alcohol intake increased, the drivers were willing to drive through progressively narrower gaps and had increasing confidence in their ability to do so. This study demonstrates the paradoxical effects of alcohol that render driving so hazardous—one's ability to drive is impaired while one's confidence in this ability is increased.

A common aftereffect of intoxication is the hangover, consisting of nausea, fatigue, headache, and thirst. The causes of hangovers are unknown, and there is nothing known to facilitate recovery.

Long-Term Effects

Excessive drinking during a period of years is associated with several diseases, including heart disease, liver cirrhosis, and muscular diseases. Excessive drinking is also associated with malnutrition because the metabolism of alcohol yields nonnutritional energy. Organic brain syndromes associated with malnutrition include Wernicke's syndrome and Korsakov's psychosis; these syndromes are discussed in Chapter 17.

The habitual use of alcohol can lead to physical dependency. Once the individual is dependent, abstinence leads to severe withdrawal symptoms known as delirium tremors (DTs). Early symptoms include muscular tremors, insomnia, irritability, and terrifying dreams. As abstinence continues, hallucinations, illusions, and profound fears may occur. For example, an individual may believe that bugs or snakes are crawling over his body, react with terror, and attempt to escape from the vermin. The DTs usually last between three and five days and constitute a withdrawal syndrome that is more severe and that involves a greater risk of death than does withdrawal from heroin and other narcotics. It has been hypothesized that at least some of the withdrawal symptoms associated with alcohol dependency result from the nervous system's habituation to the depressant effects of alcohol; in this view, as the alcohol blood levels decline, the central nervous system becomes hyperactive (see Ray, 1972).

Stages of Alcoholism

Based on a questionnaire study of 2000 members of Alcoholics Anonymous, Jellinek (1952, 1960) described four phases of becoming an alcoholic.

1. *Prealcoholic symptomatic phase.* The prospective alcoholic begins drinking for social reasons. In contrast to others, however, the prealcoholic experiences a rewarding relief and, in the course of six months to two years, the prealcoholic increasingly relies on alcohol to reduce tensions until he reaches the stage of daily drinking. Although he does not yet regularly drink to the point of intoxication, he nevertheless drinks heavily, especially as his body develops a tolerance for alcohol.

2. *Prodromal phase.* The onset of this phase is marked by the occurrence of blackouts or amnesia for recent events. During this stage the prealcoholic becomes preoccupied with alcohol; for example, he may drink before he goes to a party for fear that he will not get enough alcohol at the party. He becomes an avid drinker, gulping down his first drinks. Although his alcohol consumption is considerable, it is not yet conspicuous to others because he usually does not drink to the point of intoxication. According to Jellinek, the prodromal period may last anywhere from six months to five years.

3. *Crucial phase.* Any drinking at this point is believed by Jellinek to start a chain reaction that is experienced by the drinker as a physical demand for alcohol. Alcohol is consumed until the drinker is too intoxicated or too sick to continue. Although the individual has lost the control to stop once he has started, he can still control starting. During the crucial phase, the alcoholic rationalizes his drinking behavior and is unaware of the physical need for his drinking. For example, he may say that he drinks because he wants to and that he does not lose his control. As his drinking becomes increasingly conspicuous to his family and others, an entire system of rationalization may develop. The drinker blames others for his troubles, thereby progressively isolating himself. Aggressive attitudes toward others may develop. As the alcoholic fights to recover, there are alternating periods of total abstinence, bouts of drunkenness, and drinking at night to the point of intoxication.

4. *Chronic phase.* The alcoholic becomes regularly intoxicated during the day and on weekdays. During these binges he becomes incapacitated. A tolerance reversal occurs in that small amounts of alcohol can bring about intoxication. Drinking takes on an obsessive character, and the system of rationalization is abandoned as the drinker comes to accept defeat in his battle against alcoholism.

It is important to appreciate that Jellinek's phases are based largely on a subjective interpretation of questionnaire data and, as such, may not be valid. Drinking habits vary so much across individuals that it is questionable whether a stage process in becoming an alcoholic actually exists. In this regard a study by Marlatt, Demming, and Reid (1973) challenges Jellinek's notion that alcoholics lose control over their drinking once they have begun to drink. These investigators found that a "primer drink" of alcohol did not have differential effects on the subsequent drinking behavior of alcoholics versus social drinkers.

Theories of Etiology

Sociological Theories

The prevalence of alcoholism varies considerably as a function of religion and culture. For example, Americans, northern French, Poles, northern Russians, Swedes, and Swiss have relatively high rates of alcoholism, whereas southern French, Greeks, Italians, Jews, Portuguese, and Spaniards have relatively low rates (NIMH, 1972). In an attempt to explain these differences, Bales (1959) proposed three ways in which culture can influence the prevalence of alcoholism:

1. The greater the extent to which a culture promotes tension, the greater is the likelihood that its members will seek out alcohol as a drug capable of bringing relief from anxiety.

2. Culture can affect the rate of alcoholism by instilling attitudes toward liquor. For example, Snyder (1958) found that among college students, the intoxication rate of ascetic Protestants and Mormons is much higher than that of Jewish students, and Gusfield (1970) and Skolnick (1958) found that drinking problems are less prevalent among Jewish students than among Protestant students. Mizruchi and Perrucci (1970) explained these findings in terms of the prescriptive nature of Jewish teachings concerning alcohol. Specifically, although the Jewish religion permits drinking, it does so only under certain circumstances and it prohibits excessive drinking. In contrast, many Protestant sects prohibit drinking entirely. Thus when a Jew decides to drink, there are norms to guide his behavior and to exert an influence toward moderation; however, when a Protestant decides to drink, religious norms have ceased to affect behavior because the individual has already violated religious teachings.

3. According to Bales (1959), a third way in which culture can affect alcoholism rates is through specification of a substitute means of reducing tension. For example, in oriental cultures that permit the use of narcotics as an acceptable means of anxiety reduction, alcoholism tends to occur at a lower rate.

Learning Theory

One learning theory hypothesis explains alcoholism as a learned habit reinforced by fear reduction. In a widely cited study, Conger (1951) found that alcohol reduced the tendencies of rats to avoid electric shock but did not enhance their tendencies to approach food. Because fear mediates avoidance responses but not approach responses, this study has been interpreted as support for the learning theory view; moreover, this interpretation is consistent with clinical impressions that people often begin to drink to avoid tensions and anxieties.

An important aspect of the learning theory view is that the immediate effects of a response are more important for learning than are the delayed consequences of a response. (See Chapter 7.) Thus if drinking alcohol leads to an immediate reduction in anxiety but later has aversive consequences such as a hangover, unpleasant intoxication, loss of a job, or social embarrassment, the learning theory hypothesis still predicts that the immediate anxiety reduction is sufficient to reinforce drinking.

Psychodynamic Theories

McCord and McCord (1964) reviewed three psychodynamic theories of the causes of alcoholism:

1. The Freudian psychoanalytic view is that alcoholism is a means of releasing repressed oral dependent and homosexual wishes. There is little objective evidence to support this hypothesis.

2. Menninger (1938) suggested that alcoholism is an expression of a self-destructive tendency and is resorted to in a desperate effort to avoid even greater self-destruction. Again, there is little objective evidence to support this hypothesis.

3. Adler maintained that alcoholism is an expression of a drive to obtain power and superiority. This view was revived recently by McClelland, Davis, Kalin, and Wanner (1972), who found some support for the notion that alcohol enhances feelings of power and achievement in males. However, the hypothesis that alcoholics drink to obtain power is largely unsubstantiated.

Psychosocial Correlates of Adolescent Drinking

A critical question for psychological theories of alcoholism concerns the cause of the initiation of heavy drinking habits, a reasonable assumption being that once habitual drinking has begun, physical dependency plays a major role in its maintenance. In a review of the literature relevant to adolescent drinking habits, Braucht, Brakarsh, Follingstad, and Berry (1973) reported that, depending on the community, approximately 30 to 80 per cent of graduating high school seniors have established drinking habits. The prevalence of problem drinking in this population was estimated as between 2 and 6 per cent. These reviewers summarized the research literature on sociocultural correlates:

> In summary, the research literature concerning the sociocultural correlates of adolescent problem drinking focuses on three interrelated variables: parental models, peer models and sanctions, and religious affiliation. The most common variety of adolescent problem drinker would seem to come from a home where parents are high users of alcohol and would seem to belong to peer groups in which high alcohol use is also encouraged. Furthermore, such individuals likely have rather loose religious affiliations with one of the abstinence-oriented religions. Unfortunately, however, there has been little reported research into the relationship of adolescent problem drinking to such basic sociocultural variables as race, socioeconomic status, and living conditions [1973, p. 94].

A number of studies have attempted to identify personality correlates of adolescent problem drinkers. Braucht, Brakarsh, Follingstad, and Berry (1973) have summarized this literature:

> In summary, there appears to be substantial agreement that adolescent problem drinkers are individuals lacking in personal controls, as evidenced by relatively high aggressiveness and impulsiveness. At the same time, there exists some evidence which indicates that adolescent problem drinkers have some basic neurotic tendencies which form a coherent cluster of traits: relatively low self-esteem, high anxiety, depression, and a general lack of success in the attainment of life goals.
>
> There are some basic areas of disagreement concerning the existence of two basic conflicts within the personality of the adolescent problem drinker: independence and sex-role conflicts [1973, pp. 95–96].

Sex Role Identity

Wilsnack (1973) tested the hypothesis that alcoholic women would describe themselves as being as feminine as nonalcoholic women on conscious measures of femininity but would reveal themselves to be less feminine on unconscious measures of femininity. The conscious measures of femininity consisted of an attitude scale and an adjective checklist and, largely as predicted, the alcoholic women were either typically feminine or more feminine than were the controls. On both a questionnaire and a projective test measure, however, the alcoholic women gave responses that were rated as more masculine than were the responses of the controls. The investigator interpreted these results as evidence for an association between an unconscious sex role disturbance and female alcoholism. Further research, however, is needed to ascertain whether or not these interesting results can be substantiated.

Treatment of Alcoholism

Although it is difficult to do, many alcoholics have successfully learned to control their drinking. Accurate estimates of successful treatment outcomes are unavailable, but some psychotherapists have claimed success in as many as 60 per cent of their alcoholic patients (NIMH, 1972). This figure seems high and is probably applicable only to alcoholics most suitable for psychotherapy. The important point is that given sufficient motivation to kick the habit, help is available and successful outcome is possible.

An important source of help is a voluntary organization known as Alcoholics Anonymous (AA). Founded in 1935, AA chapters now exist throughout the country. In order to join, an individual need only contact a local AA chapter. The basic approach is that of providing group support to help the alcoholic through a program of rehabilitation. Although the organization was originally founded on the notion that only someone who has been an alcoholic can help another alcoholic, this attitude is no longer rigidly held, and today there exists much greater cooperation between the AA organization and professional workers in the area.

SUMMARY

Personality disorders are deeply ingrained, characteristic styles of inappropriate behavior. They are distinguished from neuroses in that the personality disorder describes a life-long pattern of maladaptive behavior, while the neurosis is conceptualized as a reaction to stress occurring during a particular life period. Personality disorders are distinguished from psychoses in that they are less maladaptive and occur in the absence of hallucinations, delusions, and mood and thought disorders.

The personality disorder that has received the most research attention is psychopathy (also called sociopathy and antisocial personality). Neurotic psychopathy is indicated when antisocial behavior is associated with neurotic guilt, depression, or anxiety. Subcultural (or dyssocial) psychopathy is indicated when antisocial behavior occurs in the context of a social group that reinforces and values such behavior. Primary, or true, psychopathy is markedly different from these other two syndromes.

Cleckley's 16 clinical features of primary psychopathy describe a ruthless, selfish individual who seems to have no conscience and who experiences little guilt. The primary psychopath is repeatedly engaging in antisocial acts, often to gratify immediate whims, and he typically has a long history of trouble with the law. Psychopaths are also pathological liars. Nevertheless, many psychopathic persons can be endearing on first impression; they may possess many social skills, know just what to say to get somebody to like them, and can lie with such sincerity that it seems as if they believe what they are saying when they are saying it. Psychopaths are promiscuous, and an unusually high proportion of psychopaths are heavy drinkers.

Although the causes of psychopathy are unknown, parental rejection, cortical underarousal, and a deficit in learning how to avoid physical punishment all seem to have an important etiologic role.

Several personality disorders other than psychopathy also have been discussed. The schizoid personality is characterized by a life pattern of detachment from close interpersonal relationships. These individuals have managed to adjust by organizing their life in a manner that minimizes interpersonal contact. They are frequently described as shy and cold. The passive-aggressive personality is characterized by a life pattern of aggression expressed in passive and unrecognizable forms. The compulsive personality is characterized by a life pattern of ritualistic behavior and by an extreme concern with morality and rightness. These individuals are often described as excessively rigid.

Alcoholism is indicated by a persistent and largely uncontrollable drinking problem that interferes with the drinker's health, interpersonal relations, and/or ability to work. The prevalence of alcoholism in the United States has been estimated to be between 5 and 9 million people. Alcohol is the most abused drug in this country.

Excessive drinking during a long period of time is associated with heart disease, liver cirrhosis, muscular disease, and Wernicke-Korsakov's syndrome.

A critical question for psychological theories of alcoholism concerns the antecedent conditions for the initiation of heavy drinking habits, a reasonable assumption being that once habitual drinking has begun, physical dependency plays a major role in its maintenance. Research on the sociocultural correlates of adolescent drinking suggests that adolescent problem drinkers tend to come from a home where the parents are high users of alcohol and tend to belong to peer groups in which high alcohol use is encouraged. Research on the psychological correlates of adolescent problem drinkers suggests that these individuals are lacking in personal controls, as indicated by relatively high aggressive behavior and by impulsiveness, and that they tend to have low self-esteem. Adolescent problem drinkers also tend to be anxious or depressed people with a general lack of success in the attainment of their life goals.

There are several different approaches to the treatment of alcoholism. Generally, alcoholism is difficult to treat even though successful outcomes are possible. A voluntary organization known as Alcoholics Anonymous (AA) has had some success in the treatment of large numbers of alcoholics.

Chapter 14

Depression, Mania, and Suicide

Depressive disorders are perhaps the most distressful, and certainly among the most common, maladies that afflict mankind. Although man has shown and experienced melancholic states since antiquity, it is only during the past decade or so that we have begun to develop scientific insights into the basic mechanisms involved.

AKISKAL AND MCKINNEY (1973, p. 20)

The subjective or consciously experienced aspect of an emotion considered apart from its physiological or somatic aspect is called affect. The term *affect* is roughly equivalent to the term *feeling* and somewhat similar in meaning to the term *mood.* The disorders discussed in this chapter are usually classified as affective (or mood) disorders in the belief that the most salient aspect of the disorders is the presence of inappropriate mood.

Pathological moods are either depressive or manic in character and can be viewed as forming a continuum from sad to elated. Even though depression and mania are classified as affective disorders, their symptoms also occur along cognitive and behavioral (motor) dimensions. *Depression* is indicated by feelings of sadness, a negative self-image (e.g., *I am a sinner*), and either an unusually retarded or agitated level of behavioral activity. *Mania* is indicated by feelings of euphoria; an overly positive view of one's worth, power, or ability; flight of ideas; and hyperactivity. In both depression and mania the degree of sadness or euphoria present is out of proportion to life circumstances.

Instances of depression and mania vary considerably in terms of the degrees to which inappropriate mood is stable or alternates with other moods. The manic-depressive syndrome is characterized by mood swings. These mood swings may be any of three types: fluctuations between depression and normal mood, between depression and mania, or between mania and normal mood. Mood swings between depression and normal mood are by far the most prevalent type of manic-depression.

Depression may constitute the most prevalent form of psychopathology (Secunda, Katz, Friedman, & Schuyler, 1973). Woodruff, Goodwin, and Guze (1974) summarized cross-cultural data that suggest that at least 5 per cent of men and 9 per cent of women will suffer from clinically significant episodes of primary depression (primary depression is depression in persons with no previous psychiatric history other than affective disorder). Depressive mood also occurs throughout the entire spectrum of psychopathology and is especially associated with anxiety neurosis, hypochondriasis, a number of organic brain syndromes, marital adjustment (Coleman & Miller, 1975), and possibly alcoholism. A survey by the National Institute of Mental Health (1973) found that 17.5 per cent of 445,115 people receiving psychological treatment had been diagnosed as suffering some type of depression. Depression is especially prevalent among college students, particularly freshman (Bosse, Croghan, Greenstein, Katz, Oliver, Powell, & Smith, 1975). Mania, however, is rarely seen in clinical practice (Buss, 1966).

HISTORY

The earliest known description of depression as a psychological disorder was made by Hippocrates in about 400 B.C. (Jelliffe, 1931). Hippocrates attributed the disorder to a movement of black bile into the brain in a manner that "darkened" the spirits. The term *melancholia* originally meant black bile, and Hippocrates used this term as a means of referring to what we today call the depressive disorders. Physicians explained melancholia in terms of black bile for centuries despite the absence of any evidence to support this erroneous hypothesis. Hippocrates also described mania as a clinical syndrome.

About five hundred years later, in A.D. 80, the physician Aretaeus described the melancholic person as "sad, dismayed, sleepless. . . . They become thin by their agitation and loss of refreshing sleep. . . . At a more advanced stage, they complain of a thousand futilities and desire death" (as quoted in Beck, 1967, p. 4). Aretaeus is also remembered for having delineated different types of depressive syndromes ("Those affected with melancholia are not every one of them affected according to one particular form . . ."), including the manic-depressive syndrome ("If at any time a relaxation takes place, in most cases hilarity supervenes") (as quoted in Woodruff, Goodwin, & Guze, 1974, p. 4).

Platter, writing in Europe in the late sixteenth century, described melancholia as a "kind of mental alienation in which imagination and judgment are so perverted that without any cause the victims become very sad and fearful" (Diethelm & Hefferman, 1965, p. 15). The first influential European treatise devoted solely to the topic of melancholia was Burton's *Anatomy of Melancholy* published in 1651 (Kenyon, 1965). This book distinguished several types of melancholia, including hypochondriacal melancholia. The term *manic-depressive* insanity was introduced in 1684 by Bonet, and in 1851 the Frenchman Falret described the salient aspect of this syndrome as that of cyclic mood swings either between depression and remission (normal mood) or between depression and mania. Falret reported that the manic-depressive syndrome is more prevalent in women (Woodruff et al., 1974).

Kraepelin (1923) distinguished two major types of functional psychosis: dementia praecox (today considered a form of schizophrenia), and manic-depressive insanity. (See Chapters 2 and 15.) The primary basis for the distinction was prognosis; Kraepelin hypothesized that dementia praecox is a progressively deteriorating disorder and that manic-depression is episodic and nondeteriorating. A metabolic etiology was postulated for both disorders.

SIGNS OF DEPRESSION AND MANIA

As mentioned previously, the signs of depression and mania vary along affective, cognitive, behavioral (motor), and physical dimensions. The affective signs of depression include feelings of sadness, apathy, anxiety, and anger. The most commonly reported complaint by depressives is feelings of sadness (Beck, 1972; Woodruff et al., 1974). A significant proportion of depressives are visibly nervous, and some are interpersonally hostile.

The cognitive signs of depression include a negative self-concept, hopelessness, and indecisiveness. Negative evaluations of oneself range from ideas of failure in mild cases (*I let everyone down*), to ideas of unworthiness in moderately severe cases (*I am no good*), to ideas of worthlessness in severe cases (*I don't deserve to live; I loathe myself*) (Beck, 1967). Suicidal thoughts are very common, although they occur with varying degrees of seriousness. Depressives show an exaggerated tendency to blame themselves, and they approach tasks expecting to fail. Hopelessness is another common sign—depressives complain that life is futile or report that they do not care what happens.

The behavioral signs of depression include crying, withdrawal, agitation, and retardation. Crying spells are common in about half the cases and they provide one of the few outlets of relief in severe cases. Withdrawal from social environments (often accompanied by excessive brooding and preoccupation) can occur in varying degrees. Retarded depression is characterized by lethargy and inactivity, whereas agitated depression is characterized by visible nervousness. Agitated depressives bemoan their fate, worry, pace, and may wring their hands. "They ask for reassurance, they beg for help, yet nothing satisfies them" (Woodruff et al., 1974, p. 11). As Buss (1966) noted, however, whether retarded or agitated in motor movements, the depressive shows a low level of meaningful accomplishments. Both retarded and agitated depressives have difficulty concentrating on tasks for sustained periods of time.

Common physical complaints associated with depression are insomnia, fatigue, abdominal pains, constipation, and feelings of being ill (Beck, 1967; Woodruff et al., 1974).

Seligman (1975) reported the case of a middle-aged woman who often cried. She reported that it was a struggle for her just to keep going. When the therapist suggested that she was a good-looking woman and might want to go out to buy a new dress, she replied: "That's just too hard for me. I'd have to take the bus across town and I'd probably get lost. Even if I got to the store, I couldn't find a dress that would fit. What would be the use anyway, since I'm really so unattractive" (Seligman, 1975, pp. 1–2). She indicated that she brooded often over whether her life was worth living and had contemplated suicide. Leon (1974) reported a case of an agitated depressive who eventually required hospitalization. At various times she displayed the following symptoms: she began to awake at 4 in the morning and had difficulty falling back asleep, she sat in her chair for hours during the day, she cried often and repeatedly bemoaned that there was no purpose to life, she was indecisive, she wished she were dead, and she "communicated in a rambling, sometimes hard to follow manner and she often wrung her hands" (Leon, 1974, p. 284). She complained of "the shakes" and suffered from delusions of guilt concerning her husband's death.

The common symptoms of depression as described by Schuyler (1974) appear in Table 14-1. Excellent clinical descriptions of the signs of depression are provided by both Beck (1967) and Buss (1966).

The signs of mania are in many instances the opposites of those of depression. The predominant mood is euphoria even though life circumstances are insufficient to justify the exaggerated feelings of well-being and happiness. Hyperactivity is evident as the manic seems to dash from one task to another, starting many but completing few. Rapid speech also occurs, and thought associations may be tangential. The manic is excessively optimistic about the future and often produces grandiose plans of one type or another. An excessively positive self-image is evident and frequently is perceived by others as vanity. The manic seems to have boundless energy and does not require much sleep. Delusions of grandeur and fantasies of omnipotence are sometimes present, and occasionally the presence of these symptoms renders it difficult to distin-

TABLE 14-1
Symptoms and Signs of Depression

Emotional Signs			
Sadness	Guilt	Anxiety	Anger
Diurnal mood variation			
Physical Signs			
Sleep disorder	Eating loss	Weight loss	
Weakness	Constipation	Easy fatigability	
Menstrual irregularity	Impotence-frigidity	Pain	
Diminished sexual drive			
Behavioral Signs			
Crying	Retardation	Withdrawal	Agitation
Hallucinations			
Cognitive Signs			
Negative self-concept	Negative view of world		
Self-blame	Self-criticism	Indecisiveness	
Helplessness	Hopelessness	Worthlessness	
Delusions	Negative expectations		

Adapted from tables presented by D. Schuyler, *The Depressive Spectrum.* New York: Jason Aronson Publishers, 1974, with the permission of the author and the publisher.

guish mania from schizophrenia. Manics are impulsive. Psychodynamic theories view mania as a desperate attempt to avoid depression.

Kleinmuntz (1974) reported a case of a 56-year-old dentist who awoke one morning believing himself to be the most gifted dental surgeon in the world (p. 234). He developed grandiose schemes for servicing as many patients as possible. By morning he had invited construction firms to bid on the costs of expanding his facilities, but by evening he had become impatient at the "delays" and started to tear down the walls himself. McNeil (1967) reported a case of a man who had become so manic he had to be hospitalized. The symptoms were hyperactivity, a grandiose scheme to make millions, and overtalkativeness.

CLASSIFICATION OF DEPRESSIVE DISORDERS

Depressive reactions vary in severity and in the type of behavior and thought exhibited. The diversity of symptomatology has led to numerous attempts to distinguish meaningful subtypes of depression but as yet no classification system has been universally accepted.

Normal Grief and Psychopathological Depression

The criteria used to distinguish between normal and pathological depression are the depth of the depression, the duration of the depressive episode, and the extent to which the depressive reaction is associated with guilt, feelings of worthlessness, delusions, and/or hallucinations. Temporary grief reactions to a major loss are considered normal and even healthy. A psychopathological condition is considered when the grief reaction leads to excessive self-dislike, inordinate self-blame, or to a prolonged preoccupation with one's problems. A psychopathological condition is also considered when a grief reaction continues long after its initial onset.

Exogenous (Reactive) and Endogenous Depression

Exogenous depression refers to depressive episodes that are caused by factors from outside the body, including infections and psychological causes. The disorder is diagnosed when a depressive episode has an acute onset and appears to be a reaction to some loss or stressful event, such as the death of a loved one or the loss of a job. Endogenous depression refers to depressive episodes that are caused by factors from inside the body; that is, endogenous depression suggests either a biochemical or a genetic etiology. The disorder is diagnosed when a depressive episode does not appear to be a reaction to any salient life circumstances, as often occurs when the onset of depression is insidious. Because the distinction between exogenous and endogenous depression is based on whether or not the depressive episode appears to be a reaction to some life circumstance, exogenous depression is also called *reactive* depression.

The exogenous-endogenous distinction is problematical for a number of reasons. One problem is that the distinction theoretically suggests much more than is justified on the basis of the diagnostic criteria. Specifically, the concept of exogenous depression implies that depressive episodes that occur in reaction to life circumstances are caused by exogenous (or psychological) factors. It is quite possible, however, that such episodes of depression are caused by both psychological and biological factors. Similarly, there is insufficient reason to assume that what is called endogenous depression is actually caused by biochemical and/or genetic factors. It is hazardous to infer exogenous or endogenous etiologies on the basis of whether or not a depressive episode appears to be a reaction to some life circumstance.

Another important problem with the distinction between exogenous and endogenous depression is that it is vague. For example, suppose that a person arrives at a clinic complaining of feelings of sadness that began three months following the death of an uncle. Is the three-month delay too long to consider the depressive episode a reaction to the loss? Is the client's recall accurate and complete (perhaps the uncle died five months ago and the client lost a job one week prior to the depressive episode)? Even in cases in which a depressive episode occurs within a few days after a major loss, it is still possible that the association between the loss and the depression was merely coincidental (Mendels, 1970). Because of these problems, differential diagnosis between endogenous and exogenous depression is often a subjective enterprise.

Finally, there is evidence that the distinction between exogenous and endogenous depression is unreliable. Winokur and Pitts (1964) studied the cases of 75 people who were admitted to a hospital with the diagnosis of exogenous (reactive) depression. At the time of discharge, however, the diagnosis had been changed for all but 12 of the 75 cases studied. In 45 cases, moreover, the diagnosis was changed from exogenous to endogenous depression.

Neurotic and Psychotic Depression

In actual practice the distinction between neurotic and psychotic depression is often the same distinction as that between exogenous and endogenous depression—specifically, neurotic (or exogenous) depression is diagnosed when the depressive episode seems to be a reaction to some environmental loss, and psychotic depression is diagnosed when the depressive episode does not appear to be a reaction to some environmental loss (Martarano & Nathan, 1972). Theoretically, however, the two distinctions differ in that the distinction between neurotic and psychotic depression is based on symptomatology whereas the distinction between exogeneous and endogenous depression is based on inferred etiology. Under this view, neurotic depression is diagnosed when depressive episodes occur in the context of neurotic symptoms such as nervousness and tension, whereas psychotic depression is diagnosed when depressive episodes occur in the context of psychotic symptoms such as extreme withdrawal, delusions, and hallucinations.

Continuity Versus Discontinuity Theory

A long-standing controversy exists between continuity theorists who consider depression a unitary disorder that occurs in various degrees of severity and discontinuity theorists who distinguish among different types of depression. Under continuity theory the distinction between neurotic and psychotic depression is based on the severity of the symptoms. Neurotic depression is regarded as the less severe form of the disorder. Under discontinuity theory, however, neurotic and psychotic depression are maintained to be qualitatively different from one another. The crucial issue in the debate is whether the differences between neurotic and psychotic depression are quantitative or qualitative.

Beck (1967) tested the continuity and discontinuity hypotheses by analyzing psychiatrists' ratings of 50 persons diagnosed as suffering neurotic depression and of 50 other persons diagnosed as suffering psychotic depression. Two ratings were obtained. First, the psychiatrists rated whether each of 17 clinical signs was present or absent in each case. Second, they rated whether each of the 17 clinical signs was present or absent to a severe degree. Discontinuity theory predicts that the clinical signs present in neurotic depression should differ from those present in psychotic depression. Continuity theory predicts that the same clinical signs should be present in both neurotic and psychotic depression but that psychotic depression should be associated with the presence of these signs to a more severe degree. As shown in the left-hand column of Table 14-2, Beck found that all 17 signs of depression were present in both neurotic and psychotic depression; as shown in the right-hand column of the

TABLE 14-2
Frequency of Clinical Features in Neurotic Depressive Reaction (NDR) and Psychotic Depressive Reaction (PDR)*

Clinical Feature	Feature Present		Present to Severe Degree	
	NDR(%) (n = 50)†	*PDR*(%) (n = 50)	*NDR*(%) (n = 50)	*PDR*(%) (n = 50)
Sad faces	86	94	4	24
Stooped posture	58	76	4	20
Speech: slow, etc.	66	70	8	22
Low mood	84	80	8	44
Diurnal variation of mood	22	48	2	10
Hopelessness	78	68	6	34
Conscious guilt	64	44	6	12
Feeling inadequate	68	70	10	42
Somatic preoccupation	58	66	6	24
Suicidal wishes	58	76	14	40
Indecisiveness	56	70	6	28
Loss of motivation	70	82	8	48
Loss of interest	64	78	10	44
Fatigability	80	74	8	48
Loss of appetites	48	76	2	40
Sleep disturbance	66	80	12	52
Constipation	28	56	2	16

* From A. T. Beck, *Depression: Clinical, Experimental and Theoretical Aspects*. New York: Harper, 1967. Reprinted by permission of the author and publisher.
† n = No. of patients.

table, psychotic depression is a more severe disorder. These findings support continuity theory.

Some investigators have suggested that one qualitative difference between neurotic and psychotic depression is the presence of delusions in psychotic depression and their absence in neurotic depression. Although it has been suggested that this difference supports discontinuity theory and disconfirms continuity theory, the analysis is unconvincing. A delusion is simply a firmly held irrational belief. Irrational ideas are present in both neurotic and psychotic depression, although they are present to a more severe degree in psychotic depression.

Proponents of discontinuity theory claim support for their position both from factor analytic studies of symptomatology and from therapy outcome studies. The factor analytic studies have analyzed numerous case descriptions and self-reports of depressed persons in order to evaluate the extent to which different symptoms tend to occur together. The results of these studies have been interpreted by some as objective evidence for the existence of a neurotic and a psychotic syndrome (Eysenck, 1970; Grinker, Miller, Sabshin, Nunn, &

Nunnally, 1961; Kiloh & Garside, 1963; Mendels, 1970; Mendels & Cochrane, 1968). These studies suggest that neurotic depression is associated with a salient precipitating cause, self-pity, insomnia, depression worse in the evening than in the morning, sudden onset of depression, and neurotic symptoms such as hypochondriasis, feelings of inadequacy, obsessions, immaturity, and hysteria. These studies also reported that psychotic (endogenous) depression is associated with motor retardation, weight loss, previous depressive attacks, depression worse in the morning, and early awakening. Beck (1967) has advised caution in interpreting data from the factor analytic studies, however, in part because different test questions may yield different results. Eysenck (1970), however, has argued that the factor analytic data available thus far consistently support a distinction between neurotic and psychotic depression.

Proponents of the discontinuity position also claim support from clinical reports that different therapies have different degrees of effectiveness for neurotic and psychotic depression. Electroconvulsive therapy (see Chapter 5), for example, is reported to be more effective for psychotic depression than for neurotic depression, and some drugs are reported to be more effective for neurotic depression than for psychotic depression. The evidence for the differential effects of treatment is inconclusive. Moreover, the suggested differences in response to treatments do not permit inferences of distinct disorders with differing etiologies. It is quite possible that severe forms of a disorder respond to techniques different from those of less severe forms.

The continuity-discontinuity debate seems likely to continue until knowledge of etiologies is more conclusive. The continuity position would be confirmed if neurotic and psychotic depression have common etiologies; the discontinuity position would be confirmed if they have different etiologies.

Primary and Secondary Depression

Robins and Guze (1972) and Winokur (1972) have proposed that depression should be classified as primary versus secondary. Primary depression is diagnosed when depressive episodes occur in persons with no previous history of psychopathology except for previous episodes of mania or depression. The primary category provides a group that is symptomatically pure for depression (Winokur, 1973). Secondary depression is diagnosed when depressive episodes occur in persons with a previous history of psychopathology other than depression or mania. The primary-secondary nosology is employed by some diagnosticians but has yet to be widely accepted.

Bipolar and Unipolar Depression

The bipolar and unipolar distinction is based on the presence or absence of recurrent manic episodes. Bipolar mood disorder is diagnosed when depressive and manic episodes occur or only when manic episodes occur (Perris, 1966; Woodruff et al., 1974). Unipolar mood disorder is diagnosed when manic episodes do not occur. Both Schuyler (1974) and Winokur (1973) have suggested that bipolar and unipolar depression should be considered subcategories of primary depression.

Research on bipolar and unipolar depression suggests that the distinction is

TABLE 14-3
American Psychiatric Association Mood Disorder Categories

1. Psychoses not attributed to physical conditions listed previously
   A. Major affective disorders
      1. Involutional melancholia
      2. Manic-depressive illness, manic type
      3. Manic-depressive illness, depressed type
      4. Manic-depressive illness, circular type
      5. Manic-depressive illness, circular-manic type
      6. Manic-depressive illness, circular-depressed type
      7. Other major affective disorders
   B. Other psychoses: psychotic depressive reaction
2. Neuroses
   A. Depressive
   B. Neurasthenic
3. Personality disorders: cyclothymic personality

useful. There is evidence that bipolar depression runs in families to a greater degree than does unipolar depression (Akiskal & McKinney, 1973; Perris, 1966). Mendelwicz (1974) found that physical illness was more prevalent in the lives of bipolar patients who were studied than it was in the lives of unipolar patients. Although the research on personality correlates of bipolar and unipolar depression is sparse, some initial evidence suggests that the bipolar group, as compared to the unipolar group, is often in better contact with reality, less depressed, and more likely to make socially desirable responses. In other words, the bipolar depression is in most (although not all) instances a less severe condition than is unipolar depression.

DSM-II Classification System

As outlined in Table 14-3, DSM-II classifies depressive syndromes as either a functional psychosis, a neurosis, or a personality disorder.

Involutional Melancholia

Involutional melancholia is defined as depression occurring during the "change of life" (involutional) period of either female menopause or male climacteric. Physiological changes during this period include a sharp decrease in sex hormones and a consequent loss of reproductive capacity and general energy. The symptoms present in involutional melancholia are usually those of agitated depression: tension, guilt, anxiety, insomnia, and a loss of appetite. The severity of the condition ranges from a mild loss of interest in family and social relationships to a severe self-preoccupation characterized by withdrawal and difficulty handling routine responsibilities. Delusions and hallucinations may be present in more severe cases. DSM-II defines involutional melancholia as a psychotic syndrome. In cases free of delusions and hallucinations, the psychotic symptom is withdrawal (a loss of interest in others and in the environment).

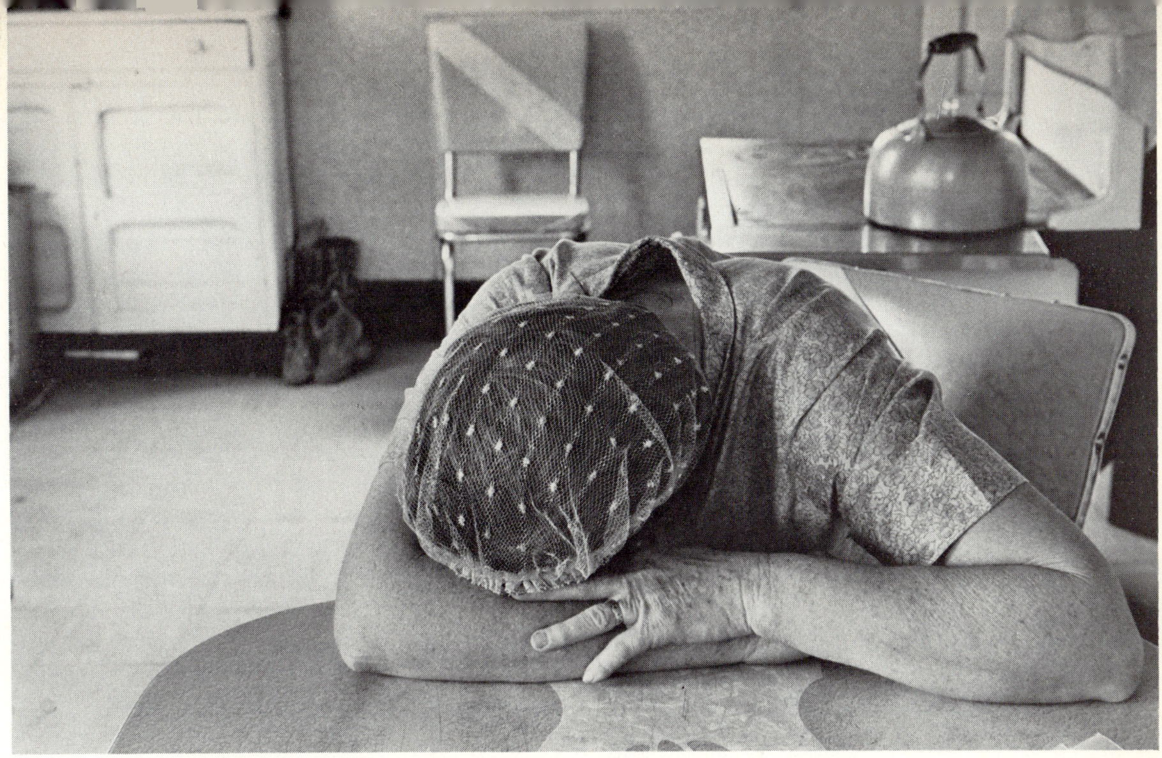

Involutional melancholia is depression associated with the "change of life" period. The signs of depression during this period are indistinguishable from the signs of depression during earlier life periods. This has led some theorists to conclude that the category of involutional melancholia is unnecessary. (Photo by Burk Uzzle; Magnum Photos, Inc.)

Because the symptoms of involutional melancholia closely resemble those of agitated depression in younger people (Martarano & Nathan, 1972), there has been debate on the merits of considering involutional melancholia as a distinct disorder. The force behind the notion that involutional melancholia is a distinct disorder has been the assumption of a biochemical etiology related to the physiological changes of the involutional period. Specifically, the presumption has been that the occurrence of depression during the involutional period in individuals whose prior life adjustment has been adequate suggests that the depressive episode was somehow triggered by hormonal changes. This presumption is speculative because the involutional period is for some people also associated with psychological stress. Men must adjust to retirement, possible feelings of becoming useless, changes in physical abilities and appearance, and the possibility of death. Many women must adjust to the children having left home, changes in appearance, and the loss of their reproductive abilities. In brief, there is no more reason to assume that involutional melancholia is attributable to hormonal changes than there is to assume that such reactions are attributable to the same combinations of biological factors and psychological stress that produce agitated depression in younger persons. There is even evidence from therapy research that involutional melancholia is not attributable to hormonal changes. Specifically, if involutional melancholia were attributable to hormonal imbalances, we should expect that it could be treated successfully by hormonal injections. The available evidence, however, indicates that hormonal therapy is ineffective in counteracting involutional depression (Beck, 1967). Thus because the symptomatology of involutional melancholia is not distinct from agitated depression in younger persons, there presently does not exist sufficient reason to consider involutional melancholia a distinct syndrome even though it is so considered under DSM-II.

Manic-Depressive Reactions

Kraepelin conceived of the manic-depressive syndrome as a form of psychosis that consisted of episodic attacks of either depression or mania. The occurrence and subsequent remission of the attacks gave the appearance of mood swings and was contrasted sharply with dementia praecox in which there was thought to be a gradual deterioration of the patient's condition; Kraepelin thus distinguished between manic-depressive psychosis and dementia praecox on the grounds that one syndrome shows progressive deterioration and the other shows episodic attacks and periods of remission. The validity of this distinction has been questioned because some cases of manic-depression do not remit and some cases of dementia praecox (schizophrenia) do.

The salient diagnostic feature of the manic-depressive syndrome is the presence of mood swings. These swings may be from depression to normal mood (manic-depression–depressed type) from mania to normal mood (manic-depression–manic type) or from depression to mania (manic-depression–circular types). Thus the manic-depression syndrome can be diagnosed in cases in which mania is not present, as in the example of mood swings between depression and normal mood.

The manic-depression category has been criticized on the grounds of vagueness and invalidity. The category is vague because the degree and number of mood swings required to diagnose the syndrome are unspecified. Some clinicians diagnose the syndrome when there is only a single attack of mania, whereas others require two or more attacks. Some diagnose the syndrome when only mild mania (*hypomania*) is present, whereas others require that a more severe mood change be present. Some require only one or two episodes of depression, whereas others require a more cyclic and repetitive pattern. It is also unclear how long after a depressive episode a manic episode can occur and still be considered part of a mood swing. In addition to these ambiguities, the validity of the diagnostic concept of a manic-depressive syndrome has been questioned (Cameron, 1963; Loftus, 1960; Zilboorg, 1933). Today the bipolar-unipolar distinction, which is based on the presence or absence of mania, is gradually replacing the manic-depression–other-depression distinction, which is based on the presence or absence of mood swings (Ariete, 1959; Beck, 1967; Schuyler, 1974).

Neurotic Depression

DSM-II's definition of neurotic depression does not differ substantially from the concept discussed previously. In summary, neurotic depression is characterized by the absence of psychotic symptoms (delusions and hallucinations) and by the presence of neurotic symptoms (expressions of guilt, anxiety, and lack of self-worth). DSM-II specifies two subtypes of neurotic depression called depressive and neurasthenic. The neurasthenic neurosis is characterized by depression and complaints of tiredness and fatigue. This syndrome was discussed in Chapter 10 as an anxiety neurosis. Episodes of anxiety, depression, and neurasthenic fatigue often alternate in the same people rendering differential diagnosis somewhat of a subjective enterprise. Which syndrome is diagnosed usually depends on which episode is most severe or salient.

Cyclothymic and Asthenic Personality

DSM-II defines two personality disorders on the basis of life patterns of mood. The cyclothymic personality type displays a life pattern of cyclic alternations of depressive and manic moods. These mood swings are mild; when severe mood swings occur, the diagnosis is much more likely to be manic depression. The cyclic mood changes may occur on a daily basis or once every year or so. The asthenic personality is defined by a chronic lack of energy and enthusiasm. The person is often too tired to enjoy life. Both the cyclothymic and asthenic personality syndromes are vague and are diagnosed infrequently.

DEMOGRAPHIC CORRELATES

Many studies have evaluated the prevalence of depression as a function of demographic correlates such as sex, race, and social class (see e.g., Schuyler, 1974). The following may be said in summary of these studies:

1. The most consistent demographic correlate of depression is sex. Many more women than men suffer manic-depression, and this finding is remarkably stable across the different populations studied (Coleman & Miller, 1975; Weissman & Klerman, 1976).
2. Although depression was once thought to be more prevalent among whites than blacks, race does not appear to be associated with a higher or lower prevalence of depression (see Schuyler, 1974).
3. Some studies have reported that depressive psychosis is more prevalent among upper-class people (e.g., Faris & Dunham, 1939; Malzberg, 1956), whereas others found depressive psychosis more prevalent among lower socioeconomic classes (Hollingshead & Redlich, 1958; Langner & Michael, 1963). Thus there appears to be no consistent relation between depressive psychosis and socioeconomic class.

ETIOLOGY OF DEPRESSION: THEORY AND RESEARCH

The etiology of depression is unknown. The upsurge of research activity in the last two decades, however, has produced a number of important findings.

Psychoanalytic Theory of Depression

The psychoanalytic theory of depression underwent several important changes during the period of 1911 to 1945. Abraham (1911, 1916), who wrote the first psychoanalytic treatise on depression, introduced the concept of anger turned against the self. Freud's (1917) analysis followed Abraham's account generally, except that Freud also proposed a hypothesis of object loss. Cameron (1963) and Fenichel (1945), however, focused on the etiological importance of low self-esteem. The attempt here is to provide an integrated account of the various psychoanalytic theories of depression.

Predisposing Personality Factors

As emphasized in Chapter 6, a fundamental hypothesis of psychoanalysis is that early childhood experiences lead to the development of personality factors that influence adult behavior. More specifically, the individual is hypothesized to progress through five stages of psychosexual development during the period of infancy through adolescence. In order of occurrence, the five stages are the oral, anal, Oedipal, latency, and genital stages. Either excessive or insufficient gratification at any of the first four developmental stages is postulated to lead to personality needs that predispose the individual to psychopathology by limiting the range of life situations to which the individual can adapt.

The personality factors that psychoanalysts have postulated to be associated with depression are dependency, anger, and low self-esteem (an inadequate self-concept characterized by a basic sense of unworthiness and inadequacy). Psychoanalytic theory suggests that excessive dependency needs are maladaptive consequences of adjustment during the oral stage of development, that excessive hostility toward others is usually a maladaptive consequence of either the oral or anal stage of development, and that low self-esteem can be a maladaptive consequence of childhood experiences during any stage of development.

The oral stage of development occurs during the first year of life and, hence, during a period when the infant is dependent on the parents for food, protection, and attention. Psychoanalytic theory postulates that the infant equates gratification of these needs with love. Insufficient gratification is perceived by the infant as a lack of love and this is further interpreted as an indication that he or she is unworthy of love. Thus, psychoanalytic theory suggests that insufficient gratification of dependency needs is one way in which low self-esteem develops. It is further postulated, moreover, that insufficient gratification of dependency needs creates a life-long need for dependent relationships, as if the adult is trying to compensate psychologically for a lack of gratification of dependency needs as a child.

Excessive gratification of oral stage needs is also postulated to lead to an excessive need for dependent relations. The infant who is excessively gratified finds the oral stage so pleasurable that he or she is reluctant to move on to the anal stage of development. This reluctance to move on to the anal stage of development is called an oral fixation. (See Chapter 6.)

Psychoanalytic theory also proposes that hostility is associated with depression. This postulate is designed to account for the self-deprecation that is

Psychodynamic theorists have reported that depression can sometimes lead to overeating. Food can function as a symbol of love, and depression is seen as often resulting from a real or imagined loss of love. Of course, there are many other reasons why a person may overeat. (Photo by Shalmon Bernstein; Magnum Photos, Inc.)

found in severe depression as well as for the anger toward others that is found in mild depression. Psychoanalytically, the origin of this anger is in either the oral or the anal stage of development. Aggression that stems from the oral stage is either a natural consequence of the frustration of basic needs (insufficient gratification) or a natural consequence of the frustration of desires to be independent (excessive gratification of dependency needs). Aggression that stems from the anal developmental stage is seen as a natural consequence of parental impositions as occur, for example, in toilet training.

Low self-esteem and hostility also can occur as a consequence of maladjustment during the Oedipal developmental stage (see Erickson, 1950), and as a natural consequence of failure to attract members of the opposite sex during adolescence (genital stage).

Precipitating Events

Life presents for all of us a number of rejections by other people and inevitable setbacks in our achievement strivings. The individual who has an internal definition of self-worth can cope with these setbacks and find substitute ways to gratify his or her needs. The individual who has an external definition of self-worth, however, has difficulty overcoming setbacks. Psychoanalytic theory maintains that people who have low self-esteem rely on others for their definition of self-worth (*I am worthy only if other people love me and approve of me*) and hence have difficulty coping with setbacks, criticism, and loss. As Cameron put it: "The adult who becomes neurotically depressed is one who has always needed a great deal of emotional support to shore up his own sagging self-esteem. To lose love, or even to be threatened with its loss, is for him to experience an attack upon the most vulnerable part of his personality system" (1963, p. 415).

Freud (1917) hypothesized that loss of a love object leads to depression in predisposed individuals. The loss may be real or imagined. An example of an imagined loss is provided by the case of a depressed adolescent who reported that his parents went away for an entire summer even though they in fact did not do so. A less obvious example of an imagined loss is provided by a person who earns a grade of B, interprets this as a failure, and then imagines that his (or her) parents no longer love him (or her).

Cameron (1963) has summarized a much broader list of factors that precipitate depression than those discussed by Freud. Cameron's list includes all of the following: loss of love or emotional support; personal and economic failure; loss of power, prestige, property, or money; and waning strength, health, youth, or beauty. Another possible precipitating event is success that implies new responsibilities; Cameron explained that success can arouse unconscious guilt feelings that one is unworthy of the success and that this can lead to self-punishment (depression) in order to alleviate the guilt.

Dynamics

The psychoanalytic theory of depression proposes that precipitating events (e.g., loss, failure, criticism, and success) combine with predisposing personality factors (dependency, low self-esteem, an external definition of self-worth, hostility, and guilt) to produce depression. The manner in which these interacting factors lead to depression is, according to various psychoanalytic theorists, roughly as follows.

1. *Anger turned against the self.* Abraham (1911) proposed that frustration of dependency needs in adulthood leads to a partial regression to the oral stage of development. This regression is associated with an arousal of oral conflicts between dependency needs and hostility toward those who gratify dependency needs. Because the expression of the hostility toward others would further frustrate dependency needs by eliciting rejection from others, the hostile impulses are released against the self. This turning of anger against the self is seen as resulting in self-hatred and low mood (depression).

2. *Incorporation of a lost love object.* Freud (1917) proposed that object loss leads to a partial regression to the oral developmental stage in a desperate effort to regain the lost love object. As the developmental period of infancy, the oral stage is one in which the concept of self is still in its formative process. By partially regressing back to this stage, the individual can unconsciously incorporate the lost love object into the self-concept (ego)—that is, through a process called incorporation and partial regression to the oral stage of development, the discrimination between the self and the lost love object is partially lost. One consequence of this incorporation is that any hostility toward the lost love object is then directed against the self. Freud maintained that depressed people have ambivalent love-hate feelings toward the lost love object that precipitated the depressive reaction.

Evaluation

The psychoanalytic theory of depression has been widely criticized on the grounds that it remains unsubstantiated some 60 years after it was proposed (Akiskal & McKinney, 1973; Davison & Neale, 1974). In evaluating the psychoanalytic position, however, it seems important to distinguish between the different levels of hypothesis. (See Chapter 6.) One level of hypothesis concerns the personality traits associated with depression. These hypotheses have been subjected to empirical investigation and thus far have been supported fairly well. Another level of hypothesis concerns the precipitating events that elicit depression. These hypotheses are largely supported by clinical observations although in some instances systematic research has also been conducted (see below). A third level of hypothesis concerns the origin of the predisposing personality traits in childhood experiences. In Chapter 6 some cross-cultural evidence was reviewed that supported the general notion that childhood experiences can lead to adult personality traits, but the specifics of the psychoanalytic theory of development have yet to be confirmed and are difficult to investigate. Finally, a fourth level of hypothesis concerns the dynamics by which depression results from precipitating events and from predisposing personality factors. These hypotheses are the weakest ones in the theory. Notions of incorporation of lost love objects, for example, seem metatheoretical and superfluous. It is this metatheoretical level of hypothesis that has been most responsible for the barrage of criticism leveled against psychoanalytic theory. It seems important to keep in mind, however, that other aspects of the theory are much more defensible even though it cannot be concluded that any significant aspect of the theory has been proven.

Research on Premorbid Personality Factors

The premorbid (pre-illness) personality factors of depression are those personality traits that tend to be true of depressives prior to the time at which they became depressed. One of the best ways to evaluate such traits is to study a high-risk population to observe which personality characteristics are associated with the people who do and who do not succumb to depression. Unfortunately, high-risk studies of depression are unavailable.

Social Achievement Strivings and Dependency

Cohen, Baker, Cohen, Fromm-Reichmann, and Weigert (1954) summarized the case histories of 12 people diagnosed as manic-depressive. All 12 had received intensive psychoanalytic therapy lasting from one to five years; the findings of the Cohen et al. investigation are based entirely on interpretations of interviews with the patients and their families. According to Cohen et al., the families of the manic-depressives had been set apart from their social environment as different. In some cases the perceived social difference was based on membership in a minority group (e.g., Jewish); in other instances it was based on economic status (either poorer or richer than the other families in the neighborhood); and in still other instances it was based on parental problems (e.g., father a drunkard). The family's social difference led either to an attempt to improve its status or (in socially prestigious families) to an attempt to maintain it. The burden of fulfilling the family's hope for winning or maintaining social prestige usually fell on the shoulders of the more capable or attractive child; this child was thus presented with either a high set of achievement standards or high standards of behavioral conduct designed to win approval from others. Cohen et al. stressed the child's adoption of high achievement or social strivings as an important predisposing factor in manic-depression. The investigators also reported that all of the manic-depressive clients studied had a history of at least one significant dependent relation. Thus high achievement or social strivings and dependency were suggested to be two personality factors associated with manic-depression.

The Cohen et al. findings should be regarded as very tentative because they were based on uncontrolled observations and subjective interpretations of clients' retrospective accounts of their lives. Some subsequent studies have confirmed the basic findings of Cohen et al., whereas other subsequent studies have found that high achievement strivings may predispose people to psychopathology in general rather than to depression in particular. For example, Gibson (1958) found that high prestige striving was more characteristic of a group of families of manic-depressives than it was of a group of families of schizophrenics. Gibson also reported that, compared to schizophrenics, the manic-depressives showed more concern for social approval and had experienced more envy and competitiveness from their siblings. Becker, Spielberger, and Parker (1963), however, found that the value of high achievement was associated more with psychiatric groups than with normals and that no particular type of psychiatric group showed high achievement strivings significantly more than any other. This study also found a correlation between high achievement values and social class, a finding that casts doubt on the interpretation of the previous studies that did not control for social class variables.

Monnelly, Woodruff, and Robins (1974) evaluated levels of social achievement strivings in 25 males hospitalized for bipolar depression and in 21 males hospitalized for unipolar depression. The hypothesis that bipolar (manic-) depression is associated with high social strivings was not supported for the samples as a whole. The results revealed, however, that bipolar patients who had a previous hospitalization showed higher social concern than did unipolar patients with a similar history. The study failed to find, however, any support for the hypothesis that bipolar patients had been singled out for achievement by their parents—specifically, there was no difference in social achievement values between the bipolar patients and their own siblings.

Naditch, Gargan, and Michael (1975) administered personality and mood scales to a sample of 547 men in army basic training. Self-reported low mood was found to correlate with discrepancy between achievement strivings and accomplishment, but the correlation was small ($r = 0.10$). The study also found that self-reported low mood was positively correlated with anxiety ($r = .29$) and with perceived helplessness ($r = .19$), and that low mood was negatively correlated with denial ($r = 0.29$). That is, the higher the use of denial, the higher the level of self-reported mood.

In summary, high achievement and social strivings have been frequently reported to be associated with depression, particularly bipolar or manic-depression. The possibility of such an association is difficult to evaluate because the available studies have generally failed to control for social class variables; moreover, there are insufficicent data to judge whether high achievement strivings are associated with depression in particular or with psychopathology in general. Under these circumstances it seems best to conclude that more research is needed to resolve the issues.

Self-esteem

The available evidence supports the hypothesis that depressives have low-self-esteem compared with other psychiatric groups (Flippo & Lewinsohn, 1971; Laxer, 1964). Coleman (1975), moreover, has found that inducing mildly depressed and nondepressed college students to say positive sentences to themselves temporarily elevated mood, whereas inducing these subjects to say negative sentences to themselves temporarily depressed mood.

Hostility

By awakening subjects at various points in their sleep, Hauri (1976) was able to obtain dream reports from 11 adults who had fully recovered from an episode of reactive depression and from 11 controls with no history of psychiatric consultation. The dream reports were rated by trained assistants who had not been informed whether the dream was obtained from the group of previously depressed people or from the control group. Compared to the control group, the previously depressed group reported dreams showing more masochism, more hostility in the environment, more inanimate objects exerting physical control, and more concern with the past. The findings are in basic agreement with data reported by Beck and Ward (1961) and by Kramer, Whitman, Baldride, and Lansky (1966). Hauri interpreted his findings as suggesting the existence of an underlying personality disturbance that predisposes people to reactive (neurotic) depression so that recovery from a depressive episode need not be associated with improvement of the personality disorder. Although this particular interpretation remains hypothetical, Hauri's impressive study does provide solid support for the association of dreams of masochism and hostility with reactive depression.

Schless, Mendels, Kipperman, and Cochrane (1974) also found that hostility and depression are associated. Specifically, hostility directed toward the self was found to be prevalent in a group of 37 depressed people. Moreover, those people who expressed hostility toward self were more depressed than were those people who expressed hostility toward others. This finding is consistent with clinical observations that hostility toward others is a defense against depression. Under this view, people who are argumentative and hostile toward others are sometimes trying to avoid becoming depressed. When this defense breaks down, relatively severe depression associated with masochistic behaviors and ideas occurs.

In conclusion, there is solid evidence that hostility and depression are associated. More research is needed, however, to specify the nature of this association in greater detail.

Social Separation Studies

Separation from social units is one particular type of loss that has been studied systematically. Research with both animal and human subjects indicates that maternal separation can result in severe depression, particularly in infants and young children.

Anaclitic Depression

Spitz (1949) observed a two-phase (protest-despair) reaction by human infants to hospitalizations that separated them from their mothers for a prolonged period. The infants were between the ages of 3 and 12 months. The initial phase of the reaction to maternal separation was characterized by agitation and seemed to constitute a protest to the separation. This protest phase was followed by a despair phase characterized by extreme withdrawal and lack of interest in the environment, unresponsiveness, and, in some cases, by a sharp reduction in appetite and food intake. Separation also retarded the maturational development of the infants; the depressive reaction, however, remitted following reunion with the mother. Spitz termed this syndrome *anaclitic depression* and noted that it occurred in about 15 per cent of the infants studied.

An important question is whether anaclitic depression is associated only with infants or whether a similar phenomenon also can be observed in older children and in adults (see Rie, 1966). Observations reported by Bowlby (1960, 1969) suggested that some older children show a depressive reaction to prolonged maternal separation. Similar to the Spitz findings, Bowlby reported that the initial reaction to maternal separation was a protest phase characterized by agitation and crying and that this protest phase was followed by a despair phase characterized by apathetic withdrawal. Bowlby, however, also reported that a third phase can occur; this third phase, called *detachment,* consisted of the rejection of the mother after the mother and child were reunited. This persistence of the depressive (withdrawal) reaction beyond the point of reunification with the mother had been largely (although not entirely) absent in the Spitz studies.

Although parental separation does not seem to lead to depressive reactions in any noteworthy number of adults, this may be because adults are much less dependent on their parents for social support than are infants and young children. It is possible that some adults are predisposed to react depressively to prolonged separation from their families or to separation from all other people. Systematic research bearing on these questions is currently unavailable.

Animal Studies

Research on infant monkeys has proven capable of producing a monkey analogue of anaclitic depression and of permitting systematic investigation of the conditions under which the phenomenon occurs and its generality to other age groups. Seay, Hansen, and Harlow (1962) and Seay and Harlow (1965) have shown that the typical infant monkey reaction to maternal separation follows the protest-despair process described by Spitz. The protest phase is characterized by high levels of vocalization and motor activity, whereas the despair stage is characterized by inactivity, social withdrawal, and a lack of social play. The despair reaction remits following reunification with the mother.

If infant monkeys are raised with peers and without their mothers, they react to peer separation with protest followed by despair. Suomi, Harlow, and Domek (1970) separated a group of infants from each other a total of 20 times in a period of six months. Each separation period lasted four days, and each was found to evoke the protest-despair reaction. Interestingly, the protest-despair reaction did not attenuate during repeated separations—the infants protested and then became depressed in reaction to the twentieth separation almost as much as they had in reaction to the first separation. Similar to the Spitz finding, the despair reactions terminated on unifications with the peers. Maturational arrest also occurred; the monkeys who had experienced separations were three months old at the start of the study and nine months old at its conclusion. Although normal monkeys typically show considerable maturational development during this age period, the monkeys who had experienced repeated separations showed an immature behavioral repertoire at nine months of age similar to their behavior at three months of age.

One issue currently being subjected to empirical investigation is whether the detachment phase described by Bowlby (1960, 1969) occurs in monkeys and, if so, under what conditions of separation. It is recalled that the detachment phase consists of a persistence of the withdrawal reaction beyond the point of reunification so that the individual continues to reject the mother or the peer. The initial animal studies failed to find any evidence of a detachment phase. Data obtained by Suomi (1973), however, suggest that a detachment phase can occur, but whether it does so depends in part on the extent to which the separation chambers are physically confining. In this study peer-raised infant monkeys were separated from one another and placed in a highly confining physical environment that resembled a long vertical pit. The results revealed that the monkeys showed a typical protest-despair reaction and that the withdrawal reaction of the protest phase persisted beyond the point of reunification. This detachment reaction contrasts sharply with the typical remittance of the withdrawal reaction following reunification in monkeys who are separated and placed in boxlike cages.

As mentioned previously, an important question is the extent to which the depressive reaction to social separation is associated with young age (particularly infancy). Although there is a paucity of data with humans pertaining to this question, the early monkey studies failed to find depressive reactions to separation with animals beyond the age of infancy at the time of separation. Considerable caution, however, is indicated before drawing the conclusion that depressive reactions to social separation are associated only with infants and young children, particularly in light of some suggestive data reported by Suomi, Eisele, Grady, and Harlow (1975). In this study, family reared, young adult monkeys were separated from their families and housed either with friends, with both friends and strangers, or alone. The results indicated that the only monkeys to show a depressive reaction were those who had been housed alone during the period of separation. These results suggest that depressive reactions to social separations can occur in young adult monkeys. The investigators, however, warned against definitive interpretation of their findings because of the small number of monkeys studied.

Summary

Research with both animal and human infants indicates that separation from the mother can result in a severe depressive reaction. A similar phenomenon, moreover, has been reported for separation from peers in monkeys raised with peers and without their mothers. Although the depressive reaction usually remits following reunification with the mother or peers, circumstances seem to exist under which a detachment phase occurs consisting of the persistence of the withdrawal reaction beyond the point of reunification. Depressive reactions to social separation occur more readily in infants and young children, although certain types of social separations may also lead to depressive reactions in adults.

Beck's Cognitive Triad Hypothesis

As mentioned previously, there are affective, cognitive, psychomotor, and motivational dimensions to depression. Most theorists during this century have viewed the affective disturbances as constituting the fundamental problem and the other signs of depression as secondary consequences of the disturbance in affect. Beck (1967) has questioned this traditional view and has proposed that depression and mania are fundamentally cognitive disorders. Under Beck's view, the affective, psychomotor, and motivational disturbances of depression are secondary consequences of a primary cognitive disturbance. The following exemplifies this position:

> If the patient were rejected, he would experience negative affect. Similarly, if he simply *thought* he was rejected, he would experience the same negative affect. I concluded that the way an individual structures his experience determined his mood. Since the depressed person consistently makes negative conceptualizations, he is prone to have a consistently negative mood [Beck, 1967, p. 261].

Beck (1967) described the predisposing conditions in depression as a primary triad of cognitive patterns. One such pattern is a tendency to interpret interactions with the environment as representing defeat, deprivation, or disparagement. The person exaggerates minor setbacks as total failures, accepts responsibility for failure, and is reluctant to accept responsibility for success. Failure is anticipated. A second cognitive pattern is that of low self-esteem—a tendency to view oneself as inadequate, unworthy of love, or otherwise defective in physical, mental, or moral attributes. A third cognitive pattern is that of helplessness and hopelessness—depressed people tend to view their suffering as interminable and see the future as a life of unending hardship and failure. As a result of this triad of cognitive patterns, the individual is seen as unusually vulnerable to stresses such as criticisms, setbacks in achievement goals, loss of love, and deprivation.

Evaluation

Beck's theory can be viewed as consisting of two types of hypotheses. One type concerns the nature of the cognitive deficits in depression. An example of such a hypothesis is that depressives are more likely than normals to accept responsibility for failures and less likely than normals to accept responsibility for success. The other type of hypothesis is that the specific cognitive deficits Beck enumerated are the primary causes of depression. The former type of hypothesis concerning the nature of the cognitive deficits is testable, but the latter type concerning the fundamental nature of the disorder does not lend itself to empirical testing.

The cognitive, affective, and motivational components of a behavior can be distinguished by abstraction, but the real-world referents for these abstractions are often the same event. Depressed mood, low motivation, and cognitions of unworthiness occur together. If someone said, "I am an unworthy, rotten person and I hate myself" and "I am in a good mood now that I realize that I hate myself," we would suspect that the person was inaccurately reporting his or her feelings. Negative cognitions about oneself and low mood go together because they are two aspects of the same psychological event. Theories that propose that one of these aspects causes the other are probably untestable. The value of Beck's theory may not be his hypothesis that cognitions are the fundamental problem, but rather his hypotheses of the nature of the cognitive deficits associated with depression. (See Staats, 1975, for a discussion of an A-R-D sytem that, in essence, views cognitive, emotional, and motivational aspects of behavior as three components of the same event.)

Learned Helplessness

Seligman and his colleagues have proposed that the central feature of reactive depression is a fatalistic belief that there is nothing one can do to control the important events in one's life (Miller & Seligman, 1973; Seligman, 1975; Seligman, Klein, & Miller, 1974). The theory proposes that depressed people believe rewards and punishments are independent of their behavior. Believing that important rewards and punishments will occur regardless of what one does or does not do, depressed people show little motivation to initiate voluntary behavior. The theory further proposes that any experience that facilitates the belief that one is helpless to control the important events in one's life causes depression. Seligman has called this theory the *learned helplessness* model of depression.

Although extensive research into helplessness is a relatively recent development, the notion that helplessness is a central feature of depression is not new. Bibring (1953) had hypothesized that the central feature of depression is the subjective feeling of helplessness or powerless in relation to important narcissistic goals. Grinker et al. (1961) isolated a "hopelessness" factor as a basic theme of depression, and Beck (1967) found that the more severe the depression, the greater were feelings of hopelessness. The recent upsurge of interest in helplessness, however, is attributable largely to experimental findings that many animals exposed to inescapable traumatic events become extremely passive and give up trying to escape.

Animal Studies

The early reports of a learned helplessness phenomenon came from investigations of avoidance-escape learning with dogs in a shuttle box. A shuttle box consists of two compartments each having a grid floor that can be electrified. The compartments are separated from one another by a barrier that can be jumped. In the typical experiment, the onset of a signal is followed by electric shock in the compartment with the animal. The animal is supposed to learn to escape the shock by jumping over the barrier. Seligman (1973) described the behavior of a typical experimentally naive dog in a shuttle box: "at the onset of the first electric shock, the dog defecates, urinates, howls, and runs around frantically until it accidentally scrambles over the barrier and escapes the shock. On the next trial, the dog, running and howling, crosses the barrier more quickly. This pattern continues until the dog learns to avoid shock altogether" (p. 44).

In a series of experiments, Seligman and his colleagues found that prior exposure to inescapable shock resulted in dogs who would lie down and passively accept shock when later placed in a shuttle box (e.g., Overmier & Seligman, 1967; Seligman & Maier, 1967). These experiments consisted of two separate phases. During the pretreatment phase, one group of dogs was restrained in a hammock and administered inescapable and moderately painful electric shock. At first the dogs would become agitated and try to escape from the hammock, but eventually they became calm and more passive. Depending on the particular study, the control group either received no pretreatment with shock, fewer trials of inescapable shock in the hammock, or trials of escapable shock. During the second phase of the experiments, the dogs were placed in a shuttle box. The results indicate that approximately two thirds of more than 150 dogs who had received helplessness training (inescapable shock in the hammock) failed to learn to avoid shock when later placed in the shuttle box. Seligman interpreted these findings as indicating that the dogs had given up trying to escape shock when they were restrained in the hammock; the dogs' expectation that there was nothing they could do to avoid shock transferred from the hammock (where it was true) to the shuttle box (where the assumption was false).

Research on learned helplessness in animals indicates that the phenomenon occurs in dogs, cats, rats, and even fish (Seligman, 1975). The effect depends on prior exposure to *uncontrollable* shock rather than on exposure to shock per se. The effect dissipates over time—testing in the shuttle box several days following training in the hammock is too long a delay to observe the helplessness phenomenon in a significant proportion of the dogs tested.

Studies with Nondepressed Humans

Following demonstrations of the helplessness phenomenon in animals, investigators evaluated the possibility that a similar phenomenon occurs in humans. Some research relevant to this question had already been reported. Zeaman and House (1960) found that retarded children exposed to prolonged failure were unable to solve problems they had been able to solve prior to exposure to failure. Glass and Singer (1972) demonstrated that exposure to uncontrollable noise can impair persistence and quality of performance on experimental tasks.

A series of recent studies has demonstrated that exposure to uncontrollable outcomes such as unpleasant noise or failures can impair subsequent performance on experimental tasks (e.g., Dweck & Reppucci, 1973; Hiroto & Seligman, 1975; Roth & Kubal, 1975). Dweck and Reppucci (1973) exposed children to a series of failures on puzzles administered by one experimenter and to a series of successes on puzzles administered by another experimenter. Following this training, it was found that the children required more time to solve puzzles when they were administered by the failure experimenter than by the success experimenter even though the problems were objectively similar. The investigators interpreted this finding as suggesting that the children learned to be helpless over the control of failure in the presence of the failure experimenter; specifically, they learned that success and failure were independent of effort. Thus they did not try as hard in the presence of the failure experimenter and, hence, they took more time to solve the puzzles. Hiroto and Seligman (1975) reported four experiments in which prior experience with an uncontrollable outcome impaired subsequent performance on an experimental task. One of these studies employed three groups, two of which were exposed to unpleasant tones prior to engaging in the experimental task. Of these two groups, one could terminate the unpleasant tone by performing a simple response (escapable group), and the other could not (helpless group). The college students in the helpless group and escapable group were paired so that termination of the tone by an escapable subject also terminated the tone for his helpless partner (yoking procedure). Thus, students in both the escapable and helpless groups received identical experiences with the unpleasant tone, except that students in the helpless group could do nothing that affected tone termination and those in the escapable group could. Following this training, all subjects were told that the tones would come on from time to time and that there was something they could do to try to terminate the tone. On one trial the escape response was to slide a door to the right, on the next trial the escape response was to slide the door to the left, and so on. The purpose of the study was to evaluate whether prior exposure to an uncontrollable and unpleasant tone would impair subsequent learning to escape the tone when escape was possible. The results indicate that, compared to the controls, students in the helpless group required more trials to learn to escape the tone. The investigators interpreted this finding as a demonstration of learned helplessness in college students.

Attributions and Expectancies

To summarize, the learned helplessness phenomenon consists of an impairment in learning to avoid unpleasant events such as loud tones and failures on experimental tasks. This impairment is caused by prior exposure to an uncontrollable event. The helplessness model postulates that this deficit in avoidance learning is caused by cognitions (beliefs) that one's behavior is unrelated to important events in one's life. Cognitions of helplessness are also postulated to cause depression.

If depressed people tend to believe that their behavior is unrelated to success or failure, they should show little change in their tendency to expect future success after having experienced a series of successful performances. In order to test this prediction, Miller and Seligman (1973) had nondepressed and very mildly depressed college students perform one task that seemed to require skill and another task that appeared to be a matter of chance. The experiment was arranged so that a series of successes on the tasks was guaranteed without the students realizing that task outcomes had been rigged for success. As a consequence of this training, nondepressed students showed a greater expectancy change than depressed students on the skill task but not on the chance task, presumably because the depressed students were less likely to attribute success to their effort or ability and more likely to attribute success to external factors. These findings, however, offer only tentative support for the learned helplessness model, in part because the level of depression of college students in the depressed group was very mild and actually within normal limits.

Although both Beck's cognitive model and Seligman's learned helplessness model propose that depression is a cognitive disorder, the two models differ in regard to predictions concerning the reactions of depressed people to failure. Beck's model assumes that depressed people tend to blame themselves for failure while not taking much credit for success; however, Seligman's model assumes that depressed people tend to perceive *both* success and failure as irrelevant to their behavior. Unfortunately, there is little data bearing on these issues, but what evidence does exist is more consistent with Beck's model than with Seligman's. Clinical observations suggest that depressed people tend to take too much responsibility for negative events—they blame themselves for deaths of loved ones, for achievement setbacks, and for interpersonal shortcomings. In an experimental investigation, moreover, Rizley (1976) found that depressed college students attributed failure to themselves more than did nondepressed college students. Interpretation of this finding, however, is complicated. The nondepressed students attributed success more than failure to themselves, whereas the depressed students showed no differences in attributions of success and failure. Perhaps the results indicate that the nondepressed students cared more about the experimental outcomes than did the depressed so that, being invested in the study, they defensively accepted more credit for success than for failure.

Evaluation

The following comments are offered in evaluation of the learned helplessness model of depression.

1. Although helplessness in humans consists of impaired (or delayed) learning of escape responses from aversive events, many depressed people actually show a high frequency of escape responses designed to alleviate their suffering (Ferster, 1973). These escape responses include talking to others about

their problems, complaining, seeking therapy, and in some cases, suicide. Although these responses are usually ineffective in producing a viable solution to problems, they nevertheless suggest that many depressed people have not given up trying to escape from their misery. Low rates of escape responses do seem to characterize some relatively severe forms of retarded depression, however, and it may be that the helplessness model is more applicable to these cases.

2. *According to the helplessness model, depressed people are supposed to believe that their behavior is unrelated to what happens to them. Depressed people, however, seem to believe instead that negative events are their own fault.*

3. Learned helplessness in animals, learned helplessness in college students, and depression appear to be three distinct phenomena. The differences among these phenomena appear more impressive than the similarities. For example, learned helplessness in animals is characterized by inactivity, whereas learned helplessness in humans is characterized by a temporary delay in learning to escape or to avoid unpleasant events. Unlike helpless dogs, helpless humans are not inactive—they do not lie down in a state of immobility. In fact, helpless children seem to emit many active responses designed to avoid achievement situations. Finally, there are important differences between helplessness and depression. For example, depression is associated with sobbing, whereas helplessness is not. Some recent data, however, suggest that helplessness in college students is associated with low mood and nervousness (Gatchel, Paulus, & Maples, 1975; Miller & Seligman, 1975). But low mood and nervousness occur so frequently and are so easy to produce in college students in laboratory experiments that it is unclear if these experiments are relevant to clinically significant depression.

4. *Even if helplessness is not an analogue of clinical depression, it is still an important phenomenon.* Helplessness in children is an especially important educational problem. Finally, Seligman and his colleagues have attracted a large number of investigators to the area of depression. This development could prove significant even if the learned helplessness model of depression proves to be largely invalid.

Reinforcement Theory of Depression

Ferster (1966, 1973) proposed that there exist a number of ways in which people become depressed so that no single etiology exists. Under this view, depression can result from any of the following events: (1) a high level of exposure to aversive events or to the need to avoid aversive events (e.g., life is a chore of avoiding possible failures); (2) a low level of positive reinforcement; (3) a sudden change in the environment resulting from the loss of a discriminative stimulus that controls a large amount of behavior (e.g., retirement, death of a loved one); (4) exposure to reinforcement schedules that require a large amount of work or effort to earn reinforcement; and (5) the expression of anger that annoys other people and thus deprives one of a significant source of positive reinforcement. Lazarus (1968) has expressed a theoretical position similar to Ferster's.

There is some tentative evidence that supports the reinforcement theory of depression. Lewinsohn and Libet (1972) found that depressives tended to engage less in pleasant activities than did nondepressives, suggesting that low levels of reinforcement may be related to depression. Wener and Rehm (1975) found that college students who performed an experimental task for a low level of reinforcement reported lower mood, had lower self-confidence, and performed more poorly than did college students who performed the same task for a high level of reinforcement. These findings suggest that low levels of positive reinforcement can induce temporary and very mild signs of depression.

Evaluation

The reinforcement theory of depression may prove to have considerable validity, but as yet much more research is needed to test the theory. Apart from the paucity of directly relevant studies, some investigators have reported data that could prove problematic for the theory. Hammen and Glass (1975), for example, found that instructing mildly depressed college students to engage in interesting activities did not elevate their mood level. Although this finding is inconsistent with expectation under the reinforcement theory, the study concerns the treatment of depression and is not directly relevant to hypotheses about how depression actually develops. Moreover, Lewinsohn (1975) has questioned the measures employed in the Hammen and Glass (1975) study.

Biochemical Hypotheses

Before considering some biochemical hypotheses of depression, it is necessary to review some basic knowledge about the nervous system. Neurons are separated by small spaces called synapses. An impulse moves along a neuron by electrical energy, but the impulse does not jump the gap to other neurons. Rather, the impulse releases a chemical substance that transverses the synapses and causes an electrical reaction in the receptor neuron. The substances released into the synapses are called neurotransmitters, and they include acetylcholine, norepinephrine, dopamine, and serotonin. It is believed that any particular nerve cell releases only one type of neurotransmitter. Neurons that release acetylcholine are termed *cholinergic,* whereas neurons that release either norepinephrine or dopamine are called *adrenergic.* Generally, the cholinergic system is thought to decrease neural activity in receptor neurons, and the adrenergic system is thought to increase such activity.

The group of neurotransmitters that has most frequently been hypothesized to have an etiological role in depression is the biogenic amines of the adrenergic system. Two types of amines are distinguished on the basis of their biochemical structure: the *catecholamines* (including norepinephrine and dopamine) and the *idoleamines* (including serotonin). Although there is evidence implicating both the catecholamines and the idoleamines in depression, the neurotransmitter that has received the most research attention is the catecholamine norepinephrine.

The norepinephrine hypothesis proposes that at least some types of depression are caused by deficiencies in the amount of norepinephrine at or near nerve cell endings in the adrenergic system and that mania is caused by an excess of norepinephrine at these sites. The evidence for this hypothesis consists of two sets of findings that may be summarized as follows:

1. *Drugs that are effective in the treatment of depression probably increase the supply of brain norepinephrine available for neural transmission.* The two classes of drugs that effectively alleviate depression are the tricyclic antidepressants and the MAO inhibitors (Cole, 1964; Kopin, 1964). There is evidence that the tricyclic antidepressants increase the amount of norepinephrine recovered from the synapse following its release for the purpose of neural transmission (see Bunney & Davis, 1965). There is evidence that MAO causes the chemical breakdown of norepinephrine; hence, drugs that inhibit the action of MAO should increase the supply of norepinephrine. Thus, one likely consequence of the two classes of drug that alleviate depression is an increase in the supply of norepinephrine available for neural transmission.

2. *Two drugs (reserpine and methyldopa) that seem to cause depression (or at least sedation) in a small but consistent proportion of hypertensive patients treated probably deplete the supply of norepinephrine in the brain* (see Bunney & Davis, 1965).

Evaluation

The evidence for the norepinephrine hypothesis (more commonly referred to as the *catecholamine hypothesis*) is far from conclusive for the following reasons.

1. Neither norepinephrine nor any other amine has been directly implicated as a causal agent in depression. The nature of the evidence is largely circumstantial and correlational.
2. Although norepinephrine depletion seems to be an important correlate of depression, depression may also be correlated with deficits in other neurotransmitters including serotonin (see Robins & Hartman, 1972). Other biochemical abnormalities that may correlate with depression include abnormalities in the available supply of glucose (Mueller, Heninger, & MacDonald, 1972) and steroids (see Schuyler, 1974).
3. Drugs believed to increase the brain supply of norepinephrine do not alleviate depression in all cases treated. Why these antidepressant drugs should be effective in only some cases is unclear under the catecholamine hypothesis, but future evidence could potentially explain this fact in a manner consistent with the hypothesis.

Imbalance Theory

Although Davis and his colleagues were early advocates of the norepinephrine hypothesis, they subsequently modified their view toward a theory that stresses an imbalance between the adrenergic and cholinergic systems (Davis,

1975a; Janowsky, Davis, El-Yousef, Sekerke, 1972). As mentioned previously, biogenic amines facilitate certain central nervous system functions, whereas cholinergic substances inhibit these same central nervous system functions. Davis's imbalance theory proposes that the critical factor in depression is the ratio of adrenergic to cholinergic substances at critical sites in the central nervous system. As a recently proposed theory, more research is needed to evaluate its validity.

Comment

Biochemical research on depression in particular and on abnormal behavior in general has led to so many exciting possibilities that did not bear fruit that today many observers regard the field with a measure of skepticism. This skepticism has been reinforced by numerous biochemical findings that either failed to replicate or were eventually attributed to dietary differences between the disturbed and nondisturbed populations studied. The inaccessibility of the brain to biochemical research has forced investigators to rely on largely indirect and circumstantial attacks on the basic questions (see Schuyler, 1974). Despite this history, there is a growing body of solid evidence suggesting that progress is being made.

The identification of biochemical mediators of depression would not necessarily mitigate the importance of psychological research. All behavior is biochemically mediated, as is proven conclusively by the facts that there can be no behavior in the absence of the central nervous system, and that the actions of the central nervous system are biochemical in nature. The identification of a biochemical etiology of depression may only provide the most immediate cause of a depressive episode. For example, if neurotransmitter imbalance were found to cause depression, we would still need to explain what caused the neurotransmitter imbalance. Such explanations would likely need to take account of psychological factors.

Genetic Studies

Most of the research on genetic factors in depression has been concerned with the manic-depressive syndrome, but recently a number of studies have appeared on other types of depression as well (see, e.g., Winokur, 1972). Solid evidence suggests that there is a genetic component to manic-depression. It has been observed for some time that manic-depression runs in families, and reviews of the available literature indicate a substantially higher concordance rate for monozygotic twins as compared with dizygotic twins (Kraepelin, 1923; Rosenthal, 1970). Perris (1966), moreover, reported that the relatives of bipolar depressives were more likely to develop bipolar than unipolar depression, and that the relatives of unipolar depressives were more likely to develop unipolar than bipolar depression. Although these data are not quite conclusive, the overall evidence for a genetic component to manic-depression is impressive (see Rosenthal, 1970). Presently, however, the evidence is too sparse to draw any conclusion in regard to possible genetic components in the less severe forms of depression.

Toward a Unified Hypothesis

Akiskal and McKinney (1973) have attempted to integrate the various areas of research on depression. Their theory proposes that the common factor underlying the depressive syndrome is a reversible disorder of neurological mechanisms believed to control the reinforcement process. These so-called pleasure centers are located in the hypothalamus which is located in the diencephalon part of the forebrain. Akiskal and McKinney propose that "depression must be understood as occurring on several levels simultaneously rather than as having a one-to-one, direct relationship with a single chemical event in the brain, and that a multiplicity of genetic, developmental, pharmacological, and interpersonal factors converge on the forebrain and lead to a reversible, functional derangement of the mechanism of reinforcement" (1973, p. 21). As shown in Figure 14-1, Akiskal and McKinney's unified hypothesis specifically proposes that object loss, interpersonal frustration (social separation), helplessness, and

Figure 14-1
A multidisciplinary model of the pathogenesis of depressive disorders. [From H. S. Akiskal and W. T. McKinney, Jr. Depressive Disorders: Toward a Unified Hypothesis. *Science,* 1973, Vol. 182, p. 26. Printed by permission of authors and publisher. Copyright 1973 by the American Association for the Advancement of Science.]

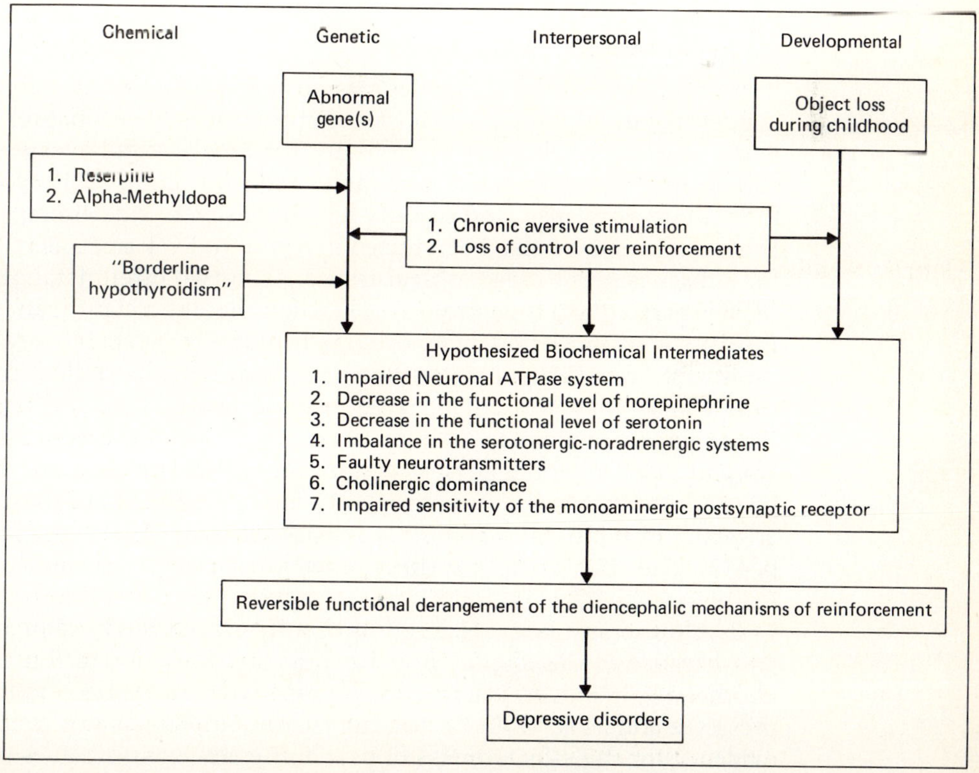

depletion of biogenic amines all result in an impairment of functioning in the so-called pleasure, or reinforcement, centers of the brain.

The Akiskal and McKinney model is an important contribution, in part because it reminds us that depression is probably a result of personality, experiential, genetic, biochemical, and neurological factors interacting with one another, so that depression is unlikely to prove explicable in terms of any single set of factors. The specifics of the model, however, should be regarded as highly theoretical for two reasons. First, there is insufficient evidence that an impairment in neurological functioning at the so-called pleasure centers of the brain is a common etiological factor in depression. Second, as we have seen, the evidence for each of the contributing factors cited by the unified hypothesis (object loss, personality, biochemistry, genetics, and frustration) permits varying degrees of confidence that the factor is important in the etiology of depression. Despite these sobering remarks designed to remind us that we are still a long way from a unified theory of depression, Akiskal and McKinney's vision that such a theory will ultimately prove necessary has considerable merit to it.

TREATMENT OF DEPRESSION

Severe depression usually is treated by either antidepressant drugs or electroconvulsive therapy (ECT), although tranquilizers also are used in some cases. The two clinical classes of antidepressant drugs effective in alleviating depression are the tricyclic antidepressants and the MAO inhibitors; the tricyclic antidepressants (particularly imipramine) are generally more effective than are the MAO inhibitors (Davis, 1975b). Both imipramine and ECT are significantly more effective in alleviating depression than is placebo treatment but neither is effective in all, or even almost all, of the cases. (See Chapter 5.) In deciding which treatment is most appropriate for any particular case, the following should be considered. ECT acts faster than imipramine, is associated with a higher rate of relapse, and usually has more severe side effects (Davis, 1975b). Ethical issues have also been raised in regard to ECT treatment. (See Chapter 5 for a discussion of these ethical issues.) The two circumstances under which ECT is particularly suggested are (1) when there is a significant risk of suicide, ECT may be preferred over drug treatment because it usually produces a more rapid recovery; and (2) when drug treatment has failed, there is a 50 per cent chance that the person will respond favorably to ECT (Davis, 1975b).

Behavior therapy may include relaxation training in cases of agitated depression. In cases in which anxiety is not a significant factor, some behavior therapists encourage their clients to spend a larger proportion of their daily schedule engaging in relatively pleasant activities (Lazarus, 1968; also see Yates, 1970, p. 417). The effectiveness of these procedures has yet to be evaluated systematically.

Psychotherapy is exceedingly difficult with severely depressed people, in part because of the client's hopelessness and low motivation to recover. Psychotherapy, however, is a reasonable mode of treatment for many neurotic depressives and as an addition to drug treatment. This is not to imply that solid evidence for the effectiveness of psychotherapy exists (it does not) but merely to note the absence of any clearly superior alternative to bolster the effects of drug treatment.

Fortunately, depression is episodic and hence usually remits without formal treatment. A significant proportion of cases, moreover, respond to placebo treatment (Davis, 1975b). Reliance on spontaneous recovery is not indicated, however, in part because drug treatment and ECT can be effective and in part because of the risk of suicide.

SUICIDE

The possibility of suicide is often a major concern in depression even though many depressed people do not commit suicide and many people who did commit suicide did not do so out of depression. In recent years we have witnessed an upsurge of research activity on suicide, but as yet very little is known about the causes of suicide and what can be done to prevent it. Much of the available research is concerned with identifying correlates of suicide that would enable clinicians to evaluate risk and consequently engage in prophylactic therapy.

Frequency of Suicide

Accurate estimates of the frequency of suicide are difficult to obtain although "ballpark" figures are available. Many of these estimates are based on official records of death made by local medical or government officials. These records are subject to errors that result from the difficulty of discerning whether a given death was accidental or suicidal and from a desire not to attribute death to suicide in order to save the family from social stigma and unnecessary guilt. Official records are thus widely believed to underestimate the true rate of suicide. Nevertheless, estimates based on official records indicate that suicide ranks as the eleventh greatest cause of death and as the third greatest cause of death for people between the ages of 20 and 30 (Schuyler, 1974). Official records suggest that 25,000 Americans commit suicide each year, but as many as 75,000 may actually do so (Schuyler, 1974). Another 200,000 to 250,000 people unsuccessfully attempt suicide each year (Litman & Wold, 1974; Renshaw, 1973). Litman and Wold (1974) reported that each year approximately 250,000 people communicate intentions to commit suicide but do not actually attempt to do so. Leonard and Flinn (1972) found that in a sample of college students and Air Force personnel in basic training, 18 per cent reported having made a serious suicide gesture or at least having given serious consideration to such action.

Suicide rates are relatively constant across socioeconomic groups within the United States, but they differ across sex, age group, and nations (Stengel, 1962; Schuyler & Beck, 1972). Approximately three times as many men commit suicide as women; many more women than men, however, unsuccessfully attempt suicide. Suicide is more frequent for people older than 40, whereas unsuccessful attempts are more frequent among people younger than 40. Approximately 15.6 per cent of all deaths in the United States are attributable to suicide; the rate is 7.1 for Italy, 19.6 for Australia, and 33.9 for Hungary (Schuyler,

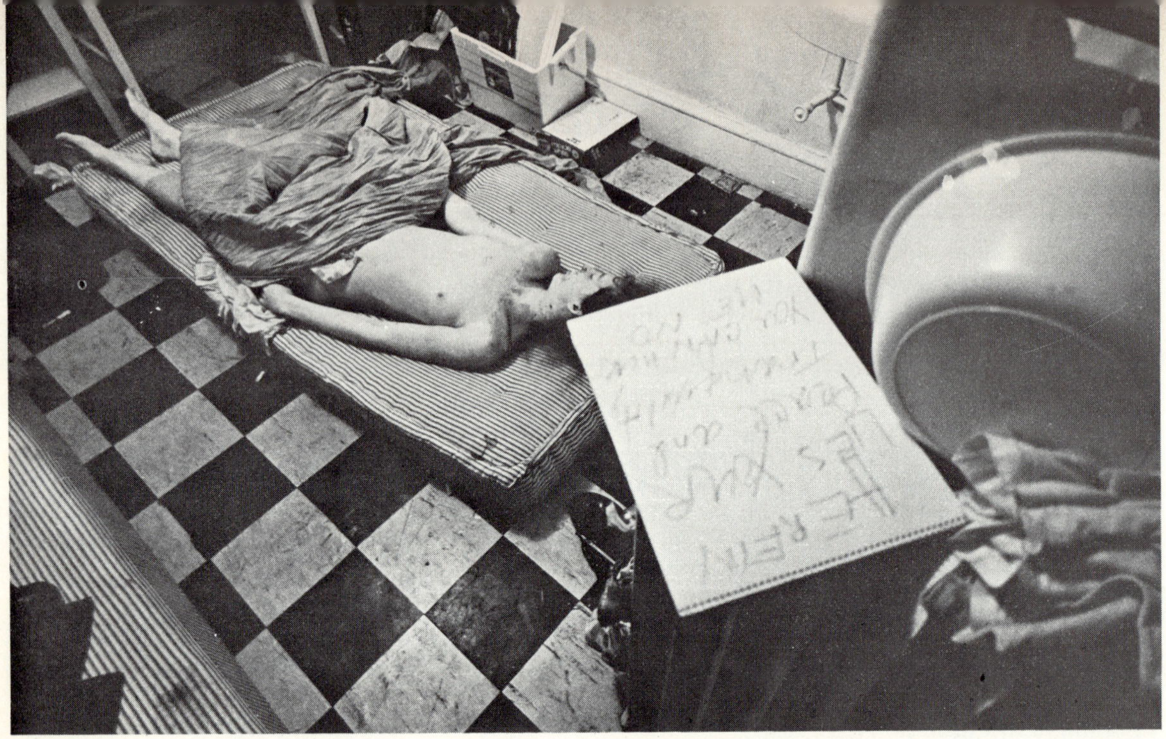

Suicide ranks as the third greatest cause of death for people between the ages of 20 and 30. (Photo by Leonard Freed; Magnum Photos, Inc.)

1974). Generally, countries with higher levels of poverty and lower levels of industrialization tend to have higher suicide rates.

As mentioned previously, not all people who commit suicide are depressed and many depressives do not commit suicide. Nevertheless, the frequency of suicide is much greater among depressives than for any other psychiatric group. Beck (1967) reported that manic-depressives commit suicide at a rate 500 times the national average, and Temoche, Pugh, and McMahon (1964) reported that depressives commit suicide at a rate three times that of schizophrenics and alcoholics.

Predictors of Suicide

Although no particular suicidal personality can be specified, many investigators have tried to identify factors that predict suicide. Schuyler and Beck (1972) described the most frequent suicide case as falling into a composite category of male, over 40, separated, widowed or divorced, unemployed or retired, and living in an urban area. This composite is consistent with the view that the typical person who commits suicide is depressed and socially isolated. Litman and Wold (1974) reported three features that are characteristic of the depressed individual who commits suicide: somatic problems (e.g., appetite loss and fatigue), disturbed affect (feelings of helplessness and worthlessness), and social isolation. Some of the other predictive factors suggested by Litman and Wold are age, maleness, extended period of depression, rejection of help, and previous suicide attempts or threats. A previous attempt is particularly indicative of a possible future attempt. Moss and Hamilton (1956) report that 90 per cent of suicide attempters have recurring thoughts of suicide, and Shniedman and Farberow (1957) found that 75 per cent of those who committed suicide had made a previous attempt. Sometimes an unsuccessful suicide attempt is seen as further evidence of lack of worth (*I can't even commit suicide right*) and this increases the desire for another attempt.

The greatest period of danger appears to be shortly after discharge from treatment. Both Shneidman and Farberow (1957) and Wheat (1960) found high rates of suicide among depressives who had recently been discharged from an in-patient unit. At the time of discharge, the amount of social support is reduced and the stress of adjustment to the outside environment is maximal.

Most people who committed suicide had threatened to do so or at least gave some sort of signal of their thoughts of death (Litman & Wold, 1974; Seiden, 1966). These signals vary from a direct statement of intention to writing "die" on a toilet wall. The message is usually conveyed in a manner that identifies the sender; along with suicide threats, such messages are commonly assumed to be a "cry for help." In some cases, however, the intent of the message, or the actual suicide, may be a real desire to hurt others or to rejoin a loved one (Schuyler, 1974).

Blatt and Ritzler (1974) compared the Rorschach protocols of 12 people who committed suicide with 12 matched controls who did not. Of the 19 measures analyzed, the only significant differences between the two groups were in the number of themes suggesting transparency (e.g., a room divided into two by a glass partition, layers of clothing perceptible through a sheer fabric) and the number of responses suggesting that the image seen in the inkblot is being seen from a cross-sectional perspective. These findings should be regarded as tentative, however, in part because of the small number of subjects. Of the 19 measures analyzed, moreover, two significant findings could occur as a consequence of random variations. Nevertheless, the Blatt and Ritzler findings could prove useful if they withstand systematic replication.

Suicide Motivation

Although there are many possible reasons why a person may commit suicide, it is often difficult to specify the motivation for any particular case. Shneidman and Farberow (1970) developed a procedure called the *psychological autopsy* in which investigators gather whatever information they can to evaluate intent to commit suicide and possible motivation. Such information may consist of a suicide note, a report of a crisis telephone call made prior to suicide, and interviews with relatives and friends. The quality of information obtained varies considerably depending on the case.

The following is a partial list of some of the major reasons for suicides.

1. *Escape from suffering.* Beck (1963) suggested that suicide thoughts and intentions are related to hopelessness, and Schuyler (1974) suggested that hopelessness may be the best predictor of suicide. The person who has no hope of solving major problems and foresees a life of unending suffering may turn to suicide as the only avenue of escape.

Findings that suicide rates are higher for depressed people under stress support the hypothesis that escape is one major reason for suicide. Two groups considered to be engaged in stressful vocations are physicians and college students. Physicians have a suicide rate nine times that of the non-medical population. Seiden (1966) considers college life to be highly stressful. He reported that college students have a significantly higher rate of suicide than their non-college peers (Bruyn & Seiden, 1965). An extensive study of 23 suicide cases that occurred at the University of California at Berkeley during a ten-year span was conducted by Seiden (1966). He found that among college students suicide rates were greater for students engaged in graduate study than in undergraduate study and that three times as many male students as female students committed suicide. Furthermore, 50 per cent of those who committed suicide had some previous psychiatric or mental health contact and that the most frequent time for suicide was at the beginning of the semester. Consistent with previous studies, Seiden also found that most of those who committed suicide had given several warnings of their intent and that they had shown symptoms of depression. Thus college students seem to have special problems to solve, but when these problems seem hopelessly insoluble and stressful, suicide is a possible outcome.

Suicidal persons may forsee a life of unending suffering in part because they are deficient in solving their problems (Rosenberg & Latimer, 1956; Shneidman, 1969). Levenson and Neuringer (1971) compared adolescents who had expressed suicidal intent with psychiatric patients who had not, and found that the suicidal group was less able to solve math and map problems. This finding was interpreted as suggesting that a limited ability to solve problems may be one factor associated with suicide. Helplessness also may be related to risk-taking behavior in the sense that people who are not solving their problems may be willing to take greater risks to achieve a solution. Experimenters have obtained data that suggest that suicide attempters are more willing to gamble (win more at risk of losing more) especially when they are depressed (Adams, Giffen, & Garfield, 1973; Kochansky, 1973).

2. *Retaliation against others.* Some people seem to commit suicide in order to make others feel guilty for their death. The irrational thought process can be as childish as, *I'll kill myself and then they will be sorry.* The child or psychotic person may even relish the thought of observing the anguish and guilt caused to the other person without fully realizing that he or she will not be alive to derive pleasure from the inflicted suffering. Shneidman reported a suicide note from a 35-year-old divorced woman that began with, "You have killed me. I hope you are happy in your heart, 'If you have one which I doubt.' *Please* leave Rover with Mike. Also leave my baby alone. If you don't I'll haunt you the rest of your life and I mean it and I'll do it" (1968, p.6).

3. *Attempt to gain attention or fame.* Suicides differ considerably in how likely they are to gain public attention. People who jump off of a tall building after threatening to do so before a crowd, and people who throw themselves in front of a train, are more likely to make the newspapers than are the people who drug themselves quietly. One possible motivation for suicide, then, is to gain attention.

4. *Altruism.* Some suicides seem motivated to help others (Durkheim, 1897) as in the case of a father who kills himself so that his family can collect on a life insurance policy. Other examples of altruistic motives include the Buddhist monks who burned themselves in public places in order to protest against the South Vietnamese government in the late 1960s and early 1970s.

5. *Compliance with cultural norms.* Sometimes suicides occur because a society or a religion values it and instills these values in selected groups of people. An example of this type of suicide is provided by the Japanese kamikaze pilot during World War II.

Suicide and Other Self-destructive Acts

A number of psychodynamic theorists have viewed suicide as an extreme example of aggression turned inward. Menninger (1938), for example, proposed that suicide and alcoholism should be regarded as self-destructive acts falling along a continuum of severity. The available evidence, however, suggests that if suicide and alcoholism are associated, it is probably because each is associated with depression. Even on this latter point, however, it should be noted that an association between alcoholism and depression has not been firmly established. The vast majority of depressives are not alcoholic, and many alcoholics do not show overt depressive features. In brief, Menninger's suggestion that drug abuse and suicide are related is based largely on theoretical psychodynamic considerations and has yet to be supported by solid empirical evidence. Nevertheless, it is plausible to assume that many depressives turn to alcohol and other drugs as a means of escaping from their misery.

SUMMARY

Pathological moods are either depressive or manic in character. Depression is among the most common forms of abnormality, whereas mania is relatively rare.

The signs of depression and mania vary along affective, cognitive, behavioral (motor), and physical dimensions. Common signs of depression are listed in Table 14-1. The signs of mania are generally the opposite of those of depression.

A number of classification systems for subtyping depression have been proposed. Two of the more commonly used distinctions are between exogenous and endogenous depression and between neurotic and psychotic depression. Theoretically, the exogenous-endogenous distinction is based on etiology. Exogenous depression refers to depression caused by factors from outside the body, and endogenous depression refers to depression caused by factors from within the body. This distinction is problematic because there exists no solid empirical basis on which to infer exogenous or endogenous etiologies. Theoretically, the neurotic-psychotic distinction is based on symptomatology. Neurotic depression is depression associated with neurotic symptoms (anxiety), and psychotic depression is depression associated with psychotic symptoms (withdrawal, delusions, and hallucinations). Despite theoretical differences between the exogenous-endogenous and the neurotic-psychotic distinctions, the operational definitions of exogenous and neurotic depression are essentially the same, as are the operational definitions of endogenous and psychotic depression. Either exogenous or neurotic depression may be diagnosed when the depressive episode has an acute onset in an apparent reaction to some precipitating environmental event; either endogenous or psychotic depression may be diagnosed when the depressive episode has a chronic onset. Thus, despite differences in theoretical implications, the important presupposition of both distinctions is that two broad syndromes of depression can be distinguished based on whether or not the depressive episode has an acute onset in an apparent reaction to some precipitating event.

A long-standing controversy exists between the continuity and discontinuity theories of depression. Continuity theory maintains that the differences between neurotic and psychotic depression are quantitative. Under this view, psychotic depression is maintained to be a more severe disorder than is neurotic depression. Discontinuity theory maintains that neurotic and psychotic depression are qualitatively different. Studies that found the same symptoms in both neurotic and psychotic depression support continuity theory. Support for discontinuity theory comes from factor analytic studies of symptomatology and from therapy outcome studies.

Two distinctions that seem to be increasing in popularity are those between primary and secondary depression and between unipolar and bipolar depression. Primary depression occurs in persons with no previous psychiatric history other than depression or mania; secondary depression occurs in persons with a previous history of psychopathology other than depression or mania. Bipolar mood disorder is diagnosed either when both depressive and manic phases occur or when only manic phases are present; unipolar mood disorder is diagnosed when manic episodes do not occur.

DSM-II classifies depressive syndromes as either a functional psychosis, a neurosis, or a personality disorder. Involutional melancholia and manic depression are classified as psychotic syndromes. Involutional melancholia is defined as depression occurring during female menopause or male climacteric. There presently does not exist sufficient reason to consider involutional melancholia a distinct syndrome even though it is so considered under DSM-II. The salient diagnostic feature of the manic-depressive syndrome is the presence of mood swings. These swings may be from depression to normal mood, from mania to normal mood, or from depression to mania.

Demographic studies indicate that in the United States many more women than men are diagnosed as depressed and that race and socioeconomic status are probably not associated with depression.

The psychoanalytic theory of depression proposes that real or imagined precipitating events (e.g., failure, loss, criticism, stressful success) interact with predisposing personality traits (dependency, low self-esteem, hostility, high achievement and social strivings) to produce depression. The predisposing personality traits are hypothesized to be consequences of early childhood experiences. The hypothesized dynamics by which depression actually occurs differ depending on the theorist. Abraham (1911) proposed that frustration of dependency needs leads to a partial regression to the oral stage of development and to the arousal of oral conflicts between dependency needs and hostility toward those who gratify dependency needs. Because the expression of hostility toward others would further frustrate dependency needs by causing rejection from others, the hostile impulses are turned inward and released against the self. Freud (1917) proposed that the individual regresses partially to the oral stage of development in order to incorporate the lost love object; in individuals who have ambivalent love-hate feelings toward the lost love object, incorporation of the object into the ego results in the release of hostility against the self.

The psychoanalytic theory of depression has been widely criticized. It is important to distinguish, however, between different levels of hypothesis in psychoanalytic theory. One level of hypothesis concerns the personality traits associated with depression. The available evidence can be summarized as follows: (1) low self-esteem is clearly associated with depression; there is solid but less conclusive evidence that hostility is associated with depression; and there are some interesting hypotheses that interpersonal hostility is often a defense against depression; (2) there is some evidence that dependency may be associated with depression, but much more research is needed to evaluate this possibility; and (3) the evidence pertaining to possible associations between high achievement and social strivings and depression is contradictory and problematic. Another level of hypothesis within psychoanalytic theory concerns the precipitating events that lead to depression. These hypotheses are largely supported by clinical observations. A third level of hypothesis concerns the origin of the predisposing personality traits in childhood experiences. Although there exists some cross-cultural data suggesting that early childhood experiences can lead to adult personality traits, the specifics of the psychoanalytic theory of development have yet to be confirmed and are difficult to test empirically. Finally, a fourth level of hypothesis concerns the dynamics by which depression results from predisposing personality factors interacting with precipitating events. These dynamic hypotheses are the weakest ones in the psychoanalytic theory of depression and have been criticized as being metatheoretical and empirically untestable.

Separation from social units is one particular type of loss that has been studied systematically. Research with both animal and human infants indicates that separation from the mother can result in a severe (protest-despair) depressive reaction. A similar phenomenon, moreover, has been reported for separation from peers in monkeys raised with peers and without their mothers. Although the depressive reaction usually remits following reunification with the mother or the peers, circumstances may exist under which a detachment phase occurs. This detachment phase consists of a continuance of the withdrawal reaction beyond the point of reunification with the mother or the peers. Depressive reactions to social separation occur more readily in infants and children, although certain types of social separations may also lead to depressive reactions in adults.

Both Beck (1967) and Seligman and his colleagues (Seligman, 1975) have proposed that depression is essentially a cognitive disorder. Beck described a triad of cognitive patterns hypothesized to characterize depression; specifically, he proposed that depressives have an overly negative view of their environment, themselves, and the future. Seligman's learned helplessness model proposes that depression is caused by a belief that one is helpless to control the important events in one's life. This model also maintains that exposures to uncontrollable traumatic events cause learned helplessness and depression. Evidence supporting the learned helplessness model comes from both animal and human studies. The animal studies have shown that exposure to uncontrollable, unpleasant events (such as electric shock) can cause an impairment in subsequent avoidance learning and an extreme passivity in the face of trauma. The human studies have demonstrated that exposure to an uncontrollable, unpleasant event (e.g., an unpleasant tone or failure) can cause a temporary delay in subsequent learning to avoid unpleasant events as well as low mood and mild hostility.

Beck's model proposes that depressives attribute failure to themselves, whereas Seligman's model proposes that depressives tend to view their behavior as unrelated to success and failure. The preliminary evidence available thus far supports Beck's view that depressives tend to blame themselves for negative events more than do nondepressives. Much more evidence, however, is needed to evaluate both Beck's and Seligman's hypotheses.

Ferster's (1966, 1973) reinforcement theory of depression proposes that depression may result from any of the following events: (1) a high level of exposure to aversive events or to the need to avoid aversive events; (2) a low level of positive reinforcement; (3) a sudden change in the environment resulting in the loss of a discriminative stimulus that controls a large amount of behavior; (4) exposure to reinforcement schedules that require a large amount of work to earn reinforcement; and (5) expressions of interpersonal anger in a manner that annoys other people. There is some evidence to support this theory as well as some evidence that may prove problematic for the theory. More research is needed to evaluate the theory properly.

Depression seems to be associated with a number of biochemical abnormalities. Norepinephrine, serotonin, acetylcholine, glucose, and various steroids all have been hypothesized to have an etiological role in depression. The norepinephrine (or catecholamine) hypothesis maintains (1) that at least some types of depression are caused by deficiencies in the amount of norepinephrine at or near nerve cell endings in the adrenergic system and (2) that mania is caused by an excess of norepinephrine at these sites. The imbalance hypothesis proposes that the critical biochemical factor in depression is the ratio of adrenergic (especially norepinephrine) to cholinergic (acetylcholine) neurotransmitter substances at critical sites in the central nervous system. There is evidence to support these hypotheses, but as yet the hypotheses are far from proven.

The hypothesis that manic-depression has a genetic component is virtually proven. There is insufficient evidence, however, to draw any conclusions regarding a possible genetic component to other types of depression, particularly neurotic (reactive) depression.

Aksikal and McKinney (1973) attempted to integrate the various areas of research on the causes of depression by proposing a unified hypothesis. This theory maintains that the common etiological factor in the depressive syndromes is a reversible disorder of neurological mechanisms believed to control the reinforcement process. Although the theory does serve to remind us that a complete account of depressive etiology will probably need to take into account psychological, biochemical, genetic, and neurological factors, the specifics of the model are far from proven.

Severe depression is usually treated by either antidepressant drugs or ECT. Behavior therapy may include relaxation training and encouraging clients to spend a greater proportion of their time in relatively pleasant activities. Psychotherapy is particularly difficult with severely depressed people.

Anywhere between 25,000 and 75,000 Americans commit suicide each year. Although no particular suicidal personality has been identified, many investigators have attempted to identify factors that predict suicide. Previous suicide attempts, depression, hopelessness, social isolation, maleness, and being a college student are all associated with increased risk of suicide. Although some people threaten suicide to gain attention, most people who actually committed suicide had in one way or another communicated either their intent or their concern with death. All factors considered, however, it is hazardous to try to predict who will and who will not commit suicide.

Much of the theoretical work on suicide is concerned with suicide motivation. Perhaps the most typical motivation for suicide is to escape or to avoid suffering. Other motives for suicide may include an attempt to gain attention or fame, altruism, and compliance with cultural norms.

Chapter 15

The Schizophrenic Syndromes

Schizophrenia has attracted scientists in disciplines ranging from molecular biology and mathematics to anthropology, sociology, and the science of ecology. New techniques and developments in related and unrelated sciences have been applied to schizophrenic patients and to this area of research. Almost every conceivable model for explaining the various inexplicable aspects of schizophrenia has been investigated, not only for the patient but even for the observer, in an attempt to explain the phenomena in question. Nonetheless, the information collected has turned out to be more useful to the sciences mentioned than to the unraveling of the mystery that is schizophrenia.

SALZINGER (1973, p. 5)

The term *schizophrenia* refers to a heterogeneous group of psychotic thought disorders that collectively constitute one of the most prevalent forms of psychopathology in the United States today. Schizophrenia is an extremely disabling disorder, often indicated by bizarre behavior, disordered thoughts, and inappropriate moods. Two chapters are devoted to a discussion of these disorders. Because the reader may not have a concrete understanding of what schizophrenic behaviors are like, our discussion begins with two case histories.

CASE HISTORIES

Emile Kraepelin, the great German psychiatrist, collected thousands of detailed case histories from individuals suffering from psychotic thought disorders. The first case history provided is from one of Kraepelin's (1896) lectures; the second case history is from Leonard Eron's files.

Schizophrenia with Hebephrenic Symptoms

The case history that follows is from E. Kraepelin, Dementia Praecox (Insanity of adolescence), in C. E. Goshen (Ed.), Documentary History of Psychiatry, *New York: Philosophical Library Inc., 1967, pp. 200–210, and is reprinted with permission of the publisher. The material is not set off in smaller print because of its length.*

Gentlemen: You have before you today a strongly built and well-nourished man, aged twenty-one, who entered the hospital a few weeks ago. He sits quietly looking in front of him, and does not raise his eyes when he is spoken to, but evidently understands all our questions very well, for he answers quite relevantly, though slowly and often only after repeated questioning. From his brief remarks, made in a low tone, we gather that he thinks he is ill, without getting any more precise information about the nature of the illness and its symptoms. The patient attributes his malady to the onanism he has practised since he was ten years old. He thinks that he has thus incurred the guilt of a sin against the sixth commandment, has very much reduced his power of working, has made himself feel languid and miserable, and has become a hypochondriac. Thus, as the result of reading certain books, he imagined that he had a rupture and suffered from wasting of the spinal cord, neither of which was the case. He would not associate with his comrades any longer, because he thought they saw the result of his vice and made fun of him. The patient makes all these statements in an indifferent tone, without looking up or troubling about his surroundings. His expression betrays no emotion; he only laughs for a moment now and then. There is occasional wrinkling of the forehead or facial spasms. Round the mouth and nose a fine, changing twitching is constantly observed.

The patient gives us a correct account of his past experiences. His knowledge speaks for the high degree of his education: indeed, he was ready to enter the University a year ago. He also knows where he is and how long he has been here, but he is only very imperfectly acquainted with the names of the people 'round him, and says that he has never asked about them. He can only give a very meagre account of the general events of the last year. In answer to our questions, he declares that he is ready to remain in the hospital for the present. He would certainly prefer it if he could enter a profession, but he cannot say what he would like to take up. No physical disturbances can be definitely made out, except exaggerated knee-jerks.

At first sight, perhaps the patient reminds you of the states of depression which we have learned to recognize in former lectures. But on closer examination you will easily understand that, in spite of certain isolated points of resemblance, we have to deal with a disease having features of quite another kind. The patient makes his statements slowly and in monosyllables, not because his wish to answer meets with overpowering hindrances, but because he feels no desire to speak at all. He certainly hears and understands what is said to him very well, but he does not take the trouble to attend to it. He pays no heed, and answers whatever occurs to him without thinking. No visible effort of the will is to be noticed. All his movements are languid and expressionless, but are made without hindrance or trouble. There is no sign of emotional dejection, such as one would expect from the nature of his talk, and the patient remains quite dull throughout, experiencing neither fear nor hope nor desires. He is not at all deeply affected by what goes on before him, although he understands it without actual difficulty. It is all the same to him who appears or disappears where he is, or who talks to him and takes care of him, and he does not even once ask their names.

This peculiar and fundamental want of any *strong feeling of the impressions of life,* with unimpaired ability to understand and to remember, is really the diagnostic symptom of the disease we have before us. It becomes still plainer if we observe the patient for a time, and see that, in spite of his good education, he lies in bed for weeks and months, or sits about without feeling the slightest need of occupation. He broods, staring in front of him with expressionless features, over which a vacant smile occasionally plays, or at the best turns over the leaves of a book for a moment, apparently speechless, and not troubling about anything. Even when he has visitors, he sits without showing any interest, does not ask about what is happening at home, hardly even greets his parents, and goes back indifferently to the ward. He can hardly be induced to write a letter, and says that he has nothing to write about. But he occasionally composes a letter to the doctor, expressing all kinds of distorted, half-formed ideas, with a peculiar and silly play on words, in very fair style, but with little connection. He begs for "a little more *allegro* in the treatment," and "liberationary movement with a view to the widening of the horizon," will "*ergo* extort some wit in lectures," and "*nota bene* for God's sake only does not wish to be combined with the club of the harmless." "Professional work is the balm of life."

These scraps of writing, as well as his statements that he is pondering over the world, or putting himself together a moral philosophy, leave no doubt that, besides the emotional barrenness, there is also a high degree of *weakness* of *judgment* and *flightiness,* although the pure memory has suffered little, if at all. We have a *mental and emotional infirmity* to deal with, which reminds us only outwardly of the states of depression previously described. This infirmity is the incurable outcome of a very common history of disease, to which we will provisionally give the name of *Dementia Praecox.*

The development of the illness has been quite gradual. Our patient, whose parents suffered transitorily from "dejection," did not go to school 'till he was seven years old, as he was a delicate child and spoke badly, but when he did he learned quite well. He was considered to be a reserved and stubborn child. Having practiced onanism at a very early age, he became more and more solitary in the last few years, and thought that he was laughed at by his brothers and sisters, and shut out from society because of his ugliness. For this reason he could not bear a looking-glass in his room. After passing the written examination on leaving school, a year ago, he gave up the *viva voce,* because he could not work any longer. He cried a great deal, masturbated much, ran about aimlessly, played in a senseless way on the piano, and began to write observations "On the Nerve-play of Life," which he cannot get on with. He was incapable of any kind of work, even physical, felt "done for," asked for a revolver, ate Swedish matches to destroy himself, and lost all affection for his family. From time to time he became excited and troublesome, and shouted out of the window at night. In the hospital, too, a state of excitement lasting for several days was observed, in which he chattered in a confused way, made faces, ran about at full speed, wrote disconnected scraps of composition, and crossed and recrossed them with flourishes and unmeaning combinations of letters. After this a state of tranquillity ensued, in which he could give absolutely no account of his extraordinary behavior.

Besides the mental and emotional imbecility, we meet with other very significant features in the case before us. The first of these is the silly, vacant *laugh,* which is constantly observed in dementia praecox. There is no joyous humor corresponding to this laugh: indeed, some patients complain that they cannot help laughing, without feeling at all inclined to laugh. Other important symptoms are *making faces* or grimacing and the fine muscular twitching in the face which is also very characteristic of dementia praecox. Then we must notice the tendency to peculiar, distorted turns of speech—*senseless playing with syllables and words*—as it often assumes very extraordinary forms in this disease. Lastly, I may call your attention to the fact that, when you offer him your hand, the patient does not grasp it, but only *stretches his own hand out stiffly to meet it.* Here we have the first sign of a disturbance which is often developed in dementia praecox in the most astounding way.

This marks the end of the direct quotation.

Henry Fisher: Chronic, Paranoid Schizophrenic

Henry Fisher, seen for the first time by a mental health professional at the age of 28, had exhibited paranoid ideas, occasional unusual behavior, and some withdrawal from social contacts since adolescence. At the age of 16, he reported being persecuted by classmates who were attempting to use sharp instruments to hurt him, and he was quite agitated and withdrawn. The episode lasted one week, was followed by a normal period about six months in duration, and then was repeated more frequently, occurring about once every two weeks and lasting for several days.

With the help and protection of his family, Henry graduated from both high school and trade school and was employed as an aircraft mechanic until he lost his job two years prior to hospital admission. In his early 20s he would imagine people were after him and would climb trees to get away from them; at work he felt spied on by the FBI and feared association with workers who had Russian-sounding names.

After losing his job he lived at home, accomplishing little and existing with no apparent direction. His chief interest was research on his family tree, and he was attempting to gather all of the possessions of a deceased uncle in order to reconstruct the family homestead. Just prior to the exacerbation of his symptoms, relatives had been trying to introduce him to an older, single woman, and he had been talking about getting married. At this time symptomatology became more severe; in the two months before he was admitted to a psychiatric hospital, Henry had four episodes of overtalkativeness, inability to sleep, irrationality, and flight of ideas. He was hospitalized because he was increasingly becoming a nuisance at home.

The admitting psychiatrist described Henry as "a tall young man who holds himself rigidly and speaks stiffly with little facial movement." He seemed tense but controlled, and he did not believe anything was wrong with him but came to the hospital voluntarily on the advice of his doctor, whom he respected. His thought content was incomprehensible. Paranoid delusions, but no hallucinations, were present. Physical and neurological examinations as well as laboratory studies were essentially negative.

Thought disturbance was evident in his responses to the Rorschach inkblots. Henry's thought associations were pedantic, pseudoscientific, inappropriately precise, redundant, and occasionally grandiose. Moreover, he was overly concerned with the symbolic significance of the stimuli. The following excerpt from his response to one Rorschach inkblot illustrates the nature of his associations as well as his tendency toward overinclusion, interpenetration of ideas, neologisms, stilted speech, and defensiveness:

> This is rather difficult. May I ask a question? Can I look at it only in the horizontal plane? The outline of a butterfly is a possibility. Before we go further, I want to mention that in high school I studied agriculture and I may take postgraduate work. My technical training gave me a mathematical background, but I don't notice any pronounced differences between halves of the inkblot. Again, I think the red-white outline is of different distinctions, the fact that red and black have different meanings in most designs. I am quite interested in colors because each color as I've carried on my learning in relation to human anatomy have their order of importance. Red represents most important and lighter shades have tendency to represent lesser important and possibly secretionary importance and lighter grey represents cavity and passages. Because I mention it, it is a blueprint which can be very complicated representing flow of gases—oxygen and nitrogen. Have to base indexes on patterns they represent. I haven't studied the designs too much but it interests me because it amazes me how you can get so much on

Schizophrenia is indicated by extremely disordered thought patterns and bizarre behavior. (Photo by Henriques; Magnum Photos, Inc.)

one piece of paper. I admire Mr. Lindbergh though I know very little about him. He's contributed to science as well as the field he's publicized in.

Diagnostic formulation indicated that Henry had a schizoid personality since early childhood. He was always withdrawn, shy, obedient, and submissive and had great difficulty in relating to his mother, a very religious person who was a primary grade teacher in the same school Henry attended. His father was a cold, distant, moralistic disciplinarian. Moreover, both parents set extremely high goals for Henry—goals he could not meet. He had an acute breakdown at the time of puberty when he was unable either to relate to his peers or to excel in his scholastic endeavors. In the protected environment furnished by his parents he was able to make a marginal adjustment; when, however, he felt that he was being pushed toward marriage and might have to assume adult responsibilities, he again suffered a breakdown and had to be hospitalized. The following story from his Thematic Apperception Test protocol reflects the extent of his apprehension about growing up and assuming adult responsibilities:

> This represents the challenge of youth—challenge we must all face towards establishing daily living through family—also presents the challenge of temptation, of becoming self-centered. The expressions show they're looking forward to greater way of living—they're looking forward to the challenge presented to everyone—life work is to further the family circle, try to meet the challenge of having children of their own, perhaps—challenge of sacrifice—point of—presents a personal challenge to me —problems of average person; when they consider marriage and relations of people as a group. Background represents home atmosphere—shelter and home and eternal challenge of striving for what is right and what we base our religion on. Religion itself is a great challenge. I feel that challenge even more because of my religious background and training.

In the hospital Henry was shy, reticent, and somewhat asocial, often sitting alone and looking out a window. When he was discharged two weeks after his admission, his parents were advised to permit him to putter around with as little strain and competition as possible and not to talk of his getting married. He was successful in fixing up an old homestead that he then rented out for a modest amount of money, and he maintained himself in this simple environment without need of further hospitalization for at least ten years.

CLASSIFICATION OF SCHIZOPHRENIC SYNDROMES

Early Classificatory Systems

During the middle of the nineteenth century, a number of prominent European theorists maintained that insanity and mental retardation were caused by a "tainted heredity" (Zilboorg & Henry, 1941). The French physician Morel (1809–1873), a leading exponent of this view, developed detailed tables of diagnostic signs for identifying the presence of hereditary weaknesses. One such weakness was the "degenerative trait"; specifically, it was postulated that in each successive generation of a degenerative line, the manifest symptoms of the tainted heredity were progressively more debilitating. In 1860 Morel applied the term *demence precoce* to a case of "stupidity" that degenerated into insanity. From this phrase, the term *dementia praecox* came into use, indicating that the disorder was an illness of youth. Other early developments included Kahlbaum's (1863) description of a deteriorating psychosis of puberty that he called paraphrenia hebetica, Kahlbaum's (1874) isolation of a disorder that he called *spannungsirrsein* (catatonia), and Hecker's delineation of a psychosis called hebephrenia (Bumke, 1932).

Toward the end of the nineteenth century, Kraepelin published case histories and statistical charts to differentiate two major categories of insanity, *dementia praecox* and *manic-depressive psychosis.* The primary basis for this distinction was that dementia praecox was believed to be incurable and to be caused by internal, constitutional factors (endogenous causation), whereas manic-depressive psychosis was believed to cure itself naturally and to be caused by external factors (exogenous causation). Three subtypes of dementia praecox were distinguished: *catatonia* (indicated by symptoms of muscular spasms, stuporous states, and occasional violence), *hebephrenia* (a puberty psychosis that rapidly deteriorates into silly, grossly inappropriate behavior), and *paranoia* (indicated by delusions of persecution). Thus Kraepelin's major contribution was to perceive the similarities among these various syndromes, classifying them as subtypes of a single disease rather than as different diseases. As impressive as Kraepelin's detailed observations were, his prognostic approach of defining disease states in terms of their eventual outcomes (curable versus incurable), and his belief that these various disorders either somehow cured themselves or could not be cured at all, were widely criticized. But of all the criticisms, the one that seems in retrospect to merit special attention was that raised by Serbski (see Zilboorg & Henry, 1941, p. 457). This critic called attention to the fact that Kraepelin's own data reported a recovery rate of about 13 per cent for patients suffering dementia praecox; these data are obviously inconsistent with Kraepelin's view of the disorder as involving irreversible, progressive deterioration.

During the early part of the twentieth century, Bleuler introduced the term *schizophrenia* to refer primarily to those disorders Kraepelin had called dementia praecox. The term *schizophrenia* is derived from words meaning "split soul"; in Bleuler's view the fundamental disease process is a loosening of thought associations, and this loosening is associated with a disintegration of personality functions. The key pathological process was seen as a lack of coordination of the various personality functions, or what Freud termed a disintegration in ego functioning. Perhaps Bleuler's most important contribution, however, was his emphasis on the heterogeneity of schizophrenic symptoms. In order to emphasize this diversity, he referred to the "group of schizophrenias" rather than to *the* schizophrenic disease. He also noted that schizophrenia occurs in varying degrees, thereby pointing to similarities in behavior between socially withdrawn, highly insensitive people who have not experienced a psychotic episode consisting of hallucinations and delusions and schizophrenics who display full-blown psychotic symptomatology.

Influenced by Freud's distinction between unconscious pathological processes and behavioral symptomatology, Bleuler (1950) conceptualized schizophrenia as consisting of fundamental and accessory symptoms. He discussed nine fundamental symptoms (Rosenthal, 1970; Zilboorg & Henry, 1941), five of which are discussed here.

1. *A loss of continuity in thought associations.* A salient characteristic of schizophrenia is the inability to focus on a single line of thought; intruding thoughts or bizarre changes in topic often characterize schizophrenic speech. For example, in the case of Henry Fisher, it is recalled that he responded in the following manner to a Rorschach inkblot. "The outline of a butterfly is a possibility. Before we go further, I want to mention that in high school I studied agriculture and I may take postgraduate work. . . . Again, I think the red-white outline is of different distinctions."

2. *The presence of emotional deterioration.* For example, in the case described by Kraepelin, a silly, vacant laugh was noted. Moreover, schizophrenics sometimes react with extremely inappropriate affect, such as laughing at sad events.

3. *Autism.* Bleuler introduced the concept of autism to refer to an escape from reality and a flight into fantasy. As such, autism is associated with an extreme form of social withdrawal and with a type of thought that is relatively free of environmental demands. The schizophrenic seems to be absorbed with his own world—afraid of or overwhelmed by social interaction. Laing (1967) refers to this as the schizophrenic's escape into the world of inner experience.

4. *Lack of initiative and interest.* Examples of this schizophrenic symptom include blank stares and sitting for hours in a stuporous state.

5. *Although the schizophrenic may be intelligent and may even be capable of feats of genius, he typically makes foolish mistakes in behavior or thinking.*

To this list of fundamental symptoms of schizophrenia, Bleuler added a number of accessory symptoms, such as hallucinations (visual or auditory "perceptions" of events or things that are not there, especially hearing nonexistent voices), delusions (irrational beliefs such as feelings of persecution or omnipotence, or the notion that one is George Washington or God), catatonia (peculiar motoric behaviors, including repetitive, stereotyped movements and mutism), and stuporous states. By combining the accessory and fundamental symptoms, Bleuler defined four subtypes of schizophrenia: paranoid, catatonic, hebephrenic, and simple schizophrenia. The major innovation here to Kraepelin's system was the addition of the simple type. This syndrome is indicated by the occurrence of the preceding defined fundamental symptoms in the absence of accessory symptoms.

Some historians have suggested that Bleuler's major contribution was to classify schizophrenia in terms of symptomatology, thus departing from Kraepelin's emphasis on prognosis as the basis of classification. But this view of Bleuler's contribution may be unfair to Kraepelin; in fact, Bleuler's classification of schizophrenia borrowed heavily from that of Kraepelin. In our view, Bleuler's major contributions were to call attention to the heterogeneity of schizophrenia, to suggest that the disorder can occur in varying degrees and without accessory symptoms, and to maintain that the onset of symptoms is not confined to adolescence but can occur at any age.

Meyer (1906, 1910) objected to the classification of schizophrenia on the basis of the symptomatology present at the time of hospitalization and proposed instead that these disorders be studied and classified on the basis of developmental history. He maintained that a longitudinal assessment of schizophrenics generally shows a gradual deterioration in psychological functioning resulting from an interaction of biological, psychological, and cultural factors. Although Meyer's influence was not as great as that of Kraepelin or of Bleuler, research described later in this chapter indicates that life history factors provide some of the best criteria for classifying schizophrenia into various subtypes.

DSM-II

In a manner reminiscent of Kraepelin's distinction between dementia praecox and manic-depressive psychosis, DSM-II distinguishes between schizophrenia and the major affective disorders. Schizophrenia is conceptualized primarily as a thought disorder, whereas the major affective illnesses are conceptualized primarily as mood disorders. DSM-II offers the following definition of schizophrenia:

> This large category includes a group of disorders manifested by characteristic disturbances of thinking, mood, and behavior. Disturbances of thinking are marked by alterations of concept formation which may lead to misinterpretation of reality and sometimes to delusions and hallucinations, which frequently appear psychologically self-protective. Corollary mood changes include ambivalent, constricted and inappropriate emotional responsiveness and loss of empathy with others. Behavior may be withdrawn, regressive and bizarre [American Psychiatric Association, 1968, 0.33].

Because the disorder is indicated by behavior so bizarre and identifiable, schizophrenia constitutes a relatively reliable global diagnostic category. Interrater reliability on diagnoses of schizophrenic versus nonschizophrenic disorders is especially high for individuals suffering psychotic episodes—that is, for individuals exhibiting hallucinations, delusions, or bizarre behavior. (See Chapter 1.) It is a little more difficult, however, to differentiate between a schizoid personality and schizophrenia prior to or following a psychotic episode; in both cases, the individual may appear withdrawn, nervous, and a little odd. Often the primary basis on which schizophrenia and schizoid personality are differentiated is the presence of some type of thought disturbance or bizarre behavior. For example, a shy 29-year-old unmarried individual who still lives with his parents and who relies on them for support might be diagnosed as schizoid, but the diagnosis is likely to be schizophrenia if the individual laughs in reaction to pain in other people or in animals or if the individual expresses bizarre ideas.

As the previous discussion indicated, schizophrenia includes an exceptionally heterogeneous group of symptoms, ranging from autism to inappropriate laughter, feelings of persecution, delusions, and hallucinations. DSM-II identifies eleven subtypes, ten of which are presented in Box 15-1. (The eleventh

BOX 15-1
DSM-II Subtypes for Schizophrenia

Simple type: Gradual withdrawal from social situations and increasing apathy to the environment; hallucinations and delusions are not present except in deteriorated states.
Hebephrenic type: Disorganized thinking and inappropriate affect (laughing, giggling, crying, baby talk) with no apparent, appropriate cause.
Catatonic type—(1) *excited:* Excessive excitement and motor activity; inappropriate affect; (2) *withdrawn:* Extreme retardation in motor and verbal behavior; inappropriate affect.
Paranoid type: Persecutory or grandiose delusions; disorganized thought processes; possible hallucinations.
Acute episode: Sudden onset of confusion, delusions, or hallucinations; if condition lingers, diagnosis may be changed to another subcategory.
Latent type: Some signs of thought disorder, occasional confusion, mild withdrawal; no obvious psychotic episode; can care for oneself.
Residual type: Some signs of thought disorder in a person who has had at least one previous psychotic episode.
Schizo-affective type: Schizophrenia is usually associated with "flat" affect; the occurrence of mood disorder in people who also show schizophrenic symptoms, therefore, is given a special diagnosis, schizo-affective type.
Childhood type: Thought disorder, hallucinations, and/or severe withdrawal prior to the age of puberty.
Chronic undifferentiated type: Mixture of behaviors associated with several of the subcategories for schizophrenia.

subtype is "other than those listed above" and does not merit our attention.) The four subtypes that have been studied most extensively are paranoid, hebephrenic, catatonic, and simple.

Paranoid Type

Paranoid schizophrenia, the most common subtype, is indicated by the presence of thought disturbance and delusions of persecution. Hallucinations, especially auditory ones, are common (Arieti, 1959). Grandiosity and associated feelings of omnipotence are sometimes present. Moreover, paranoid schizophrenics are frequently suspicious, as exemplified in the following interchange reported by Kleinmuntz:

> Doctor: Can I get you to join the group therapy session this afternoon? You know, Herbert, you're the only holdout from among the guys on your ward.
> Patient: So be it doc, so be it. You're not gonna get me in one of those crazy groups. I got enough troubles keeping away from those guys as is.
> Doctor: Why do you want to do that?
> Patient: They're fixing to get rid of me. [1974, p. 267]

A phenomenological aspect of schizophrenia is confusion. These people, in warning of the coming of the Great Confusion, seem to be predicting mass paranoid schizophrenia. (Photo by Charles Gatewood; Magnum Photos, Inc.)

In paranoid schizophrenia, the onset of symptomatology may occur at any time between adolescence and the fifth decade of life (Arieti, 1959). Research on the distinction between paranoid and nonparanoid schizophrenia is discussed later in this chapter.

Hebephrenic Type

The hebephrenic type of schizophrenia is associated with grandiose delusions and with inappropriate affect, including laughter, giggling, and smiling. Hypochondriacal ideas and preoccupation with body image are common (Arieti, 1959). The patient's condition sometimes deteriorates to an extremely regressed state that may include bedwetting, sloppy personal habits, and screaming. It is often difficult to distinguish between hebephrenic and paranoid types of schizophrenia (Arieti, 1959).

Catatonic Type

The catatonic type of schizophrenia is readily distinguishable from the other types. In addition to hallucinations and delusions, catatonic schizophrenia is associated with mood fluctuations between a state of agitation sometimes characterized by aimless activity and a state of extreme apathy. During this latter state, called *catatonic stupor,* the patient may assume a fixed posture for hours; he may not talk, eat, or dress himself, and he may be totally unresponsive to his environment. For example, Arieti (1959, p. 463) reported a case of a 24-year-old male who had been brooding excessively about his life. A few days after admission to the hospital, he was found in a statuesque pose with his legs contorted in an awkward position. In this position, he was unresponsive to those who attempted to talk to him, his face revealed no emotion, and he had to be fed by others.

Simple Schizophrenia

Simple schizophrenia usually begins during adolescence and develops gradually. The individual progressively withdraws from his social environment, becoming apathetic, listless, and indifferent. He may avoid dating, refuse to go to school or to work, and possibly even refuse to leave home. Hallucinations and delusions are usually absent. Furthermore, this form of schizophrenia is generally less debilitating than are the other types.

Evaluation of DSM-II Subtypes

Although, as noted previously, there is good reliability in diagnosing gross psychotic syndromes, agreement among different diagnosticians on schizophrenia subcategory classifications (interrater reliability) is generally very low for the DSM-II system. This is largely because there is considerable overlapping in symptomatology among the categories. An interesting study by Blashfield (1973) found that the system has the greatest reliability where classification

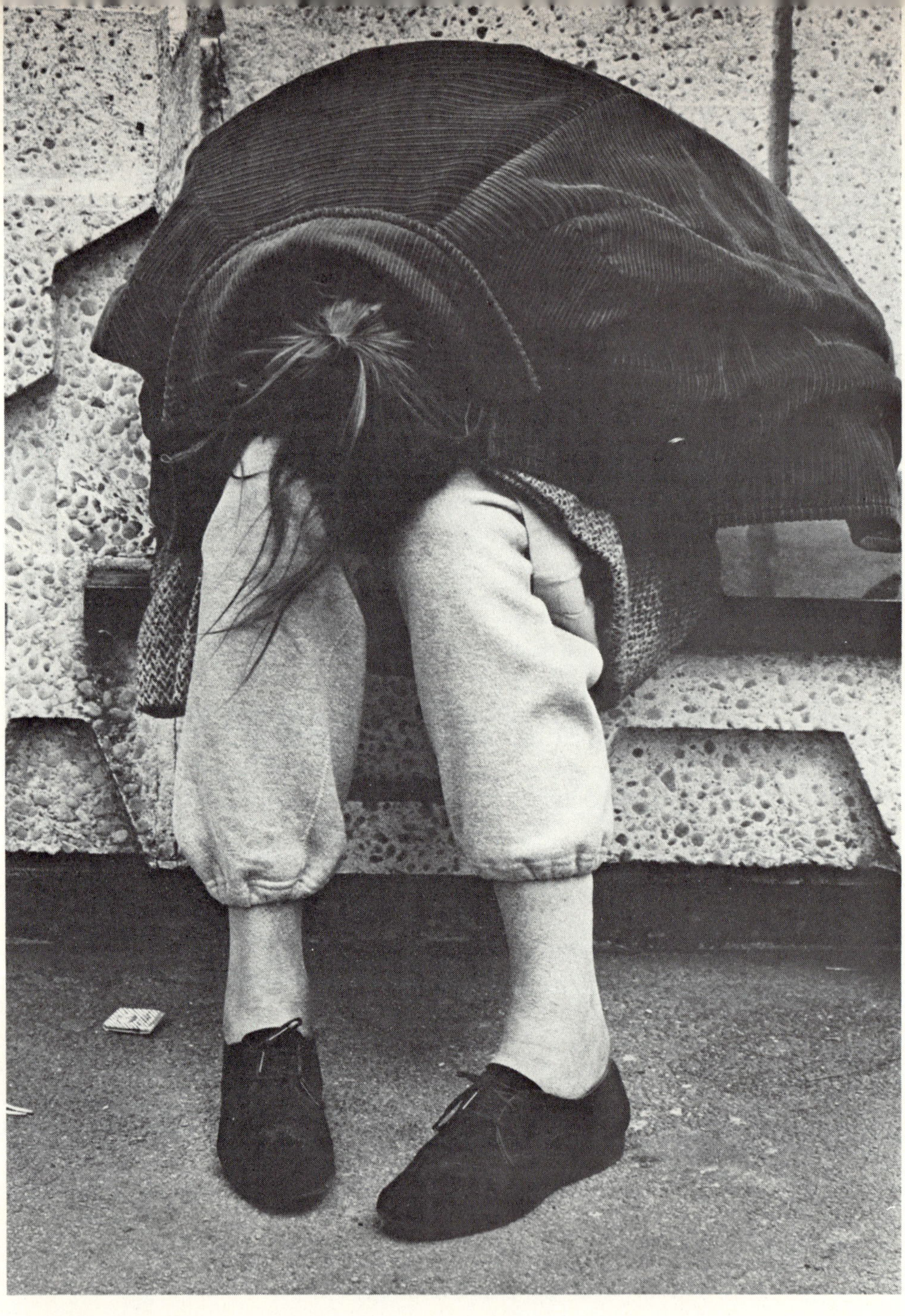

Catatonic schizophrenia is often characterized by a complete withdrawal and loss of responsiveness to one's environment. (Photo by Dave Healey; Magnum Photos, Inc.)

categories describe the most unusual behaviors; that is, the system seems most reliable for those subtypes that occur least frequently. In addition to low interrater reliability, the subcategories lack demonstrated validity, having failed to result in unambiguous differences in prognosis or in indicated treatment. In brief, there appears to be little value to the DSM-II subcategories of schizophrenia (Blashfield, 1973; Phillips & Draguns, 1971; Zubin, 1967) even though the system is widely used.

Factor Analytic Research

The trend in classification has been toward greater objectivity both in the assessment of the patient's behavior (see Gunderson, Autry, Mosher, & Buchsbaum, 1974) and in the construction of the subtype categories. By feeding coded case-history data into a computer programmed to perform a factor analysis, investigators have been able to isolate ten major clusterings, or dimensions, of schizophrenia (Lorr, 1966, 1968; Lorr & Klett, 1969; Lorr, McNair, Klett, & Lasky, 1962; Martorano & Nathan, 1972; Wittenborn, 1955; Wittenborn & Smith, 1964). By rating patients along these dimensions and by analyzing these data, the investigators have attempted to identify actual subtypes of schizophrenia. Thus far this factor-analytic work has yielded a number of subtype categories, and these categories have been shown to have satisfactory reliability. The system, however, is used rarely, in part because it is complicated, in part because it is new, and in part because it has yet to be shown to be valid. This work is nevertheless promising and eventually may produce a valid classification system.

Classificatory Distinctions in Research Studies

In an effort to specify psychological deficits associated with schizophrenia, researchers have compared the performance of schizophrenic and normal persons on a variety of experimental tasks. Results have often been contradictory. In some studies significant differences have been found between the average scores of schizophrenics and normals on an experimental task; in other studies schizophrenic subjects have done as well as normals on the same or similar experimental tasks for which other research showed differences. How can such inconsistent results be accounted for? A hypothetical example will be considered. Suppose an investigator is interested in demonstrating that schizophrenics are deficient in their ability to communicate with others. Furthermore, suppose that a study is devised in which each subject must describe an object from a set of three objects so that someone listening to this description can correctly identify the object described. The number of correct identifications by the listener is interpreted as an objective measure of the speaker's ability to communicate. The hypothetical results of such a study are presented in Table 15-1. An inspection of the results provided in display A of Table 15-1 suggests that all of the normal subjects performed well on the task, obtaining scores between 7 and 10, and that some schizophrenics did as well as the normals, whereas other schizophrenics did very poorly. The variability within the schizophrenic group is so great that the finding of a lower average performance for schizophrenics is difficult to interpret. Suppose, however, that some

TABLE 15-1
Hypothetical Results of Study Comparing Performances of Schizophrenic and Normal Subjects on a Laboratory Task

	Display A		Display B		
	Normal	Schizophrenic	Normal	Schizophrenic Type X	Schizophrenic Type Y
	7	8	7	3	8
	7	3	7	1	10
	9	10	9	2	7
	8	1	8	1	9
	10	7	10	2	9
	7	9	7		
	8	2	8		
	8	9	8		
	7	1	7		
	10	2	10		
Mean	8.10	5.20	8.10	1.80	8.60
Standard deviation	1.20	3.71	1.20	0.84	1.14

independent classificatory distinction can be made within the schizophrenic group so that we can distinguish between schizophrenia type X and schizophrenia type Y in a manner shown in display B of Table 15-1. If the X–Y distinction significantly reduces the within-group variance, as it does in display B, then the investigator can reasonably conclude that communication deficits are associated with type X schizophrenia but not with type Y schizophrenia.

Research investigators use the classificatory distinctions of process and reactive schizophrenia, paranoid and nonparanoid schizophrenia, and acute and chronic schizophrenia. In general, the popularity of these distinctions is attributable to the reduction in within-group variability obtained in experiments in which they are employed and to the consequent increase in the interpreta bility of the results of these experiments.

Reactive and Process Schizophrenia

As noted previously, Meyer was the earliest theorist of this century to suggest that schizophrenia be classified on the basis of life history factors rather than on the basis of symptoms exhibited at the time of hospitalization. It was not until the 1950s, however, that a schizophrenic's adjustment prior to the onset of symptomatology, called *premorbid* (predisease) adjustment, was used as an important basis for classifying schizophrenia (Feffer & Phillips, 1953; Kantor, Wallner, & Winder, 1953). The classificatory distinction that is based on premorbid adjustment differentiates reactive and process schizophrenia (Kantor & Herron, 1966).

In *reactive schizophrenia* symptoms are believed to develop in response to some life stress or crisis. Hence the reactive schizophrenic is an individual who shows relatively normal psychosocial adjustment prior to the onset of symptomatology—he shows normal physical health, has normal siblings, is accepted by his family, adjusts well to school, and shows a relatively normal degree of interest in others, in school activities, and in the opposite sex (Kantor et al., 1953). Although a psychotic episode typically occurs during adolescence or early adulthood, symptom onset is typically acute, and the individual usually responds well to treatment. In contrast, *process schizophrenia* is believed to develop gradually and not in reaction to any temporary or identifiable life stress or crisis. The process schizophrenic shows a poor premorbid psychosocial adjustment. He may be rejected by his family, have an overprotective mother, be introverted as a child, adjust poorly to school, or show little interest in school. In brief, social withdrawal during the developmental years is much greater in process schizophrenia than in reactive schizophrenia.

Some investigators tend to view the reactive-process distinction as dichotomous, whereas others tend to view it as defining two end points on a continuum. Those who view the distinction as an "either-or" dichotomy generally do so because they suspect that reactive schizophrenia is precipitated by environmental factors and that process schizophrenia is determined more by biological factors. Those who view the reactive-process distinction as continuous (e.g., Garmezy & Rodnick, 1959) usually do so because they believe that very few schizophrenics can be classified as pure reactive schizophrenics or as pure process schizophrenics; rather, these theorists maintain that most schizophrenics can be classified at some point between these extremes.

As noted previously, the process-reactive distinction has received wide acceptance because of its demonstrated value in many research studies. Specifically, many early studies compared normals and schizophrenics on a variety of experimental tasks. Typically, the schizophrenics would show a wide range of performances on these tasks (see Bellak, 1948, pp. 445–447), thereby rendering interpretation of the results very difficult. By classifying schizophrenic subjects along the reactive-process continuum, however, it has often been possible to obtain more consistent results.

A number of studies have confirmed clinical impressions that reactive schizophrenia is a less severe disorder than process schizophrenia. Compared to process schizophrenics, reactive schizophrenics exhibit a higher level of thought process (Kilburg & Siegel, 1973), superior ability to perform abstract tasks (Watson, 1973), more reaction to environmental threat (Sappington, 1975), and better integrated perceptions (Kantor & Herron, 1966). Moreover, Phillips (1953) reported that reactive schizophrenics respond better to treatment than do process schizophrenics, whereas Depue and Dubicki (1974) found that withdrawn (largely process) schizophrenics are hospitalized at a younger age and spend more of their lives in a psychiatric facility than do nonwithdrawn (largely reactive) schizophrenics.

DeWolfe (1974) discussed the possibility that qualitative differences exist in thought deficits shown by process and reactive schizophrenics. In this theoretical view, process schizophrenia is characterized by poor cognitive development, idiosyncratic thought, and an underresponsiveness to task demands. On the other hand, reactive schizophrenia is characterized by a fragmentation of relatively normal thinking resulting from stress or acute disturbance; this fragmentation of normal thinking is expressed by an overresponsiveness to task relevant information and to task demands. This model further allows for process schizophrenics to show thought fragmentation when they are under stress. As DeWolfe noted, this theory is tentative and requires more extensive testing.

A number of scales have been devised to assess schizophrenia along the reactive-process dimension, the most widely used of these being the Phillips Scale of Premorbid Adjustment (Phillips, 1953). Items on this scale concern recent sexual life, adolescent sexual life, and social aspects of sexual life. Garfield (1967) suggested that the Phillips scale is redundant, measuring little more than whether or not the individual is married; however, Farina (1967) has disagreed with this view. Other scales are available (Ullmann & Giovannoni, 1964; Wittman, 1944; Zigler & Phillips, 1962). For example, an abbreviated form of the Phillips scale with good reliability and validity has been developed by Harris (1975). The original five-section scale is reduced to two sections: premorbid sexual adjustment and premorbid personal-social adjustment.

An important methodological issue was recently raised by Wagener and Hartsough (1974). These investigators noted that in studies comparing the performances of process schizophrenics and normals on experimental tasks, deficits observed in the disturbed subjects may be attributable to premorbid adjustment rather than to schizophrenia. The appropriate control condition for such studies would be to compare the performances of process schizophrenics to those of process normals—that is, to compare schizophrenics low in social competency to normals low in social competency. In addition to raising this methodological issue, Wagener and Hartsough have presented data exemplifying its importance, thereby demonstrating that their point is more than speculation.

Paranoid and Nonparanoid Schizophrenia

Delusions of persecution, called *paranoia,* sometimes occur in conjunction with schizophrenic symptomatology and sometimes occur in the absence of such symptomatology. There has been a century of energetic debate on whether people who exhibit both paranoid and schizophrenic symptoms should be considered to suffer from a subtype of schizophrenia (e.g., paranoid schizophrenia) or from a distinct form of paranoia. As noted previously, DSM-II distinguishes a paranoid schizophrenic subtype. In this regard, it is noteworthy that Orgel (1957) found a high interrater reliability (0.95) in differentially diagnosing schizophrenics as paranoid or nonparanoid.

Cameron (1943, 1959) has provided one of the few theoretical accounts of delusions in paranoid thinking. He proposed that as a result of inadequate social learning and social development, the paranoid individual has a limited ability to understand how others think and feel. Under conditions of stress, the paranoid's ability to understand how others think and feel is further impaired, forcing him to rely on his own idiosyncratic interpretation of events. According to Cameron, this may "culminate in a conviction that he himself is the focus of a community of persons who are united in a conspiracy of some kind against him. It is this supposed functional community of real persons whom the patient can see and hear, and of other persons whom he imagines, that we call 'the paranoid pseudo-community'" (1959, p. 53). Cameron thus views the delusional system as a replacement for accurate social understanding and, once this system is formed, he sees the paranoid as reacting to a "pseudocommunity" consisting of real and imagined persons. Moreover, Cameron has suggested that the delusional system becomes a self-fulfilling prophecy; that is, once the individual treats others with distrust and attacks imagined enemies, others begin to react to him in ways that appear to confirm the delusions. Perhaps for this reason delusional systems are relatively resistant to change.[1]

The reactive–process distinction discussed previously is based on premorbid history, whereas the paranoid–nonparanoid distinction is based on symptomatology at the time of hospitalization. The question thus arises as to whether the two distinctions are related; specifically, do paranoid schizophrenics tend to have premorbid histories different from those of nonparanoid schizophrenics? In this regard psychodynamic considerations suggest that paranoids should have relatively good premorbid histories because paranoid defenses avoid a more diffuse disintegration of personality functioning by focusing anxiety on an external object or person. Empirical studies seem to provide some tentative support for this hypothesis. Although Johannsen, Friedman, Leitschuh, and Ammons (1963) found no differences in premorbid social competence between paranoids and nonparanoids, Goldstein, Held, and Cromwell (1968) and Zigler and Levine (1973) found evidence of higher levels of premorbid social competence for paranoid as compared to nonparanoid schizophrenics.

Both clinical and laboratory evidence generally support the notion that the deficits associated with paranoid schizophrenia tend to be less severe than those associated with nonparanoid schizophrenia (Broen, 1968; Deckner & Cromwell, 1970; Payne & Hewlett, 1960). For example, Youkilis and DeWolfe (1975) found that on a forced-choice word association test paranoid schizophrenics gave significantly fewer responses of the type that children produce than nonparanoid schizophrenics; this finding was interpreted as supporting a regression theory of schizophrenia.

If paranoid symptoms constitute a projection of anxiety onto others, then a paranoid should tend to deny that he is anxious even when objective evidence indicates the presence of such anxiety. In order to test this hypothesis, Shean, Faia, and Schmaltz (1974) exposed paranoids and nonparanoids to emotionally arousing slides (e.g., homicide victims, heterosexual activity, and nudes). Physiological measures were obtained to assess the extent to which the slides actually aroused the subjects. Compared to nonparanoid schizophrenics,

[1] See Chapter 19 (Abnormal Behavior in "Normal" People) for research suggesting a functional relation between delusions and prejudices.

paranoid-reactive schizophrenics tended to underrate their emotional arousal. This finding is consistent with clinical impressions that paranoids project anxiety onto others rather than acknowledge their own feelings.

Acute and Chronic Schizophrenia

The distinction between acute and chronic schizophrenia is based on how fast the schizophrenic condition develops. In acute schizophrenia, symptoms may appear in a matter of weeks; in chronic schizophrenia, symptoms gradually develop during the course of several years. The prognosis for acute schizophrenia is substantially better than that for chronic schizophrenia. Also, some evidence suggests that chronic schizophrenics show greater deficits in focusing attention on experimental tasks (Broen, 1968; Silverman, 1964a, 1964b).

The most frequently used operational definitions of acute and chronic schizophrenia presuppose that the speed of symptom onset can be inferred from the length and number of hospitalizations (Strauss, 1973). For example, three widely used operational definitions of acute schizophrenia are (1) the patient was recently admitted to a hospital for the first time; (2) the patient is a first admission to a hospital and has been there for less than a year; (3) the patient has been admitted to a hospital on several occasions but the total length of hospitalization is short (Strauss, 1973).

The distinction between acute and chronic schizophrenia has been criticized by many psychologists. One problem is that the various operational definitions yield inconsistent diagnostic results. Under one operational definition Jones is diagnosed as an acute schizophrenic, whereas under another Jones is diagnosed as a chronic schizophrenic. These inconsistencies make it difficult to interpret contradictory research findings because the meaning of the acute-chronic distinction differs across studies.

Another problem is that the validity of the acute-chronic distinction is questionable—that is, it is unclear whether the length of hospitalization is a valid measure of the length of illness. As Strauss (1973) commented, the effectiveness of drug treatment means that many patients no longer require lengthy hospitalization even though they are still schizophrenic. Thus some patients who have brief stays in a hospital should be diagnosed as drug-responsive, chronic schizophrenics rather than as acute schizophrenics.

Finally, the acute–chronic distinction is confounded with the process–reactive distinction and with the paranoid–nonparanoid distinction. Compared to chronic patients, acute schizophrenics tend to have a better premorbid adjustment and are more likely to have paranoid symptoms. Consequently, in many studies reporting differences between acute and chronic schizophrenics, the differences may be attributable to differences in premorbid adjustment or to differences in symptomatology.

Although these criticisms indicate a need for an improved operational definition of the distinction between acute and chronic schizophrenia, it should be noted that the attractiveness of the distinction is partially related to notions that schizophrenia is not a static disorder and that its developmental aspects merit study. In this context, the thrust of the preceding criticisms is that investigators utilizing the acute-chronic distinction have generally failed to study the developmental history of schizophrenia; instead they have produced a series of inconsistent findings that are often difficult to interpret. With appropriate adjustments to the criticisms that have been raised, the acute-chronic distinction may yet prove to be valuable.

Summary

Schizophrenia is a psychotic thought disorder characterized by difficulty in maintaining a single line of thought, bizarre associations, autism (social withdrawal and flight into fantasy), inappropriate affect, delusions, hallucinations, and a lack of responsiveness to the environment. Although schizophrenia is relatively easy to distinguish from other disorders discussed in this book, the extraordinary heterogeneity of symptoms shown by schizophrenics has led to several major attempts to identify various schizophrenic subtypes. One of the earliest of such attempts was made by Kraepelin, who distinguished among hebephrenic, catatonic, and paranoid psychotic thought disorders. To this list, Bleuler added simple schizophrenia. DSM-II defines eleven subtypes, but this system lacks adequate reliability and validity.

In recent years we have witnessed attempts to construct a classificatory system based on factor analytic techniques. The initial results from this work seem promising.

In order to reduce within-group variability and thereby increase the interpretability of research findings, three distinctions are widely used in experimental research. The reactive-process distinction is basically a distinction between schizophrenics with good and poor premorbid social adjustment. The paranoid–nonparanoid distinction is basically a distinction between schizophrenics who do and do not exhibit delusions. Both of these distinctions have some demonstrated validity; in general, reactive and paranoid schizophrenics are less disturbed than are process and nonparanoid schizophrenics, respectively. A distinction between acute and chronic schizophrenia is also used, although the various operational definitions of chronicity have been criticized in recent years.

INCIDENCE AND PREVALENCE

Incidence refers to the rate at which new cases develop, whereas prevalence refers to the proportion of the population who suffer from a disorder at any given time. Precise estimates of the incidence and prevalence of schizophrenia are difficult to obtain because of the absence of standard procedures for diagnosing the disorder. There is, however, little doubt that schizophrenia is an important mental health problem that occurs in both sexes throughout the world. Schizophrenia has occurred throughout history.

Overall Incidence and Prevalence in the United States

The incidence of schizophrenia in the United States has been estimated at about 150 cases per 100,000 (Crocetti & Lemkau, 1967). The prevalence of schizophrenia has been estimated variously as between 3 and 4 per cent of the general population (e.g., Heston, 1970). Many more people show schizophrenic-like symptoms even though they never have experienced a psychotic episode requiring hospitalization (Grinker & Holzman, 1973). Koh and Peterson (1974), for example, found that 18 per cent of a population of Caucasian college students with no history of psychiatric treatment could be diagnosed as mildly schizophrenic on the basis of the MMPI.

Incidence and Prevalence by Social Class

Hollingshead and Redlich (1957) reported that the incidence of schizophrenia per 100,000 population is more than three times greater for extreme lower-class Americans than for extreme upper-class Americans. They also reported a prevalence rate that is eight times greater for extreme lower-class Americans than for extreme upper-class Americans. Similar findings were obtained by Srole, Langner, Michael, Opler, and Rennie (1962) in a study of midtown Manhattan.

Although schizophrenia is associated with low socioeconomic status, especially in urban areas (Clausen & Kohn, 1959), the theoretical significance of this finding is unclear. We do not know whether schizophrenics tend to be downwardly mobile because of their schizophrenia or whether the stresses of low socioeconomic status have a causal role in the development of schizophrenia (Rosenthal, 1970). Studies relevant to this issue have obtained inconsistent results (Dunham, 1965; Hollingshead & Redlich, 1957; Lystad, 1957; Turner & Wagonfeld, 1967). On the one hand, some studies found that the fathers of schizophrenics have occupations higher in pay and in status than those held by patients (Goldberg & Morrison, 1963; Turner & Wagonfeld, 1967). This finding suggests that people who become schizophrenic tend to drift into socioeconomic groups of lower status than that of their parents. On the other hand, Langner and Michael (1963) found a correlation between the degree of stress in lower-class life and the occurrence of schizophrenia. This finding suggests that such stress may have an etiologic role. Perhaps both hypotheses are true—that is, schizophrenics may tend to drift into lower-class life and, as they do, the stresses of that life may exacerbate their disturbance.

Cross-Cultural Studies

Although schizophrenia has been observed in populations throughout the world, widely varying incidence rates have been reported for different cultures (Murphy, 1968), with the higher rates usually reported for the more industrialized countries (Leighton, Lambo, Hughes, Leighton, Murphy, & MacKline, 1963; Lin, 1953). The significance of these studies is unclear because of a lack of uniformity in diagnostic procedures. For example, hospital statistics indicate that psychotic mood disorders are much more common in London than in New York, while schizophrenia is more common in New York than in London (Gunderson et al., 1974). This difference seems to be a result of different diagnostic practices rather than a consequence of the influence of cultural factors on schizophrenia. Specifically, it has been found that when shown the same videotapes of patient interviews, New York psychiatrists are more likely than are British psychiatrists to diagnose schizophrenia (Cooper, Kendell, Gurland, Sharp, Copeland, & Simon, 1972). In an effort to solve this problem of inconsistent diagnostic practices across cultures, the World Health Organization has sponsored a nine-country study from which a uniform system for diagnosing schizophrenia seems to be emerging (Gunderson et al., 1974).

Hospitalization Trends in the United States

During the first half of this century, the prognosis for chronic schizophrenia was so poor that many chronic schizophrenics were hospitalized for the remainder of their lives. As a consequence, schizophrenics came to occupy an increasing proportion of the beds in mental hospitals. This was true even during the period of 1922 to 1942, when the rate of new admissions to mental hospitals for schizophrenia was relatively constant. Following World War II, a sharp rise occurred in the rate of admission for schizophrenia of males between the ages of 20 and 30. Thus by 1950, more than half of all hospital beds for mental patients, and more than one fifth of all hospital beds in the United States (including those for physical illnesses), were occupied by schizophrenics (Pugh & MacMahon, 1962).

Since the 1950s two developments have led to a decline in the number of schizophrenics being hospitalized. One development, discussed in Chapter 5, was the discovery of tranquilizer drugs. These drugs are sufficiently effective that many backward residents of state and county mental hospitals could be discharged. The other development, discussed in detail in Chapter 9, was the emergence of the community mental health movement. This movement challenged the notion that a troubled individual is best cared for when hospitalized and advocated family and community care whenever possible. As a consequence of these developments, the following trends can be noted.

1. *Decline in the number of schizophrenic residents in state and county hospitals.* During the period 1962 to 1969, there occurred a 31 per cent decrease in resident schizophrenic patients in United States state and county hospitals and a 10 per cent decrease in schizophrenic patients admitted for the first time (Mosher, Gunderson, & Buchsbaum, 1973). Furthermore, 1970 and 1971 are the first two years on record in which the number of discharges exceeded the number of admissions (Bethel & Redick, 1972). The National Institute of Mental Health (NIMH) surveys hospital admission rates every four or five years. In the latest bulletin (NIMH, 1973) 529,379 admissions for schizophrenia and 38,809 admissions for other psychotic disorders were reported for 1971; moreover, psychotic disorders accounted for 22.3 per cent of all hospital admissions. However, the figure of more than one-half million admissions for schizophrenia probably underestimates the real number of admissions because the NIMH survey did not include residential centers for children, Veteran's Administration hospital out-patient clients, and some clinics for which appropriate data were unavailable. Most schizophrenics admitted to hospitals are between the ages of 20 and 40 (Yolles & Kramer, 1969).

2. *Increased reliance on out-patient care.* The number of patients receiving out-patient care more than doubled between 1966 and 1973 (Gunderson, Autry, Mosher, & Buchsbaum, 1974). However, approximately 62 per cent of all schizophrenics treated still receive in-patient care.

3. *Increased number of readmissions.* The reduction in the average length

of stay for schizophrenics who are hospitalized and the increased reliance on out-patient care have been correlated with a growing number of readmissions to hospitals (Gunderson et al., 1974; Taube & Rednick, 1973). Thus, available statistics indicate that today many schizophrenics periodically are admitted to hospitals for brief stays. One factor that may be contributing to the increasing number of readmissions is that many schizophrenics receive minimal care once admitted (Gunderson et al., 1974).

COGNITIVE DEFICITS IN SCHIZOPHRENIA

Hunt and Cofer (1944) introduced the term *psychological deficit* to refer to performance differences between psychiatric patients and normals on a variety of intellectual tasks. Here we shall use the term more generally to refer to any performance deficiency or abnormal behavior that can be demonstrated under laboratory conditions. A cognitive deficit, then, is either an abnormality of thought processes or a deficiency in performance on tasks that evaluate the use of symbolic processes.

Five categories of cognitive deficits in schizophrenia are

1. Presence of delusions.
2. Deficits in conceptual processes.
3. Deficits in speech and communication.
4. Deficits in short-term memory.
5. Deficits in memory processing.

Delusions

Delusional thinking is present in the overwhelming majority of schizophrenics. Lucas, Sansbury, and Collins (1962), for example, found paranoid delusional thinking in 71 per cent of a sample of 405 schizophrenics. The older the patient at the time of onset of schizophrenic symptomatology, the greater was the prevalence of paranoid delusions. Delusions of grandiosity were reported in 44 per cent of the cases, and hypochondriacal delusions were reported in 20 per cent of the cases.

Deficits in Conceptual Thinking

A considerable amount of research activity has been devoted to specifying the manner in which schizophrenics are deficient in conceptual processes.

Regressed Thinking

As originally proposed, the regression hypothesis maintained that schizophrenic thought represents a partial regression to the primary process thinking that is characteristic of infantile thought processes (see Federn, 1952; Fenichel, 1945; Kasanin, 1946). More recently, however, the hypothesis has been modified to propose that, compared to thought processes in the nonschizophrenic adult, thought processes in the adult schizophrenic are more similar to those found in children and/or infants (e.g., Arieti, 1959; Klorman &

Chapman, 1969; Lewin, 1951). Although there is little support for the regression theory of schizophrenia, an important exception is a recent study by Youkilis and DeWolfe (1975). These investigators operationally defined regression as the similarity between an adult's responses and those usually given by children on a word association test. The study found that such similarity was greater for nonparanoid schizophrenics than for paranoid schizophrenics. The investigators noted, however, that their findings are not definitive and that what is needed to confirm the regression hypothesis are longitudinal studies comparing adult schizophrenics' responses with their own responses as children.

Deficiency in Logical Deductions

Von Domarus (1946), and later Arieti (1959), proposed that schizophrenics are deficient in the ability to reason logically. The essence of this hypothesis is that normal people infer identity from identical subjects, whereas schizophrenics infer identity from identical predicates. For example, given the information *All people born in the United States are Americans* and *Jones was born in the United States,* the logical conclusion is to infer that *Jones is an American.* This inference is based on Aristotelian logic and is an example of what Von Domarus believed to be characteristic of reasoning in the normal adult. Suppose, however, that the following information is given: *All presidents of the United States were born Americans* and *Jones was born in America.* Here there is an equivalence of predicates, and the information given does not permit the inference that *Jones is president of the United States.* Von Domarus provided evidence that schizophrenics show a greater tendency than normals to draw this conclusion. Unfortunately, research attempts to replicate Von Domarus's results have been complicated by findings that normal people often do not think in accordance with the principles of formal logic. Thus 30 years after it was originally proposed, Von Domarus's hypothesis remains largely unsubstantiated and is regarded today as too vague to permit experimental testing (Salzinger, 1973).

Deficiency in Abstraction

Concrete concepts refer to physical properties of stimuli, whereas abstract concepts refer to functional properties of stimuli. For example, the concept of red refers to a physical property of many objects, and the concept of a writing instrument refers to a functional property of objects such as pens and pencils. Suppose someone were asked to group three objects: a red pen, a blue pencil, and a red ball. Grouping the pen and ball together would suggest a concrete form of conceptual thought, whereas grouping the pen and pencil together would suggest an abstract form of conceptual thought. Goldstein (1940) and Vigotsky (1934) suggested that both schizophrenics and brain-damaged subjects are deficient in the ability to use abstract concepts.

Although several reviewers interpreted Goldstein and Vigotsky's hypothesis as implying a loss of abstraction abilities in schizophrenics (e.g., Buss & Lang,

1965; Craig, 1973), Wright (1975) has maintained that the original hypothesis implied an impairment in abstraction rather than a total loss of such abilities. In any event, the available data indicate that schizophrenics can use abstract concepts although they do not seem to do so as often as normals (Benjamin, 1946; Bolles & Goldstein, 1938; Lothrop, 1961; see Wright, 1975). Moreover, some evidence suggests that deficiencies in abstraction vary for different types of schizophrenia. For example, Wegrocki (1940) reported abstraction deficiencies in hebephrenic schizophrenics, and Wahl and Wisher (1972) reported abstraction deficiencies in nonparanoid but not in paranoid schizophrenics. A number of studies have found greater deficiencies in abstraction for process schizophrenics as compared to reactive schizophrenics (e.g., Becker, 1956; Meichenbaum, 1969; Watson, 1973). In a review of the relevant literature, Wright (1975) concluded that there exists "strong support for the notion that schizophrenics are impaired in abstract conceptualization."

Deficiency in Nature of Thought

Some theorists maintain that the important deficiency in schizophrenic conceptual thought is not an inability to employ abstract concepts but rather the inappropriate or autistic nature of the abstractions used (Buss & Lang, 1965; Cameron, 1938; Chapman & Taylor, 1957; McGaughran & Moran, 1956; Payne & Hewlett, 1960). Payne expressed this view as follows:

> These studies then suggest that schizophrenics as a group are probably not abnormally concrete in the sense of being unable to form a new concept. They are, however, abnormal in the *type* of concepts they form. Their concepts tend to be unusual and often eccentric [1961, p. 243].

In this regard Cameron (1938, 1946) proposed that schizophrenics show a tendency toward *overinclusion*—that is, they form concepts that include irrelevant as well as relevant information. For example, the concept of "fruit" includes apples but excludes meat; classifying both apples and meat as fruit represents an overinclusive use of the concept of fruit. Because success at many problem-solving tasks requires the ability to focus on relevant material and to exclude the irrelevant, overinclusive thinking is nonadaptive. A number of studies have provided evidence of overinclusion in schizophrenia (Chapman & Taylor, 1957; Cromwell & Dokecki, 1968; Moran, 1953; Payne & Hewlett, 1960; Shakow, 1962; Yates, 1966).

Summary

To summarize, several hypotheses have been proposed to specify the deficits in schizophrenic conceptual thought. The regression hypothesis maintains that one deficit consists of the intrusion of primary process thinking into consciousness; in its modified form, however, the regression hypothesis maintains that conceptual processes in adult schizophrenics are similar to those found in earlier developmental periods. Although there is some evidence that supports this view, the regression hypothesis is far from proven.

Von Domarus's (1946) hypothesis of a deficit in formal logical processes is unsubstantiated.

There exists evidence that schizophrenics do not spontaneously use abstract concepts to as great an extent as do normals. Also, there exists solid evidence that schizophrenic patients show a greater tendency than do normals to use overinclusive concepts.

Speech and Communication Deficits

Many psychologists view speech as so closely associated with thought that disturbances of speech are generally assumed to reflect disturbances in thought (Critchley, 1964). The speech of some schizophrenics, especially hebephrenics, is sometimes incoherent and bizarre. Words and sounds may be jumbled together in a manner that is sometimes referred to as a *word salad. Neologisms*—that is, unintelligible, idiosyncratic words made by combining several words into one—are not uncommon. For example, Forrest (1969) reported that by "sniggeration," a schizophrenic patient meant "a giggle." Lehmann reported the following example of schizophrenic speech: "The Seabeach gathering homestead building upon the site of the bear mountain. Time placed of the dunced to the recovery of the setting sun, upon the streams, poling paddleboat, Mickey, Rooney, Bill. Proceeded of, to the onlivement" [1967, p. 627]. Also common are unusual word associations that seem to result from intruding throughts, as if the schizophrenic were unable to focus on a single line of reasoning. For example, Maher, McKean, and McLaughlin (1966) reported the following associations of a schizophrenic patient: "I like coffee, cream, cows, and Elizabeth Taylor."

Formal Properties of Schizophrenic Speech

Research on the formal properties of schizophrenic speech has produced at least two solid findings (Maher, 1972): (1) schizophrenics tend to reuse the same words more often than do normals, often repeating the words within a given passage or utterance, and (2) schizophrenic speech is less predictable (less redundant) than is the speech of normals. These two findings may seem inconsistent because we normally think of redundant speech as being that in which the same words are repeated. The findings, however, are consistent—because schizophrenics tend to repeat the same words inappropriately and unexpectedly, the informational content of their speech is less redundant than is the informational content of the speech of normals.

In information theory (Shannon, 1951) a redundant word is one that is predictable from the total context. For example, in the phrase, "The pitcher threw the ball, and then the batter hit the --- out of the park," the missing word (*ball*) is predictable from the context given; hence, it is redundant in that context. Effective communication requires an optimal level of redundancy, and schizophrenic speech has been shown to be less redundant than normal speech (Bertoch, 1966; Rice, 1970; Salzinger, Portnoy, & Feldman, 1964). For example, Silverman (1972) collected speech samples of 200 words from schizophrenics and from normals. The samples were edited to delete words at regular in-

A disturbed woman, carrying a photograph of President Ford and a letter, recites a continuous stream of invectives as she walks along a New York street. (Photo by Bernard Pierre Wolff; Magnum Photos, Inc.)

tervals, and the edited samples were then given to a panel of four raters who attempted to predict the missing words. The raters were able to predict the missing words more accurately for normal speech than for schizophrenic speech, thereby indicating that the schizophrenic speech was less redundant.

Another experimental paradigm for investigating schizophrenic speech includes both a speaker and a listener; the speaker's task is to describe one of *n* objects in a manner that enables the listener to identify the object. For example, a speaker might be provided with three different colored disks. When asked to describe one of the disks, the speaker might say "the red one"; if the colors of the other disks are unlike red, effective communication is likely and the listener should correctly select the disk described.

Rosenberg and Cohen (1964, 1966) proposed a two-stage model for understanding the manner in which a speaker selects labels in an experimental communication task similar to the one just described. In the first stage possible labels are sampled (e.g., *red*), and the words sampled are determined in part by the speaker's vocabulary. In the second stage of the model the sampled label is edited to test for its discriminative capacity. For example, suppose the label *red* is sampled; if all three disks are reddish in color, the word *red* does not communicate effectively because it does not permit the listener to select the correct disc. Thus, the normal speaker rejects (edits out) the word *red,* samples another label (e.g., *reddish-brown*), assesses the discriminative capacity of this word, and then either uses it or rejects it in favor of some other label. In brief, the Rosenberg-Cohen model postulates two processes: sampling and self-editing (comparison).

Utilizing an experimental paradigm of communicator and listener similar to that just described, Cohen, Nachmani, and Rosenberg (1974) were able to test three models of schizophrenic speech.

1. *The Tower of Babel model.* This model proposes that the schizophrenic samples from an idiosyncratic repertoire of descriptive terms. For example, if asked to describe a colored object, he might use a neologism such as "zoolook" or give an association such as "blood." As reviewed by Cohen et al., this model does not explain adequately the available data: "to generalize: the accumulated evidence suggests not only that schizophrenics, as a group, do not share a special language but also that the individual patient does not have an autistic language of his own" [1974, p. 7]. It should be noted, however, that this conclusion is based primarily on the study of acute schizophrenics in simple experimental situations and may not be applicable to chronic cases or to behavior in more complex situations.

2. *The impulsive speaker model.* This model assumes that the schizophrenic speaker selects from a normal repertoire of descriptors but that he tends to select the first label that comes to mind regardless of the appropriateness of that label. In other words, the schizophrenic speaker differs from the normal in that he does not edit or test the discriminative capacity of words; rather, he simply communicates whatever comes to mind. The results of the studies reviewed by Cohen et al. do not support this model.

3. *The perseverative speaker model.* This model proposes that the schizophrenic samples from a normal set of descriptors, edits, but then continually resamples the same verbal label after having rejected it as inadequate. This model was supported by some of the Cohen et al. findings but was disconfirmed by other findings. To account for their data, Cohen et al. (1974) proposed a *perseverative-chaining* model. Under this model, the schizophrenic is assumed to (1) sample a descriptor from a normal repertoire of descriptors (e.g., sample *red*); (2) edit (e.g., reject *red* because other items are also reddish); (3) sample a second label based on his associations to the rejected item rather than to the stimulus to-be-described (e.g., sample *lipstick*), and (4) edit. The sampling-editing process continues until a descriptor is selected, but the sampling is based on associations to the last descriptor sampled rather than to the object. The schizophrenic is thus hypothesized to lose sight of the task.

Summary

Schizophrenic speech is bizarre, includes neologisms, and is characterized by unusual associations. Research on the formal properties of schizophrenic speech reveals two deficits: (1) schizophrenics show a greater tendency than do normals to repeat the same words within a given passage or utterance, and (2) the informational content of schizophrenic speech is less redundant than is the informational content of normal speech—hence schizophrenic speech is less communicative. Research on simple communication processes suggests that schizophrenics show a greater tendency than do normals to get sidetracked;

that is, although their initial verbal association to an object may be appropriate, subsequent responses tend to be more of an association to the initial word selected and less of an appropriate descriptor of the object. In this regard, Cohen, Nachmani, and Rosenberg reported the following examples of normals and schizophrenics attempting to describe the differences between two colors:

> Normal Speaker: Both are salmon colored. This one, however, has more pink.
> Schizophrenic Speaker: This is the stupid color of a shit ass bowl of salmon. Mix it with mayonnaise. Then it gets tasty. Leave it alone and puke all over the fuckin' place. Puke fish [1974, p. 11].

Short-Term Memory Deficits

A number of studies have established that schizophrenics are deficient in short-term memory (Bauman & Murray, 1968; Nachmani & Cohen, 1969; Truscott, 1970). For example, if presented with a series of stimuli and then asked to recall those stimuli, schizophrenics recall fewer items than do normals. However, if presented with a series of stimulus items and then asked whether or not a particular stimulus had been presented, schizophrenics perform as well as normals (Russell, Bannatyne, & Smith, 1975). One possible explanation of these findings is that schizophrenics encode to-be-remembered material in a way that is difficult to retrieve. Studies by Koh and Peterson (1974) and by Saccuzzo, Hirt, and Spencer (1974) suggest that schizophrenics are, in fact, deficient in the initial encoding of to-be-remembered material.

Memory Processing Deficits

As mentioned previously, Koh and Peterson (1974) obtained evidence suggesting faulty encoding of to-be-remembered material as a cause of memory deficits in schizophrenia. Koh and his associates have conducted a series of related studies based on an information processing model of these deficits (Koh, in press; Koh, Kayton, & Berry, 1973; Koh, Kayton, & Peterson, 1976; Koh, Kayton, & Schwarz, 1974). This approach permits a separate evaluation of short-term and long-term memory strategies. Based on the findings from his studies, Koh concluded that schizophrenic memory deficits are a consequence of inefficient memory strategies and memory organization rather than a deficiency in memory capacity. Additional support for this hypothesis was obtained by Larsen and Fromholt (1976). One eventual outcome of this research may be the development of methods to teach efficient memory strategies to schizophrenics.

PERCEPTUAL DEFICITS ASSOCIATED WITH SCHIZOPHRENIA

Perceptual deficiencies associated with schizophrenia include a tendency to hallucinate and a deficiency in the ability to concentrate.

Hallucinations

Hallucinations are sensory perceptions of stimuli that are not there. The perception itself is typically meaningful and is often reacted to as if it were a veridical perception of reality (Sedman, 1966); unlike the tired driver who realizes that he is beginning to perceive false images on the road, the schizophrenic does not seem to realize when he is hallucinating. Moreover, schizophrenic hallucinations are sometimes experienced as very frightening.

Clinicians have reported that, in schizophrenia, auditory hallucinations are the most common; visual hallucinations are rare in mild cases but are common in severe cases; and hallucinations of touch, taste, and smell are relatively rare (see Buss, 1966). Malitz, Wildens, & Esecover (1962) reported that in groups of chronic schizophrenics, 50 per cent suffered from auditory hallucinations whereas 9 per cent suffered from visual hallucinations. The greater prevalence of auditory hallucinations is not surprising when it is considered that schizophrenia is a thought disorder and that thinking and speech processes are assumed to be related. For example, McGuigan (1966) found that behavioral correlates of speech (chin and tongue movements, breathing, and whispering) increased just prior to auditory hallucinations, as if the auditory hallucination consisted of an actual hearing of one's own voice.

Schizophrenic hallucinations may be a consequence of prolonged withdrawal from the social environment. Suedfeld (1969b) suggested that attention focuses on internal stimuli when people are exposed to an unchanging or sensory-deprived environment and that this focus on internal stimuli increases the probability of hallucinations. If this were true, we should expect that social isolation would increase the probability of hallucinations in normal subjects. In fact, anecdotal data suggest that people who are socially isolated for long periods of time (e.g., explorers and prisoners) are more likely to hallucinate. Moreover, a number of experiments on the effects of sensory deprivation seem to substantiate these anecdotal data (see Kubzansky, 1961; Suedfeld, 1969a). In the initial series of these studies (e.g., Bexton, Heron, & Scott, 1954; see Heron, 1957), college students were paid to lie on a couch for as long as possible with their eyes covered by translucent plastic, with their ears covered by earphones, and with their hands and bodies covered to minimize tactile sensations. A number of students reported hallucinations after only a few hours of sensory deprivation, suggesting that social isolation and sensory deprivation may lead to hallucinations.

One possible alternative explanation of the sensory deprivation studies is that the students who reported hallucinations did so in response to the implicit social demands of the experimental situation. This hypothesis maintains that the procedure of requiring students to wear plastic glasses, earphones, and gloves creates an implicit demand that something strange be reported; the students, expecting strange experiences, may tend to report such experiences as a consequence of their expectations rather than as a consequence of sensory deprivation per se. Applying this line of reasoning to schizophrenia, Ullmann and Krasner (1969) suggested that schizophrenics may sometimes hallucinate because of an implicit social demand to do so; that is, because the socially defined role of schizophrenia includes hallucinatory experiences, the schizophrenics may have such experiences because, like most people, they tend to behave in socially expected ways. Some experimental data indicate that a social demand for hallucinatory experiences can, in fact, elicit verbal reports of hallucinations in normal college students (e.g., Sarbin, Juhasz, & Todd, 1971). For example, if given a chemically inert pill and told that the pill usually causes hallucinations, at least some people would be more likely to report hallucinations than if they had been told nothing about the pill's effects.

As noted in Chapter 5, a number of drugs (e.g., mescaline and LSD) induce hallucinations if taken in sufficient dosages. Although such findings suggest that schizophrenic hallucinations may be caused by biochemical factors, Feinberg (1962) noted the following differences between drug-induced visual hallucinations in normal subjects and visual hallucinations in schizophrenics: (1) drug-induced hallucinations generally develop more gradually than do schizophrenic hallucinations; (2) drug-induced hallucinations seem unrelated to the subject's emotional state, whereas schizophrenic hallucinations are often accompanied by emotional excitement; (3) drug-induced hallucinations are usually distortions of the external environment, whereas schizophrenic hallucinations are "superimposed" onto the external environment; and (4) drug-induced visual hallucinations are more likely to occur when the individual's eyes are closed, whereas schizophrenic visual hallucinations tend to occur when the individual's eyes are open. In sum, it is unclear whether or not drug-induced hallucinations provide a model for schizophrenic hallucinations.

Attention Deficits

Schizophrenics have been reported to be deficient in their ability to concentrate on a line of reasoning and to attend to the demands of a task at hand. These observations suggest a deficiency in attention and in concentration. The literature on attentional deficits in schizophrenia is voluminous, in part because the phenomenon lends itself to laboratory investigation and in part because attention deficits are one of the most salient of all schizophrenic symptoms. One of the most widely used measures for investigating attention deficits is reaction time. This measure is simply the time a subject takes to perform a correct response in reaction to the onset of a stimulus. For example, two groups of subjects, schizophrenics and normals, might be instructed to press a button as soon as a light stimulus is presented. If the schizophrenics respond more slowly than do the normals, this finding can be attributed to a deficit in the ability to attend to the onset of the light stimulus. In addition to simple reaction time paradigms such as the one just described, a number of more complex paradigms have been used. For example, subjects might be instructed to press a blue button when a red light comes on and to press a red button when a blue light comes on.

Compared to normals, schizophrenics are slower in performing simple motor responses (e.g., button presses) in reaction to the onset of a stimulus (Huston, Shakow, & Riggs, 1937; Rappaport, 1967; Shakow, 1962). Moreover, Karras (1967, 1973) has demonstrated that schizophrenics are slower in their reaction time to stimulus onset than are other psychiatric groups. Given that attention deficits in schizophrenics are well documented, the question arises as to how these deficits might best be understood. Both Karras (1967) and Yates (1966) suggested that the deficit is a result of a slow rate of information processing. Yates hypothesized that a slow rate of information processing is related to a limited capacity for short-term memory (e.g., Yates & Korboot, 1970). A recent study by Korboot and Damiani (1976) supports this view with data obtained on a signal detection task. Additional research, however, is still needed to clarify the status of Yates's interesting hypothesis.

The hypothesis that schizophrenics show attention deficits because they are more distractible than are normals has been extensively investigated (e.g., Chapman & McGhie, 1962). In this view, the slow reaction time of schizophrenics is attributable to the occurrence of responses that compete with attention to the task at hand. Two major views have been proposed concerning the nature of the hypothesized responses that interfere with attention in schizophrenia. Broen (1968), Mednick (1958), and Mednick and Schulsinger (1968) proposed that the interfering response is anxiety. Mednick proposed that schizophrenics have a very low threshold for anxiety and consequently respond anxiously to many more stimuli than do normals. Mednick and Schulsinger (1968) further proposed that the schizophrenic's hypothesized predisposition to respond anxiously to many environmental stimuli is related to organic brain damage in the hippocampus region of the brain. Although this view may have been plausible at the time it was proposed, Kessler and Neale (1974) maintain that the hippocampus does not function in the manner suggested by Mednick and Schulsinger.

Chapman, Chapman, and Miller (1964) suggested that attention deficits in schizophrenics are caused by a tendency to utilize the same dominant responses somewhat independently of the environmental context or demands. That is, a dominant response intrudes into the schizophrenic's thought, thereby resulting in an incorrect or a delayed response. Suppose, for example, that schizophrenics and normals are asked to say *red* as soon as a black stimulus is presented and to say *black* as soon as a red stimulus is presented. In the opinion of Chapman et al. (1964), both schizophrenics and normals tend to have a dominant response in the sense that most individuals tend to think of black when presented a black stimulus and to think of red when presented a red stimulus. Whereas the normal can respond as instructed (e.g., say *black* to red), the schizophrenic tends to overgeneralize his dominant response pattern, thus saying *black* to black and *red* to red; hence, he is slower to suppress this response in order to comply with the experimental instruction. This hypothesis of overgeneralization in schizophrenia has received some support from laboratory studies (e.g., Chapman et al., 1964; Mourer, 1973), but future research is needed to clarify its status.

In laboratory studies of attention deficits, subjects are generally required to perform some task in which there is an implicit assumption of good (correct) versus bad (incorrect) performance. Thus poor performance on such tasks may reflect an oversensitivity to the possibility of failure, and this oversensitivity should interfere with performance and lead to the very failure that is feared. This position is elaborated by Rodnick and Garmezy's (1957) *social censure hypothesis.* Garmezy (1966) defines censure as any signal suggesting criticism or disapproval. The basic notion is that schizophrenics overreact to and withdraw from censure and thus perform poorly on tasks that provide such cues. Although this hypothesis received some early support, Van Dyke and Routh (1973) found that both schizophrenic and nonschizophrenic subjects improved their performances in response to a tone that indicated poor performance. Because these results are the opposite of what is predicted by the social censure hypothesis, Van Dyke and Routh proposed a major revision. They proposed that performance deficits are unlikely when censure is contingent on performance because the subjects will realize that they can avoid censure by improving their performance. They also proposed that the effects of noncontingent censure depend on whether the subject falsely assumes that the censure is contingent on performance or accurately perceives the absence of any relation.

Time Judgments

A number of studies have reported that schizophrenics overestimate elapsed time (e.g., Broadhurst, 1968; Goldstone & Goldfarb, 1962; Wright, Goldstone, & Boardman, 1962), with female patients showing a greater tendency to overestimate time than male patients. There is no adequate explanation of these empirical findings.

Summary

To summarize, clinical observations suggest that schizophrenics are deficient in the ability to concentrate on a line of reasoning and to attend to the demands of the task at hand. Experimental studies have confirmed the existence of an attention deficit in schizophrenia. The hypothesis that this deficit is simply a result of a slow rate of information processing is supported by some data but is in conflict with other data. The hypothesis that this deficit is caused by some type of competing (or intruding) response is viable, but the nature of the interfering response is as yet unclear. It should be noted that there may be several such competing responses. Rodnick and Garmezy's social censure hypothesis proposes that anxiety elicited by cues associated with social censure interferes with performance on experimental tasks. This may sometimes occur, but the available evidence does not consistently support the notion that schizophrenics are particularly sensitive to social censure cues. Finally, schizophrenics show a greater tendency than do normals to overestimate elapsed time, but as yet it is unclear what significance to attribute to this reliable finding.

DEFICITS IN INTERPERSONAL RELATIONSHIPS

A number of theorists have proposed that schizophrenics fear interpersonal relationships and that this fear explains several other schizophrenic symptoms (e.g., Sullivan, 1953). Some attempts to study the interpersonal behavior of schizophrenics consisted of observations of performance on an experimental task under conditions in which another person either was or was not present. For example, Berkowitz (1964) compared the reaction time performances of chronic schizophrenics and nonschizophrenics under three conditions of contact with an experimenter: no contact; contact with an aloof and unresponsive experimenter; and contact with a warm and accepting experimenter. The schizophrenic patients showed the slowest reaction times with the warm and accepting experimenter. This finding is consistent with clinical theories of schizophrenia; that is, it suggests that because schizophrenics avoid interpersonal contact, the warm and accepting experimenter elicited the greatest demand for such contact and, hence, the greatest degree of anxiety. The poor performance under this condition is explicable in terms of interfering anxiety. Similarly, Gelburd and Anker (1970) found that the absence of an experimenter can function as a positive reinforcer for improving performance in schizophrenics. In this study, the subjects performed better in order to escape from the presence of an experimenter. The hypothesis that schizophrenics fear interpersonal relationships is further supported in a study by Gorelick (1970). This investigator asked schizophrenics to select from descriptions in a questionnaire a partner with whom they would like to work and socialize. She found that the schizophrenics were reluctant to expose themselves to social contacts. Furthermore, Thornton and Gottheil (1971) found that when asked to group human figures, schizophrenics placed the figures at greater distances from one another than did normals. In conclusion, the hypothesis that schizophrenics tend to avoid interpersonal contact has been substantiated.

SELF-OTHER BOUNDARIES

A notion implicit in the concept of regression is that of faulty development, for it is deficiencies in development that are presumed to determine the course of regression (see Chapters 5 and 10). In this regard, increasing attention has been given to inadequate development among schizophrenics in the formation of psychological boundaries (e.g., Zucker, 1958; Landis, 1970). Blatt and Ritzler (1974) and Quinlan and Harrow (1974) have delineated three types of psychological boundaries:

1. *Self-other boundaries* that permit the individual to distinguish between "I" and others. This concept includes body boundaries—for example, the distinction between where one's arm extends and where it ends.
2. *Intrapsychic boundaries* that permit the organization of conscious and unconscious material. A breakdown in these boundaries may result from the intrusion of unconscious material into consciousness.
3. *Interobject boundaries* that permit the individual to distinguish one object from another.

There is some evidence that boundary confusion is positively correlated with degree of psychopathology (Federn, 1952; Landis, 1970).

It has been suggested that schizophrenia is associated with an inadequate development of self-other and intrapsychic boundaries. Evidence for self-other boundary confusion is provided by the bizarre bodily sensations reported by schizophrenics, including feelings that one's body is falling apart, that one's chest is touching one's back, that one's arms are inching up into to one's body, and that part of one's body is made of wood (Angyal, 1936; Buss, 1966). Evidence of intrapsychic boundary confusion is provided by observations of intruding thoughts and fantasies.

Although a number of instruments have been used to assess the presence of boundary confusion, perhaps the instrument used most extensively for this purpose is the Rorschach. For example, Quinlan and Harrow (1974) administered the Rorschach to 171 psychiatric in-patients, 48 of whom were schizophrenics experiencing a psychotic episode. Compared to other groups of patients, the schizophrenics showed more contaminations (Rorschach responses in which two percepts are arbitrarily or incongruously combined, as in *a bear with a chicken's head*). These findings were interpreted as supporting the hypothesis that schizophrenics give Rorschach responses that indicate boundary disturbances.

SUMMARY

The summary for this chapter is combined with that for Chapter 16.

Chapter 16

The Possible Etiologies of Schizophrenia

STEVEN REISS, ROLF A. PETERSON,

and PATRICK O'NEILL

> Suppose that you were required to write down a procedure for selecting an individual from the population who would be diagnosed as schizophrenic by a psychiatric staff; you have to wager $1,000 on being right; you may not include in your selection procedure any behavioral fact, such as a symptom or trait, manifested by the individual. What would you write down? So far as I have been able to ascertain, there is only one thing you could write down that would give you a better than even chance of winning such a bet—namely, "Find an individual *X* who has a schizophrenic identical twin.
>
> MEEHL (1973, pp. 135–136)

The central question with which this chapter is concerned is "Why do some people behave in ways that are schizophrenic when others do not?" The model with which we shall pursue this question posits a two-step process:

1. Predisposition(s) to schizophrenic behavior are inherited.
2. Individuals who have inherited a predisposition to schizophrenia will become schizophrenic only when exposed to certain environmental and cultural factors.

This chapter, then, is concerned primarily with possible biological and environmental causes of schizophrenia; additionally, treatment approaches are discussed at the conclusion of the chapter.

THE GENETICS OF SCHIZOPHRENIA

Both Kraepelin and Bleuler believed that schizophrenia is a genetic disorder, although neither could offer convincing evidence to support this belief. During the last fifty years, however, considerable evidence has been obtained supporting the hypothesis of a genetic predisposition to schizophrenia. This evidence comes from three types of studies: (1) studies assessing familial morbidity rates; (2) twin studies; and (3) adoption studies.

Familial Morbidity Rates

A familial morbidity rate is a measure of the extent to which a particular disorder tends to occur in families. In order to assess these rates, a researcher begins with at least two groups of individuals, schizophrenics and nonschizophrenics, and then assesses the extent to which their relatives are schizophrenic or nonschizophrenic. The individuals who provide the starting point are variously called index cases or probands. Thus the purpose of familial morbidity studies of schizophrenia is to assess the presence or absence of schizophrenia in the relatives of schizophrenic and nonschizophrenic probands. Often such research is complicated by difficulties in locating and in obtaining accurate life-history information.

Table 16-1 presents Rosenthal's (1970) summary of 14 studies of familial morbidity rates for schizophrenia. This table reveals the following information:

1. The incidence of schizophrenia is much greater among the parents and siblings of schizophrenics than it is among the parents and siblings of nonschizophrenics. This finding confirms clinical impressions that schizophrenia tends to run in families.

TABLE 16-1
Morbidity-Risk Estimates for Parents and Siblings of Schizophrenic Index Cases

Study	Age of Risk	Number of Probands	Risk Estimates, Per Cent: Parents	Sibs	Sibs-Parents Ratio	General Population
Brugger, 1928	15–40	85	4.3	10.3	2.4:1	1.53
Bleuler, 1930	20–40	100	2.0	4.9	2.5:1	
Schulz, 1932	15–40	660	2.6	6.7	2.6:1	0.76
Luxenburger, 1936	15–40	128	11.7	7.6	0.65:1	0.85
Smith, 1936	15–40	200	1.2	3.3	2.8:1	
Galatschjan, 1937	15–40	214	4.9	14.0	2.9:1	
Strömgren, 1938	20–40	195	0.7	6.7	9.6:1	0.48
Kallmann, 1938	15–45	1,047	2.7	7.5	2.8:1	0.35
Bleuler, 1941	15–40	100	5.6	10.4	1.9:1	1.53
Kallmann, 1946	15–45	691	9.2	14.3	1.6:1	
Böök, 1953	15–50	80	12.0	9.7	0.81:1	2.85
Slater, 1953	15–40	158	4.1	5.4	1.3:1	
Hallgren-Sjögren, 1959	20–40	247	0.2	5.7	28.5:1	0.83
Garrone, 1962	15–70	227	7.0	8.6	1.2:1	2.40

From D. Rosenthal, *Genetic theory and abnormal behavior.* New York: McGraw-Hill Book Co., 1970, p. 109. Reprinted by permission of author and publisher.

2. The various studies, however, have reported substantially different morbidity-risk rates for the siblings as well as for the parents of schizophrenics. For example, Hallgren and Sjögren (1959; see Table 16-1) reported a morbidity-risk rate of 0.2 for parents, whereas Böök (1953) reported a comparable rate of 12.0. These variations are currently inexplicable (Rosenthal, 1970) and may reflect methodological differences in diagnosing schizophrenia, variations across cultures in the distribution of schizophrenic genes, or differences in environmental factors that, when combined with a genetically determined predisposition, lead to schizophrenic behavior.

3. The available data do not support single-gene theories of schizophrenia. If schizophrenia were determined by a single dominant gene, the expected morbidity rate for siblings would approximate 50 per cent.[1] Yet the highest such rate reported in Table 16-1 is 14.3, a figure that does not approximate the 50 per cent rate. Moreover, under a single-recessive-gene theory, the expected morbidity rate for siblings would be 25 per cent, a figure that is still much too high for the data reported in Table 16-1. To explain these data in

[1] Similarly, under a single-dominant-gene hypothesis, the morbidity risk for parents of probands should approximate 50 per cent. All schizophrenics, however, do not marry and have children; those who do are, as a group, less severely disturbed than those who do not. Thus the parent sample may be biased in favor of lower morbidity rates (Rosenthal, 1970).

terms of genetics, it is necessary to assume that schizophrenia is determined by the inheritance of more than one gene and/or that environmental factors somehow account for the reduced rates.

Twin Studies

Findings that schizophrenia tends to occur more frequently among relatives of schizophrenics than among relatives of nonschizophrenics can be explained by environmental factors. For example, a child born to a schizophrenic parent not only is exposed to a psychotic parental model but also is more likely to have at least one parent hospitalized periodically. It is possible that these environmental factors, rather than a genetic predisposition, account for the findings of a higher morbidity rate among the families of schizophrenics. In an effort to control environmental factors more fully, investigators have assessed the concordance rates for identical and for fraternal twins who were reared in the same family. It will be recalled that a twin pair is concordant for schizophrenia if both members of the pair are schizophrenic, whereas a twin pair is discordant if one member has schizophrenia and the other does not.

The early twin studies found concordance rates as high as 75 per cent for identical twins, thereby providing important support for the hypothesis of a genetic etiology (Luxenburger, 1934; Kallmann, 1946). Although more recent studies have tended to report lower rates, these lower rates are still sufficiently high to provide impressive support for a genetic factor.[2] For example, Allen, Cohen, and Pollin (1972) studied 16,000 pairs of male twins who served in the United States armed forces. In 420 pairs, one or both members of the pair were diagnosed as schizophrenic. These investigators found concordance in 26 of 95 identical twin pairs and in only six of 125 fraternal twin pairs; thus the concordance rates for identical and fraternal twins were 27.4 and 4.8 per cent, respectively. Other recent studies found concordance rates of 38 (Kringlen, 1967), 48 (Fischer, Harvald, & Hauge, 1969), and 50 (Shields, 1972) for identical twins, figures considerably higher than those found in these studies for fraternal twins.

The twin studies provide considerable support for the hypothesis of a genetic factor because both identical and fraternal twins tend to share similar environments—that is, they are usually reared in the same home. These studies, however, do not rule out environmental factors completely because it is possible that parents and significant others in the environment behave more similarly to identical twins who look alike than to fraternal twins who may not look alike.

Adoption Studies

As noted previously, findings of higher morbidity rates for the families of schizophrenics can be explained by environmental factors related to living in a family with a schizophrenic member. One way to control for such environ-

[2] More recent studies found generally lower concordance rates for schizophrenia in identical twins because of improved sampling procedures and more objective methods of diagnosing schizophrenia in co-twins.

mental factors is to assess morbidity rates for children reared apart from their schizophrenic biological parents. Because these children would not be reared by a schizophrenic parent, under the environmental hypothesis they should be no more likely to become schizophrenic than adopted children who have non-schizophrenic biological parents. Under the genetic hypothesis, however, these children would still be genetically related to a schizophrenic parent and hence should be predisposed to schizophrenia.

Two studies on children reared apart from their schizophrenic parents provide substantial evidence for the genetic hypothesis. Heston (1966, 1970) studied 47 persons who were offsprings of schizophrenic mothers and who had been reared by an adopted family or in an orphanage. Fifty subjects, selected from the same orphanages, served as controls. At the time of follow-up, 10.6 per cent of the subjects with schizophrenic mothers were diagnosed as schizophrenic, whereas none of the controls were so diagnosed. Moreover, as compared to children in the control group, much higher percentages of children with schizophrenic mothers were diagnosed as mentally defective, psychopathic, or neurotic. Heston concluded, "The importance of genetic factors in the development of schizophrenia has now been established beyond reasonable dispute, although it is clear that environment too plays its etiologic role" [1970, p. 255].

Equally impressive support for the genetic hypothesis was provided by Rosenthal, Wender, Kety, Welner, and Schulsinger (1971), who conducted an exhaustive study of children adopted in Denmark between 1924 and 1947. These investigators found that being biologically related to a schizophrenic is associated with increased risk of schizophrenia even when the individual has had no personal contact with the schizophrenic relative. In a recent article, however, these authors had this to say:

> Several studies taken together clearly indicate that many schizophrenics have an important genetic contributant. Further studies of this sort may more clearly define the boundaries of the spectrum, but will not elucidate its mechanism. Comparing the situation to that of studies of retardation in the nineteenth century, one must expect that further progress will be made only by attempting to define homogeneous subgroups, some of which have specific biological etiologies, and exploring the biological attributes of these subgroups.
>
> These adoption studies may be compared crudely to that in which a kite was flown and an electric spark was discovered. They are provocative and, I think, exciting; but one can anticipate further progress only on the basis of careful study of electricity and not by the use of bigger and higher flying kites [Wender, Rosenthal, Rainer, Greenhill, & Sarlin, in press].

Conclusion

The available evidence strongly supports the hypothesis that, at the very least, a predisposition to schizophrenia is inherited. This, however, does not tell us which types of schizophrenic deficits are genetically determined and which are not. For example, in the previous chapter it was noted that one well-documented deficiency in schizophrenia is an attention deficit indicated by slow reaction times. Yet the available evidence suggests that this deficit is unrelated to genetic factors, although it may be related to having disturbed parents (Van Dyke, 1972; Zahn, Rosenthal, Pollin, & Mosher, 1972; see Gunderson et al., 1974). These findings exemplify just how incomplete our current knowledge is. Although we can conclude that there is a genetic predisposition to schizophrenia, we do not know which deficiencies are related to genetic factors.

Another important unanswered question is whether genetic involvement is greater in different types of schizophrenia; for example, is genetic involvement greater in chronic or process schizophrenia than in acute or reactive schizophrenia? For an excellent summary of genetic research on schizophrenia, the interested reader can consult David Rosenthal (1970), *Genetic Theory and Abnormal Behavior.*

BIOCHEMICAL RESEARCH IN SCHIZOPHRENIA

Since the early 1950s there have been scores of reports of various biochemical differences in the urine of hospitalized schizophrenics and of normals. Many of these findings, however, resulted from differences that are unrelated to the presence or absence of schizophrenia. For example, many biochemical differences in urine samples from hospitalized schizophrenics and normals result from greater tendencies on the part of schizophrenics to eat improperly, to receive drug treatment, to exercise infrequently, and to suffer from emotional stress (Kety, 1969).

The Transmethylation Hypothesis

The transmethylation hypothesis proposes that schizophrenics manufacture within their bodies hallucinogenic substances like LSD-25 and mescaline and that the presence of these substances in the brain causes schizophrenia (Blaschko, 1959; Kety, 1969; Osmond & Smythies, 1952; Woolley, 1962; Woolley & Shaw, 1954). Specifically, this hypothesis proposes the following:

1. Dopamine, norepinephrine, epinephrine, and serotonin are biochemicals found in the brain. Because these substances are involved in the transmission of nerve impulses, they are called *neurotransmitters.*

2. These neurotransmitters have a chemical structure so similar to LSD-25 or to mescaline that a defect in the metabolic processes that normally produce these substances could result instead in the production of hallucinogenic substances. The metabolic process in which this defect is hypothesized to occur is called the *transmethylation process.*

An early experimental test of the transmethylation hypothesis was possible as a result of the work conducted by Hoffer and Osmond (Hoffer & Osmond, 1962, 1964, 1966, 1968; Hoffer, Osmond, & Smythies, 1954). As early as 1952 these investigators treated schizophrenia with the vitamin niacin. Because niacin is a methyl acceptor, Hoffer and Osmond reasoned that the introduction of this vitamin might partially correct the hypothesized disorder in methylation processes and hence result in an alleviation of psychotic symptoms. The results of niacin treatment, however, are at best ambiguous—although Hoffer and Osmond have reported the treatment to be effective, others have failed to confirm these findings (Ashby, Collins, & Bassett, 1960; Ban & Lehmann, 1970). Moreover, a series of studies by the Canadian Mental Health Association suggests that niacin treatment may increase psychotic symptoms (Ban, 1971).

Although the niacin studies offer no reliable support for the transmethylation hypothesis, other studies do in fact support this hypothesis. If methylation processes are pathologic in schizophrenics, the introduction of drugs that stimulate these processes should produce an increase in psychotic symptoms. Some evidence suggests that L-dopa in fact has this predicted effect (Pollin, Cardon, & Kety, 1961; Smythies & Antun, 1970).

Conclusive evidence for the transmethylation hypothesis can come only from the discovery in schizophrenics of a hallucinogenic biochemical that is produced by an identified metabolic disorder. In this regard, Friedhoff and Van Winkle (1962) reported finding a hallucinogenic compound in the urine of 15 of 19 schizophrenics but not in the urine of any of 14 normal controls. This compound has been variously referred to as the pink spot and as 3,4-dimethoxyphenethylamine (DMPEA), and its discovery confirmed Harly-Mason's 1952 prediction of its existence. Although some studies support the hypothesis that DMPEA may have an important role in schizophrenia (e.g., Bourdillon et al., 1965; Boulton et al., 1967), others have failed to confirm these findings (e.g., Faurbye & Pind, 1964; Pennell, Pawlus, Saravis, & Scrimshaw, 1965). More recent research, however, seems to support the importance of DMPEA. It has been shown, for example, that liver extracts can enzymatically transform substances very similar to DMPEA into mescaline (Gunderson et al., 1974).

The available research has established the viability of the transmethylation hypothesis; specifically, it has been shown that the necessary biochemical ingredients for the metabolism of hallucinogenic substances exist in the human brain. What remains to be demonstrated is that methylating enzymes are found only in schizophrenics or are found in abnormal amounts in schizophrenics, and that a hallucinogenic substance is actually produced in schizophrenics in unusual amounts (Gunderson et al., 1974).

The Taraxein Hypothesis

Heath proposed that schizophrenia results from a substance he called taraxein (Heath, 1954, 1960; Heath, Cohen, Silva, Leach, & Cohen, 1959; Heath, Martens, Leach, Cohen, & Angel, 1957). He claimed to have isolated taraxein from the blood of schizophrenics and to have produced schizophrenic-like behavior in nonschizophrenic prisoners by injecting taraxein into their bloodstreams. Other investigators have failed to replicate Heath's findings even when using taraxein prepared in Heath's laboratory (Robins, 1957) or according to Heath's directions (Siegel, Niswalder, Sachs, & Stavros, 1959). The investigation of taraxein is continuing with results both positive (Heath, Guschwan, & Coffey, 1970) and negative (Mosher & Feinsilver, 1970) in regard to its possible etiologic role in schizophrenia.

Muscle Enzyme Research

One of the more promising lines of current biochemical research in schizophrenia is the study of a serum muscle enzyme called *creatine phosphokinase* (CPK). This enzyme is found in skeletal muscles and in the heart and brain.

Elevated CPK levels have been detected in many patients suffering from acute psychosis; moreover, CPK levels have been found to decline with remission of the psychotic symptoms. About 25 per cent of the close relatives of acutely psychotic patients show small but persistent elevations in CPK levels as well as a hyperactive CPK response to exercise. Meltzer (1969) reported that CPK elevation preceded by a few days the first clinical detection of psychosis and that this elevation was highest during the first week of a psychotic episode. He also found that in some psychotic patients CPK levels were 20 times higher than the upper limit found in normals and that in acutely psychotic patients there was a high positive correlation between increases in CPK, psychotic behavior, and sleep disturbance. Some of these findings have been replicated by others (see Gunderson et al., 1974). In brief, Meltzer's hypothesis—that muscle enzyme abnormalities in psychotic patients may lead to a better understanding of the factors that cause schizophrenia—is a viable one worthy of continued study.

THE FAMILIES OF SCHIZOPHRENICS

The search for environmental factors that lead to schizophrenia has focused on the study of family interactions. This line of research, initiated in response to a 1948 article by Fromm-Reichmann, has proceeded from the study of individuals to the study of total interaction patterns within the families of schizophrenics.

The Mothers of Schizophrenics

Fromm-Reichmann (1948) introduced the extraordinarily influential concept of a schizophrenogenic mother—that is, of a type of mother who engenders in her children a predisposition to schizophrenia. According to Fromm-Reichmann, the schizophrenogenic mother is domineering, rejecting, immature, and lacking in self-confidence. In the 1950s countless studies were done on the personality characteristics of mothers of schizophrenics (e.g., Abrahams & Varon, 1953; Galvin, 1956; Hill, 1955; Mark, 1953; Reichard & Tillman, 1950; Rodnick & Garmezy, 1957; Thomas, 1955; Tietze, 1949), and it was widely reported that the mothers of schizophrenics (1) tend to be disturbed (either neurotic or psychotic) and (2) tend to foster dependency in their children by being overprotective, domineering, and restrictive. It was also hypothesized that the combination of a domineering mother and a passive father leads to schizophrenia. Unfortunately, the studies on which these findings and hypotheses are based have been criticized as methodologically questionable (e.g., Fontana, 1966; Jacob, 1975). Moreover, Klebanoff (1959) has reported data suggesting that maternal overprotection is not specific to mothers of schizophrenics but instead is a behavioral tendency found in mothers of many disturbed children. Thus it is possible that mothers tend to react to children who have problems by overprotecting them. In summary, although clinicians have widely reported that schizophrenics have overprotective or domineering mothers, investigators have been unable to establish conclusively the existence of this or any other trait as being characteristic of the mothers of schizophrenics (Fontana, 1966).

Marital Schism and Marital Skew

During the 1950s Lidz and his associates undertook a decade-long study of the families of 14 young, upper-class schizophrenics (e.g., Lidz, 1973; Lidz, Cornelison, Fleck, & Terry, 1957; Fleck, 1960). As a result of this work, two types of families were identified. One type of family, called a *schismatic family,* was characterized by chronic strife and by controversy between the parents. Fleck (1960) hypothesized that in these families the child has difficulty identifying with one parent without incurring the wrath of the other. The other type of family in which the young schizophrenics were found to live was called a *skewed family.* In these families the parents are able to avoid overt conflict but only at the expense of some disturbance in family relationships; for example, a skewed family may avoid overt conflict if a weak, ineffectual father acquiesces to the demands of a domineering mother. All of the families studied by Lidz were found to be either schismatic or skewed.

The Lidz study was clearly one of the more ambitious research projects of the 1950s, but the absence of a control group and the subjective nature of the data render the results highly tenuous. For example, one finding that emerged from this work is that male schizophrenics tend to come from skewed families with a passive, ineffectual father and a disturbed, engulfing mother. In his review of relevant literature, however, Fontana (1966) found no reliable support for this finding.

Double-Bind Hypothesis

In 1956 Bateson and his colleagues introduced the double-bind hypothesis as an explanation of schizophrenic behavior (Bateson, Jackson, Haley, & Weakland, 1956). A *double-bind* is essentially a no-win situation in which an individual is damned regardless of what he does. Specifically, Bateson et al. (1956) defined a double-bind situation as including all of the following:

1. The situation must include at least two people (e.g., mother and child or mother, father, and child), one of whom is called the victim (e.g., the child).
2. The victim is told either (a) "if you do behavior X, I will punish you" or (b) "if you do not do behavior X, I will punish you." This communication is called the *primary negative injunction.*
3. Through nonverbal or more subtle means (e.g., tone of voice, gesture), the victim receives a contradictory message (e.g., do not listen to the prohibition). This communication is called the *secondary injunction.* The secondary injunction may or may not be given by the same individual who gave the primary injunction; for example, the mother may give the primary injunction and the father may give the secondary injunction.
4. The victim cannot escape from the double-bind.

Thus conflicting messages, threat of punishment, and inescapability are the basic ingredients of the double-bind situation hypothesized to engender schizophrenia. For example, Bateson et al. (1956) reported that Zen Buddhist priests employ a double-bind with their pupils. They hold a stick over a pupil's head and say fiercely: "If you say this stick is real, I will strike you with it. If you say this stick is not real, I will strike you with it. If you fail to say anything, I will strike you with it."

Bateson et al. (1956) proposed that children exposed to inescapable, conflicting commands from parents while under threat of punishment tend to develop schizophrenic symptoms. Specifically, any of the following behaviors might be learned in defense against double-bind communications:

1. A child exposed to conflicting commands may learn to insist on greater clarity in communications from others. An associated tendency to take all communications seriously and to be suspicious of others may also develop. Such learning is hypothesized to lead to paranoid symptoms.
2. A child exposed to conflicting commands may learn to dismiss them as not being serious. Overgeneralization of this learning may lead to hebephrenic symptoms in which the schizophrenic misperceives important matters as being inconsequential or as appropriate subjects for humor.
3. A child exposed to conflicting commands may simply learn to shut off the communication and to withdraw from interpersonal situations. Overgeneralization of this learning may lead to catatonic symptoms.

The double-bind hypothesis is intuitively attractive, but its scientific merits are questionable. In a recent review of the relevant literature, Schuham concluded: "The research literature fails to support the assumptions and predictions of the theory. . . . The tenets of the double-bind hypothesis require further limitation, clarification, and operationalization for it to become a reliable phenomenon capable of empirical validation" [1967, p. 409].

Communication Patterns

Although the specific predictions of the double-bind hypothesis have not been confirmed, Jacob's review of the literature indicates that most methodologically adequate investigations have found that normal families communicate more clearly and more effectively than do the families of schizophrenics (see Mishler & Waxler, 1968):

> Specifically normal families and parents were judged higher on attention and communication adequacy than were schizophrenic families and parents (Behrens, Rosenthal, & Chodoff, 1968); normal families produced more valid and explicit information than schizophrenic families (Ferreira & Winter, 1968); schizophrenic families were rated as more confused and produced TAT stories reflecting more vagueness and incompleteness than normal families (Friedman & Friedman, 1970); schizophrenic versus normal and nonschizophrenic disturbed children achieved fewer correct answers when instructions were communicated by parents (Haley, 1968); mothers of nonorganic schizophrenic children were judged to reflect more "perplexity" than mothers of organic schizophrenic children and mothers of normal children (Meyers & Goldfarb, 1961); and schizophrenic families were differentiated from normal controls along the dimension of amorphous-fragmented communications (Morris & Wynne, 1965) [1975, p. 54].

THEORIES OF GENERAL ETIOLOGY OF SCHIZOPHRENIA

A number of theorists posit an interaction between genetic and environmental factors in the etiology of schizophrenia (e.g., Rado, 1956). For example, Shields (1972) has proposed that a predisposition to schizophrenia is determined by a number of genes; the genes involved are not rare mutants but rather are normal variants circulating widely in the population. The greater the number of such genes an individual inherits, the lower is his threshold for developing schizophrenia. In this view an individual who inherits a high threshold for schizophrenia will not become schizophrenic even if exposed to unusual levels of environmental stress; furthermore, an individual who inherits a low threshold for schizophrenia will become schizophrenic if exposed to high levels of environmental stress, and an individual who inherits a very low threshold for schizophrenia will become schizophrenic in almost any real-world environment. Thus whether or not schizophrenia occurs depends on an interaction between the degree to which the individual is predisposed to develop the disorder and the level of environmental stress to which he is exposed.

In a widely cited article entitled *Schizotaxia, Schizotypy, and Schizophrenia,* Meehl (1962) also proposed that schizophrenia is caused by an interaction of genetic and environmental factors. Specifically, he suggested that when a defect of the central nervous system, called *schizotaxia,* is inherited, the individual may, as a consequence of social learning, become predisposed to schizophrenia. Following Rado (1956), Meehl applied the term *schizotype* to the personality organization that develops. In this view, schizotaxia always leads to a schizotype personality organization, but this personality organization only predisposes the individual to schizophrenia. Whether or not the schizotype becomes schizophrenic depends on environmental factors, the most important of which is the mother's behavior.

Mednick's Anxiety Conditioning Theory

Mednick (1958) proposed that the preschizophrenic is hypersensitive to emotionally arousing stimuli. Based on this hypothesis, Mednick further postulated a cycle of events in which the preschizophrenic comes to fear many environmental and cognitive stimuli. Specifically, autonomic hypersensitivity should facilitate both a Pavlovian conditioning of anxiety to environmental stimuli and a generalization of this learning to other neutral cues. Having learned to respond anxiously to many environmental stimuli, the preschizophrenic becomes increasingly anxious, and this anxiety leads to still further conditioning of anxiety to environmental cues. Moreover, as the level of anxiety increases, thoughts begin to race through the preschizophrenic's mind, and these thoughts also become associated with anxiety. Eventually, the preschizophrenic learns to think in unusual or in tangential ways in order to avoid the anxiety associated with normal thoughts. The basic notion, then, is that schizophrenic thinking represents conditioned avoidance responses reinforced by anxiety reduction and that the etiologic condition for this learning is autonomic hypersensitivity.

During the 1960s in Denmark, Mednick and Schulsinger (1968) and Mednick (1970) conducted a long-term, longitudinal study designed to obtain data relevant to the possible antecedents of schizophrenia and to their theory of anxiety conditioning. Two large groups of mothers were identified—those who were chronic schizophrenics and hence whose children were considered high risks for schizophrenia, and those who were normal and hence whose children were considered low risks for schizophrenia. Moreover, the normal and schizophrenic mothers were matched on a number of socioeconomic variables. At the start of the study, the average age of the children in each group was approximately 15 years. A battery of tests was administered, and the investigators then kept track of the children who did and who did not develop schizophrenia. The initial results produced a number of correlates of the children who subsequently developed schizophrenia, including findings of birth complications during the period when the mother was pregnant with the child, of psychological deficits in calming down once excited, and of psychological deficits in word association tasks.

Although the finding that the preschizophrenics had difficulty calming down once excited is consistent with Mednick's theory that preschizophrenics are hyperactive to emotionally arousing stimuli, a critical issue is whether preschizophrenics acquire conditioned anxiety responses more readily than do normals. Some early studies found evidence supporting this prediction (e.g., Pfaffman & Schlosberg, 1936; Spence & Taylor, 1953), but other studies failed to find any differences between schizophrenics and normals in the acquisition of conditioned anxiety responses. In their longitudinal study, Mednick and Schulsinger found that, compared to high-risk children who did not become disturbed, those who did (1) learned avoidance responses more readily, (2) showed higher-magnitude GSR responses, and (3) more readily acquired conditioned GSR responses. Because the GSR is a measure of anxiety, these results were interpreted as support for Mednick's theory that schizophrenia results from the pervasive conditioning of anxiety first to external and then to internal stimuli. More recent studies, however, have found that schizophrenics do not show a generalized hypersensitivity to emotionally arousing stimuli but instead show autonomic hypersensitivity to some stimuli and not to others (e.g., Zahn, Rosenthal, Pollin, & Mosher, 1972; see Magaro, 1973). The weight of the evidence at the present time provides inconsistent support for Mednick's theory.

Cameron's Psychoanalytic Theory

Cameron's (1963) psychoanalytic theory of schizophrenia posits that the basic cause of this disorder is inadequate development of the ego. Specifically, the preschizophrenic is seen as having failed to establish adequate self–other boundaries. He does not have a self-identity that is independent of his parents, nor does he discriminate adequately between internal and external stimuli. The antecedent condition for this pathological development is hypothesized to be parental behavior during the infant's first year of life. Specifically, the mother either fails to provide comfort and gratification or smothers the child in a manner that fosters almost total dependency. In both cases the seeds of hostility are planted, and the child develops neither an identity of his own nor trust in other people.

Having failed to establish an adequate self-identity and basic trust in others that would permit normal social interactions, the preschizophrenic child resorts to fantasy to satisfy his ungratified sexual and aggressive id impulses. These impulses are repressed, however, because the child fears further parental rejection. Moreover, the child behaves passively in order not to anger his parents and incur further rejection, and he withdraws in order to avoid any possible conflicts with his parents or others. In this manner the child maintains a borderline adjustment, quietly conforming to parental demands that cannot be avoided. If no other factors induce stress, the individual might manage to survive at this level. Psychoanalytic theory, however, posits that the family continues to subject the preschizophrenic child to stress in the form of maternal domination, double-bind communications, and hostility among family members. Moreover, the family pattern of a dominant mother and a weak father is hypothesized to encourage in the male child an opposite-sex identification with the mother, from which flow homosexual feelings toward the father. Although the cross-sex identification is approved by the parents, the homosexual impulses are disapproved of and the child represses them.

In late adolescence, the preschizophrenic is threatened both by the social expectation of his becoming an independent person and by the social expectation of dating members of the opposite sex. Because these expectations threaten the preschizophrenic's very identity with the mother, from whom he inadequately distinguishes himself, the individual becomes frightened of personality disintegration and of a loss of control over his homosexual impulses. These overwhelming fears lead to an extreme withdrawal from the social environment and to a regressive return to parental protection. If the withdrawal and regression continue, the defective ego permits the individual to lapse into a state of total psychotic (primary process) thought. The individual, now schizophrenic, avoids all stress by his failure to recognize reality, and he gratifies id impulses by fantasy and infantile behavior. Even though these behaviors appear to the observer to be self-destructive, they are seen by psychoanalysts as a protective response designed to prevent action on overwhelmingly hostile impulses to kill the parents for smothering development and for inhibiting homosexual impulses (Cameron, 1963).

As noted previously, some evidence supports the hypothesis that schizophrenics tend to have domineering mothers. In general, however, Cameron's theory lacks adequate empirical verification.

TREATMENT OF SCHIZOPHRENIA

Even though no specific causal factor of schizophrenia has yet been identified, partially effective treatment procedures have been developed.

Drug Treatment

A number of phenothiazine drugs (major tranquilizers) have been effective in producing symptomatic relief sufficient to shorten greatly the length of time of hospitalization. As noted in Chapter 5, there are considerable individual differences in reactions to drug treatment, and long-term maintenance on drugs is often indicated. Present research on the possible side effects of the long-term use of phenothiazines suggests that an irreversible muscular disorder called tardive dyskinesia occurs in between 1 and 41 per cent of the patients treated (Gunderson et al., 1974). For just how long and at what dosages various phenothiazines can be safely employed is currently under investigation.

Token Economies

Token economies have been introduced into many mental hospital wards to teach chronic schizophrenics various social behaviors. In a control group assessment of the effects of token economy treatment with chronic schizophrenics, Maley, Feldman, and Ruskin found evidence of generalized psychological improvement in the treated group:

> These results indicate that token economy patients, as compared to custodial-care patients, exhibited more appropriate mood states, were more cooperative, and engaged in more communication with better developed skills. Token economy patients did not show as much "psychotic behavior," such as unusual motor activity, confusion, anxiety, and bizarreness. The token economy patients were seen as being more socially appropriate and desirable in that they were rated higher in their ability to function on low-level jobs, were rated in less need of hospitalization, and rated as more likeable in so far as people would desire to spend time talking and being with them. All of these findings demonstrate that token-economy treated patients were more sociable, less withdrawn and afraid of people, and more likely to be able to interact with others in a "normal" manner [1973, p. 143].

Although it is clear that token economies are effective in helping schizophrenics to function better in hospital environments, an important and largely unanswered question is to what extent such improvements persist following discharge from the hospital.

Psychotherapy

Many varieties of psychodynamic therapies have been employed to treat schizophrenia. In addition to psychoanalysis, Sullivan's (1953) interpersonal therapy was popular during the 1950s, and Laing's (1967) experiential therapy received widespread attention during the late 1960s. There is insufficient objective evidence to draw any firm conclusions regarding the effects of these various therapies. It should be noted, however, that the general impression among clinicians is that psychodynamic therapy is largely ineffective with psychotics.

SUMMARY: CHAPTERS 15 AND 16

The term *schizophrenia* refers to a heterogeneous group of psychotic thought disorders that collectively constitute one of the most prevalent forms of psychopathology in the United States today. The disorder is characterized by thought disturbance, delusions, apathy, social withdrawal, and bizarre behavior. Auditory and, to a lesser extent, visual hallucinations are common.

Although schizophrenia is relatively easy to distinguish from other syndromes discussed in this book, the extraordinary heterogeneity of schizophrenic behaviors has led to many attempts to construct a classificatory system of subtypes of schizophrenia. During the nineteenth century, clinical observers described disorders we would today call catatonia, paranoia, and hebephrenia. Toward the end of the nineteenth century, Kraepelin published volumes of case histories and of statistical charts to support his hypothesis that catatonia, paranoia, and hebephrenia are best considered as subtypes of a single disorder rather than as separate disorders. He chose the term *dementia praecox* to refer to the disorder he described; the word *praecox* indicates a puberty disorder. During the early part of the twentieth century, Bleuler introduced the term *schizophrenia;* this term derives from words meaning "split soul." In Bleuler's view, the fundamental disease process in schizophrenia is a loosening of thought associations, and this loosening is associated with a disintegration of personality functions. Bleuler also introduced the concept of autism to refer to an escape from reality and a flight into fantasy, and he added a fourth subtype, called simple schizophrenia, to Kraepelin's system. Perhaps Bleuler's most important contribution was his emphasis on the heterogeneity of schizophrenic syndromes. Although Bleuler himself saw schizophrenia as a distinct disorder, today many observers suggest that schizophrenic behaviors are so heterogeneous that they are several disorders rather than one. Another early theorist was Meyer, who proposed in 1906 that schizophrenia should be studied and classified on the basis of its developmental history rather than on the basis of the symptomatology present at the time of hospitalization. Meyer, however, was too far ahead of his time to have the impact on the field that his ideas merited.

DSM-II defines eleven subtypes of schizophrenia (see Table 15-1). The paranoid type, which is most prevalent, is indicated by the presence of delusions; the hebephrenic type is associated with inappropriate affect, including a tendency to take lightly matters that others consider serious; the catatonic type is associated with mood fluctuations between states of aimless activity and of extreme apathy (including stupor); simple schizophrenia is indicated by social withdrawal, apathy, and the absence of hallucinations and delusions. The common element to these various disorders is thought disturbance. The DSM-II subcategories are of limited value because they lack adequate reliability and validity. In recent years, quantitatively oriented investigators have attempted to construct a subclassification system of schizophrenia by employing factor-analytic techniques. The initial results from this work are promising, but more validity research is still needed for a meaningful evaluation of the factor-analytic categories.

Three distinctions among schizophrenics have been made by researchers because these distinctions reduce within-group performance variations (see Table 15-2), thereby increasing the interpretability of research studies. The reactive-process distinction is a distinction between schizophrenics with good and poor premorbid social adjustment. The paranoid-nonparanoid distinction is a distinction between schizophrenics who do and who do not exhibit delusions. Both of these distinctions have some demonstrated validity; in general, reactive and paranoid schizophrenics are less disturbed than are process and nonparanoid schizophrenics, respectively. A distinction between acute and chronic schizophrenia is also made although the various operational definitions of chronicity have been criticized in recent years.

The prevalence of schizophrenia in the United States has been estimated to be about 3 per cent of the population. However, many more people show pronounced schizophrenic traits or schizoid personality structure—these people are excessively shy, insensitive, withdrawn, and cold, and they have a rich fantasy life. It has been found repeatedly that schizophrenia is most prevalent in the lowest socioeconomic groups, but it is unclear whether this is because schizophrenics tend to drift into the lower classes or because they tend to grow up in poverty. The incidence of schizophrenia has also been found to vary across cultures; the significance of these findings, however, is unclear because of a lack of uniformity in diagnostic procedures. For example, it has been shown that when presented with videotapes of the same patients, New York psychiatrists diagnosed schizophrenia more frequently than did London psychiatrists. Nevertheless, it is doubtful if differences in diagnostic procedures alone could account for all of the findings of different incidence and prevalence rates across cultures. In this regard, it is possible that the greater stress associated with living in urban, industrialized societies and/or in poverty has an etiologic role in schizophrenia.

Hunt and Cofer (1944) introduced the term *psychological deficit* to refer to performance differences between psychiatric patients and normals on an experimental task. The literature on psychological deficits in schizophrenia is voluminous. The following possible deficits were reviewed in Chapter 15:

1. Several theories have been proposed to specify the nature of the deficit in schizophrenic conceptual processes. The regression hypothesis proposes that this deficit consists of the intrusion of primary process thinking, whereas Von Domarus's (1946) hypothesis proposes that this deficit consists of illogical reasoning processes. Neither of these hypotheses has been substantiated. On the other hand, there exists evidence that schizophrenics do not spontaneously use abstract concepts to as great an extent as do normals. Also, there exists solid evidence that schizophrenic patients show a greater tendency than do normals to employ overinclusive concepts.

2. Schizophrenic speech is bizarre, includes neologisms, and is characterized by unusual associations. Research on the formal properties of schizophrenic speech reveals two deficits: (a) schizophrenics show a greater tendency than do normals to repeat the same words within a given passage or utterance, and (b) the informational content of schizophrenic speech is less redundant than that of normal speech—hence schizophrenic speech is less communicative. Research on simple communication processes suggests that schizophrenics show a greater tendency than do normals to get sidetracked; that is, although their initial verbal association to an object may be appropriate, subsequent responses tend to be more of an association to the initial word selected and less of an appropriate descriptor of the object.

3. A number of studies have established that schizophrenics are deficient in short-term memory. One possible explanation of these findings is that schizophrenics encode to-be-remembered material in ways that are difficult to retrieve.

4. Perceptual deficits in schizophrenia include a tendency to hallucinate, a deficiency in attention, and a deficit in time judgments. It has been hypothesized that social withdrawal leads to hallucinations. Although a series of studies conducted during the 1950s found that sensory deprivation increased hallucinatory experiences in college students, these studies are open to alternative explanations that the experimental procedures created social demand for unusual experiences. Another strategy for studying hallucinations is to evaluate the effects of hallucinogenic drugs. Feinberg (1962) has noted several differences between drug-induced and schizophrenic hallucinations, thus implying that the former is at best an approximate model of the latter.

Perhaps the most salient psychological deficit in schizophrenics is their impaired ability to concentrate on a line of reasoning or to attend to the demands of a task at hand. This deficiency in attention has been demonstrated in both simple and complex reaction time experiments. Yates proposed that attention deficiencies in schizophrenia are related to a limited capacity for short-term memory. Chapman et al. (1964), however, favor a competing response hypothesis in which intruding thoughts result in delayed reactions to the onset of stimuli. Rodnick and Garmezy's (1957) social censure hypothesis proposes that schizophrenics overreact to, and withdraw from, censure cues (any signal suggesting criticism or disapproval) and that this reaction results in poor performances on experimental tasks, including reaction-time tasks. Recent evidence provides inconsistent support for the hypothesis that attentional deficits are related to short-term memory; the competing response hypothesis is viable, but the nature of any such interfering responses is unclear; and the social censure hypothesis requires reformulation in light of recent data.

Little is known about the causes of schizophrenia. The available evidence strongly supports the hypothesis that a predisposition to schizophrenia is inherited. Specific genetic factors, however, have not been identified. Nor is there much evidence relating genetic factors to specific psychological deficits.

Biochemical research on the causes of schizophrenia has revealed so many false leads, and has been associated in recent years with so many exaggerated claims, that many investigators approach this literature with considerable caution. Nevertheless, in less than three decades a number of significant findings have emerged. It has been shown, for example, that the necessary biochemical ingredients for the metabolism of hallucinogenic substances exist in the human brain. These findings support the viability of the transmethylation hypothesis that schizophrenics manufacture within their bodies hallucinogenic substances like LSD-25 and mescaline, and that the presence of these substances causes schizophrenia. It has yet to be demonstrated, however, that schizophrenics actually metabolize hallucinogenic substances and that they do so to a degree greater than normals. Another promising line of biochemical research is the study of a serum muscle enzyme called CPK.

Fromm-Reichmann's 1948 publication of the concept of a schizophrenogenic mother stimulated an extraordinary number of studies on the families of schizophrenics. The available research has generally failed to establish that the mothers of schizophrenics tend to have a particular type of personality; however, there are many reports that these mothers tend to be domineering and overprotective of their children. It was also hypothesized that the combination of a domineering mother and a passive father is a cause of schizophrenia, but this hypothesis lacks support from methodologically adequate studies. The notion of a single type of mother or a single type of mother-father combination appears to be oversimplistic. For this reason, research has increasingly focused on the study of larger units of family interaction patterns. In the 1950s, an influential longitudinal study on total family interaction patterns was conducted by Lidz and his colleagues. As a consequence of its subjective methodology, this work failed to produce any reliable empirical findings; however, it led to a theoretical distinction between schizophrenic families in which there is overt conflict (marital schism) and schizophrenic families in which imbalance in family relationships occurs as a consequence of compromises to preclude overt conflict (marital skew). Perhaps the major significance of this work is that it focused attention on overall family dynamic patterns.

Bateson's (1956) double-bind hypothesis also focused attention on family dynamics. This hypothesis posits that children exposed to inescapable, conflicting commands from parents while under threat of punishment tend to develop schizophrenic symptoms. That is, they either (1) tend to demand greater clarity in communication (hypothesized to be an antecedent condition of paranoid suspicion); (2) tend to dismiss the communication by not taking it seriously (hypothesized to be an antecedent condition of hebephrenic symptoms); or (3) tend to withdraw and shut off communication completely (hypothesized to be an antecedent condition of catatonic symptoms). The double-bind hypothesis is vague and difficult to test, and recent reviewers have concluded that it needs revision.

Perhaps the most significant advance in family research has been the development of an objective methodology for studying family interaction patterns. It is now clear that family behavior is affected by the following variables: sex of the schizophrenic, family economic status, family cultural and religious background, family size, and age of family members (Jacobs, 1975). At the very least, then, a study needs to control for these sources of variance if it is to identify a family dynamic associated with the presence of a schizophrenic member. In addition to such controls, methodologically adequate studies need to sample families in an adequate manner and should rely on coded observational data rather than on patients' retrospective accounts of family interactions. Because few studies conducted prior to 1965 meet the criteria for methodological adequacy, the findings from these studies are questionable.

Methodologically adequate studies of family interaction patterns have generally failed to confirm the many findings of the less objective studies reported during the 1950s and the early 1960s. One important exception to this general rule is the finding that in schizophrenics' families, communications tend to be more ambiguous and less effective than in nonschizophrenics' families.

Four theories of general etiology were noted in this chapter: Shields's genetic-environmental stress theory, Meehl's schizotaxia-schizotype theory, Mednick's theory of autonomic hyperreactivity and anxiety conditioning, and Cameron's psychoanalytic theory. A current trend in research designed to test theories of general etiology is the longitudinal study of high-risk children. Mednick and Schulsinger (1968), who reported the first objective high-risk study, found a number of correlational antecedents of schizophrenia including the following: birth complications during the period when the mother was pregnant with the child (Mednick, 1970), psychological deficits in calming down once excited, psychological deficits in word association tasks, high-magnitude GSR responses, and an unusually rapid acquisition of conditioned GSR responses. More recent laboratory studies, however, have found that schizophrenics do not show a generalized hypersensitivity to emotionally arousing stimuli but instead show autonomic hypersensitivity to only some stimuli. A number of studies of high-risk children are currently in progress.

During the last 25 years we have witnessed considerable progress in the treatment of schizophrenia. A number of drugs have been shown to produce significant symptomatic relief, and behavior therapy has been shown to be partially effective in establishing social behaviors in hospitalized, chronic schizophrenics. Psychotherapy is generally believed to be of limited value with psychotic patients.

A topic closely related to schizophrenia is fantasy. Fantasy and dream research are discussed at the end of Chapter 20.

Chapter 17

Organic Brain Syndromes

ALFRED W. KASZNIAK and STEVEN REISS

the study of the various disturbances of the higher cortical functions accompanying local brain lesions is . . . highly complex. It would be wrong, however, to suppose that such an investigation is thereby impossible or that the role of the local lesion in the disturbance of the higher mental processes cannot be defined. Experience shows that, despite all these complications, the psychological investigation of the higher cortical functions has a role in the topical diagnosis of brain lesions and that it is a method that can be used for these purposes in neurological and neurosurgical practice.

LURIA (1966, p. 93)

The diseases discussed in this chapter are grouped together on the basis of etiology. Organic brain syndromes are impairments in psychological functioning that result from either disease, damage, or injury to the brain. The symptoms vary considerably, depending on the nature of the problem, the area of the brain affected, the age of the patient, and in some types of diseases the premorbid personality of the patient. A number of symptoms, however, clinically suggest the possible presence of damage or injury to the brain. These symptoms include:

1. Disorientation of time, place, or person.
2. Impairment of recent memory.
3. Global impairment of intellectual functions.
4. Perceptual deficits.
5. Impairment of speech or speech comprehension.
6. Neurological symptoms such as convulsions, jerking of muscle groups, and many other motor abnormalities.

HISTORICAL PERSPECTIVE

One of the early debates in medicine concerned the location of the sites of reason and emotion (Critchley, 1969). Some ancients held these sites to be in the liver, others argued for the spleen, but most agreed that the heart is the all-important organ providing the biological basis for consciousness. The view that the heart is the seat of emotions was expressed in the Bible in passages such as, "And let none of you imagine evil in your hearts against his neighbor" (Zechariah 8:17) and "A merry heart doth good like medicine" (Proverbs 17:22). Even today we refer to compassionate people as "having a good heart." There appears to have been no clear point in history at which the brain assumed its present place of importance. In the fifth century B.C., Hippocrates proposed that the brain is the organ of the intellect and the heart the organ of the senses (Luria, 1966). Galen proposed, in the second century B.C., that a fluid circulated within the ventricles of the brain and that this fluid somehow gave rise to mental processes. With relatively minor modifications, Galen's beliefs persisted throughout the Middle Ages.

A resurgence of scientific interest in the brain occurred in the early nineteenth century as a consequence of the theories of Gall and Spurzheim (Boring, 1950). These theorists maintained that each personality trait is controlled by its own unique region of the brain, so that the larger the brain region, the greater is the extent to which the personality trait is present. Understanding another person's personality was reduced to studying the contours of the skull for clues to the sizes of the various brain regions. An overly optimistic person, for example, was expected to have an enlargement of the skull over brain region 17 (see Figure 17-1), whereas a person skilled in calculation was believed to have an enlargement of the skull over brain region 29. This attempt to correlate skull contours with personality and intellectual traits came to be known as *phrenology.* Today we know that skull contours are not related to any meaningful personality traits; in other words, phrenology is erroneous.

Gall's theory was important because it stimulated research that eventually led to some important findings. Foremost among these findings are the discoveries of two brain regions that control speech behavior. In 1861 Broca found a lesion in the brain of a patient who had developed a speech disturbance. (The lesion was in the posterior third of the inferior frontal gyrus; see Figure 17-2.) Later that same year, Broca discovered a similar lesion in the brain of another patient who suffered from a similar speech disturbance. Broca's discovery stimulated additional research, and in 1874 Wernicke published a case in which a brain lesion was associated with a disturbance in the ability to understand speech. (The lesion was in the posterior third of the superior temporal gyrus.) Today lesions in or near "Broca's area" are recognized as causally related to certain dysfunctions of expressive speech, and lesions in or near "Wernicke's area" are recognized as causally related to dysfunctions of speech comprehension.

Clinical neuropsychology is a relatively new discipline that attempts to correlate damage to specific brain areas with specific patterns of abnormal behavior (see Benton, 1969; Miller, 1972; Reitan & Davison, 1974). This chapter is an introduction to clinical neuropsychology.

NEUROLOGICAL DISEASES[1]

Eight categories of basic diseases of the central nervous system are reviewed here.

1. Vascular diseases.
2. Traumatic diseases.
3. Infectious diseases.
4. Neoplasms.
5. Degenerative diseases.
6. Nutritional deficiencies.
7. Toxic diseases.
8. Epilepsy.

Vascular Diseases of the Cerebral Hemispheres

A diminution in the supply of blood to an area of the brain can deprive the neurons in this area of the nutrients and oxygen needed for normal func-

[1] The description of the various diseases in this chapter follows that provided by Curtis, Jacobson, and Marcus (1972) and the other reports that are cited.

Figure 17-1
The "Powers and Organs of the Mind" according to phrenology. (From E. G. Boring, *A history of experimental psychology.* New York: Appleton-Century-Crofts, 1950. Reprinted with permission of the publisher.)

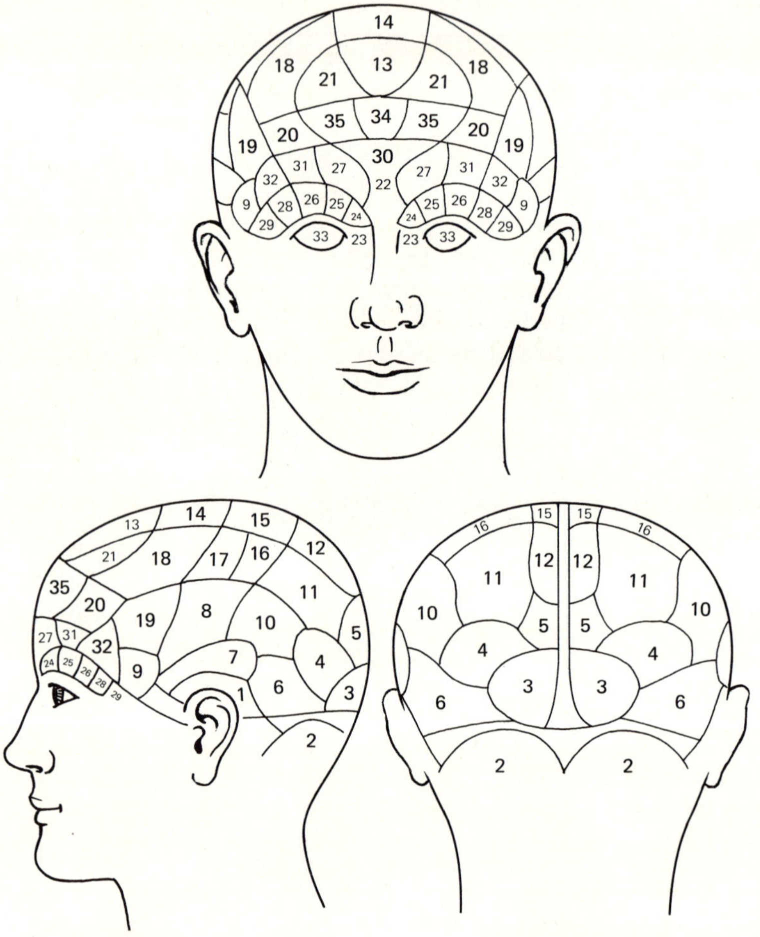

AFFECTIVE FACULTIES

PROPENSITIES

? Desire to live
* Alimentiveness
1 Destructiveness
2 Amativeness
3 Philoprogenitiveness
4 Adhesiveness
5 Inhabitiveness
6 Combativeness
7 Secretiveness
8 Acquisitiveness
9 Constructiveness

SENTIMENTS

10 Cautiousness
11 Approbativeness
12 Self-Esteem
13 Benevolence
14 Reverence
15 Firmness
16 Conscientiousness
17 Hope
18 Marvelousness
19 Ideality
20 Mirthfulness
21 Imitation

INTELLECTUAL FACULTIES

PERCEPTIVE

22 Individuality
23 Configuration
24 Size
25 Weight and Resistance
26 Coloring
27 Locality
28 Order
29 Calculation
30 Eventuality
31 Time
32 Tune
33 Language

REFLECTIVE

34 Comparison
35 Causality

An artist's caricature of phrenology's thesis that the contours of the skull reveal personality traits. (Reprinted with permission of Historical Pictures Services, Inc., Chicago, Illinois.)

Figure 17-2
Left cerebral hemisphere with the approximate locations of Broca's and Wernicke's areas.

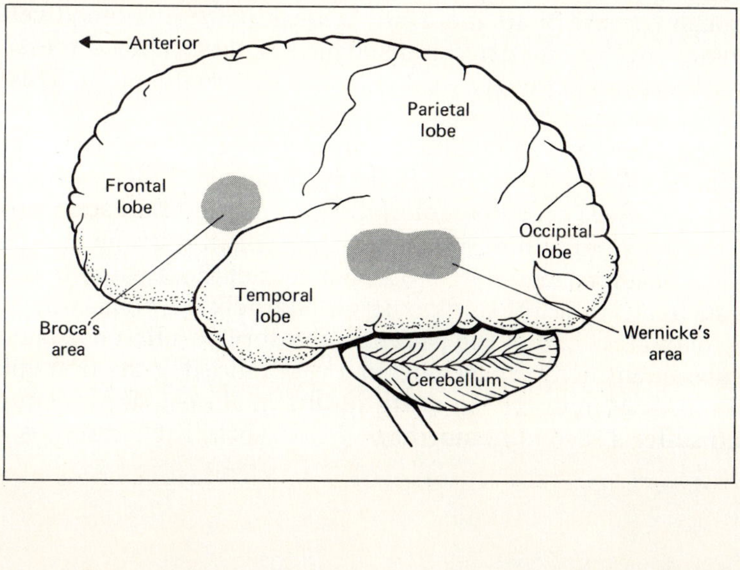

tioning. Such a diminution is usually caused either by an obstruction in a blood vessel or by a rupture of a blood vessel. The psychological effects of these vascular problems depend on the particular brain area affected and on the age of the patient.

Cerebral Ischemia ("Stroke")

The accumulation of fatty material in a blood vessel feeding a brain region can deprive this region of an adequate supply of nutrients and of oxygen; when this occurs, the affected brain area is said to suffer cerebral ischemia, and the individual is said to suffer from ischemic-occlusive disease. The ischemic episode can be brief or prolonged. Brief episodes usually produce a temporary impairment of normal psychological functioning; in prolonged episodes, however, the affected neurons may die, possibly causing a permanent impairment of psychological functioning. Compared to other cerebrovascular problems, ischemic-occlusive disease has the highest incidence.

Cerebral Embolism

An embolus is, in most cases, a fragment of thrombus (blood clot) that has become detached from a larger thrombus within the heart. When the embolus breaks loose from the thrombus, it usually travels in the blood stream until it reaches a point where the diameter of the vessel is smaller than the size of the embolus. Hence emboli will often lodge in the smaller cerebral vessels, thereby creating a blockage of blood flow similar to that found in ischemic-occlusive disease.

Intracerebral Hemorrhage

A third variety of cerebral vascular disease is intracerebral hemorrhage. There are several ways in which hemorrhages (bleeding) within the brain can occur, including (1) as a complication of a circulatory disorder (e.g., leukemia), (2) through rupture of an aneurysm (a weak point in a blood vessel), and (3) as a consequence of repetitive and sudden changes in blood pressure in which the vessels are progressively weakened and eventually burst. This latter condition occurs in some individuals with hypertension.

When hemorrhaging does occur, it most typically occurs at the base of the brain. Blood from this area flows into the ventricles of the brain (see Figure 17-3) and places considerable pressure on the brain-stem structures that are crucial for maintaining vital functions (e.g., breathing and heart rate). Death occurs in approximately 15 to 22 per cent of those patients with a first episode of such bleeding (Nishioka, 1966; Skultely & Nishioka, 1966). Moreover, approximately half of the patients who survive a first episode of bleeding have a subsequent hemorrhage within a year following the first episode (Curtis, Jacobson, & Marcus, 1972); death results in almost 80 per cent of those patients who suffer a second hemorrhage (McKissock, Richardson, & Walsh, 1962).

Traumatic Disease

A severe blow to the head (trauma) can impair psychological functioning by temporarily displacing neurons or by rupturing blood vessels. Although death can result if the bleeding is undiagnosed, the long-term prognosis of most cases of severe head injury is good. Miller and Stern (1965) re-examined 92 survivors of severe head injury from three to 40 years after the initial trauma. Some degree of intellectual impairment was present in only about 11 per cent of these patients. In a study of patients in Japan, intellectual impairment was observed in only about 2 per cent of 1,168 cases of head trauma that did not penetrate the skull (Oto, 1969). In those relatively few cases of head injury in which lasting intellectual impairment occurs, it has been hypothesized that the cause may be a permanent disruption of nerve fibers resulting from a shearing action of the skull against the brain (Strich, 1969). Another factor that appears to be related to residual intellectual impairment following head trauma is the length of time the patient remains unconscious following the blow. Van der Zwan (1969) reported that in patients who suffered at least three weeks of posttraumatic unconsciousness, some degree of intellectual deficit was observable in the majority of the survivors whom he examined. Yet, even in these cases, a socially disabling impairment of intellectual functioning was rare.

Figure 17-3
A sagital section of the human brain showing the ventricles, or cavities. These cavities are filled with cerebrospinal fluid under normal conditions, and the infusion of blood during intracerebral hemorrhage causes the ventricles to become swollen with a consequent increase of pressure on internal structures.

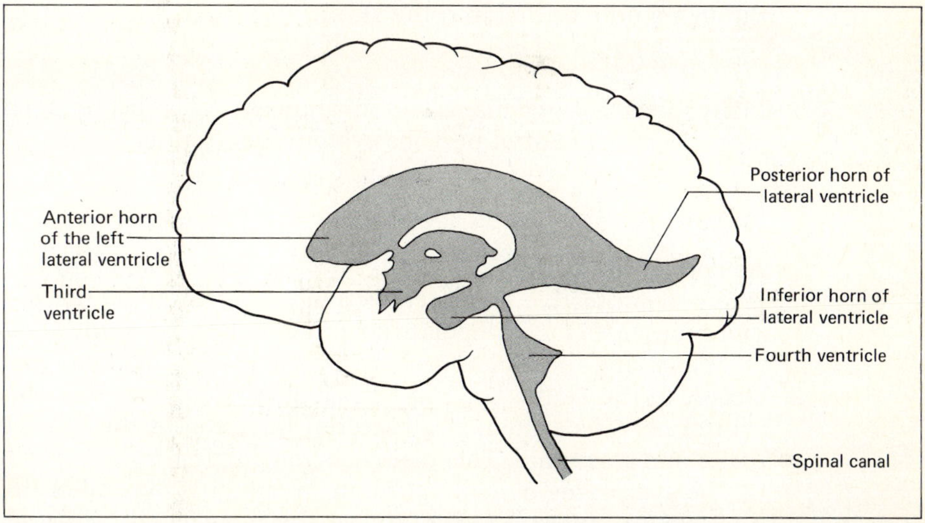

Cerebral Concussion

A concussion is indicated by a general disorientation, or dazed feeling, following injury to the head; this symptom may last for a few minutes or for several hours. Memory for the events occurring during this period of disorientation is usually impaired, and sometimes memory for events occurring minutes, hours, or days before the injury is also impaired. An occasional complication is the postconcussion syndrome, consisting of recurrent episodes of headache and dizziness. Although the actual physiological explanation of concussion is unclear, it appears that the forcing of the cerebral cortex against the hard surfaces of the skull produces a transient dysfunction of the involved neurons.

Contusions and Lacerations

A *contusion* is a local area of swelling and capillary hemorrhage resembling a bruise; contusions most typically occur directly under the site of the blow to the skull and across from this site. A *laceration* of the brain is an actual tear in the surface of the cortex. Contusions and lacerations are often accompanied by the same symptoms as those noted for concussions; however, specific disturbances in sensation and/or in muscular behavior may also occur.

Hematoma

If a severe blow to the head ruptures an artery or vein, blood may collect above or below the outermost covering of the brain. Such a gathering of blood, called a *hematoma,* compresses the underlying brain tissue, thereby disrupting normal functioning. As greater amounts of blood leak into this area, a progressively greater portion of the brain is compressed and the patient feels increasingly confused and disoriented; if untreated, eventual coma and death may occur. A hematoma is properly treated by suctioning off the collected blood through a hole drilled into the skull.

Infections

Many infectious organisms and substances such as bacteria, viruses, fungi, and protozoa affect central nervous system functioning.

Meningitis

As shown in Figure 17-4, the cortical tissue of the brain is covered by three layers of protective tissue collectively referred to as the *meninges.* The *pia mater* provides the immediate covering of the cortex, the *arachnoid* covers the pia mater, and the *dura mater* covers the arachnoid and is the protective layer closest to the skull. The most frequently occurring infectious disease of the central nervous system is a bacterial infection of the space between the pia mater and arachnoid. This disease is known as *purulent* (pus-like) *meningitis.*

The symptoms of acute purulent meningitis depend on the age of the patient. Infants under the age of six usually show fever, decreased activity, drowsiness, failure to take feedings, and occasional vomiting. The older infant or child typically shows severe stiffness of the neck, fever, convulsions, and in the later stages, coma. In the older child and adult, common symptoms during the early stages of meningitis are bodily aches, upper respiratory infection, and low fever. As the infection progresses, chills, vomiting, severe headache, and stiffness of the neck occur. With further progression of the disease the patient becomes drowsy and may eventually enter a coma.

The early diagnosis of meningitis is crucial because death is the typical outcome in untreated cases. Prior to the discovery of antibiotic drugs, the mortality rate for patients having meningitis was approximately 90 per cent. Today, with specific drugs available for the treatment of specific infecting organisms, this rate is under 10 per cent (Swartz & Dodge, 1965).

The psychological aftereffects of meningitis are more severe in children than in adults, perhaps because in children the disease can impair later intellectual development (Johnson, 1960). For example, in a study of 99 patients with meningitis resulting from bacterial infection, permanent intellectual impairment was observed in only three cases, notably all children (Dodge & Swartz, 1965). Lorber (1961) has reported a long-term follow-up of 100 children who recovered from meningitis resulting from a tuberculous infection. Of the 100 children, 23 showed severe neurological and behavioral aftereffects, with six of these children being profoundly mentally retarded.

Figure 17-4
The meninges covering the brain.

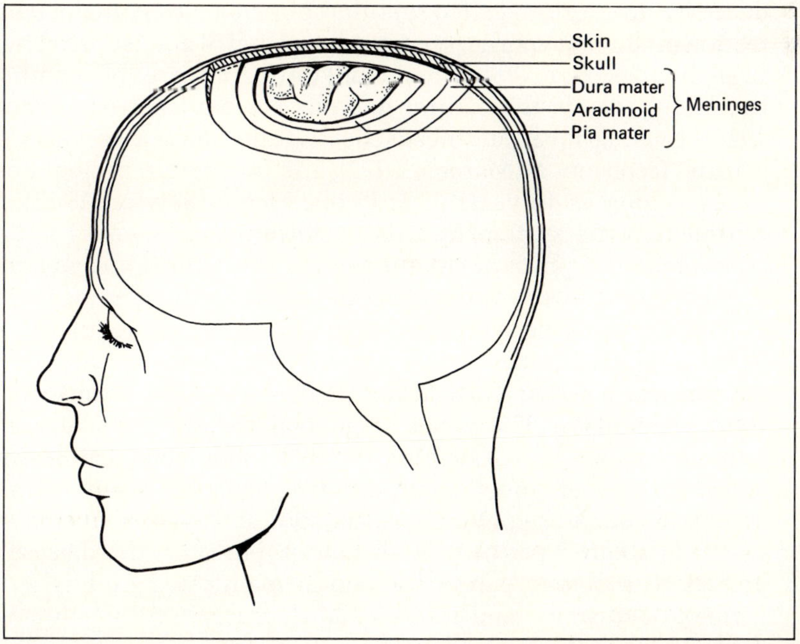

Encephalitis refers to an infection of the brain region. Its symptoms depend on the type of infection (viral or bacterial), on the area affected, and on the age of the patient. Encephalitis occurs in both acute and chronic forms.

The clinical syndrome in most cases of acute viral encephalitis includes the sudden onset of vomiting, headache, drowsiness, stiffness of the neck, convulsions, and possibly coma. The aftereffects of the disease, however, are usually greater in children than in adults (Merritt, 1967). Postencephalitic behaviors shown by children can include hyperactivity, impulsivity, distractibility, and aggression; fortunately, these behaviors can be treated by the administration of amphetamines (Levy, 1959; see Chapter 5). The most serious aftereffect in children who survive, however, is mental retardation. During the 1950s, encephalitis produced approximately 5 per cent of all institutionalized cases of mental retardation (Jervis, 1959). In general it appears that the older the child at the time of onset of the disease, the less severe is any intellectual impairment that might result.

The aftereffects of acute viral encephalitis are typically less severe in adults. Adult postencephalitic patients occasionally become more impulsive and aggressive, but they usually retain fully the capacity for insight and self-criticism (Brill, 1959).

Although viral encephalitis is relatively rare, it occurs with great frequency during periods of viral epidemics. For example, a form of viral encephalitis occurred in epidemic proportions during the period 1916 to 1926 (Wilkins & Brody, 1968).

Chronic encephalitis, although less common than acute forms, can be produced by a bacterium called syphilis spirochete (*treponema pallidum*). This infection produces syphilis (see Chapters 2 and 5) and is spread by sexual contact. In slightly less than 30 per cent of all untreated cases of syphilis, the spirochete bacterium infects the central nervous system (Merritt, Adams, & Solomon, 1946), causing fever and headaches within about two years of the infection (Curtis, Jacobson, & Marcus, 1972); the incubation period, however, is sometimes as long as 40 years (U.S. Public Health Service, 1962). Infection of the central nervous system by this bacterium is known as neurosyphilis. Two types of neurosyphilis are *meningovascular syphilis* and *general paresis*. In the former disease, the syphilis spirochete attacks the meninges and the arteries of the brain, producing symptoms similar to those of meningitis. In the latter and more disabling disease, the syphilis spirochete directly invades the brain, causing death to the cortical neurons invaded and a consequent reduction in total brain mass. The onset of general paresis is usually gradual, initially marked by symptoms such as errors in judgment, carelessness in personal appearance, and mood alternations (Wilson, 1954). Other neurological symptoms such as convulsions, incoordination, and slurred speech may also occur. In about 5 per cent of all neurosyphilitics, the disease eventually progresses to a classic paretic psychosis manifested by euphoria, overactivity, paranoid delusions, and intellectual deterioration (Freedman, Kaplan, & Sadock, 1972).

BOX 17-1
Accurate Diagnosis of Brain Disease

Because cerebral disease can lead to emotional behaviors resembling both neurotic and psychotic syndromes, an individual suffering central nervous system disease is occasionally misdiagnosed as a neurotic or psychotic. The necessity for accurate diagnosis is exemplified by the case of George Gershwin, the famed composer. Gershwin was treated by psychoanalysis for more than two years, many of his symptoms having been diagnosed as related to early childhood experiences. He finally died of a brain tumor that would have been operable had the original diagnosis been correct.

Early mental health investigators believed there was an "organic brain syndrome" common to most types of cerebral disease and hence searched for a single test that would be indicative of this disorder (see Davison, 1974). The test resulting from this search is the Bender Visual-Motor Gestalt Test. (See Chapter 4.) This test, which requires the copying of geometric designs, is probably a valid indicator of cerebral disease in the sense that certain test performances are useful in the diagnosis of cerebral diseases, particularly those involving the right parietal lobes (see Garron & Cheifetz, 1965). There exists, however, no single organic brain syndrome, and hence there are many cerebral diseases that do not affect the right parietal lobe, perceptual-motor functioning, or performance on the Bender. Although certain performances on the Bender suggest cerebral disease, a normal performance on this test does not permit the assumption of the absence of cerebral disease, and an inadequate performance is not necessarily due to cerebral lesion.

One diagnostic approach used today consists of a battery of tests originally developed by Halstead (1947) and subsequently modified by Reitan (1966). Filskov and Goldstein (1974) used this test battery in a study of 89 patients suffering from different types and locations of cerebral disease. It was found that the test battery predicted both the locus and the type of pathology better than any other single laboratory test such as the EEG, X rays, or a brain-scan test. Reitan's test battery, however, should not be employed as the sole diagnostic procedure. Rather, its appropriate role is as a screening instrument to be followed by other techniques when the test results confirm the initial suspicion of cerebral disease.

Prior to the discovery of penicillin, syphilis accounted for 10 to 20 per cent of admissions to state hospitals for the mentally ill (Freedman, Kaplan, & Sadock, 1972). However, the number of new cases of syphilis-caused brain syndromes has greatly decreased since the use of pencillin to treat the early stages of the disease. As of 1962, syphilis accounted for less than 1 per cent of all first admissions to psychiatric hospitals (U.S. Public Health Service, 1962).

Encephalitis can also occur when pus containing an infectious agent spreads to the brain. The infectious pus can come from a number of places within the body and can enter the brain through any one of several pathways (Liske & Weikers, 1964). The infected brain neurons die, and the body defends against the further spread of the infection by encapsulating the infected area with connective tissue, thereby forming what is commonly called an abcess. The encapsulated abcess, however, grows within the brain, compressing the adjacent brain structures and interfering with normal functioning. If untreated, the expansion of the encapsulated pus continues until the neurons of the brain stem are compressed. Because the brain stem controls the vital functions of breathing and heart functioning, compression of this area by a growing abcess eventually causes death.

The treatment of a brain abcess consists of surgical drainage and of total removal of the encapsulated mass. Administration of an appropriate antibiotic is also indicated (Loeser & Scheinberg, 1957). Despite the success of surgical and antibiotic treatment in saving the lives of abcess patients, a reduction of intellectual abilities may persist (Tarkkanen, 1963).

Tumors

A tumor (neoplasm) is new growth within the body; tumors can develop within the brain itself, within the meninges coverings of the brain, or within the body, spreading to the brain via the bloodstream. The symptoms depend both on the location of the tumor and on the degree of malignancy. If a malignant tumor is located in an accessible part of the brain or its coverings, neurosurgery is indicated; otherwise, radiation or drug treatment may be attempted.

Degenerative Diseases

Degenerative diseases involve a slow, progressive, physical deterioration of cells within the nervous system. Although the etiology of most degenerative disorders is poorly understood, genetic factors seem to play an especially important role in the development of some of these diseases. The symptoms of most degenerative diseases usually do not begin to appear until the patient is in his forties or fifties; occasionally, however, symptoms begin to appear when the patient is in his twenties or thirties.

Alzhemier's Disease

Alzhemier's disease is a degeneration of *all* areas of the cerebral cortex, especially the frontal and temporal lobes. The affected cells actually die. The initial symptoms resemble those found in neurotic disorders and include anxiety, depression, restlessness, and sleep difficulties. Sometimes visual hallucinations occur (Haase, 1971). Memory for recent events also deteriorates and, as the disease advances, there is a progressive deterioration in all intellectual faculties. The onset of Alzhemier's disease usually occurs between the ages of 45 and 60 although rare cases of earlier onset have been recorded (McMenemey, 1966). The causes of the disease seem to be related to genetic factors (Pratt, 1967), and no treatment exists that can halt the progressive degenerative process. Special X-ray techniques of the cerebral ventricles (see Figure 17-3) are helpful in diagnosing Alzhemier's disease because as the total brain mass decreases, the size of the ventricles increases (Taveras & Wood, 1964).

Pick's Disease

This syndrome is a rare degenerative disease of circumscribed areas of the brain, particularly the frontal areas. It is very similar to Alzhemier's disease in terms of age of onset, symptomatology, and a possible genetic etiology. No known treatment exists.

Parkinson's Disease

The basic neuropathology of this disease appears to be a loss of neurons within the basal ganglia (see Figure 17-5). Symptoms typically include movement abnormalities such as a rhythmical, alternating tremor of the extremities, eyelids, and tongue, along with a rigidity of the muscles and a slowness of movement (Wilkins & Brody, 1969). The slowness of movement is called *akinesia.*

Although this disease was originally thought to involve only a disorder of movement without intellectual deterioration (Parkinson, 1817), it is now recognized that there is some association between global intellectual impairment and Parkinson's disease (Pollock & Hornabrook, 1966). Garron, Klawans, and Narin (1972) have systematically studied the intellectual functioning of a group of 47 Parkinson's patients and a group of controls matched for age, sex, education, area of residence, and social background. A correlation between the degree of impaired intelligence and the presence of a Parkinson motor symptom (akinesia) was obtained for older subjects. It thus appears that intellectual deterioration is associated with Parkinsonism when the disease occurs late in life.

The cells lost in Parkinson's disease contain a neurochemical called *dopamine,* and the motor disturbances associated with this disorder seem to be caused primarily by deficiencies in dopamine. Today the treatment of choice is the administration of a precursor of dopamine called L-dopa. This drug decreases tremors and muscular rigidity and can alleviate symptoms of slowed movement. The administration of L-dopa may also improve intellectual func-

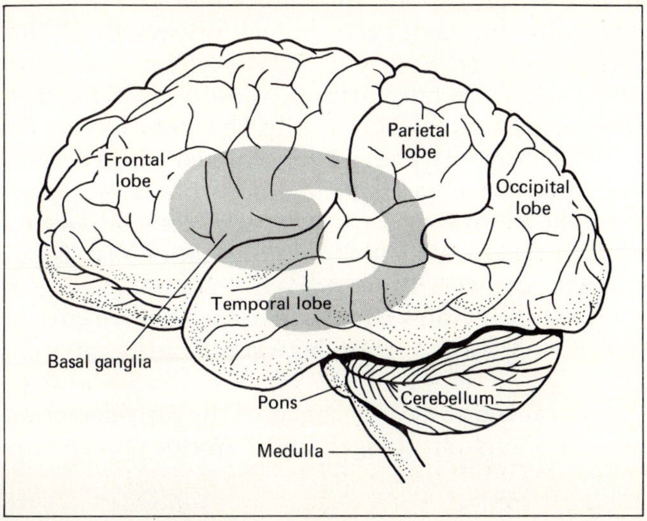

Figure 17-5
Left cerebral hemisphere.

tioning in some patients (Meier & Martin, 1970); however, the reliability of this effect is unclear (Boshes, Blonsky, Arbit, & Klein, 1969). There have been some reports that L-dopa may have emotional side effects. Of 104 patients with Parkinson's disease, Klawans and Garvin (1969) observed during the early stages of L-dopa treatment four instances of lethargy, seven of sleeplessness and agitation, three of confusion, and two of paranoid psychosis. However, Cheifetz, Garron, Leavitt, Klawans, and Garvin (1971) found no adverse effects of L-dopa treatment in 34 patients treated for Parkinsonism. One difference between these two studies that might account for the discrepant findings is that in the former study, in which emotional side effects were found, some of the patients had a prior history of psychiatric illness, whereas in the latter study, in which no side effects were found, none of the patients had such a history. Hence, L-dopa may tend to have emotional side effects primarily in patients with a prior history of emotional disturbance; further research is needed to assess this possibility.

Huntington's Chorea

The symptoms of Huntington's chorea, which usually begin to appear when the patient is in his thirties or forties, typically consist of involuntary jerky movements of the face, tongue, and extremities. These movements are rapid and irregular. Intellectual impairment, particularly of memory for recent events, and severe emotional disturbance can also occur. One large survey found that approximately half of the patients with Huntington's chorea developed psychosis at some point in the illness; 25 per cent of these cases were indistinguishable from schizophrenia in their behavioral manifestations (Heathfield, 1967).

Huntington's chorea is determined by a single dominant gene—50 per cent of the offspring of an afflicted parent will inherit the disease (Pratt, 1967). The development of the disease is slow, but degeneration is progressive; death usually occurs approximately 15 years following the onset of the symptoms (Haase, 1971). Although no present medical procedure can reverse the degenerative process, major tranquilizers can be administered to alleviate choreatic movements.

Some recent evidence raises the possibility that Huntington's chorea is pathophysiologically and biochemically the opposite of Parkinsonism (see Klawans, 1970). Parkinson's disease is associated with a deficiency of the neurochemical dopamine, whereas Huntington's chorea is a genetic disease associated with either an excess of, or an excessive sensitivity to, dopamine. The evidence for this hypothesis is that administration of L-dopa alleviates motor symptoms in patients with Parkinson's disease but induces motor symptoms in patients with Huntington's chorea. Investigators are currently exploring the possibility of this opposite relation between Huntington's chorea and Parkinson's disease.

Another area of current research concerns the early detection of Huntington's chorea. Klawans, Paulsson, Rengel, and Barbeau (1972) administered low to moderate doses of L-dopa to the asymptomatic offspring of patients with Huntington's chorea. Approximately a third of these individuals developed choreatic movements—it was assumed that these offspring would later develop Huntington's chorea because L-dopa increases choreatic movements in individuals suffering from this disease.

Nutritional Deficiencies

Both acute and chronic deficiencies in nutrients can cause brain dysfunction. The symptomatology caused by nutritional deficiencies, especially deficiencies of the vitamins niacin and thiamin, resembles that seen in the degenerative diseases of the central nervous system (Curtis, Jacobson, & Marcus, 1972). Both niacin and thiamin are part of the vitamin B complex.

Malnutrition is highly prevalent among alcoholics (U.S. Department of Health, Education, and Welfare, 1971). This is especially true of skid row alcoholics, but even upper class alcoholics tend to be malnourished because the high caloric content of alcohol reduces their hunger for other, more nutritional foods.

Pellagra

The early behavioral signs of pellagra include irrational fears, depression, agitation, hallucinations, disorientation, and intellectual deterioration (Spillane, 1947). Diarrhea and a reddening of the skin also occur. Brain neurons degenerate in untreated cases, eventually producing a condition similar to that seen in Alzcheimer's disease (Aita, 1964). The syndrome is caused by a deficiency of nicotinic acid; all of the symptoms are rapidly reversed if nicotinic acid or nicotinomide is administered prior to significant neuron degeneration in the brain.

Beriberi

This syndrome is indicated by fatigue, weakened muscles, extreme lassitude, irritability, and insomnia. The fatigue associated with this disorder is expressed by the name *beriberi,* which means "I cannot" (Coleman, 1972). The symptoms result from a deficiency in thiamin and are treated by the administration of this vitamin. The syndrome was once common in the Far East because diets of polished rice do not provide needed quantities of thiamin.

Wernicke-Korsakoff Encephalopathy

The symptoms associated with Wernicke's syndrome include the sudden onset of drowsiness, paralysis of eye movements, and an inability to walk (Brody & Wilkins, 1968). This syndrome is associated with a severe deficiency of thiamin and responds well to prompt administration of this vitamin. Korsakoff's psychosis is primarily a memory disorder and is most typically caused by a deficiency of thiamin, with the consequent development of lesions within the limbic system of the brain (Victor, Adams, & Collins, 1971). Sometimes

Wernicke's syndrome progresses into Korsakoff's psychosis. Chronic alcoholics are particularly susceptible to this disorder.

Based on the available data, the following can be said about the intellectual and perceptual-motor deficiencies associated with Korsakoff's psychosis.

1. Afflicted individuals retain normal abilities in long-established skills such as writing, verbal facility, and the performance of simple motor acts. They also retain a normal ability to repeat immediately a series of spoken digits (Brion, 1969).

2. The most noticeable intellectual impairment is of memory, especially memory for the recent, although not the immediate, past. During the initial stages of the syndrome, the patient may respond to questions of memory by providing factually incorrect statements rather than by admitting that he cannot recall what happened. This propensity for generating factually incorrect statements, called *confabulation,* is much less common in the chronic phase of the syndrome (Talland, 1965). Apparently, the Korsakoff psychotic is at first incompletely aware of his memory impairment—if challenged on the accuracy of confabulated statements, he can become very indignant and may insist that he remembers correctly.

Toxic Diseases

A large number of toxic substances affect the central nervous system. Contact with these agents often produces an acute brain syndrome characterized by disturbances of perception, cognition, and social behavior and by emotional instability (Haase, 1971). In some instances a permanent impairment of general intelligence occurs.

Lead poisoning is representative of organic brain syndromes that result from the ingestion of toxic metals. Adults might ingest lead as a consequence of exposure to industrial substances or by eating contaminated food. Lead intoxication can produce an acute brain syndrome in adults characterized by irritability, memory impairment, confusion, and drowsiness. Convulsions are also common, and some individuals may progress into coma (Aring & Trufant, 1953). Neurophysiologically, lead poisoning causes the excretion of large amounts of fluid into the intercellular tissue spaces of the brain, a condition called edema. In children such excretions are massive, producing unconsciousness and convulsions.

Even with immediate treatment designed to reduce brain edema, the mortality rates from lead poisoning are high (Wilson, 1954). Adults who survive often suffer from paralysis in the hands and in the extremities as a consequence of damage to peripheral motor nerves, but they tend to recover from the initial cognitive and emotional effects of intoxication. In children who survive, however, permanent intellectual impairment is common, with some cases showing marked mental retardation (Chisolm & Kaplan, 1968; Wiener, 1970); in still other cases perceptual-motor deficiencies may be evident. For example, Bradley and Baumgartner (1958) studied 18 children, aged two to five, who had been treated for lead encephalopathy. Although none of these children suffered intellectual impairment as measured by global IQ, perceptual-motor deficiencies were found on the Draw-a-Person test and on the Bender Visual-Motor Gestalt test. (See Chapter 4.)

Epilepsy

Epilepsy is an organic disorder characterized by random discharges from a hyperexcitable aggregate of neurons in the brain (Pincus & Tucker, 1974). It is unclear whether such discharges, called seizures, result from a decrease in inhibitory input into the affected area, as suggested by the work of Spencer and Kandel (1969), or from an increase in excitatory input into the affected area, as Creutzfeld (1973) has concluded. It is also possible that each of these hypotheses is correct, depending on the location of the hyperexcitable aggregate of neurons (see Brazier, 1974; Eccles, 1964, 1966).

The occurrence of epileptic attacks is often unpredictable—they may occur as infrequently as once or twice in a lifetime or as frequently as hundreds of times. In between seizures the epileptic typically exhibits normal psychological functioning. There are many different types of seizures. Some of these are minor, occur in almost everyone, and typically do not interfere with normal functioning. Other types of seizures, however, are accompanied by unconsciousness and thus pose a serious hazard to the afflicted individual, even though the seizure itself might last for only a few seconds or minutes. The true incidence of epilepsy is unknown. Based primarily on survey data and on army draftee induction records, however, various estimates of the annual incidence of epilepsy in the United States have been reported. One such estimate has placed the incidence of epilepsy at 19.8 cases per 100,000 (Ervin, 1967).

The many types of epilepsy are classified in two ways. One classificatory distinction is based on etiology—whether epilepsy is a result of brain injury or disease (*symptomatic epilepsy*) or a result of unknown etiology (*idiopathic epilepsy*). The other classificatory distinction is based on the type of seizure. Although we shall discuss a number of seizures, the three types that have attracted the greatest attention among psychologists are *grand mal, petit mal,* and *psychomotor* seizures. Only psychomotor seizures have been shown to be associated with severe emotional and behavioral complications.

Symptomatic Epilepsy

Symptomatic epilepsy refers to the development of epilepsy following brain injury or identifiable disease (e.g., trauma, tumor, encephalitis, or toxic disease). Watson (1952), for example, found that in a large group of World War II veterans who sustained penetrating shrapnel injuries to the head, 41.6 per cent developed epilepsy within three years of the injury. The high prevalence of epilepsy in this group seems largely attributable to the tissue damage caused by the injury from the sharp projectiles. In contrast, Jennett (1962) found epilepsy in only about 5 per cent of 1,000 individuals who suffered a head injury caused by blunt objects. After studying this latter group for a four-year period, Jennett suggested that the following factors increase the risk of epilepsy following a head injury from a blunt object:

1. Patients who suffered prolonged periods of unconsciousness associated with head injury were more likely to have posttraumatic epilepsy.
2. Patients who had seizures associated with acute injury had a 25 to 33 per cent risk of posttraumatic epilepsy.

3. Patients who developed hematomas due to trauma had a 25 to 33 per cent risk.
4. Patients with skull fractures that penetrated the dura mater had a 50 per cent risk, whereas those with simple fractures that did not penetrate the meninges showed only a 3 per cent risk.

In patients who did not show any of these characteristics, only 1 per cent had epilepsy, a prevalence figure that is only slightly above that reported for the general population. Thus posttraumatic epilepsy seems more likely to occur in individuals who suffer actual structural damage of the cerebral cortex. The fact that not every individual with structural damage of the cerebral cortex developes epilepsy, however, indicates that other factors also play a determining role.

Idiopathic Epilepsy

Idiopathic epilepsy refers to seizure disorders caused by unknown factors.

The available evidence suggests that genetic factors play an important role in at least some varieties of idiopathic epilepsy. For example, Metrakos and Metrakos (1961) found abnormal EEG patterns characteristic of epilepsy in 20 of 40 siblings of epileptics between the ages of 4.5 and 7.5. This finding suggests that the EEG abnormality found in epilepsy is transmitted by a single dominant gene. Several twin studies have also provided support for the hypothesis of inheritance of epilepsy. Inouye (1960), for example, found that, of the identical twins he studied in which one member had an EEG abnormality suggesting epilepsy, 77 per cent of the other members also had an EEG abnormality. In contrast, the corresponding rate for fraternal twins was only 22 per cent.

Grand Mal Epilepsy

In addition to the classification of epilepsy as symptomatic or idiopathic, epilepsy is subclassified in accordance with the type of seizure. Grand mal epilepsy is characterized by seizures consisting of stereotyped motor activity and a total loss of consciousness. Warning symptoms, called an *aura,* often precede an oncoming attack. These symptoms may consist of sensations of not feeling well, dizziness, numbness, or tingling. The actual seizure begins with a *tonic stage* during which breathing stops and the body stiffens. Unless supported, the individual will fall to the floor. This is followed by a *clonic stage* in which there is rhythmic shaking of the trunk and extremities. During this stage, there is danger that the tongue will be swallowed or bitten, and frothy saliva usually gathers at the mouth. The entire seizure may last for one or two minutes; occasionally, a second tonic-stage–clonic-stage sequence occurs. Cessation of the convulsion is typically followed by an impairment of consciousness consisting of headache, drowsiness, and confusion; these symptoms, called postictal confusion, may last from several minutes to several days.

Petit Mal Seizures

Petit mal (small illness) seizures, which are markedly different from grand mal seizures, are characterized by a loss of awareness during which there is no motor activity other than blinking or rolling up the eyes. These seizures usually last less than ten seconds. Because muscle tonus is not lost during petit mal seizure, the individual does not fall to the ground. These seizures occur primarily in children and are rare in persons older than 15 years of age (Pincus & Tucker, 1974).

Focal Seizures

Focal seizures are characterized by rhythmic shaking of a particular area of the body. They sometimes start in the distal part of an extremity (e.g., hand) and move proximally (e.g., toward the shoulder and trunk). This marching effect, known as *Jacksonian March,* may be caused by the spread of electrical disturbances from the focus of hyperexcitable neurons in the cortex to neighboring neurons within the sensory or motor areas of the cortex. Penfield and his associates have demonstrated that both the sensory and the motor areas of the cortex are topographically organized in terms of their connections to various body areas (Penfield & Rasmussen, 1950). As shown in Figure 17-6, a focal electrical disturbance near the finger area of the motor cortex could spread upward and could progressively involve the hand, arm, shoulder, trunk, and legs in march-like fashion. In patients older than 10 years of age, the occurrence of focal seizures is generally related to tumor, vascular disease, or trauma in the side of the brain opposite the affected side of the body (Pincus & Tucker, 1974).

Figure 17-6
Topographical organization of the motor cortex.

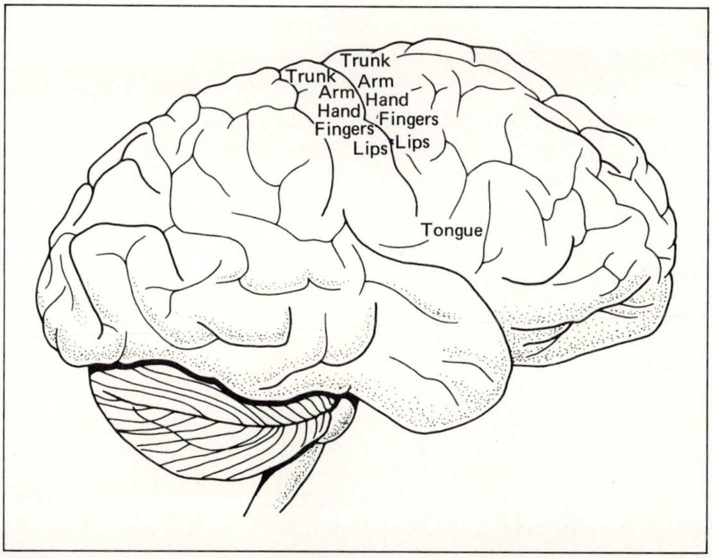

Minor Motor Seizures

Minor motor seizures are characterized by relatively brief and undramatic motor disturbances. The brain disorders associated with these seizures may be severely debilitating even though the observable motor disturbances during seizures are relatively minor. There are three types of minor motor seizures: (1) infantile spasms, (2) akinetic seizure, and (3) myoclonic jerks.

Infantile spasms consist of a sudden extension or flexion of the body and are often accompanied by crying. These spasms occur primarily in infants between the ages of three and seven months and are generally accompanied by extremely abnormal EEG activity. Most children with infantile spasms become seriously retarded (Pincus & Tucker, 1974). The spasms are associated with several diseases of the central nervous system including encephalitis and congenital malformations of the central nervous system.

Another type of minor motor seizure is the akinetic seizure in which the child falls to the floor because of the sudden relaxation of the antigravity muscles.

In a third variety of minor motor seizures, called myoclonic jerks, a seizure occurs in a small group of muscles. Myoclonic jerks typically occur in healthy individuals as they are falling asleep; occasionally their occurrence is indicative of a serious central nervous system problem.

Psychomotor Seizure

Psychomotor seizures result from abnormal electrical discharges usually, although not always, originating from the temporal lobes. Symptoms accompanying psychomotor seizures often resemble those found in hysteria or psychosis. The EEG can conclusively establish the presence of this disorder although it cannot conclusively rule out a diagnosis of psychomotor epilepsy. Most people with psychomotor seizures report distinct subjective experiences during the seizure, including alternations of mood, anxiety, compulsive thoughts of a disturbing nature, feelings of *déjà vu,* visual distortions such as micropsia (everything appearing very small) and macropsia (everything appearing very large), dreamlike states or sensations similar to those of alcohol intoxication, hallucinations of taste and smell, and abdominal pain (Pincus & Tucker, 1974). Especially notable during a psychomotor seizure are repetitive and inappropriate motor behaviors such as lipsmacking, swallowing, and gagging—these repetitive behaviors are called automatisms. During seizures some psychomotor patients assume bizarre postures resembling those seen in catatonic schizophrenia; some enter fugue states in which they perform complicated and seemingly purposeless acts and later have no remembrance of these actions.

Treatment

The extent to which an epileptic disorder interferes with the ability to lead a normal life varies considerably, depending on the nature of the seizure, on the frequency of seizures, and on the individual's emotional reaction to being epileptic. In general, most epileptics lead normal lives. Julius Caesar, Vincent Van Gogh, and Napoleon were all epileptics.

Treatment for each of the various types of epilepsy primarily consists of the administration of drugs known to have anticonvulsive effects (e.g., dilantin). Although most seizure disorders respond to some combination of medications, a few people have such severe seizures that they cannot be controlled pharmacologically. In some of these cases, surgical excision of the affected brain tissue may help; in other cases of intractable seizures, surgical separation of the right and left hemispheres of the brain has been performed in an effort to prevent abnormal electrical activity in one hemisphere from spreading to the other (Bogen & Vogel, 1962).

SOME SPECIFIC BEHAVIORAL SYNDROMES

Aphasia

Aphasia is an impairment or loss of some language ability, including (1) an impairment or loss of the ability to express oneself through written or spoken language, and/or (2) an impairment or loss of the ability to comprehend written or spoken language. These deficits are caused either by lesions in the language areas of the brain or by other varieties of central nervous system disease. When a lesion is involved, the exact symptoms depend on the locus of the lesion in the brain. We shall consider first some research pertaining to the locus of the lesion and then consider the various behavioral manifestations of impaired language functions that can result.

Locus of Language Control

In their original discoveries associating specific brain lesions with language deficits, both Broca (1861) and Wernicke (1874) suggested that the locus of lesions associated with aphasia is in the left cerebral hemisphere. Piercy (1964), however, suggested that the locus of the lesion may differ, depending on whether the individual is right-handed or left-handed. He found that 98 per cent of the cases of aphasia in right-handed individuals are associated with lesions of the left hemisphere. But for aphasia in left-handed people, Zangwill (Wyke, 1971) found that 54.9 per cent had lesions in the left cerebral hemisphere, whereas 29.2 per cent had lesions in the right cerebral hemisphere. These data suggest that aphasia is primarily associated with lesions in the left cerebral hemisphere, but that in 2 per cent of the patients who are right-handed, and in 29.2 per cent of the patients who are left-handed, aphasia is associated with lesions in the right cerebral hemisphere.

Behavioral Manifestations

Although there are several types of aphasic syndromes, the two most frequently observed types are Broca's aphasia and Wernicke's aphasia (see Benson, 1967, for convincing evidence distinguishing between Broca's and Wernicke's aphasia).

BOX 17-2
Brain Damage in Children: Some Common Misconceptions

Children are susceptible to many central nervous system diseases and, as in adults, the behavioral manifestations of such diseases depend on the nature of the disease and on the area of the brain affected. Thus the phrase *brain-damaged child* is misleading insofar as it suggests the existence of a single unitary disorder common to all children with cerebral disease. Commenting on the misleading nature of this phrase, Birch stated: "The essential inadequacy of the term *brain damage* for purposes of [diagnostic] classification derives from the contradiction between its singular form and the plurality of content which it seeks to embrace" (1964, p. 6).

Another misconception of brain damage in children is the belief that lesions incurred early in life are less damaging than those incurred later in life. This generalization is oversimplistic and misleading (Geschwind, 1974). Sometimes children are more likely than adults to recover from cerebral disease, sometimes they are no more likely than adults to recover, and sometimes they are less likely to recover. For example, it has been estimated that 34 per cent of adult patients suffering aphasia due to missile wounds directly over Broca's or Wernicke's area tend to recover lost language skills (Luria, 1970), but almost all children who become aphasic prior to the age of three recover language functioning (Lenneberg, 1967). In motor paralysis of one side of the body resulting from brain damage, however, children are no more likely to recover than are adults. Moreover, children who survive meningitis typically suffer more severe aftereffects than do adults who had the disease.

In *Broca's aphasia,* the individual typically shows little speech production. When he does speak, words are emitted slowly, with great effort, and with poor articulation. Moreover, he fails to produce grammatically correct sentences—word endings and various connectors may be omitted. There is usually, however, an ability to understand spoken and written language.

In sharp contrast to Broca's aphasia, the speech output in *Wernicke's aphasia* is often rapid and effortless, and in many cases the rate of word production exceeds that of normals. But often this verbiage makes little sense. Errors in word usage, called *paraphasias,* occur. For example, "spoot" may be substituted for "spoon," and "cup" may be substituted for "dish." Geschwind (1970a) provided the following example of speech in a Wernicke aphasic: "I was over in the other one, and then after they had been in the department, I was in this one."

These two types of aphasic disturbances are seen in patients suffering from a variety of disease states that have local effects on the brain (e.g., tumors and focal infections), but they are particularly prominent in patients suffering ischemic-occlusive disease ("stroke") of the middle cerebral artery (see Geschwind, 1970b). Broca's aphasia tends to be produced by tissue destruction in the frontal-temporal region, whereas Wernicke's aphasia occurs as a consequence of lesions of the posterior-superior temporal area (see Figure 17-2). For a complete review of the literature on the location of these lesions, see Hécaen and Angelergues (1964), *Disorders of Language.*

Another misconception that merits clarification is that hyperactivity in children is the result of *minimal brain damage.* As noted in Chapter 5, the label "minimal brain damage" has been generously applied to hyperactive and to problem children by many physicians even though the meaning of this label is obscure. Although hyperactivity and distractibility are associated with some types of brain disease (e.g., encephalitis), many hyperactive, distractible children show no evidence of organic brain damage. Commenting on the term *minimal brain damage,* Benton wrote:

> The confusion is inherent in the term itself. A child is observed to show hyperactivity, distractibility, motor awkwardness, instability in behavioral level, or perceptual handicap. These disabilities are relatively minor as compared to global retardation of frank cerebral palsy. Then by a process of neurological mythmaking, the relatively minor behavioral manifestations are transformed into relatively minor brain abnormality. There is, of course, no justification for doing this. On the one hand, all these behavioral disabilities may have come about because of faulty nurture (using this term in its broadest sense). On the other hand, they may be the expression of major (not minimal) brain damage [1974, p. 50].

Today the term *learning disability* is used to refer to children of normal intelligence who have learning problems in school but who do not show any demonstrable evidence of organic brain damage. Although the notion of a learning disability is vague, the term at least does not suggest any particular cause of the problem.

Apraxia

De Ajuriaguerra and Tissot (1969) define apraxia as the inability to perform complex intentional acts even though the muscle systems through which these actions are carried out are intact. Such a definition covers a very broad range of possible behaviors. There is, for example, apraxia for walking and apraxia for dressing. The present focus, however, is on *constructional apraxia.* This disorder has been defined as "a difficulty in putting together one-dimensional units so as to form two-dimensional figures or activities" (Critchley, 1953, p. 172). Constructional apraxia is thus indicated by difficulties in drawing, in constructing figures with matchsticks or cubes, or in assembling puzzles. Even though constructional apraxia has been defined operationally in terms of motor behavior, part of the problem is perceptual. Thus Brain viewed constructional apraxia as "the outcome of a disintegration of the visual and kinesthetic elements in spatial perception" (1961, p. 149).

There is general agreement that the lesions responsible for constructional apraxia are located within the parietal-temporal-occipital region of the cerebral hemispheres. In 123 cases studied, Hécaen, De Ajuriaguerra, and Massonnett (1951) found involvement of the parietal lobe in 51 cases, the occipital lobe in 39 cases, and the temporal lobe in 33 cases. In this study 53 cases showed left hemisphere lesions and 69 showed right-sided lesions.

There seem to be qualitative differences in constructional apraxia resulting from right or left hemisphere damage. As shown in Figure 17-7, when asked to copy a geometric figure, patients with right-sided damage tend to leave out the left field. In severe cases these patients may not recognize the left side of their bodies as belonging to them. Patients with right-sided damage also make errors in spatial locations of drawings they are copying. In patients with left-sided lesions, however, there tends to be an oversimplification of the figure being copied.

Senile Dementia

Senile dementia refers to the gradual deterioration of intellectual functioning that is associated with old age. Although all intellectual functions are affected, the impairment is particularly severe for short-term memory (Kaszniak, Garron, Fox, Huckman, & Ramsey, 1975; Kral, 1969).

Senile dementia is associated with cortical atrophy. (Cortical atrophy refers to the physical deterioration of the neurons in the brain; the cortical mass actually shrinks.) As a general rule, the greater the degree of cortical atrophy, the greater the severity of the deficits in intellectual functioning (Kaszniak et al., 1975; Roth, Tomlinson, & Blessed, 1967; Willanger, Thygesen, Nielsen, & Petersen, 1968). There are, however, some exceptions to this general rule. Willanger et al. (1968), for example, did not find significant evidence of dementia in 22 per cent of their subjects who showed marked cerebral atrophy. It has been suggested that the effects of cortical atrophy on intellectual functioning depend in part on the individual's premorbid history, physical health, socioeconomic status, and on situational factors (Kiev, Chapman, Guthrie, & Wolff, 1962; Wang & Busse, 1971).

Figure 17-7
Original forms from the Bender Visual-Motor Gestalt test, and the attempts of a patient with a right parietal lobe lesion to copy these forms. Note the spatial disorganization of form 1 and the neglect of the left side of form 2. In this patient the right parietal lobe lesion was caused by a "stroke."

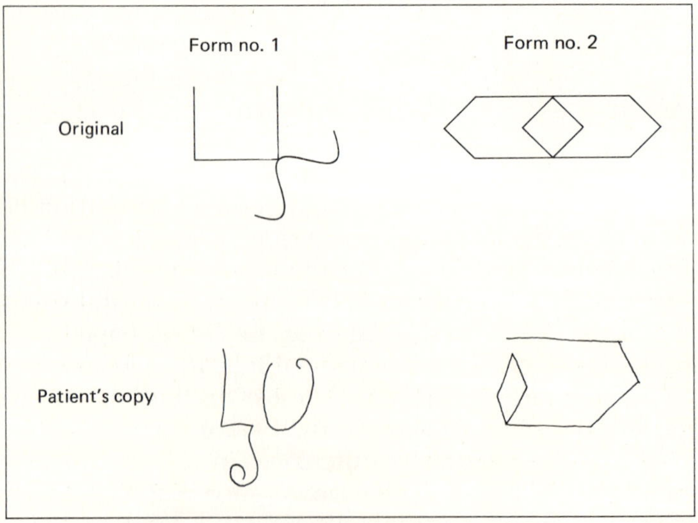

EMOTIONAL DISTURBANCE ASSOCIATED WITH BRAIN SYNDROME

A number of emotional disturbances are associated with organic brain syndromes. Such reactions, however, tend to vary considerably, depending on the individual.

Depression

The most common mood change associated with organic brain injury is depression. Sometimes depressive moods occur as a direct physiological consequence of organic brain damage. More typically, however, the depression seems to result from a recognition of one's disability and of its consequence for one's life (Horenstein, 1970). Depression is a typical reaction to any severely disabling disease.

Geschwind (1970b) noted that persons suffering from classical Broca's aphasia typically show a grief reaction to their sudden disability, whereas those suffering from Wernicke's aphasia tend to become euphoric. He suggested that depressive reactions are associated with Broca's aphasia because these individuals are typically aware of their disability and that depressive reactions are not associated with Wernicke's aphasia because these individuals are typically unaware of their disability.

If depressive reactions associated with organic brain syndrome are usually a consequence of the patient's recognition of his disability, then it would be expected that, in general, the greater the severity of the disability, the greater the severity of the depressive reaction. Some replicated support for this correlation has been found by Anderson and Hanvit (1950) and by Williams (1952).

Denial

Particularly in individuals with obsessive-compulsive traits and a history of defensive denial, a common response to disability resulting from organic brain syndrome is denial of the illness (Weinstein & Kahn, 1955). For example, the individual might refuse to purchase a wheelchair because he is confident he will walk again even though he has been unable to do so for months. It also has been suggested that younger and more active patients may be more likely to deny their disability than older patients who have already adjusted to a life of reduced activity (Ullman, 1962).

Some Syndrome Specific Reactions

In addition to emotional reactions to the loss of ability and to the fact of one's illness, some emotional reactions appear to be directly related to disease or to the injury of particular brain structures. For example, tumors of the anterior midline and of the hypothalamus are associated with attacks of increased excitability that build into severe rage and undirected aggression (Poeck, 1969).

There exists some evidence associating psychomotor epilepsy with psychotic-like reactions. Guerrant, Anderson, Fischer, Weinstein, Jaros, and Deskins (1962) studied 32 patients with psychomotor epilepsy, 26 patients with grand mal epilepsy of idiopathic origin, and 26 patients with a variety of chronic psychological disorders that did not involve any organic brain disease. These groups were matched for age, sex, social class, and education, although the psychomotor epilepsy subjects were receiving more anticonvulsive medication than were those with grand mal epilepsy. Independent diagnosis by two psychiatrists revealed psychosis in 20 per cent of the psychomotor epileptics but in only 4 per cent of the grand mal epileptics. The question arises as to how this finding of a relatively high prevalence of psychosis among psychomotor patients might be understood. One possible explanation is suggested by findings that psychomotor epileptics who tend to show psychotic symptoms also tend to have damaged or diseased tissue either within the limbic structures or in the temporal lobes; in fact, Slater, Beard, and Glithero (1963) found that 80 per cent of 69 epileptics who showed psychotic-like behavior had either damage within the limbic structures or EEG abnormality over the temporal lobes. Thus damage to these structures might produce both psychomotor epilepsy and psychotic-like behavior. Meier (1969) was able to provide direct support for this hypothesis. He administered the MMPI to psychomotor epileptics with EEG abnormalities over the anterior-temporal lobe and obtained profiles similar to those provided by anxious acute schizophrenics. Following surgical removal of the diseased tissue, however, these same individuals provided MMPI profiles more similar to those provided by normals. It thus appears that pathophysiological disturbances of the limbic system or the temporal lobes can cause psychotic personality disturbances associated with psychomotor epilepsy.

Emotional Reactions in Children

In his review of the literature on the emotional effects of brain injury in children, Shaffer (1973) concluded that children suffering from brain injury or epilepsy are more likely to develop emotional problems as a consequence of such diseases. The children who seemed most likely to develop such problems were those who suffered from psychomotor epilepsy or from structural damage that caused seizures.

PREVENTION AND REMEDIATION

The manner in which cerebral diseases can sometimes be prevented depends on the particular disease. For example, children living in slum environments sometimes peel and eat paint off the walls; because the paint contains lead, these children may suffer organic brain damage resulting from the ingestion of a toxic substance. Prevention of such tragedies requires public concern and action to eradicate social conditions that permit the existence of poorly maintained buildings with peeling paint. Prevention of ischemic-occlusive disease (stroke) would include the early detection and treatment of hypertension (high blood pressure) because this disease greatly increases the probability of a stroke (Bauer, 1967).

Once a brain syndrome has developed, several treatment approaches are available depending on the particular syndrome. Some of these approaches to the treatment of specific brain syndromes have already been discussed.

TABLE 17-1
Organic Brain Syndromes

Syndrome	Neurological Aspects	Behavioral Manifestations
VASCULAR DISEASES	Disorders of some of the blood vessels supplying the brain	Depends on affected area
Ischemic-occlusive disease	Adequate supply of blood to a brain area blocked by deposits of cholesterol	
Cerebral embolism	Adequate supply of blood to a brain area blocked by a clot of blood	
Intracerebral hemorrhage	Bleeding of a blood vessel within the brain	
TRAUMATIC SYNDROMES	Severe blow to head resulting in an impairment of psychological functioning	Depends on affected area
Concussion	Believed to involve a temporary dysfunction of brain neurons thrust against the hard coverings of the brain	Disorientation, dazed feeling, possible headache, impaired memory for events prior to trauma
Contusions and lacerations	Capillary swellings and actual tearing of brain tissue	Depends on affected area
Hematoma	Gathering of blood above or below the outermost covering of the brain	Confusion and disorientation; eventual coma and death if untreated
INFECTIOUS DISEASES OF THE CNS	Any infection of the body that affects CNS functioning	Depends on infection and on area affected
Meningitis	Infection of the coverings (meninges) of the brain	In older children and in adults: bodily aches and low fever; followed by chills, vomiting, severe headache, stiff neck; followed by drowsiness and coma; eventual death
Encephalitis	Direct invasion of the brain by an infectious substance	Depends on infectious substance and on affected area
Acute viral encephalitis	Viral encephalitis with acute (sudden) onset of symptoms	In adults: vomiting, headache, drowsiness, stiff neck, convulsion, possible coma
Chronic encephalitis (e.g., general paresis)	Encephalitis with gradual onset of symptoms; usually a bacterium infection (e.g., syphilis spirochete)	Judgment errors, sloppy appearance, mood alternations, convulsions, slurred speech, muscular incoordination, death.

(Continued)

TABLE 17-1 *(Continued)*

Syndrome	Neurological Aspects	Behavioral Manifestations
Purulent encephalitis	Direct infection of brain neurons produced by the spread of pus into the brain region; typically, brain injury following trauma provides the entry through which the pus travels; abcess develops and expands	Depends on affected area; possible death
TUMORS (NEOPLASMS)	A new growth in the body	Depends on affected area
DEGENERATIVE DISEASES	A slow, progressive physical deterioration of the CNS; usually but not always associated with advancing age; probably inherited	
Alzhemier's disease	Degeneration of *all* areas of the cerebral cortex—total cortical mass progressively decreases	Initially: memory impairment, anxiety, restlessness, depression; eventually: deterioration of all intellectual faculties and death
Pick's disease	Rare degenerative disease of specific brain areas	Similar to Alzhemier's disease
Parkinson's disease	Degeneration of neurons within the basal ganglia area of the brain; seems to be caused by a loss of the neurochemical dopamine	Motor dysfunction called *akinesia:* tremors of the extremities, slow movement, muscular rigidity; impairment of global intelligence
Huntington's chorea	Degeneration of a number of brain areas; caused by inheritance of a single dominant gene; possible excessive production of dopamine as a result of this gene	Involuntary, spasmodic jerking of the face, tongue, and extremities; impaired memory for recent events and overall deterioriation in intelligence; severe emotional disturbance; death
NUTRITIONAL DEFICIENCIES	Brain dysfunction or damage caused by deficiencies in nutrients	
Pellagra	Deficiency of nicotinic acid	Irrational fear, disorientation, agitation, depression, hallucination
Beriberi	Deficiency of thiamin	Extreme fatigue, weakened muscles, irritability
Wernicke's syndrome	Deficiency of thiamin	Drowsiness, inability to walk
Korsakoff's psychosis	Suspected deficiency of thiamin and consequent damage to limbic system; associated with chronic alcoholism	Impaired memory for recent events, confabulation, deficient integration of sequential information

TOXIC SYNDROMES	Invasion of CNS by noninfectious, toxic substance (e.g., metals)	Depends on amount and nature of toxin ingested; can include severe disturbances in perception, cognition, social and emotional behavior; coma and death possible
EPILEPSY	An organic disorder characterized by the occurrence of random discharges from an hyperexcitable aggregate of neurons. Called symptomatic epilepsy if results from brain injury or disease. Called idiopathic epilepsy if etiology is unknown. Idiopathic epilepsy is probably inherited.	Depends on types of seizure
Grand mal	Type of seizure	Total loss of consciousness, fall to ground, incontinence, postictal confusion. Two stages: tonic (breathing stops, body stiffens), and clonic (shaking of trunk and extremities)
Petit mal	Type of seizure	No motor activity, loss of awareness
Focal seizures	Type of seizure	Rhythmic shaking of a small-muscle group; sometimes this shaking marches up from an extremity
Psychomotor seizure	Type of seizure	Apparent consciousness during seizure; automatisms (repetitive behaviors); psychosis seen in many psychomotor patients
APHASIA	Damage to any area of the brain controlling functions necessary for the use or understanding of language	Impaired ability to use and/or to comprehend written or spoken language
Broca's aphasia	Lesions in Broca's area of the brain	Little speech production; speech often grammatically incorrect; can understand language and speech
Wernicke's aphasia	Lesions in Wernicke's area of the brain	Excessive, but often unintelligible, speech production; difficulty understanding speech of others
CONSTRUCTIONAL APRAXIA	Damage to parietal, occipital, or temporal lobes	Difficulty in constructing or reproducing figures

A number of educational retraining programs have been created to help patients either recover or improve lost skills. The most extensively developed of these retraining programs are the language retraining programs for aphasics (see Eisenson, 1973). For a discussion of other remediation programs, the interested reader can consult Luria, Naydin, Tsvetkova, and Vinarskaya (1969), *Disorders of Higher Nervous Activity.*

Although damage to the brain is irreversible due to the lack of regeneration of cerebral neurons, in many cases the associated behavioral deficits need not be permanent. One of the tasks of clinical neuropsychology is to provide a better understanding of the neurological and psychological aspects of such behavioral syndromes so that more effective treatment programs can be developed.

SUMMARY

Organic brain syndromes are impairments in psychological functioning that result from either disease, damage, or injury to the brain. The symptoms vary considerably, depending on the nature of the problem, the area of the brain affected, the age of the patient, and in some types of diseases, the premorbid personality of the patient. There is no such thing as a single organic brain syndrome with a common set of symptoms, as was once believed to exist. Rather, there is a highly complex brain that can malfunction in any of numerous ways for any of numerous reasons.

A number of symptoms suggest the *possible* presence of some type of brain disease or brain injury, particularly when their occurrence does not seem to be a consequence of emotional stress. These symptoms include disorientation in time and space, impairment of recent memory, dementia (global impairment of intelligence), impairment of perceptual and constructional abilities, impairment of either speech production or comprehension, and neurological motor symptoms.

Because some organic brain syndromes are associated with behaviors similar to those seen in psychotic disorders, it is sometimes difficult to diagnose organic brain pathology. Sometimes positive findings on X-ray tests, EEG recordings, and the Bender Visual-Motor Gestalt Test can conclusively establish the presence of an organic brain syndrome; however, negative findings on these tests do not necessarily rule out the presence of brain pathology. An especially useful screening tool is a test battery originally developed by Halstead (1947) and subsequently modified by Reitan (1966).

Table 17-1 summarizes the diseases discussed in this chapter.

Some organic brain diseases are associated with psychotic behaviors, as in the example of psychomotor epilepsy.

Depression and denial are common reactions in patients suffering brain disease. In most instances depression seems to be a reaction to the awareness of one's disability rather than a direct physiological consequence of the disease itself.

Chapter 18

Mental Retardation

We shall never comprehend the behavior of the retarded if we assume that every behavior he manifests is the immutable product of his low intelligence. Furthermore, we must disavow the overly simplistic idea that all retardates manifest a highly similar pattern of behavior which is determined by their common defect.

ZIGLER (1968, p. 535)

The syndromes discussed in this chapter have subnormal intellectual ability in common as a salient diagnostic feature. Moreover, in these syndromes intellectual impairment leads to difficulties in adapting to the social environment. Our discussion begins with a historical perspective of how the retarded have been viewed by scientists and by the public, beginning with the eighteenth century debates on the nature of intelligence.

One of the oldest controversies in psychology concerns the relative importance of hereditary versus environmental factors in the development of intelligence. Those adopting the hereditary position have tended to express a pessimistic view of the possibilities of educating the retarded, whereas those adopting the environmental view have tended to be more optimistic. An early empirical test of these positions began in 1798, when a twelve-year-old boy named Victor was found living in wild and savage-like conditions in the forests of Aveyron, France. The famous French psychiatrist Pinel pronounced the child congenitally retarded, predicting that he would always be retarded. However, in an effort to demonstrate that the child's deficiencies were a product of environmental rather than hereditary factors, Itard undertook the task of extensive education. Although the child made marked progress during the first nine months of treatment, he required supervision for his entire life, and Itard terminated treatment after five and one-half years. Itard regarded his attempt to educate Victor as a failure, and his experience was interpreted by many as support for the view that intelligence and mental retardation are genetically determined.

During Itard's time and through much of the nineteenth century, most genetic hypotheses about the causes of mental retardation were variations of degeneration theory. This theory maintained that mental retardation, psychosis, epilepsy, and immorality are caused by different forms of a single, degenerative trait that is inherited. In Morel's formulation of degeneration theory, "the first generation of a degenerative line might be merely nervous, the second would tend to be neurotic, the third psychotic, while the fourth consisted of idiots who would tend not to reproduce and so lead to extinction of the line" (Sarason & Doris, 1969, p. 211). Implicit in this view is the notion that mental retardation and insanity are merely two forms of the same illness. Support for degeneration theory consisted primarily of "pedigree studies" in which it was found that mental retardation, insanity, and criminality tended to occur in families from one generation to the next.

Sarason and Doris (1969) have noted that degeneration theorists initially regarded the retarded as unfortunate recipients of a "tainted heredity." Thus the social attitude associated with degeneration theory was initially a humane one. The advent of Darwin's theory of survival of the fittest, however, changed this social attitude. Instead of being viewed as unfortunate victims of heredity, the retarded came to be viewed as members of an inferior race who, by natural law, ought not survive. Attempts to prevent the development of retardation through the control of hereditary factors (*eugenics*) were made in the late nineteenth century. Galton, the father of the eugenic movement, advocated that early marriages be encouraged in highly intelligent and creative people; if this occurred, people of superior abilities would outbreed people of normal and subnormal abilities. Apart from the obvious ethical and value assumptions, the major underlying scientific assumption of Galton's eugenic writings was that intelligence has been shown to be an inheritable ability subject to "natural selection." This assumption, however, had not, and still has not, been proven.

By the early twentieth century the retarded were regarded as a menace to society. Many prominent scientists believed that mental retardates are moral idiots who are genetically predisposed to delinquency, prostitution, and lewdness. For example, Fernald, a prominent medical authority on mental retardation, is reported to have made the following remarks in a 1912 speech:

> Every feeble-minded person, especially the high-grade imbecile, is a potential criminal needing only the environment and opportunity for the development and expression of his criminal tendencies. . . . Feeble-minded women are almost invariably immoral. . . . It has been truly said that feeble-mindedness is the mother of crime, pauperism, and degeneracy [Garfield, 1963, p. 571].

Such views received seemingly strong support when the newly developed Stanford-Binet intelligence test was administered to convicted criminals. The initial results from these studies suggested that between 60 and 90 per cent of all delinquents are mentally retarded (Pintner, 1923). In a recent review, Beier (1964) found that estimates of criminality among the retarded have ranged from 0.5 to 55 per cent. The early studies, in which the very high prevalence rates were found, defined mental retardation in terms of a mental age below one's chronological age; the later studies, in which much lower prevalence rates were found, defined mental retardation in terms of an IQ below 70. Thus one reason for the initial findings of a high correlation between mental retardation and delinquency was the inappropriate use of an overly sensitive, MA definition of mental retardation. Another reason for the initial findings was the failure to use appropriate control groups. Intelligence test scores reflect in part an individual's education; because deliquency is relatively high in lower socioeconomic areas in which schools are of low quality, it is not especially surprising that a relatively large percentage of delinquents tend to have below-average IQs. Delinquents do not appear to have IQs significantly below those of nondelinquents of similar socioeconomic background (D.C. Department of Public Health, 1966). If they do, the difference is much smaller than was originally believed (Menolascino, 1974). There is no convincing evidence that mental retardation causes criminality. Nevertheless, the intelligence test, introduced during an era when the retardate was regarded as a menace to society, was initially employed to provide "scientific evidence" of the dangerousness of mental retardates.

Today it is widely believed that an individual's intelligence is a product of both hereditary and environmental factors, although the relative importance of each is still controversial. In one view the individual's genetic composition is seen as determining a range of possible IQs, whereas environmental experiences determine whether the individual functions toward the lower, middle, or higher limits of his capacity (e.g., Zigler, 1968). In some types of mental retardation genetic factors have been shown to cause the deficiency. In other types of retardation the role of genetic as well as other biological factors is still unclear.

Extensive research interest on the nature and the causes of mental retardation is a relatively recent occurrence. The National Association of Retarded Children, which was formed in 1950 by concerned parents, has played an important role in securing improved services and in encouraging federal and state governments to support research. President Kennedy greatly expanded the federal government's commitment to the retarded. The last decade has been a period of unprecedented research activity on mental retardation, its various causes, and methods of treatment. An unusual aspect of this research effort is its exemplary interdisciplinary nature—psychologists, neurologists, educators, nutritionists, physical therapists, and geneticists all have made recent contributions.

This chapter is an introduction to clinical and experimental research on the nature and the causes of mental retardation.

CLASSIFICATION OF MENTAL RETARDATION

Mental retardation is indicated by subnormal intelligence and by problems in social adaptation (Heber, 1961). This formal definition raises at least three issues: (1) the definition and measurement of intelligence, (2) the definition and measurement of social adaptation, and (3) the relative weights that should be given to intellectual versus social deficiencies in the diagnosis of mental retardation.

IQ Criterion and Level of Retardation

IQ scores obtained from the Stanford-Binet and WISC-R (see Chapter 4) are typically used to assess subnormal intellectual functioning. At least two problems associated with the use of standardized intelligence tests merit consideration. One problem is that IQ scores are performance measures that reflect, in addition to intellectual ability, the individual's motivation to answer the questions and his educational and cultural background. Subjective interpretation is required to assess the extent to which the subject was motivated to answer the questions; in the case of the retarded, it is often difficult to infer with confidence the extent to which test performances are affected by motivational factors. Another important problem associated with the use of intelligence tests is the misuse of IQ scores as explanations of behavior (Sarason & Doris, 1969). For example, if a retarded child has a temper tantrum or behaves in a "stupid" manner, many people would tend to explain such behavior in terms of the child's low intelligence. As Sarason and Doris (1969) have noted, however, this explanation is either inadequate or incomplete because all children with the same low IQ do not behave in the same way. The subnormal IQ is only one of several diagnostic signs of mental retardation; it is not an explanation of retardates' behavior.

IQ scores are basically measures of scholastic ability; these scores are valid predictors of achievement in school. The IQ test samples only a limited range of intellectual behaviors; specifically, it samples intellectual behavior in structured situations in which there are correct and incorrect responses. The IQ test does not measure creative intelligence (divergent thinking).

DSM-II defines five degrees of severity of intellectual subnormality: borderline (IQ range: 83 to 68), mild (IQ range: 67 to 52), moderate (IQ range: 51 to 36), severe (IQ range: 35 to 20), and profound (IQ less than 20). The classification of mental retardation into these categories is independent of etiology. To some extent, the various levels of retardation are arbitrarily defined. For example, it is misleading to suggest that an IQ of 52 indicates a different level of severity (mild retardation) than does an IQ of 51 (moderate retardation). Moreover, the distinction between severe and profound retardation seems especially unreliable and pointless—these individuals are largely nonverbal and hence their IQs are often unobtainable. Nevertheless, the classification of mental retardation on the basis of degree of intellectual impairment has some practical significance for psychoeducational planning.

Borderline and Mild Retardation

Together, these groups are roughly equivalent to the special education category of *educable.* The overwhelming majority of educable retardates show no physical anomalies and no obvious signs of gross central nervous system damage. Most children in this category attend special education classes in public schools and are capable of leading relatively useful lives, including employment in many types of simple jobs.[1]

Moderate Retardation

This category corresponds roughly to the special education category of *trainable.* Many trainable retardates show physical anomalies and physical pathology including brain damage, metabolic disorders, and genetic disorders. Trainable retardates rarely attain intellectual levels greater than that of the average seven-year-old and, hence, usually require some type of supervision for life. Educational efforts focus on training social and motor skills rather than on academic subjects.

Severe and Profound Retardation

This group shows a wide range of central nervous system damage and of physical anomalies. Communication skills are minimal; motor skills are also poor. The severely and profoundly retarded require lifetime supervision, but reinforcement therapy techniques can be employed to teach some self-help skills.

[1] Many jobs in our industrial society are not intellectually demanding. It has been estimated that at least 118 occupations require a mental age of five to 12 (Beckman, 1930; Burr, 1925).

Social Quotient (SQ) and the Social Adaptation Criterion

As noted previously, although DSM-II defines mental retardation solely in terms of subnormal intelligence, the American Association on Mental Deficiency also requires a consequent problem in social adjustment. This might be indicated by deficiencies in self-care skills such as dressing oneself, as might be evident in a severely retarded child, or by a difficulty in holding down a job, as is sometimes seen in mildly to moderately retarded adults.

The diagnosis of subnormal social skills in young children is sometimes based partially on results obtained from the Vineland Social Maturity Scale (Doll, 1953). This scale provides for ratings of various behaviors such as the extent to which a child pulls off his own socks, uses pencils, or tells time; a social quotient (SQ) statistic can be obtained from these ratings. There is evidence, however, that IQ and SQ tests largely measure the same basic traits. One study, for example, found the correlation between Stanford-Binet mental age and the Vineland Scale social age to be 0.72 (Saslow, 1961).

Adams, McIntosh, and Weade (1973) evaluated some of the consequences of defining severity of retardation in terms of IQ alone versus in terms of SQ alone. A specific purpose of the study was to compare the percentages of Caucasian and black retarded children who would be considered severely or profoundly retarded when IQ served as the sole criterion for classification and when SQ served as the sole criterion. As shown in Table 18-1, when IQ was considered as the sole criterion, many more blacks than Caucasian children were classified as severely or profoundly retarded. However, when SQ was considered as the sole criterion, the percentages of black and Caucasian children classified as severely or profoundly retarded were approximately equal. These data suggest that the inclusion of social adaptability (SQ) into the formal definition of mental retardation should result in the classification of more Caucasians and fewer blacks as severely or profoundly retarded.

IQ and SQ

Although the formal definition of mental retardation requires an assessment of both intelligence and social adaptability, it is unclear exactly how data from these two sources should be combined to arrive at a final diagnosis. In actual practice this problem often does not arise because most psychologists continue to diagnose mental retardation in terms of IQ alone (Adams, 1973). That this procedure results in a disproportionate number of retarded blacks is well recognized, for blacks generally perform lower than whites on IQ tests (Jensen, 1974). It is possible, if not probable, that the lower average IQ of blacks as compared to whites reflects the fact that, on the average, whites adjust better to the intellectual demands of a white society. If our society were rooted in black culture and if our intelligence tests were developed by blacks and were validated against black norms, whites would obtain lower IQ's than blacks. Because the IQ test is a measure of adjustment to the intellectual demands of a particular society, the general finding that blacks score lower than whites is not necessar-

TABLE 18-1
Per Cent of Subjects Classified Severely or Profoundly Retarded in a Study by Adams, McIntosh, and Weade (1973)

Criterion For Classification	Caucasian	Black
IQ alone	25.4	50.0
SQ alone	51.0	60.0

ily an indication that the tests are discriminatory but may be a reflection of the fact that our society is discriminatory.

INCIDENCE

A conservative estimate of the number of people whose IQ is below 70 is 3 per cent of the population. This means that in the United States approximately 6.5 million people are mentally retarded. Of these, approximately 200,000, or less than 4 per cent of the retarded, reside in institutions (Report of the American Medical Association, 1965). Approximately 92 per cent of all persons with IQs of 70 or less have IQs between 50 and 70 (see Dingman & Tarjan, 1960).

TYPES OF MENTAL RETARDATION

Cultural-Familial Retardation

Cultural-familial retardation, comprising about 75 per cent of all retardates, is indicated by the following:

1. The level of retardation is mild or is at least in the high moderate range.
2. At least one parent or sibling is also mentally retarded.
3. There is no *known* damage to the central nervous system. This does not mean that biological causation can be ruled out, nor does it mean that biological causation is unlikely. It simply means that we can distinguish between mental retardates in whom there is compelling evidence of physiological damage and those in whom such damage does not exist, or at least is impossible to detect given current means of assessing such damage.

The overwhelming majority of cultural-familial retardates are from the lowest socioeconomic classes. Hence they have been called "culturally deprived" and "socially deprived." The concept of cultural deprivation is, however, vague—some children labeled "culturally deprived" are from cultures other than the dominant culture of the child's society, whereas others so labeled have been exposed to sterile environments. Nevertheless, there is little doubt that most cultural-familial retardates come from backgrounds of poverty.

An interesting aspect of cultural-familial retardation is that it is usually difficult to detect until after the child enters school. One possible explanation of this, proposed by Sarason and Doris (1969), is that the child has learned to adapt to a particular culture at home and that this learning is in some important way incompatible with scholastic learning. When viewed in terms of the culture of the home, the child's behavior is not problematic; problems arise only when the child is taken out of his native culture and placed in some other culture such as that of the school. For example, a child whose family is on welfare might learn to associate the word *draw* with "drawing a welfare check" (Sarason & Doris, 1969). This learning makes sense in the context of the child's home, but the association is not the usual meaning of *draw* as used by teachers.

Possible cultural conflict is only one plausible means by which cultural-familial retardation might be promoted. Another plausible causal condition is lack of educational stimulation in the home. The cultural-familial retardate typically has a parent who also has a low IQ. In an investigation that controlled for a poverty background by studying 88 mothers living in a city slum, Heber (1970) found that the probability that a child's IQ would decrease as he grew older was highly related to his mother's IQ. In children whose mothers had near average IQs, IQ remained relatively stable as the child grew older; however, in children whose mothers had IQs below 80, IQ tended to decrease as the child grew older. These results can be explained in terms of a possible genetic factor, a lack of education provided by the mother, incompatible education provided by the mother, or a combination of these factors.

Identifying the causes of cultural-familial mental retardation is difficult because there are many ways in which a correlation between poverty and low IQ can be explained. In addition to cultural conflict, it is possible to explain such correlations in terms of inadequate schooling, motivational deficiencies, and malnutrition. Perhaps all of these factors are important.

The possibility that inadequate schooling can lead to mental retardation is suggested by Ginzberg and Bray's (1953) study of World War II rejectees. Approximately 4 per cent of the men tested, or 716,000 people between the ages of 18 and 37, were rejected by the army on grounds of intellectual incompetence. The national average of a 4 per cent rejection rate is, however, misleading, for in some states the rate was as high as 14 per cent and in others it was as low as one-half per cent. In general, rejection rates were high for states with low-quality educational programs. Ginzberg and Bray noted that "the regional patterning of the rejections indicates that the screening assessed primarily the individual's educational background" (1953, p. 41). The rate for rejections of blacks was approximately six times greater than that for whites, but this statistic is misleading because black rejection rates in some regions were lower than white rejection rates in other regions. The rejection rates for both whites and blacks generally co-varied with economic conditions of the region and with the extent to which the region funded its programs of public education.

The correlation between poverty and subnormal scholastic performance may be mediated in part by motivational factors. Some evidence suggests that children from disadvantaged homes tend to have poor self-concepts and a low sense of mastery (e.g., Kagan, 1970). In such children expectation of failure is high and expectation of success is low. Hence these children may learn less in school and may perform poorly because they expect failure and do not try.

Retarded young people at work in a community based occupational training program. (Photo by Hiroji Kubota; Magnum Photos, Inc.)

The preceding hypotheses on the nature of cultural-familial retardation have in common the theoretical identification of a psychological cause. Plausible biological hypotheses, however, also merit consideration. For example, poverty is correlated with malnutrition, which in extreme cases produces neurological damage. Even in much milder cases malnutrition may produce hormonal imbalances that affect intellectual functioning. There is considerable evidence that malnutrition is correlated with intellectual deficiency (e.g., Cabak & Najdanvic, 1965; Chase & Martin, 1970) even though the extent to which malnutrition actually causes retardation is still unclear (Warren, 1970).

Cultural-Familial Retardation as the Lower End of the IQ Distribution

It has been suggested that cultural-familial retardation is simply the low end of the normal distribution of intelligence (Achenbach, 1974). The upper portion of Figure 18-1 shows the expected distribution of IQ scores. This normal curve suggests that, because some scores must necessarily fall at the lower end of the IQ distribution, some people have subnormal IQs for statistical reasons—that is, to understand statistical subnormality, it is necessary to understand the nature of intelligence and the factors responsible for normal variations in intellectual abilities. However, as shown in Figure 18-1, the actual prevalence of mental retardation is greater than that suggested by the normal curve (Dingman & Tarjan, 1960). This excess is particularly great at IQ levels below

50. Thus, in addition to statistical subnormality related to nonpathological variations in intelligence, some people have low IQs as a result of other factors (e.g., accidents and diseases).

Down's Syndrome (Mongolism)

Down's syndrome was first described by Down in 1866 and independently in the same year by Seguin (Sarason & Doris, 1969). Down referred to this disorder as mongolism, in part because several physical anomalies suggested an appearance superficially resembling Mongols and in part because he believed mental retardation to result from a degeneration of one's racial type.

Down's syndrome is associated with a number of physical anomalies including delicate skin, a protruding belly, and eyes that slant up and outward. Because mongoloid children often appear especially cute, people tend to respond to them in affectionate ways. However, because the adult's appearance is less attractive, some mongoloids have difficulty adjusting to the loss of attention as they grow older. The adult mongol is usually under 5 feet tall (Bender, 1956).

Figure 18-1
Expected and actual distribution of IQ scores. Adapted from T. Achenbach, *Developmental psychopathology,* p. 228. Copyright 1974, The Ronald Press Company, New York. Printed with permission of author and publisher.

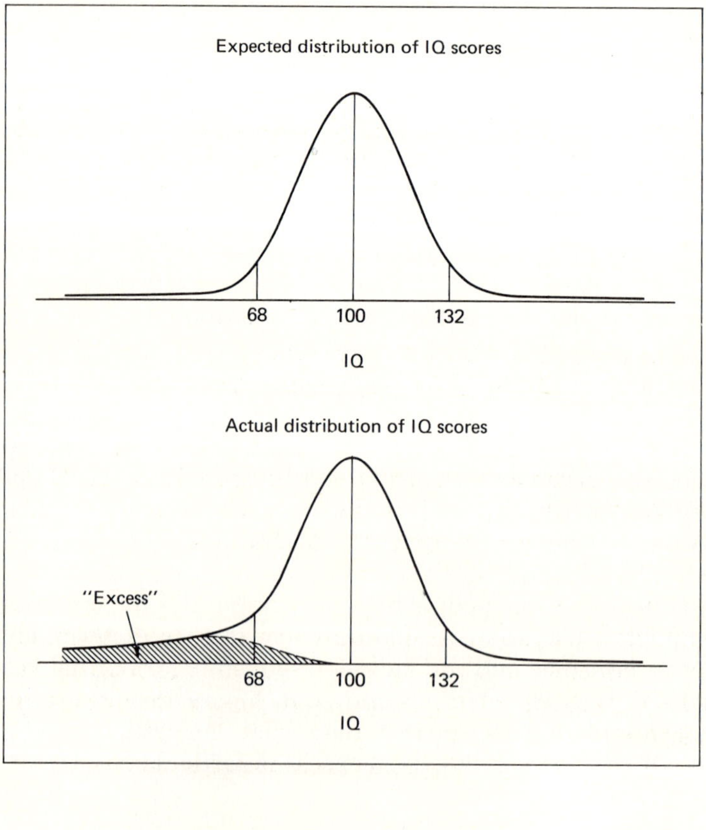

Although the IQs of mongoloids vary across the entire range of subnormality, most have IQs below 50. The disorder is thus associated with moderate to severe retardation, even though some mongoloids have IQs in the 60s and a few have IQs higher than 70.

The incidence of mongolism has been estimated to be between 0.5 and 4 births per thousand (see Sarason & Doris, 1969). There is, however, a high correlation between maternal age and a mongoloid birth (Gruenberg, 1966; Penrose, 1962). For mothers under 30 years of age, the incidence is under 2 births per thousand, but for mothers between the ages of 35 and 39, the incidence is about 8.5 per thousand (Benda, 1960). In mothers over 40 the incidence is as high as 39 births per thousand.

Lejeune, Gautier, and Turpin (1959) were the first to demonstrate that mongolism is caused by chromosomal abnormalities. Cytological studies of mongoloid cells typically reveal 47 chromosomes, one more than the normal complement of 46. The mongoloid chromosomal abnormality is called *trisomy-21* because the extra chromosome is associated with the number 21 autosome. (See Figure 5-3 on p. 102.) In addition to trisomy-21, mongolism is occasionally caused by chromosomal translocutions (see Chapter 5).

Leukemia of both chronic and acute varieties is associated with the deletion of material from chromosome 21. Because mongolism results from an anomaly of the same chromosome, it is not surprising that leukemia and mongolism are positively correlated (Hurst, 1972).

Phenylketonuria (PKU)

PKU is a metabolic disorder that is transmitted by a single rare recessive gene (Jervis, 1939). Untreated cases rarely attain IQs at or above 70 (Sarason & Doris, 1969). The estimated incidence of this disorder is 1 birth per 10,000 (Koch, Acosta, Fishler, Schaeffler, & Wohlers, 1967). As discussed in Chapter 5, diet therapy can prevent brain damage and intellectual subnormality if the disorder is detected and treated within the first few weeks of life. The testing of newborns for PKU is now routine.

Cretinism

Cretinism is another disorder suspected of being caused by a single recessive gene (Achenbach, 1974). Cretinism results from a thyroid deficiency and is easily recognized within the first four weeks of life (Pickering & Fisher, 1958). If untreated, the disorder becomes progressively worse; the cretin looks much like an aged, wrinkled person by the time of adolescence (Hutt & Gibby, 1965). Cretins are usually dwarfs less than 3 feet tall. If the disorder is treated very early in life, however, most of the undesirable symptoms can be prevented.

Other Organic Syndromes

Virtually all retardates with IQs in the severe and profound ranges show compelling evidence of organic pathology. There are many types of organic pathologies that cause mental retardation; only a few of these are mentioned in this chapter.

In addition to chromosomal abnormalities and genetic defects, central nervous system damage leading to mental retardation can be caused by infectious disease, tumors, poisons such as lead and carbon monoxide, radiation, and accidents. For example, rubella (German measles) is likely to produce central nervous system damage if contracted by the mother within the first three months of pregnancy.

There are several rare disorders characterized by abnormal size and weight of the brain and head. *Microcephaly* refers to an unusually small cranium and is often associated with moderate to severe levels of intellectual deficiency. Some cases of microcephaly seem to be caused by a recessive gene (American Psychiatric Association, 1968). *Hydrocephaly* refers to an enlargement of the head caused by an accumulation of excessive cerebrospinal fluid. In some cases the disorder is congenital, whereas in other cases it is caused by diseases and tumors acquired later in life. Afflicted individuals usually die; in congenital cases death usually occurs in childhood.

EXPERIMENTAL RESEARCH COMPARING RETARDATES AND NORMALS ON INTELLECTUAL TASKS

Developmental Versus Defect Theories

Developmental theory proposes that IQ is primarily a measure of rate of intellectual development. In this view, the retardate progresses through normal stages of intellectual development but does so at a slower rate and without achieving a normal level of development. Zigler expressed this view as follows:

> If we approach the cognitive differences between these two individuals [one has an IQ of 70, the other has an IQ of 100] from a developmental view, as Piaget and the Geneva group have done (Inhelder, 1968), we can observe that the retarded individual progresses through the same sequence of early stages of cognitive development as does the individual of average intellect, but the retarded individual does so at a slower rate. Thus, the essential difference between the retarded individual and the individual of average intellect appears to be a difference in the rate of cognitive development as well as in the ultimate or final level of cognition achieved [1973, p. 233].

In contrast to developmental theory, defect theory proposes that the intellectual functioning of retardates is defective beyond that attributable to slow development. This view was expressed by Luria: "Child psychiatry, just as the science which is engaged in the education of abnormal children, is now confronted with a fundamental task; it must learn to *qualify the basic defect* and still more to approximate to the analysis of *its underlying mechanisms*" [1963, p. 353]. Luria proposed that the basic defect shown by retardates is a failure to use verbalization to organize behavior and to solve problems. One consequence of this deficiency is the absence of "any creative, intellectual activity" (1963, p. 383). Luria further hypothesized that the cause of this defect is a weakness in the nervous system.

Spitz (1963) has proposed a neurological defect theory of mental retardation that is variously called field theory and cortical satiation theory. This theory postulates that retardates have a deficiency in recovering from neural stimulation; specifically, it is postulated that the brain cells of retardates require more time to recover from a previous impulse.[2] The cortical satiation theory is supported primarily by figural aftereffect experiments on subjects whose mental retardation is of organic etiology; the applicability of this theory to the cultural-familial retardate is unclear and has been questioned by data obtained by Carlson and Michalson (1973).

Controlling for (MA)

In order to understand the paradigm for tests of the developmental position, it is helpful to review the relations among MA (mental age), CA (chronological age), and IQ. In Chapter 4 it was noted that the MA formula for IQ is IQ = MA/CA × 100. Compare the following:

$$\frac{\text{MA: 5 years}}{\text{CA: 10 years}} \times 100 = \text{IQ} = 50$$

$$\frac{\text{MA: 5 years}}{\text{CA: 5 years}} \times 100 = \text{IQ} = 100$$

In these examples both children have an MA of five years. This means that the intellectual functioning of both children is the same as that of an average five-year-old child. In the case of a ten-year-old child, an MA of five years indicates retardation, but in the case of a five-year-old, an MA of five years indicates normal intellectual development. According to developmental theorists, both children are in the same cognitive stage of development and are thus expected to perform similarly on intellectual tasks, given equal motivation to perform well. According to defect theorists, the intellectual functioning of the retarded child with an MA of five years is deficient compared to that of the normal child with an MA of five years. Thus by comparing normal and retarded children of equal MAs, the researcher attempts to specify the nature of the intellectual deficiencies shown by retardates; because MA is controlled for, these deficiencies are not attributable to slow development.

A review of the experimental literatures comparing MA-matched groups of normals and subnormals on intellectual tasks indicates generally inferior performances for retardates. The retardates' inferior performances are particularly evident on tasks requiring the spontaneous use of verbal mediators and on tasks of short-term memory. The following is an introduction to the relevant experimental literatures.

Discrimination Learning

Many studies have compared the performance of retardates and normals on discrimination tasks in order to evaluate whether retardates are deficient in this type of learning and, if so, to specify the nature of the deficiency. At issue here is the manner in which retardates learn to behave differently to different stimuli. For example, children learn to discriminate among colors, forms, shapes,

[2] The impedance hypothesized by Spitz's theory is not the refractory phase of neural impulses.

letters, words, and people. Researchers have investigated whether retardates learn such discriminations more slowly than normals, whether they make more errors, and whether their deficiencies are related to the use of ineffective learning strategies.

Psychologists have created a number of simple experimental paradigms for studying discrimination learning. For example, a child might be seated in front of a panel on which two stimuli flash; the child's task is to select the stimulus that leads to reward. Suppose that the following two stimuli flash on the screen on trial 1:

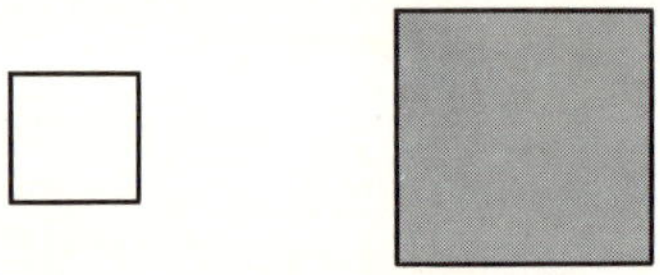

These stimuli differ along three dimensions: shade (dark or light), size (larger or smaller), and position (right or left). If the experimenter is always going to dispense reward for selection of the larger stimulus, size is called the relevant dimension, and shade and position are called the irrelevant dimensions. On trial 1, the child will obtain reward if he selects the larger stimulus, the darker stimulus, or the stimulus on the right. Suppose, however, that the following stimuli are presented on trial 2:

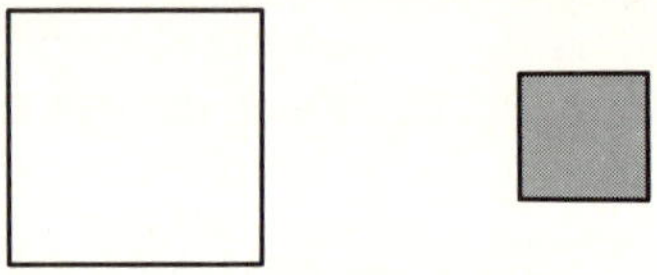

If on trial 1 the child happened to earn reward by responding to the irrelevant dimensions of shade or position, on trial 2 the child would respond incorrectly, because in this instance the selection of the stimulus on the right or the darker stimulus does not also imply the selection of the larger stimulus. Over repeated trials of selecting one of two stimuli and discovering which one leads to reward, the child eventually learns that size is the relevant dimension and that the larger of the two stimuli is the correct response.

When matched for chronological age, retardates usually learn discrimination tasks more slowly than do normals (e.g., Lent, Holvoet, Ferneti, Keilitz, & Tucker, 1973). When matched for mental age, some studies have found no differences in discrimination learning between retardates and normals (e.g., Achenbach & Zigler, 1968; Balla & Zigler, 1964; O'Connor & Hermelin, 1959), whereas others have found inferior performances for retardates (e.g., House & Zeaman, 1958; Lobb, 1972; Lutkus & Trabasso, 1974; Zeaman & House, 1967). It is possible that the studies reporting no differences included tasks that were too simple. However, a recent study by Gruen and Berg (1973), in which task complexity was varied, found no differences between MA-matched groups of retardates and normals.

Zeaman and House's (1963) attentional theory is based on a two-process analysis of discrimination learning. The first process is learning to attend to the relevant dimension (e.g., size); the second process is learning to discriminate within the relevant dimension (e.g., the larger versus the smaller size). Originally, attentional theory proposed that the retardate assessed only one dimension at a time, but in a recent revision Zeaman (1973) rejected this "one-look" model in favor of a "multiple-look" model. In the revised theory, the number of dimensions a subject can attend to on any single trial is determined by his intelligence. Because less intelligent subjects are hypothesized to be limited in the number of dimensions they can attend to on any given trial, the theory provides an explanation for why retardates require more trials to learn simple discrimination tasks. A recent study by Ullman (1974) partially supported this "limited breadth of attention" model.

Paired-Associate Learning

A number of studies have evaluated the possibility that retardates sometimes are deficient in learning because, compared to normals, they fail to use their language capacity to maximum advantage. One paradigm for evaluating this possibility is called the paired-associate paradigm. The typical paired-associate task first presents the subject with a list of paired words, such as man–dog and tree–apple; later it tests for learning by presenting the first word of the pair in order to observe whether the subject can recall the second word.

Several investigators have proposed that one specific deficit in the intellectual functioning of retardates is their relative inability to use verbal mediators (e.g., Milgram, 1973). For example, recall of *man–dog* and *tree–apple* is aided by remembering short sentences such as "The man pets the dog" and "The tree grows apples." The assumption of a deficiency in the use of verbal mediators implies that, compared to normals at the same MA level, retardates are less likely to use the strategy of constructing short sentences to remember associations between two words. Although a deficiency in the use of verbal mediators has not been proven, some supporting evidence has been reported (Jensen & Rohwer, 1963; Luria, 1963).

If retardates do not generate verbal mediational strategies on their own, the question arises as to whether or not they can be taught such strategies. In a study directed toward this question, Wanschura and Borkowski (1974) explicitly trained retardates to use verbal mediators to aid recall in paired-associate learning. The results indicated that moderately and severely retarded children can learn mediational strategies but that the long-term retention of these experimentally taught strategies is poor.

Memory

Several studies have been reported suggesting deficiencies in the memory processes of retardates. Some investigators have reported observations of a spontaneous loss of learning in mentally retarded subjects (e.g., Barrett & Lindsley, 1962; Ellis, 1963; Hayes, 1969; Ross & Ross, 1973). Perhaps the clearest evidence of inferior performances on memory tasks, however, comes from comprehensive studies of retardates and normals on tasks of short-term memory (Butterfield, Wambold, & Belmont, 1973; Ellis, 1970). Apparently, retarded people are deficient in short-term memory in part because they fail to rehearse spontaneously the material to be remembered. However, recent evidence suggests that special training techniques (see Butterfield et al., 1973) can be used to improve considerably short-term memory in the retardate.

There is some evidence that recall in retardates is deficient because they do not spontaneously cluster stimuli into groups. For example, in trying to remember the names Einstein, Kennedy, Washington, Skinner, Eisenhower, and Freud, recall is aided by clustering these stimuli into groups of presidents (Kennedy, Washington, and Eisenhower) and scientists (Einstein, Skinner, and Freud). Several studies have reported that retardates are deficient in the spontaneous use of clustering strategies (Osborn, 1960; Rossi, 1964; Riegel & Taylor, 1974).

As noted, the deficiency in memory processes found in retardates seems to be related to the failure to use spontaneously rehearsal and clustering strategies. It should be emphasized that this deficiency does not necessarily indicate that, given equal learning, the potential for memory in retardates is less than that of normals. In fact, a number of the studies cited suggest that recall in retardates can be improved to normal levels by teaching strategies of rehearsal and of organizing material. Unfortunately, this educational task may require that memory strategies be taught for each of the different types of material to be remembered—that is, the retardate does not seem to acquire the capacity to transfer spontaneously a recall strategy from one type of material to another type of material.

Complex Problem-Solving and Conceptual Behavior

In his review of the literature on conceptual behavior in the retarded, Rosenberg drew the following conclusion:

> It would be difficult to attempt to characterize the problem-solving and conceptual behavior of mental defectives from the research reported to date with any high degree of reliability. There should be little doubt, however, of the existence of a relationship between problem-solving and/or conceptual behavior and IQ and MA. The relationship, nevertheless, is a very complex one, the details of which will have to be worked out in future research. It is also clear that under certain conditions, some mental defectives are capable of problem solving, abstract learning, abstract performance, and generalization despite evidence of an inability to identify verbally the relevant dimensions of similarity. These results should act as a stimulus for those workers interested in education and training to search for the variables which facilitate and interfere with problem-solving and conceptual behavior [1963, p. 459].

Since Rosenberg's review, there has been an increase in research activity on abstraction and on higher mental processes in retardates (see Milgram, 1973), but it is still true that most research has focused on the study of simple learning processes. An important exception to this general rule, however, is the high interest in conceptual processes among the few investigators concerned with the relevance of Piaget's theory to mental retardation (Schmid-Kitsikis, 1973; Woodward, 1963). Piaget's theory postulates a series of thought structures, or developmental-cognitive stages, through which the normal child progresses. The view of retardates as progressing through these stages at a slower rate suggests that retardates think in accordance with the cognitive structures of younger children and that Piaget's description of these structures is of considerable relevance for understanding mental retardation. However, the relevant literature on the applicability of Piaget's theory to mental retardation is sparse and inconclusive (see Inhelder, 1963; Robinson, 1974).

Motivational Factors

Performances on intellectual tasks are affected by motivational as well as by intellectual factors. An experimental finding that retardates show inferior performances on an intellectual task is, thus, theoretically explicable in terms of subnormal intellectual ability, inferior motivation to perform, or both. Having surveyed some of the major findings concerning the relative performances of retardates and normals on intellectual tasks, we turn our attention to a survey of the motivational factors that interfere with intellectual functioning in the mentally retarded.

Observations that retarded children are more distractible and have shorter attention spans than normals have been reported for quite some time (Ribot, 1890). Similarly, it has long been recognized that on intellectual tasks retardates tend to perseverate by repeatedly making the same mistake; Lewin (1936) considered this tendency to perseverate evidence that *cognitive rigidity* is a specific defect characteristic of thought in retarded people. It is possible, however, to explain both the greater distractibility and the tendency to perseverate in terms of motivational factors. Specifically, Zigler and his colleagues (see Zigler, 1968, 1973) have hypothesized an excessive need for adult social interaction in the institutionalized, mentally retarded child. Thus, when brought to an experimental room, the institutionalized retardate is motivated more to maintain social interactions with the experimenter than to solve the task. Consequently, the retardate is more distractible (looks more at the experimenter) and appears to have a shorter attention span. Additionally, the retardate may perseverate on learning tasks in order to prolong the experiment and hence to increase social contact with the experimenter.

The hypothesis that institutionalized retardates are more motivated than normals to interact with experimenters is supported by studies indicating that institutionalized retardates are subjected to relatively high degrees of social deprivation (e.g., Clarke & Clarke, 1954; Zigler, 1961). In general, social deprivation increases motivation for social interaction. This support is, however, indirect—additional research is needed to evaluate whether the institutionalized retardate tends to perform poorly on experimental tasks because of heightened social motivation.

Expectancy for Failure

Cromwell (1963) has reported that, compared to normals, retardates tend to approach tasks with an expectation of failure. Consequently, retardates may learn less than normals in part because they expect to fail and hence do not try to succeed—that is, expectation of failure is a self-fulfilling prophecy leading to failure. For example, Zeaman and House (1960) found that retardates exposed to prolonged failure were unable to solve problems they had been able to solve prior to exposure to failure. Dweck and Reppucci (1973), who extended the Zeaman and House (1960) finding to normals, showed that lack of effort in solving problems after repeated failure is correlated with cognitive assumptions concerning the futility of trying and inadequate ability (e.g., *I might as well not try because I can't do this; I am unlucky so there's no point in trying*). Thus, it appears that retardates learn to expect failure and assume that success, when it occurs, is unrelated to their effort or ability.

Outerdirectedness

Turnure and Zigler (1964) reasoned that the retardate's long history of failure may encourage him to distrust his own abilities and to rely instead on external sources of information. These investigators called the tendency to rely on external sources of information outerdirectedness. In an experimental test, Turnure and Zigler (1964) assessed the extent to which normals and retardates matched for MA imitated adult and peer models. Prior to testing for imitation, the children played games under conditions of success and failure. Hypothesis 1 was that retardates, having had a greater history of failure, would be more outerdirected in that they would be more imitative than normals. Hypothesis 2 was that both retarded and normal children would be more imitative following failure than following success. The results supported both hypotheses. Additional support for the outerdirectedness hypothesis was obtained in studies by Achenbach and Zigler (1968), by Sanders, Zigler, and Butterfield (1968), and by Turnure (1973).

EMOTIONAL DISTURBANCE AND MENTAL RETARDATION

As noted earlier in this chapter, degeneration theorists considered insanity and mental retardation as variations of the same disease. Even the great Pinel regarded mental retardation as a form of insanity. Esquirol (1772–1840), a student of Pinel, was among the first to distinguish clearly between the two types of disorders. Esquirol (1845) observed that in insanity normal intellectual functioning is lost, whereas in mental retardation normal intellectual functioning is never achieved.

The intellectually retarded show a wide range of emotional disturbances similar to those found in the intellectually normal (see Garfield, 1963). The occurrence of both mental retardation and emotional disturbance in the same individual raises the question of how the two are related. On the one hand, the occurrence of emotional disturbance, particularly in young children, can interfere with intellectual functioning. The prolonged occurrence of emotional disturbance may even produce subnormal IQs in otherwise borderline or below average individuals. On the other hand, the intellectually subnormal individual may be likely to develop emotional problems as a consequence of his recognition of his low abilities and of the stigma of being labeled mentally retarded. The relation between mental subnormality and emotional disturbance is thus complex because either problem can cause the other.

Psychosis and Mental Retardation

Sarason and Gladwin stated:

> Practically every major psychotic symptom which has been described in the nondefective patient has also been noted in many of the defective cases. There appears to be little justification for the generalization that when psychosis occurs in a mentally defective individual it is necessarily less "complex" than when found in the nondefective individual [1958, p. 179].

The case of Annette presented in Chapters 7 and 9 provides an example of a mentally retarded child who suffered from a severe emotional disturbance. Annette's violent screaming and excessive dependency on adults seemed psychotic in nature and interfered with her intellectual functioning even though her mental retardation could not be entirely attributed to her emotional problems.

There is a paucity of significant research on severe emotional disturbance and mental subnormality. The available literature consists primarily of demographic studies that document relatively high incidences of emotional disturbance in severely retarded, institutionalized children (e.g., Angus, 1948; Payne, 1968; see Garfield, 1963), of case histories, and of theoretical debates as to whether the nature of psychosis is qualitatively different in intellectually normal and subnormal people (e.g., Bourne, 1955; O'Gorman, 1954).

Adjustment Problems

Several factors create special psychological difficulties for retardates (Hutt & Gibby, 1965). First, the subnormal must face the reality of his retardation. The recognition of lower intellectual abilities and the history of failure on intellectual tasks predispose the intellectually subnormal to feelings of worthlessness, mild depression, and helplessness. Second, as the retardate grows older, he falls farther behind his friends and is increasingly excluded from social groups. Although his psychological need for companionship is as great as that of the intellectually normal child, it is more difficult for him to fulfill this need. The frustration of basic social needs, and the exclusion from groups, may predispose some retardates to feelings of anger and rebellion. Third, the family life to which the retardate must adjust may be complicated by parental guilt. Some parents of retarded children show evidence of unconscious guilt for having brought a child into the world with subnormal abilities. One prevalent form of expression of this guilt is parental overprotection. For example, rather than encourage self-help skills, the parents might continue to dress and to feed the child at inappropriate ages. Such patterns of parental behavior encourage a dependent style of interpersonal interaction in the child. Other parents express unconscious guilt by denying the child's disabilities. Many clinicians have encountered parents of retarded children who look forward to the day when their child will enter Dartmouth, Harvard, or Yale. Parental defensive reactions such as overprotection and denial create obvious adjustment difficulties for the child.

BOX 18-1
The Idiot Savant and Infantile Autism

The idiot savant is a retardate who shows superior ability in a narrow intellectual area. The idiot savant has been characterized as suffering from an impairment of the ability to think abstractly. This syndrome occurs both in individuals in whom there is no discernible central nervous system pathology and in individuals in whom there is demonstrable central nervous system pathology, although the former is more typical. Perhaps the clearest description of the idiot savant was provided by Scheerer, Rothman, and Goldstein (1945) as a result of their observations of an eleven-year-old boy, L. Although his IQ was 50, L. could play melodies on the piano by ear, could rapidly manipulate simple numbers, and had a remarkable ability to recall dates, names, places, and times. Nevertheless, L.'s abstract abilities were impaired: He could not reason, understand the concept of causation, or comprehend symbols; he could only learn and recall what was situationally concrete.

The causes of the idiot savant condition are obscure, but a number of hypotheses have been proposed. For example, La Fontaine and Benjamin (1971) have noted that a prominent feature of the idiot savant is the discrepancy between one particular skill and other abilities that are on a subnormal level. In this regard, normals also show a range in abilities in different skills—what characterizes the idiot savant is the degree of this range. Hoffman (1971) has hypothesized that the idiot savant's unusual skill in one area is aided by his ability to ignore interfering stimuli and hence to concentrate on a narrow range of stimuli. However, the most intriguing hypothesis about the idiot savant syndrome is that it is essentially the same syndrome that Kanner (1943) called infantile autism.

As described by Kanner, infantile autism is a psychotic disorder characterized by (1) a lack of responsivity to the environment during infancy; for example, autistic children do not assume an anticipatory posture when picked up and are withdrawn; (2) retarded acquisition of speech; at least initially, speech is echolalic; (3) an impairment of abstraction ability; and (4) a tendency to show startle reactions to auditory or moving stimuli. Like the idiot savant syndrome, autism is more prevalent in males. Some autistic children show a phenomenal ability for memorizing concrete events.

Kanner classified infantile autism as an emotional disturbance because he assumed that the intellectual abnormalities could be understood in terms of a basic emotional pathology characterized by a desire for aloneness and sameness. It is possible, however, to interpret many of the behaviors associated with infantile autism as emotional reactions to impaired intelligence (see Rimland, 1964, and Scheerer et al., 1945, for comments on the relation between infantile autism and the idiot savant). It is also possible to regard infantile autism as both an emotional disturbance and a form of mental retardation. Controversy over the nature of infantile autism and the idiot savant syndrome is likely to continue for quite some time.

Stereotypy

Baumeister and Forehand defined stereotypy as "highly consistent and repetitious motor or posturing behavior, the adaptive consequences of which, if any, are not immediately apparent" [1973, p. 56]. Stereotyped behavior includes rhythmic hand waving, rhythmic shoulder rocking, gazing at a hand, and the repeated rubbing of fingers.

The prevalence of stereotypy among institutionalized retarded boys is very high. For example, Berkson and Davenport (1962) found that more than two thirds of the institutionalized retarded boys in their sample engaged in some type of stereotypy. This study also found a positive correlation between length of institutionalization and stereotypy and a negative correlation between IQ and stereotypy. Thus the low-IQ male who has been institutionalized for a long period of time is the retardate most likely to show frequent stereotyped behavior.

There are several plausible theories of stereotypy. One view, which can be called the self-stimulatory hypothesis, posits an optimal level of sensory stimulation such that people seek to increase stimulation when sensory input is below this optimal level. The institutionalized retardate may receive insufficient stimulation from his sterile environment; moreover, some types of organic defects may lower the overall level of sensory input. Such individuals may engage in stereotypic behavior to increase the level of sensory stimulation. The self-stimulatory hypothesis thus proposes that stereotypic behavior is maintained because it increases the level of sensory input. Another hypothesis proposes that stereotypic behavior is a form of anxiety and tension reduction (e.g., Brody, 1960; Gerard, 1957; Lourie, 1959). Still another hypothesis suggests a relation between stereotypy and arousal level (Berkson & Mason, 1964). There is evidence to support each of these theories (see Baumeister & Forehand, 1973).

Stereotypy is more frequent in blind than in sighted retardates (Berkson & Davenport, 1962; Guess, 1966). This observation is consistent with the general theoretical notion that stereotypy is maintained by self-stimulation in a sensory-deprived individual. Berkson (1973) tested the hypothesis that blindness causes stereotypy by experimentally blinding seven monkeys and by comparing their behavior to seven sighted controls. Both the blind and the sighted animals were raised in social isolation. The results indicated that both groups developed stereotypic movements at approximately the same rate; that is, rearing in social isolation was sufficient to produce stereotyped movements in monkeys, and blinding the monkeys prior to social isolation did not increase the level of stereotypy. These results do not support the hypothesis that blindness causes stereotypy, and the reasons why blind retardates tend to show more stereotypy are still unclear.

Self-mutilating Behavior

Self-mutilating behavior has been observed to occur in several small, specialized populations (Bachman, 1972; Lester, 1972; Ressman & Butterworth, 1952). Violent head banging, tantrums, and biting and scratching are the most prevalent forms of self-mutilation in institutionalized retarded children.

Several theories of self-mutilation have been proposed. Levy (1944) hypothesized that head banging is a stereotyped behavior performed to increase sensory input. Skinner (1953) postulated that self-mutilation is learned either when it leads to the avoidance of even more aversive consequences or when the aversive self-mutilation has previously been paired with a source of positive reinforcement. Although there is little evidence concerning the actual ways in which retardates learn self-mutilating behavior, reinforcement therapists have shown that electric shock punishment suppresses the frequency of self-injurious behavior (e.g., Napolitan & Peterson, 1972; Lovaas & Simmons, 1969; Tate & Baroff, 1966).

PREVENTION, REMEDIATION, AND CARE

In the last two decades we have witnessed unprecedented progress in our knowledge concerning the prevention and remediation of mental retardation. Begab has summarized the current situation: "Undoubtedly, we have much still to learn about mental retardation, but in certain aspects of the problem at least, we have only to apply what we already know. We can indeed significantly reduce the incidence and prevalence of mental retardation" [1974, p. 529].

Prevention

There are several ways to prevent mental retardation. It is possible to prevent metabolic disorders such as PKU and cretinism if treatment begins within the first few weeks of life. Based on the established correlation of mother's age and mongolism, programs of public education can encourage parents to have their children prior to age 40. Genetic counseling is available to provide parents with information concerning the probability of having a mentally deficient child, but unfortunately such counseling can be given only to parents who have already had a retarded child.

Prevention of mental retardation caused by toxic agents can be facilitated by programs of public education and by more effective means of pollution control. The tragic cases of children who eat crumbling paint from the walls of slum houses and who consequently become mentally retarded are unnecessary (Byers, 1959). Equally unnecessary are reported cases of retarded children born to mothers who during pregnancy ate high amounts of shellfish from mercury-infested waters (Takeuchi & Matsumoto, 1969).

Compensatory Education

Compensatory education attempts to prevent developmental defects that interfere with educational progress in the disadvantaged, preschool child. The most ambitious of such attempts is Project Head Start (e.g., Hellmuth, 1969). The many Head Start centers have differed in purpose, philosophy, and technique, and this extraordinary diversity has precluded a meaningful evaluation of the effectiveness of the Head Start effort. Thus the extent to which Head Start programs may have prevented mental retardation or borderline intellectual performance is unclear.

The Milwaukee Project (Heber, Garber, Harrington, & Hoffman, 1972) is one of the most successful attempts to prevent cultural-familial mental retardation. This project provided an experimental evaluation of a comprehensive program of early education. The 50 subjects were newborns who were high risks for mental retardation; that is, all subjects were from disadvantaged neighborhoods, and all had mothers whose IQs were under 70. The subjects were randomly assigned to experimental and control groups. From the fourth week of life, the experimental subjects received a structured program of sensory and language stimulation that emphasized achievement motivation, problem-solving skills, and interpersonal relations. The children received this training on a daily basis and are now of school age; additionally, the mothers of experimental subjects received training in homemaking and in child care. The project differed from previous compensatory education programs in the young age of its subjects and in its comprehensiveness. The results showed striking differences in the levels of intellectual functioning between experimental and control subjects. At the age of five years and six months, the mean Stanford-Binet IQ was 125 and 92 for experimental and controls, respectively.

The Milwaukee Project demonstrates the effectiveness of early and comprehensive intervention in the prevention of cultural-familial retardation. However, we are still a long way from its large-scale prevention.

Special Education

In theory, the special education class seems to provide a reasonable structure for educating the mentally subnormal child. Because a retardate learns at a slower rate, he should not be subjected to the demands of a regular class. Moreover, because special curricular materials and techniques are needed, the retardate should be taught in small classes by specially trained teachers. In accordance with this type of educational philosophy, special education classes for educable retardates have been created in most schools across the country. In recent years, however, there has been an increasing tendency to question the desirability of the self-contained special education class. Concern has focused on those aspects of the special class that may encourage stigmatization and rejection of the child. For example, placement in a special class requires that the child be labeled retarded. Both the retardate and his normal peers may tend to view attendance in the special class as degrading. Additionally, some teachers may assume that the child is incapable of significant learning because he is retarded; the child is thus taught less and learns less. To remedy these problems, many special educators are advocating "mainstreaming," or the placement of retardates in regular classes.

One empirical issue raised by the special education class is peer reaction to retardates in regular classes. The available research suggests that acceptability of educable retardates in regular elementary school classes depends primarily on the extent to which the individual engages in deviant behavior (e.g., Johnson & Kirk, 1950) and on the individual's social class (e.g., Monroe & Howe, 1971); in general, acceptance does not appear to depend on academic performance. In recent studies, Gottlieb and Budoff (1973) found that retardates were rejected more in an open-space class than in a traditional classroom environment, whereas Sheare (1974) found that educable retardates were liked more when integrated into regular classes than when in special classes. The debate between those who favor mainstreaming and those who favor special classes is likely to continue in the foreseeable future.

An art therapy class in a mental retardation unit. The patients are being encouraged to plan and draw a large mural. (Photo by Burk Uzzle; Magnum Photos, Inc.)

Institutionalization

The overwhelming majority of mentally retarded people do not require institutionalization; as noted previously, less than 4 per cent of all retardates in the United States receive institutional care. Overcrowded wards and sterile environments are still prevalent in many large state institutions. In some states (e.g., Connecticut), efforts have been made to decentralize state care by constructing statewide community-based residential centers. The residential center is much smaller in both population and size than is the state institution and provides both in-patient and out-patient services. In addition to being a seemingly superior alternative to the large state institution, the cost effectiveness of most residential centers is one reason for their increasing popularity.

It has been generally assumed that the effects of institutionalization are deleterious. Institutions, however, differ considerably from one another, thus rendering generalizations hazardous (Klaber, 1969). The general assumption of deleterious effects seems most appropriate for institutions in which the care is mostly custodial and in which drugs are freely dispensed to control deviant behavior. Some investigators, however, have reported positive effects of institutionalization on IQ (Clarke & Clarke, 1953; Zigler, Balla, & Butterfield, 1968). In a longitudinal, cross-institutional investigation, Balla, Butterfield, and Zigler (1974) found that the effects of institutionalization varied with the individual's preinstitutional life experiences, the environment of the particular institution, and the sex and diagnosis of the individual. The size of the institution, which in this study varied from 383 to 2,012, and the population density of the residential unit, which varied from 32 to 87, were not found to be related to any child behaviors. The investigators concluded that "the effects associated with residing in one institution rather than in another, independent of all factors, were surprisingly few in number" [1974, p. 542]. These results not only indicate the need for additional objective assessments of the effects of institutionalization but also suggest that the general conclusion of pervasive deleterious effects may be an exaggeration.

Reinforcement Therapy

Reinforcement therapy techniques have been found applicable to many problems of the mentally retarded. Reinforcement therapy has been successful in establishing social skills (e.g., Bendebba, 1973), motor skills such as tricycle riding (Peterson & McIntosh, 1973), self-help skills such as toilet training (e.g., Azrin & Foxx, 1971) and proper eating (e.g., Barton, Guess, Garcia, & Baer, 1970), and speech and language (e.g., Baer & Guess, 1971; Sailor, Guess, & Baer, 1973). Reinforcement therapy has been demonstrated to be at least partially effective in cases of tantrums (e.g., Reiss & Redd, 1970), stereotypic behavior (e.g., Azrin, Kaplan, & Foxx, 1973), self-mutilating behavior (e.g., Lovaas & Simmons, 1969), and many other management problems. The literature on reinforcement therapy with the mentally subnormal is voluminous, and virtually all of the studies demonstrate that appropriate behavioral changes are possible.

Reinforcement therapy has been applied in institutions and in special education classes. One especially well-implemented program in an institution is Sidman's program at the W. E. Fernald State School in Waltham, Massachusetts. This program has demonstrated remarkable long-term behavioral improvement in severely retarded children.

An important aspect of reinforcement therapy with the mentally retarded is the rapid occurrence of visible changes in behavior. Many have doubted the ability of retardates to learn, so that the visible demonstration of progress does much to change attitudes about the capabilities of retardates. Although the gains from reinforcement therapy programs are usually modest in terms of the progress made by normal children—that is, the children still remain obviously retarded—genuine progress in both intellectual and social behavior is almost always possible by the proper application of reinforcement therapy techniques.

SUMMARY

According to the American Association on Mental Retardation (AAMD), mental retardation should be diagnosed on the basis of low intelligence and related social problems. IQ scores obtained from the Stanford-Binet and WISC-R are typically used to assess intelligence; SQ scores obtained from the Vineland Social Maturity Scale are typically used to assess social competence. In actual practice, however, mental retardation is often diagnosed almost exclusively in terms of low intelligence. The correlation between scores on tests of intelligence and scores on tests of social competence is relatively high (Goldschmid & Domino, 1965; Saslow, 1961), thereby suggesting that diagnosis on the basis of intelligence alone will often yield the same diagnosis as that on the basis of both intelligence and social problems. However, Adams, McIntosh, and Weade (1973) found that black retarded children, compared to white retarded children, tend to score higher on tests of social competence than on tests of intelligence. Thus diagnosis solely on the basis of low IQ scores results in the classification of a greater number of black children as severely or profoundly retarded than does diagnosis on the basis of both low IQ and low SQ scores. Approximately 3 per cent of the population has an IQ below 70.

The mentally retarded are an extremely heterogeneous group of people. Cultural-familial retardation is diagnosed on the basis of three criteria: mild retardation, at least one parent or sibling who is also retarded, and the absence of demonstrable central nervous system damage. The overwhelming majority of cultural-familial retardates are from the lowest socioeconomic classes. Down's syndrome is caused by a chromosomal disorder called trisomy-21. PKU and cretinism are metabolic disorders believed to be transmitted by a single recessive gene. In addition to chromosomal abnormalities and genetic defects, central nervous system damage leading to mental retardation can be caused by infectious diseases, tumors, poisons, radiation, and accidents.

Historically, social values and advances in biology have influenced scientific theories on the nature of mental retardation. Degeneration theories held that mental retardation, insanity, epilepsy, and immorality are various expressions of a common, inheritable degenerative process. Early proponents of this theory regarded the retarded as unfortunate recipients of a tainted inheritance. Later nineteenth-century proponents of the theory, however, maintained that, by natural law, degenerative lines were unfit to survive. By the early twentieth century, retardates were regarded as potential criminals and as moral deviates who constituted a menace to society. Fortunately, a more humane and enlightened attitude prevails at the present time.

Some evidence suggests that mental retardation might be associated with juvenile delinquency, although the degree of association is small. There is no direct evidence, however, that mental retardation causes antisocial behavior. Rather, the association, if any, is probably a consequence of the fact that both mental retardation and juvenile delinquency are associated with poverty backgrounds. The overwhelming majority of mental retardates are not delinquents.

The developmental-defect controversy has stimulated a considerable amount of laboratory research. Developmental theory maintains that the retardate progresses through the same stages of cognitive development as does the intellectually normal child, except that the retardate does so more slowly and never achieves the same ultimate level of intellectual functioning. Defect theory maintains that the intellectual processes that are characteristic of mental retardation are defective in ways other than slow development. On the whole, the available data favor defect theory, although the evidence is often inconsistent and there is still merit to the developmental position.

Experimental research comparing retardates and normals matched for MA suggests that retardates are deficient in the ability to generate spontaneously verbal mediators and in the ability to generate spontaneously recall strategies in tasks of short-term memory. Moreover, Zeaman (1973) has recently postulated that retardates are deficient in the ability to attend to multiple dimensions of a discrimination task. It is possible that some of the findings that retardates exhibit inferior performances on intellectual tasks are attributable to motivational factors. For example, Cromwell (1963) has reported that, compared to normals, retardates tend to approach tasks with an expectation of failure. Turnure and Zigler (1964) introduced the concept of outerdirectedness to refer to the retardate's seemingly greater tendency to rely on external sources of information.

The retarded exhibit a wide range of emotional disturbances similar to those found in the intellectually normal. The occurrence of emotional disturbance and intellectual subnormality in the same individual raises the questions of whether the two are related and, if so, in what manner. Sometimes severe emotional disturbance may exacerbate intellectual subnormality, and sometimes mental retardation presents special adjustment problems that increase the likelihood of emotional disturbance. Examples of these special adjustment problems include parental over-protection, rejection by peers, and restricted dating opportunities. Finally, it is possible that mental retardation and emotional disturbance can sometimes occur in the same individual without there being any direct causal relation between the two disorders.

Stereotypy has been defined as repetitious motor or posturing behavior that has no apparent adaptive benefits. The prevalence of stereotypy among institutionalized, retarded boys is very high, with one study finding that more than two-thirds of the subjects engaged in some type of stereotypy. One theoretical explanation of stereotypy is the self-stimulatory hypothesis; this hypothesis maintains that stereotyped behaviors are performed to increase sensory input from chronically underaroused levels.

In recent years we have witnessed considerable progress in our knowledge concerning the prevention and treatment of mental retardation. One major development in the area of prevention is the Milwaukee Project in which a comprehensive program of early intervention was found to prevent below average IQs in a group of disadvantaged children. One major development in the area of psychoeducation has been the application of reinforcement therapy techniques to mental retardation.

Chapter 19

Abnormal Behavior in "Normal" People[1]

CHARLES L. GRUDER, SHARON GURWITZ, and STEVEN REISS[1]

Normal men have killed perhaps 100,000,000 of their fellow normal men in the last fifty years.

LAING (1967, p. 11)

The behaviors discussed in this chapter include mass hysteria at a rock and roll concert or a revival meeting, prejudice (sexism and racism), negative self-evaluations of one's worth as a person, and cigarette smoking. All of these behaviors can be regarded as psychopathological. All occur in relatively well-adjusted people although they also occur in people suffering from the disorders described in Chapters 10 through 17. Some of these behaviors are unusual, whereas others are relatively common.

In Chapter 3 abnormality was defined as a family resemblance of three attributes: (1) the presence of irrationality, (2) the presence of anxiety or suffering, and (3) interpersonal maladaptation. The greater the number of attributes present and/or the greater the extent to which any single attribute is present, the more clearly is the behavior abnormal (psychopathological). So defined, at least some abnormal behaviors can and do occur in people who would be judged by most of us to be perfectly normal. In fact, it is a rare person who does not occasionally exhibit behavior that is irrational, leads to unnecessary suffering, and/or is maladaptive. So-called normal people are thus not normal under all circumstances in which they might find themselves.

One way to distinguish between abnormal behavior in relatively well-adjusted people and abnormal behavior in maladjusted people is to assess the extent to which the behavior interferes with normal life functioning. The behaviors discussed in this chapter can occur in "normal" people because they generally do not interfere with the individual's ability to lead a normal life. This is because the abnormal behavior either represents a transient reaction to a temporary situation (e.g., abnormal behavior in certain gatherings) or does not occur in sufficient frequency or intensity to be debilitating (e.g., prejudice).

The fact that we all occasionally behave in a "crazy" or psychopathological manner does *not* suggest that we are on the brink of developing a debilitating psychological disorder. The notion that there is a "fine line between sanity and insanity" is misleading. People possess many personality and characterological strengths that permit them to adjust and to function under both favorable and adverse circumstances. It generally requires prolonged exposure to highly stressful situations before emotional disorders develop; moreover, even when such disorders do develop, the capacity in most persons for coping and recovery is considerable and should not be underestimated.

HYSTERICAL BEHAVIOR IN GROUPS

The notion of abnormal behavior in normal people is especially applicable to a number of group phenomena. The Beatles, for example, were once capable of eliciting emotional frenzy and hysterical behavior in millions of otherwise

[1] Charles L. Gruder wrote the sections of this chapter on abnormal behavior in groups, self-esteem, and smoking; Sharon B. Gurwitz wrote the section on prejudice and stereotyping; and Steven Reiss organized and edited these contributions.

normal teenagers. Similar states of emotional frenzy occur at religious revival meetings in which some participants become "possessed" and lie on the floor in a stuporous state of religious intoxication. Hitler was capable of eliciting similar reactions in some of his followers and was successful in creating the mass delusion that Aryans are a superior race. Two dramatic examples of abnormal behavior in groups will be considered here. One example is an account of a religious festival in which a half-million people cheer as thousands engage in acts of self-mutilation. The other example is that of an epidemic of a disease that did not even exist.

Two Examples: The Shiite Festival and the June Bug Epidemic

The Shiites are an Islamic religious sect predominant in Iran and Yemen and with strong representation in India and in Iraq. The great Shiite Festival is held to commemorate the passion of a Prophet who suffered a violent and bloody death as the culmination of his persecution by a cruel secular leader. In reading the following account of this festival, it is important to keep in mind that most of the people involved led what we would consider to be normal lives.

> 500,000 people, seized with madness, cover their heads with ashes and beat their foreheads on the ground. They want to give themselves up in torture, to commit suicide in groups, or to mutilate themselves with a refined cruelty. The guilds follow each other in procession. Composed of men who have retained a glimmer of reason—the human instinct of self-preservation—their members are dressed in ordinary fashion.
>
> A great silence descends. Men in white shirts advance in hundreds, their faces turned ecstatically to heaven.
>
> Of these men, several will be dead by evening, and many more mutilated and disfigured; their shirts, red with blood, will be their shrouds. They are beings who have already ceased to belong to this world. Their coarsely made shirts leave only face and hands visible: faces of martyrs, hands of murderers.
>
> With encouraging shouts, and infecting them with their own madness, others hand them swords. Their excitement becomes murderous; they turn round and round, brandishing over their heads the weapons they have been given. Their shouts dominate the shouts of the crowd. To be able to bear what they are going to suffer they have to work themselves into a state of catalepsy. With the steps of automata they advance, retreat and move sideways in no apparent order. In time with each step they strike their heads with their jagged swords. Blood flows and their shirts become scarlet. The sight of the blood brings the confusion in the minds of these voluntary martyrs to a climax. Some of them collapse, striking themselves haphazardly with their swords. In their frenzy they have cut through veins and arteries, and they die where they fall before the police have time to carry them to an ambulance installed behind the closed shutters of a shop.
>
> The crowd, insensible to the blows of the police, close over them and drag them to another part of the town where the massacre continues. As they are carried past, the raging crowd rages more and more fiercely. There is not one man who retains the balance of his mind. Those who lack the courage for massacre offer kola to others, inciting them with the drug and with curses.
>
> The martyrs take off their shirts, which are now regarded as blessed, and give them to those who carry them. Others, who were not at first among the voluntary victims, suddenly, in the general commotion, discover their thirst for blood. They ask for weapons, tear their clothes off, and wound themselves haphazardly.
>
> Sometimes there is a gap in the procession when one of the participants falls down

The aftermath at Woodstock rock festival. (Photo by Burk Uzzle; Magnum Photos, Inc.)

exhausted. But the gap is only momentary. The crowd immediately closes over the wretched man and kicks him and tramples on him. No destiny is accounted more beautiful than to die on the feast-day of Ashura, when the gates of all eight paradises stand wide open for the saints, and everyone seeks to enter there.

Soldiers on duty, who are supposed to take charge of the wounded and maintain order, are infected with the frenzy of the crowd and tear off their uniforms and join in the bloodshed.

The madness seizes the children, even very young ones. Beside a fountain, a mother, drunk with pride, hugs a child who has just mutilated himself. Another woman comes running, shouting, "He has gouged out an eye. In a few minutes he will put out the other." The parents watch it with delight.[2]

Similar accounts of frenzied violence in groups have been recorded throughout history.

Another interesting example of abnormal behavior in groups has been termed *hysterical contagion* (Kerckhoff & Back, 1968). In Chapter 10 it was noted that a hysterical conversion symptom refers to a loss of a bodily function in the absence of any organic damage that could account for this loss. Thus in hysterical blindness the individual behaves as if he were blind and reports being unable to see even though he does not suffer from any demonstrable

[2] From *Crowds and Power* by Elias Canetti. Copyright © 1960 by Claassen Verlag Hamburg. English translation copyright © 1962 by Victor Gollancz Ltd. Reprinted by permission of The Viking Press and Victor Gollancz.

organic problem. Hysterical contagion refers to the spread of hysterical conversion symptoms from one individual to another as if the conversion symptom were caused by a communicable infection.

A fascinating example of hysterical contagion is the "June bug" epidemic that broke out in June 1962 in a small southern city (Kerckhoff & Back, 1968). This epidemic lasted several days and affected 9 per cent of the women working in a textile mill. These women, who believed they suffered an infection from bites by insects contained in a shipment of cloth from England, experienced symptoms such as nausea, pain, fainting, and fits. An extensive medical investigation, however, revealed that there never was a June bug. Instead of suffering from a physical disease, the women were apparently suffering hysterical reactions to stress in their jobs.

Explanations of Abnormal Behavior in Groups

At least three distinguishable, though overlapping, views have been offered as explanations of psychopathological behavior in groups. These views may be termed instinct theory, convergence theory, and conformity theory.

Instinct Theory

Based on the view that the normal personality is a product of instinctual forces, moral faculties, and intelligence, many early theorists maintained that psychopathological behavior in groups results from the direct expression of primitive instincts (Allport, 1924; Durkheim, 1933; Freud, 1921; Hobbes, 1651; Le Bon, 1885; Machiavelli, c. 1512; Martin, 1920; McDougall, 1920; Ross, 1908; Trotter, 1919). Le Bon (1885) posited the following three overlapping forces as responsible for the release of primitive instincts in groups:

1. *A sense of intoxicating power* is imparted to individuals in a crowd so that they are willing to act in unusual ways without fear. Hence, an individual who fears retaliation for violence when alone is less afraid of retaliation when in a group.
2. *A sense of social contagion* is imparted to individuals in a crowd; that is, the individual, in a heightened state of emotionality, identifies with the group's expression of primitive instincts and loses his own individuality. Tarde (1903) referred to this phenomenon as a heightened tendency for imitation, McDougall (1920) called it *primitive sympathy,* and Allport (1924) called it *social facilitation.*
3. Persons become more *suggestible* in crowds or groups. Trotter (1919) posited the existence of a "herd instinct" in part to account for this heightened suggestibility.

Instinct theory is associated with the notion that the individual "loses himself in the crowd"—that is, the normal self-control mechanisms somehow cease to be effective, thereby permitting the release of instinctual forces. Zimbardo recently emphasized the importance of the notion of a loss of self-control, even though he did not expound a theory of instincts. He termed the loss of self-control *deindividuation,* defined as "a complex, hypothesized process in which a series of antecedent social conditions lead to changes in perception of self and others, and thereby to a lowered threshold of normally restrained behavior. Under appropriate conditions, what results is the 'release' of behavior in violation of established norms of appropriateness" (1969, p. 251). Zimbardo posited three antecedent conditions that lead to deindividuation. Each of these conditions can be present in group situations.

1. *Anonymity.* A number of theorists have identified fear of retaliation as a major force preventing the expression of aggression. Anonymity facilitates a breakdown in this control mechanism because persons who cannot be identified need not fear retaliation. One possible reason, then, why crowds may sometimes turn violent is that the individuals within the crowd do not fear retaliation for their own violent behavior because they suspect that they cannot be identified as having committed violent acts.
2. *Reduction in the sense of personal responsibility.* Another psychological control mechanism is guilt. The more people who engage in any particular act, the less likely is any one individual to feel personally responsible for the act and, hence, the less likely is the act to be inhibited by guilt. Thus people in crowds may engage in otherwise socially unacceptable behavior because they feel little personal responsibility for their behavior. Another example of a reduction of personal responsibility in group situations is the legal electrocution in which three men simultaneously throw different switches—only one of which is operational—in order to prevent awareness of who actually took the condemned man's life.
3. *Heightened emotionality.* Heightened emotionality fosters deindividuation in two ways: It leads to an altered time perspective in which the individual lives for the moment, and it results in a diminished capacity for realistic perception for self-awareness.

As noted, all three of these antecedent conditions can exist in groups. Thus when a group situation facilitates anonymity, diffusion of personal responsibility, and heightened emotionality, Zimbardo's theory suggests that deindividuation tends to occur and that individuals are likely to engage in socially disapproved behaviors. In support of this theory several studies suggest that deindividuation facilitates verbal expression of hostility (e.g., Cannavale, Scarr, & Pepitone, 1970; Festinger, Pepitone, & Newcomb, 1952; Singer, Brush, & Lublin, 1965).

Convergence Theory

Convergence theory is based on the possibility that some gatherings selectively attract particular types of individuals (Milgram & Toch, 1969; Turner, 1964). Some rock and roll concerts, for example, may attract people who, for one reason or another, enjoy and expect to engage in public displays of nudity or who tend to engage in violent behavior. As Milgram and Toch (1969) suggested, convergence theory need not be interpreted as an explanation of unusual behavior in all groups—it might be useful in explaining unusual behavior in only some groups or in only some individuals within a group.

Conformity Theory

In social situations most people tend to conform to established modes of expected behavior called norms (e.g., Asch, 1951, 1956; Sherif, 1935). Most people, for example, are not usually violent, in part because nonviolence is a norm in our society; similarly, Americans who believe in a two-party political system and Russians who believe in a one-party political system are people whose beliefs represent the established norms of their respective societies. *Conformity* may be defined as a change in behavior or beliefs in the direction of a group norm. Conformity theory suggests that in some gatherings new norms may emerge that conflict with, or at least are different from, the established norms of the society at large. Thus, although nonviolent behavior is the norm for Iranian society in general, at a Shiite Festival a new norm of violence may emerge. Participants in a Shiite Festival who engage in violence may be conforming to the new, emergent norm of the subgroup in which they are participating. Under conformity theory, then, unusual crowd behavior is a direct consequence of the emergence in the crowd of new norms regarding acceptable behavior and of conformity to these norms by persons who are uncertain how to behave in the crowd.

PREJUDICE

Sexism, racism, and other forms of stereotyping have inflicted on certain groups considerable degrees of human suffering.

Stereotypes and Prejudices

When someone categorizes a person as belonging to a group, and when his expectations about what that particular person is like are based on his ideas about what members of that group in general are like, he is using a stereotype. A *stereotype* has been defined as "an exaggerated belief associated with a category" (Allport, 1954, p. 187) and as "an overgeneralization—the attribution of identical characteristics to any person in a group, regardless of the actual variation among members of that group" (Aronson, 1972, p. 173). A person who holds stereotypes about different groups is likely to prejudge the members of those groups; that is, he draws conclusions about the individual group members even though he may not have had any personal contact with them. Although it is possible to have positive prejudices (e.g., *Jews are intelligent*), psychologists have focused on stereotypes and prejudices in which a negative opinion about others is drawn.

It is obvious on the basis of everyday experience that people in our society have stereotyped beliefs about many ethnic groups. An important line of experimental research on this phenomenon was begun in 1933 by Katz and Braly. These investigators prepared a list of 84 adjectives and asked a large group of Princeton students to indicate which traits they considered most characteristic of each of the following ten groups: Germans, Italians, Negroes, Irish, English, Jews, Americans, Chinese, Japanese, and Turks. They found a very high degree of agreement among their subjects in the traits they used to describe each of the groups, suggesting that the students had responded on the basis of culturally shared stereotypes rather than on the basis of personal experience with members of the various groups. About 35 years later, Karlins, Coffman, and Walters (1969) repeated the Katz and Braly study, again by asking a large group of Princeton students to indicate which adjectives characterized the ten ethnic groups. The comparisons between the results of the 1933 study and the 1969 study were very interesting. Whereas the traits assigned to a number of the groups were considerably more favorable in the later study, the uniformity of the stereotypes increased for almost all groups from 1933 to 1969. That is, in the more recent study there was even higher agreement among the subjects as to what traits to attribute to the various ethnic groups, even though the stereotypes in this study were more positive than were the stereotypes in the 1933 study. It is unclear how much of this increased favorability is attributable to a general change in stereotypes over time, how much is attributable to the students' feeling that it is "socially undesirable" to say negative things about ethnic groups, and how much is attributable to the changed composition of the Princeton student body. Nevertheless, the fact remains that students' impressions of the various groups were very standard, suggesting general stereotypes elicited by the ethnic group names.

Ethnic groups are not the only groups in our society that are reacted to in terms of stereotypes. For example, there exists considerable evidence that sex-role stereotypes are still very prevalent despite recent attempts to change or eliminate them. Broverman, Vogel, Broverman, Clarkson, and Rosenkrantz, after conducting a series of experiments on this topic, concluded that "despite the apparent fluidity of sex-role definition in contemporary society as contrasted with the previous decades, our own findings to date confirm the existence of pervasive and persistent sex-role stereotypes" (1972, p. 64). They found that a great many traits are thought to characterize one sex more than the other. For example, males are thought to be more aggressive, independent, objective, and dominant than females; females are thought to be more passive, talkative, tactful, and gentle than males. These investigators also found differences in the social desirability of the characteristics designated as masculine and feminine—more often than not, those characteristics considered "masculine" are also considered to be more socially desirable.

Expectancies and Perception

Stereotyping involves the categorization or labeling of another individual. Although it is natural and necessary for people to use categories in thinking about others, a question arises concerning the extent to which the categorization of others interferes with the accuracy of perceptions. It has been maintained, for example, that stereotyping creates expectations and that these expectations sometimes cause people to perceive what they expect to perceive. For example, Hastorf and Cantril (1954) studied the reaction of students to a football game between Dartmouth and Princeton. The game was rough, both sides were angry, and there was disagreement as to what had happened during the game. A week after the game, the researchers administered a questionnaire to undergraduates at both institutions. Other groups of students at both schools were shown a movie of the game and were asked to check any infractions of the rules they saw. There were differences between Dartmouth and

Princeton students on both measures. On the questionnaire, more than two thirds of the Princeton students and about one fourth of the Dartmouth students rated the game as "rough and dirty." Eighty-six per cent of the Princeton students, but only 36 per cent of the Dartmouth students, thought that Dartmouth had started the rough play. When viewing the film, Princeton students reported that the Dartmouth team made more than twice as many infractions as the Princeton team (9.8 vs. 4.3), whereas Dartmouth students reported seeing equal numbers of infractions by both teams (4.4 vs. 4.2). Thus the students saw (and honestly believed they saw) what they wanted to see.

In addition to affecting perceptions of social events, expectancies can also affect perceptions of other people. A number of studies have found support for the notion that the first information one receives about another person creates expectancies that influence one's perceptions of subsequent information (e.g., Anderson, 1965; Asch, 1946; Luchins, 1957). For example, Asch (1946) presented college student subjects with both positive and negative information about a stranger. If expectancies bias one's overall assessment, then the subjects who receive the positive information first and then the negative information would tend to form a more positive impression of the person than would those who receive the negative and then the positive information. However, if expectancies do not bias interpersonal impressions, then the subjects' impressions should not be affected by the order in which the positive and negative information is presented. Asch found that the information presented first was more important in determining the subjects' impressions; this *primacy effect* supports the hypothesis that expectancies influence impressions of other people.

Early impressions of another person can influence behavior toward the person. Kelley (1950) investigated this issue in the context of a college classroom. Students in several sections of a psychology course were informed that their regular instructor was out of town and that a guest lecturer would conduct the day's class. Before meeting him, the students were given written information that described such factors as the instructor's educational background and teaching experience. Additionally, some of the students were told that "people who know him consider him to be a rather cold person, industrious, critical, practical, and determined," whereas others were told that "people who know him consider him to be a very warm person, industrious, critical, practical, and determined." Thus all students had identical background information about the instructor, except that some expected him to be "rather cold" and others expected him to be "very warm." They then heard the same lecture by the same person.

The study found that the two groups of students responded differently to the instructor in two important ways. First, those students who expected the instructor to be "warm" consistently rated him more favorably than those students who expected him to be "cold." The students who expected him to be warm rated him as more considerate of others, more informal, more sociable, more popular, better natured, more humorous, and more humane. Second, the frequency with which the students took part in the discussion led by the instructor was affected by their expectations of the type of person he would be.

Fifty-six per cent of the students who expected him to be a warm person entered the discussion, whereas only 32 per cent of the students who expected him to be a cold person did so.

Even psychologists and psychiatrists, who have received extensive training in analyzing behavior in an objective manner, are susceptible to biased opinions resulting from expectations created by labels. Temerlin (1968), for example, tape recorded an interview with a professional actor who was trained to portray a mentally healthy man and then played the tape recording to groups of psychiatrists, clinical psychologists, and graduate students in clinical psychology. Shortly before hearing the tape, some of the subjects were told that a prestigious person (a well-known psychologist or board-certified psychiatrist) had said that the patient was a very interesting man because he looked neurotic but actually was quite psychotic. The control group of subjects heard the tape-recorded interview without first hearing any suggested diagnosis. Whereas not one of the subjects in the control group thought the man interviewed was psychotic, a number of subjects who had heard the opinion of the prestigious psychologist or psychiatrist said that they too thought the man was psychotic. It was also found that different groups responded differently to having another person label the man as psychotic: 60 per cent of the psychiatrists diagnosed the man as psychotic, whereas only 28 per cent of the clinical psychologists and 11 per cent of the graduate students did so. Temerlin thus suggested that not only are psychologists and psychiatrists susceptible to label bias, but also that they are more susceptible than are lay persons. Sushinsky and Wener (1975), however, failed to substantiate Temerlin's suggestion that professionals are *more* susceptible than are lay persons to label bias. In this investigation, both lay and professional subjects were found to be influenced in their judgments of mental health by prestigious suggestions.

Expectations Based on Physical Attractiveness

One stereotype that has been studied increasingly in the last few years is the physical attractiveness stereotype. It has been found repeatedly that "what is beautiful is good" (Dion, Berscheid, & Walster, 1972)—that is, physically attractive people are rated as likely to possess more positive personality traits and have more positive life experiences than are people who are unattractive. Physically attractive people have been rated as being more sensitive, kind, interesting, strong, poised, modest, sociable, outgoing, and sexually warm and responsive than physically unattractive people (Berscheid & Walster, 1974). It also has been found that the very same act can be evaluated differently, depending on the physical attractiveness of the person performing it. Dion (1972) described an incident to adults in which a seven year-old child committed a transgression (e.g., throwing rocks at a dog). Along with the description of the transgression, the subjects were given some background information about the child, including a picture. If the picture showed an unattractive child, the subjects attributed more chronic negative behavioral dispositions to the child and thought there was a greater probability of the transgression being committed again in the future than if the picture showed an attractive child. Landy and Sigall (1974) showed that the impact of physical attractiveness is not restricted to ratings of children's behavior. Subjects were asked to evaluate an essay that was supposedly written by a college student for a freshman English class. If the picture of the author of the essay showed a physically attractive person, the essay was rated as being of higher quality than if the picture showed a physically unattractive person. The physical attractiveness stereotype appears to be very common, at least among college students; many people, however, are unaware that physical attractiveness affects their interpersonal judgments of others.

Unfortunately, there exists little research relating the physical attractiveness stereotype to interpersonal judgments of people suffering from neurotic or psychotic reactions. It is not uncommon for such people to dress in sloppy ways and to take little interest in their physical appearance. Because many troubled people are less attractive than they would be if they took a greater interest in their appearance, it seems possible that they are susceptible to biases resulting from the physical attractiveness stereotype and hence that negative traits are attributed to them partially on the basis of appearance.

Sex-Role Stereotypes

There is abundant evidence that many people believe that men and women differ in ways other than anatomy and that those attributes which are stereotypically considered masculine are more often perceived as socially desirable. Of particular interest is the possibility of a double standard in assessments of the mental health of males and females. Broverman, Broverman, Clarkson, Rosenkrantz, and Vogel (1970) sent a scale consisting of 122 items, each describing two opposite poles of a personality dimension (e.g., active-passive), to three groups of mental health professionals. One group was instructed to "think of normal, adult men and then indicate on each item the pole to which a mature, healthy, socially competent adult man would be closer." A second group was given similar instructions except that they were asked to describe a "mature, healthy, socially competent adult woman." A third group was asked to describe a "healthy, mature, socially competent adult person." The sex of the person to be described by this third group was not specified.

The results indicated that the professionals held a double standard of mental health for men and for women; that is, the traits they assigned to a mentally healthy male were different from the traits they assigned to a mentally healthy female, and these differences paralleled the sex-role stereotypes of our society. The investigators summarized their results:

> clinicians are more likely to suggest that healthy women differ from healthy men by being more submissive, less independent, less adventurous, more easily influenced, less aggressive, less competitive, more excitable in minor crises, having their feelings more easily hurt, being more emotional, more conceited about their appearance, less objective, and disliking math and science. This constellation seems a most unusual way of describing any mature, healthy individual [1970, pp. 4–5].

While the clinicians' ideas of a mentally healthy male differed from their ideas of a mentally healthy female, there were no differences between their descriptions of a mentally healthy adult, sex unspecified, and their descriptions of a mentally healthy male. There were, however, differences between their descriptions of a mentally healthy adult, sex unspecified, and their descriptions of a mentally healthy female. Thus the general standard of mental health seems to be a masculine standard. When a man has what are considered to be stereotypically masculine qualities, he is considered mentally healthy. When a woman has these same qualities, she is not considered mentally healthy—even though these are qualities that meet clinicians' general standards of mental health. As the authors note, this double standard for men and women may stem from the clinicians' acceptance of an "adjustment" notion of mental health, meaning that health consists of good adjustment to one's environment. In this view a well-adjusted female would be one who fulfills society's expectations of what a female is supposed to be:

> In our society, men and women are systematically trained, practically from birth on, to fulfill different social roles. An adjustment notion of health, plus the existence of different norms of male and female behavior in our society, automatically lead to a double standard of health. Thus, for a woman to be healthy, from an adjustment viewpoint, she must adjust to and accept the behavioral norms for her sex, even though these behaviors are generally less socially desirable and considered to be less healthy for the generalized competent, mature adult [Broverman et al., 1970, p. 6].

Mental health practitioners are human, like the rest of us; hence it should not be too surprising that they are subject to the same biases that affect the judgments of other "normal" people. Still, it should be noted that clinicians are in unusually powerful positions to influence other people's behavior. Their sex-role stereotypes and their sex-specific notions of mental health can play important roles in the goals they set for their clients and in the way therapy proceeds.

Therapy, of course, is experienced by a relatively small percentage of people in our society. Thus it is important to consider other consequences of sex-role stereotypes that are likely to have more general effects. Many of the personal characteristics that are stereotypically considered both masculine and socially desirable seem to reflect competency. The masculine "competency" attributes include being independent, objective, active, competitive, logical, skilled in business, worldly, adventurous, able to make decisions easily, self-confident, always acting as a leader, and ambitious (Broverman et al., 1972). These traits are thought to characterize men; a relative absence of these traits characterizes the stereotypic perception of women. If people generally hold these stereotypes, then we should anticipate that expectations for, and evaluations of, the accomplishments of women will be lower than those for men. A variety of studies, some of which are discussed here, have shown that this is indeed the case.

Prejudices and stereotypes are held not only by people outside of the stereotyped group but also by members of the group itself. Thus there are blacks who are prejudiced against blacks, Jews who are prejudiced against Jews, and women who are prejudiced against women. In a study that addressed this issue, Goldberg (1968) tested the proposition that women would evaluate the accomplishments of other women as being inferior to the accomplishments of men. This investigator prepared summaries of articles from professional journals in each of six fields. Female undergraduates were asked to read each article; to evaluate it for value, persuasiveness, and profundity; and to rate the author for writing style, professional competence, professional status, and ability to sway the reader. All the subjects read the same six articles; the only difference in the information provided to the subjects was the names of the authors (e.g., John T. McKay versus Joan T. McKay). Each subject read three articles by "men" and three articles by "women."

Goldberg found that his female subjects were biased against the female authors. The subjects consistently found an article more valuable and its author more competent when the author was a man. Interestingly, the subjects preferred the article supposedly written by the male in all six professional fields, including the fields of dietetics and elementary school teaching, fields that are traditionally associated with women. These results demonstrated that women tend to view other women in terms of our society's stereotype for females.

Is the work of women always underrated relative to the work of men? Pheterson, Kiesler, and Goldberg (1971) designed an experiment to assess when this negative evaluation does and does not occur. In this study, college women were shown slides of eight unfamiliar modern art paintings and were asked to evaluate each one. When a painting was described as having been entered in an art contest, the female subjects judged the painting as more competent, and the artist as having a better artistic future, if they thought the painting was done by a man than if they thought it was done by a woman. These results replicate the Goldberg (1968) finding. When, however, the painting was described as having already won a prize in an art contest, the subjects' ratings of the painting and the painter were unaffected by the painter's sex. These results suggest that the work of a woman is devalued by other women until it has received some special distinction. Receiving that distinction, however, is likely to be especially difficult for women because people are biased against their work from the beginning.

Even when women achieve a position in what has previously been considered a masculine domain of competence, their stereotype-based problems may not be over. Touhey (1974) provided subjects with information describing one of five professions (architect, college professor, lawyer, physician, and scientist) and asked them to rate the prestige and desirability of the profession they read about. At the end of the occupational descriptions given to some subjects was the prediction that the occupation would have a sharply increasing proportion of women practitioners during the next 30 years. For example, subjects receiving information about physicians were told that approximately 7 per cent of the physicians in the United States now are women, that current patterns of recruitment indicate that the percentage of women physicians will increase to 35 per cent during the next 15 years, and that in 25 to 30 years the majority of physicians will be women. Both male and female subjects who received the information predicting that the proportion of women in a profession would increase rated that profession as less prestigious and less desirable than subjects not receiving this information. These findings suggest that negative stereotypes about women are so powerful that the expectation of large numbers of them in high-status occupations can affect how prestigious and desirable these occupations are rated.

The Persistence of Stereotypes

Like some of the irrational beliefs of neurotics (see Chapter 10), stereotypes are self-perpetuating and hence resistant to change. This persistence of stereotypic behavior can be explained in at least three ways. One explanation is that stereotypes create self-fulfilling prophecies. A second explanation is that prejudiced people tend to avoid contact with members of the group against whom they are prejudiced; hence, they have a restricted opportunity to discover information that is inconsistent with their prejudices. A third explanation is that people tend to interpret new, disconfirming information in a manner consistent with their prejudices.

When a belief or attitude or prediction leads one to behave in a way that actually causes the belief, attitude, or prediction to come true, a self-fulfilling prophecy is said to have occurred. If people's stereotypes lead them to expect that members of a particular group will behave in certain ways, their own behavior can influence the stereotyped group's behavior in ways that confirm the stereotype. For example, the prejudice that blacks are superior athletes but are not especially intelligent can (1) encourage blacks to develop their athletic abilities but not their intellectual abilities and (2) discourage discrimination against blacks in sports while encouraging discrimination against blacks in professions thought to require a high degree of intelligence. This could have the effect of many more successful black athletes than black intellectuals. When this happens, people see their stereotypes confirmed and hence continue to hold the stereotypes, perhaps more firmly than before. It should be noted that people are usually unaware that by their expectations they are in part causing confirmation of their prejudices.

There are many ways in which self-fulfilling prophecies can affect the maintenance of sex-role stereotypes. Socializing agents encourage girls and boys to conform to these stereotypes. Teachers in elementary schools treat boys and girls differently in ways that are consistent with stereotypes (Sears & Feldman, 1966). Children's books present boys and girls and men and women almost exclusively in highly stereotyped ways, suggesting few options other than the adventurous, competent male and the retiring, domestic female (Weitzman, Eifler, Hokada, & Ross, 1972). There is also evidence that parents respond differently to male and female infants (Moss, 1967). In one relevant study, Goldberg and Lewis (1969) observed mothers interacting with their infants when the children were six months and 13 months of age. If mothers stereotypically assume that girls are weaker and more dependent than boys, they might be expected to hold girls and to talk to them more than boys. Goldberg and Lewis in fact found this to be the case—the mothers of six-month-old daughters touched their infants and talked to them more often than did the mothers of sons. Of particular interest in this investigation, however, was the manner in which these early differences in parental behavior might have led to later differences

Individual prejudices can combine with group frenzy to produce mass violence. This is a scene after a recent busing disturbance in Charlestown, Massachusetts. (Photo by Alex Webb; Magnum Photos, Inc.)

in the children's behavior toward the parents. In this regard, it was found that boys and girls showed striking differences in their behavior toward their mothers when they were observed at 13 months, and that these differences suggested that the parent's expectancies regarding sex differences may have created self-fulfilling prophecies. Specifically, at 13 months of age, girls behaved in a more dependent fashion in that they were more reluctant to leave their mothers, touched their mothers more, and vocalized more to their mothers, as compared to boys. These findings support the possibility that children's behavior becomes consistent with the stereotypes their parents hold and that parents then continue to hold the stereotypes.

Another possible explanation for the persistence of stereotypes is that people are likely to avoid contact with persons against whom they are prejudiced. Newcomb (1947) elaborated on this notion by discussing cases in which someone with an initially hostile attitude toward another person restricts his communications and contact with that person; this may encourage the preservation of the hostile attitude because the person is prevented from learning new information that could change the attitude. It is not unusual for "perfectly normal" people to place themselves in this type of vicious cycle in which they continue to maintain their prior beliefs because they do not acquire new information, and in which they do not acquire new information because they are biased by their prior beliefs. Although this cycle may explain some instances of persistent stereotypes, it is nevertheless obvious that people sometimes encounter information that is inconsistent with their prejudices. When this occurs, a person might modify his stereotype or, as often occurs, might deny, misperceive, or rationalize the discrepant information in a manner that maintains the stereotype.

In a study that investigated reactions to unexpected information, Haire and Grunes (1950) provided college students with lists of characteristics of a factory worker and asked them to relate their impressions in a paragraph. The characteristics given to one group of students were: works in a factory, reads a newspaper, goes to movies, average height, cracks jokes, strong, and active. The impressions of students given this list were generally quite similar. Typically, they described the man as a likeable, uncomplicated, "typical American Joe" who was interested in sports and who was not very intelligent. The list given to a second group of students was the same as that given to the first group, except that the word *intelligent* was included as one of the man's characteristics. Intelligence was not part of the students' stereotype of factory workers, and Haire and Grunes were interested to see how the students' impressions of this man would be affected by the inclusion of *intelligent* in the list. The subjects reacted to the unexpected trait in a number of ways. One common response was to interpret the man's intelligence in such a way that it did not create strong conflicts with the general stereotype of workingmen (e.g., *he lacks initiative to do anything useful with his intelligence*). Another type of response used by a few people was to deny the man's intelligence despite the fact that it was listed (e.g., *intelligence not notable even though it is stated*). Some subjects explicitly stated that there was a conflict between their stereotype and the trait of intelligence without trying to integrate the two (e.g., *the traits seem to be conflicting . . . most factory workers I have heard about aren't too intelligent*). Finally, some subjects did use the information about the man's intelligence to form an impression of him that was different from the usual sterotype of a factory worker. Even here, however, it often seemed that they were permitting their impressions to deviate from the common stereotype as little as possible. This study and others indicate that people are resistant to changing their prejudices even when they receive fairly clear disconfirmations.

Another reason why stereotypes may be resistant to change is that people can interpret many ambiguous situations as evidence for their prejudices. For example, Rosenhan (1973) has observed how difficult it can be for someone who has been labeled schizophrenic to "overcome the tag." Behavior that would appear perfectly normal and not be questioned in most settings can be seen as quite deviant and as consistent with popular theories of schizophrenic reaction if performed by someone previously labeled as schizophrenic. One interesting anecdote reported by Rosenhan took place when a psychiatrist and a group of psychiatric residents observed patients sitting outside the hospital cafeteria entrance half an hour before lunchtime. To Rosenhan, this behavior could easily be explained by the fact that there are very few things to anticipate in a psychiatric hospital setting besides eating. To the psychiatrist, however, the residents waiting near the cafeteria before lunch was a behavior characteristic of the oral-acquisitive nature of the schizophrenic syndrome. Hence what may have been a perfectly normal behavior was interpreted as consistent with the psychiatrist's understanding that the individuals were schizophrenic.

SUMMARY

It is efficient and seemingly necessary, in terms of human information processing capabilities, for people to use categories in their perceptions of objects and persons. As we have seen, however, there are certain consequences of this categorization process that can be problematic. Once we use categories and form expectations about what instances of those categories will be like, we are susceptible to a number of psychological biases. Our expectations may color the way we interpret new information, and they may influence the type of new information we receive. When we perceive this new information as confirming our expectations, we may hold these expectations more firmly than ever before. It is easy to fall into the cycle of believing a stereotype because it is confirmed and having it confirmed because evidence is interpreted in light of the stereotype. It is because of this cycle that prejudices and stereotypes persist in the absence of few rational reasons to maintain them.

HIGH AND LOW SELF-ESTEEM

Self-esteem refers to an individual's evaluation of his own worth as a person. People who are insecure are generally said to have low self-esteem. In general, low self-esteem is associated with feelings of depression and shame.

Conceptions of Self-esteem

James (1892) was one of the earliest psychologists to discuss self-esteem. He proposed that a person's judgment of his worth is a function of his accomplishments relative to what he claims to do well. Thus a person who takes pride in his abilities in music but not in mathematics would, according to James, suffer a much larger loss of self-esteem if he performed poorly at a concert than if he performed poorly on a mathematics examination. If the person did not pride himself at all in mathematics, a poor performance on an examination might not affect his self-esteem at all. James expressed this position by proposing that self-esteem is a ratio of one's accomplishments to one's pretensions.

More recently, a number of psychologists investigated self-esteem as a process of self-evaluation (see Brissett, 1972; Crowne & Stephens, 1961). Expressing a position similar to that held by James, Rosenberg (1965, 1967) suggested that the process of evaluating one's worth can be analyzed as involving three steps. First, the individual selects the dimensions along which he judges himself (e.g., judgments of athletic or scholastic ability). Second, the individual evaluates himself along these dimensions (e.g., *I am a lousy athlete and a poor student*). Third, the individual interprets this evaluation in terms of his self-worth (e.g., *So what if I'm a lousy athlete and a poor student—I'm still a worthwhile human being*).

One important question concerns the extent to which one's evaluation of one's worth (global self-esteem) is affected by one's evaluation of specific abilities. The available literature suggests that a considerable degree of independence exists among different types of self-evaluation. Rosenberg (1967), for example, found that although the college students he surveyed believed that good

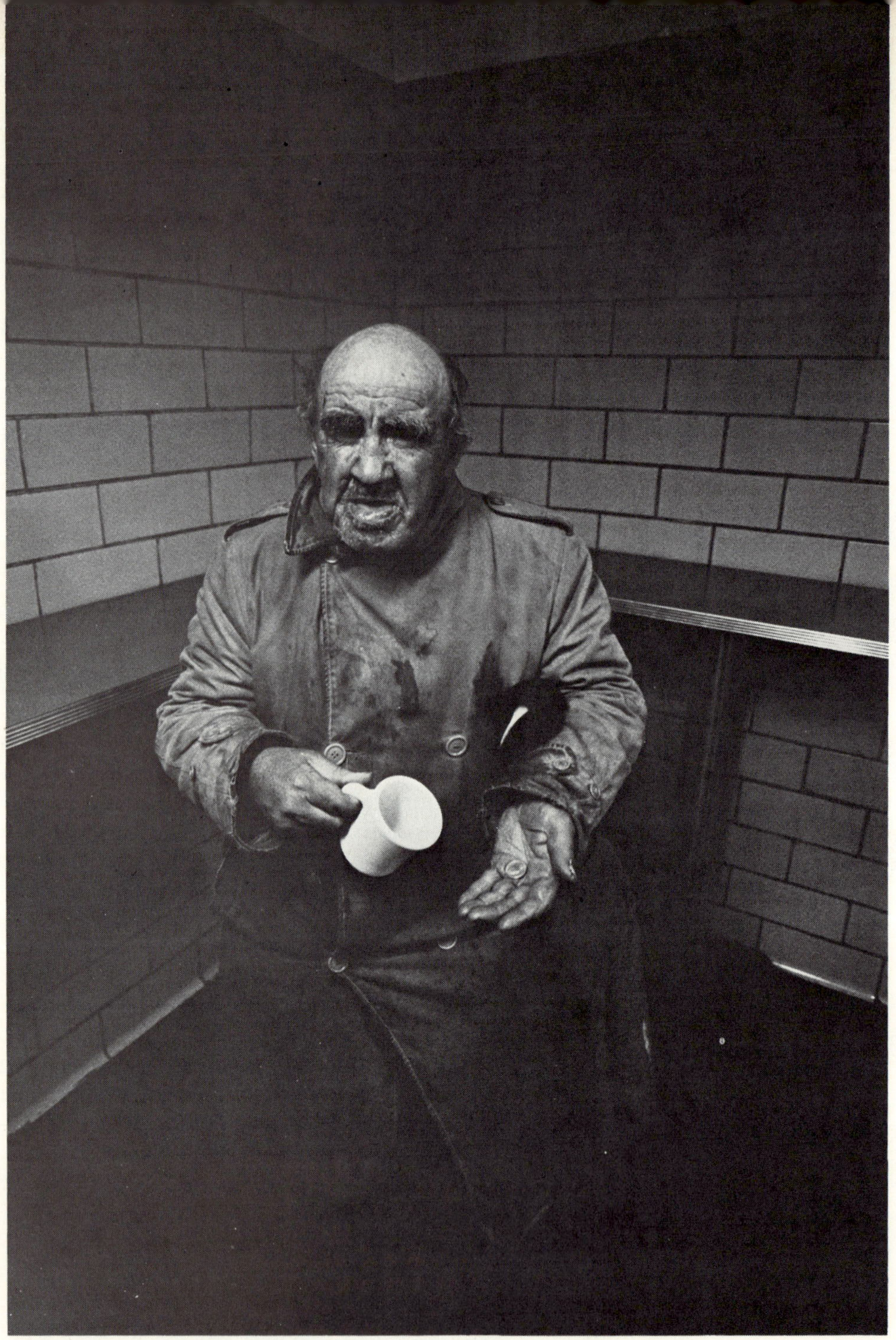

Indicating a low self-esteem, this patron of a Salvation Army Free Kitchen shows all the money he has when asked about his worth as a person. (Photo by Leonard Freed; Magnum Photos, Inc.)

grades are generally associated with being a good student, they did not believe that grades are associated with being logical, reasonable, imaginative, original, or having sound judgment. Borislow (1962) asked underachievers and achievers (1) to rate themselves as students and (2) to respond to questions comprising a scale of self-esteem. He found that underachievers and achievers did not differ in global self-esteem and that this was true for students who valued scholastic achievement as well as for those who did not. When asked to evaluate themselves *as students,* however, achievers reported higher self-esteem than did underachievers, and this was true both for students who valued scholastic achievement and for those who did not. These data suggest that a person's overall evaluation of his worth is relatively stable and is not easily affected by scholastic performance. Wyer (1965), however, found that male college freshmen who had higher grades tended to have higher global self-esteem. For female college freshmen, Wyer did not find any statistically reliable relations between grades and global self-evaluations. Wyer's findings are thus in apparent disagreement with those reported by Borislow insofar as they suggest that in males global self-esteem is associated with scholastic performance.

Thus, the concept of self-esteem as a process of self-evaluation is complicated because a person's self-evaluations vary considerably, depending on what the person is asked to evaluate (see Diggory, 1966; Diggory & Magaziner, 1959). If asked to evaluate himself on a specific skill, the person generally provides a judgment as to how successful he is at tasks requiring that skill. Such judgments can be altered experimentally by providing the subject with feedback indicating success or failure (e.g., Diggory & Magaziner, 1959). However, global self-esteem, or a person's overall evaluation of himself, is far more stable and resistant to change.

Whereas some psychologists have conceived of self-esteem as a process of self-evaluation, others have conceived of self-esteem as an inner sense of one's self-worth. Sullivan (1953), for example, discussed self-esteem in terms of a need for interpersonal security. In this view, self-worth is enhanced by sensing one's own power to act to avoid interpersonal insecurity. This conception of self-esteem is related to White's (1959) notion of competence motivation in which self-worth is enhanced by a sense of mastery of the environment, by having executive control over one's own behavior, and by being effective in causing desired effects.

Rogers (1950, 1951; Rogers & Dymond, 1954) discussed self-esteem in terms of the individual's need to have positive regard for the self. As noted in Chapter 9, Rogers distinguished between the real and ideal selves by asking people to describe themselves twice—once as they believed they actually are and again as they would like to be. This distinction between a real and an ideal self is similar to James's distinction between one's accomplishments (real self) and one's pretensions (ideal self). James, however, focused on the ratio of the real to the ideal self as the determinant of self-esteem, whereas Rogers focused on the discrepancy between the real and ideal selves. For Rogers, the greater the discrepancy between the real and ideal selves, the lower is the self-esteem, and the greater is the degree of maladjustment.

Self-esteem and Maladjustment

Many clinical observers have commented on the relation between low self-esteem and psychopathology. Freud, for example, wrote "whoever holds and expresses to others . . . [a low] opinion of himself . . . is ill, whether he speaks the truth or is more or less unfair to himself" (1959 p. 156). More recently, Ellis (1962) suggested that a negative view of one's worth is irrational. But of all recent theorists, none placed as great an emphasis on the importance of self-esteem for psychological adjustment as Carl Rogers.

An impressive number of studies have found a positive correlation between self-esteem and psychological adjustment, with a high proportion of persons with low self-esteem showing signs of psychological maladjustment (see Byrne, 1974; Feder, 1968). Although many of these studies operationally defined self-esteem in terms of a discrepancy between real and ideal selves, a variety of indexes have been employed to measure adjustment. The most frequently employed measures of adjustment have been structured and unstructured personality inventories and interviews (Bills, 1954; Hanlon, Hofstaetter, & O'Conner, 1954; Kaplan & Pokorny, 1969; Murstein, 1961; Smith, 1958; Smith & Teevan, 1971; Turner & Vanderlippe, 1958). In at least one study, adjustment as measured by the California Psychological Inventory was found to be correlated with self-esteem (Gergen & Morse, 1967). Self-esteem has also been reported to be correlated with professionally diagnosed psychopathology (Chase, 1957; Davids & Lawton, 1961; Piers, 1972; Youngleson, 1973).

Although self-esteem appears to be related to psychological adjustment, it may not be the case that those persons having high self-esteem are well-adjusted, whereas those having very low self-esteem are maladjusted. Rather, a number of studies have found evidence consistent with the intriguing hypothesis of a curvilinear relation between self-ideal discrepancy and psychological adjustment (Block & Thomas, 1955; Chodorkoff, 1954, Cole, Oetting, & Miskimins, 1969; Friedman, 1955; Hillson & Worchel, 1957; Kamano,

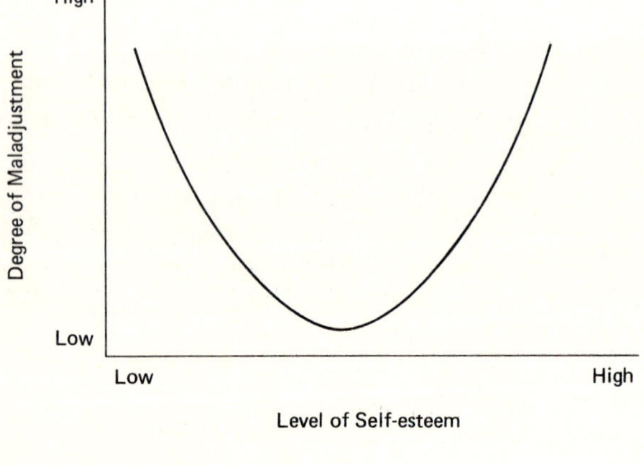

Figure 19-1
Hypothesized curvilinear relationship between self-esteem and maladjustment.

1961). The hypothesis of a curvilinear relation, as shown in Figure 19-1, is that people with a small self-ideal discrepancy (unusually high self-esteem) and people with a large self-ideal discrepancy (unusually low self-esteem) are psychologically maladjusted.

Hewitt and Goldman (1974) recently investigated the proposition that two groups of people obtain high self-esteem scores; one group, said to have *true high self-esteem,* is characterized by an honest acceptance of themselves as they really are, whereas the other group, said to have *socially desirable high self-esteem,* is characterized by describing themselves as possessing socially desirable characteristics in order to fulfill a need for social approval. Socially desirable, high self-esteem may be viewed as a defensive cover-up of one's true feelings—these people may really have a low opinion of themselves but report a highly favorable opinion in order to keep themselves from facing the disturbing nature of their true feelings. Thus, both people with socially desirable high self-esteem and those with low self-esteem should react defensively to evaluations of themselves by others, whereas people with an inner definition of their worth (true high self-esteem) should not react defensively to evaluations from others. Hewitt and Goldman (1974) tested this hypothesis by comparing the reactions of three groups of subjects: (1) college students with low self-esteem and a low need for social approval (low self-esteem group); (2) college students with high self-esteem and a high need for social approval (socially desirable high self-esteem group); and (3) college students with high self-esteem and a low need for social approval (true high self-esteem group). This study used a self-ideal discrepancy measure of self-esteem and the Marlowe-Crowne Social Desirability Scale to measure need for social approval (Crowne & Marlowe, 1964). All subjects were exposed to positive and negative evaluations made by others. As predicted, socially desirable high-self esteem and low-self-esteem subjects increased their liking for a positive evaluator and decreased their liking for a negative-evaluator, whereas true high-self-esteem subjects did not. Hewitt and Goldman suggested that socially desirable, high-self-esteem persons may in fact be persons with low self-esteem who use repressive defenses to deny undesirable traits in describing themselves.

The considerations reviewed thus far suggest that persons with low self-esteem, and at least some persons with high self-esteem, are less well adjusted than are persons with moderate self-esteem, even though the former groups are maladjusted in different ways. In some situations, therefore, we might expect highs and lows to behave similarly because they are both maladjusted, whereas in other situations we might expect them to behave differently because they use different psychological defenses.

Hendrick and Page (1970) found that college students with high and low self-esteem were more extreme in their evaluations of others than were subjects with moderate self-esteem. Specifically, compared to moderates, highs and lows liked a person who agreed with them and disliked a person who disagreed with them. The investigators suggested that persons with moderate self-esteem might be better able to tolerate conflicting opinions because they are better adjusted. Johnson, Gormly, and Gormly (1973) replicated Hendrick and Page's results insofar as they found that subjects with high self-esteem exhibited the most marked response to a stranger, liking him more when he agreed with them and disliking him more when he disagreed with them.[3]

In conclusion, the hypothesis of a curvilinear relation between self-esteem and psychological adjustment has been supported by several studies. The hypothesis, however, is far from proven, and the exact relation between self-esteem and psychological adjustment remains to be elucidated by future research.

Rejection of Success

Many investigators have reported observations of people who avoid or reject success (e.g., Barker, Dembo, Lewin, & Wright, 1943; Haimowitz & Haimowitz, 1966; Ovesey, 1962). For example, some people develop neuroses when they learn of a forthcoming promotion; in such cases, the neurotic symptoms often have the consequence of preventing the person from being promoted (e.g., a man develops a phobia for flying and hence cannot accept a big promotion that requires extensive travel). Rejection of success is a surprising phenomenon because we normally think of success as something every individual desires. Success, however, elicits anxiety in many people, especially when it is unexpected.

There are several plausible ways in which success can become associated with anxiety and hence be avoided or rejected. For example, in people brought up to think of themselves as unworthy and as unimportant, success can elicit feelings of guilt. Thus a student awarded a fellowship to Harvard might feel that he does not deserve the award as much as do some of his friends. Another possible explanation of success avoidance is that success can heighten a fear of failure. Thus the student awarded a fellowship to Harvard might fear that he cannot succeed at so prestigious a school and hence might prefer to go somewhere else.

Cognitive consistency theory provides another possible explanation of success rejection or avoidance. This theory maintains that people accept information that supports their self-concept (consistency) and reject information that conflicts with their self-concept (inconsistency). Thus success is discrepant information for people with low self-esteem; that is, when successful, these people tell themselves *I generally do things very poorly* and *This time I performed extremely well.* According to consistency theory, people with low self-esteem reject or avoid success because the cognition *I am successful* is inconsistent with their self-concept.

Maracek and Mettee (1972) tested the consistency hypothesis in a study with female college students. The experimental task consisted of two blocks of ten trials during which subjects matched geometric figures on a display board. After the first block of ten trials, all subjects were given positive feedback (success) regarding their performance on the experimental task. From consistency theory, Maracek and Mettee reasoned that low self-esteem subjects who were certain of their low self-esteem and who were made to feel personally

[3] For discussion of the possible curvilinear nature of the relation between self-esteem and susceptibility to social influence, see McGuire (1968), "Personality and Susceptibility to Social Influence."

responsible for the initial success would attempt to avoid future positive feedback by making more errors on the second set of ten experimental trials than they had made on the first set of ten trials. In contrast, high self-esteem subjects were predicted to perform at least as well on the second set of experimental trials as they had performed on the first set. Furthermore, success avoidance was *not* predicted for low self-esteem subjects who were encouraged to think performance on the task was a matter of luck or who were not certain of their low self-esteem. For these low self-esteem subjects success was not hypothesized to be discrepant with self-image (that is, there is no discrepancy between *I have poor abilities* and *I did well on task A, which is a game of chance and simply a matter of luck*). The results supported the predictions made from consistency theory—only in subjects who were certain of their low abilities and who felt responsible for their initial success did positive feedback lead to deteriorated performance on the second set of ten trials.

Jones (1973) has recently reviewed research relevant to the consistency theory of self-esteem. As defined by Jones, the *consistency view* is that persons respond to evaluative information about the self to avoid, reduce, or eliminate inconsistency with the stable self-image. For example, the high self-esteem person does not acknowledge failure and the low self-esteem person rejects success. Jones contrasted the consistency view with what may be called the self-enhancement position. This position assumes that people seek to improve themselves even if it creates inconsistency. As Jones presents it, the basic tenet of the self-enhancement view is that "the individual has a need to enhance his self-evaluation and to increase, maintain, or confirm his feelings of personal satisfaction, worth, and effectiveness" (1973, p. 186). Thus, the self-enhancement hypothesis predicts that both high and low self-esteem subjects should avoid failure and seek success. The results of ten of the 16 studies Jones reviewed supported the self-enhancement theoretical position. At this point, then, we can best conclude that both the cognitive consistency and the self-enhancement hypotheses enjoy some experimental support and provide possible explanations of the differences in behavior among persons with high, low, and moderate self-esteem.

CIGARETTE SMOKING

Smoking is well regarded as a complex chain of behaviors such as purchasing cigarettes, inhaling and exhaling smoke, smelling the smoke, and flicking ashes. Different people exhibit different habits of smoking—for example, some are chain smokers, others smoke primarily in social situations, and still others smoke primarily after dinner or with coffee. Eysenck (1973) and Guilford (1966) have suggested that different people smoke for different reasons and that, in order to be successful, treatment programs will have to take into account differences in the habits of individual smokers. Smoking is an exceptionally persistent habit. It has been estimated that less than 20 per cent of all American smokers ever quit (Bernstein, 1970) and that only about 25 per cent of those who try to quit are successful for as long as six months (Hunt & Matarazzo, 1973).

Physiological Factors

Although there are many reasons why an individual might begin to smoke, a number of theorists have suggested that, once a person has begun, the habit is maintained by physical dependence on the drug nicotine (e.g., Jarvik, 1970). This drug is found in tobacco and is inhaled when a person smokes. The addiction theory of smoking is, however, controversial—there exists evidence for and against it. Perhaps the strongest evidence for an addiction theory is the incredible persistence of smoking habits under conditions in which people want to quit—with the possible exception of certain compulsive and stereotypic behaviors, the only other behaviors known to be so persistent are those related to drug dependency (e.g., alcoholism and drug addiction). Other evidence for an addiction theory suggests that nicotine produces tolerance so that, following its repeated use, greater dosages are required to produce the same effects. However, the defining characteristic of an addiction is the occurrence of withdrawal symptoms when drug use is terminated. The controversy over whether or not cigarette smoking is an addiction has thus focused on whether smoking cessation produces any consistent withdrawal symptoms. Recently, Brecher (1972) maintained that the cessation of smoking consistently produces nervousness, drowsiness, or headaches; cessation also produces a craving for cigarettes sometimes called nicotine hunger. However, except for nicotine hunger, these symptoms are neither especially pronounced nor always present. Moreover, it is unclear whether these symptoms can be properly termed withdrawal symptoms because they can be produced by cessation of any compulsive behavior. Thus, although it is reasonable to conclude that nicotine plays some important role in the maintenance of smoking habits, it has yet to be established that cigarette smoking can be properly regarded as a physical addiction.

Psychological Factors

Smoking is an extremely well-practiced habit. The individual who smokes two packs of cigarettes a day has been estimated to puff smoke between 120,000 and 146,000 times a year (Hunt & Matarazzo, 1970; Jarvik, 1970). On the assumption that cigarette inhalation has primary reinforcing properties, the consistent association of many environmental stimuli with smoking can result in the establishment of many secondary reinforcers—that is, the smell, taste, feel, and look of a cigarette can become reinforcing, thereby strengthening further the complex chain of behaviors in the smoking habit. Moreover, in addition to learning habits of smoking, the heavy smoker is not practicing and hence not learning habits of nonsmoking (Logan, 1973). Thus the smoking habit may be very persistent because (1) it is well practiced, (2) it has been reinforced countless times, and (3) the individual has not practiced and learned habits of nonsmoking.

Some research on the psychological factors in smoking has focused on the personality characteristics that distinguish smokers from nonsmokers (e.g., Eysenck, 1973; Hill, 1970; Hunt & Matarazzo, 1970). It has been suggested, for example, that compared to nonsmokers, smokers tend to exhibit poor mental health, to have stronger oral needs, to be impulsive, and to believe that their lives are guided more by luck and fate. There is, however, little evidence for

Smoking is an exceptionally persistent habit despite strong appeals to reason that the behavior is injurious. (Photo by Alex Webb; Magnum Photos, Inc.)

such speculations (Smith, 1970). By contrast, some evidence exists supporting the notion that smokers tend to be more antisocial and extraverted than nonsmokers (Smith, 1970).

Herman (1974) reported an interesting study suggesting a possible personality difference between light and heavy smokers. This study investigated the hypothesis that light smokers usually smoke in reaction to specific situational cues (e.g., at a party, during an office coffee break), whereas heavy smokers usually smoke when they feel an urge. That is, stimulus control of the smoking habit was hypothesized to be external for light smokers (e.g., visibility of cigarettes) and internal for heavy smokers (e.g., nicotine deprivation). Herman tested this hypothesis in a study that varied both initial level of nicotine deprivation and visibility of cigarettes. In order to vary the initial level of nicotine deprivation, both light and heavy smokers were prevented from smoking for 30 minutes, after which some smoked a cigarette with high nicotine content, others smoked a cigarette with low nicotine content, and still others did not smoke at all. The subjects then listened to music in a room in which cigarettes high in nicotine content were either quite obviously visible or were barely visible. The time subjects took before smoking their first cigarette and the number of cigarettes smoked were measured. As predicted, light smokers were influenced more by whether cigarettes were obviously or barely visible and heavy smokers were influenced more by nicotine deprivation.

Nesbitt's Paradox

Nesbitt (1973) identified the following paradoxical effects of smoking: The physiological effects of smoking are arousing, yet most smokers describe the psychological effects of their habit as relaxing. There exists some evidence that nicotine is physiologically arousing in the sense that it increases heart rate (Jarvik, 1970; Nesbitt, 1973). There also exists evidence that most smokers report their habits to be psychologically relaxing (Ikard, Green, & Horn, 1968). At least three plausible theories can be offered in explanation of this paradox.

1. *Compulsive behavior hypothesis.* Smoking can be regarded as a compulsive behavior. (See Chapter 10.) As occurs in the cessation of other compulsive behaviors, cessation of smoking typically produces anxiety and tension. Thus even though nicotine may be a mild, physiological stimulant, the smoker may know that he will experience much more arousal if he does not smoke; hence he learns to consider smoking relaxing.

2. *Optimal arousal level hypothesis.* People are probably subjectively relaxed when physiological arousal is at some optimal level. When physiological arousal is below this level, the individual is subjectively lethargic; when physiological arousal is above this level, the individual is subjectively alert (see Berlyne, 1960). It is possible that smokers and nonsmokers tend to have different optimal levels of physiological arousal so that the stimulation provided by nicotine actually functions to relax the smoker. This difference in the optimal levels of physiological arousal for subjective feelings of relaxation may be a consequence of the smoking habit itself or, as Eysenck (1973) has suggested, of genetically determined differences in extraversion-introversion.

3. *Attribution hypothesis.* A third explanation of this paradox begins with the premise that smokers have learned to attribute nicotine arousal to cigarettes (Nesbitt, 1973; see Schachter, 1973). It is further assumed that, as a consequence of such attributions, when smokers encounter other arousing stimuli, they tend to attribute some of this arousal to smoking and thus attribute less of it to internal stimuli or to unknown factors. For example, if a smoker became aroused when worrying over an exam, theoretically he would tend to attribute part of this arousal to smoking, and hence he would subjectively believe that he is less worried over the exam than he would be if he were not smoking. In this sense, smoking might be regarded as subjectively relaxing.

Treatment

In recent years behavior therapists have investigated a number of treatments for heavy smoking. These investigators have employed systematic desensitization to reduce anxiety supposedly cueing smoking (e.g., Wagner & Bragg, 1970), systematic desensitization to disrupt associations between anxiety-cueing stimuli and smoking (e.g., Morganstern & Ratcliff, 1969), various self-control procedures (e.g., Nolan, 1968; Roberts, 1969), and a variety of aversion techniques, including threatened loss of money (Elliot & Tighe, 1968), mild electric shock punishment contingent on smoking (e.g., Berecz, 1972; Steffy, Meichenbaum, & Best, 1970), and forced oversmoking (e.g., Lichtenstein, Harris, Birchler, Wahl, & Schmahl, 1973; Resnick, 1968; Schmahl, Lichtenstein, & Harris, 1972). Initially, these procedures typically produce a dramatic reduction in cigarette consumption for most smokers, but within five to 20 weeks most clients return to between 60 and 80 per cent of their pretreatment level of smoking (see Bernstein, 1970; Hunt & Matarazzo, 1973). The only treatment procedures that appear to produce results superior to those just described are the forced oversmoking procedures.

Forced oversmoking treatment involves instructing the client to smoke at a very high rate, such as once every six seconds, until he can no longer tolerate another inhalation. This procedure is repeated when the client reports that he can tolerate smoking again. As the procedure is repeated a number of times, the client eventually refuses to smoke and treatment is discontinued. Booster (retraining) sessions may be planned to strengthen the treatment effect. The rationale for forced oversmoking procedures is that they condition an unpleasant affect to all aspects of the smoking habit so that nonsmoking becomes more pleasurable than smoking.

The initial results from evaluations of oversmoking procedures suggest that these techniques may prove to be valuable aids in smoking cessation programs. For example, both Schmahl et al. (1972) and Lichtenstein et al. (1973) have reported that more than 60 per cent of their clients were abstinent at six month follow-ups. *The procedure, however, should not be attempted on one's own and should be used, if at all, only under professional supervision. This is because many professionals have expressed concern that oversmoking is hazardous to one's physical health, possibly increasing the risk of heart failure.*

SUMMARY

The material presented in this chapter indicates that abnormal behavior is not necessarily unusual—millions of people have low self-esteem, are prejudiced, or smoke. What is unusual, however, is the debilitating presence of abnormal behavior.

An especially interesting form of abnormal behavior is hysterical behavior in groups. Two examples of such behavior were considered. In one example, the Shiite Festival, a half million people cheer as thousands engage in acts of self-mutilation. In the other example, the June bug epidemic, a hysterical disorder spread from one female factory worker to another as if an infectious disease were present. Three general theories have been proposed to account for such behaviors. *Instinct theory* is generally associated with the notion that the individual "loses himself in the crowd"—that is, the normal self-control mechanisms somehow cease to be effective, thereby permitting the release of instinctual forces. A modern version of this theory—one that does not, however, include an elaborate theory of instinctual forces—is Zimbardo's theory of deindividuation. This theory proposes that when group situations facilitate anonymity, diffusion of personal responsibility, and heightened emotionality, individuals within the group are likely to engage in socially disapproved behavior. Another theory of hysterical behavior in groups is called *convergence theory.* This theory proposes that certain gatherings selectively attract people who normally engage in socially disapproved behavior. *Conformity theory* suggests that new norms emerge within a crowd and that, when these norms conflict with the norms of society, individuals within the crowd who engage in socially disapproved behavior are simply conforming to the new norms of the crowd.

Another abnormal behavior considered in this chapter is prejudice. An essential component of human thought is categorization—we categorize and label both objects (e.g., "table") and people (e.g., "woman," "black," "American"). However, when we use categories too rigidly or when we overgeneralize from them—as in the example of categorizing a person as a woman and then assuming that her scholarly and professional work is of low quality—we are using a stereotype and are prejudging the people whom we view stereotypically.

Stereotypes can have powerful influences on the way we expect other people to behave and even on the way we perceive behavior. For example, stereotypes about men and women have led to a double standard of mental health in which the mentally healthy female differs from the mentally healthy male by being more submissive, less competitive, less adventurous, more emotional, and more conceited. Thus even though mental health professionals have been trained to judge people as mentally healthy in accordance with supposedly objective criteria, research indicates that mental health professionals are biased in their view of what constitutes a mentally healthy male and female.

Similar to the irrational beliefs of neurotics, stereotypes are self-perpetuating and extremely resistant to change. Three explanations for the persistence of stereotypes were considered: (1) the *self-fulfilling prophecy* hypothesis (prejudice actually leads to conditions that make the prejudice come true, as in the example of treating female infants as if they were fragile, bringing them up to be dependent, and then referring to consequent dependency behaviors as evidence that females are really dependent by nature); (2) the *minimal contact* hypothesis (people maintain their prejudices because they do not acquire new information about those against whom they are prejudiced, and they do not acquire new information because they are biased and avoid contact with members of the stereotyped group); and (3) the *cognitive consistency* hypothesis (people interpret ambiguous information as evidence for their prejudices).

Many definitions of self-esteem have been proposed; it seems clear that global self-esteem (overall judgment of self-worth) is not related to self-evaluations of specific abilities in any simple manner. In fact, many self-evaluations of specific abilities seem independent of global self-esteem, although they are usually related to prior success in tasks requiring that ability.

An especially intriguing hypothesis is that persons with low self-esteem and at least some persons with high self-esteem are less well adjusted than are persons with moderate self-esteem. That is, people who report highly favorable opinions about themselves can be divided into those with true high self-esteem and those with socially desirable high self-esteem. The latter group appears to report highly favorable self-evaluations as a defense against recognition of their true feelings of inadequacy. Experimental evidence supporting this distinction between socially desirable and true self-esteem was reviewed.

Smoking is well regarded as a complex chain of behaviors that is notable for its extraordinary persistence—it has been estimated that only about 25 per cent of those who try to quit are successful for as long as six months. Physiological theories of smoking generally propose that the smoking habit is maintained by physical addiction to the drug nicotine. Although some evidence supports this view, the defining condition of physical addiction is the occurrence of withdrawal symptoms following cessation of drug use, and it has yet to be shown that the cessation of cigarette smoking produces any consistent withdrawal symptoms other than those associated with the cessation of any compulsive behavior. Psychological theories of smoking generally maintain that smoking is a habit maintained by practice, reinforcement, and the nonpractice of nonsmoking behaviors. Personality differences between smokers and nonsmokers have also been studied; presently, some evidence suggests that smokers tend to be more antisocial and extraverted than nonsmokers. Thus far, the most effective treatment technique for smoking seems to be the forced oversmoking techniques. Forced oversmoking, however, has the disadvantage of being dangerous to the client's health.

Chapter 20

Some Topics Closely Related to the Study of Abnormal Behavior: Aggression and Fantasy

LEONARD D. ERON

and CHARLES L. GRUDER[1]

We are known for our violence, we Americans. The creative violence with which we haul down the good for what we fancy as better. The cruel violence with which we have treated red men and black men. The intoxicating violence of our music and art. The absurd violence of our comics and cartoons. The organized violence of our athletic and corporate games. The coarse violence of our speech, even our jokes.

And now we have come violently to disagree about the nature of our violence in Vietnam or Dallas or Watts or Hiroshima. We seek the primitive within ourselves and bemoan the failure of affluence to civilize. Our young deplore the violence of the old and are tempted to use violence against them. The old deplore the ferocity of the young and are tempted to use violence to suppress them.

FRANKEL (1968, p. v)

The behaviors discussed in this chapter are aggression and fantasy. As the opening quotation suggests, aggression is one of the major social problems facing our society. In this chapter several theories of aggressive behavior are reviewed, and each theory is shown to be associated with different practical implications for controlling aggression. Two especially important issues are the manner in which aggressive behavior is learned in childhood and how various parental practices might facilitate or discourage aggressive tendencies as the child grows older. Because of the importance of these issues, this chapter presents in detail the conclusions of a ten-year study on aggression by Eron, Walder, and Lefkowitz (1971).

Although aggression under some circumstances can be regarded as abnormal, aggression under many other circumstances is best regarded as a normal behavior. Fantasy is also best regarded as a normal behavior. Nevertheless, for reasons presented in the text of this chapter, our knowledge of both aggression and fantasy is relevant to our understanding of abnormal behavior.

AGGRESSIVE BEHAVIOR

In popular parlance the term *aggression* can have positive connotations, as in the example of an aggressive business executive, as well as negative connotations, as in the example of a violent murderer. In this chapter, we refer to aggression only in its negative sense—that is, only as destructive and socially disapproved behavior. So defined, aggression includes malicious gossiping and verbal insults as well as violent behaviors that physically harm other people.

Case Example of a Highly Aggressive Child

Ronald was first seen professionally when he was eight years old and in the second grade. His teacher, who described him as "a likable and happy-go-lucky child," had referred him to the school psychologist because of immature behavior and poor work habits. He had repeated first grade, but the teacher felt he was brighter than group tests indicated. Ronald was the youngest of three children. His brother, age 11, was out of the home at a special school for emo-

---

[1] Leonard D. Eron wrote the section of this chapter on aggression. Charles L. Gruder and Leonard D. Eron wrote the section of this chapter on fantasy. Steven Reiss organized portions of the chapter.

tionally disturbed youngsters and his sister, age 12, was progressing normally in school. Ronald had been sickly from infancy, having suffered from severe attacks of asthma until the previous year. The parents reported that because the attacks were so frightening they had overindulged him. However, the father, who had to hold two jobs in order to support the family, did not spend much time with the children. The mother's primary complaint about Ronald was that he was always hungry and "would eat from morning to night."

An individually administered intelligence test indicated that Ronald was of average ability. He was, however, one year retarded in reading, due perhaps to a disturbance in spatial orientation that was apparent in the way he handled test materials. It was noted that he was impulsive and did not go about problem solving in any planful way, relying solely on trial and error. He was uncritical of his own performance.

Ronald was next seen by a psychologist when he was 12 years old and in the sixth grade. At this time, he was failing in school, reading at a second-grade level, and was a management problem in his class. He talked back to the teacher, provoked fights, and was constantly making noise. He was not allowed to go to the lavatory with his classmates because he would get into fights with them. Ronald was also having difficulty on the school bus and in the neighborhood, continually getting into fights with other boys by taunting them and egging them on. The parents did not seem to be concerned about the boy's behavior. The father never appeared for a parent interview and the mother said it was the school's problem, not hers. She usually took the boy's part and accused the school officials of picking on her son.

By coincidence, Ronald was a subject in the longitudinal study of aggression to be described later in this chapter. It has been possible to retrieve the parent interviews conducted when Ronald was nine years old and his own interview when he was 19. In the third grade Ronald was already seen by his peers as one of the most aggressive boys in class, doing things that bother others, starting a fight over nothing, saying mean things, not obeying the teacher, and pushing other children. At the same time the father and mother indicated that Ronald was disobedient at home, that he annoyed and pestered them, had a bad temper, and used foul language. They did not approve of a number of things that he did, giving many indications of a rejecting attitude toward Ronald and little indication that they understood him or were concerned about him. They related having had many arguments between themselves that did not settle anything; they moved around a lot so that Ronald continually had to find new friends. These behaviors and occurrences created a very frustrating situation at home that probably instigated Ronald to be aggressive both there and at school. The father related using many physical punishments when Ronald was aggressive, including spanking him severely and washing out his mouth with soap, thus adding to the youngster's frustration and providing the model of an aggressive adult. Other aggressive models were furnished on Ronald's favorite TV programs, "Maverick," "Have Gun Will Travel," and "The Three Stooges." The parents indicated that Ronald showed few signs of internalized standards of behavior such as feeling sorry after he disobeyed, worrying about telling a fib or a lie, or confessing when he had done something naughty. Thus, according to information furnished by his parents at that time, Ronald at age nine was experiencing many instigations to aggression at home, had a physically punitive father as well as other aggressive models, and showed little indication of having developed a conscience.

At the time Ronald was interviewed at the age of 19, he was on probation for three years for petty larceny. A few weeks after the interview he was picked up by the police and charged with "criminal mischief in the third degree" and one week later with "criminal possession of drugs, fourth degree." During the interview it was revealed that he had dropped out of high school in the tenth grade, but he insisted that he expected to go to graduate school so that he could eventually do research in "brain biology." He said he engaged in many aggressive behaviors. On the MMPI he had high scores on a pattern of scales characteristic of recalcitrant delinquents (scales 4, 8, and 9—psychopathic deviate, schizophrenia, and mania, respectively). He continued to prefer violent television programs and thought that "Mod Squad," "Mannix," and "Dragnet" were very realistic in showing what police work is really like.

Theories of Aggression

Two categories of theory have been proposed concerning the causes of aggressive behavior. One general position is that people are naturally aggressive. The other general position is that people are born with the potential to act aggressively but whether they do so depends on their subsequent experience.

Psychoanalytic Theory

It will be recalled from Chapter 6 that Freud (1922) postulated the presence in all individuals of two drives or instincts: Eros, the life instinct, and Thanatos, the death instinct. According to this theory, every person is born with a fixed amount of energy directed toward destructiveness, and this energy must inevitably be expressed in one form or another. If aggressive energy is blocked or inhibited in its direct external expression, it will then be expressed indirectly. If all external expression is prevented, aggression is turned inward on the individual himself (Menninger, 1938). Depression, for example, has been hypothesized to represent a form of aggression turned against the self.

Psychoanalytic theory posits that aggression can be released vicariously. In this view, a person can release aggressive energy by having a fantasy of being aggressive, by watching violent television programs or violent sports, by reading about fierce warriors, or by acting the part of a killer in a play. The vicarious release of aggressive energy is called *catharsis;* psychoanalytic theory proposes that the greater the extent to which a person can release aggressive energy in fantasy through catharsis, the less is the extent to which it is necessary for him to express aggression directly in real life. This hypothesis, however, is not supported by the available experimental data (Bandura, 1965; Berkowitz, 1969; Hokanson, 1970). For example, the psychoanalytic notion of catharsis suggests that a child who watches violent television programs is not likely to engage in aggressive behavior. The relevant experimental data, however, suggest the opposite—that is, that the direct viewing of violent television programs and other instances of aggression tends to increase aggressive behavior (e.g., Eron, Huesmann, Walder, & Lefkowitz, 1972).

There exists little experimental support for the psychoanalytic theory of aggression as an innate force continually seeking expression. What evidence there is for such theorizing comes primarily from the accounts of psychoanalytically oriented therapists of their patients' revelations. Although some psychoanalysts believe that these data suggest that aggression is innate, few experimentally oriented psychologists concur.

Ethological Theory

Ethologists such as Robert Ardrey (1966), Konrad Lorenz (1966), and N. Tinbergen (1968) have attempted to understand human aggression as a trait inherited from our animal ancestry. In lower animals aggression is instinctive and hence is controlled primarily by inherited factors. Moreover, lower animals have inherited inhibitory mechanisms that constrain aggression toward other animals of the same species; thus aggression among animals of the same species is relatively rare. Ethologists have hypothesized that through evolution humans have inherited aggressive instincts without also having inherited effective inhibitory mechanisms; hence aggression among humans is much more common than is aggression among other like species of animals. Lorenz (1966) wrote that man has "in his hand the atom bomb, the product of his intelligence, [and] in his heart the aggression drive inherited from his anthropoid ancestors, which this same intelligence cannot control. . . ."

The ethological view of innate aggression has been widely criticized (Hinde, 1967; Lefkowitz, Eron, Walder, & Huesmann, 1976; Montagu, 1968). It has been noted that the postulates of ethological theory have not been demonstrated by the methods of experimental science. Moreover, there exists conclusive evidence that aggressive behavior is often learned and is subject to situational influences; yet these facts have not been adequately incorporated into ethological theory. Because of these and other considerations, the theorizing of ethologists about innate aggression has not gained much credibility among psychologists and behavioral scientists.

Biological Hypotheses

Some theories ascribe aggressive behavior to structural and physiological anomalies within the organism. These theories trace aggressive behavior to chromosomal anomalies, sex hormones, and central nervous system damage.

One of the most dramatic claims is that of a causal relation between an XXY chromosomal pattern (an extra male chromosome) called *karyotype* and aggression in men. Jarvik, Klodin, and Matsuyama (1973) have provided evidence that the incidence of the karyotype pattern is 15 times greater among apprehended criminals than in the general population. Nevertheless, this finding does not establish that karyotype causes aggression. The occurrence of this karyotype is also associated with lower intelligence and with excessive tallness; thus the obtained correlation between karyotype and aggression might be due to these factors or to some still undiscovered third variable that causes both the aggression and the anomalous chromosomal structure. Even if the XXY chromosomal pattern were a cause of aggression, its occurrence is so infrequent (one out of every 1,000 births) that it could not provide an explanation of most instances of aggression.

Some biologically oriented investigators have attempted to identify specific brain centers that control aggressive behavior. It is currently believed that the areas of the brain that control aggression are located in the temporal lobes and in subcortical structures known as the limbic system. Experimental studies have shown that stimulation of these areas via implanted electrodes can result in increased or in decreased aggression, depending on the exact areas of stimulation (Delgado, 1965). In man, injury to these brain areas can lead to a wide range of aggressive behavior, including temper tantrums, irritability, fighting, and violence. However, the exact relation between these centers of the brain and aggression is incompletely understood.

It has been consistently reported that males engage in more aggressive behavior than females. This finding is true for all ages and all species that have been studied. In this context it is not surprising that considerable evidence exists suggesting that male aggressiveness has a biological component associated with male sex hormones (e.g., Maccoby & Jacklin, 1971; Young, Goy, & Phoenix, 1964). However, that males are more aggressive than females may also be a result of differing social roles and learning experiences in the life history of males and females.

Frustration-Aggression Hypothesis

The Yale studies on aggression (Dollard, Doob, Miller, Mowrer, & Sears, 1939) started an extended line of inquiry that initially concerned a possibly unlearned, innate relation between frustration and aggression. In its original formulation the frustration-aggression hypothesis proposed:

1. All frustration inevitably leads to some type of aggressive response.
2. A necessary antecedent condition of all aggression is frustration.

Miller (1941) clarified this position by noting that, although aggression is a frequent response to frustration, frustration may also lead to other responses. Thus Miller wrote, "Frustration produces instigations to a number of different types of responses, one of which is an instigation to some form of aggression" (1941, p. 338). The strength of this instigation to aggression was said to vary with the following three factors:

1. *The greater the magnitude of the response frustrated, the greater the instigation to aggression.* For example, if a male high school student were refused a date by his steady girl friend, this would produce a greater instigation to aggressive behavior than if he were refused a date by a girl he had just met. Presumably, the approach tendency toward the steady girl friend is a response of greater magnitude than is the approach tendency toward a girl whom he had never dated.

2. *The greater the degree of interference with the response, the greater is the frustration and hence the greater is the instigation to aggressive behavior.* For example, a youngster digging in the sand with two shovels would be less annoyed, and thus less impelled toward aggressive behavior, if one shovel rather than both were taken away.
3. *The greater the number of responses frustrated, the greater is the instigation to aggressive behavior.* This is the principle of a cumulative effect of separate frustrations. For example, a young executive who was reprimanded by his boss for a business deal that fell through, and who then lost a bet on the World Series, subsequently fell and scraped his knee on the way to the water cooler, and finally missed his commuter train, would be more annoyed on arriving home to find dinner late than would another man who had experienced only one of these frustrating occurrences during the day.

Other studies have found that aggression is more likely when the frustrating event appears arbitrary (Pastore, 1952) and when it is unexpected (Berkowitz, 1962).

It is important to recognize that the frustration-aggression hypothesis does not specify the specific aggressive behaviors that will occur as a consequence of frustration; the hypothesis simply predicts that some type of aggressive behavior will occur. In regard to the issue of what type of aggressive response will occur, the Yale theorists proposed that this depends on the following factors:

1. *The greater the instigation to aggression, the more likely is physical aggression.* For example, if a man is deliberately pushed aside by another individual while both are in line waiting to buy tickets to an athletic event, he is more apt to respond with physical aggression than he would be if the other individual accidentally stepped on his toe.
2. *The greater the possibility of retaliation, the less likely is physical aggression.* For example, if a young boy knows from past experience that he will be punished severely for hitting his younger sister, he will tend to refrain from doing this.
3. *The probability of physical aggression is affected by characteristics of the potential target and the possibility of displacement to other people or objects.* Thus a young boy frustrated by his teacher or mother is more likely to take it out on his younger sister than he is to attack his teacher or mother.

The frustration-aggression hypothesis thus provides a number of limitations on how and with what intensity aggression will be expressed in response to frustration. As noted by Miller, an instigation to some form of aggression is only one of several different responses possible to frustration. In a hierarchy of responses produced by a specific frustrating situation, if aggression is the strongest component, then it is the most likely response to occur. However, other responses incompatible with aggression may also be instigated; if these responses are stronger than the instigation to aggression, they will occur first. Thus, although aggression is a very likely response to frustration, it is not the only one; other responses to frustration that have been investigated are regression, withdrawal, and constructive striving.

Despite the fact that the causes of aggression are not completely understood, there is little doubt that many of the expressions of aggressive behavior are learned. (Photo by Bruce Davidson; Film Photos, Inc.)

Social Learning Theory

Buss (1961) has proposed one of several reinforcement theories of aggression that abandon the notion that frustration is a necessary antecedent to aggression. Aggression, according to Buss, occurs primarily if it has instrumental value; that is, if the individual gets what he wants by an aggressive act, eliminates an annoyance, or fends off an attack. This view proposes that aggression is a function of its consequences; when the consequences are reinforcing, aggressive behavior patterns are learned, but when the consequences are not reinforcing or are punishing, aggressive behavior patterns are not learned.

Bandura and his colleagues (e.g., Bandura, 1973; Bandura & Walters, 1965) have investigated the manner in which aggressive behavior patterns are acquired through observational learning (modeling). Many experimental studies have shown that children and adults are more likely to behave aggressively after having observed aggression by others. Imitation of a model's aggression is especially likely if the model is in some way rewarded for aggressive acts. When the model's aggressive behavior is punished, however, the observer is unlikely to imitate the model. Similar findings have been reported in field studies. For example, Eron et al. (1972) found that the observation of television violence by young children has the effect of increasing the frequency of the children's aggressive behavior.

In general, laboratory studies with children have demonstrated convincingly that aggressive behavior is facilitated when rewarded (e.g., Patterson, Littman, & Bricker, 1967). The effects of punishment on aggression, however, are less clear. The animal literature suggests that the effects of punishment depend on many variables, including the nature of the punishment procedure, the intensity of the punishment, the type of aggressive behavior punished, the organism's prior learning history, and the availability of an alternative, nonpunished response (see Chapter 7). The animal literature indicates that the effects of punishment may be to decrease or to increase the frequency of the punished response, depending on the preceding variables. Experimental studies of the effects of punishment on aggression in young children have generally indicated that such behavior is inhibited when punished (e.g., Chasdi & Lawrence, 1955). Field studies of real-life behavior, however, have not been as uniform in their results. A general finding of these field studies is that parental punishment for aggressive behavior increases aggression in children (Bandura & Walters, 1959; Eron, Walder, Toigo, & Lefkowitz, 1963; Sears, Maccoby, & Levin, 1957). These findings may be explicable in terms of a modeling hypothesis. The parent who punishes a child may be furnishing the child with an aggressive model to imitate; thus, although the child's aggression at home is inhibited, the child is more aggressive elsewhere as a consequence of imitating the parental model.

Aggression-Anxiety Hypothesis

Punishment for aggression in children can be assumed to result in the conditioning of anticipatory anxiety to cues of aggression. Hence when the child is subsequently provoked, anxiety in the form of fear of retaliation might occur; in order to reduce this anxiety, the child might not aggress. In this view anxi-

The Iowa Aggression Machine used in the Peterson (1971) study. The subject believes that she can punish incorrect responses of another subject in another room by pressing one of the buttons.

ety functions as a signal of impending danger if one engages in aggressive behavior. Such anxiety may be termed *aggression anxiety.*

Aggression anxiety has been formally defined as a hypothetical construct that can explain the inhibition of aggressive behavior under conditions in which such behavior has been instigated. So defined, aggression anxiety has been invoked to explain in part why some children are highly aggressive and others are rarely aggressive. Highly aggressive children have been hypothesized to be low in aggression anxiety—that is, they do not fear retaliation for aggression; low aggressive children have been hypothesized to be high in aggression anxiety—that is, they anticipate punishment for aggressive behavior.

Peterson (1971) investigated the effects of threat of retaliation on two types of eight-year-old boys—those who were rated by their peers as being highly aggressive and those who were rated by their peers as having a low frequency of aggressive behavior. The experimenter informed each child that another boy was playing a game in another room and that, when the boy in the other room made a mistake, the subject could punish him by pressing one of a graded series of buttons corresponding to louder and louder sounds. The louder the sound button pressed, the more aggressive the response. (The peer in the other room did not exist—nevertheless, the subject thought he was really punishing another child.) Half of the subjects were placed in a retaliation situation in which they were told that after they punished their partners, the partners would have the opportunity to punish them. The other half were placed in a nonretaliation situation; these subjects were told that when they finished punishing their partners the experiment would be over. As Figure 20-1 shows, the results indicate important differences between high- and low-aggressive children in reaction to the retaliation versus nonretaliation conditions. The highly aggressive children were more aggressive under threat of retaliation than under no threat, whereas the children who were low in aggression were more aggressive under no threat of retaliation than under threat. The aggression-anxiety hypothesis explains these data as follows:

1. Threat of retaliation elicited aggression anxiety in the children with low aggression, thereby inhibiting aggression.
2. Threat of retaliation did not elicit aggression anxiety in the highly aggressive children because these children do not fear retaliation. In fact, the results suggest that threat of retaliation actually functions to increase aggression in highly aggressive children.

An anecdotal example of how behaviors can be learned to avoid aggression anxiety is provided by Dick Gregory (1964) in his book *Nigger.* Writing about his childhood experiences in St. Louis, Gregory says that he learned to be a stand-up comic and raconteur while under threat of retaliation. When cornered by stronger, more belligerent peers, he avoided punishment by doing something to make his potential attackers laugh. Thus his comic behavior was originally learned because it reduced and avoided anxiety over punishment.

Findings of increased inhibition of aggression with increased probability of retaliation have been reported in studies with college students (e.g., Buss, 1961; Edwards, 1967) and with nursery school children (e.g., Patterson, Littman, & Bricker, 1967). These findings suggest that the relation between anticipation of punishment and aggressive behavior develops early in life and is maintained at least through early adulthood.

Figure 20-1
The intensity of aggression under conditions of threat and no threat of retaliation in high- and low-aggressive children. (From R. A. Peterson, Aggression as a function of expected retaliation and aggression level of target and aggressor. *Developmental Psychology,* Vol. 5, 1971, p. 165. Printed by permission of author and American Psychological Association.)

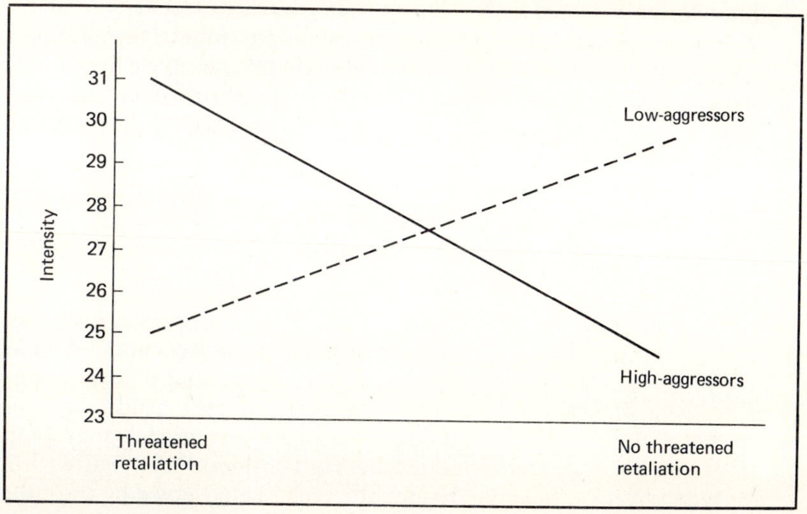

Theories of Social Control

Thus far we have considered several theories of aggression primarily from the scientific perspective of understanding why aggression occurs and why some people are more aggressive than others. It should be noted that each of these theories has been associated with a particular view on how society might best deal with the problem of controlling violence. Although the scientific merits of the various theories actually have little to do with the associated social programs, it is nevertheless of interest to consider just what types of practical advice have emerged.

It may be recalled that ethologists have proposed that it is human nature to behave aggressively, attempting to destroy that which is annoying or threatening. This view supports a fear of one's fellowman and could be used to justify social programs designed to inhibit impulses to respond aggressively, or at least to channel impulses in nondestructive directions. If such measures are unsuccessful, then isolation, incarceration, and more extreme forms of punishment can be seen as appropriate methods for containing and for controlling violence. The ultimate eventuality might be a constant concern with attack stemming from the belief that man is innately aggressive; hence extreme precautions against being victimized could be seen as essential. In this context a garrison social structure could develop.

The theory that aggressive behavior is the result of structural and physical anomalies has been employed to argue that massive screening programs are necessary to identify people who are predisposed toward violence. Corrective procedures such as psychosurgery, drug therapy, or even specific learning regimes to compensate for a deficiency due to a defective apparatus would then be instituted. This point of view is epitomized in the following quotation:

> In order to reverse the trend of human violence, we must set certain basic standards of behavior (e.g., "golden rule" or "Ten Commandments") that any individual with a normal brain can follow. In addition, we need to find some way to detect those individuals with brain abnormalities who are unlikely to be able to follow those standards. In other words, we need to develop an "early warning test" of limbic brain function to detect those humans who have a low threshold for impulsive violence, and we need better and more effective methods of treating them once we have found out who they are. Violence is a public health problem, and the major thrust of any program dealing with violence must be toward its prevention—a goal that will make a better and safer world for us all [Mark & Ervin, 1970, p. 160].

The theory that aggressive behavior is learned leads to an educational model of prevention and control of violence. The following quotation exemplifies this approach:

> A parent or teacher who wishes to reduce the frequency of an aggressive behavior may consider various ways of doing it: (1) The amount of instigation to aggression may be reduced. Bickering between parents, criticizing the child, and not nurturing the child are instigations that can be reduced. (2) Aggressive models may be made less available to the child. Some parents and teachers tell children to be gentle while they themselves are aggressive. Parents may reduce the violence observed by the child, whether on TV,

in the disciplinary practices of the parents, in the parents' social and occupational behaviors in general, or in the actions of people in low and high places in government. (3) Nonaggressive models may be made more available to the child. Parents may attempt to present nonviolent behaviors on TV, in their disciplinary practices, in their general social and occupational behaviors, and in their government. (4) Finally, the consequences of aggression and of nonaggression can be programmed so that decreasing amounts of aggression and increasing amounts of nonaggression will occur.

To be an effective disciplinarian, the parent must systematically present to his child a wide variety of consequences of aggression. The parent who presents only negative, noxious consequences offers an aggressive role model (as noted above), cannot punish by withholding positive consequences, and cannot easily strengthen nonaggressive behaviors. Although such an extreme parent is probably very rare (if he exists at all), a parent who is an approximation of this hypothetical specialist in negative discipline will be unable to control behaviors efficiently and will instill behaviors in the child that serve merely to avoid punishment. Such avoidance behaviors will be in evidence just as long as the parent is present and is strong enough to punish; only with luck will they be strengthened and routinely maintained by nonparental reinforcing agents. Any time the parent is not present or if, even when present, he no longer punishes, the suppressed behaviors will emerge.

The parent who presents both positive and negative consequences of aggression offers both an aggressive and a nonaggressive role model, can punish both by presenting noxious consequences and by withdrawing positive ones, and can more easily strengthen nonaggressive behaviors. Such a parent is in a position to control behaviors efficiently and to develop behaviors in the child that serve to gain positive consequences as well as to avoid negative ones. It is obvious that behaviors responsive to both positive and negative controls are more likely to be desirable behaviors than are those under only negative controls.

Another general benefit for the parent who dispenses an adequate number of positive consequences is that his child will work to please him. This implies that the child will copy not only the parent's disciplining but also the parent's rules and instructions about how he should behave (referred to as internalization). This will serve to control the child's behavior in situations where the parent is not present, e.g., in school.

In addition to providing a broad range of variety of consequences, the parent must arrange for the child to receive these consequences in a generally systematic way so that the child, by behaving either well or badly, can influence the kind and amount of positive and negative consequences dispensed by the parent (and in this sense control the parent). Also the parents must set requirements for the child that are appropriate to his development in order to ensure that he is most often successful in behaving well and learning through trial and success. Such a state of affairs keeps the chronic instigation to aggression down to a minimal level.[2]

Childhood Learning and Aggression

More than twenty years ago Eron and his colleagues embarked on a research program designed to study aggressive behavior in all of the third-grade children in a semirural county in New York State (875 children in 38 classrooms) as well as their mothers and fathers (Eron, Laulicht, Walder, Farber, & Spiegel, 1961). One part of this study related the aggressive behavior of children as ob-

[2] From L. D. Eron, L. O. Walder, and M. M. Lefkowitz, *Learning of Aggression in Children* (Boston: Little, Brown, 1971), pp. 165–167; (New York: Pergamon Press, Inc., 1976). Reprinted with permission of the authors and publishers.

served in school to the antecedents of such behavior as reflected in the child-rearing practices of the parents. The measure of aggression was a peer-nomination procedure in which every child in a class rated every other child on ten items of aggressive behavior. The reliability and validity of this measure have been demonstrated in a number of studies (Eron et al., 1971; Walder, Abelson, Eron, Banta, & Laulicht, 1961). The parents' interview was a closed-ended, precoded questionnaire, individually administered in a face-to-face situation. The interview was designed to obtain information on four types of antecedent conditions: instigation to aggression, reinforcement, identification, and sociocultural variables. Instigation referred to conditions in the home that were likely to be frustrating to the child and thus spark aggressive behavior. Reinforcement referred to contingent responses by the parent to the child's aggression. Identification has two aspects: internalization of parental standards and modeling the behavior of significant adults. These can either inhibit or facilitate aggressive behavior. Social-class variables were also studied because they were hypothesized to affect behavior in a variety of ways.

Ten years later a follow-up study was done in which approximately 50 per cent of the original subjects were reinterviewed and asked to rate again each other's aggression.

All of the major findings were consistent with the hypothesis that aggression can be learned by a child from his interaction with the environment. It was also found that aggression as measured in childhood is a good predictor of aggression in young adulthood; that is, aggression is a relatively stable characteristic of the individual.

Each of the four classes of antecedent variables mentioned was found to be related to the aggression of the child in the third grade. In general the more frustrating the conditions at home, the more aggressive the child was in school; for example, children who had been rejected at home tended to be highly aggressive. It was also found that the more the child was punished for aggression at home and the less he identified with either or both parents, the more aggressive he was in school. One of the major instigators to aggression in children seems to be a general lack of favorable support from both parents which in turn tends to reduce the effectiveness of any punishment the parent administers in order to discourage aggressive behavior.

Although each of the antecedent variables studied was found to be related to aggression in the third grade, ten years later only two of these variables—identification and social class—were associated with aggression. Both rejection by the parents and parental punishment, which, as noted, related to the childrens' aggression in third grade, ten years later no longer affected the subjects' aggression. However, measures of identification that related to aggression at age eight continued to be related to aggression at age 19. These measures included internalization, such as the extent to which the child manifested guilt and confessed when he or she committed transgressions, and measures of modeling, such as how much the youngster's behavior resembled either or both of his or her parents' behavior. Moreover, social-class variables measured in the third grade continued to have an effect on aggression when the subjects were 19 years old. Especially important were fathers' occupational status (the higher the status the occupation reflected, the more aggressive the subjects) and mobility orientation (the more ambitious the father, the more aggressive the son at age 19).

These findings suggest that the effects of punishment and frustration influence aggression at the time they occur but do not last long beyond that period. As the child grows older and spends less time in the home, these variables no longer seem to have much effect. The early models of behavior to which the child is exposed as he is growing up, however, continue to have an effect on his behavior.

Television Violence

The Eron et al. study (1972) found that one of the best predictors of how aggressive a boy will be at ages 18 and 19 is the amount of violence on the television programs he preferred when he was eight years old. Through the use of a number of sophisticated statistical techniques it was demonstrated that the most plausible interpretation of these data is that early viewing of violent television *causes* later aggression (Eron, Heusmann, Walder, & Lefkowitz, 1972). This direct positive relation between violence of preferred programs and later aggression is true only for boys; for girls there were indications that viewing television may lead to less aggression.

Why might there be this differential effect of television violence for boys and girls? One possible explanation is that there are far fewer aggressive females on television for a girl to imitate than there are aggressive males for a boy to imitate. Furthermore, girls are usually the victims, rather than the perpetrators, of aggression on television; hence the more programs girls watch, the more exposed they are to female models who are harmed by aggressive acts.

Psychopathology

During the follow-up phase of this project, each subject who appeared for reinterviewing 10 years later was administered a personality questionnaire, the MMPI; scores on this instrument were related to measures of aggression taken at both stages of the investigation and to the child-rearing data obtained when the subjects were in the third grade. Not only was there a relation between psychopathology and aggression at both periods, but parent child-rearing variables that did not relate to aggression in the follow-up period did relate to psychopathology at that time (Eron, Lefkowitz, Walder, & Huesmann, 1974). This was especially true of rejection by the parent when the child was in the third grade, which was significantly related to psychopathology in the young adult 10 years later. However, the relation is not a direct one. It seems that the lowest psychopathology scores were obtained by those 19-year-olds who at age eight had been moderately rejected. Those who had very high or very low scores on rejection at age eight were the ones who scored highest on the psychopathology scale at age 19.

An examination of the content of the rejection scale suggests a reasonable

BOX 20-1
Summary of Findings of Eron, Walder, and Lefkowitz Study and Lefkowitz, Eron, Walder, and Huesmann Study

1. Aggression measured when children are eight years old is positively correlated with aggression measured 10 years later.
2. Children who are physically aggressive also tend to be verbally aggressive and to express aggression in various indirect ways. In other words, different modes of expressing aggression go together.

These two findings, that aggressive behavior is consistent over time and across situations, would indicate that aggression has the qualities of a trait. This does not mean necessarily that it is inherited or biological. These are probably behaviors that are learned early and generalize readily, probably because the pay-off is so good.

3. Eight-year-old boys are consistently more aggressive than eight-year-old girls over all situations. The difference is even more pronounced 10 years later. Although biological (e.g., hormonal) factors may account for a portion of the variance, differing socialization experiences for boys and girls are very important and can easily overcome any biological predispositions.
4. Punishment has a complicated relation to aggression. In general, the more boys are punished for aggression, the more aggressive they are. However, for a special subset of boys who identify closely with their fathers, punishment works to inhibit aggressive behaviors.
5. The upward mobility strivings of parents is one of the best predictors of aggres-

interpretation for this finding. The rejection items concern behaviors in the child that the parent feels are worthy of change: e.g., Do you think Johnny is too forgetful? Are you satisfied with Johnny's manners? Are you pleased with the quality of Johnny's schoolwork? Parents who obtain very low scores on this scale, indicating that they feel their child needs little improvement, are possibly communicating unrealistic evaluations to their child; parents in the middle classification, who indicate that there are some areas in which the child can improve his behavior, are perhaps communicating a more realistic image; parents with high scores are saying the child can never measure up to their standards, thus communicating a very negative evaluation. Thus it would seem that parents in the moderate range on this rejection scale have reasonable expectations for their children, training them not to expect universal approval from everyone they interact with, but also not encouraging them to adopt a defeatist attitude about their competencies. It would seem that a little rejection has positive effects. Siegelman has reported that "male and female college students with personality traits frequently associated with creativity, tended to describe both parents as more rejecting than loving when growing up" (1973, p. 43).

The Eron et al. study also found that boys who are anxious about expressing aggression at the age of eight tend to have *low* MMPI psychopathology scores at the age of 19. A possible explanation of this finding concerns the nature of the aggression-anxiety scale. Specifically, items on this scale reflect a tendency

sion. The most aggressive of all subjects are those whose fathers have high occupational status but low educational achievement.
6. The violence of television programs preferred by boys when they are eight years old is the best single predictor of aggression 10 years later. This relation is independent of IQ, social status, parental aggression, or the original aggression level of the youngster. Eight-year-old boys with low aggression who watch violent television are significantly more aggressive 10 years later than highly aggressive eight-year-olds who watch nonviolent television.
7. There is a tendency for girls who watch violent television at eight years of age to be less aggressive 10 years later than girls who watch nonviolent television. This may be due to the fact that female models on television have in the past been the victims, not the perpetrators, of aggression.
8. Aggression is related to psychopathology. Highly aggressive males engage in more schizophrenic-like and compulsive behaviors than boys with low aggression.
9. Highly aggressive females are more masculine in their attitudes and interests, whereas females low in aggression tend to withdraw from social interaction more than do highly aggressive females.
10. Rejection by parents at the age of eight is related to aggression at that age but not to aggression 10 years later. However, rejection at the age of eight is strongly related to the extent of psychopathology 10 years later.

From Eron, L. D., Walder, L. O. and Lefkowitz, M. M. *Learning of Aggression in Children,* Boston: Little, Brown, 1971; and Lefkowitz, M. M., Eron, L. D., Walder, L. O. and Huesmann, L. R. *Growing Up to Be Violent,* New York: Pergamon, 1976.

to try to facilitate interpersonal relations (e.g., "Who says excuse me even when they have not done anything bad?"; "Who will never fight even when picked on?"). Such boys care about their interactions with others and have probably learned techniques that help them get along well with others. Consequently, they are more apt to gain gratifications from interpersonal relations and not develop the maladaptive, defensive behaviors that are tapped by the MMPI items.

The results of the Eron et al. study are summarized in Box 20-1.

FANTASY

Hallucinations and the excessive reliance on fantasy as a psychological escape from reality are associated with psychotic disorders (see Chapter 15). Thus even though dreaming and daydreaming frequently occur in normal people and by themselves must be considered normal behavior, a knowledge of fantasy behavior and its functions is relevant to our understanding of some forms of abnormality.

Interpretation of Dreams

The notion that dreams are psychologically meaningful and can be interpreted to reveal inner feelings has been expressed since antiquity. An early expression of this view appeared in Plato's *Republic:* "in every one of us, even those who seem most respectable, there exists desires, terrible in their untamed lawlessness, which reveal themselves in dreams" (p. 297). In more recent times Freud (1900) and Jung (Jacobi, 1951) have expressed this view in great detail and related it to abnormal behavior. In Freud's view a fantasy is a disguised expression of a repressed wish—it is a means for the personality to satisfy the unacceptable, instinctive demands of the id.

Psychoanalytic theory distinguishes between the manifest and the latent content of dreams. The *manifest content* is the surface meaning of the dream as revealed in the imagery of the dream or in the dream report. For example, in a dream of climbing a mountain, the visual imagery of the climb is the manifest content. The *latent content* of a dream is its hidden, unconscious meaning. Psychoanalytic theory maintains that all dreams are wishfulfilling; hence the latent content always consists of these hypothesized, unconscious wishes. The translation of a dream from its manifest to its latent content is called the interpretation of the dream. Freud stated that the interpretation of dreams provides the royal road to understanding the unconscious. For example, the manifest content of climbing a mountain would typically be interpreted as a desire for sexual intercourse because in psychoanalytic theory climbing is an unconscious symbol for sexual intercourse.

Although many theorists still maintain that dream content can be interpreted to reveal hidden desires, this position is unproven and is generally unpopular among experimental scientists.

Fantasy in Normal and Disturbed Persons

An extensive body of research has investigated whether or not the fantasy productions of disturbed and nondisturbed people differ in any systematic way. Few consistent findings have thus far emerged from this line of inquiry, particularly in regard to those studies that used projective tests to measure fantasy productions. The recent use of more objective techniques, particularly in sleep research, seems to offer much more promise in identifying possible differences in fantasy productions between disturbed and nondisturbed populations.

Projective techniques such as the Rorschach and the TAT (see Chapter 4) have been extensively employed to study fantasy in normal and disturbed persons. The available data, however, indicate that these procedures are of limited value. It can be concluded from reviews of findings obtained on the TAT (Eron, 1950, 1959, 1972; Jensen, 1959) and the Rorschach inkblots (Cronbach, 1948; Eysenck, 1959; Shaffer, 1959; Zubin, Eron, & Schumer, 1965) that these procedures are not useful in identifying categories of psychopathology. The tests have been found seriously lacking in both reliability and validity; they do not often distinguish between normal and disturbed persons.

A growing number of investigators are focusing their efforts on the objective study of dreams and daydreams rather than on fantasy elicited by the TAT or Rorschach (e.g., Cartwright, 1972; Dement, 1955; Koresko, Snyder, & Feinberg, 1963). Cartwright (1972), for example, studied the bizarreness of fantasy in dream reports of schizophrenics and of normals (see Chapter 15) and found that in normals fantasy tended to occur primarily during periods of sleep when there were rapid eye movements (REM), whereas in schizophrenics bizarre fantasy occurred in a much wider range of mental states. This finding should lead us to expect differences between schizophrenics and normals in the content of daydreams. In this regard, Cazavelon and Epstein (1966) found that although schizophrenics and normals reported daydreaming equally often, the content of their daydreams differed. The daydreams of schizophrenics contained more manifestly pathological content and more references to mysticism and strange controlling forces than the daydreams of normals, which contained more references to anxiety and problem-solving themes. Psychiatric inpatients with various diagnoses have also been found to report different patterns of daydreaming than hospitalized medical patients and nonhospitalized controls (Streissguth, Wagner, & Wechsler, 1969). The psychiatric patients reported more daydreams and daydream content that was more improbable, ideational, and affect-laden. Virtually no relations between daydreaming styles and psychopathological symptoms were found, however, in a study of psychiatric outpatients (Starker & Singer, 1975).

Research with normal adolescents who differed in personality has revealed some differences in the fantasy of their free associations (Rychlak, 1972, 1973). The fantasies of anxious college students included more ideas and images than those of less anxious students. Compared with normal high school students, slightly troubled students reported more negative ideas and images and tended not to think positively about the future.

It seems that a person's fantasies reflect, to some degree, other characteristics of that person's behavior. Such manifestations in fantasy, however, are not always apparent, nor do they seem to be particularly revealing of personality dynamics.

Continuity Between Dreams and Daydreams

The continuity hypothesis maintains that play, night dreams, and daydreams are the same type of activity and that they serve the same basic functions (Klinger, 1971). Some support for this hypothesis has been obtained by Singer and his colleagues. Singer (1966) observed that both daydreams and night dreams tend to occur when the individual is alone and with minimal stimulation from the external environment. Singer and Antrobus (1963, 1972) found that people's daydreams and night dreams tend to express similar themes; that is, people whose daydreams express enjoyable themes tend to have night dreams that express enjoyable themes, and people whose daydreams express negative themes tend to have night dreams that express negative themes.

One prediction of the continuity hypothesis is that a person deprived of night dreams should have more daydreams or other fantasy experiences during the subsequent day. Attempts to test this hypothesis have evaluated the effects of REM sleep deprivation. Dreams occur much more frequently during sleep periods in which there are rapid eye movements (REM) than during sleep periods in which there are no rapid eye movements (NREM) (Foulkes, 1962, 1966). Thus, one way to test the hypothesis that night dream deprivation increases fantasy experiences during the next day is to awaken people during REM sleep and then to evaluate the amount of daydreaming during the next day.

Studies that evaluated the effects of REM sleep deprivation on subsequent fantasy production have obtained inconsistent findings. Some studies have found that REM sleep deprivation increases daydreaming and other fantasy activities (Agnew, Webb, & Williams, 1967; Dement, 1960; Dement & Fisher, 1963; Sampson, 1966), whereas other studies have failed to find such effects (e.g., Kales, Hoedemaker, Jacobson, Wyatt, Kupfer, Scott, Robinson, & Snyder, 1964; Vogel, 1968). Thus, these studies fail to provide consistent support for the continuity hypothesis' prediction that deprivation in one type of fantasy (night dreams) causes an increase in other types of fantasy (daydreams).

FANTASY AND OVERT AGGRESSION

In this chapter two behaviors were discussed—aggression and fantasy—that are common among normal individuals but that also serve as distinguishing features of some types of abnormality when they are present to an excessive degree or under inappropriate circumstances. Before closing we should mention that these two behaviors are often related insofar as aggression is often expressed in fantasy. The question thus arises as to whether the expression of aggression in fantasy resembles an individual's overt behavior (the greater the fantasized expression of aggression, the more aggressive is the individual) or whether fantasy compensates for real-life aggression in a manner suggested by the notion of catharsis (the greater the fantasized expression of aggression, the less aggressive is the individual). As noted previously, the available data do not support the hypothesis of catharsis; instead they suggest that the greater the fantasized expression of aggression, the more likely is the individual to engage in overt aggression.

The relation of fantasy aggression to overt aggression suggests that projective techniques may be employed to predict aggressive behavior under a variety of conditions. For example, if a patient tells many violent stories in response to TAT type pictures, can the psychologist predict that the patient will engage in such behaviors in real life? Again, the weight of the evidence indicates that there is a positive relation between these fantasy productions and the needs, attitudes, and behavior of the narrator. In one study (Pittluck, 1950), however, it is suggested that it is not a simple matter of one-to-one translation from fantasy production to overt behavior. Pittluck found that there was a positive relation between the amount of aggressive behavior expressed overtly and in TAT stories, but that this relation was modified by the amount of anxiety associated with the fantasized expression of aggression. Pittluck used as her behavioral measure reports by attendants and nurses of the spontaneous aggressive behavior of patients in a psychiatric hospital ward and found that more aggressive responses on the TAT were associated with more aggressive behavior on the ward. However, the aggressive responses on the TAT had to be considered in relation to defensive mechanisms in the stories, such as rejection or denial of the aggression. By use of such mechanisms the aggressive response becomes a compromise between aggressive impulses and the anxiety opposing their expression. Pittluck found the tendency to use these mechanisms was negatively related to the tendency to be aggressive on the ward. However, patients who used more unmodified, primitive responses in fantasy tended to be more aggressive on the ward. She concluded, therefore, that aggressive fantasy can provide direct clues to overt aggressive behavior if the measures evaluate not the absolute frequency of aggressive content but the extent to which such content is free from defensive modification.

SUMMARY

Several theories of aggression were considered in this chapter. Psychoanalytic theory posits the existence of an innate aggressive drive, Thanatos, that must inevitably be expressed in one form or another. This view is associated with the hypothesis of catharsis; this hypothesis proposes that the greater the extent to which a person can release aggressive energy in fantasy, the less is the extent to which it is necessary for him to express aggression directly in real life. The available data do not support this hypothesis.

Ethologists have attempted to understand human aggression as a trait inherited from our animal ancestry. In this view (e.g., Lorenz, 1966) our evolution has resulted in the inheritance of aggression instincts but not in the inheritance of inhibitory mechanisms that tend to preclude aggression among like-species individuals. There is little evidence to support this theory of innate aggression.

Several biological hypotheses of aggressive behavior were reviewed. Claims that an XXY chromosomal pattern, called karyotype, causes aggression are supported by some evidence, but this karyotype pattern occurs too infrequently to provide an explanation for the overwhelming majority of instances of aggressive behavior. It has been consistently found that males are more aggressive than are females, and there is considerable evidence suggesting that male aggressiveness has a biological component associated with male sex hormones.

Dollard et al. (1939) proposed that (1) frustration is an innate elicitor of some types of aggression, and that (2) a necessary antecedent of all aggression is frustration. In this view frustration elicits a number of responses, only one of which is aggression. Whether frustration will actually lead to aggression depends in part on whether, in addition to some form of aggression, frustration also elicits a competing response sufficient to inhibit aggression. The factors theoretically specified as affecting the strength of instigation to aggression and the nature of the aggressive response were presented. The frustration-aggression hypothesis has led to a number of informative studies on aggression, and there is little doubt that aggression is a usual response to frustration. Nevertheless, the assumption that frustration is an *innate* and *necessary* elicitor of some form of aggression is largely unsupported.

In recent years social learning theories of aggression have gained increasing acceptance among psychologists; these theories reject the notion that aggression is an innate drive or an innate response to frustration and propose instead that aggressive behavior is learned. Buss (1961) proposed that aggression occurs primarily if it has instrumental value—that is, if the individual gets what he wants by an aggressive act. During the 1960s, Bandura and his colleagues made a substantial contribution in their systematic, empirical study of observational learning of aggressive behavior. This work has demonstrated that aggression is often learned through imitating models, and it has led to an identification of some of the variables that affect such learning.

One specific area of experimental investigation has concerned the effects of threat of retaliation on aggressive behavior. The aggression-anxiety hypothesis proposes that the effects of such threat depend in part on the extent to which the individual has learned to feel anxious or guilty over expressing aggression. Peterson (1971) found that threat of retaliation increased aggression in highly aggressive children who presumably are low in aggression anxiety and decreased aggression in children low in aggression who presumably are high in aggression anxiety.

Each of the various theories of aggression has become associated with social policies for controlling aggression and violence. The ethological view of instinctive aggression is associated with policies based on a constant fear of one's fellowman; the biological view that aggression is related to physical anomalies is associated with policies of massive screening to identify individuals predisposed toward violence and with policies of corrective treatment for those identified; social-learning theories are associated with policies designed to educate people to behave nonaggressively.

The results of the Eron et al. longitudinal study on childhood learning and aggression were presented in detail. Some of the major findings from this study are that (1) one of the best predictors of how aggressive a boy would be at ages 18 and 19 was the violence of the television programs he preferred at the age of eight; (2) variables measuring instigation to aggression, reinforcement of aggression, identification with parents, and social status were related to aggression at the age of eight; and (3) variables measuring identification and social status at the age of eight were related to aggression at ages 18 and 19, but variables measuring instigation to aggression and reinforcement of aggression at the age of eight were not related to aggression at ages 18 and 19.

One research topic that has received extensive study concerns possible differences in the fantasy productions of normal and disturbed persons. Studies employing projective techniques have proven of limited value in investigating such differences, and more recent investigators have focused on the study of dreams rather than on the study of fantasy productions elicited by the TAT or Rorschach. Some recent evidence suggests that bizarre fantasy is more confined to REM sleep in normals than in schizophrenics. Moreover, there is accumulating evidence that a person's fantasy reflects other characteristics of the person's behavior, even though such fantasy may not be particularly revealing of that person's personality dynamics.

References

1. The Classification of Abnormal Behavior Patterns

ALLPORT, G. W. *Personality: A psychological interpretation.* New York: Holt, Rinehart, and Winston, 1937.

American Psychiatric Association. *Diagnostic and statistical manual of mental disorders* (1st ed.). Washington, D.C.: American Psychiatric Association, 1952.

American Psychiatric Association. *Diagnostic and statistical manual of mental disorders* (2nd ed.). Washington, D.C.: American Psychiatric Association, 1968.

BAKER, R. P., & DREGER, R. M. The preschool behavioral classification project: An initial report. *Journal of Abnormal Child Psychology,* 1973, *1,* 88–120.

Committee on Child Psychiatry. *Psychopathological disorders in childhood: Theoretical considerations and a proposed classification.* Vol. 6 (Report 62). Group for the Advancement of Psychiatry, 1966.

CROCETTI, G. M., SPIRO, H. R., LEMKAU, P. V., & SIASSI, J. Multiple models and mental illness: A rejoinder to "Failure of a moral enterprise: Attitudes of the public toward mental illness" by T. R. Sarbin and J. C. Mancuso. *Journal of Consulting and Clinical Psychology,* 1972, *39,* 1–5.

CROWN, S. "On being sane in insane places": A comment from England. *Journal of Abnormal Psychology,* 1975, *84,* 453–455.

ERON, L. D. (Ed.) *The classification of behavior disorders.* Chicago: Aldine, 1966.

EYSENCK, H. J. Classification and the problem of diagnosis. In H. J. Eysenck (Ed.), *Handbook of abnormal psychology.* New York: Basic Books, 1961.

FARBER, I. E. Sane and insane: Constructions and misconstructions. *Journal of Abnormal Psychology,* 1975, *84,* 589–620.

FEINSTEIN, A. *Clinical judgment.* Baltimore: Williams & Wilkins, 1967.

FERSTER, C. B. Classification of behavioral pathology. In L. Krasner & L. P. Ullmann (Eds.), *Research in behavior modification.* New York: Holt, Rinehart, and Winston, 1967.

GARLAND, L. H. The problem of observer error. *Bulletin of the New York Academy of Medicine,* 1960, *36,* 570–584.

GLIDEWELL, J. C. The prevalence of maladjustment in elementary schools. Mimeographed report prepared for the Joint Commission on Mental Health of Children, December, 1967.

GROSSMAN, M. Insurance reports as a threat to confidentiality. *American Journal of Psychiatry,* 1971, *128,* 96–100.

HEBER, R. Manual on terminology and classification in mental retardation. *American Journal of Mental Deficiency* (Monograph supplement), 1961.

KANFER, F. H., & SASLOW, G. Behavioral diagnosis. In C. M. Franks (Ed.), *Behavior therapy: Appraisal and status.* New York: McGraw-Hill, 1969.

LANGER, E. J., & ABELSON, R. P. A patient by any other name . . . : Clinician group differences in labelling bias. *Journal of Consulting and Clinical Psychology,* 1974, *42,* 4–9.

MASLOW, A. Cognition of the particular and of the generic. *Psychological Review,* 1948, *55,* 22–40.

MENNINGER, K. The psychiatric diagnosis. *Bulletin of Menninger Clinic,* 1959, *23,* 226–239.

MILLON, T. *Modern psychopathology: A biosocial approach to maladaptive learning and functioning.* Philadelphia: W. B. Saunders, 1969.

MILLON, T. Reflections on Rosenhan's "On being sane in insane places." *Journal of Abnormal Psychology,* 1975, *84,* 456–461.

National Institute of Mental Health. *Information Publication No. 5027.* Washington, D.C.: U.S. Government Printing Office, 1970.

PETERSON, D. R. *The clinical study of social behavior.* New York: Meredith, 1968.

ROGERS, C. *Client-centered therapy.* Boston: Houghton Mifflin, 1951.

ROSENHAN, D. L. On being sane in insane places. *Science,* 1973, *180,* 365–369.

ROSENHAN, D. L. The contextual nature of psychiatric diagnosis. *Journal of Abnormal Psychology,* 1975, *84,* 462–474.

SHAW, C. R., & LUCAS, A. R. *The psychiatric disorders of childhood* (2nd ed.). New York: Appleton-Century-Crofts, 1970.

SPITZER, R. L. On pseudoscience in science, logic in remission, and psychiatric diagnosis: A critique of Rosenhan's "On being sane in insane places." *Journal of Abnormal Psychology,* 1975, *84,* 442–452.

SPITZER, R. L., & FLEISS, J. L. A reanalysis of the reliability of psychiatric diagnosis. *British Journal of Psychiatry,* 1974, *125,* 341–347.

SUINN, R. M. *Fundamentals of behavior pathology.* New York: John Wiley and Sons, 1970.

SUSHINSKY, L. W., & WENER, R. Distorting judgments of mental health. *Journal of Nervous and Mental Disease,* 1975, *161,* 82–89.

TEMERLIN, M. K. Suggestion effects in psychiatric diagnosis. *Journal of Nervous and Mental Disease,* 1968, *147,* 349–353.

ULLMANN, L. P., & KRASNER, L. (Eds.) *Case studies in behavior modification.* New York: Holt, Rinehart, and Winston, 1965.

ULLMANN, L. P., & KRASNER, L. *A psychological approach to abnormal behavior.* Englewood Cliffs, N.J.: Prentice-Hall, 1969.

WEINER, B. "On being sane in insane places": A process (attributional) analysis and critique. *Journal of Abnormal Psychology,* 1975, *84,* 433–441.

WOODRUFF, R. A., GOODWIN, D. W., & GUZE, S. B. *Psychiatric diagnosis.* New York: Oxford University, 1974.

World Health Organization. *International classification of diseases adapted for use in the United States* (8th ed.). Washington, D.C.: U.S. Government Printing Office, 1968. (Public Health Service Publication No. 1693.)

ZIGLER, E., & PHILLIPS, L. Psychiatric diagnosis: A critique. *Journal of Abnormal Psychology,* 1961, *63,* 607–618.

ZUBIN, J. Classification of behavior disorders. *Annual Review of Psychology,* 1967, *18,* 373–406.

ZUBIN, J., SALZINGER, K., FLEISS, J. L., GURLAND, B., SPITZER, R. L., ENDICOTT, J., & SUTTON, S. Biometric approach to psychopathology: Abnormal and clinical psychology—statistical, epidemiological, and diagnostic approaches. *Annual Review of Psychology,* 1975, *26,* 621–671.

2. Historical Perspectives and Legal Issues

ALEXANDER, F. G., & SELESNICK, S. T. *The history of psychiatry.* New York: Harper & Row, 1966.

BOCKOVEN, J. S. *Moral treatment in American psychiatry.* New York: Springer, 1963.

BORING, E. G. *A history of experimental psychology.* New York: Appleton-Century-Crofts, 1957.

BROOKS, A. D. *Law, psychiatry, and the mental health system.* Boston: Little, Brown, 1974.

DEWHURST, K. *Dr. Thomas Sydenham.* Berkeley: University of California Press, 1966.

ENNIS, B., & SIEGEL, L. *The rights of mental patients.* New York: Avon Books, 1973.

GALDSTON, I. (Ed.) *Historic derivations of modern psychiatry.* New York: McGraw-Hill, 1967.

HENDERSON, D. K., & GILLESPIE, R. D. *A textbook of psychiatry for students and practitioners.* London: Oxford University Press, 1946.

HUNTER, R., & MACALPINE, I. *The construction and government of lunatic asylums and hospitals for the insane by John Conolly, M.D.* London: Dawsons of Pall Mall, 1968.

LIVERMORE, J. M., MALMQUIST, C. P., & Meehl, P. E. On the justification for civil commitment. *University of Pennsylvania Law Review,* 1968, *117,* 75–96.

LIVERMORE, J. M., & MEEHL, P. E. The virtues of M'Naghten. *Minnesota Law Review,* 1967, *51,* 789–856.

MOWRER, O. H. Sin, the lesser of two evils. *American Psychologist,* 1960, *15,* 301–305.

MURPHY, G. *An historical introduction to modern psychology.* New York: Harcourt Brace Jovanovich, 1929.

RIESE, W. The neuropsychologic phase in the history of psychiatric thought. In I. Galdston (Ed.), *Historic derivations of modern psychiatry.* New York: McGraw-Hill, 1967.

ROSEN, G. *Madness in society.* Chicago: University of Chicago Press, 1968.

SCHNECK, J. M. *A history of psychiatry.* Springfield, Ill.: Charles C. Thomas, 1960.

SCHNEIDER, J. Civil commitment of the mentally ill. *American Bar Association Journal,* 1972, *58,* 1059–1063.

SELLING, L. S. *Men against madness.* New York: Garden City Books, 1943.

SZASZ, T. S. *The myth of mental illness.* New York: Harper & Row, 1961.

SZASZ, T. S. *The manufacture of madness.* New York: Harper & Row, 1970.

VEITH, I. Psychiatric nosology: From Hippocrates to Kraepelin. *American Journal of Psychiatry,* 1957, *114,* 385–391.

WATSON, J. B. Psychology as the behaviorist views it. *Psychological Review,* 1913, *20,* 158–177.

3. The Concept of Abnormality

AYER, A. J. *The problem of knowledge.* Baltimore: Penguin Books, 1959.

ADAMS, H. D. Mental illness or interpersonal behavior. *American Psychologist,* 1964, *19,* 191–197.

AUSUBEL, D. L. Personality disorder is disease. *American Psychologist,* 1961, *16,* 69–74.

COLEMAN, J. C. *Abnormal psychology and modern life.* Glenview, Ill.: Scott, Foresman, 1972.

ELLIS, A. *Reason and emotion in psychotherapy.* New York: Lyle Stuart, 1962.

ELLIS, A. Should some people be labelled mentally ill? *Journal of Consulting Psychology,* 1967, *31,* 435–446.

GERT, B. *The moral rules: A rational foundation for morality.* New York: Harper & Row, 1970.

LONDON, P., & ROSENHAN, D. The meaning of abnormality. In P. London & D. Rosenhan (Eds.), *Foundations of abnormal psychology.* New York: Holt, Rinehart, and Winston, 1968.

MOWRER, O. H. Sin, the lesser of two evils. *American Psychologist,* 1960, *15,* 301–305.

REDLICH, F. C. The concept of normality. *American Journal of Psychotherapy,* 1952, *7,* 551–576.

REISS, S. A critique of Thomas S. Szasz' "myth of mental illness." *American Journal of Psychiatry,* 1972, *128,* 1081–1085.

SARASON, S. B. *The psychological sense of community: Prospects for a community psychology.* San Francisco: Jossey-Bass, 1974.

SZASZ, T. S. *The myth of mental illness.* New York: Harper & Row, 1961.

SZASZ, T. S. *The manufacture of madness.* New York: Harper & Row, 1970.

ULLMANN, L. P., & KRASNER, L. *A psychological approach to abnormal behavior.* Englewood Cliffs, N.J.: Prentice-Hall, 1969.

WEGROCKI, H. G. A critique of statistical and cultural concepts of abnormality. *Journal of Abnormal and Social Psychology,* 1939, *34,* 166–178.

WERRY, J. S. Psychotherapy—a medical procedure? *Canadian Psychiatric Association Journal,* 1965, *10,* 278–281.

WHITE, R. W. *The abnormal personality.* New York: Ronald Press, 1964.

WITTGENSTEIN, L. *Philosophical investigations.* New York: Macmillan, 1953.

4. Psychological Assessment

ADAMS, J. The contribution of the psychological evaluation to psychiatric diagnosis. *Journal of Personality Assessment,* 1972, *36,* 561–566.

ALLPORT, G. W. The trend in motivational theory. In B. I. Murstein (Ed.), *Handbook of projective techniques.* New York: Basic Books, 1965.

ANASTASI, A. *Psychological testing* (4th ed.). New York: Macmillan, 1976.

BENDER, L. *A visual motor gestalt test and its clinical use.* New York: American Orthopsychiatric Association, 1938.

BENJAMIN, A. *The helping interview.* Boston: Houghton Mifflin, 1969.

BINET, A., & SIMON, T. Méthodes nouvelles pour le diagnostic du niveau intellectuel des anormaux. *L'Année Psychologique,* 1905, *11,* 191–244.

BUROS, O. K. *The seventh mental measurement yearbook.* Highland Park, N.J.: Gryphon, 1972.

CRENSHAW, D. A., BOHN, S., HOFFMAN, M. R., MATHEUS, J. M., & OFFENBACH, S. G. The use of projective methods in research: 1947–1965. *Journal of Projective Techniques and Personality Assessment,* 1968, *32,* 3–9.

DAHLSTROM, W. G., WELSH, G. S., & DALSTROM, L. E. *An MMPI handbook: Clinical interpretation* (Vol. 1, rev. ed.). Minneapolis: University of Minnesota Press, 1972.

DANA, R. H. A review of the TAT. In O. K. Buros (Ed.), *The seventh mental measurement yearbook.* Vol. 1. Highland Park, N.J.: Gryphon, 1972, 457–460.

DOLE, A. A. The vocational sentence completion blank in counseling. *Journal of Counseling Psychology,* 1958, *5,* 200–205.

EICHMAN, W. J. A review of the Minnesota Multiphasic Personality Inventory computerized scoring and interpreting services. In O. K. Buros (Ed.), *The seventh mental measurement yearbook.* Vol. 1. Highland Park, N.J.: Gryphon, 1972, 250–253.

ERON, L. D. A review of the TAT. In O. K. Buros (Ed.), *The seventh mental measurement yearbook.* Vol. 1. Highland Park, N.J.: Gryphon, 1972, 460–462.

ERON, L. D., & CHERTKOFF, S. O. Psychological tests in clinical practice. In L. E. Abt & B. F. Reiss (Eds.), *Progress in clinical psychology.* Vol. 7. New York: Grune and Stratton, 1966.

FORER, B. R. A structured sentence completion test. *Journal of Projective Techniques,* 1950, *14,* 15–29.

GARFIELD, S. L., & KURTZ, R. M. Attitudes toward training in diagnostic testing: A survey of directors of internship training. *Journal of Consulting and Clinical Psychology,* 1973, *40,* 350–355.

GILBERSTADT, H., & DUKER, J. *A handbook for clinical and actuarial MMPI interpretation.* Philadelphia: W. B. Saunders, 1965.

GOLDBERG, P. A. A review of sentence completion methods in personality assessment. In B. I. Murstein (Ed.), *Handbook of projective techniques.* New York: Basic Books, 1965, 788–821.

GOLDE, P., & KOGAN, N. A sentence completion procedure for assessing attitudes toward old people. *Journal of Gerontology,* 1959, *14,* 355–360.

HARRIS, D. B. A review of the draw-a-person. In O. K. Buros (Ed.), *The seventh mental measurement yearbook.* Vol. 1. Highland Park, N.J.: Gryphon, 1972. 401–404.

KITAY, P. M. A review of the Bender Gestalt. In O. K. Buros (Ed.), *The seventh mental measurement yearbook.* Vol. 1. Highland Park, N.J.: Gryphon, 1972. 394–395.

KLEINMUNTZ, B., & ALEXANDER, L. B. Computer program for the Meehl-Dahlstrom MMPI profile roles. *Educational and Psychological Measurement,* 1962, *22,* 193–199.

LONEY, J. Clinical aspects of the Loney draw-a-car test: Enuresis and encopresis. *Journal of Personality Assessment,* 1971, *35,* 265–274.

LYMAN, H. B. A review of the WAIS. In O. K. Buros (Ed.), *The seventh mental measurement yearbook.* Vol. 1. Highland Park, N.J.: Gryphon, 1972, 788–790.

MACHOVER, K. *Personality projection in the drawing of the human figure.* Springfield, Ill.: Charles C. Thomas, 1949.

MARKS, P. A., & SEEMAN, W. *The actuarial description of personality: An atlas for use with the MMPI.* Baltimore: Williams & Wilkins, 1963.

MATARAZZO, J. D. Wechsler's measurement and appraisal of adult intelligence. Baltimore: Williams & Wilkins, 1972.

MCCLELLAND, D. C. Testing for competence rather than for "intelligence." *American Psychologist,* 1973, *28,* 1–14.

MEEHL, P. E. Why I don't go to case conferences. In P. E. Meehl (Ed.), *Psychodiagnosis: Selected papers.* Minneapolis: University of Minnesota Press, 1973.

MURRAY, H. A. *Manual for the thematic apperception test.* Cambridge, Mass.: Harvard University Press, 1943.

MURRAY, H. A. Uses of the thematic apperception test. In B. I. Murstein (Ed.), *Handbook of projective techniques.* New York: Basic Books, 1965, 425–432.

MURSTEIN, B. I. (Ed.) *Handbook of projective techniques.* New York: Basic Books, 1965.

RAPAPORT, D., GILL, M. M., & SCHAFER, R. *Diagnostic psychological testing.* New York: International Universities Press, 1968.

RORSCHACH, H. *Psychodiagnostics.* New York: Grune and Stratton, 1921.

ROTTER, J. B., & RAFFERTY, J. E. *The Rotter Incomplete Sentences Blank, College Form: Manual.* New York: The Psychological Corporation, 1950.

ROTTER, J. B., & WILLERMAN, B. The incomplete sentences test as a method of studying personality. *Journal of Consulting Psychology,* 1947, *11,* 43–48.

SCHULBERG, H. C., & TOLOR, A. The use of the Bender–Gestalt in clinical practice. *Journal of Projective Techniques,* 1961, *25,* 347–351.

STOTSKY, B. A., & LAWRENCE, J. F. Various Rorschach indices as discriminators of marked and little conceptual disorganization among schizophrenics. *Journal of Consulting Psychology,* 1955, *19,* 189–193.

SULLIVAN, H. S. *The psychiatric interview.* New York: W. W. Norton, 1954.

TENDLER, A. D. A preliminary report on a test for emotional insight. *Journal of Applied Psychology,* 1930, *14,* 123–136.

TERMAN, L. M. *The measurement of intelligence.* Boston: Houghton Mifflin, 1916.

TERMAN, L. M., & MERRILL, M. A. *Measuring intelligence.* Boston: Houghton Mifflin, 1937.

TERMAN, L. M., & MERRILL, M. A. *Stanford–Binet Intelligence Scale.* Boston: Houghton Mifflin, 1960.

WECHSLER, D. *WAIS manual: Wechsler Adult Intelligence Scale.* New York: The Psychological Corporation, 1955.

WECHSLER, D. *Manual for the Wechsler Intelligence Scale for Children.* New York: The Psychological Corporation, 1974.

ZUBIN, J., ERON, L. D., & SCHUMER, F. *An experimental*

approach to projective techniques. New York: John Wiley and Sons, 1965.

5. The Biological Approach

BERRY, H. K. Phenylketonuria: Diagnosis, treatment, and long–term management. In G. Farrell (Ed.), *Congenital mental retardation.* Austin: University of Texas Press, 1969.

BOWDEN, C. L., & MADDUX, J. F. Methadone maintenance: Myth and reality. *American Journal of Psychiatry,* 1972, *129,* 435–439.

CALDWELL, A. E. *Origins of psychopharmacology: From CPZ to LSD.* Springfield, Ill.: Charles C. Thomas, 1970.

CAMPBELL, D. The psychological effects of cerebral electroshock. In H. J. Eysenck (Ed.), *Handbook of abnormal psychology.* New York: Basic Books, 1961.

DEUTSCH, J. A., & DEUTSCH, D. *Physiological psychology.* Homewood, Ill.: Dorsey, 1973.

DOLE, V. P., & NYSWANDER, M. A medical treatment for diacetylmorphine (heroin) addiction. *Journal of the American Medical Association,* 1965, *193,* 646–650.

EYSENCK, H. J. (Ed.) *Handbook of abnormal psychology.* New York: Basic Books, 1961.

FRIEDMAN, S., MOORE, B. E., RANGER, C. O., & RUSSMAN, C. A progress study of lobotomized and control patients. *American Journal of Psychiatry,* 1951, *108,* 10–18.

GLASER, G. H. (Ed.) *EEG and behavior.* New York: Basic Books, 1963.

GOODMAN, L. S., & GILLMAN, A. *The pharmacological basis of therapeutics.* New York: Macmillan, 1975.

HEBB, D. O. *A textbook of psychology.* Philadelphia: W. B. Saunders, 1966.

HIMWICH, H. E., KETY, S. S., & SMYTHIES, J. R. (Eds.) *Amines and schizophrenia.* Elmsford, N.Y.: Pergamon, 1967.

KALINOWSKY, L. B., & HIPPIUS, H. *Pharmacological, convulsive, and other somatic treatments in psychiatry.* New York: Grune and Stratton, 1969.

KARDENER, S. H. EST and the M.D. *Diseases of the Nervous System,* 1970, *31,* 110–115.

KNOX, E. W. An evaluation of the treatment of phenylketonuria with diets low in phenylanine. *Pediatrics,* 1960, *26,* 1–11.

KRIEGER, I. The energy metabolism in infants with growth failure due to maternal deprivation, undernutrition, or causes unknown. *Pediatrics,* 1966, *38,* 63–76.

LEHNINGER, A. L. *Bioenergetics.* New York: W. A. Benjamin, 1965.

LENNARD, H. L., EPSTEIN, L. J., & ROSENTHAL, M. S. The methadone illusion. *Science,* 1972, *176,* 881–884.

LEWIS, D. J., & MAHER, B. A. Electroconvulsive shock and inhibition: Some problems considered. *Psychological Review,* 1966, *73,* 388–392.

LILIENFELD, A. M. *Epidemiology of mongolism.* Baltimore: Johns Hopkins Press, 1969.

LYNN, E. L., & RACY, J. The resolution of pathological grief after electroconvulsive therapy. *Journal of Nervous and Mental Disease,* 1969, *148,* 165–169.

MARKS, J., & PARE, C. M. B. (Eds.) *The scientific basis of drug therapy in psychiatry.* Elmsford, N.Y.: Pergamon, 1965.

MCNAIR, D. M., KAHN, J., DROPPLEMAN, L. F., & FISHER, S. Patient acquiescence and drug effects. In K. Rickels (Ed.), *Non-specific factors in drug therapy.* Springfield, Ill.: Charles C. Thomas, 1968.

PATTERSON, A. S. *Electrical and drug treatments in psychiatry.* New York: Am. Elsevier, 1963.

RAY, O. S. *Drugs, society, and human behavior.* St. Louis: C. V. Mosby, 1972.

SALZMAN, I. An evaluation of shock therapy. *American Journal of Psychiatry,* 1947, *103,* 669–679.

SARGANT, W., & SLATER, E. *Physical method of treatment in psychiatry.* Baltimore: Williams & Wilkins, 1963.

SHAGASS, C. *Evoked brain potentials in psychiatry.* New York: Plenum, 1972.

SZASZ, T. S. *The manufacture of madness.* New York: Harper & Row, 1970.

TROUTON, D., & EYSENCK, H. J. The effects of drugs on behavior. In H. J. Eysenck (Ed.), *Handbook of abnormal psychology.* New York: Basic Books, 1961.

VANDERNBERG, S. G. Contributions of twin research to psychology. *Psychological Bulletin,* 1966, *66,* 327–352.

WARREN, N. Malnutrition and mental development. *Psychological Bulletin,* 1973, *80,* 324–328.

WEPPNER, R. S., STEPHENS, R. C., & CONRAD, H. T. Methadone: Some aspects of its legal and illegal use. *American Journal of Psychiatry,* 1972, *129,* 451–455.

WILLETT, R. A. The effects of psychosurgical procedures on behavior. In H. J. Eysenck (Ed.), *Handbook of abnormal psychology.* New York: Basic Books, 1961.

WILLIAMS, H. R. Low and high methadone maintenance: Treatment of hard core heroin addicts. In S. Einstein (Ed.), *Methadone maintenance.* New York: Marcel, Dekker, 1971.

6. The Psychoanalytic Approach

ADLER, A. *The practice and theory of individual psychology.* New York: Harcourt Brace Jovanovich, 1927.

BERGIN, A. E. Further comments on psychotherapy research and therapeutic practice. *International Journal of Psychiatry,* 1967, *3,* 317–323.

BERGIN, A. E. The evaluation of therapeutic outcomes. In A. E. Bergin & S. L. Garfield (Eds.), *Handbook of psychotherapy and behavior change.* New York: John Wiley and Sons, 1971.

BRENNER, C. *An elementary textbook of psychoanalysis.* New York: International Universities Press, 1955.

CAMERON, N. *Personality development and psychopathology.* Boston: Houghton Mifflin, 1963.

CARTER, R. B. *On the pathology and treatment of hysteria.* London: John Churchill, 1853.

COLBY, K. M. *A primer for psychotherapists.* New York: Ronald Press, 1951.

DREIKURS, R. *Fundamentals of Adlerian psychology.* Chicago: Alfred Adler Institute, 1953.

ERICKSON, E. H. *Childhood and society.* New York: W. W. Norton, 1950.

EYSENCK, H. J. The effects of psychotherapy: An evaluation. *Journal of Consulting Psychology,* 1952, *16,* 319–324.

FENICHEL, O. *The psychoanalytic theory of neurosis.* New York: W. W. Norton, 1945.

FINE, R. *The development of Freud's thought.* New York: Jason Aronson, 1973.

Ford, D. H., & Urban, H. B. *Systems of psychotherapy.* New York: John Wiley and Sons, 1963.
Freud, A. *The psychoanalytic treatment of children.* New York: International Universities Press, 1946.
Freud, S. *A general introduction to psychoanalysis.* New York: Washington Square Press, 1924.
Freud, S. *New introductory lectures on psychoanalysis.* New York: W. W. Norton, 1933.
Grinker, R. R. A philosophical appraisal of psychoanalysis. In J. H. Masserman (Ed.), *Science and psychoanalysis.* New York: Grune and Stratton, 1958.
Hartmann, H. (1939) *Ego psychology and the problem of adaptation.* New York: International Universities Press, 1948.
Hartmann, H., Kris, E., & Loewenstein, R. M. Comments on the formation of psychic structure. *Psychoanalytic Study of the Child,* 1946, *2,* 11–38.
Horney, K. *The neurotic personality of our time.* New York: W. W. Norton, 1937.
Jones, E. Mother-right and the sexual ignorances of savages. *International Journal of Psychoanalysis,* 1925, *6,* 108–130.
Jung, C. G. *Psychology of the unconscious.* New York: Dodd, Mead, 1952.
Kardiner, A. *The individual and his society: The psychodynamics of primitive social organization.* New York: Columbia University Press, 1939.
Lazarus, A. A. *Behavior therapy and beyond.* New York: McGraw-Hill, 1971.
Lion, J. R., & Pasternak, S. A. Countertransference reactions to violent patients. *American Journal of Psychiatry,* 1973, *130,* 207–210.
Luborsky, L., & Spence, D. Quantitative research on psychoanalytic therapy. In A. E. Bergin & S. L. Garfield (Eds.), *Handbook of psychotherapy and behavior changes.* New York: John Wiley and Sons, 1971.
Malinowski, B. *Sex and repression in savage society.* London: Humanities Press, 1927.
Martin, D. G. *Introduction to psychotherapy.* Belmont, Calif.: Brooks/Cole, 1971.
Meltzoff, J., & Kornreich, M. *Research in psychotherapy.* New York: Atherton, 1970.
Monroe, R. L. *Schools of psychoanalytic thought.* New York: Dryden, 1955.
Rogers, L. S. An adult neurotic. In A. Burton & R. Harris (Eds.), *Clinical studies of personality.* New York: Harper & Row, 1955.
Salzman, L. Feminine psychology revisited, circa 1970. *American Journal of Psychoanalysis,* 1971, *31,* 121–133.
Stoller, R. J. Overview: The impact of new advances in sex research on psychoanalytic theory. *American Journal of Psychiatry,* 1973, *130,* 241–259.
Storr, A. *C. G. Jung.* New York: Viking, 1973.
Sullivan, H. S. *The interpersonal theory of psychiatry.* New York: W. W. Norton, 1953.
Sullivan, H. S. *The psychiatric interview.* New York: W. W. Norton, 1954.
Veith, I. *Hysteria: The history of a disease.* Chicago: University of Chicago Press, 1965.
White, R. W. *The abnormal personality.* New York: Ronald Press, 1964.
Whiting, J. M., & Child, I. L. (1953) *Child training and personality.* New Haven, Conn.: Yale University Press, 1966.

7. Social Learning Theory

Adams, J. Change on 16 fear factors during psychiatric hospitalization. *Journal of Behavior Therapy and Experimental Psychiatry,* 1972, *3,* 91–95.
Allport, G. W. Effect: A secondary principle of learning. *Psychological Review,* 1946, *53,* 335–347.
Altman, K. Effects of cooperative response acquisition of social behavior during free play. *Journal of Experimental Child Psychology,* 1971, *12,* 387–395.
Ascher, L. M., & Cautela, J. R. Covert negative reinforcement: An experimental test. *Journal of Behavior Therapy and Experimental Psychiatry,* 1972, *3,* 1–5.
Ayllon, T. Intensive treatment of psychotic behavior by stimulus satiation and food reinforcement. *Behavior Research and Therapy,* 1963, *1,* 53–61.
Ayllon, T., & Azrin, N. *The token economy: A motivational system for therapy and rehabilitation.* New York: Appleton-Century-Crofts, 1968.
Azrin, N. H., & Lindsley, O. R. The reinforcement of cooperation between children. *Journal of Abnormal and Social Psychology,* 1956, *52,* 100–102.
Azrin, N. H., & Nunn, R. G. Habit-reversal: A method of eliminating nervous habits and tics. *Behavior Research and Therapy,* 1973, *2,* 619–628.
Bandura, A. *Principles of behavior modification.* New York: Holt, Rinehart, and Winston, 1969.
Bandura, A., Blanchard, E. B., & Ritter, B. The relative efficacy of desensitization and modeling approaches for inducing behavioral, affective, and attitudinal changes. Unpublished manuscript, Stanford University, 1968.
Bandura, A., Grusec, J. E., & Menlove, F. L. Some social determinants of self-monitoring reinforcing systems. *Journal of Personality and Social Psychology,* 1967, *5,* 449–455.
Bandura, A., & Menlove, F. L. Factors determining vicarious extinction of avoidance behavior through symbolic modeling. *Journal of Personality and Social Psychology,* 1968, *8,* 99–108.
Bandura, A., & Walters, R. H. *Social learning and personality development.* New York: Holt, Rinehart, and Winston, 1963.
Banuazizi, A. Modification of an autonomic response by instrumental learning. Paper presented at the eighth annual meeting of the Psychonomic Society, Chicago, October, 1967.
Barber, T. X. An empirically-based formulation of hypnotism. *American Journal of Clinical Hypnosis,* 1969, *12,* 100–130.
Barlow, D. H., Reynolds, E. J., & Agras, W. S. Gender identity change in a transsexual. *Archives of General Psychiatry,* 1973, *28,* 569–576.
Barton, E. S., Guess, D., Garcia, E., & Baer, D. M. Improvement of retardates' mealtime behaviors by timeout procedures using multiple baseline techniques. *Journal of Applied Behavior Analysis,* 1970, *3,* 77–84.
Bernstein, D. A. Modification of smoking behavior: An evaluative review. *Psychological Bulletin,* 1969, *71,* 418–440.

BERNSTEIN, D. A., & BEATY, W. E. The use of *in vivo* desensitization as part of a total therapeutic intervention. *Journal of Behavior Therapy and Experimental Psychiatry,* 1971, *2,* 259–265.

BERNSTEIN, D. A., & PAUL, G. L. Some comments on therapy analogue research with small animal "phobias." *Journal of Behavior Therapy and Experimental Psychiatry,* 1971, *2,* 225–237.

BIJOU, S. W., & BAER, D. M. *Child development I. A systematic and empirical theory.* New York: Appleton-Century-Crofts, 1961.

BIJOU, S. W., & REDD, W. H. Child behavior therapy. In *The American handbook of psychiatry.* New York: Basic Books, 1974.

BLACK, A. H. The direct control of neural processes by reward and punishment. *American Scientist,* 1973, *59,* 236–245.

BLANCHARD, E. B., & YOUNG, L. D. Clinical applications of biofeedback training. *Archives of General Psychiatry,* 1974, *30,* 573–589.

BLEECKER, E. R., & ENGEL, B. T. Learned control of ventricular rate in patients with atrial fibrillation. *Psychosomatic Medicine,* 1973, *35,* 161–175.

BOOTZIN, R. B. *Behavior modification and therapy: An introduction.* Cambridge, Mass.: Winthrop Publishers, 1975.

BOSTOW, D. E., & BAILEY, J. Modification of severe disruptive and severe aggressive behavior using brief timeout and reinforcement procedures. *Journal of Applied Behavior Analysis,* 1969, *4,* 201–214.

BREGER, L., & MCGAUGH, J. L. Critique and reformulation of "learning-theory" approaches to psychotherapy and neurosis. *Psychological Bulletin,* 1965, *63,* 338–358.

BUDZYNSKI, T., STOYVA, J., ADLER, C., & MULLANEY, D. EMG biofeedback and tension headache: A controlled outcome study. *Psychosomatic Medicine,* 1973, *35,* 484–496.

CALLAHAN, E. J., & LEITENBERG, H. Aversion therapy for sexual deviation: Contingent shock and covert desensitization. *Journal of Abnormal Psychology,* 1973, *81,* 60–73.

CAUTELA, J. R. Treatment of compulsive behavior by covert sensitization. *Psychological Record,* 1966, *16,* 33–41.

CAUTELA, J. R., & KASTENBAUM, R. A. A reinforcement survey schedule for use in therapy, training and research. *Psychological Reports,* 1967, *20,* 239–240.

CAUTELA, J. R., KASTENBAUM, R. A., & WINCZE, J. P. The use of the fear survey schedule and the reinforcement survey schedule to survey possible reinforcing and aversive stimuli among juvenile offenders. *Journal of Genetic Psychology,* 1972, *121,* 255–261.

CHURCH, R. M. The varied effects of punishment on behavior. *Psychological Review,* 1963, *70,* 369–402.

COLEMAN, J. C. *Abnormal psychology and modern life.* Glenview, Ill.: Scott, Foresman, 1972.

COREY, J. R., & SHAMOW, J. The effects of fading on the acquisition and retention of oral reading. *Journal of Applied Behavior Analysis,* 1972, *5,* 311–315.

CORTE, H. E., WOLF, M. M., & LOCKE, B. J. A comparison of procedures for eliminating self-injurious behavior of retarded adolescents. *Journal of Applied Behavior Analysis,* 1971, *4,* 201–213.

COSSAIRT, A., HALL, R. V., & HOPKINS, B. L. The effects of experimenter's instructions, feedback, and praise on teacher praise and student attending behavior. *Journal of Applied Behavior Analysis,* 1973, *6,* 89–100.

DAVISON, G. C., & NEALE, J. M. *Abnormal psychology: An experimental clinical approach.* New York: John Wiley and Sons, 1974.

DICARA, L. Learning in the autonomic nervous system. *Scientific American,* 1970, *222,* 30–39.

DOLLARD, J., & MILLER, N. E. *Personality and psychotherapy.* New York: McGraw-Hill, 1950.

DRABMAN, R. S., SPITALNIK, R., & O'LEARY, K. D. Teaching self-control to disruptive children. *Journal of Abnormal Psychology,* 1973, *82,* 10–16.

EISLER, R. M., HERSEN, M., & MILLER, P. M. Effects of modeling on components of assertive behavior. *Journal of Behavior Therapy and Experimental Psychiatry,* 1973, *4,* 1–6.

ELLIS, A. *Reason and emotion in psychotherapy.* New York: Lyle Stuart, 1962.

ENGEL, B. T., & MELMON, K. L. Operant conditioning of heart rate in patients with cardiac arrythmias. *Conditioned Reflex,* 1968, *3,* 130.

EYSENCK, H. J. The effects of psychotherapy: An evaluation. *Journal of Consulting Psychology,* 1952, *16,* 319–324.

EYSENCK, H. J. Psychiatric diagnosis as a psychological and statistical problem. *Psychological Reports,* 1955, *1,* 3–17.

EYSENCK, H. J. Classification and the problem of diagnosis. In H. J. Eysenck (Ed.), *Handbook of abnormal psychology.* New York: Basic Books, 1961.

EYSENCK, H. J. A note on the alleged nonexistence of individual differences in reminiscence. *Psychological Bulletin,* 1973, *80,* 243–244.

FERSTER, C. B. Positive reinforcement and behavioral deficits of young children. *Child Development,* 1961, *32,* 437–456.

FERSTER, C. B., & DEMYER, M. K. A method for the experimental analysis of the behavior of autistic children. *The American Journal of Orthopsychiatry,* 1962, *32,* 89–98.

FERSTER, C. B., & SKINNER, B. F. *Schedules of reinforcement.* New York: Appleton-Century-Crofts, 1957.

FOXX, R. M., & AZRIN, N. H. Restitution: A method of eliminating aggressive disruptive behavior of retarded and brain damaged patients. *Behavior Research and Therapy,* 1972, *10,* 15–27.

FOXX, R. M., & AZRIN, N. H. Dry pants: A rapid method of toilet training children. *Behavior Research and Therapy,* 1973, *11,* 435–442.

GOLDIAMOND, I. The maintenance of ongoing fluent verbal behavior and stuttering. *Journal of Mathematics,* 1962, *1,* 57–95.

GOLDIAMOND, I. Stuttering and fluency as manipulatable operant response classes. In L. Krasner & L. P. Ullmann (Eds.), *Research in behavior modification.* New York: Holt, Rinehart, and Winston, 1965.

GOLDSTEIN, A. P., MARTENS, J., HUBBEN, J., VAN BELLE, H. A., SCHAAF, W., WIERSMA, H., & GOEDHART, A. The use of modeling to increase independent behavior. *Behavior Research and Therapy,* 1973, *11,* 31–42.

HALL, R. V., LUND, D., & JACKSON, D. Effects of teacher

attention on study behavior. *Journal of Applied Behavior Analysis,* 1968, *1,* 1–12.

HOMME, L., CSANYI, A. P., GONZALES, M. A., & RECHS, J. R. *How to use contingency contracting in the classroom.* Champaign, Ill.: Research Press, 1969.

HORTON, L. E. Generalization of aggressive behavior in adolescent delinquent boys. *Journal of Applied Behavior Analysis,* 1972, *5,* 233–246.

JACOBSON, E. *Progressive relaxation.* Chicago: University of Chicago Press, 1938.

JAFFE, P. G., & CARLSON, P. M. Modelling therapy for test anxiety: The role of model affect and consequences. *Behavior Research and Therapy,* 1972, *10,* 329–339.

JONES, M. C. A laboratory study of fear: The case of Peter. *Pedagogical Seminary,* 1924, *31,* 308–315.

KANFER, F. H., & MARSTON, A. R. Human reinforcement: Vicarious and direct. *Journal of Experimental Psychology,* 1963, *65,* 292–296.

KANFER, F. H., & PHILLIPS, J. S. *Learning foundations of behavior therapy.* New York: John Wiley and Sons, 1970.

KAZDIN, A. E. Response cost: The removal of conditioned reinforcers for therapeutic change. *Behavior Therapy,* 1972, *3,* 533–546.

KAZDIN, A. E., & BOOTZIN, R. The token economy: An evaluative review. *Journal of Applied Behavior Analysis,* 1972, *5,* 343–372.

KIMMEL, H. D., & HILL, F. A. Operant conditioning of the GSR. *Psychological Reports,* 1960, *7,* 555–562.

LADER, M., & MATHEWS, A. A physiological model of phobic anxiety and desensitization. *Behavior Research and Therapy,* 1968, *6,* 411–421.

LANG, P. J., & LAZOUIK, A. D. Experimental desensitization of a phobia. *Journal of Abnormal and Social Psychology,* 1963, *66,* 519–529.

LAZARUS, A. A. In support of technical eclecticism. *Psychological Reports,* 1967, *21,* 415–416.

LAZARUS, A. A. *Behavior therapy and beyond.* New York: McGraw-Hill, 1971.

LAZARUS, A. A. "Hypnosis" as a facilitator in behavior therapy. *International Journal of Clinical and Experimental Hypnosis,* 1973, *21,* 25–31.

LAZARUS, A. A., & RACHMAN, S. The use of systematic desensitization in psychotherapy. In H. J. Eysenck (Ed.), *Behavior therapy and the neuroses.* Elmsford, N.Y.: Pergamon, 1960.

LEVIS, D. J. Implosive therapy: A critical analysis of Morganstern's review. *Psychological Bulletin,* 1974, *81,* 155–158.

LICHTENSTEIN, E., HARRIS, D. E., BIRCHLER, G. R., WAHL, J. M., & SCHMAHL, D. P. Comparison of rapid smoking, warm smoky air, and attention placebo in the modification of smoking behavior. *Journal of Consulting and Clinical Psychology,* 1973, *40,* 92–98.

LISINA, M. I. The role of orientation in the transformation of involuntary into voluntary reactions. In A. V. Zaporozhets (Ed.), *The development of voluntary movements.* Moscow: 1960.

LONDON, P. The end of ideology in behavior modification. *American Psychologist,* 1972, *27,* 913–920.

LOPICCOLO, J., STEWART, R., & WATKINS, B. Case study: Treatment of erectile failure and ejaculatory incompetence with homosexual etiology. *Journal of Behavior Therapy and Experimental Psychiatry,* 1972, *3,* 233–236.

LOVAAS, O. I., BERBERICH, J. P., PERLOFF, B. F., & SCHAEFFER, B. Acquisition of imitative speech by schizophrenic children. *Science,* 1966, *151,* 705–707.

LOVAAS, O. I., KOEGEL, R., SIMMONS, J. Q., & LONG, J. S. Some generalization and follow-up measures on autistic children in behavior therapy. *Journal of Applied Behavior Analysis,* 1973, *6,* 131–164.

LOVITT, T. C., & ESVELDT, K. A. The relative effects on math performance of single- versus multiple-ration schedules: A case study. *Journal of Applied Behavior Analysis,* 1970, *3,* 261–270.

MANN, R. A. The behavior-therapeutic use of contingency contracting to control an adult behavior problem: Weight control. *Journal of Applied Behavior Analysis,* 1972, *5,* 99–109.

MANNO, B., & MARSTON, A. R. Weight reduction as a function of negative covert reinforcement (sensitization) versus positive covert reinforcement. *Behavior Research and Therapy,* 1972, *10,* 201–207.

MCREYNOLDS, W. T., & COLEMAN, J. Token economy: Patient and staff changes. *Behavior Research and Therapy,* 1972, *10,* 29–34.

MEICHENBAUM, D. H. Cognitive modification of test anxious college students. *Journal of Consulting and Clinical Psychology,* 1972, *39,* 370–380.

METTEE, D. R. Rejection of unexpected success as a function of the negative consequences of accepting success. *Journal of Personality and Social Psychology,* 1971, *17,* 332–341.

MILLER, N. E., & DICARA, L. Instrumental learning of heart rate changes in curarized rats: Shaping and specificity to discriminative stimuli. *Journal of Comparative and Physiological Psychology,* 1967, *63,* 12.

MILLER, S., & KONORSKI, J. On a particular type of conditioned reflex. *Proceedings of the Biological Society,* 1928, *99,* 1155–1157.

MORGANSTERN, K. P. Implosive therapy and flooding procedures: A critical review. *Psychological Bulletin,* 1973, *79,* 318–334.

MOWRER, O. H. A stimulus-response analysis of anxiety and its role as a reinforcing agent. *Psychological Review,* 1939, *46,* 553–565.

MUSICO, M. Lower reinforcement and superior performance in two retarded children with impoverished self-esteem. Unpublished manuscript, Smith College, 1971.

O'CONNOR, R. D. Relative efficacy of modeling, shaping, and the combined procedures for modification of social withdrawal. *Journal of Abnormal Psychology,* 1972, *79,* 327–334.

OELSNER, L. U.S. bars crime fund use on behavior modification. *New York Times,* February 15, 1974, p. 54.

OHMAN, A., ERIXON, G., & LOFBERG, J. Potentially phobic stimuli as conditioned stimuli in GSR conditioning. *Journal of Abnormal Psychology,* 1975.

O'LEARY, K. D., & DRABMAN, R. Token reinforcement programs in the classroom: A review. *Psychological Bulletin,* 1971, *4,* 379–398.

O'LEARY, K. D., POULOS, P. W., & DEVINE, V. T. Tangible reinforcers: Bonuses or bribes. *Journal of Consulting and Clinical Psychology,* 1972, *38,* 1–8.

Orne, M. T. The nature of hypnosis: Artifact and essence. *Journal of Abnormal and Social Psychology,* 1959, *58,* 277–299.

Paul, G. L. *Insight vs. desensitization in psychotherapy.* Palo Alto: Stanford University Press, 1966.

Peterson, R. A., & McIntosh, E. Teaching tricycle riding. *Mental Retardation,* 1973, *11,* 32–34.

Peterson, R. A. The natural development of nocturnal bladder control. *Developmental Medicine and Child Neurology,* 1971, *13,* 730–734.

Premack, D. Toward empirical behavior laws. I: Positive reinforcement. *Psychological Review,* 1956, *66,* 219–233.

Rackensperger, W., & Feinberg, A. M. Treatment of a severe hand-washing compulsion by systematic desensitization: A case report. *Journal of Behavior Therapy and Experimental Psychiatry,* 1972, *3,* 123–127.

Reiss, S. Transfer effects of success and failure training from one reinforcing agent to another. *Journal of Abnormal Psychology,* 1973, *82,* 435–445.

Reiss, S., & Redd, W. H. Generalization of the control of screaming behavior in an emotionally disturbed retarded female. *APA Proceedings,* 1970, 741–742.

Reiss, S., & Sushinsky, L. W. Overjustification, competing responses, and the acquisition of intrinsic interest. *Journal of Personality and Social Psychology,* 1975, *31,* 1116–1125.

Reiss, S., & Sushinsky, L. W. The competing response hypothesis of decreased play effects: A reply to Lepper and Greene. *Journal of Personality and Social Psychology,* 1976, *33,* 233–244.

Reppucci, N. D., & Reiss, S. Effects of operant treatment with disruptive and normal elementary school children. *APA Proceedings,* 1970, 743–744.

Rescorla, R. A., & Wagner, A. R. A theory of Pavlovian conditioning: Variations in the effectiveness of reinforcement and nonreinforcement. In A. Black & W. Prokasy (Eds.), *Classical conditioning II.* New York: Appleton-Century-Crofts, 1972.

Rizley, R. C., & Reppucci, N. D. Pavlovian conditioned inhibitory processes in behavior therapy. In B. A. Maher (Ed.), *Progress in experimental personality research,* 1975, in press.

Rosenzweig, S. Preferences in the repetition of successful and unsuccessful activities as a function of age and personality. *Journal of Genetic Psychology,* 1933, *42,* 423–441.

Ross, D. M., Ross, S. A., & Evans, T. A. The modification of extreme social withdrawal by modeling with guided participation. *Journal of Behavior Therapy and Experimental Psychiatry,* 1972, *2,* 273–279.

Salter, A. *Conditioned reflex therapy.* New York: Creative Age, 1949.

Sarbin, T. R. Role theoretical interpretation of psychological change. In P. Worchel & C. Byrne (Eds.), *Psychological change.* New York: John Wiley and Sons, 1964.

Sarbin, T. R. Hypnosis as a behavior modification technique. In L. Krasner & L. P. Ullmann (Eds.), *Research in behavior modification.* New York: Holt, Rinehart, and Winston, 1965.

Sarbin, T. R., & Coe, W. C. *Hypnosis: A social psychological analysis of influence communication.* New York: Holt, Rinehart, and Winston, 1972.

Schwartz, M. L., & Hawkins, R. P. Applications of delayed reinforcement procedures to the behavior of an elementary school child. *Journal of Applied Behavior Analysis,* 1970, *3,* 85–96.

Seligman, M. E. P. On the generality of the laws of learning. *Psychological Review,* 1970, *77,* 406–418.

Seligman, M. E. P. *Helplessness: On depression, development, and death.* San Francisco: W. H. Freeman, 1975.

Seligman, M. E. P., Maier, S. F., & Geer, J. H. Alleviation of learned helplessness in the dog. *Journal of Abnormal Psychology,* 1968, *73,* 256–262.

Serber, M. Teaching the nonverbal components of assertive therapy. *Journal of Behavior Research and Experimental Psychiatry,* 1972, *3,* 179–183.

Sherman, A. R. Real-life exposure as a primary therapeutic factor in the desensitization treatment of fear. *Journal of Abnormal Psychology,* 1972, *79,* 19–28.

Sidman, M. *The tactics of scientific research.* New York: Basic Books, 1961.

Skinner, B. F. *Walden two.* New York: Macmillan, 1948.

Skinner, B. F. *Science and human behavior.* New York: Macmillan, 1953.

Skinner, B. F. Behaviorism at fifty. In T. Wann (Ed.), *Behaviorism and phenomenology.* Chicago: University of Chicago Press, 1966.

Skinner, B. F. *Beyond freedom and dignity.* New York: Knopf, 1971.

Solomon, R. L. Punishment. *American Psychologist,* 1964, *19,* 239–253.

Staats, A. W. A case in and a strategy for the extension of learning principles to problems of human behavior. In L. Krasner & L. P. Ullmann (Eds.), *Research in behavior modification.* New York: Holt, Rinehart, and Winston, 1965.

Staats, A. W. *Social behaviorism.* Homewood, Ill.: Dorsey, 1975.

Stampfl, T. G. Implosive therapy, part I: The theory. In S. G. Armitage (Ed.), *Behavior modification techniques in the treatment of emotional disorders.* Battle Creek, Mich.: V. A. Publications, 1967.

Stampfl, T. G., & Levis, D. J. Essentials of implosive therapy: A learning-theory-based psychodynamic behavioral therapy. *Journal of Abnormal Psychology,* 1967, *72,* 496–503. (a)

Stampfl, T. G., & Levis, D. J. Phobic patients: Treatment with the learning theory approach of implosive therapy. *Voices: The Art and Science of Psychotherapy,* 1967, *3,* 23–27. (b)

Stuart, R. B. Operant-interpersonal treatment for marital discord. *Journal of Consulting and Clinical Psychology,* 1969, *33,* 675–682.

Stuart, R. B. A three-dimensional program for the treatment of obesity. *Behavior Research and Therapy,* 1971, *9,* 177–186.

Sushinsky, L. W. Expectation of future treatment, stimulus satiation, and smoking. *Journal of Consulting and Clinical Psychology,* 1972, *39,* 343.

Thorndike, E. L. Animal intelligence. *Psychological Review Monograph Supplement,* 1898, *2,* no. 4.

Trexler, L. D., & Karst, T. O. Rational-emotive therapy,

placebo, and no-treatment effects on public-speaking anxiety. *Journal of Abnormal Psychology,* 1972, *79,* 60–67.

Trotter, S., & Warren, J. Behavior modification under fire. In *APA Monitor.* Washington, D.C.: American Psychological Association, 1974.

Trowill, J. A. Instrumental conditioning of the heart rate in the curarized rat. *Journal of Comparative and Physiological Psychology,* 1967, *63,* 7–11.

Ullmann, L. P., & Krasner, L. (Eds.) *Case studies in behavior modification.* New York: Holt, Rinehart, and Winston, 1965.

Vukelich, R., & Hake, D. F. Reduction of dangerously aggressive behavior in a severely retarded resident through a combination of positive reinforcement procedures. *Journal of Applied Behavior Analysis,* 1971, *4,* 215–225.

Wagner, M. R. A case of public masturbation treated by operant conditioning. *Journal of Child Psychology and Psychiatry,* 1968, 61–65.

Watson, L. S. Application of operant conditioning techniques to institutionalized profoundly retarded children. *Mental Retardation Abstracts,* 1967, *4,* 1–18.

Watson, J. B., & Raynor, R. Conditioned emotional reactions. *Journal of Experimental Psychology,* 1920, *3,* 1–14.

Weiner, H. Some effects of response cost upon human operant behavior. *Journal of the Experimental Analysis of Behavior,* 1962, *5,* 201–208.

Weinman, B., Gelbart, P., Wallace, M., & Post, M. Inducing assertive behavior in chronic schizophrenics: A comparison of socioenvironmental, desensitization, and relaxation therapies. *Journal of Consulting and Clinical Psychology,* 1972, *39,* 246–252.

Weiss, T., & Engel, B. T. Operant conditioning of heart rate in patients with premature ventricular contractions. *Psychosomatic Medicine,* 1971, *33,* 301–320.

Weitzenhoffer, A. M. Behavior therapeutic techniques and hypnotherapeutic methods. *American Journal of Clinical Hypnosis,* 1972, *15,* 71–82.

Williams, C. D. The elimination of tantrum behavior by extinction procedures. *Journal of Abnormal and Social Psychology,* 1959, *59,* 269.

Wilson, G. T., & Davison, G. C. Processes of fear reduction in systematic desensitization: Animal studies. *Psychological Bulletin,* 1971, *76,* 1–14.

Wincze, J. P. A comparison of systematic desensitization and "vicarious extinction" in a case of frigidity. *Journal of Behavior Therapy and Experimental Psychiatry,* 1971, 2, 285–289.

Wisocki, P. A. The successful treatment of a heroin addict by covert conditioning techniques. *Journal of Behavior Therapy and Experimental Psychiatry,* 1973, *4,* 55–61.

Wolf, M. M., Risley, T., & Mees, H. L. Application of operant conditioning procedures to the behavior problems of an autistic child. *Behavior Research and Therapy,* 1964, *1,* 305–312.

Wollersheim, J. P. Effectiveness of group therapy based upon learning principles in the treatment of overweight women. *Journal of Abnormal Psychology,* 1970, *76,* 462–474.

Wolpe, J. *Psychotherapy by reciprocal inhibition.* Palo Alto: Stanford University Press, 1958.

Wolpe, J. The instigation of assertive behavior: Transcripts from two cases. *Journal of Behavior Therapy and Experimental Psychiatry,* 1970, *1,* 141–151.

Wolpe, J., & Lazarus, A. A. *Behavior therapy techniques: A guide to the treatment of neuroses.* Elmsford, N.Y.: Pergamon, 1966.

Yates, A. J. The application of learning theory to the treatment of tics. *Journal of Abnormal and Social Psychology,* 1958, *56,* 175–182.

Yates, A. J. *Behavior therapy.* New York: John Wiley and Sons, 1970.

8. Phenomenology

Butler, J. M., & Haigh, G. V. Changes in the relation between self-concepts and ideal concepts, consequent upon client-centered counseling. In C. R. Rogers & R. F. Dymond (Eds.), *Psychotherapy and personality change.* Chicago: University of Chicago Press, 1954.

Cherniss, C. Personality and ideology: A personological study of women's liberation. *Psychiatry,* 1972, *35,* 109–125.

Frankl, V. E. *Man's search for meaning: An introduction to logotherapy.* New York: Washington Square Press, 1963.

Frankl, V. E. Logotherapy. *Israel Annals of Psychiatry and Related Disciplines,* 1967, *5,* 142–155.

Giovacchini, P. L. Treatment of marital disharmonies: The classical approach. In B. L. Greene (Ed.), *The psychotherapies of marital disharmony.* New York: Free Press, 1965.

Greene, B. L. *The psychotherapies of marital disharmony.* New York: Free Press, 1965.

Hartley, M. W. A Q-technique study of changes in the self-concept during psychotherapy. Unpublished doctoral dissertation, University of Chicago, 1951.

Jackson, D. D. The question of family homeostasis. *Psychiatry Quarterly Supplement,* 1957, *31,* 79–90.

Kubie, L. S. Psychoanalysis and marriage: Practical and theoretical issues. In V. E. Eisenstein (Ed.), *Neurotic interaction in marriage.* New York: Basic Books, 1956.

Laing, R. D. *The politics of experience.* New York: Pantheon, 1967.

Laing, R. D., Phillipson, H., & Lee, A. R. *Interpersonal perception.* New York: Springer, 1966.

Maslow, A. H. *Motivation and personality.* New York: Harper & Row, 1954.

Maslow, A. H. (Ed.) *New Knowledge in human values.* New York: Harper & Row, 1959.

Maslow, A. H. *Toward a psychology of being.* New York: Van Nostrand, 1962.

May, R. *Existential psychology.* New York: Random House, 1960.

May, R. *Psychology and the human dilemma.* New York: Van Nostrand, 1967.

Murstein, B. I. Stimulus-value-role: A theory of marital choice. *Journal of Marriage and the Family,* 1970, *32,* 465–481.

Murstein, B. I. Perceived congruence among premarital couples as a function of neuroticism. *Journal of Abnormal Psychology,* 1973, *81,* 22–26.

Napier, A. The primary task. In A. Ferber, M. Mendelsohn, & A. Napier (Eds.), *The book of family therapy.* New York: Science House, 1972.

Patterson, C. H. *Theories of counseling and psychotherapy.* New York: Harper & Row, 1973.

Ricks, D. F., & Wessman, A. E. Winn: A case study of a happy man. *Journal of Humanistic Psychology,* 1966, *6,* 2–16.

Rogers, C. R. Some observations on the organization of personality. *American Psychologist,* 1947, *2,* 358–368.

Rogers, C. R. (1951) *Client-centered therapy.* Boston: Houghton Mifflin, 1965.

Rogers, C. R. A theory of personality. In S. Koch (Ed.), *Psychology: A study of a science.* New York: McGraw-Hill, 1959.

Rogers, C. R. *On becoming a person.* Boston: Houghton Mifflin, 1961.

Rogers, C. R., & Dymond, R. F. *Psychotherapy and personality change.* Chicago: University of Chicago Press, 1954.

Satir, V. M. *Conjoint marital therapy.* In B. L. Greene (Ed.), *The psychotherapies of marital disharmony.* New York: Free Press, 1965.

Satir, V. M. *Conjoint family therapy.* Palo Alto, Calif.: Science and Behavior Books, 1967.

Snyder, W. U. The case of Robert Winslow Smith. In W. U. Snyder (Ed.), *Casebook of nondirective counseling.* Boston: Houghton Mifflin, 1947.

Stephenson, W. *The study of behavior: Q-technique and its methodology.* Chicago: University of Chicago Press, 1953.

Yalom, I. D., & Lieberman, M. A. A study of encounter group casualties. *Archives of General Psychology,* 1971, *25,* 16–30.

9. Community Psychology and Community Mental Health

Albee, G. W. *Mental health manpower trends.* New York: Basic Books, 1959.

Albee, G. W. The relation of conceptual models to manpower needs. In E. L. Cowen, E. A. Gardner, & M. Zax (Eds.), *Emergent approaches to mental health problems.* New York: Appleton-Century-Crofts, 1967.

Argyris, C. T-groups for organizational effectiveness. *Harvard Business Review,* 1964, *42,* 60–74.

Arnhoff, F. N., Rubenstein, E. A., Shriver, B., & Jones, D. R. The mental health fields: An overview of manpower growth and development. In F. N. Arnhoff, E. A. Rubenstein, & J. C. Speisman (Eds.), *Manpower for mental health.* Chicago: Aldine, 1969.

Arnhoff, F. N., Rubenstein, E. A., & Speisman, J. C. (Eds.) *Manpower for mental health.* Chicago: Aldine, 1969.

Bellak, L., & Small, L. *Emergency psychotherapy and brief psychotherapy.* New York: Grune and Stratton, 1965.

Benne, K. D. History of the t-group in the laboratory setting. In L. P. Bradford, J. R. Gibb, & K. D. Benne (Eds.), *T-group theory and laboratory method.* New York: John Wiley and Sons, 1964.

Bennis, W. G. Changing organizations. *Journal of Applied Behavioral Science,* 1966, *2,* 247–263.

Bunker, D. R. Individual applications of laboratory training. *Journal of Applied Behavioral Science,* 1965, *1,* 131–148.

Campbell, J. P., & Dunnette, M. D. Effectiveness of t-group experiences in managerial training and development. In H. A. Hornstein, B. B. Bunker, W. W. Burke, M. Gindes, & R. J. Lewicki (Eds.), *Social intervention.* New York: Free Press, 1971.

Caplan, G. *Principles of preventive psychiatry.* New York: Basic Books, 1964.

Cherniss, C. New settings in the university: Their creation, problems and early development. Unpublished doctoral dissertation, Yale University, 1972.

Cowen, E. L. Social and community interventions. In P. H. Mussen & M. R. Rosenzweig (Eds.), *Annual Review of Psychology,* 1973, *24,* 423–472.

Cowen, E. L., Gardner, E. A., & Zax, M. (Eds.) *Emergent approaches to mental health problems.* New York: Appleton-Century-Crofts, 1967.

Denner, B., & Price, R. H. (Eds.) *Community mental health.* New York: Holt, Rinehart, and Winston, 1973.

Fairweather, G. W. (Ed.) *Social psychology in treating mental illness: An experimental approach.* New York: John Wiley and Sons, 1964.

Fairweather, G. W. *Methods for experimental social innovation.* New York: John Wiley and Sons, 1967.

Freed, H. M., Schroder, D. J., & Baker, B. Community participation in mental health services: A case of factional control. In L. Miller (Ed.), *Mental health in rapid social change.* Jerusalem, Israel: Jerusalem Academic Press, 1970.

Goffman, E. The moral career of the mental patient. *Psychiatry,* 1959, *22,* 123–142.

Goldenberg, I. I. *Build me a mountain: Youth, poverty, and the creation of a new setting.* Cambridge, Mass.: MIT Press, 1971.

Goldman, A. R., Bohr, R. H., & Steinberg, T. A. On posing as mental patients: Reminiscences and recommendations. *Professional Psychology,* 1970, *1,* 427–434.

Golembiewski, R. T. *Renewing organizations: The laboratory approach to planned change.* Itasca, Ill.: Peacock Publishers, 1972.

Goodman, G. An experiment with companionship therapy: College students and troubled boys—assumptions, selections and design. *American Journal of Public Health,* 1967, *57,* 1772–1777.

Graziano, A. Clinical innovation and the mental health power structure: A social case history. *American Psychologist,* 1969, *24,* 10–13.

Gruver, G. G. College students as therapeutic agents. *Psychological Bulletin,* 1971, *76,* 111–127.

Guerney, B. G. (Ed.) *Psychotherapeutic agents.* New York: Holt, Rinehart, and Winston, 1969.

Hornstein, H. A., Bunker, B. B., Burke, W. W., Gindes, M., & Lewicki, R. J. (Eds.) *Social intervention.* New York: Free Press, 1971.

Huessy, H. R. (Ed.) *Mental health with limited resources: Yankee ingenuity in low-cost programs.* New York: Grune and Stratton, 1966.

Joint Commission on Mental Health of Children. *Crisis in child mental health: Challenge for the 1970s.* New York: Harper & Row, 1970.

Joint Commission on Mental Illness. *Action for mental health.* New York: Basic Books, 1961.

Kelly, J. G. Ecological constraints on mental health services. *American Psychologist,* 1966, *21,* 535–539.

Kelly, J. G. Towards an ecological conception of preventive interventions. In J. W. Carter (Ed.), *Research contributions from psychology to community mental health.* New York: Behavioral Publications, 1968.

Kelly, J. G. Naturalistic observations in contrasting social environments. In E. P. Willems & H. L. Raush (Eds.), *Naturalistic viewpoints in psychological research.* New York: Holt, Rinehart, and Winston, 1969.

Leighton, D. C. Distribution of psychiatric symptoms in a small town. *American Journal of Psychiatry,* 1956, *112,* 716–723.

Mendel, W. M., & Rapport, S. Determinants of the decision for psychiatric hospitalization. *Archives of General Psychiatry,* 1969, *20,* 321–328.

Miles, M. B. Learning processes and outcomes in human relations training: A clinical experimental study. In E. Schein & W. Bennis (Eds.), *Personal and organizational change through group methods: The laboratory approach.* New York: John Wiley and Sons, 1965.

Miller, D. L., & Schwartz, M. County lunacy commission hearings: Some observations of commitments to a state mental hospital. *Social Problems,* 1966, *14,* 26–35.

Nichols, R. S. The influence of economic and administrative factors on the type and quality of care given to persons with psychological disease. *Working Papers in Community Mental Health,* 1963, *1,* 1–34.

O'Neill, P. Role and responsibility: The psychologist and the delivery of mental health services. Unpublished paper, Yale University, 1973.

O'Neill, P. Self-esteem and behavior of girls with convergent and divergent cognitive abilities. Unpublished doctoral dissertation, Yale University, 1974.

Reiss, S. Educational and psychological effects of open-space education in Oak Park, Illinois. Unpublished technical report, University of Illinois at Chicago Circle, 1974.

Reiss, S., & Dyhdalo, N. Persistence, achievement, and open-space environments. *Journal of Educational Psychology,* 1975, *67,* 506–513.

Reppucci, N. D., & Saunders, J. T. Social psychology of behavior modification: Problems of implementation in natural settings. *American Psychologist,* 1974, *29,* 649–660.

Rioch, M. J. Changing concepts in the training of therapists. *Journal of Consulting Psychology,* 1966, *30,* 290–292.

Rosenhan, D. L. On being sane in insane places. *Science,* 1973, *179,* 250–258.

Ryan, W. (Ed.) *Distress in the city.* Cleveland: Case-Western University, 1969.

Sarason, S. B. *The creation of settings and the future societies.* San Francisco: Jossey-Bass, 1972.

Scheff, T. J. Decision roles, types of error, and their consequences in medical diagnosis. *Behavioral Science,* 1963, *8.*

Scheff, T. J. The societal reaction to deviance: Ascriptive elements in the psychiatric screening of mental patients in a midwestern state. *Social Problems,* 1964, *11,* 401–413.

Schein, E. H. *Process consultation: Its role in organization development.* Reading, Mass.: Addison-Wesley, 1969.

Schmuck, R. A., Runkel, P. J., Saturen, S. L., Martell, R. L., & Derr, C. B. *Handbook of organization development in schools.* Washington, D.C.: National Press Books, 1972.

Senf, G. M. Testimony before subcommittee on handicapped of the Committee on Labor and Public Welfare, U.S. Senate, 93rd Cong., March 23, 1973. Washington, D.C.: U.S. Government Printing Office, 1973.

Silberman, C. E. *Crisis in the classroom.* New York: Random House, 1970.

Smith, M. B., & Hobbs, N. The community and the community mental health center. *American Psychologist,* 1966, *21,* 499–509.

Spielberger, C. D. A mental health consultation program in a small community with limited professional mental health resources. In E. L. Cowen, E. A. Gardner, & M. Zax (Eds.), *Emergent approaches to mental health problems.* New York: Appleton-Century-Crofts, 1967.

Srole, L., Langner, T. S., Michael, S. T., Opler, M. K., & Rennie, T. A. C. *Mental health in the metropolis.* Vol. 1. New York: McGraw-Hill, 1962.

Szasz, T. S. *The manufacture of madness.* New York: Harper & Row, 1970.

Szasz, T. S. *The age of madness.* Garden City, N.Y.: Anchor Books, 1973.

Valiquet, I. M. Contribution to the evaluation of a management development program. Unpublished master's thesis, Massachusetts Institute of Technology, 1964.

Walberg, H. J., & Thomas, S. C. Open education: An operational definition and validation in Great Britain and in the United States. *American Educational Research Journal,* 1972, *9,* 197–208.

Wenger, D. L., & Fletcher, C. R. The effect of legal counsel on admissions to a state mental hospital: A confrontation of professions. *Journal of Health and Human Behavior,* 1969, *10,* 66–72.

Wineman, D., & James, A. The advocacy challenge to schools of social work. *Social Work,* 1969, *14,* 23–32.

Zax, M., & Cowen, E. L. *Abnormal psychology.* New York: Holt, Rinehart, and Winston, 1972.

10. The Neurotic Syndromes

Abse, D. W. Hysteria. In S. Arieti (Ed.), *American handbook of psychiatry.* Vol 1. New York: Basic Books, 1959.

Brady, J. P., & Lind, D. L. (1961) Experimental analysis of hysterical blindness. In L. P. Ullmann & L. Krasner (Eds.), *Case studies in behavior modification.* New York: Holt, Rinehart, and Winston, 1965.

Brown, F. W. Heredity in the psychoneurosis. *Proceed-*

ings of the Royal Society of Medicine, 1942, *35,* 785–790.

Buss, A. H. *Psychopathology.* New York: John Wiley and Sons, 1966.

Cameron, N. *Personality development and psychopathology.* Boston: Houghton Mifflin, 1963.

Cannon, W. B. *Bodily changes in pain, hunger, fear, and rage.* New York: Appleton-Century-Crofts, 1929.

Carr, A. T. Compulsive neurosis: A review of the literature. *Psychological Bulletin,* 1974, *81,* 311–318.

Cattell, R. B., & Scheier, I. H. *The meaning and measurement of neuroticism and anxiety.* New York: Ronald Press, 1961.

Chodoff, P., & Lyons, H. Hysteria, the hysterical personality and hysterical conversion. *American Journal of Psychiatry,* 1958, *114,* 734–740.

Chrzanowski, G. Neurasthenia and hypochondriasis. In S. Arieti (Ed.), *American handbook of psychiatry.* Vol. 1. New York: Basic Books, 1959.

Coleman, J. C. *Abnormal psychology and modern life.* Glenview, Ill.: Scott, Foresman, 1972.

Dixon, J., de Moncheau, D., & Sandler, J. Patterns of anxiety: The phobias. *British Journal of Psychology,* 1957, *30,* 3–40.

Dmitruk, V. M. "Experimental neurosis" in cats: Fact or artifact? *Journal of Abnormal Psychology,* 1974, *83,* 97–105.

Dollard, J., & Miller, N. E. *Personality and psychotherapy.* New York: McGraw-Hill, 1950.

Eisenberg, L. School phobia: A study in the communication of anxiety. *American Journal of Psychiatry,* 1958, *114,* 712–718.

Ellis, A. *Reason and emotion in psychotherapy.* New York: Lyle Stuart, 1962.

Eysenck, H. J. *The dynamics of anxiety and hysteria.* London: Routledge and Kegan Paul, 1957.

Eysenck, H. J. *Handbook of abnormal psychology.* New York: Basic Books, 1961.

Eysenck, H. J., & Prell, D. B. The inheritance of neuroticism: An experimental study. *Journal of Mental Sciences,* 1951, *97,* 441–467.

Fisher, C. The self, the sense of self, and perception. *Psychoanalytic Study of the Child,* 1959, *14,* 81–109.

Freud, S. (1895) Obsessions and phobias: Their psychic mechanisms and their etiology. In S. Freud, *Collected papers.* Vol 1. New York: Basic Books, 1959.

Gillespie, R. D. Hypochondria: Its definition, nosology, and psychopathology. *Guy's Hospital Report,* 1928, *78,* 408–460.

Glover, E. *On the early development of mind.* New York: International Universities Press, 1956.

Grinker, R. R., & Spiegel, J. P. Brief psychotherapy in war neurosis. *Psychosomatic Medicine,* 1944, *6,* 123.

Jacobson, E. Depersonalization. *Journal of American Psychoanalytic Association,* 1959, *7,* 581–610.

Janet, P. *The major symptoms of hysteria.* New York: Macmillan, 1924.

Jenkins, R. L. The varieties of children's behavioral problems and family dynamics. *American Journal of Psychiatry,* 1968, *124,* 1440–1445.

Johnson, A. M., Falstein, E. I., Szurek, S. A., & Svendson, M. School phobia. *American Journal of Orthopsychiatry,* 1941, *11,* 701–702.

Kardiner, A. Traumatic neuroses of war. In S. Arieti (Ed.), *American handbook of psychiatry.* Vol. 1. New York: Basic Books, 1959.

Kennedy, W. A. School phobia: Rapid treatment of 50 cases. *Journal of Abnormal Psychology,* 1965, *70,* 285–289.

Kenyon, F. E. Hypochondriasis: A survey of some historical, clinical, and social aspects. *British Journal of Psychiatry,* 1965, *38,* 117.

Lader, M. H. Palmer skin conductance measure in anxiety and phobic states. *Journal of Psychosomatic Research,* 1967, *11,* 271–281.

Laughlin, H. P. *The neuroses.* Washington, D.C.: Butterworths, 1967.

Maddi, S. R. The existential neurosis. *Journal of Abnormal Psychology,* 1967, *72,* 311–325.

Martin, B. *Anxiety and neurotic disorders.* New York: John Wiley and Sons, 1971.

Masserman, J. H. *Behavior and neurosis.* Chicago: University of Chicago Press, 1943.

McKinley, J. C., & Hathaway, S. R. A multiphasic personality schedule (Minnesota). II. A differential study of hypochondriasis. *Journal of Psychology,* 1940, *10,* 255–268.

McKinley, J. C., & Hathaway, S. R. The Minnesota multiphasic inventory. V. Hysteria, hypomania and psychopathic deviate. *Journal of Applied Psychology,* 1944, *28,* 153–174.

McNeil, E. B. *Neuroses and personality disorders.* Englewood Cliffs, N.J.: Prentice-Hall, 1970.

Merbaum, M., & Hefez, A. Some personality characteristics of soldiers exposed to extreme war stress. *Journal of Consulting and Clinical Psychology,* 1976, *44,* 1–6.

Mowrer, O. H. A stimulus-response analysis of anxiety and its role as a reinforcing agent. *Psychological Review,* 1939, *46,* 553–565.

O'Connor, J. P. A statistical test of psychoneurotic syndromes. *Journal of Abnormal and Social Psychology,* 1953, *48,* 581–584.

Pasamanick, B. A survey of mental disease in an urban population. IV. An approach to total prevalence rates. *Archives of General Psychiatry,* 1961, *5,* 151–155.

Pavlov, I. P. *Lectures on conditioned reflexes.* New York: International Publishers, 1928.

Philips, D. L. The "true prevalence" of mental illness in a New England state. *Community Mental Health Journal,* 1966, *2,* 35–40.

Portnoy, I. The anxiety states. In S. Arieti (Ed.), *American handbook of psychiatry.* Vol. 1. New York: Basic Books, 1959.

Prince, M. *The dissociation of a personality.* New York: Longmans, 1905.

Pronko, N. H. *Abnormal psychology.* Baltimore: Williams & Wilkins, 1963.

Purtell, J. J., Robins, E., & Cohen, M. E. Observations on the clinical aspects of hysteria. A quantitative study of 50 hysteria patients and 156 control subjects. *Journal of the American Medical Association,* 1951, *146,* 902–909.

Rado, S. Obsessive behavior: So-called obsessive-compulsive neurosis. In S. Arieti (Ed.), *American handbook of psychiatry.* Vol. 1. New York: Basic Books, 1959.

Redlich, F. C., & Freedman, D. X. *The theory and practice of psychiatry.* New York: Basic Books, 1966.

Riese, W. The pre-Freudian origins of psychoanalysis. In J. H. Masserman (Ed.), *Science and psychoanalysis.* New York: Grune and Stratton, 1958.

Rizley, R. C., & Reppucci, N. D. Pavlovian conditioned inhibitory processes in behavior therapy. In B. A. Maher (Ed.), *Progress in experimental personality research,* 1975, in press.

Rosenthal, D. *Genetic theory and abnormal behavior.* New York: McGraw-Hill, 1970.

Roth, M. The phenomenology of depressive states. *Canadian Psychiatric Association Journal,* 1959, *4,* special supplement, 32–53.

Sandler, J., & Hazari, A. The "obsessional": On the psychological classification of obsessional character traits and symptoms. *British Journal of Medical Psychology,* 1960, *33,* 113–122.

Seligman, M. E. P. On the generality of the laws of learning. *Psychological Review,* 1970, *77,* 406–418.

Seligman, M. E. P. Phobias and preparedness. *Behavior Therapy,* 1971, *2,* 307–320.

Shirvaikar, R. V. A study of hypochondriasis. *Neurology,* 1957, *5,* 44–48.

Smart, R. Conflict and conditioned aversive stimuli in the development of experimental neurosis. *Canadian Journal of Psychology,* 1965, *19,* 208–223.

Srole, L., Langner, T. S., Michael, S. T., Opler, M. K., & Rennie, T. A. C. *Mental health in the metropolis.* New York: McGraw-Hill, 1962.

Stephens, J. H., & Kamp, M. On some aspects of hysteria: A clinical study. *Journal of Nervous and Mental Disease,* 1962, *134,* 305–315.

Straus, E. W. *On obsession.* New York: Johnson Reprint Corporation, 1948.

Swank, R. L. Combat exhaustion: A descriptive and statistical analysis of causes, symptoms, and signs. *Journal of Nervous and Mental Disease,* 1949, *109,* 475–598.

Szasz, T. S. *The myth of mental illness.* New York: Harper & Row, 1961.

Taylor, J. A. A personality scale of manifest anxiety. *Journal of Abnormal and Social Psychology,* 1953, *48,* 285–290.

Thigpen, C. H., & Cleckley, H. *The three faces of Eve.* Kingsport, Tenn.: Kingsport Press, 1954.

Veith, I. *Hysteria: The history of a disease.* Chicago: University of Chicago Press, 1965.

Waldfogel, S. Emotional crisis in a child. In A. Burton (Ed.), *Case studies in counseling and psychotherapy.* Englewood Cliffs, N.J.: Prentice-Hall, 1959.

Walters, A. Psychogenic regional pain alias hysterical pain. *Brain,* 1961, *84,* 1–18.

Westphal, C. Die agoraphobie; eine neuropathische erscheinung. *Archiv. Psychiatrie,* 1872, *3,* 138–161.

Wittenborn, J. R. Symptom patterns in a group of mental hospital patients. *Journal of Consulting Psychology,* 1951, *15,* 290–302.

Wolpe, J. *Psychotherapy by reciprocal inhibition.* Palo Alto, Calif.: Stanford University Press, 1958.

Wolpe, J., & Rachman, S. Psychoanalytic "evidence," a critique based on Freud's case of Little Hans. *Journal of Nervous and Mental Disease,* 1960, *131,* 135–147.

Woodruff, R. A., Goodwin, D. W., & Guze, S. B. *Psychiatric diagnosis.* New York: Oxford University Press, 1974.

11. Psychophysiologic Disorders and Sexual Dysfunctions

Alexander, F. *Psychosomatic medicine: Its principles and applications.* New York: W. W. Norton, 1950.

Alexander, F., & Flagg, G. W. The psychosomatic approach. In B. B. Wolman (Ed.), *Handbook of clinical psychology.* New York: McGraw-Hill, 1965.

Alexander, F., French, T. M., & Pollock, G. H. *Psychosomatic specificity.* Vol. 1. Chicago: University of Chicago Press, 1968.

Allen, C. *A textbook of psychosexual disorders.* New York: Oxford University Press, 1969.

Anon, J. S. The therapeutic use of masturbation in the treatment of sexual disorders. Paper presented at the fifth annual meeting of the Association for the Advancement of Behavior Therapy, Washington, D.C., 1971.

Ax, A. F. The physiological differentiation between fear and anger in humans. *Psychosomatic Medicine,* 1953, *15,* 433–442.

Backman, H., Kalliola, H., & Ostling, G. Placebo effect in peptic ulcer and other gastrointestinal disorders. *Gastroenterologia,* 1960, *94,* 11–20.

Baraff, A. S., & Cunningham, A. P. Asthmatic and normal children. *Journal of the American Medical Association,* 1965, *192,* 99–101.

Bogoch, A., Wilson, R., Fishman, S., Kliman, M. R., Trueman, G. E., & Norton, G. I. The stomach and duodenum. In A. Bogoch (Ed.), *Gastroenterology.* New York: McGraw-Hill, 1973.

Brady, J. V., Porter, R. W., Conrad, D. G., & Mason, J. W. Avoidance behavior and the development of gastroduodenal ulcers. *Journal of the Experimental Analysis of Behavior,* 1958, *1,* 69–72.

Buchan, D. J. Psychologic considerations in gastrointestinal disease. In A. Bogoch (Ed.), *Gastroenterology.* New York: McGraw-Hill, 1973.

Budzynski, T., Stoyva, J., & Adler, C. Feedback-induced muscle relaxation: Application to tension headaches. *Journal of Behavior Therapy and Experimental Psychiatry,* 1970, *1,* 205–211.

Cannon, W. B. The James-Lange theory of emotions: A critical examination and an alternative. *American Journal of Psychology,* 1927, *39,* 106–124.

Cruz-Coke, R., Etchenerry, R., & Nagel, R. Influence of migration on blood pressure of Easter Islanders. *Lancet,* 1964, *1,* 697–699.

Dengrove, E. Review of Masters, W. H., & Johnson, V. E., Human sexual inadequacy. *Behavior Therapy,* 1971, *2,* 112–113.

DiCara, L. V., & Miller, N. E. Instrumental learning of systolic blood pressure responses by curarized rats: Dissociation of cardiac and vascular changes. *Psychosomatic Medicine,* 1968, *30,* 489–494.

Dragstedt, L. R. A concept of the etiology of duodenal ulcer. *American Journal of Roentgenology,* 1956, *75,* 219–229.

Eich, R. H., Cuddy, R. P., & Smulyan, H. Hemodynamics in labile hypertension: A follow-up study. *Circulation,* 1966, *34,* 299–307.

Ellis, A. *The art and science of love.* New York: Lyle Stuart, 1960.

Engel, B. T., & Bickford, A. F. Response specificity: Stimulus-response and individual-response specificity in essential hypertensives. *Archives of General Psychiatry,* 1961, *5,* 478–489.

Etter, L. E., Dunn, J. P., Kammer, A. G., Osmond, L. H., & Reese, L. C. Gastroduodenal x-ray diagnosis: A comparison of radiographic techniques and interpretations. *Radiology,* 1960, *74,* 766–770.

Faulk, M. "Frigidity": A critical review. *Archives of Sexual Behavior,* 1973, *2,* 257–265.

Finkielman, S., Warcel, M., & Agrest, A. Hemodynamic patterns in essential hypertension. *Circulation,* 1965, *31,* 356–368.

Fisher, S. *The female orgasm: Psychology, physiology, fantasy.* New York: Basic Books, 1973.

Forsyth, R. P. Regional blood-flow changes during 72-hour avoidance schedules in the monkey. *Science,* 1971, *173,* 546.

Friedman, A. P. *Chronic recurring headache: Aspects of diagnosis and differentiation.* Hanover, N.J.: Sandoz, 1973.

Fuchs, K., Hoch, Z., Paldi, E., Abramovici, H., Brandes, J. M., Timor-Tritsch, J., & Kleinhaus, M. Hypnodesensitization therapy of vaginismus: Part I. "In vitro" method. Part II. "In vivo" method. *International Journal of Clinical and Experimental Hypnosis,* 1973, *21,* 144–156.

Garma, A. *Peptic ulcer and psychoanalysis.* Baltimore: Williams & Wilkins, 1958.

Gill, A. K. Pain and the healing of peptic ulcers. *Lancet,* 1947, 291.

Graham, D. Y. Psychosomatic medicine. In N. S. Greenfield & R. S. Sternbach (Eds.), *Handbook of psychophysiology.* New York: Holt, Rinehart, and Winston, 1972.

Graham, P. J., Rutter, M. L., Yule, W., & Pless, I. B. Childhood asthma: A psychosomatic disorder? Some epidemiological considerations. *British Journal of Preventive Medicine,* 1967, *21,* 78–85.

Grossman, H. J., & Greenberg, N. H. Psychosomatic differentiation in infancy. I: Autonomic activity in the newborn. *Psychosomatic Medicine,* 1957, *19,* 213–306.

Hardyck, C., Singer, M. T., & Harris, R. E. Transient changes in affect and blood pressure. *Archives of General Psychiatry,* 1962, *7,* 15–23.

Harris, R. E., & Forsyth, R. P. Personality and emotional stress in essential hypertension in man. In G. Onesti, K. E. Kim, & J. H. Moyer (Eds.), *Hypertension: Mechanisms and management.* New York: Grune and Stratton, 1973.

Hartman, W. E., & Fithian, M. A. *Treatment of sexual dysfunction: A biopsycho-social approach.* Long Beach, Calif.: Center for Marital and Sexual Studies, 1972.

Hastings, D. W. *Impotence and frigidity.* Boston: Little, Brown, 1963.

Hokanson, J. E., & Shetter, S. The effect of overt aggression on physiological tension level. *Journal of Abnormal and Social Psychology,* 1961, *63,* 446–448.

Johnson, J. *Disorders of sexual potency in the male.* Elmsford, N.Y.: Pergamon, 1968.

Kaplan, H. S. *The new sex therapy: Active treatment of sexual dysfunctions.* New York: Bruner/Mazel, 1974.

Kaplan, S. M., Gottschalk, L. A., Magliocco, E. B., Rohovit, D. D., & Ross, W. D. Hostility in verbal productions and hypnotic dreams of hypertensive patients. *Psychosomatic Medicine,* 1961, *23,* 311–322.

Keith, N. M., Wagener, H. P., & Barker, N. W. Some different types of essential hypertension: Their course and prognosis. *American Journal of Medical Science,* 1939, *197,* 332–343.

Kinsey, A. C., Pomeroy, W. B., & Martin, C. E. *Sexual behavior in the human male.* Philadelphia: W. B. Saunders, 1948.

Kinsey, A. C., Pomeroy, W. B., Martin, C. E., & Gebhard, P. H. *Sexual behavior in the human female.* Philadelphia: W. B. Saunders, 1953.

Kleegman, S. Frigidity in women. *Quarterly Review of Surgery, Obstetrics, and Gynecology,* 1959, *16,* 243–248.

Knapp, P. H., & Nemetz, S. J. Personality variations in bronchial asthma. *Psychosomatic Medicine,* 1957, *19,* 443–465.

Lacey, J. I., Bateman, D. E., & Van Lehn, R. Autonomic response specificity. *Psychosomatic Medicine,* 1953, *15,* 8–21.

Lachman, S. J. *Psychosomatic disorders: A behavioristic interpretation.* New York: John Wiley and Sons, 1972.

Lazarus, A. A. The treatment of chronic frigidity by systematic desensitization. *Journal of Nervous and Mental Disease,* 1963, *136,* 272–278.

Lazarus, A. A. *Behavior therapy and beyond.* New York: McGraw-Hill, 1971.

Lidberg, L. Social and psychiatric aspects of impotence and premature ejaculation. *Archives of Sexual Behavior,* 1972, *2,* 135–146.

Lobitz, W. I., & LoPiccolo, J. New methods in the behavioral treatment of sexual dysfunction. *Journal of Behavior Therapy and Experimental Psychiatry,* 1972, *3,* 265–271.

LoPiccolo, J. Scoring and interpretation manual for the Oregon Sex Inventory. Unpublished manuscript, University of Oregon, 1972.

Lyght, C. E. (Ed.) *The Merck manual of diagnosis and therapy.* Rahway, N.J.: Merck, 1966.

Malmo, R. B., & Shagass, C. Physiological study of symptom mechanisms in psychiatric patients under stress. *Psychosomatic Medicine,* 1949, *11,* 25–29.

Malmo, R. B., Shagass, C., & Davis, F. H. Symptom specificity and bodily reactions during psychiatric interview. *Psychosomatic Medicine,* 1950, *12,* 362–376.

Masters, W. H., & Johnson, V. E. *Human sexual inadequacy.* Boston: Little, Brown, 1970.

Masuda, M., Notske, R. N., & Holmes, T. H. Catecholamine excretion and asthmatic behavior. *Journal of Psychosomatic Research,* 1966, *10,* 255–262.

Matarazzo, J. D. An experimental study of aggression in the hypertensive patient. *Journal of Personality,* 1954, *22,* 423–447.

MENNINGER, K. A. Impotence and frigidity. *Bulletin of the Menninger Clinic,* 1937, *1,* 251–260.

MENZIES, R. Conditioned vasomotor responses in human subjects. *Journal of Psychology,* 1937, *4,* 75–120.

METCALFE, M. Demonstration of a psychosomatic relationship. *British Journal of Medical Psychology,* 1956, *29,* 63–66.

MIALL, W. E., & LOVELL, H. G. Relation between change of blood pressure and age. *British Medical Journal,* 1967, *2,* 660–664.

MIRSKY, I. A. Physiologic, psychologic, and social determinants in the etiology of duodenal ulcer. *American Journal of Digestive Diseases,* 1958, *3,* 285–314.

MITTELMAN, B., WOLFF, H. G., & SCHARF, M. Emotions and gastroduodenal functions. *Psychosomatic Medicine,* 1942, *4,* 5–61.

MOOS, R. H., & ENGEL, B. T. Psychophysiological reactions in hypertensive and arthritic patients. *Journal of Psychosomatic Research,* 1962, *6,* 227–241.

MÜLLER-WIELAND, K., & OSSENBERG, F. W. Medical management and treatment of duodenal ulcer. *Advances in Psychosomatic Medicine,* 1971, *6,* 152–168.

NECHELES, H. A blood factor in peptic ulcers. *The Sciences,* 1970, *10,* 15–16.

NEMIAH, J. C. The psychophysiologic management and treatment of patients with peptic ulcer. *Advances in Psychosomatic Medicine,* 1971, *6,* 169–185.

OBLER, M. Systematic desensitization in sexual disorders. *Journal of Behavior Therapy and Experimental Psychiatry,* 1973, *4,* 93–101.

ORGEL, S. Effect of psychoanalysis on the course of peptic ulcer. *Psychosomatic Medicine,* 1958, *20,* 117–123.

PFLANZ, M. Epidemiological and sociocultural factors in the etiology of duodenal ulcer. *Advances in Psychosomatic Medicine,* 1971, *6.*

PURCELL, K., BERNSTEIN, L., & BUKANTZ, S. C. A preliminary comparison of rapidly remitting and persistently "steroid-dependent" asthmatic children. *Psychosomatic Medicine,* 1961, *23,* 306–310.

PURCELL, K., & METZ, J. R. Distinctions between subgroups of asthmatic children: Some parent attitude variables related to age of onset of asthma. *Journal of Psychosomatic Research,* 1962, *6,* 251–258.

REISER, M. F., BRUST, A. A., & FERRIS, E. B. Life situations, emotions, and the course of patients with arterial hypertension. *Psychosomatic Medicine,* 1951, *13,* 133–139.

ROESSLER, R. L., & BROGDEN, W. J. Conditioned differentiation of vasoconstriction to subvocal stimuli. *American Journal of Psychology,* 1943, *56,* 78–86.

RUSKIN, A., BEARD, O. W., & SCHAFFER, R. L. Blast hypertension: Elevated arterial pressures in the victims of the Texas City disaster. *American Journal of Medicine,* 1948, *4,* 228–230.

SARGENT, J. D., GREEN, E. E., & WALTERS, E. D. Preliminary report on the use of autogenic feedback training in the treatment of migraine and tension headaches. *Psychosomatic Medicine,* 1973, *35,* 129–135.

SAWREY, W. L., & WEISS, J. D. An experimental method of producing gastric ulcers. *Journal of Comparative and Physiological Psychology,* 1956, *49,* 269–270.

SCHOENBERGER, J. A., STAMLER, J., & SHEKELLE, R. B. Current status of hypertension control in an industrial population. *Journal of the American Medical Association,* 1972, *22,* 559–562.

SCHULTZ, J. H., & LUTHE, W. *Autogenic therapy.* New York: Grune and Stratton, 1969.

SELYE, H. The general adaptation syndrome and the diseases of adaptation. *Journal of Clinical Endocrinology,* 1946, *6,* 117–128.

SEMANS, J. H. Premature ejaculation: A new approach. *Southern Medical Journal,* 1956, *49,* 353.

SINES, J. O., CLEELAND, C., & ADKINS, J. The behavior of normal and stomach lesion susceptible rats in several learning situations. *Journal of Genetic Psychology,* 1963, *102,* 91–94.

SMITH, D. E., ODEL, H. M., & KERNOHAN, J. W. Causes of death in hypertension. *American Journal of Medicine,* 1950, *9,* 516–527.

Society of Actuaries. Build and Blood Pressure Study. Chicago, 1959.

STAINBROOK, E. Psychosomatic medicine in the nineteenth century. *Psychosomatic Medicine,* 1952, *14,* 211–227.

United States National Center for Health Statistics. Vital and health statistics. Heart diseases in adults: United States, 1960–1962. Washington, D.C.: U.S. Government Printing Office, 1964 (PHS Publication No. 1000, S. 11, No. 6).

WEINER, H., THALER, M., REISER, M. F., & MIRSKY, I. A. Etiology of duodenal ulcer: I. Relation of specific psychological characteristics to rate of gastric secretion. *Psychosomatic Medicine,* 1957, *19,* 1–10.

WEISS, E., & ENGLISH, S. O. *Psychosomatic medicine.* Philadelphia: W. B. Saunders, 1957.

WEISS, J. M. Effects of coping behavior in different warning signal conditions on stress pathology in rats. *Journal of Comparative and Physiological Psychology,* 1971, *77,* 1–13. (a)

WEISS, J. M. Effects of punishing the coping response (conflict) on stress pathology in rats. *Journal of Comparative and Physiological Psychology,* 1971, *77,* 14–21. (b)

WEISS, J. M. Effects of coping behavior with and without a feedback signal on stress pathology in rats. *Journal of Comparative and Physiological Psychology,* 1971, *77,* 22–30. (c)

WELGAN, P. R. Learned control of gastric acid secretions in ulcer patients. *Psychosomatic Medicine,* 1974, *5,* 411–419.

WITTKOWER, E. D., & DUDEK, S. Z. Psychosomatic medicine: The mind-body-society interaction. In B. B. Wolman (Ed.), *Handbook of general psychology.* Englewood Cliffs, N.J.: Prentice-Hall, 1973.

WOLF, S., CARDON, P. V., SHEPARD, E. M., & WOLFF, H. *Life, stress and essential hypertension.* Baltimore: Williams & Wilkins, 1955.

WOLF, S., & WOLFF, H. *Human gastric function.* New York: Oxford University Press, 1947.

WOLFF, H. Headache mechanisms. *McGill Medical Journal,* 1946, *15,* 130–169.

WOLFF, H. *Headache and other head pain.* New York: Oxford University Press, 1963.

WOLPE, J. *Psychotherapy by reciprocal inhibition.* Palo Alto, Calif.: Stanford University Press, 1958.

WOLPE, J. *The practice of behavior therapy.* Elmsford, N.Y.: Pergamon, 1973.

YAGER, J., & WEINER, H. Observations in man. *Advances in Psychosomatic Medicine,* 1971, *6.*

12. Sexual Variance

ALLEN, C. *A textbook of psychosexual disorders.* New York: Oxford University Press, 1969.

APPERSON, L. B., & MCADOO, W. G. Parental factors in the childhood of homosexuals. *Journal of Abnormal Psychology,* 1968, *73,* 201–206.

BANCROFT, J. A. A comparative study of aversion and desensitization in the treatment of homosexuality. In L. E. Burns & J. L. Worsley (Eds.), *Behaviour therapy in the 1970s.* Bristol: John Wright and Sons, 1970.

BANDURA, A. *Principles of behavior modification.* New York: Holt, Rinehart, and Winston, 1969.

BANDURA, A., & WALTERS, R. H. *Social learning and personality development.* New York: Holt, Rinehart, and Winston, 1963.

BARLOW, D. H. Review of homosexual behaviour therapy and assessment. *Behavior Therapy,* 1972, *3,* 479–481.

BARLOW, D. H. Increasing heterosexual responsiveness in the treatment of sexual deviation: A review of the clinical and experimental literature. *Behavior Therapy,* 1973, *4,* 655–671.

BARLOW, D. H., REYNOLDS, E. J., & AGRAS, W. S. Gender identity change in a transsexual. *Archives of General Psychiatry,* 1973, *28,* 569–576.

BARR, R. F. Responses to erotic stimuli of transsexual and homosexual males. *British Journal of Psychiatry,* 1973, *123,* 579–585.

BENJAMIN, H. *The transsexual phenomenon.* New York: Julien Press, 1966.

BENTLER, P. M., & PRINCE, C. Personality characteristics of male transvestites. III. *Journal of Abnormal Psychology,* 1969, *74,* 140–143.

BENTLER, P. M., & PRINCE, C. Psychiatric symptomology in transvestites. *Journal of Clinical Psychology,* 1970, *26,* 434–435.

BENTLER, P. M., SHERMAN, R. W., & PRINCE, C. Personality characteristics of male transvestites. *Journal of Clinical Psychology,* 1970, *26,* 287–291.

BERGLER, E. *Homosexuality: Disease or way of life.* New York: Hill and Wang, 1957.

BIEBER, I., DAIN, H. J., DINCE, P. R., DRELLICH, M. G., GRAND, H. C., GUNDLACH, R. H., KREMER, M. W., RIFKIN, A. H., WILBUR, C. B., & BIEBER, T. B. *Homosexuality: A psychoanalytic study.* New York: Random House, 1962.

BROWN, D. G. Transvestism and sex-role inversion. In A. Ellis & A. Abarbanel (Eds.), *The encyclopedia of sexual behavior.* New York: Jason Aronson, 1973.

CAPRIO, F. S. Fetishism. In A. Ellis & A. Abarbanel (Eds.), *The encyclopedia of sexual behavior.* New York: Jason Aronson, 1973.

COHEN, M., & SEGHORN, T. Sociometric study of the sex offender. *Journal of Abnormal Psychology,* 1969, *74,* 249–255.

COLEMAN, J. C. *Abnormal psychology and modern life.* Glenview, Ill.: Scott, Foresman, 1976.

CURRAN, D., & PARR, D. Homosexuality: An analysis of 100 male cases seen in private practice. *British Medical Journal,* 1957, *103,* 797–801.

DAVISON, G. C. Elimination of a sadistic fantasy by a client-controlled counter-conditioning technique. *Journal of Abnormal Psychology,* 1968, *73,* 84–90.

DAVISON, G. C., & NEALE, J. M. *Abnormal psychology.* New York: Wiley, 1974.

DOIDGE, W. T., & HOLTZMAN, W. H. Implications of homosexuality among Air Force trainees. *Journal of Consulting Psychology,* 1960, *24,* 9–13.

EDWARDES, A., & MASTERS, R. E. L. *The cradle of erotica.* New York: Julien Press, 1963.

EHRHARDT, A. A., EPSTEIN, R., & MONEY, J. Fetal androgens and female gender identity in the early-treated adrenogenital syndrome. *Johns Hopkins Medical Journal,* 1968, *22,* 160–167.

EHRHARDT, A. A., & MONEY, J. Progestin-induced hermaphroditism: IQ and psychosexual identity in a study of ten girls. *Journal of Sex Research,* 1967, *3,* 83–100.

ELLIS, A. The effectiveness of psychotherapy with individuals who have severe homosexual problems. *Journal of Consulting Psychology,* 1956, *20,* 58–60.

EVANS, D. R. An exploratory study of emotive imagery and aversive conditioning. *Canadian Psychologist,* 1967, *8,* 162.

EVANS, R. B. Childhood parental relationships of homosexual. *Journal of Consulting and Clinical Psychology,* 1969, *33,* 129–135.

FEDERAL BUREAU OF INVESTIGATION *Uniform crime reports.* Washington, D.C.: U.S. Government Printing Office, 1971.

FELDMAN, M. P., & MACCULLOCH, M. J. *Homosexual behaviour: Therapy and assessment.* Elmsford, N.Y.: Pergamon, 1971.

FENICHEL, O. *Outline of clinical psychoanalysis.* London: Routledge, 1934.

FERENCZI, S. *Sex in psychoanalysis.* New York: Basic Books, 1914.

FISHER, G. Psychological needs of heterosexual pedophiliacs. *Diseases of the Nervous System,* 1969, *30,* 419–421.

FORD, C. S., & BEACH, F. A. *Patterns of sexual behavior.* New York: Harper & Row, 1951.

FOREL, A. H. (1907) *The sexual question.* Translated by C. F. Marshall. New York: Physicians and Surgeons Book, 1924.

FREUD, S. *A general introduction to psychoanalysis.* New York: Washington Square Press, 1924.

FREUND, K., LANGEVIN, R., ZAJAC, Y., STEINER, B., & ZAJAC, A. The transsexual syndrome in homosexual males. *Journal of Nervous and Mental Disease,* 1974, *158,* 145–153. (a)

FREUND, K., LANGEVIN, R., ZAJAC, Y., STEINER, B., & ZAJAC, A. Parent-child relations in transsexual and non-transsexual homosexual males. *British Journal of Psychiatry,* 1974, *124,* 22–23. (b)

FULMER, G. P. Testosterone levels and female-to-male transsexualism. *Archives of Sexual Behavior,* 1973, *2,* 399–400.

GAGNON, J. H., & SIMON, W. *Sexual conduct: The social sources of human sexuality.* Chicago: Aldine, 1973.

GEBHARD, P. H., GAGNON, J. H., POMEROY, W. B., & CHRISTENSON, C. V. *Sex offenders: An analysis of types.* New York: Harper & Row, 1965.

GELDER, M. G., & MARKS, I. M. Aversion treatment in transvestism and transsexualism. In R. Green & J. Money (Eds.), *Transsexualism and sex reassignment.* Baltimore: Johns Hopkins Press, 1969.

GRADY, K. L., PHOENIX, C. H., & YOUNG, W. C. Role of the developing rat testis in differentiation of the neural tissues mediating mating behavior. *Journal of Comparative and Physiological Psychology,* 1965, *59,* 176–182.

GREEN, R. Childhood cross-gender identification. *Journal of Nervous and Mental Disease,* 1968, *147,* 500–509.

GREEN, R. Attitudes toward transsexualism and sex reassignment procedures. In R. Green & J. Money (Eds.), *Transsexualism and sex reassignment.* Baltimore: Johns Hopkins Press, 1969.

GREEN, R., & MONEY, J. (Eds.) *Transsexualism and sex reassignment.* Baltimore: Johns Hopkins Press, 1969.

GREEN, R., NEWMAN, L. E., & STOLLER, R. J. Treatment of boyhood "transsexualism." *Archives of General Psychiatry,* 1972, *26,* 213–217.

HAIST, M., & HEWITT, J. The butch-fem dichotomy in male homosexual behavior. *Journal of Sex Research,* 1974, *10,* 68–75.

HATTERER, L. *Changing homosexuality in the male.* New York: McGraw-Hill, 1970.

HEDBLOM, J. H. The female homosexual: Social and attitudinal dimensions. In J. A. McCaffery (Ed.), *The homosexual dialectic.* Englewood Cliffs, N.J.: Prentice-Hall, 1972.

HEDBLOM, J. H. Dimensions of lesbian sexual experience. *Archives of Sexual Behavior,* 1973, *4,* 329–341.

HENRY, G. W., & GROSS, A. A. Social factors in case histories of 100 underprivileged persons. *Mental Hygiene,* 1938, *22,* 591–611.

HESTON, L. L., & SHIELDS, J. Homosexuality in twins: A family study and a registry study. *Archives of General Psychiatry,* 1968, *18,* 149–160.

HIRSCHFIELD, M. *Sexual anomalies and perversions: Physical and psychological development and treatment.* London: Francis Aldor, 1944.

HIRSCHFIELD, M. *Sexual anomalies.* New York: Emerson Books, 1948.

HOENIG, J. The management of transsexualism. *Canadian Psychiatric Association Journal,* 1974, *19,* 1–6.

HOENIG, J., & KENNA, J. Epidemiological aspects of transsexualism. *Psychiatric Clinica,* 1973, *6,* 65–80.

HOOKER, E. The adjustment of the overt male homosexual. *Journal of Projective Techniques,* 1957, *21,* 18–31.

HOOKER, E. Parental relations and male homosexuality in patient and nonpatient samples. *Journal of Consulting and Clinical Psychology,* 1969, *33,* 140–142.

HOFFMAN, M. *The gay world: Male homosexuality and the social creation of evil.* New York: Basic Books, 1968.

HUMPHREYS, L. *Tearoom trade: Impersonal sex in public places.* Chicago: Aldine, 1970.

JONES, J. R., & SAMINY, J. Plasma testosterone levels and female transsexualism. *Archives of Sexual Behavior,* 1973, *2,* 251–256.

JOST, A. The role of fetal hormones in prenatal development. *Harvey Lectures,* Series 55, 1961, 201–226.

JUNKE, N., HAHN, E., LINDBERGH, J. O., & BRASSEUR, F. *Sex and love today.* New York: Vala Publishing, 1967.

KALLMANN, F. J. Twin and sibship study of overt male homosexuality. *American Journal of Human Genetics,* 1952, *4* 136–146.

KANFER, F., & PHILLIPS, J. *The learning foundations of behavior therapy.* New York: John Wiley and Sons, 1970.

KARLEN, A. *Sexuality and homosexuality.* New York: W. W. Norton, 1971.

KATCHADOURIAN, H. A., & LUNDE, D. T. *Fundamentals of human sexuality.* New York: Holt, Rinehart, and Winston, 1972.

KETTERER, W. A. Homosexuality and venereal disease. *Medical Aspects of Human Sexuality,* 1971, *5,* 119.

KINSEY, A. C., POMEROY, W. B., & MARTIN, C. E. *Sexual behavior in the human male.* Philadelphia: W. B. Saunders, 1948.

KINSEY, A. C., POMEROY, W. B., MARTIN, C. E., & GEBHARD, P. *Sexual behavior in the human female.* Philadelphia: W. B. Saunders, 1953.

KOHLENBERG, R. J. Treatment of a homosexual pedophiliac using in vivo desensitization: A case study. *Journal of Abnormal Psychology,* 1974, *83,* 192–195.

KOLB, L. C. *Modern clinical psychiatry.* Philadelphia: W. B. Saunders, 1973.

KOLODNY, R. C., MASTERS, W. H., HENDRYX, J., & TORO, G. Plasma testosterone and semen analysis in male homosexuals. *New England Journal of Medicine,* 1971, *285,* 1170–1174.

KRAFFT-EBING, R. V. (1886) *Psychopathia sexualis.* New York: Putnam, 1965.

LACEY, W. K. *The family in classical Greece.* New York: Cornell University Press, 1968.

LANG, T. Studies on the genetic determination of homosexuality. *Journal of Nervous and Mental Disease,* 1940, *92,* 55–64.

LONDON, L. S., & CAPRIO, F. S. *Sexual deviations.* Washington, D.C.: Linacre Press, 1951.

LONEY, J. Background factors, sexual experiences, and attitudes toward treatment in two "normal" homosexual samples. *Journal of Consulting and Clinical Psychology,* 1972, *38,* 57–75.

LONEY, J. Family dynamics in homosexual women. *Archives of Sexual Behavior,* 1973, *2,* 343–350.

LORAINE, J. A., ADAMOPOULOS, D. A., KIRKHAM, K. E., ISMAIL, A. A., & DORE, G. A. Patterns of hormone excretion in male and female homosexuals. *Nature,* 1971, *234,* 552–554.

MARGOLESE, M. S. Homosexuality: A new endocrine correlate. *Hormones and Behaviour,* 1970, *1,* 151.

MARKS, J. M., & GELDER, M. G. Transvestism and fetishism: Clinical and psychological changes during faradic aversion. *British Journal of Psychiatry,* 1967, *113,* 711–729.

MARQUIS, J. Orgasmic reconditioning: Changing sexual object choice through controlling masturbation fantasies. *Journal of Behavior Therapy and Experimental Psychiatry,* 1970, *1,* 263–271.

Marshall, D. S., & Suggs, R. C. *Human sexual behavior.* New York: Basic Books, 1971.

Masters, W. H., & Johnson, V. E. *Human sexual response.* Boston: Little, Brown, 1966.

Masters, W. H., & Johnson, V. E. *Human sexual inadequacy.* Boston: Little, Brown, 1970.

McCary, J. L. *Human sexuality.* New York: Van Nostrand, 1973.

McGuire, R. J., Carlisle, J. M., & Young, B. G. Sexual deviations as conditioned behavior: A hypothesis. *Behaviour Research and Therapy,* 1965, *2,* 185–190.

Miller, P. M., Bradley, J. B., Gross, R. S., & Wood, G. Review of homosexuality research (1960–1966) and some implications for treatment. *Psychotherapy: Theory, Research and Practice,* 1968, *5,* 3–6.

Millon, T. *Modern psychopathology.* Philadelphia: W. B. Saunders, 1969.

Mischel, W. A social-learning view of sex differences in behavior. In E. Maccoby (Ed.), *The development of sex differences.* Palo Alto: Stanford University Press, 1966.

Mohr, J. W., Turner, R. E., & Jerry, M. B. *Pedophilia and exhibitionism.* Toronto: University of Toronto Press, 1964.

Money, J. Sexual dimorphism and homosexual gender identity. *Psychological Bulletin,* 1970, *74,* 425–440.

Money, J. Prefatory remarks on outcome of sex reassignment in 24 cases of transsexualism. *Archives of Sexual Behavior,* 1971, *1,* 163–165.

Money, J. Sex reassignment therapy in gender identity disorders. In H. L. P. Resnik & M. E. Wolfgang (Eds.), *Sexual behaviors: Social, clinical, and legal aspects.* Boston: Little, Brown, 1972.

Money, J., & Brennan, J. G. Sexual dimorphism in the psychology of female transsexuals. *Journal of Nervous and Mental Disease,* 1968, *147,* 487–499.

Money, J., & Pollitt, E. Cytogenetic and psychosexual ambiguity: Klinefelter's syndrome and transvestism compared. *Archives of General Psychiatry,* 1964, *11,* 589–595.

Money, J., & Primrose, C. Sexual dimorphism and dissociation in the psychology of male transsexuals. *Journal of Nervous and Mental Disease,* 1968, *147,* 472–486.

Myrick, F. Attitudinal differences between heterosexually and homosexually oriented males and between covert and overt male homosexuals. *Journal of Abnormal Psychology,* 1974, *83,* 81–86.

Neumann, F., & Elger, W. Permanent changes in gonadal function and sexual behavior as a result of early feminization of male rats by treatment with an antiandrogenic steroid. *Endokrinologie,* 1966, *50,* 209–225.

Ovesey, L., Gaylin, W., & Hendin, H. Psychotherapy of male homosexuality. *Archives of General Psychiatry,* 1963, *9,* 19–31.

Pauly, I. Male psychosexual inversion: Transsexualism. *Archives of General Psychiatry,* 1965, *13,* 172–181.

Pauly, I. Current status of the change of sex operation. *Journal of Nervous and Mental Disease,* 1968, *47,* 460–471.

Pomeroy, W. B. Parents and homosexuality: I. *Sexology,* 1966, March, 508–511.

President's Commission on Law Enforcement and Administration of Justice. *The challenge of crime in a free society.* Washington, D.C.: U.S. Government Printing Office, 1967.

Prince, V. *The transvestite and his wife.* Los Angeles: Argyle Books, 1967.

Prince, V., & Bentler, P. M. Survey of 504 cases of transvestism. *Psychological Reports,* 1972, *31,* 903–917.

Pritchard, M. Homosexuality and genetic sex. *Journal of Mental Sciences,* 1962, *108,* 616–623.

Raboch, J., & Nedoma, K. Sex chromatin and sexual behavior. A study of 36 men with female nuclear pattern and of 194 homosexuals. *Psychosomatic Medicine,* 1958, *20,* 55–59.

Rachman, S. Sexual fetishism: An experimental analogue. *Psychological Record,* 1966, *16,* 293–296.

Rachman, S., & Hodgon, R. J. Experimentally-induced "sexual fetishism": Replication and development. *Psychological Record,* 1968, *18,* 25–27.

Randall, J. Preoperative and postoperative status of male and female transsexuals. In R. Green & J. Money (Eds.), *Transsexualism and sex reassignment.* Baltimore: Johns Hopkins Press, 1969.

Redlich, F. C., & Freedman, D. X. *The theory and practice of psychiatry.* New York: Basic Books, 1966.

Reinisch, J. M. Fetal hormones, the brain, and human sex differences: A heuristic, integrative review of the recent literature. *Archives of Sexual Behavior,* 1974, *3,* 51–90.

Rekers, G. A., & Lovaas, O. J. Behavioral treatment of deviant sex-role behaviors in a male child. *Journal of Applied Behavior Analysis,* 1974, *7,* 173–190.

Revitch, E., & Weiss, R. G. The pedophiliac offender. *Diseases of the Nervous System,* 1962, *23,* 73–78.

Rimland, B. Psychogenesis versus biogenesis: The issues and the evidence. In S. C. Plog & R. B. Edgerton (Eds.), *Changing perspectives in mental illness.* New York: Holt, Rinehart, and Winston, 1969.

Rooth, G. Exhibitionism outside Europe and America. *Archives of Sexual Behavior,* 1973, *4,* 351–363.

Rosen, E., Fox, R. E., & Gregory, I. *Abnormal psychology.* Philadelphia: W. B. Saunders, 1972.

Saghir, M. T., & Robins, E. Homosexuality: I. Sexual behavior of the female homosexual. *Archives of General Psychiatry,* 1969, *20,* 192–201.

Saghir, M. T., & Robins, E. *Male and female homosexuality: A comprehensive investigation.* Baltimore: Williams & Wilkins, 1973.

Saghir, M. T., Robins, E., & Walbran, B. Homosexuality: II. Sexual behavior of the male homosexual. *Archives of General Psychiatry,* 1969, *21,* 219–229.

Salzman, L. *Developments in psychoanalysis.* New York: Grune and Stratten, 1962.

Siegelman, M. Parental background of male homosexuals and heterosexuals. *Archives of Sexual Behavior,* 1974, *3,* 3–17. (a)

Siegelman, M. Parental background of homosexual and heterosexual women. *British Journal of Psychiatry,* 1974, *124,* 14–21. (b)

SIECUS. *Sexuality and man.* New York: Sex Information and Education Council of the United States, 1970.

Slater, E. The sibs and children of homosexuals. In D. R. Smith & W. A. Davidson (Eds.), *Symposium on nuclear sex.* New York: Interscience Publishers, 1958.

Smith, D. K. Transsexualism, sex reassignment surgery and the law. *Cornell Law Review*, 1971, *56*, 963–1009.
Socarides, C. W. *The overt homosexual.* New York: Grune and Stratton, 1968.
Socarides, C. W. Homosexuality—basic concepts and psychodynamics. *International Journal of Psychiatry*, 1972, *10*, 118–125.
Spitzer, R. L. A proposal about homosexuality and the APA nomenclature: Homosexuality as an irregular form of sexual behavior and sexual orientation disturbance as a psychiatric disorder. In R. J. Stoller, J. Marmor, I. Bieber, R. Gold, C. W. Socarides, R. Green, & R. L. Spitzer, A symposium: Should homosexuality be in the APA nomenclature? *American Journal of Psychiatry*, 1973, *130*, 1207–1216.
Steiner, B. W., Zajac, A. S., & Mohr, J. W. A gender identity project: The organization of a multidisciplinary study. *Canadian Psychiatric Association Journal*, 1974, *19*, 7–12.
Stephan, W. G. Parental relationships and early social experiences of activist male homosexuals and male heterosexuals. *Journal of Abnormal Psychology*, 1973, *82*, 506–513.
Stevenson, I., & Wolpe, P. Recovery from sexual deviations through overcoming nonsexual neurotic responses. *American Journal of Psychiatry*, 1960, *116*, 737–742.
Stoller, R. J. *Sex and gender.* New York: Science House, 1968.
Stoller, R. J. Etiological factors in female transsexualism: A first approximation. *Archives of Sexual Behavior*, 1972, *2*, 47–64.
Stoller, R. J. Male transsexualism: Uneasiness. *American Journal of Psychiatry*, 1973, *130*, 536–539.
Thompson, N., McCandless, B., & Strickland, B. Personal adjustment of male and female homosexuals and heterosexuals. *Journal of Abnormal Psychology*, 1971, *78*, 237–240.
Thompson, N., Schwartz, D., McCandless, B., & Edwards, D. Parent-child relationships and sexual identity in male and female homosexuals and heterosexuals. *Journal of Consulting and Clinical Psychology*, 1973, *41*, 120–127.
Ullmann, L. P., & Krasner, L. *A psychological approach to abnormal behavior.* Englewood Cliffs, N.J.: Prentice-Hall, 1969.
Walinder, J. Transsexualism: Definition, prevalence and sex distribution. *Acta Psychiatricia Scandinavia*, 1968, *203*, 255–258.
Weinberg, M. S., & Williams, C. J. *Male homosexuals: Their problems and adaptations.* New York: Oxford University Press, 1974.
Wickramasekera, I. The application of learning theory to the treatment of a case of sexual exhibitionism. *Psychotherapy: Theory, Research and Practice*, 1968, *5*, 108–112.
Wilson, G. T., & Davison, G. C. Behavior therapy and homosexuality: A critical perspective. *Behavior Therapy*, 1974, *5*, 16–28.
Witzig, J. S. The group treatment of male exhibitionists. *American Journal of Psychiatry*, 1968, *125*, 75–81.
Wolff, C. *Love between women.* New York: Harper & Row, 1971.
Wolpe, J. *Psychotherapy by reciprocal inhibition.* Palo Alto: Stanford University Press, 1958.
Yates, A. J. *Behavior therapy.* New York: John Wiley and Sons, 1970.

13. Personality Disorders, Psychopathy, and Alcoholism

Baldwin, A. L., Kalhorn, J., & Breese, F. H. Patterns of parental behavior. *Psychological Monographs*, No. 3, 1945.
Bales, R. F. Cultural difference in rate of alcoholism. In R. G. McCarthy (Ed.), *Drinking and intoxication.* New York: Free Press, 1959.
Bandura, A., & Walters, R. *Adolescent aggression.* New York: Harper & Row, 1959.
Bogen, E. The human toxicology of alcohol. In H. Emerson (Ed.), *Alcohol and man.* New York: Macmillan, 1932.
Braucht, G. N., Brakarsh, D., Follingstad, D., & Berry, K. L. Deviant drug use in adolescence: A review of psychosocial correlates. *Psychological Bulletin*, 1973, *79*, 92–106.
Cameron, N. *Personality development and psychopathology.* Boston: Houghton Mifflin, 1963.
Campagna, A. F., & Harter, S. Moral judgment in sociopathic and normal children. *Journal of Personality and Social Psychology*, 1975, *31*, 199–205.
Chafetz, M. E. Alcoholism. In A. M. Freedman & H. I. Kaplan (Eds.), *Comprehensive textbook of psychiatry.* Baltimore: Williams & Wilkins, 1967.
Chesno, F. A., & Kilmann, P. R. Effects of stimulation intensity on sociopathic avoidance learning. *Journal of Abnormal Psychology*, 1975, *84*, 144–150.
Cleckley, H. M. Psychopathic states. In S. Arieti (Ed.), *American handbook of psychiatry.* New York: Basic Books, 1959.
Cleckley, H. M. *The mask of insanity.* St. Louis: C. V. Mosby, 1964.
Conger, J. J. The effects of alcohol on conflict behavior in the albino rat. *Quarterly Journal of Studies on Alcohol*, 1951, *12*, 1–29.
Eron, L. D., Walder, L. D., & Lefkowitz, M. M. *Learning of aggression in children.* Boston: Little, Brown, 1971.
Goldberg, L. Quantitative studies on alcohol tolerance in man. *Acta Physiologica. Scandinavica*, 1943, *1*, Supplement 16.
Gray, K. C., & Hutchison, H. C. The psychopathic personality: A survey of Canadian psychiatrists' opinions. *Canadian Psychiatric Association Journal*, 1964, *9*, 452–461.
Greer, S. Study of parental loss in neurotics and sociopaths. *Archives of General Psychiatry*, 1964, *11*, 177–180.
Gregory, I. Studies on parental deprivation in psychiatric patients. *American Journal of Psychiatry*, 1958, *115*, 432–442.
Gusfield, J. The structural context of college drinking. In G. L. Maddox (Ed.), *The domesticated drug: Drinking among collegians.* New Haven, Conn.: College and University Press, 1970.
Hare, R. D. *Psychopathy: Theory and research.* New York: John Wiley and Sons, 1970.

Hill, D., & Watterson, D. Electroencephalographic studies of the psychopathic personality. *Journal of Neurology and Psychiatry,* 1942, *5,* 47–64.

Jellinek, E. M. Phases of alcohol addiction. *Quarterly Journal of Studies on Alcohol,* 1952, *13,* 673–684.

Jellinek, E. M. *The disease concept of alcoholism.* New Haven, Conn.: Hillhouse Press, 1960.

Jenkins, R. L., & Hewitt, L. Types of personality structure in child guidance clinics. *American Journal of Orthopsychiatry,* 1944, *14,* 84–94.

Johns, J. H., & Quay, H. C. The effect of social reward on verbal conditioning in psychopathic and neurotic military offenders. *Journal of Consulting Psychology,* 1962, *26,* 217–220.

Jurkovic, G. J., & Prentice, N. M. Dimensions of moral interaction and moral judgment in delinquent and nondelinquent families. *Journal of Consulting and Clinical Psychology,* 1974, *42,* 256–262.

Keller, M. The definition of alcoholism and the estimation of its prevalence. In D. J. Pittman & C. R. Snyder (Eds.), *Society, culture and drinking patterns.* New York: John Wiley and Sons, 1962.

Kohlberg, L. Development of moral character and moral ideology. *Review of child development research.* Vol. 1. New York: Russell Sage Foundation, 1964.

Kohlberg, L. Stage and sequence: The cognitive-developmental approach of socialization. In D. A. Goslin (Ed.), *Handbook of socialization theory and research.* Chicago: Rand McNally, 1969.

Kurtines, W., & Greif, E. B. The development of moral thought: Review and evaluation of Kohlberg's approach. *Psychological Bulletin,* 1974, *81,* 453–470.

Lykken, D. T. A study of anxiety in the sociopathic personality. *Journal of Abnormal and Social Psychology,* 1957, *55,* 6–10.

Marlatt, G. A., Demming, B., & Reid, J. B. Loss of control drinking in alcoholics: An experimental analogue. *Journal of Abnormal Psychology,* 1973, *81,* 233–241.

McClelland, D. C., Davis, W. N., Kalin, R., & Wanner, E. *The drinking man.* New York: Free Press, 1972.

McCord, W., & McCord, J. *The psychopath: An essay on the criminal mind.* New York: Van Nostrand, 1964.

McNeil, E. B. *The quiet furies: Man and disorder.* Englewood Cliffs, N. J.: Prentice-Hall, 1967.

Menninger, K. *Man against himself.* New York: Harcourt Brace Jovanovich, 1938.

Millon, T. *Modern psychopathology.* Philadelphia: W. B. Saunders, 1969.

Mischel, W. Preference for delayed reinforcement and social responsibility. *Journal of Abnormal and Social Psychology,* 1961, *62,* 1–7.

Mizruchi, E. H., & Perrucci, R. Prescription, proscription and permissiveness: Aspects of norms and deviant drinking behavior. In G. L. Maddox (Ed.), *The domesticated drug: Drinking among collegians.* New Haven, Conn.: College and University Press, 1970.

National Institute of Mental Health. *Alcohol and alcoholism.* Washington, D.C.: U.S. Government Printing Office, 1972.

Oltman, J., & Friedman, S. Parental deprivation in psychiatric conditions, III. *Diseases of the Nervous System,* 1967, *28,* 298–303.

Page, J. D. *Psychopathology: The science of understanding deviance.* Chicago: Aldine, 1971.

Partridge, G. E. A study of 50 cases of psychopathic personality. *American Journal of Psychiatry,* 1928, *7,* 953–973.

Peterson, D. R., & Becker, W. C. Family interaction and delinquency. In H. C. Quay (Ed.), *Juvenile deliquency: Research and theory.* New York: Van Nostrand, 1965.

Pritchard, J. C. *A treatise on insanity.* Philadelphia: Haswell, Barrington and Haswell, 1835.

Quay, H. C. Psychopathic personality as pathological stimulation seeking. *American Journal of Psychiatry,* 1965, *122,* 180–183.

Ray, O. S. *Drugs, society, and human behavior.* St. Louis: C. V. Mosby, 1972.

Rosenquist, C. M., & Megaree, E. I. *Delinquency in three cultures.* Austin: University of Texas Press, 1969.

Schachter, S., & Latané, B. Crime, cognition and the autonomic nervous system. In M. R. Jones (Ed.), *Nebraska symposium on motivation.* Lincoln: University of Nebraska Press, 1964.

Shagass, C., & Schwartz, M. Observations on somatosensory cortical reactivity in personality disorders. *Journal of Nervous and Mental Disease,* 1962, *135,* 44–51.

Skolnick, J. H. Religious affiliation and drinking behavior. *Quarterly Journal of Studies on Alcohol,* 1958, *19,* 452–470.

Skrzypek, G. J. The effects of perceptual isolation and arousal on anxiety, complexity preference, and novelty preference in psychopathic and neurotic delinquents. *Journal of Abnormal Psychology,* 1969, *74,* 321–329.

Snyder, C. R. *Alcohol and the Jews.* New York: Free Press, 1958.

Wanberg, K. W., & Horn, J. L. Alcoholism symptom patterns of men and women: A comparative study. *Quarterly Journal of Studies on Alcohol,* 1970, *31,* 40–61.

Wiesen, A. E. Differential reinforcing effects of onset and offset of stimulation on the operant behavior of normals, neurotics, and psychopaths. (Doctoral dissertation, University of Florida) Ann Arbor, Mich.: University Microfilms, 1965, No. 65-9625.

Wilsnack, S. C. Sex role identity in female alcoholism. *Journal of Abnormal Psychology,* 1973, *82,* 253–261.

14. Depression, Mania, and Suicide

Abraham, K. (1911) Notes on the psychoanalytic investigation and treatment of manic-depressive insanity and allied conditions. In K. Abraham, *Selected papers on psychoanalysis.* New York: Basic Books, 1960.

Abraham, K. (1916) The first pregenital stage of libido. In K. Abraham, *Selected papers on psychoanalysis.* New York: Basic Books, 1960.

Adams, R. L., Giffen, R. B., & Garfield, F. Risk taking among suicide attempters. *Journal of Abnormal Psychology,* 1973, *82,* 262–267.

Akiskal, H. S., & McKinney, W. T. Depressive disorders: Toward a unified hypothesis. *Science,* 1973, *182,* 20–28.

Arieti, S. Manic-depressive psychosis. In S. Arieti (Ed.), *American handbook of psychiatry,* Vol. 1. New York: Basic Books, 1959.

Beck, A. T. Thinking and depression: I. Idiosyncratic content and cognitive distortions. *Archives of General Psychiatry,* 1963, *9,* 324–454.

Beck, A. T. *Depression: Clinical, experimental, and theoretical aspects.* New York: Harper & Row, 1967.

Beck, A. T. *Depression.* Philadelphia: University of Pennsylvania Press, 1972.

Beck, A. T., & Ward, C. H. Dreams of depressed patients: Characteristic themes in manifest content. *Archives of General Psychiatry,* 1961, *5,* 462–467.

Becker, J., Spielberger, C. D., & Parker, J. B. Value achievement and authoritarian attitudes in psychiatric patients. *Journal of Clinical Psychology,* 1963, *19,* 57–61.

Bibring, E. The mechanism of depression. In P. Greenacre (Ed.), *Affect disorders: Psychoanalytic contribution to their study.* New York: International Universities Press, 1953.

Blatt, S. J., & Ritzler, B. A. Suicide and the representation of transparency and cross-sections on the Rorschack. *Journal of Consulting and Clinical Psychology,* 1974, *42,* 280–287.

Bosse, J. J., Croghan, L. M., Greenstein, M. B., Katz, N. W., Oliver, J. M., Powell, D. A., & Smith, W. R. Frequency of depression in the freshman year as measured in a random sample by a retrospective version of the Beck Depression Inventory. *Journal of Consulting and Clinical Psychology,* 1975, *43,* 746–747.

Bowlby, J. Grief and mourning in infancy and early childhood. *Psychoanalytic Study of the Child,* 1960, *15,* 9–52.

Bowlby, J. *Attachment and loss.* Vol. 1. New York: Basic Books, 1969.

Bruyn, H. B., & Seiden, R. H. Student suicide: Fact or fancy? *Journal of the American College Health Association,* 1965, *14,* 69–77.

Bunney, W. E., & Davis, J. M. Norepinephrine in depressive reactions. *Archives of General Psychiatry,* 1965, *13,* 483–494.

Buss, A. H. *Psychopathology.* New York: John Wiley and Sons, 1966.

Cameron, N. *Personality development and psychopathology.* Boston: Houghton Mifflin Company, 1963.

Cohen, M. B., Baker, G., Cohen, R. A., Fromm-Reichmann, F., & Weigert, E. V. An intensive study of twelve cases of manic-depressive psychosis. *Psychiatry,* 1954, *17,* 103–137.

Cole, J. O. Therapeutic efficacy of antidepressive drugs. *Journal of the American Medical Association,* 1964, *190,* 448–462.

Coleman, R. E. Manipulation of self-esteem as a determinant of mood of elated and depressed women. *Journal of Abnormal Psychology,* 1975, *84,* 693–700.

Coleman, R. E., & Miller, A. G. The relationship between depression and marital maladjustment in a clinic population: A multitrait–multimethod study. *Journal of Consulting and Clinical Psychology,* 1975, *43,* 647–651.

Davis, J. M. Critique of single amine theories: Evidence of a cholinergic influence in the major mental illness. In D. X. Freedman (Ed.), *Research on Nervous and Mental Diseases,* Vol. 54. New York: Raven Press, 1975. (a)

Davis, J. M. Tricyclic antidepressants. L. Simpson (Ed.), *Textbook of psychotropic drugs.* New York: Plenum, 1975. (b)

Davison, G. C., & Neale, J. M. *Abnormal psychology.* New York: John Wiley and Sons, 1974.

Diethelm, O., & Hefferman, T. Felix Platter and psychiatry. *Journal of the History of Behavioral Science,* 1965, *1,* 10–23.

Durkheim, E. (1897) *Suicide.* (Translated by J. A. Spaulding & G. Simpson.) New York: Free Press, 1951.

Dweck, C. S., & Reppucci, N. D. Learned helplessness and reinforcement responsibility in children. *Journal of Personality and Social Psychology,* 1973, *25,* 109–116.

Erickson, E. H. *Childhood and society.* New York: W. W. Norton, 1950.

Eysenck, H. J. The classification of depressive illness. *British Journal of Psychiatry,* 1970, *117,* 241–250.

Faris, R. E. L., & Dunham, H. W. *Mental disorders in urban areas: An ecological study of schizophrenia and other psychoses.* Chicago: University of Chicago Press, 1939.

Fenichel, O. *The psychoanalytic theory of neurosis.* New York: W. W. Norton, 1945.

Ferster, C. B. Animal behavior and mental illness. *Psychological Record,* 1966, *28,* 857–870.

Ferster, C. B. A functional analysis of depression. *American Psychologist,* 1973, *28,* 857–870.

Flippo, J. R., & Lewinsohn, P. M. Effects of failure on the self-esteem of depressed and nondepressed subjects. *Journal of Consulting and Clinical Psychology,* 1971, *36,* 151.

Freud, S. (1917) Mourning and melancholia. In E. Jones (Ed.), *The collected papers of Sigmund Freud.* New York: Basic Books, 1959.

Gatchel, R. J., Paulus, P. B., & Maples, C. W. Learned helplessness and self-reported affect. *Journal of Abnormal Psychology,* 1975, *84,* 732–734.

Gibson, R. W. The family background and early life experience of the manic-depressive patient: A comparison with the schizophrenic patient. *Psychiatry,* 1958, *21,* 71–90.

Glass, D. C., & Singer, J. E. *Urban stress: Experiments on noise and social stressors.* New York: Academic Press, 1972.

Grinker, R., Miller, J., Sabshin, M., Nunn, R., & Nunnally, J. *The phenomena of depressions.* New York: Hoeber, 1961.

Hammen, C. L., & Glass, D. R. Depression, activity, and evaluation of reinforcement. *Journal of Abnormal Psychology,* 1975, *84,* 718–721.

Hauri, P. Dreams in patients remitted from reactive depression. *Journal of Abnormal Psychology,* 1976, *85,* 1–10.

Hiroto, D. S., & Seligman, M. E. P. Generality of learned helplessness in man. *Journal of Personality and Social Psychology,* 1975, *31,* 311–327.

Hollingshead, A. B., & Redlich, F. C. *Social class and mental illness.* New York: John Wiley and Sons, 1958.

Janowsky, D. S., Davis, J. M., El-Yousef, M. K., & Sekerke, H. J. A cholinergic-adrenergic hypothesis of mania and depression. *Lancet,* 1972, 632–635.

JELLIFFE, S. E. Some historical phases of the manic-depressive synthesis. *Association for Research on Nervous and Mental Processes,* 1931, *11,* 3–47.

KENYON, F. E. Hypochondriasis: A survey of some historical, clinical and social aspects. *British Journal of Psychiatry,* 1965, *38,* 308–325.

KILOH, L. G., & GARSIDE, R. F. The independence of neurotic depression and endogenous depression. *British Journal of Psychiatry,* 1963, *109,* 451–463.

KLEINMUNTZ, B. *Essentials of abnormal behavior.* New York: Harper & Row, 1974.

KOCHANSKY, G. E. Risk taking and hedonic mood stimulation in suicide attempters. *Journal of Abnormal Psychology,* 1973, *81,* 80–86.

KOPIN, I. J. Storage and metabolism in catecholamines; the role of monoamineoxidase. *Pharmacological Review,* 1964, *16,* 179–164.

KRAEPELIN, E. *Textbook of psychiatry.* New York: Macmillan, 1923.

KRAMER, M., WHITMAN, R. M., BALDRIDGE, W., & LANSKY, L. Dreaming in the depressed. *Canadian Psychiatric Association Journal,* 1966, *11,* 178–192.

LANGNER, T. S., & MICHAEL, S. T. Life stress and mental health: The midtown Manhattan study. New York: Free Press, 1963.

LAXER, R. M. Self-concept changes of depressive patients in a general hospital treatment. *Journal of Consulting Psychology,* 1964, *28,* 214–219.

LAZARUS, A. A. Learning theory and the treatment of depression. *Behavior Research and Therapy,* 1968, *6,* 83–89.

LEON, G. R. *Case histories of deviant behavior: A social learning analysis.* Boston: Holbrook Press, 1974.

LEONARD, C. V., & FLINN, D. E. Suicidal ideation and behavior in youthful nonpsychiatric populations. *Journal of Consulting and Clinical Psychology,* 1972, *38,* 366–371.

LEVENSON, M., & NEURINGER, C. Problem-solving behavior in suicidal adolescents. *Journal of Consulting and Clinical Psychology,* 1971, *37,* 433–436.

LEWINSOHN, P. M. Engagement in pleasant activities and depression level. *Journal of Abnormal Psychology,* 1975, *84,* 729–731.

LEWINSOHN, P. M., & LIBET, J. Pleasant events, activity schedules, and depressions. *Journal of Abnormal Psychology,* 1972, *79,* 291–295.

LITMAN, R. E., & WOLD, C. T. Masked depression and suicide. In S. Lesse (Ed.), *Masked depression.* New York: Jason Aronson, 1974.

LOFTUS, T. A. *Meaning and methods of diagnosis in clinical psychiatry.* Philadelphia: Lea, 1960.

MALZBERG, B. Mental disease in relation to economic status. *Journal of Nervous and Mental Disease,* 1956, *123,* 256–261.

MARTORANO, R. D., & NATHAN, P. E. Syndromes of psychosis and nonpsychosis: Factor analysis of a systems analysis. *Journal of Abnormal Psychology,* 1972, *80,* 1–10.

MCNEIL, E. B. *The quiet furies.* Englewood Cliffs, N.J.: Prentice-Hall, 1967.

MENDELS, J. *Concepts of depression.* New York: John Wiley and Sons, 1970.

MENDELS, J., & COCHRANE, C. The nosology of depression: The endogenous reactive concept. *American Journal of Psychiatry,* 1968, *124,* 1–11.

MENDELWICZ, J. A genetic contribution toward an understanding of affective equivalents. In S. Lesse (Ed.), *Masked depression.* New York: Jason Aronson, 1974.

MENNINGER, K. (1938) *Man against himself.* New York: Harcourt Brace Jovanovich, 1965.

MILLER, W. R., & SELIGMAN, M. E. P. Depression and the perception of reinforcement. *Journal of Abnormal Psychology,* 1973, *82,* 62–73.

MILLER, W. R., & SELIGMAN, M. E. P. Depression and learned helplessness in man. *Journal of Abnormal Psychology,* 1975, *84,* 228–238.

MONNELLY, E. P., WOODRUFF, R. A., & ROBINS, L. Manic-depressive illness and social achievement in a public hospital sample. *Acta Psychiatrica Scandinavica,* 1974, *50,* 318–325.

MOSS, L. M., & HAMILTON, D. M. Psychotherapy in the suicidal patient. *American Journal of Psychiatry,* 1956, *112,* 814–820.

MUELLER, P. S., HENINGER, G. R., & MACDONALD, R. K. Studies on glucose utilization and insulin sensitivity in affective disorders. In T. A. Williams, M. M. Katz, & J. A. Shield (Eds.), *Recent advances in the psychobiology of the depressive illness.* Washington, D.C.: U.S. Government Printing Office, 1972.

NADITCH, M. P., GARGAN, M. A., & MICHAEL, L. B. Denial, anxiety, locus of control, and the discrepancy between aspirations and achievement as components of depression. *Journal of Abnormal Psychology,* 1975, *84,* 1–9.

National Institute of Mental Health. *Utilization of mental health facilities—1971. DHEW* Publication No. NIH-74-657. Washington, D.C.: U.S. Government Printing Office, 1973.

OVERMIER, J. B., & SELIGMAN, M. E. P. Effects of inescapable shock upon subsequent escape and avoidance learning. *Journal of Comparative and Physiological Psychology,* 1967, *63,* 23–33.

PERRIS, C. A study of bipolar (manic-depressive) and unipolar recurrent depressive psychoses. *Acta Psychiatrica Scandinavica,* 1966, *44,* Supplement 194.

RENSHAW, D. C. Depression in the 1970s. *Diseases of the Nervous System,* 1973, *34,* 241–245.

RIE, H. E. Depression in childhood. *Journal of the American Academy of Child Psychiatry,* 1966, *5,* 653–685.

RIZLEY, R. The perception of causality in depression: An attributional analysis. Unpublished doctoral dissertation, Yale University, 1976.

ROBINS, E., & GUZE, S. B. Classification of affective disorders: The primary-secondary, the endogenous-reactive, and the neurotic-psychotic concepts. In T. A. Williams, M. M. Katz, & J. A. Shields (Eds.), *Recent advances in the psychobiology of the depressive illnesses.* Washington, D.C.: U.S. Government Printing Office, 1972.

ROBINS, E., & HARTMAN, B. K. Biochemical theories of mental disorder. In F. Albers (Ed.), *Basic neurochemistry.* Boston: Little, Brown, 1972.

ROSENBERG, P. H., & LATIMER, R. Suicide attempts by children. *Mental Hygiene,* 1956, *50,* 354–359.

ROSENTHAL, D. *Genetic theory and abnormal behavior.* New York: McGraw-Hill, 1970.

ROTH, S., & KUBAL, L. Effects of noncontingent reinforcement on tasks of differing importance: Facilitation and learned helplessness. *Journal of Personality and Social Psychology,* 1975, *32,* 680–691.

SCHLESS, A. P., MENDELS, J., KIPPERMAN, A., & COCHRANE, C. Depression and hostility. *Journal of Nervous and Mental Disorders,* 1974, *159,* 91–100.

SCHUYLER, D. *The depressive spectrum.* New York: Jason Aronson, 1974.

SCHUYLER, D., & BECK, A. T. The assessment of suicidal intent. In R. Litman (Ed.), *Proceedings of the Sixth International Congress for Suicide Prevention.* Ann Arbon: Edwards, 1972.

SEAY, B., HANSEN, E. W., & HARLOW, H. F. Mother-infant separation in monkeys. *Journal of Child Psychology and Psychiatry,* 1962, *3,* 123–132.

SEAY, B., & HARLOW, H. F. Maternal separation in the rhesus monkey. *Journal of Nervous and Mental Disease,* 1965, *140,* 434–440.

SECUNDA, S. K., KATZ, M. M., FRIEDMAN, R. J., & SCHUYLER, D. *Special report, 1973: The depressive disorders.* Washington, D.C.: U.S. Government Printing Office, 1973.

SEIDEN, R. Campus tragedy: A study of student suicide. *Journal of Abnormal and Social Psychology,* 1966, *71,* 389–399.

SELIGMAN, M. E. P. Fall into helplessness. *Psychology Today,* June, 1973.

SELIGMAN, M. E. P. *Helplessness: On depression, development, and death.* San Francisco: W. H. Freeman, 1975.

SELIGMAN, M. E. P., KLEIN, D. C., & MILLER, W. Depression. In H. Leitenberg (Ed.), *Handbook of behavior therapy.* Englewood Cliffs, N.J.: Prentice-Hall, 1974.

SELIGMAN, M. E. P., & MAIER, S. F. Failure to escape traumatic shock. *Journal of Experimental Psychology,* 1967, *74,* 1–9.

SHNEIDMAN, E. S. Classification of suicidal phenomena. *Bulletin of Suicidology.* Washington, D.C.: U.S. Government Printing Office, 1968.

SHNEIDMAN, E. S. Logical analysis. In G. Gerbner, O. K. Holsti, K. Krippendoff, W. J. Paisley, & P. J. Stone (Eds.), *The analysis of communication content.* New York: John Wiley and Sons, 1969.

SHNEIDMAN, E. S., & FARBEROW, N. L. Clues to suicide. In E. S. Shneidman & N. L. Farberow (Eds.), *Clues to suicide.* New York: McGraw-Hill, 1957.

SHNEIDMAN, E. S., & FARBEROW, N. L. A psychological approach to the study of suicide notes. In E. S. Shneidman, N. L. Farberow, & R. E. Litman (Eds.), *The psychology of suicide.* New York: Jason Aronson, 1970.

SPITZ, R. A. Anaclitic depression—an inquiry into the genesis of psychiatric conditions in early childhood. *Psychoanalytic Study of the Child,* 1949, *2,* 313–342.

STAATS, A. W. *Social behaviorism.* Homewood, Ill.: Dorsey, 1975.

STENGEL, E. Recent research into suicide and attempted suicide. *American Journal of Psychiatry,* 1962, *118,* 725–727.

SUOMI, S. J. Repetitive peer separation of young monkeys: Effects of vertical chamber confinement during separations. *Journal of Abnormal Psychology,* 1973, *81,* 1–10.

SUOMI, S. J., EISELE, C. D., GRADY, S. A., & HARLOW, H. F. Depressive behavior in adult monkeys following separation from family environment. *Journal of Abnormal Psychology,* 1975, *84,* 576–578.

SUOMI, S. J., HARLOW, H. F., & DOMEK, C. J. Effect of repetitive infant-infant separation of young monkeys. *Journal of Abnormal Psychology,* 1970, *76,* 162–172.

TEMOCHE, A., PUGH, T. F., & MCMAHON, B. Suicide rates among current and former mental institution patients. *Journal of Nervous and Mental Disorders,* 1964, *136,* 124–130.

WEISSMANN, M. M., & KLERMAN, G. L. Sex differences and the epidemology of depression. Unpublished manuscript, Department of Psychiatry, School of Medicine, Yale University, New Haven, Connecticut, 1976.

WENER, A. E., & REHM, L. P. Depressive affect: A test of behavioral hypotheses. *Journal of Abnormal Psychology,* 1975, *84,* 221–227.

WHEAT, W. D. Motivational aspects of suicide in patients during and after psychiatric treatment. *Southern Medical Journal,* 1960, *53,* 273–278.

WINOKUR, G. Family history studies VIII: Secondary depression is alive and well, and. . . . *Diseases of the Nervous System,* 1972, *33,* 94–99.

WINOKUR, G. The types of affective disorder. *Journal of Nervous and Mental Disorders,* 1973, *156,* 82–96.

WINOKUR, G., & PITTS, F. N. Affective disorder: I. Is reactive depression an entity. *Journal of Nervous and Mental Disease,* 1964, *138,* 541–547.

WOODRUFF, R. A., GOODWIN, D. W., & GUZE, S. B. *Psychiatric diagnosis.* New York: Oxford University Press, 1974.

YATES, A. J. *Behavior therapy.* New York: John Wiley and Sons, 1970.

ZEAMAN, D., & HOUSE, B. J. Approach and avoidance in the discrimination learning of retardates. In D. Zeaman et al. (Eds.), *Learning and transfer in mental defectives.* Progress Report No. 2, National Institute of Mental Health, 1960.

ZILBOORG, G. Manic-depressive psychosis. In S. Lorand (Ed.), *Psychoanalysis today: Its scope and function.* New York: Covici, Friede, 1933.

15 and 16. The Schizophrenic Syndromes and the Possible Etiologies of Schizophrenia

ABRAHAMS, J., & VARON, E. J. *Maternal dependency and schizophrenia: Mother and daughter in a therapeutic group.* New York: International Universities Press, 1953.

ALLEN, M., COHEN, S., & POLLIN, W. Schizophrenia in veteran twins: A diagnostic review. *American Journal of Psychiatry,* 1972, *128,* 939–945.

American Psychiatric Association. *Diagnostic and statistical manual of mental disorders (DSM-II).* Washington, D.C.: APA, 1968.

ANGYAL, A. The experience of the body-self in schizophrenia. *Archives of Neurology and Psychiatry,* 1936, *35,* 1029–1053.

ARIETI, S. Schizophrenia: The manifest symptomatology, the psychodynamic and formal mechanisms. In S. Arieti (Ed.), *American handbook of psychiatry.* Vol. 1. New York: Basic Books, 1959.

ASHBY, W. R., COLLINS, G. H., & BASSETT, M. The effects

of nicotinic acid, nicotinamide, and placebo on the chronic schizophrenic. *Journal of Mental Science,* 1960, *106,* 1555–1559.

Ban, T. A. Canadian niacin study. II. *Schizophrenia Bulletin,* 1971, *4,* 6–7.

Ban, T. A., & Lehmann, H. E. Nicotinic acid in the treatment of schizophrenia. *Canadian Psychiatric Association Journal,* 1970, *15,* 499–500.

Bateson, G., Jackson, D. D., Haley, J., & Weakland, J. Toward a theory of schizophrenia. *Behavioral Science,* 1956, *1,* 251–264.

Bauman, E., & Murray, D. J. Recognition versus recall in schizophrenia. *Canadian Journal of Psychology,* 1968, *22,* 18–25.

Becker, W. C. A genetic approach to the interpretation and evaluation of the process-reactive distinction in schizophrenia. *Journal of Abnormal and Social Psychology,* 1956, *53,* 229–236.

Behrens, M., Rosenthal, H., & Chodoff, P. Communication in lower class families of schizophrenics. *Archives of General Psychiatry,* 1968, *18,* 689–696.

Bellak, L. *Dementia praecox.* New York: Grune and Stratton, 1948.

Bender, L. A visual motor gestalt test and its clinical use. *American Orthopsychiatric Association Research Monograph,* 1938, No. 3.

Benjamin, J. D. A method for distinguishing and evaluating formal thought disorders in schizophrenia. In J. S. Kasanin (Ed.), *Language and thought in schizophrenia.* Berkeley: University of California Press, 1946.

Berkowitz, H. Effects of prior experimenter-subject relationships on reinforced reaction time of schizophrenics and normals. *Journal of Abnormal and Social Psychology,* 1964, *69,* 522–530.

Bertoch, D. J. Encoder-decoder variables, level of response uncertainty and verbal redundancy of psychiatric patients. Unpublished doctoral dissertation, University of Utah, 1966.

Bethel, H., & Redlick, R. W. *Statistical note 60: Provisional patient movement and administrative data, state and county mental hospital inpatient services, July 1, 1970 to June 20, 1971.* Rockville, Md.: National Institute of Mental Health, 1972.

Bexton, W. H., Heron, W., & Scott, T. H. Effects of decreased variation in the sensory environment. *Canadian Journal of Psychology,* 1954, *8,* 70–76.

Blaschko, H. The development of current concepts of catecholamine formation *Pharmacological Review, 1959, 11,* 307–316.

Blashfield, R. An evaluation of the DSM-II classification of schizophrenia as a nomenclature. *Journal of Abnormal Psychology,* 1973, *82,* 382–389.

Blatt, S. J., & Ritzler, B. A. Thought disorder and boundary disturbances in psychosis. *Journal of Consulting and Clinical Psychology,* 1974, *42,* 370–381.

Bleuler, E. *Dementia praecox or the group of schizophrenias.* New York: International Universities Press, 1950.

Bolles, M., & Goldstein, K. A study of schizophrenic patients. *Psychiatric Quarterly,* 1938, *12,* 42–65.

Böök, J. A. A genetic and neuropsychiatric investigation of a North-Swedish population with special regard to schizophrenia and mental deficiency. *Acta Genetica,* 1953, *4,* 1–139.

Boulton, A. A., Pollitt, R. J., & Majer, J. R. Identity of a urinary "pink spot" in schizophrenia and Parkinson's disease. *Nature,* 1967, *215,* 132–134.

Bourdillon, R. E., Clarke, C. A., Ridges, A. P., Sheppard, P. M., Harper, P., & Leslie, S. A. "Pink spot" in the urine of schizophrenics. *Nature,* 1965, *208,* 453–455.

Broadhurst, A. Time estimation related to personality, cognitive speed and schizophrenia. *Life Sciences,* 1968, *8,* 69–78.

Broen, W. E. *Schizophrenia: Research and theory.* New York: Academic Press, 1968.

Bumke, O. *Handbuch der geisteskrankheiten. Vol. 9. Die schizophrenie.* Berlin: Springer, 1932.

Buss, A. H. *Psychopathology.* New York: John Wiley and Sons, 1966.

Buss, A. H., & Lang, P. J. Psychological deficits in schizophrenia. I. Affect, reinforcement, and concept attainment. *Journal of Abnormal and Social Psychology,* 1965, *70,* 2–24.

Cameron, N. Reasoning, regression and communication in schizophrenics. *Psychological Monographs,* 1938, *50,* Whole No. 221.

Cameron, N. The paranoid pseudo-community. *American Journal of Sociology,* 1943, *49,* 32–38.

Cameron, N. Experimental analysis of schizophrenic thinking. In J. S. Kasanin (Ed.), *Language and thought in schizophrenia.* Berkeley: University of California Press, 1946.

Cameron, N. The paranoid pseudo-community revisited. *American Journal of Sociology,* 1959, *65,* 52–58.

Cameron, N. *Personality development and psychopathology: A dynamic approach.* Boston: Houghton Mifflin, 1963.

Chapman, L. J., Chapman, J. P., & Miller, G. A. A theory of verbal behavior in schizophrenia. In B. A. Maher (Ed.), *Progress in experimental personality research.* Vol. 1. New York: Academic Press, 1964.

Chapman, L. J., & McGhie, A. A comparative study of disordered attention in schizophrenia. *Journal of Mental Science,* 1962, *108,* 487–500.

Chapman, L. J., & Taylor, J. A. The breadth of deviate concepts used by schizophrenics. *Journal of Abnormal and Social Psychology,* 1957, *54,* 118–123.

Clausen, J. A., & Kohn, M. L. Relation of schizophrenia to the social structure of a small city. In B. Pasamanick (Ed.), *Epidemiology of mental disorder.* Washington, D.C.: American Association for the Advancement of Science, 1959.

Cohen, B. D., Nachmani, G., & Rosenberg, A. Referent communication disturbances in acute schizophrenia. *Journal of Abnormal Psychology,* 1974, *83,* 1–13.

Cooper, J. E., Kendell, R. E., Gurland, B. J., Sharp, L., Copeland, J. R.M., & Simon, R. *Psychiatric diagnosis in New York and London: A comparative study of mental hospital admissions.* New York: Oxford University Press, 1972.

Craig, R. J. Interpersonal competition, overinclusive thinking, and schizophrenia. *Journal of Consulting and Clinical Psychology,* 1973, *40,* 9–14.

Critchley, M. The neurology of psychotic speech. *British Journal of Psychiatry,* 1964, *110,* 353–364.

Crocetti, G. M., & Lemkau, P. V. Schizophrenia: II. Epidemiology. In A. M. Freeman & H. I. Kaplan (Eds.), *Comprehensive textbook of psychiatry.* Baltimore: Williams & Wilkins, 1967.

Cromwell, R. L., & Dokecki, P. R. Schizophrenic language: A disattention interpretation. In S. Rosenberg & J. H. Koplin (Eds.), *Developments in applied psycholinguistics research.* New York: Macmillan, 1968.

Deckner, D. W., & Cromwell, R. L. Commonality of word association process in schizophrenia as a function of premorbid adjustment chronicity and premorbid status. *Psychological Reports,* 1970, *26,* 503–509.

Depue, R. A., & Dubicki, M. D. Hospitalization and premorbid characteristics in withdrawn and active schizophrenics. *Journal of Consulting and Clinical Psychology,* 1974, *42,* 628–632.

De Wolfe, A. S. Are there two kinds of thinking in process and reactive schizophrenics? *Journal of Abnormal Psychology,* 1974, *83,* 285–290.

Dunham, H. W. *Community and schizophrenia: An epidemiological analysis.* Detroit: Wayne State University Press, 1965.

Farina, A. A note on "prognostic scales in schizophrenia." *Journal of Consulting Psychology,* 1967, *31,* 98.

Faurbye, A., & Pind, K. Investigation on the occurrence of the dopamine metabolite 3,4-dimethoxyphenylethylamine in the urine of schizophrenics. *Acta Psychiatrica Scandinavica,* 1964, *40,* 240–243.

Federn, P. *Ego psychology and the psychoses.* New York: Basic Books, 1952.

Feffer, M., & Phillips, L. Social attainment and performance under stress. *Journal of Personality,* 1953, *22,* 284–297.

Feinberg, I. A comparison of the visual hallucinations in schizophrenia with those induced by mescaline and LSD-25. In L. J. West (Ed.), *Halluncinations.* New York: Grune and Stratton, 1962.

Fenichel, O. *The psychoanalytic theory of neurosis.* New York: W. W. Norton, 1945.

Ferreira, A., & Winter, W. Decision-making in normal and abnormal two-child families. *Family Process,* 1968, *7,* 17–36.

Fischer, M., Havald, B., & Hauge, M. A. Danish twin study of schizophrenia. *British Journal of Psychiatry,* 1969, *115,* 981–990.

Fleck, S. Family dynamics and origin of schizophrenia. *Psychosomatic Medicine,* 1960, *22,* 333–343.

Fontana, A. F. Familial etiology of schizophrenia: Is a scientific methodology possible? *Psychological Bulletin,* 1966, *66,* 214–227.

Forrest, T. Treatment of the father in family therapy. *Family Process,* 1969, *8,* 106–118.

Friedhoff, A. J., & Van Winkle, E. Isolation and characterization of a compound from the urine of schizophrenics. *Nature,* 1962, *194,* 897–898.

Friedman, C., & Friedman, A. Characteristics of schizogenic families during a joint family story-telling task. *Family Process,* 1970, *9,* 333–354.

Fromm-Reichmann, F. Notes on the development of schizophrenia by psychoanalytic psychotherapy. *Psychiatry,* 1948, *11,* 267–277.

Galvin, J. Mothers of schizophrenics. *Journal of Nervous and Mental Disorders,* 1956, *123,* 568–570.

Garfield, S. A further note on "prognostic scales in schizophrenia." *Journal of Consulting Psychology,* 1967, *31,* 99.

Garmezy, N. The prediction of performance in schizophrenia. In P. H. Hoch & J. Zubin (Eds.), *Psychopathology of schizophrenia.* New York: Grune and Stratton, 1966.

Garmezy, N., & Rodnick, E. H. Premorbid adjustment and performance in schizophrenia: Implications for interpreting heterogeneity in schizophrenia. *Journal of Nervous and Mental Disease,* 1959, *129,* 450–466.

Gelburd, A. S., & Anker, J. A. Humans as reinforcing stimuli in schizophrenic performance. *Journal of Abnormal Psychology,* 1970, *75,* 195–198.

Goldberg, E. M., & Morrison, S. L. Schizophrenia and social class. *British Journal of Psychiatry,* 1963, *109,* 785–802.

Goldstein, K. *Human nature in the light of psychopathology.* Cambridge: Harvard University Press, 1940.

Goldstein, M. J., Held, J. M.,& Cromwell, R. L. Premorbid adjustment and paranoid-nonparanoid status in schizophrenia. *Psychological Bulletin,* 1968, *70,* 382–386.

Goldstone, S., & Goldfarb, J. L. Time estimation and psychopathology. *Perceptual and Motor Skills,* 1962, *15,* 28.

Gorelick, L. E. Affiliation among schizophrenics: A new test of the "social censure" hypothesis. Unpublished doctoral dissertation, Ohio State University, 1970.

Grinker, R. R., & Holzman, P. S. Schizophrenic pathology in young adults. *Archives of General Psychiatry,* 1973, *28,* 168–175.

Gunderson, J. G., Autry, J. H., Mosher, L. R., & Buchsbaum, S. Special report: Schizophrenia, 1974. *Schizophrenia Bulletin,* 1974.

Haley, J. Testing parental instructions of schizophrenic and normal children. *Journal of Abnormal Psychology,* 1968, *73,* 559–565.

Hallgren, B., & Sjögren, T. A clinical and genetico-statistical study of schizophrenia and low-grade mental deficiency in a large Swedish rural population. *Acta Psychiatrica Scandinavica,* 1959, Supplement 140.

Harris, J. G. An abbreviated form of the Phillips rating scale of premorbid adjustment in schizophrenia. *Journal of Abnormal Psychology,* 1975, *84,* 129–137.

Heath, R. G. *Studies in schizophrenia.* Cambridge: Harvard University Press, 1954.

Heath, R. G. A biochemical hypothesis on the etiology of schizophrenia. In D. D. Jackson (Ed.), *The etiology of schizophrenia.* New York: Basic Books, 1960.

Heath, R. G., Cohen, S. B., Silva, F., Leach, B. E., & Cohen, M. Administration of taraxein in humans. *Diseases of the Nervous System,* 1959, *20,* 106–208.

Heath, R. G., Guschwan, A. F., & Coffey, J. W. Relation of taraxein to schizophrenia. *Diseases of the Nervous System,* 1970, *31,* 391–395.

Heath, R. G., Martens, S., Leach, B. E., Cohen, M., & Angel, C. Effect on behavior in humans with the administration of taraxein. *American Journal of Psychiatry,* 1957, *114,* 14–24.

Heron, W. The pathology of boredom. *Scientific American,* 1957, 2–6.

Heston, L. L. Psychiatric disorders in foster home reared children of schizophrenic mothers. *British Journal of Psychiatry,* 1966, *112,* 819–825.

Heston, L. L. The genetics of schizophrenic and schizoid disease. *Science,* 1970, *167,* 249–256.

Hill, L. *Psychotherapeutic interaction in schizophrenics.* Chicago: University of Chicago Press, 1955.

Hoffer, A., & Osmond, H. Some schizophrenic recoveries. *Diseases of the Nervous System,* 1962, *23,* 204–210.

Hoffer, A., & Osmond, H. Treatment of schizophrenia with nicotinic acid: A 10 year follow-up. *Acta Psychiatrica Scandinavica,* 1964, *40,* 171–189.

Hoffer, A., & Osmond, H. Nicotinamide adenine dinucleotide (NAD) as a treatment for schizophrenia. *Journal of Psychopharmacology,* 1966, *1,* 79–95.

Hoffer, A., & Osmond, H. Nicotinamide adenine dinucleotide in the treatment of chronic schizophrenic patients. *British Journal of Psychiatry,* 1968, *114,* 915–917.

Hoffer, A., Osmond, H., & Smythies, J. Schizophrenia: A new approach. II. Result of a year's research. *Journal of Mental Science,* 1954, *100,* 29–45.

Hollingshead, A. B., & Redlich, F. C. *Social class and mental illness.* New York: John Wiley and Sons, 1957.

Hunt, J. M., & Cofer, C. N. Psychological deficit. In J. M. Hunt (Ed.), *Personality and the behavior disorders.* New York: Ronald Press, 1944.

Huston, P. C., Shakow, D., & Riggs, L. A. Studies of motor functions in schizophrenia: II. Reaction time. *Journal of General Psychology,* 1937, *16,* 39–82.

Jacob, T. Family interaction in disturbed and normal families: A methodological and substantive review. *Psychological Bulletin,* 1975, *82,* 33–65.

Johannsen, W. J., Friedman, S. H., Leitschuh, T. H., & Ammons, H. A. A study of certain schizophrenic dimensions and their relationship to double alternative learning. *Journal of Consulting Psychology,* 1963, *27,* 375–382.

Kahlbaum, K. L. *Gruppierung der psychischen krankheiten.* Danzig: Kafemann, 1863.

Kahlbaum, K. L. *Die katatonie oder das spannungsirresein.* Berlin: Hirschwald, 1874.

Kallmann, F. J. The genetic theory of schizophrenia. *American Journal of Psychiatry,* 1946, *103,* 309–322.

Kantor, R. E., & Herron, W. G. *Reactive and process schizophrenia.* Palo Alto, Calif.: Science and Behavior Books, 1966.

Kantor, R. E., Wallner, J., & Winder, C. Process and reactive schizophrenia. *Journal of Consulting Psychology,* 1953, *17,* 157–162.

Karras, A. The effect of stimulus-response complexity on the reaction time of schizophrenics. *Psychonomic Science,* 1967, *7,* 75–76.

Karras, A. Effects of competing and complex responses on the reaction time of acute psychiatric groups. *Journal of Abnormal Psychology,* 1973, *82,* 134–183.

Kasanin, J. S. The disturbance of conceptual thinking in schizophrenia. In J. S. Kasanin (Ed.), *Language and thought in schizophrenia.* Berkeley: University of California Press, 1946.

Kessler, P., & Neale, J. M. Hippocampal damage and schizophrenia: A critique of Mednick's theory. *Journal of Abnormal Psychology,* 1974, *83,* 91–96.

Kety, S. S. Biochemical hypotheses and studies. In L. Bellak & L. Loeb (Eds.), *The schizophrenic syndrome.* New York: Grune and Stratton, 1969.

Kilburg, R. R., & Siegel, A. W. Formal operations in reactive and process schizophrenia. *Journal of Consulting and Clinical Psychology,* 1973, *40,* 371–376.

Klebanoff, L. B. Parental attitudes of mothers of schizophrenic, brain-injured, retarded, and normal children. *American Journal of Orthopsychiatry,* 1959, *24,* 445–454.

Kleinmuntz, B. *Essentials of abnormal psychology.* New York: Harper & Row, 1974.

Klorman, R., & Chapman, L. J. Regression and schizophrenic thought disorder. *Journal of Abnormal Psychology,* 1969, *74,* 199–204.

Koh, S. D. Remembering of verbal material by schizophrenic young adults. In S. Schwartz (Ed.), *Language and cognition in schizophrenia.* Hillsdale, N.J.: Lawrence Erlbaum, in press.

Koh, S. D., Kayton, L., & Berry, R. Mnemonic organization in young nonpsychotic schizophrenics. *Journal of Abnormal Psychology,* 1973, *81,* 299–310.

Koh, S. D., Kayton, L., & Peterson, R. A. Affective encoding and consequent remembering in schizophrenic young adults. *Journal of Abnormal Psychology,* 1976, *85,* 156–166.

Koh, S. D., Kayton, L., & Schwarz, C. The structure of word storage in the present memory of nonpsychotic schizophrenics. *Journal of Consulting and Clinical Psychology,* 1974, *42,* 879–887.

Koh, S. D., & Peterson, R. A. Perceptual memory for numerousness in "nonpsychotic schizophrenics." *Journal of Abnormal Psychology,* 1974, *83,* 215–226.

Korboot, P., & Damiarri, H. Auditory processing speed and signal detection in schizophrenia. *Journal of Abnormal Psychology,* 1976, in press.

Kraepelin, E. *Psychiatrie.* Lepzig: Johann Ambrosius Barth, 1896.

Kringlen, E. *Heredity and environment in the functional psychoses.* London: Heinemann, 1967.

Kubzansky, P. E. The effects of reduced environmental stimulation on human behavior: A review. In A. D. Biderman & H. Zimmer (Eds.), *The manipulation of human behavior.* John Wiley and Sons, 1961.

Laing, R. D. *The politics of experience.* New York: Pantheon, 1967.

Landis, B. Ego boundaries. *Psychological Issues,* 1970, *6* (Monograph 24).

Langner, T. S., & Michael, S. T. *Life stress and mental health.* Beverly Hills: Glencoe, 1963.

Larsen, S. F., & Fromholt, P. Mnemonic organization and free recall in schizophrenia. *Journal of Abnormal Psychology,* 1976, *85,* 61–65.

Lehmann, H. E. Schizophrenia: IV. Clinical features. In A. M. Freeman & H. L. Kaplan (Eds.), *Comprehensive textbook of psychiatry.* Baltimore: Williams & Wilkins, 1967.

Leighton, A. H., Lambo, T. A., Hughes, C. C., Leighton,

D. C., Murphy, J. M., & MacKline, D. B. Psychiatric disorder in West Africa. *American Journal of Psychiatry,* 1963, *120,* 521–525.

Lewin, K. Field theory in social science. New York: Harper & Row, 1951.

Lidz, T. *The origin and treatment of schizophrenic disorders.* New York: Basic Books, 1973.

Lidz, T., Cornelison, A., Fleck, S., & Terry, D. Intrafamilial environment of the schizophrenic patient. I. The father. *Psychiatry,* 1957, *20,* 329–342.

Lin, T. Y. A study of the incidence of mental disorder in Chinese and other cultures. *Psychiatry,* 1953, *16,* 313–336.

Lorr, M. (Ed.) *Explorations in typing psychotics.* Elmsford, N.Y.: Pergamon, 1966.

Lorr, M. A typology for functional psychotics. In M. M. Katz, J. O. Cole, & W. E. Barton (Eds.), *The role and methodology of classification in psychiatry and psychopathology.* Chevy Chase, Md.: National Institute of Mental Health, 1968.

Lorr, M., & Klett, C. J. Psychotic syndromes across cultures. *Journal of Abnormal Psychology,* 1969, *74,* 531–543.

Lorr, M., McNair, D. M., Klett, C. J., & Lasky, J. J. Evidence of ten psychotic syndromes. *Journal of Consulting Psychology,* 1962, *26,* 185–189.

Lothrop, W. W. A critical review of research on the conceptual thinking of schizophrenics. *Journal of Nervous and Mental Science,* 1961, *132,* 118–126.

Lucas, C. J., Sansbury, P., & Collins, J. G. A social and clinical study of delusions in schizophrenia. *Journal of Mental Science,* 1962, *108,* 747–758.

Lystad, M. M. Social mobility among selected groups of schizophrenics. *American Sociological Review,* 1957, *22,* 288–292.

Magaro, P. A. Skin conductance basal level and reactivity in schizophrenia as a function of chronicity, premorbid adjustment, diagnosis, and medication. *Journal of Abnormal Psychology,* 1973, *81,* 270–281.

Mahar, B. The language of schizophrenia: A review and interpretation. *British Journal of Psychiatry,* 1972, *120,* 3–17.

Mahar, B., McKean, K. O., & McLaughlin, B. Studies in psychotic language. In P. J. Stone et al. (Eds.), *The general inquirer: A computer approach to content analysis.* Cambridge: MIT Press, 1966.

Maley, R. F., Feldman, G. L., & Ruskin, R. S. Evaluation of patient improvement in a token economy treatment program. *Journal of Abnormal Psychology,* 1973, *82,* 141–144.

Malitz, S., Wildens, B., & Esecover, H. A comparison of drug induced hallucinations with those seen in spontaneously occurring psychoses. In L. J. West (Ed.), *Hallucinations.* New York: Grune and Stratton, 1962.

Mark, J. C. The attitudes of mothers of male schizophrenics toward child behavior. *Journal of Abnormal and Social Psychology,* 1953, *48,* 185–189.

Martorano, R. D., & Nathan, P. E. Syndromes of psychosis and nonpsychosis: Factor analysis of a systems analysis. *Journal of Abnormal Psychology,* 1972, *80,* 1–10.

McGaughran, L. S., & Moran, L. J. "Conceptual level" vs. "conceptual area" analysis of object sorting behavior of schizophrenic and nonpsychotic groups. *Journal of Abnormal and Social Psychology,* 1956, *52,* 43–50.

McGuigan, F. J. Covert oral behavior and auditory hallucinations. *Psychophysiology,* 1966, *3,* 421–428.

Mednick, S. A. A learning theory approach to research in schizophrenia. *Psychological Bulletin,* 1958, *55,* 316–327.

Mednick, S. A. Breakdown in individuals at high-risk for schizophrenia: Possible predispositional perinatal factors. *Mental Hygiene,* 1970, *54,* 50–63.

Mednick, S. A., & Schulsinger, F. Some premorbid characteristics related to breakdown in children with schizophrenic mothers. In D. Rosenthal & S. S. Katz (Eds.), *The transmission of schizophrenia.* Elmsford, N. Y.: Pergamon, 1968.

Meehl, P. E. Schizotaxia, schizotypy, and schizophrenia. *American Psychologist,* 1962, *17,* 827–838.

Meehl, P. E. *Psychodiagnosis: Selected papers.* Minneapolis: University of Minnesota Press, 1973.

Meichenbaum, D. H. Validational study of marital status and the self-report scale for process-reactive schizophrenia. *Journal of Consulting and Clinical Psychology,* 1969, *33,* 351–356.

Meltzer, H. Muscle enzyme release in the acute psychoses. *Archives of General Psychiatry,* 1969, *21,* 102–112.

Meyer, A. Fundamental conceptions of dementia praecox. *British Medical Journal,* 1906, *2,* 757.

Meyer, A. The dynamic interpretation of dementia praecox. *American Journal of Psychology,* 1910, *21,* 385.

Meyers, D. F., & Goldfarb, W. Studies of perplexity in mothers of schizophrenic children. *American Journal of Orthopsychiatry,* 1961, *31,* 551–564.

Mishler, E., & Waxler, N. *Interaction in families: An experimental study of family processes and schizophrenia.* New York: John Wiley and Sons, 1968.

Moran, L. J. Vocabulary knowledge and usage among normal and schizophrenic subjects. *Psychological Monographs,* 1953, *67,* Whole No. 370.

Morris, G., & Wynne, L. Schizophrenic offspring and parental styles of communication. *Psychiatry,* 1965, *28,* 19–44.

Mosher, L. R., & Feinsilver, D. Special report on schizophrenia. U.S. Dept. of Health, Education, and Welfare, Public Health Service, Health Services and Mental Health Administration, National Institute of Mental Health, April, 1970.

Mosher, L. R., Gunderson, J. G., & Buchsbaum, S. Special report on schizophrenia: 1972. *Schizophrenia Bulletin,* 1973, *7,* 10–52.

Mourer, S. A. A prediction of patterns of schizophrenic error resulting from semantic generalization. *Journal of Abnormal Psychology,* 1973, *81,* 250–254.

Murphy, H. B. M. Cultural factors in the genesis of schizophrenia. In D. Rosenthal & S. S. Kety (Eds.), *The transmission of schizophrenia.* Elmsford, N.Y.: Pergamon, 1968.

Nachmani, G., & Cohen, B. D. Recall and recognition free learning in schizophrenics. *Journal of Abnormal Psychology,* 1969, *74,* 511–516.

National Institute of Mental Health. Utilization of mental health facilities 1971. DHEW Publication No.

NIH-74-657, Superintendent of Documents. Washington, D.C.: U.S. Government Printing Office, 1973.
ORGEL, S. A. Differential classification of hebephrenic and paranoid schizophrenics from case material. *Journal of Clinical Psychology,* 1957, *13,* 159–161.
OSMOND, H., & SMYTHIES, J. Schizophrenia: A new approach. *Journal of Mental Science,* 1952, *98,* 309–315.
PAYNE, R. W. Cognitive abnormalities. In H. J. Eysenck (Ed.), *Handbook of abnormal psychology.* New York: Basic Books, 1961.
PAYNE, R. W., & HEWLETT, J. H. G. Thought disorder in psychotic patients. In H. J. Eysenck (Ed.), *Experiments in personality, psychodiagnostics and psychodynamics.* London: Routledge and Keegan Paul, 1960.
PENNELL, R. B., PAWLUS, C., SARAVIS, C. A., & SCRIMSHAW, G. Further characterization of a human plasma component which influences animal behavior. *Transactions of the New York Academy of Science,* 1965, *28,* 47–58.
PFAFFMAN, C., & SCHLOSBERG, H. The conditioned knee jerk in psychotic and normal individuals. *Journal of Psychology,* 1936, *1,* 201–206.
PHILLIPS, L. Case history data and prognosis in schizophrenia. *Journal of Nervous and Mental Disorders,* 1953, *117,* 515–525.
PHILLIPS, L., & DRAGUNS, J. G. Classification of the behavior disorders. *Annual Review of Psychology,* 1971, *22,* 447–482.
POLLIN, W., CARDON, P. V., & KETY, S. S. Effects of amino acid feedings in schizophrenic patients treated with iproniazid. *Science,* 1961, *133,* 104–105.
PUGH, T. F., & MACMAHON, B. *Epidemiologic findings in United States mental hospital data.* Boston: Little, Brown, 1962.
QUINLAN, D. M., & HARROW, M. Boundary disturbances in schizophrenia. *Journal of Abnormal Psychology,* 1974, *83,* 533–541.
RADO, S. *Psychoanalaysis of behavior: Collected papers.* New York: Grune and Stratton, 1956.
RAPPAPORT, M. Competing voice messages: Effects of message load and drugs on the ability of acute schizophrenics to attend. *Archives of General Psychiatry,* 1967, *17,* 97–103.
REICHARD, S., & TILLMAN, C. Patterns of parent-child relationships in schizophrenia. *Psychiatry,* 1950, *13,* 247–257.
RICE, J. Disordered language as related to autonomic responsivity and the process-reactive distinction. *Journal of Abnormal Psychology,* 1970, *76,* 50–54.
ROBINS, E. Discussion of paper by R. G. Heath. In H. A. Abramson (Ed.), *Neuropharmacology.* New York: Josiah Macy Jr. Foundation, 1957.
RODNICK, E. H., & GARMEZY, N. An experimental approach to the study of motivation in schizophrenia. In M. R. Jones (Ed.), *Nebraska symposium on motivation: 1957.* Lincoln: University of Nebraska Press, 1957.
ROSENBERG, S., & COHEN, B. D. Speakers' and listeners' processes in a word-communication task. *Science,* 1964, *145,* 1201–1203.
ROSENBERG, S., & COHEN, B. D. Referential processes of speakers and listeners. *Psychological Review,* 1966, *73,* 208–231.
ROSENTHAL, D. *Genetic theory and abnormal behavior.* New York: McGraw-Hill, 1970.
ROSENTHAL, D., WENDER, P., KETY, S., WELNER, J., & SCHULSINGER, F. The adopted-away offspring of schizophrenics. *American Journal of Psychiatry,* 1971, *128,* 307–310.
RUSSELL, P. N., BANNATYNE, P. A., & SMITH, J. F. Associative strength as a mode of organization in recall and recognition: A comparison of schizophrenics and normals. *Journal of Abnormal Psychology,* 1975, *84,* 122–128.
SACCUZZO, D. P., HIRT, M., & SPENCER, T. J. Backward masking as a measure of attention in schizophrenics. *Journal of Abnormal Psychology,* 1974, *83,* 512–522.
SALZINGER, K. *Schizophrenia: Behavioral aspects.* New York: John Wiley and Sons, 1973.
SALZINGER, K., PORTNOY, S., & FELDMAN, R. Verbal behavior in schizophrenics and some comments toward a theory of schizophrenia. Paper presented at the annual meeting of the American Psychological Association, 1964.
SAPPINGTON, J. Psychometric correlates of defensive style in process and reactive schizophrenia. *Journal of Consulting and Clinical Psychology,* 1975, *43,* 154–156.
SARBIN, T. R., JUHASZ, J. B., & TODD, P. The social psychology of "hallucinations." *Psychological Record,* 1971, *21,* 87–93.
SCHUHAM, A. I. The double-bind hypothesis a decade later. *Psychological Bulletin,* 1967, *68,* 409–416.
SEDMAN, G. A comparative study of pseudohallucinations, imagery and true hallucinations. *British Journal of Psychiatry,* 1966, *112,* 9–17.
SHAKOW, D. Segmental set: A theory of the formal psychological deficit in schizophrenia. *Archives of General Psychology,* 1962, *6,* 1–17.
SHANNON, C. E. Prediction and entropy of printed English. *Bell System Technological Journal,* 1951, *30,* 50–64.
SHEAN, G., FAIA, C., & SCHMALTZ, E. Cognitive appraisal of stress and schizophrenic subtype. *Journal of Abnormal Psychology,* 1974, *83,* 523–528.
SHIELDS, J. Concepts of heredity for schizophrenia. *Annual Review of the Schizophrenic Syndrome,* 1972, *2,* 319–336.
SIEGEL, M., NISWALDER, G. D., SACHS, E., & STAVROS, D. Tarexein, fact or artifact? *American Journal of Psychiatry,* 1959, *115,* 819–820.
SILVERMAN, G. Psycholinguistics of schizophrenic language. *Psychological Medicine,* 1972, *2,* 254–259.
SILVERMAN, J. The problem of attention in research and theory in schizophrenia. *Psychological Review,* 1964, *71,* 357–379. (a)
SILVERMAN, J. Scanning-control mechanism and "cognitive filtering" in paranoid and nonparanoid schizophrenia. *Journal of Consulting Psychology,* 1964, *28,* 385–393. (b)
SMYTHIES, J. R., & ANTUN, F. The biochemistry of psychosis. *Scottish Medical Journal,* 1970, *15,* 34–40.
SPENCE, K. W., & TAYLOR, J. A. The relation of conditioned response strength to anxiety in normal, neurotic, and psychotic subjects. *Journal of Experimental Psychology,* 1953, *45,* 265–277.
SROLE, L., LANGNER, T. S., MICHAEL, S. T., OPLER, M. K., &

Rennie, T. A. C. *Mental health in the metropolis: The midtown manhattan study.* New York: McGraw-Hill, 1962.

Strauss, M. E. Behavioral differences between acute and chronic schizophrenics: Course of psychosis, effects of institutionalization, or sampling biases? *Psychological Bulletin,* 1973, *79,* 271–279.

Suedfeld, P. Introduction and historical background. In J. P. Zubek (Ed.), *Sensory deprivation: Fifteen years of research.* New York: Appleton-Century Crofts, 1969. (a)

Suedfeld, P. Theoretical formulation: II. In J. P. Zubek (Ed.), *Sensory deprivation: Fifteen years of research.* New York: Appleton-Century-Crofts, 1969. (b)

Sullivan, H. S. *The interpersonal theory of psychiatry.* New York: W. W. Norton, 1953.

Taube, C. A., & Rednick, R. W. *Utilization of mental health resources by persons diagnosed with schizophrenia.* Rockville, Md.: National Institute of Mental Health, 1973.

Thomas, B. C. Mother-daughter relationship and social behavior. Unpublished doctoral dissertation, Catholic University, 1955.

Thornton, C. C., & Gottheil, E. Social schemata in schizophrenic males. *Journal of Abnormal Psychology,* 1971, *77,* 192–195.

Tietze, T. A study of mothers of schizophrenic patients. *Psychiatry,* 1949, *12,* 55–65.

Truscott, I. P. Contextual constraint and schizophrenic language. *Journal of Consulting and Clinical Psychology,* 1970, *35,* 189–194.

Turner, R. J., & Wagonfeld, M. O. Occupational mobility and schizophrenia. *American Sociological Review,* 1967, *32,* 104–113.

Ullmann, L. P., & Giovannoni, J. M. The development of a self-report measure of the process-reactive continuum. *Journal of Nervous and Mental Disease,* 1964, *138,* 38–42.

Ullmann, L. P., & Krasner, L. *A psychological approach to abnormal behavior.* Englewood Cliffs, N.J.: Prentice-Hall, 1969.

VanDyke, J. L. Electrodermal functioning in adopted-away offspring of schizophrenics: A study of inherited diathesis in schizophrenia. Unpublished doctoral dissertation, George Washington University, 1972.

VanDyke, W. K., & Routh, D. Effects of censure on schizophrenic reaction time: Critique and reformulation of the Garmezy censure-deficit model. *Journal of Abnormal Psychology,* 1973, *82,* 200–206.

Vigotsky, L. S. Thought in schizophrenia. *Archives of Neurology and Psychiatry,* 1934, *31,* 1063–1077.

Von Domarus, E. The specific laws of logic in schizophrenia. In J. S. Kasanin (Ed.), *Language and thought in schizophrenia.* Berkeley: University of California Press, 1946.

Wagener, J. M., & Hartsough, D. M. Social competence as a process-reactive dimension with schizophrenics, alcoholics, and normals. *Journal of Abnormal Psychology,* 1974, *83,* 112–116.

Wahl, O., & Wisher, J. Schizophrenic thinking as measured by developmental tests. *Journal of Nervous and Mental Disease,* 1972, *155,* 232–244.

Watson, C. G. Abstract thinking deficit and autism in process and reactive schizophrenics. *Journal of Abnormal Psychology,* 1973, *82,* 399–403.

Wegrocki, J. J. Generalizing ability in schizophrenia. *Archives of Psychology,* 1940, *36,* 254.

Wender, P. H., Rosenthal, D., Rainer, J., Greenhill, L., & Sarlin, B. Schizophrenics' adopting parents: Psychiatric status. Quoted in J. Zubin, Vulnerability: A new view of schizophrenia. *Journal of Abnormal Psychology,* 1976, in press.

Wittenborn, J. R. *Wittenborn psychiatric rating scales.* New York: Psychological Corporation, 1955.

Wittenborn, J. R., & Smith, B. K. A comparison of psychotic dimensions in male and female hospital patients. *Journal of Nervous and Mental Disease,* 1964, *138,* 375–382.

Wittman, P. A scale for measuring prognosis in schizophrenic patients. *Elgin State Hospital Papers,* 1944, *4,* 20–33.

Woolley, D. W. *The biochemical bases of psychoses.* New York: John Wiley and Sons, 1962.

Woolley, D. W., & Shaw, E. A biochemical and pharmacological suggestion about certain mental disorders. *Science,* 1954, *119,* 587–588.

Wright, D. J., Goldstone, S., & Boardman, W. K. Time judgment and schizophrenia: Step intervals as a relevant contextual factor. *Journal of Psychology,* 1962, *54,* 33–38.

Wright, D. M. Impairment in abstract conceptualization in schizophrenia. *Psychological Bulletin,* 1975, *82,* 120–127.

Yates, A. J. Psychological deficit. In P. R. Farnsworth (Ed.), *Annual Review of Psychology,* 1966.

Yates, A. J., & Korboot, P. Speed of perceptual functioning in chronic nonparanoid schizophrenics. *Journal of Abnormal Psychology,* 1970, *76,* 453–461.

Yolles, S. F., & Kramer, M. Vital statistics of schizophrenia. In L. Bellak & L. Loeb (Eds.), *The schizophrenic syndrome.* New York: Grune and Stratton, 1969.

Youkilis, H. D., & De Wolfe, A. S. The regression hypothesis and scales classification of schizophrenia, *Journal of Abnormal Psychology,* 1975, *84,* 36–40.

Zahn, T. P., Rosenthal, D., Pollin, W., & Mosher, L. Psychophysiological responsivity in schizophrenia. In *Annual Report, Mental Health Intramural Research Programs, Division of Clinical and Behavioral Research, and Division of Biological and Biochemical Research. Vol. 2.* Bethesda, Md.: National Institute of Mental Health, 1972.

Zigler, E., & Levine, J. Premorbid adjustment and paranoid-nonparanoid status in schizophrenia: A further investigation. *Journal of Abnormal Psychology,* 1973, *82,* 189–199.

Zigler, E., & Phillips, L. Social competence and the process-reactive distinctions in psychopathology. *Journal of Abnormal and Social Psychology,* 1962, *65,* 215–222.

Zilboorg, G., & Henry, G. W. *A history of medical psychology.* New York: W. W. Norton, 1941.

Zubin, J. Classification of the behavior disorders. *Annual Review of Psychology,* 1967, *18,* 373–406.

Zucker, L. *Ego structure in paranoid schizophrenia.* Springfield, Ill.: Charles C. Thomas, 1958.

17. Organic Brain Syndromes

AITA, J. A. *Neurological manifestations of general diseases.* Springfield, Ill.: Charles C. Thomas, 1964.

ANDERSEN, A. L., & HANVIT, L. J. The differential effect of frontal and parietal lesions on MMPI profiles. *Journal of Clinical Psychology,* 1950, *6,* 177–180.

ARING, C. D., & TRUFANT, S. A. Effects of heavy metals on the central nervous system. *Proceedings of the Association for Research on Nervous and Mental Disease,* 1953, *32,* 463–470.

BAUER, R. B. Evaluation of the stroke patient with respect to associated diseases. In W. S. Fields, W. A. Spencer, & H. G. Warren (Eds.), *Stroke rehabilitation.* St. Louis: Green, 1967.

BENSON, D. F. Fluency in aphasia: Correlation with radioactive scan localization. *Cortex,* 1967, *3,* 373–394.

BENTON, A. L. (Ed.) *Contributions to clinical neuropsychology.* Chicago: Aldine, 1969.

BENTON, A. L. Clinical neuropsychology of childhood: An overview. In R. M. Reitan & L. A. Davison (Eds.), *Clinical neuropsychology: Current status and applications.* Washington, D.C.: Winston & Sons, 1974.

BIRCH, H. G. The problem of "brain damage" in children. In H. G. Birch (Ed.), *Brain damage in children.* Baltimore: Williams & Wilkins, 1964.

BLINDERMAN, E. E., WEIDNER, W., & MARKHAM, C. H. The pneumoencephalogram in Huntington's chorea. *Neurology,* 1964, *14,* 601–612.

BOGEN, J. E., & VOGEL, P. J. Cerebral commissurotomy: A case report. *Bulletin of the Los Angeles Neurological Society,* 1962, *27,* 169.

BORING, E. G. *A history of experimental psychology.* New York: Appleton-Century-Crofts, 1950.

BOSHES, B., BLONSKY, E. R., ARBIT, J., & KLEIN, K. Effect of L-dopa on individual symptoms of parkinsonism. *Transactions of the American Neurological Association,* 1969, *94,* 229–231.

BRADLEY, J. E., & BAUMGARTNER, R. J. Subsequent mental development of children with lead encephalopathy as related to type of treatment. *Journal of Pediatrics,* 1958, *53,* 311–315.

BRAIN, W. R. *Speech disorders: Aphasia, apraxia, and agnosia.* Washington, D.C.: Butterworths, 1961.

BRAZIER, M. A. B. The search for the neuronal mechanisms in epilepsy: An overview. *Neurology,* 1974, *24,* 903–911.

BRION, S. Korsakoff's syndrome: Clinico-anatomical and physiopathological considerations. In G. A. Talland & N. C. Waugh (Ed.), *The pathology of memory.* New York: Academic Press, 1969.

BROCA, P. Remarques sur le siège de la faculté du langage articale suivies d'une observation d'aphemie. *Bulletin Sociéte Anatomique de Paris,* 1861, *36,* 331.

BRODY, I. A., & WILKINS, R. H. Neurological classics IX: Wernicke's encephalopathy. *Archives of Neurology,* 1968, *19,* 228–232.

CHEIFETZ, D. I., GARRON, D. C., LEAVITT, F., KLAWANS, H. L., & GARVIN, J. S. Emotional disturbance accompanying the treatment of parkinsonism with L-dopa. *Clinical Pharmacology and Therapeutics,* 1971, *12,* 56–61.

CHISOLM, J. J., & KAPLAN, E. Lead poisoning in childhood —comprehensive management and prevention. *Journal of Pediatrics,* 1968, *73,* 942–950.

COLEMAN, J. C. *Abnormal psychology and modern life.* Glenview, Ill.: Scott, Foresman, 1972.

CREUTZFELDT, O. D. Synaptic organization of the cerebral cortex and its role in epilepsy. In A. M. B. Brazier (Ed.), *Epilepsy: Its phenomena in man.* New York: Academic Press, 1973.

CRITCHLEY, M. *The parietal lobes.* London: Arnold, 1953.

CRITCHLEY, M. Disorders of higher nervous activity: Introductory remarks. In P. J. Vinken & G. W. Bruyn (Eds.), *Handbook of clinical neurology.* Vol. 3. *Disorders of higher nervous activity.* Amsterdam: North-Holland Publishing Company, 1969.

CURTIS, B. A., JACOBSON, S., & MARCUS, E. M. *An introduction to the neurosciences.* Philadelphia: W. B. Saunders, 1972.

DAVISON, L. A. Introduction. In R. M. Reitan & L. A. Davison (Eds.), *Clinical neuropsychology: Current status and applications.* Washington, D.C.: Winston & Sons, 1974.

DE AJURIAGUERRA, J., & TISSOT, R. The apraxias. In P. J. Vinken & G. W. Bruyn (Eds.), *Handbook of clinical neurology. Vol 4. Disorders of speech, perception, and symbolic behavior.* Amsterdam: North-Holland Publishing Company, 1969.

DODGE, P. R., & SWARTZ, M. N. Bacterial meningitis: A review of selected aspects. II. Special neurologic problems, postmeningitis complications and clinicopathological correlations. *New England Journal of Medicine,* 1965, *272,* 1003–1009.

ECCLES, J. C. *The physiology of synapses.* New York: Academic Press, 1964.

ECCLES, J. C. *The brain and conscious experience.* New York: Springer, 1966.

EISENSON, J. *Adult aphasia: Assessment and treatment.* New York: Appleton-Century-Crofts, 1973.

ERVIN, F. R. Brain disorders. IV: Associated with convulsions. In A. M. Freedman & H. I. Kaplan (Eds.), *Comprehensive textbook of psychiatry.* Baltimore: Williams & Wilkins, 1967.

FILSKOV, S. B., & GOLDSTEIN, S. G. Diagnostic validity of the Halstead-Reitan neuropsychological battery. *Journal of Consulting and Clinical Psychology,* 1974, *42,* 382–388.

FREEDMAN, A. M., KAPLAN, H. I., & SADOCK, B. J. *Modern synopsis of comprehensive textbook of psychiatry.* Baltimore: Williams & Wilkins, 1972.

GARRON, D. C., & CHEIFETZ, D. I. Comment on "Bender Gestalt discernment of organic pathology." *Psychological Bulletin,* 1965, *63,* 197–200.

GARRON, D. C., KLAWANS, H. L., & NARIN, F. Intellectual functioning of persons with idiopathic parkinsonism. *Journal of Nervous and Mental Disease,* 1972, *154,* 445–452.

GESCHWIND, N. The organization of language and the brain. *Science,* 1970, *170,* 940–944. (a)

GESCHWIND, N. Language disturbances in cerebrovascular disease. In A. L. Benton (Ed.), *Behavioral change in cerebrovascular disease.* New York: Harper & Row, 1970. (b)

GESCHWIND, N. Late changes in the nervous system: An overview. In D. G. Stein, J. J. Rosen, & N. Butters (Eds.),

Plasticity and recovery of function in the central nervous system. New York: Academic Press, 1974.
GUERRANT, J., ANDERSON, W. W., FISCHER, A., WEINSTEIN, M. R., JAROS, R. M., & DESKINS, A. *Personality in epilepsy.* Springfield, Ill.: Charles C. Thomas, 1962.
HAASE, G. R. Diseases presenting as dementia. In C. E. Wells (Ed.), *Dementia.* Philadelphia: Davis, 1971.
HALSTEAD, W. C. *Brain and intelligence.* Chicago: University of Chicago Press, 1947.
HEATHFIELD, K. W. G. Huntington's chorea: Investigation into the prevalence of this disease in the area covered by the North East Metropolital Regional Hospital Board. *Brain,* 1967, *90,* 203.
HÉCAEN, H., & ANGELERGUES, E. Localization of symptoms in aphasia. In *Disorders of language: A CIBA foundation symposium.* London: Churchill, 1964.
HÉCAEN, H., DE AJURIAGUERRA, J., & MASSONNETT, J. Les troubles visuoconstructifs par lésion parieto-occipital droite. Rôle des perturbations vestibulaires. *Encéphale,* 1951, *40,* 122–179.
HORENSTEIN, S. Effects of cerebrovascular disease on personality and emotionality. In A. L. Benton (Ed.), *Behavioral change in cerebrovascular disease.* New York: Harper & Row, 1970.
INOUYE, E. Observations on forty twin index cases with chronic epilepsy and their co-twins. *Journal of Nervous and Mental Disease,* 1960, *130,* 401–408.
JENNETT, W. B. *Epilepsy after blunt head injuries.* London: Heinemann Medical Books, 1962.
JOHNSON, E. M. A study of psychological findings of one hundred children recovering from purulent meningitis. *Journal of Clinical Psychology,* 1960, *16,* 55–58.
KASZNIAK, A. W., GARRON, D. C., FOX, J. H., HUCKMAN, M. S., & RAMSEY, R. G. Relation between dementia and cerebral atrophy as measured by computerized tomography. Paper presented at the annual meeting of the American Academy of Neurology, May, 1975.
KIEV, A., CHAPMAN, L. F., GUTHRIE, T. C., & WOLFF, H. G. The highest integrative functions and diffuse cerebral atrophy. *Neurology,* 1962, *12,* 385–393.
KLAWANS, H. L. A pharmacologic analysis of Huntington's chorea. *European Neurology,* 1970, *4,* 148–162.
KLAWANS, H. L., & GARVIN, J. S. Observations on the treatment of parkinsonism with L-dopa. *Diseases of the Nervous System,* 1969, *30,* 737–749.
KLAWANS, H. L., PAULSSON, G. C., RENGEL, S. P., & BARBEAU, A. Use of L-dopa in the detection of presymptomatic Huntington's chorea. *New England Journal of Medicine,* 1972, *286,* 1332–1334.
KRAL, V. A. Memory disorders in old age and senility. In G. A. Talland & N. C. Waugh (Eds.), *The pathology of memory.* New York: Academic Press, 1969.
LENNEBERG, E. H. *Biological foundations of language.* New York: John Wiley and Sons, 1967.
LEVY, S. Post-encephalitic behavior disorders—a forgotten entity: A report of 100 cases. *American Journal of Psychiatry,* 1959, *115,* 1062–1067.
LISKE, E., & WEIKERS, N. J. Changing aspects of brain abscesses: Review of cases in Wisconsin, 1940 through 1962. *Neurology,* 1964, *14,* 294–300.
LOESER, E., & SCHEINBERG, L. Brain abscesses: A review of ninety-nine cases. *Neurology,* 1957, *7,* 601–609.
LORBER, J. Long-term follow-up of 100 children who recovered from tuberculous meningitis. *Pediatrics,* 1961, *28,* 778–786.
LURIA, A. R. *Higher cortical functions in man.* New York: Basic Books, 1966.
LURIA, A. R. *Traumatic aphasia.* The Hague, Netherlands: Mouton, 1970.
LURIA, A. R., NAYDIN, V. L., TSVETKOVA, L. S., & VINARSKAYA, E. N. Restoration of higher cortical function following local brain damage. In P. J. Vinken & G. W. Bruyn (Eds.), *Handbook of clinical neurology. Vol. 3. Disorders of higher nervous activity.* Amsterdam: North-Holland Publishing Company, 1969.
MCKISSOCK, W., RICHARDSON, A., & WALSH, L. Middle cerebral aneurysms: Further results in the controlled trial of conservative and surgical treatment of ruptured intracranial aneurysms. *Lancet,* 1962, *11,* 417–421.
MCMENEMEY, W. H. The dementias and progressive diseases of the basal ganglia. In W. Blackwood (Ed.), *Greenfield's neuropathology.* Baltimore: Williams & Wilkins, 1966.
MEIER, M. J. The regional localization hypothesis and personality changes associated with focal cerebral lesions and ablations. In J. N. Butcher (Ed.), *MMPI: Research developments and clinical applications.* New York: McGraw-Hill, 1969.
MEIER, M. J., & MARTIN, W. E. Intellectual changes associated with Levodopa therapy. *Journal of the American Medical Association,* 1970, *213,* 465–466.
MERRITT, H. H. *A textbook of neurology.* Philadelphia: Lea, 1967.
MERRITT, H. H., ADAMS, R. D., & SOLOMON, H. C. *Neurosyphilis.* New York: Oxford University Press, 1946.
METRAKOS, K., & METRAKOS, J. D. Genetics of convulsive disorders: II. Genetic and encephalographic studies in centrencephalic epilepsy. *Neurology,* 1961, *11,* 474–486.
MILLER, E. *Clinical neuropsychology.* Baltimore: Penguin, 1972.
MILLER, H., & STERN, G. The long-term prognosis of severe head injury. *Lancet,* 1965, *1,* 225–227.
NISHIOKA, H. Report of the cooperative study of intracranial aneurysms and subarachnoid hemorrhage, section VII: 1, Evaluation of the conservative management of ruptured intracranial aneurysms. *Journal of Neurosurgery,* 1966, *25,* 574–592.
OTO, Y. Psychiatric studies on civilian head injuries. In A. E. Walker, W. F. Caveness, & M. Critchley (Eds.), *The late effects of head injury.* Springfield, Ill.: Charles C. Thomas, 1969.
PARKINSON, J. *An essay on the shaking palsy.* London: Sherwood, Neely, & Jones, 1817.
PENFIELD, W., & RASMUSSEN, T. *The cerebral cortex of man.* New York: Macmillan, 1950.
PIERCY, M. The effects of cerebral lesions on intellectual function: A review on current research trends. *British Journal of Psychiatry,* 1964, *110,* 310–352.
PINCUS, J. H., & TUCKER, G. J. *Behavioral neurology.* New York: Oxford University Press, 1974.
POECK, K. Pathophysiology of emotional disorders associated with brain damage. In P. J. Vinken & G. W. Bruyn (Eds.), *Handbook of clinical neurology. Vol. 3. Disorders of higher nervous activity.* Amsterdam: North-Holland Publishing Company, 1969.

POLLOCK, M., & HORNABROOK, R. W. The prevalence, natural history, and dementia of Parkinson's disease. *Brain,* 1966, *89,* 429–440.

PRATT, R. T. C. *The genetics of neurological disorders.* New York: Oxford University Press, 1967.

REITAN, R. M. A research program on the psychological effects of brain lesions in human beings. In N. R. Ellis (Ed.), *International review of research in mental retardation.* Vol. 1. New York: Academic Press, 1966.

REITAN, R. M., & DAVISON, L. A. (Eds.) *Clinical neuropsychology: Current status and applications.* Washington, D.C.: Winston & Sons, 1974.

ROTH, M., TOMLINSON, B. E., & BLESSED, G. The relationship between quantitative measures of dementia and degenerative changes in the grey matter of elderly subjects. *Proceedings of the Royal Society of Medicine,* 1967, *60,* 254–258.

SHAFFER, D. Psychiatric aspects of brain injury in childhood: A review. *Developmental Medicine and Child Neurology,* 1973, *15,* 211–220.

SKULTELY, F. M., & NISHIOKA, H. Report on the cooperative study of intracranial aneurysms and subarachnoid hemorrhage, section VIII: 2, The results of intracranial surgery in the treatment of aneurysm. *Journal of Neurosurgery,* 1966, *25,* 683–704.

SLATER, E., BEARD, A. W., & GLITHERO, E. The schizophrenia-like psychosis of epilepsy. *British Journal of Psychiatry,* 1963, *109,* 95–116.

SPENCER, W. A., & KANDEL, E. R. Synaptic inhibition in seizures. In H. Jasper, A. A. Ward, & A. Pope (Eds.), *Basic mechanisms of the epilepsies.* Boston: Little, Brown, 1969.

SPERRY, R. W., GAZZANIGA, M. S., & BOGEN, J. E. Interhemispheric relationships: The neocortical commissures: Syndromes of hemisphere disconnection. In P. J. Vinken & G. W. Bruyn (Eds.), *Handbook of clinical neurology. Vol. 4. Disorders of speech, perception, and symbolic behavior.* Amsterdam: North-Holland Publishing Company, 1969.

SPILLANE, J. D. *Nutritional disorders of the nervous system.* Edinburgh: Livingstone, 1947.

STRICH, S. J. The pathology of brain damage due to blunt head injuries. In A. E. Walker, W. F. Caveness, & M. Critchley (Eds.), *The late effects of head injury.* Springfield, Ill.: Charles C. Thomas, 1969.

SWARTZ, M. N., & DODGE, P. R. Bacterial meningitis: A review of selected aspects. *New England Journal of Medicine,* 1965, *272,* 725–731.

TARKKANEN, J. V. Ontogenic brain abscess. *Acta Otolaryngologica,* 1963, Supplement 185.

TAVERAS, J. M., & WOOD, E. H. *Diagnostic neuroradiology.* Baltimore: Williams & Wilkins, 1964.

ULLMAN, M. *Behavioral changes in patients following strokes.* Springfield, Ill.: Charles C. Thomas. 1962.

U.S. Department of Health, Education, and Welfare. *Alcohol and health.* DHEW Publication No. HSM 73-9031, December, 1971.

U.S. Public Health Service. *The eradication of syphilis: A task force report to the surgeon general on syphilis control in the United States.* Washington: U.S. Government Printing Office, 1962.

VAN DER ZWAN, A. Late results from prolonged traumatic unconsciousness. In A. E. Walker, W. F. Caveness, & M. Critchley (Eds.), *The late effects of head injury.* Springfield, Ill.: Charles C. Thomas, 1969.

VICTOR, M., ADAMS, R., & COLLINS, G. *The Wernicke-Korsakoff syndrome.* Philadelphia: Davis, 1971.

WANG, H. S., & BUSSE, E. W. Dementia in old age. In C. E. Wells (Ed.), *Dementia.* Philadelphia: Davis, 1971.

WATSON, C. W. Incidence of epilepsy following craniocerebral injury, II. Three year follow-up study. *Archives of Neurology and Psychiatry,* 1952, *68,* 831–834.

WEINSTEIN, E. A., & KAHN, R. L. *Denial of illness.* Springfield, Ill.: Charles C. Thomas, 1955.

WERNICKE, C. *Der aphasische symptomenkomplex.* Berlin: Breslau, Cohn, & Weigart, 1874.

WIENER, G. Varying psychological sequelae of lead ingestion in children. *Public Health Reports,* 1970, *85,* 19–24.

WILKINS, R. H., & BRODY, I. A. Neurological classics IV: Encephalitis lethargica. *Archives of Neurology,* 1968, *18,* 324–328.

WILKINS, R. H., & BRODY, I. A. Neurological classics XVII: Parkinson's syndrome. *Archives of Neurology,* 1969, *20,* 440–445.

WILLANGER, R., THYGESEN, P., NIELSEN, R., & PETERSEN, O. Intellectual impairment and cerebral atrophy: A psychological, neurological and radiological investigation. *Danish Medical Bulletin,* 1968, *15,* 65–93.

WILLIAMS, H. L. The development of a caudality scale for the MMPI. *Journal of Clinical Psychology,* 1952, *8,* 293–297.

WILSON, S. A. K. *Neurology.* London: Butterworths, 1954.

WYKE, M. Dysphasia. *British Medical Bulletin,* 1971, *27,* 211–217.

18. Mental Retardation

ACHENBACH, T. *Developmental psychopathology.* New York: Ronald Press, 1974.

ACHENBACH, T., & ZIGLER, E. Cue-learning and problem-learning strategies in normal and retarded children. *Child Development,* 1968, *3,* 827–848.

ADAMS, J. Adaptive behavior and measured intelligence in the classification of mental retardation. *American Journal of Mental Deficiency,* 1973, *78,* 77–81.

ADAMS, J., MCINTOSH, E. I., & WEADE, B. L. Ethnic background, measured intelligence, and adaptive behavior scores in mentally retarded children. *American Journal of Mental Deficiency,* 1973, *78,* 1–6.

American Psychiatric Association. *Diagnostic and statistical manual of mental disorders* (2nd ed.). Washington, D.C.: APA, 1968.

American Medical Association. Report of the American Medical Association Conference on Mental Retardation. *Journal of the American Medical Association,* 1965, 191.

ANGUS, L. R. Schizophrenia and schizoid conditions in students in a special school. *American Journal of Mental Deficiency,* 1948, *53,* 227–238.

AZRIN, N. H., & FOXX, R. M. A rapid method of toilet training the institutionalized retarded. *Journal of Applied Behavior Analysis,* 1971, *4,* 89–99.

AZRIN, N. H., KAPLAN, S. J., & FOXX, R. M. Autism reversal: Eliminating stereotyped self-stimulation of retarded individuals. *American Journal of Mental Deficiency,* 1973, *78,* 241–248.

BACHMAN, J. A. Self-injurious behavior: A behavioral analysis. *Journal of Abnormal Psychology,* 1972, *80,* 211–224.

BAER, D. M., & GUESS, D. Receptive training of adjectival inflections in mental retardates. *Journal of Applied Behavior Analysis,* 1971, *4,* 129–139.

BALLA, D. A., BUTTERFIELD, E. C., & ZIGLER, E. Effects of institutionalization on retarded children: A longitudinal cross-institutional investigation. *American Journal of Mental Deficiency,* 1974, *78,* 530–549.

BALLA, D., & ZIGLER, E. Discrimination and switching learning in normal, familial retarded, and organic retarded children. *Journal of Abnormal and Social Psychology,* 1964, *69,* 664–669.

BARRETT, B. H., & LINDSLEY, O. R. Deficits in acquisition of operant discrimination and differentiation shown by institutionalized retarded children. *American Journal of Mental Deficiency,* 1962, *67,* 424–436.

BARTON, E. S., GUESS, D., GARCIA, E., & BAER, D. M. Improvement of retardates' mealtime behaviors by timeout procedures using multiple baseline techniques. *Journal of Applied Behavior Analysis,* 1970, *3,* 77–84.

BAUMEISTER, A. A., & FOREHAND, R. Stereotyped acts. In N. R. Ellis (Ed.), *International review of research in mental retardation.* New York: Academic Press, 1973.

BECKMAN, A. S. Minimum intelligence levels for several occupations. *Personnel Journal,* 1930, *9,* 309–313.

BEGAB, M. J. The major dilemma of mental retardation: shall we prevent it? (Some social implications of research in mental retardation). *American Journal of Mental Deficiency,* 1974, *78,* 519–529.

BEIER, D. C. Behavior disturbances in the mentally retarded. In H. Stevens & R. Heber (Eds.), *Mental retardation: A review of research.* Chicago: University of Chicago Press, 1964.

BENDA, C. E. *The child with mongolism.* New York: Grune and Stratton, 1960.

BENDEBBA, M. Contingencies management in home and school situations: A blueprint for the education of the "mildly retarded" child. *Mental Retardation,* 1973, *11,* 34–37.

BENDER, C. E. Mongolism: A comprehensive review. *Archives of Pediatrics,* 1956, *73,* 391.

BERKSON, G. Visual defect does not produce stereotyped movements. *American Journal of Mental Deficiency,* 1973, *78,* 89–94.

BERKSON, G., & DAVENPORT, R. K. Stereotyped movements of mental defectives. I. Initial survey. *American Journal of Mental Deficiency,* 1962, *66,* 849–852.

BERKSON, G., & MASON, W. A. Stereotyped movements of mental defectives. IV. The effects of toys and the character of the acts. *American Journal of Mental Deficiency,* 1964, *68,* 511–524.

BOURNE, H. Protophrenia. A study of perverted rearing and mental dwarfism. *Lancet,* 1955, *20,* 1156–1163.

BRODY, S. Self-rocking in infancy. *Journal of the American Psychoanalytic Society,* 1960, *8,* 464–491.

BURR, E. T. Minimum intellectual levels of accomplishment in industry. *Personnel Journal,* 1925, *3,* 207–212.

BUTTERFIELD, E. C., WAMBOLD, C., & BELMONT, J. M. On the theory and practice of improving short-term memory. *American Journal of Mental Deficiency,* 1973, *77,* 654–669.

BYERS, R. K. Lead poisoning: Review of the literature and report on 45 cases. *Pediatrics,* 1959, *23,* 585.

CABAK, V., & NAJDANVIC, R. Effect of undernutrition in early life on physical and mental development. *Archives of Disease in Childhood,* 1965, *40,* 532–534.

CARLSON, J. S., & MICHALSON, L. H. Methodological study of conservation in retarded adolescents. *American Journal of Mental Deficiency,* 1973, *78,* 348–353.

CHASE, H. P., & MARTIN, H. P. Undernutrition and child development. *New England Journal of Medicine,* 1970, *282,* 933–939.

CLARKE, A. D. B., & CLARKE, A. M. How constant is the IQ? *Lancet,* 1953, *265,* 877–880.

CLARKE, A. D. B., & CLARKE, A. M. Cognitive changes in the feebleminded. *British Journal of Psychology,* 1954, *45,* 173–179.

CROMWELL, R. L. A social learning approach to mental retardation. In N. R. Ellis (Ed.), *Handbook of mental deficiency* . New York: McGraw-Hill, 1963.

D.C. Public Health Advisory Committee. Report on the working party on the retarded offender: Mental retardation planning committee. Washington, D.C.: Department of Public Health, 1966.

DINGMAN, H., & TARJAN, G. Mental retardation and the normal distribution curve. *American Journal of Mental Deficiency,* 1960, *64,* 991–994.

DOLL, E. A. *Measurement of social competence: A manual for the Vineland Social Maturity Scale.* Circle Pines, Minn.: American Guidance Service, 1953.

DWECK, C. S., & REPPUCCI, N. D. Learned helplessness and reinforcement responsibility in children. *Journal of Personality and Social Psychology,* 1973, *25,* 109–116.

ELLIS, N. R. The stimulus trace and behavioral inadequacy. In N. R. Ellis (Ed.), *Handbook of mental deficiency.* New York: McGraw-Hill, 1963.

ELLIS, N. R. Memory processes in retardates and normals. In N. R. Ellis (Ed.), *International review of research in mental retardation. Vol. 4.* New York: Academic Press, 1970.

ESQUIROL, J. *Treatise on insanity.* Translated by E. K. Hunt. Philadelphia: Lea & Blanchard, 1845.

GARFIELD, S. L. Abnormal behavior and mental deficiency. In. N. R. Ellis (Ed.), *Handbook of mental deficiency.* New York: McGraw-Hill, 1963.

GERARD, M. *The emotionally disturbed child.* New York: Child Welfare League of America, 1957.

GINZBERG, E., & BRAY, D. W. *The uneducated.* New York: Columbia University Press, 1953.

GOTTLIEB, J., & BUDOFF, M. Social acceptability of retarded children in nongraded schools differing in architecture. *American Journal of Mental Deficiency,* 1973, *78,* 15–19.

GRUEN, G. E., & BERG, B. Visual discrimination learning in familial retarded and nonretarded children. *American Journal of Mental Deficiency,* 1973, *78,* 63–69.

GRUENBERG, E. M. Epidemiology of mental retardation. *International Journal of Psychiatry,* 1966, *2,* 78–129.

GUESS, D. The influence of visual and ambulation restrictions on stereotype behavior. *American Journal of Mental Deficiency,* 1966, *70,* 542–547.

HAYES, C. Short-term memory in normals and retardates

as a function of stimulus intensity and length of recall interval: A test of Ellis' S_t theory. Unpublished master's thesis, University of Iowa, 1969.

HEBER, R. A manual on terminology and classification in mental retardation. *American Journal of Mental Deficiency,* 1961 (Monograph Supplement).

HEBER, R. *Epidemiology of mental retardation.* Springfield, Ill.: Charles C. Thomas, 1970.

HEBER, R., GARBER, H., HARRINGTON, S., & HOFFMAN, C. Rehabilitation of families of risk for mental retardation. Progress Report, Social Rehabilitation Service, Department of Health, Education, and Welfare, 1972.

HELLMUTH, J. (Ed.) *Disadvantaged child.* New York: Brunner Mazel, 1969.

HOFFMAN, E. The idiot savant: A case report and a review of explanations. *Mental Retardation,* 1971, *9,* 18–21.

HOUSE, B. J., & ZEAMAN, D. Reward and nonreward in the discrimination learning of imbeciles. *Journal of Comparative and Physiological Psychology,* 1958, *51,* 614–619.

HURST, L. A. Etiology of mental disorders: Genetics. In B. B. Wolman (Ed.), *Manual of child psychopathology.* New York: McGraw-Hill, 1972.

HUTT, M. L., & GIBBY, R. G. *The mentally retarded child: Development, education and treatment.* Boston: Allyn and Bacon, 1965.

INHELDER, B. *Le diagnostic du raisonnement chez les débiles mentaux.* Neuchâtel: Delachaux et Niestlé, 1963.

INHELDER, B. *The diagnosis of reasoning in the mentally retarded.* New York: Day, 1968.

JENSEN, A. R. Interaction of level I and level II abilities with race and socioeconomic status. *Journal of Educational Psychology,* 1974, *66,* 99–111.

JENSEN, A. R., & ROHWER, W. The effect of verbal mediation on the learning and retention of paired-associates by retarded adults. *American Journal of Mental Deficiency,* 1963, *68,* 80–84.

JERVIS, G. A. A contribution to the study of the influence of heredity on mental deficiency. *Journal of Psychoasthenics,* 1939, *64,* 13–24.

JOHNSON, G. O., & KIRK, S. A. Are mentally handicapped children segregated in the regular grades? *Exceptional Children,* 1950, *17,* 65–68.

KAGAN, J. On class differences and early development. In V. H. Denenberg (Ed.), *Education of the infant and young child.* New York: Academic Press, 1970.

KANNER, L. Autistic disturbances of affective contact. *The Nervous Child,* 1943, *2,* 217–250.

KLABER, M. M. The retarded and institutions for the retarded—a preliminary research report. In S. B. Sarason & J. Doris, *Psychological problems in mental deficiency.* New York: Harper & Row, 1969.

KOCH, R., ACOSTA, P., FISHLER, D., SCHAEFFLER, G., & WOHLERS, A. Clinical observations on phenylketonuria. *American Journal of Diseases of Children,* 1967, *113,* 6–15.

LAFONTAINE, L., & BENJAMIN, G. E. Idiot savants: Another view. *Mental Retardation,* 1971, *9,* 41–42.

LEJEUNE, J., GAUTIER, M., & TURPIN, R. Les chromosomes humains en culture de tissue. *Comptes Rendus Hebdomadaires des Séances de l'Académie des Sciences* (Paris), 1959, *248,* 602.

LENT, J. R., HOLVOET, J. F., FERNETI, C. L., KEILITZ, I. & TUCKER, D. J. Direction following of retarded and nonretarded adolescents. *American Journal of Mental Deficiency,* 1973, *78,* 316–322.

LESTER, D. Self-mutilating behavior. *Psychological Bulletin,* 1972, *78,* 119–128.

LEVY, D. M. On the problem of movement restraint. *American Journal of Orthopsychiatry,* 1944, *14,* 664–671.

LEWIN, K. *A dynamic theory of personality.* New York: McGraw-Hill, 1936.

LOBB, H. Pretraining retarded and intellectually average children for discrimination learning: Nonreward vs. reward. *American Journal of Mental Deficiency,* 1972, *77,* 59–68.

LOURIE, R. S. The role of rhythmic patterns in childhood. *American Journal of Psychiatry,* 1959, *105,* 653–660.

LOVAAS, O., & SIMMONS, J. Q. Manipulation of self-destruction in three retarded children. *Journal of Applied Behavior Analysis,* 1969, *2,* 143–157.

LURIA, A. R. Psychological studies of mental deficiency in the Soviet Union. In N. R. Ellis (Ed.), *Handbook of mental deficiency.* New York: McGraw-Hill, 1963.

LUTKUS, A., & TRABASSO, T. Transitive inferences by preoperational, retarded adolescents. *American Journal of Mental Deficiency,* 1974, *78,* 599–606.

MENOLASCINO, F. J. The mentally retarded offender. *Mental Retardation,* 1974, *12,* 7–11.

MILGRAM, N. A. Cognition and language in mental retardation: Distinctions and implications. In D. K. Routh (Ed.), *The experimental psychology of mental retardation.* Chicago: Aldine, 1973.

MONROE, J. D., & HOWE, C. E. The effects of integration and social class on the acceptance of retarded adolescents. *Education and Training of the Mentally Retarded,* 1971, *6,* 20–24.

NAPOLITAN, J. L., & PETERSON, R. A. Treatment of a child with multiple stereotypies. Presented at the Clinical Roundtable, Training Parents in Behavior Modification, Association for Advancement of Behavior Therapy Convention, New York, 1972.

O'CONNOR, N., & HERMELIN, B. Discrimination and reversal learning in imbeciles. *Journal of Abnormal and Social Psychology,* 1959, *59,* 409–413.

O'GORMAN, G. Psychosis as a cause of mental defect. *Journal of Mental Science,* 1954, *100,* 934–943.

OSBORN, W. J. Associative clustering in organic and familial retardates. *American Journal of Mental Deficiency,* 1960, *65,* 331–357.

PAYNE, D. Regional cooperation in mental retardation data collection. *Mental Retardation,* 1968, *6,* 52–53.

PENROSE, L. S. *The biology of mental defect.* New York: Grune and Stratton, 1962.

PETERSON, R. A., & MCINTOSH, E. Teaching tricycle riding. *Mental Retardation,* 1973, *2,* 32–34.

PICKERING, D. E., & FISHER, D. A. Therapeutic concepts relative to hypothyroidism in childhood. *Journal of Chronic Diseases,* 1958, *7,* 242–263.

PINTNER, R. *Intelligence testing.* New York: Holt, Rinehart, and Winston, 1923.

REISS, S., & REDD, W. H. Generalization of the control of screaming behavior in an emotionally disturbed retarded female. *APA Proceedings,* 1970, 741–742.

Ressman, A. C., & Butterworth, T. Localized acquired hypertrichosis. *Archives of Dermatology and Syphillis,* 1952, *65,* 418–423.

Ribot, T. *The psychology of attention.* London: Kegan Paul, 1890.

Riegel, R. H., & Taylor, A. M. Compairson of conceptual strategies for grouping and remembering employed by EMR and nonretarded children. *American Journal of Mental Deficiency,* 1974, *78,* 592–598.

Rimland, B. *Infantile autism.* New York: Appleton-Century-Crofts, 1964.

Robinson, C. Error patterns in level 4 and level 5 object permanence training. *American Journal of Mental Deficiency,* 1974, *78,* 389–396.

Rosenberg, S. Problem-solving and conceptual behavior. In N. R. Ellis (Ed.), *Handbook of mental deficiency.* New York: McGraw-Hill, 1963.

Ross, D. M., & Ross, S. A. Cognitive training for the EMR child: Situational problem solving and planning. *American Journal of Mental Deficiency,* 1973, *78,* 20–26.

Rossi, E. L. Development of classificatory behavior. *Child Development,* 1964, *35,* 137–142.

Sailor, W., Guess, D., & Baer, D. M. Functional language for verbally deficient children: An experimental program. *Mental Retardation,* 1973, *11,* 27–35.

Sanders, B., Zigler, E., & Butterfield, E. C. Outer-directedness in the discrimination learning of normal and mentally retarded children. *Journal of Abnormal Psychology,* 1968, *73,* 368–375.

Sarason, S. B., & Doris, J. *Psychological problems in mental deficiency.* New York: Harper & Row, 1969.

Sarason, S. B., & Gladwin, T. Psychological and cultural problems in mental subnormality: A review of research. *Genetic Psychology Monographs,* 1958, *57,* 3–290.

Saslow, H. L. The comparability of the Peabody Picture Vocabulary Test and the revised Stanford-Binet, form L-M, with cerebral palsied children. *American Psychologist,* 1961, *16,* 377.

Scheerer, M., Rothman, E., & Goldstein, R. A case of "idiot savant": An experimental study of personality organization. *Psychological Monographs, 1945, 58,* No. 4.

Schmid-Kitsikis, E. Piagetian theory and its approach to psychopathology. *American Journal of Mental Deficiency,* 1973, *77,* 694–705.

Sheare, J. B. Social acceptance of EMR adolescents in integrated programs. *American Journal of Mental Deficiency,* 1974, *78,* 678–682.

Skinner, B. F. *Science and human behavior.* New York: Macmillan, 1953.

Spitz, H. H. Field theory in mental deficiency. In N. R. Ellis (Ed.), *Handbook of mental deficiency.* New York: McGraw-Hill, 1963.

Takeuchi, T., & Matsumoto, H. Minameta disease of human fetuses. In Nishimura et al. (Eds.), *Methods for teratological studies in experimental animals and man: Proceedings of the second international workshop in teratology, Kyoto, 1968.* Tokyo: Igaku Shoin, 1969.

Tate, B. G., & Baroff, G. S. Aversive control of self-injurious behavior in a psychotic boy. *Behavior Research and Therapy,* 1966, *4,* 281–287.

Turnure, J. E. Outerdirectedness in EMR boys and girls. *American Journal of Mental Deficiency,* 1973, *78,* 163–170.

Turnure, J. E., & Zigler, E. Outer-directedness in the problem-solving of normal and retarded children. *Journal of Abnormal and Social Psychology,* 1964, *69,* 427–436.

Ullman, D. G. Breadth of attention and retention in mentally retarded and intellectually average children. *American Journal of Mental Deficiency,* 1974, *78,* 640–648.

Wanschura, P. B., & Borkowski, J. G. Development and transfer of mediational strategies by retarded children in paired-associate learning. *American Journal of Mental Deficiency,* 1974, *78,* 631–639.

Warren, N. Research design for investigation of the lasting behavioral effects of malnutrition: The problem of controls. *Social Science and Medicine,* 1970, *4,* 589–593.

Woodward, M. The application of Piaget's theory to research in mental deficiency. In N. R. Ellis (Ed.), *Handbook of mental deficiency.* New York: McGraw-Hill, 1963.

Zeaman, D. One programmatic approach to retardation. Paper presented at the sixth annual program on Current Concerns in Clinical Psychology, Iowa City, Iowa, May, 1970. (Also in D. K. Routh (Ed.), *The experimental psychology of mental retardation.* Chicago: Aldine, 1973.)

Zeaman, D., & House, B. J. Approach and avoidance in the discrimination learning of retardates. In D. Zeaman et al. (Eds.), *Learning and transfer in mental defectives.* Progress Report No. 2, National Institute of Mental Health, 1960.

Zeaman, D., & House, B. The role of attention in retardate discrimination learning. In N. R. Ellis (Ed.), *Handbook of mental deficiency.* New York: McGraw-Hill, 1963.

Zeaman, D., & House, B. J. The relation of IQ and learning. In R. M. Gagne (Ed.), *Learning and individual differences.* Columbus, Ohio: Merrill, 1967.

Zigler, E. Social deprivation and rigidity in the performance of feebleminded children. *Journal of Abnormal and Social Psychology,* 1961, *62,* 413–421.

Zigler, E. Mental retardation. In P. London & D. Rosenhan (Eds.), *Foundations of abnormal psychology.* New York: Holt, Rinehart, and Winston, 1968.

Zigler, E. The retarded child as a whole person. In D. K. Routh (Ed.), *The experimental psychology of mental retardation.* Chicago: Aldine, 1973.

Zigler, E., Balla, D., & Butterfield, E. C. A longitudinal investigation of the relationship between preinstitutional social deprivation and social motivation in institutionalized retardates. *Journal of Personality and Social Psychology,* 1968, *10,* 437–445.

19. Abnormal Behavior in "Normal" People

Allport, G. W. *Social psychology.* Boston: Houghton Mifflin, 1924.

Allport, G. W. The nature of prejudice. Reading, Mass.: Addison-Wesley, 1954.

Anderson, N. H. Primacy effects in personality impression formation using a generalized order effect paradigm. *Journal of Personality and Social Psychology,* 1965, *2,* 1–9.
Aronson, E. *The social animal.* San Francisco: W. H. Freeman, 1972.
Asch, S. E. Forming impressions of personality. *Journal of Abnormal and Social Psychology,* 1946, *41,* 258–290.
Asch, S. E. Effects of group pressure in the modification and distortion of judgments. In I. H. Guetzkow (Ed.), *Groups, leadership, and men.* Pittsburgh: Carnegie, 1951.
Asch, S. E. Studies of independence and conformity: A minority of one against a unanimous majority. *Psychological Monographs,* 1956, *70,* Whole No. 416.
Barker, R. G., Dembo, T., Lewin, K., & Wright, M. E. Frustration and regression: An experiment with young children. In R. G. Barker, J. S. Kounin, & M. E. Wright (Eds.), *Child behavior and development.* New York: McGraw-Hill, 1943.
Berecz, J. Modification of smoking behavior through self-administered punishment of imagined behavior: A new approach to aversion therapy. *Journal of Consulting and Clinical Psychology,* 1972, *38,* 244–250.
Berlyne, D. E. *Conflict, arousal, and curiosity.* New York: McGraw-Hill, 1960.
Bernstein, D. A. The modification of smoking behavior: An evaluative review. In W. A. Hunt (Ed.), *Learning mechanisms in smoking.* Chicago: Aldine, 1970.
Berscheid, E., & Walster, E. Physical attractiveness. In L. Berkowitz (Ed.), *Advances in experimental social psychology. Vol 7.* New York: Academic Press, 1974.
Bills, R. E. Self-concept and Rorschach signs of depression. *Journal of Consulting Psychology,* 1954, *18,* 135–139.
Block, J., & Thomas, H. Is satisfaction with self a measure of adjustment? *Journal of Abnormal and Social Psychology,* 1955, *51,* 254–259.
Borislow, B. Self-evaluation and academic adjustment. *Journal of Counseling Psychology,* 1962, *9,* 246–253.
Brecher, E. M., & the editors of *Consumer Reports. Licit and illicit drugs.* Mount Vernon, N.Y.: Consumers Union, 1972.
Brissett, D. Toward a clarification of self-esteem. *Psychiatry,* 1972, *35,* 255–263.
Broverman, I. K., Broverman, D. M., Clarkson, F. E., Rosenkrantz, P. S., & Vogel, S. R. Sex-role stereotypes and clinical judgments of mental health. *Journal of Consulting and Clinical Psychology,* 1970, *34,* 1–7.
Broverman, I. K., Vogel, S. R., Broverman, D. M., Clarkson, F. E., & Rosenkrantz, P. S. Sex-role stereotypes: A current appraisal. *Journal of Social Issues,* 1972, *28,* 59–78.
Byrne, D. The repression-sensitization scale: Rationale, reliability, and validity. *Journal of Personality,* 1961, *29,* 334–349.
Byrne, D. *An introduction to personality: Research, theory, and applications.* Englewood Cliffs, N.J.: Prentice-Hall, 1974.
Canétti, E. (1960) *Crowds and power.* New York: Viking, 1963.
Cannavale, F. J., Scarr, H. A., & Pepitone, A. Deindividuation in the small group: Further evidence. *Journal of Personality and Social Psychology,* 1970, *16,* 141–147.
Chase, P. H. Self-concepts in adjusted and maladjusted hospital patients. *Journal of Consulting Psychology,* 1957, *21,* 495–497.
Chodorkoff, B. Adjustment and the discrepancy between the perceived and ideal self. *Journal of Clinical Psychology,* 1954, *10,* 266–268.
Cole, C. W., Oetting, E. R., & Miskimins, R. W. Self-concept therapy for adolescent females. *Journal of Abnormal Psychology,* 1969, *74,* 642–645.
Crandall, V. C. Sex differences in expectancy of intellectual and academic reinforcement. In C. P. Smith (Ed.), *Achievement-related motives in children.* New York: Russell Sage Foundation, 1969.
Crowne, D. P., & Marlowe, D. *The approval motive.* New York: John Wiley and Sons, 1964.
Crowne, D. P., & Stephens, M. W. Self-acceptance and self-evaluative behavior: A critique of methodology. *Psychological Bulletin,* 1961, *58,* 104–119.
Davids, A., & Lawton, M. J. Self-concept, mother concept, and food aversions in emotionally disturbed and normal children. *Journal of Abnormal and Social Psychology,* 1961, *62,* 309–314.
Diggory, J. C. *Self-evaluation: Concepts and studies.* New York: John Wiley and Sons, 1966.
Diggory, J. C., & Magaziner, D. E. Self-evaluation as a function of instrumentally relevant capacities. *Bulletin de l'Association Internationale de Psychologie Appliquée,* 1959, *8,* 2–19.
Dion, K. K. Physical attractiveness and evaluations of children's transgressions. *Journal of Personality and Social Psychology,* 1972, *24,* 207–213.
Dion, K. K., Berscheid, E., & Walster, E. What is beautiful is good. *Journal of Personality and Social Psychology,* 1972, *24,* 285–290.
Durkheim, E. Translated by G. Simpson. *The division of labor in society,* New York: Macmillan, 1933.
Elliot, R., & Tighe, T. J. Breaking the cigarette habit: Effects of a technique involving threatened loss of money. *Psychological Record,* 1968, *18,* 503–513.
Ellis, A. *Reason and emotion in psychotherapy.* New York: Lyle Stuart, 1962.
Eysenck, H. J. Personality and the maintenance of the smoking habit. In W. L. Dunn (Ed.), *Smoking behavior: Motives and incentives.* Washington, D.C.: Winston & Sons, 1973.
Fenichel, O. *The psychoanalytic theory of neurosis.* New York: W. W. Norton, 1945.
Festinger, L., Pepitone, A., & Newcomb, T. Some consequences of deindividuation in a group. *Journal of Abnormal and Social Psychology,* 1952, *47,* 382–389.
Freud, S. (1926) *Inhibitions, symptoms, and anxiety.* London: Hogarth, 1936.
Freud, S. (1921) *Group psychology and the analysis of the ego.* New York: Bantam, 1960.
Freud, S. Mourning and melancholia. (Translated by J. Rivière.) *Internationale Zeitschrift fur Artzliche Psychoanalyse,* 1916–1918, *4,* 288–301. In S. Freud, *Collected papers.* Vol. 4. London: Hogarth, 1959.
Friedman, I. Phenomenal, ideal, and projected conceptions of self. *Journal of Abnormal and Social Psychology,* 1955, *51,* 611–615.

GERGEN, K. J., & Morse, S. J. Self-consistency: Measurement and evaluation. *Proceedings of the seventy-fifth Annual Convention of the American Psychological Association,* 1967, *2,* 207–208.

GOLDBERG, P. A. Are women prejudiced against women? *Transaction,* April, 1968, 28–30.

GOLDBERG, S., & LEWIS, M. Play behavior in the year-old infant: Early sex differences. *Child Development,* 1969, *40,* 21–31.

GUILFORD, J. *Factors related to successful abstinence from smoking: Final report.* Los Angeles: American Institutes for Research, 1966.

HAIMOWITZ, M. L., & HAIMOWITZ, N. R. The evil eye: Fear of success. In M. L. Haimowitz & N. R. Haimowitz (Eds.), *Human development: Selected readings.* New York: Cromwell, 1966.

HAIRE, M., & GRUNES, W. F. Perceptual defenses: Processes protecting an organized perception of another personality. *Human Relations,* 1950, *3,* 403–412.

HANLON, T. E., HOFSTAETTER, P. R., & O'CONNER, J. P. Congruence of self and ideal self in relation to personality adjustment. *Journal of Consulting Psychology,* 1954, *18,* 215–217.

HASTORF, A. H., & CANTRIL, H. They say a game: A case study. *Journal of Abnormal and Social Psychology,* 1954, *49,* 129–134.

HENDRICK, C., & PAGE, H. A. Self-esteem, attitude similarity, and attraction. *Journal of Personality,* 1970, *38,* 588–601.

HERMAN, C. P. External and internal cues as determinants of the smoking behavior of light and heavy smokers *Journal of Personality and Social Psychology,* 1974, *30,* 664–672.

HEWITT, J., & GOLDMAN, M. Self-esteem, need for approval, and reactions to personal evaluations. *Journal of Experimental Social Psychology,* 1974, *10,* 201–210.

HILL, W. F. Comments on paper by Premack. In W. A. Hunt (Ed.), *Learning mechanisms in smoking.* Chicago: Aldine, 1970.

HILLSON, J. S., & WORCHEL, P. Self-concept and defensive behavior in the maladjusted. *Journal of Consulting Psychology,* 1957, *21,* 83–88.

HOBBES, T. (1651) *Leviathan.* Oxford: The Clarendon Press, 1909.

HUNT, W. A., & MATARAZZO, J. D. Habit mechanisms in smoking. In W. A. Hunt (Ed.), *Learning mechanisms in smoking.* Chicago: Aldine, 1970.

HUNT, W. A., & MATARAZZO, J. D. Three years later: Recent developments in the experimental modification of smoking behavior. *Journal of Abnormal Psychology,* 1973, *81,* 107–114.

IKARD, F. F., GREEN, D. E., & HORN, D. The development of a scale to differentiate between types of smoking as related to the management of affect. Paper presented at the annual meeting of the Eastern Psychological Association, Washington, D.C., 1968.

JAMES, W. *Psychology: Briefer course.* New York: Holt, Rinehart, and Winston, 1892.

JARVIK, M. E. The role of nicotine in the smoking habit. In W. A. Hunt (Ed.), *Learning mechanisms in smoking.* Chicago: Aldine, 1970.

JOHNSON, C. D., GORMLY, J., & GORMLY, A. Disagreements and self-esteem: Support for the competence-reinforcement model of attraction. *Journal of Research in Personality,* 1973, *7,* 165–172.

JONES, S. C. Self- and interpersonal evaluations: Esteem theories versus consistency theories. *Psychological Bulletin,* 1973, *79,* 185–199.

KAMANO, D. K. Self-satisfaction and psychological adjustment in schizophrenics. *Journal of Consulting Psychology,* 1961, *25,* 492–496.

KAPLAN, H. B., & POKORNY, A. D. Self-derogation and psychosocial adjustment. *Journal of Nervous and Mental Disease,* 1969, *149,* 421–434.

KARLINS, M., COFFMAN, T. L., & WALTERS, G. On the fading of social stereotypes: Studies in three generations of college students. *Journal of Personality and Social Psychology,* 1969, *13,* 1–16.

KATZ, D., & BRALY, K. W. Racial stereotypes of one hundred college students. *Journal of Abnormal and Social Psychology,* 1933, *28,* 280–290.

KELLEY, H. H. The warm-cold variable in first impressions of persons. *Journal of Personality,* 1950, *18,* 431–439.

KERCKHOFF, A. C., & BACK, K. W. *The June bug: A study of hysterical contagion.* New York: Appleton-Century-Crofts, 1968.

LAING, R. D. *The politics of experience.* New York: Pantheon, 1967.

LANDY, D., & SIGALL, H. Beauty is talent: Task evaluation as a function of the performers' physical attractiveness. *Journal of Personality and Social Psychology,* 1974, *29,* 299–304.

LEBON, G. (1885) *The crowd: A study of the popular mind.* London: Unwin, 1896.

LICHTENSTEIN, E., HARRIS, D. E., BIRCHLER, G. R., WAHL, J. H., & SCHMAHL, D. P. Comparison of rapid smoking, warm smoky air, and attention placebo in the modification of smoking behavior. *Journal of Consulting and Clinical Psychology,* 1973, *40,* 92–98.

LOGAN, F. Self-control as habit, drive, and incentive. *Journal of Abnormal Psychology,* 1973, *81,* 127–136.

LUCHINS, A. S. Experimental attempts to minimize the impact of first impressions. In C. I. Hovland (Ed.), *The order of presentation in persuasion.* New Haven, Conn: Yale University Press, 1957.

MACHIAVELLI, N. (1512–1526) Translated by L. Ricci. *The prince and the discourses.* New York: Random House, 1950.

MARACEK, J., & METTEE, D. R. Avoidance of continued success as a function of self-esteem, level of esteem certainty, and responsibility for success. *Journal of Personality and Social Psychology,* 1972, *22,* 98–107.

MARTIN, E. D. *The behavior of crowds.* New York: Harper & Row, 1920.

MCDOUGALL, W. *The group mind.* New York: Putnam, 1920.

MCGUIRE, W. J. Personality and susceptibility to social influence. In E. F. Borgatta & W. W. Lambert (Eds.), *Handbook of personality theory and research.* Chicago: Rand McNally, 1968.

MILGRAM, S., & TOCH, H. Collective behavior: Crowds and social movements. In G. Lindzey & E. Aronson (Eds.), *The handbook of social psychology. Vol. 4.* Reading, Mass.: Addison–Wesley, 1969.

MORGANSTERN, K. P., & RATCLIFF, R. G. Systematic desensitization as a technique for treating smoking behavior: A preliminary report. *Behavior Research and Therapy,* 1969, *7,* 397–398.

MOSS, H. Sex, age and state as determinants of mother-infant interaction. *Merrill-Palmer Quarterly,* 1967, *13,* 19–36.

MURSTEIN, B. I. The relation of the famous sayings test to self- and ideal-self-adjustment. *Journal of Consulting Psychology,* 1961, *25,* 368.

NESBITT, P. D. Smoking, physiological arousal, and emotional response. *Journal of Personality and Social Psychology,* 1973, *25,* 137–144.

NEWCOMB, T. M. Autistic hostility and social reality. *Human Relations,* 1947, *1,* 69–87.

OVESEY, L. Fear of vocational success. *Archives of General Psychiatry,* 1962, *7,* 82–92.

PHETERSON, G. I., KIESLER, S. B., & GOLDBERG, P. A. Evaluation of the performance of women as a function of their sex, achievement, and personal history. *Journal of Personality and Social Psychology,* 1971, *19,* 114–118.

PIERS, P. V. Parent prediction of children's self-concepts. *Journal of Consulting and Clinical Psychology,* 1972. *38,* 428–433.

RESNICK, J. H. Effects of stimulus satiation on the overlearned maladaptive response of cigarette smoking. *Journal of Consulting and Clinical Psychology,* 1968, *32,* 501–505.

ROBERTS, A. H. Self-control procedures in modification of smoking behavior. *Psychological Reports,* 1969, *24,* 675–676.

ROGERS, C. R. The significance of self-regarding attitudes and perceptions. In M. L. Reymert (Ed.), *Feeling and emotion: The mooseheart symposium.* New York: McGraw-Hill, 1950.

ROGERS, C. R. *Client-centered therapy.* Boston: Houghton Mifflin, 1951.

ROGERS, C. R., & DYMOND, R. (Eds.) *Psychotherapy and personality change.* Chicago: University of Chicago Press, 1954.

ROSENBERG, M. *Society and the adolescent self-image.* Princeton, N.J.: Princeton University Press, 1965.

ROSENBERG, M. Psychological selectivity in self-esteem formation. In C. W. Sherif & M. Sherif (Eds.), *Attitude, ego-involvement and change.* New York: John Wiley and Sons, 1967.

ROSENHAN, D. L. On being sane in insane places. *Science,* 1973, *179,* 250–258.

ROSS, E. A. *Social psychology,* New York: Macmillan, 1908.

SCHACHTER, S. Nesbitt's paradox. In W. L. Dunn (Ed.), *Smoking behavior: Motives and incentives.* Washington, D. C.: Winston & Sons, 1973.

SCHMAHL, D., LICHTENSTEIN, E., & HARRIS, D. D. Successful treatment of habitual smokers with warm smoky air and rapid smoking. *Journal of Consulting and Clinical Psychology,* 1972, *38,* 105–111.

SEARS, P. S., & FELDMAN, D. H. Teacher interactions with boys and girls. *National Elementary Principal,* 1966, *46,* 30–35.

SHERIF, M. A study of some social factors in perception. *Archives of Psychology,* 1935, *27,* No. 187.

SINGER, J., BRUSH, C., & LUBLIN, S. Some aspects of deindividuation: Identification and conformity. *Journal of Experimental Social Psychology,* 1965, *1,* 356–378.

SMITH, B. D., & TEEVAN, R. C. Relationships among self-ideal congruence, adjustment, and fear-of-failure motivation. *Journal of Personality,* 1971, *39,* 44–56.

SMITH, G. M. Six measures of self-concept discrepancy and instability: Their interrelationships, reliability and relations to other personality measures. *Journal of Consulting Psychology,* 1958, *22,* 101–112.

SMITH, G. M. Personality and smoking: A review of the empirical literature. In W. A. Hunt (Ed.), *Learning mechanisms in smoking.* Chicago: Aldine, 1970.

STEFFY, R. A., MEICHENBAUM, D., & BEST, J. A. Aversive and cognitive factors in the modification of smoking behavior. *Behavior Research and Therapy,* 1970, *8,* 115–125.

SULLIVAN, H. S. *The interpersonal theory of psychiatry.* New York: W. W. Norton, 1953.

SUSHINSKY, L. W., & WENER, R. Distorting judgments of mental health: Generality of the labeling bias effect. *Journal of Nervous and Mental Disease,* 1975, *161,* 82–89.

TARDE, G. (1890) Translated by E. C. Parsons. *The laws of imitation.* New York: Holt, Rinehart, and Winston, 1903.

TEMERLIN, M. K. Suggestion effects in psychiatric diagnosis. *Journal of Nervous and Mental Disease,* 1968, *147,* 349–359.

TOUHEY, J. C. Effects of additional women professionals on ratings of occupational prestige and desirability. *Journal of Personality and Social Psychology,* 1974, *29,* 86–89.

TROTTER, W. *Instincts of the herd in peace and war.* London: Benn, 1919.

TURNER, R. H. Collective behavior. In R. E. L. Faris (Ed.), *Handbook of modern sociology.* Chicago: Rand McNally, 1964.

TURNER, R. H., & VANDERLIPPE, R. H. Self-ideal congruence as an index of adjustment. *Journal of Abnormal and Social Psychology,* 1958, *57,* 202–206.

WAGNER, M. K., & BRAGG, R. A. Comparing behavior modification approaches to habit decrement—smoking. *Journal of Consulting and Clinical Psychology,* 1970, *34,* 258–263.

WEITZMAN, L. J., EIFLER, D., HOKADA, E., & ROSS, C. Sex-role socialization in picture books for preschool children. *American Journal of Sociology,* 1972, *77,* 1125–1150.

WHITE, R. W. Motivation reconsidered: The concept of competence. *Psychological Review,* 1959, *66,* 297–333.

WYER, R. S. Self-acceptance, discrepancy between parents' perceptions of their children, and goal-seeking effectiveness. *Journal of Personality and Social Psychology,* 1965, *2,* 311–316.

YOUNGLESON, M. L. The need to affiliate and self-esteem in institutionalized children. *Journal of Personality and Social Psychology,* 1973, *26,* 280–286.

ZIMBARDO, P. C. The human choice: Individuation, reason, and order versus deindividuation, impulse, and chaos. In W. J. Arnold & D. Levine (Eds.), *Nebraska symposium on motivation.* Vol. 17. Lincoln: University of Nebraska Press, 1969.

20. Some Topics Closely Related to the Study of Abnormal Behavior: Aggression and Fantasy

AGNEW, H. W., WEBB, W. B., & WILLIAMS, R. L. Comparison of stage four and 1-REM sleep deprivation. *Perceptual and Motor Skills,* 1967, *24,* 851–858.

ARDREY, R. *The territorial imperative.* New York: Atheneum, 1966.

BANDURA, A. Vicarious processes: A case of no trial learning. In L. Berkowitz (Ed.), *Advances in experimental social psychology.* Vol. 2. New York: Academic Press, 1965.

BANDURA, A. *Aggression: A social learning analysis.* Englewood Cliffs, N.J.: Prentice-Hall, 1973.

BANDURA, A., & WALTERS, R. H. *Adolescent aggression.* New York: Ronald Press, 1959.

BANDURA, A., & WALTERS, R. H. *Social learning and personality development.* New York: Holt, Rinehart, and Winston, 1965.

BERKOWITZ, L. *Aggression: A social psychological analysis.* New York: McGraw-Hill, 1962.

BERKOWITZ, L. Control of aggression. In B. M. Caldwell & H. Ricciuti (Eds.), *Review of child development research.* Vol. 3. New York: Russell Sage Foundation, 1969.

BUSS, A. H. *The psychology of aggression.* New York: John Wiley and Sons, 1961.

CARTWRIGHT, R. D. Sleep fantasy in normal and schizophrenic persons. *Journal of Abnormal Psychology,* 1972, *80,* 275–279.

CAZAVELON, J., & EPSTEIN, S. Daydreams of female paranoid schizophrenics. *Journal of Clinical Psychology,* 1966, *22,* 27–32.

CHASDI, E. H., & LAWRENCE, M. S. Some antecedents of aggression and effects of frustration in doll play. In D. McClelland (Ed.), *Studies in motivation.* New York: Appleton-Century-Crofts, 1955.

CRONBACH, L. J. A validation design for qualitative studies of personality. *Journal of Consulting Psychology,* 1948, *12,* 365–374.

DELGADO, J. M. R. Evoking and inhibiting aggressive behavior by radio stimulation in monkey colonies. *American Zoologist,* 1965, *5,* 642.

DEMENT, W. Dream recall and eye movements during sleep in schizophrenics and normals. *Journal of Nervous and Mental Disease,* 1955, *122,* 263–269.

DEMENT, W. The effect of dream deprivation. *Science,* 1960, *131,* 1705–1707.

DEMENT, W., & FISHER, C. Experimental interference with the sleep cycle. *Canadian Psychiatric Association Journal,* 1963, *8,* 400–405.

DOLLARD, J., DOOB, L. W., MILLER, N. E., MOWRER, O. H., & SEARS, R. R. *Frustration and aggression.* New Haven, Conn.: Yale University Press, 1939.

EDWARDS, N. Aggressive expression under threat of retaliation. Unpublished doctoral dissertation, University of Iowa, 1967.

ERON, L. D. A normative study of the Thematic Apperception Test. *Psychological Monographs,* 1950, *64* (Whole No. 315).

ERON, L. D. Review of the Thematic Apperception Test. In O. K. Buros (Ed.), *The fifth mental measurements yearbook.* Highland Park, N.J.: Gryphon, 1959.

ERON, L. D. Review of the Thematic Apperception Test. In O. K. Buros (Ed.), *The seventh mental measurements yearbook.* Vol. 1. Highland Park, N.J.: Gryphon, 1972.

ERON, L. D., HUESMANN, L. R., WALDER, L. O., & LEFKOWITZ, M. M. Does television violence cause aggression? *American Psychologist,* 1972, *27,* 253–263.

ERON, L. D., LAULICHT, J. H., WALDER, L. O., FARBER, I. E., & SPIEGEL, J. P. Application of role and learning theories to the study of the development of aggression in children. *Psychological Reports,* 1961, *9,* 261–334 (Monograph Supplement).

ERON, L. D., LEFKOWITZ, M. M., WALDER, L. O., & HUESMANN, L. R. Relation of learning in childhood to psychopathology and aggression in young adulthood. In A. Davids (Ed.), *Child personality and psychopathology: Current topics.* Vol. 1. New York: John Wiley and Sons, 1974.

ERON, L. D., WALDER, L. O., & LEFKOWITZ, M. M. *Learning of aggression in children.* Boston: Little, Brown, 1971.

ERON, L. D., WALDER, L. O., TOIGO, R., & LEFKOWITZ, M. M. Social class, parental punishment for aggression and child aggression. *Child Development,* 1963, *34,* 849–867.

EYSENCK, H. J. Review of the Rorschach. In O. K. Buros (Ed.), *The fifth mental measurements yearbook.* Highland Park, N.J.: Gryphon, 1959.

FOULKES, D. Dream reports from different stages of sleep. *Journal of Abnormal and Social Psychology,* 1962, *65,* 14–25.

FOULKES, D. *The psychology sleep.* New York: Scribner, 1966.

FRANKEL, M. Introduction. In D. Walker (Ed.), *Rights in conflict.* New York: Bantam, 1968.

FREEMON, F. R. *Sleep research: A critical review.* Springfield, Ill.: Charles C. Thomas, 1972.

FREUD, S. (1900) The interpretation of dreams. Vols. 4. and 5. *The complete psychological works of Sigmund Freud.* London: Hogarth, 1953.

FREUD, S. *Beyond the pleasure principle.* London: International Psychoanalytic Press, 1922.

GREGORY, D. *Nigger.* New York: Pocket Books, 1964.

HINDE, R. A. The nature of aggression. *New Society,* 1967, *9,* 302–304.

HOKANSON, J. E. Psychophysiological evaluation of the catharsis hypothesis. In E. I. Megargee & J. E. Hokanson (Eds.), *The dynamics of aggression.* New York: Harper & Row, 1970.

JACOBI, J. *The psychology of C. G. Jung.* London: Routledge & Kegan Paul, 1951.

JARVIK, L. F., KLODIN, V., & MATSUYAMA, S. S. Human aggression and the extra y chromosome: Fact or fancy. *American Psychologist,* 1973, *28,* 674–682.

JENSEN, A. R. Review of the Thematic Apperception Test. In O. K. Buros (Ed.), *The fifth mental measurements yearbook.* Highland Park, N.J.: Gryphon, 1959.

KALES, A., HOEDEMAKER, F. S., JACOBSON, A., & LICHTENSTEIN, E. L. Dream deprivation: An experimental reappraisal. *Nature,* 1964, *204,* 1337–1338.

KLINGER, E. *Structure and function of fantasy.* New York: John Wiley and Sons, 1971.

Koresko, R., Snyder, F., & Feinberg, I. "Dream time" in hallucinating and non-hallucinating schizophrenic patients. *Nature,* 1963, *199,* 1118–1119.

Lefkowitz, M. M., Eron, L. D., Walder, L. O., & Huesmann, L. R. *Growing up to be violent: A longitudinal study of the development of aggression.* Elmsford, N.Y.: Pergamon, 1975.

Lorenz, K. *On aggression.* New York: Harcourt Brace Jovanovich, 1966.

Maccoby, E. E., & Jacklin, C. N. Sex differences and their implications for sex roles. Paper presented at the American Psychological Association, Washington, D.C., September, 1971.

Mark, V. H., & Ervin, F. R. *Violence and the brain.* New York: Harper & Row, 1970.

Menninger, K. (1938) *Man against himself.* New York: Harcourt Brace Jovanovich, 1965.

Miller, N. E. The frustration-aggression hypothesis. *Psychological Review,* 1941, *48,* 337–342.

Montagu, M. F. A. The new litany of "innate depravity" or original sin revisited. In M. F. A. Montagu (Ed.), *Man and aggression.* New York: Oxford University Press, 1968.

Pastore, N. Role of arbitrariness in the frustration-aggression hypothesis. *Journal of Abnormal and Social Psychology,* 1952, *47,* 728–731.

Patterson, G. R., Littman, R. A., & Bricker, W. Assertive behavior in children: A step toward a theory of aggression. *Monograph of Society for Research in Child Development,* 1967, *32,* 5 (Serial No. 113).

Peterson, R. A. Aggression as a function of retaliation and aggression level of target and aggressor. *Developmental Psychology,* 1971, *5,* 161–166.

Pittluck, P. The relation between aggressive fantasy and overt behavior. Unpublished doctoral dissertation, Yale University, 1950.

Plato. *The republic.* Translated by F. M. Cornford. London: Oxford University Press, 1941.

Rychlak, J. F. Manifest anxiety as reflecting commitment to the psychological present at the expense of cognitive futurity. *Journal of Consulting and Clinical Psychology,* 1972, *38,* 70–79.

Rychlak, J. F. Time orientation in the positive and negative free phantasies of mildly abnormal versus normal high school males. *Journal of Consulting and Clinical Psychology,* 1973, *41,* 175–180.

Sampson, H. Psychological effects of deprivation of dreaming sleep. *Journal of Nervous and Mental Disease,* 1966, *143,* 305–317.

Sears, R. R., Maccoby, E. E., & Levin, H. *Patterns of child rearing.* Boston: Row Peterson, 1957.

Shaffer, L. J. Review of the Rorschach. In O. K. Buros (Ed.), *The fifth mental measurements yearbook.* Highland Park, N.J.: Gryphon, 1959.

Siegelman, M. Parent behavior correlates of personality traits related to creativity in sons and daughters. *Journal of Consulting and Clinical Psychology,* 1973, *40,* 43–47.

Singer, J. L. *Daydreaming.* New York: Random House, 1966.

Singer, J. L., & Antrobus, J. A. A factor analytic study of daydreaming and conceptually-related cognitive and personality variables. *Perceptual and Motor Skills,* 1963, *17,* 187–209 (Monograph Supplement 3).

Singer, J. L., & Antrobus, J. A. Daydreaming, imaginal processes and personality: A normative study. In P. Sheehan (Ed.), *The nature and function of imagery.* New York: Academic Press, 1972.

Starker, S., & Singer, J. L. Daydreaming and symptom patterns of psychiatric patients: A factor analytic study. *Journal of Abnormal Psychology,* 1975, *84,* 567–570.

Streissguth, A. P., Wagner, N., & Wechsler, J. Effects of sex, illness and hospitalization on daydreaming. *Journal of Consulting and Clinical Psychology,* 1969, *33,* 218–225.

Tinbergen, N. On war and peace in animal and man: An ethologist's approach to the biology of aggression. *Science,* 1968, *160,* 1411–1418.

Vogel, C. W. REM deprivation: III. Dreaming and psychosis. *Archives of General Psychiatry,* 1968, *18,* 312–329.

Walder, L. O., Abelson, R., Eron, L. D., Banta, T. J., & Laulicht, J. H. Development of a peer-rating measure of aggression. *Psychological Reports,* 1961, *9,* 497–556 (Monograph Supplement).

Young, W. C., Goy, R. W., & Phoenix, C. H. Hormones and sexual behavior. *Science,* 1964, *143,* 212–218.

Zubin, J., Eron, L. D., & Schumer, F. *An experimental approach to projective techniques.* New York: John Wiley and Sons, 1965.

Name Index

Subject Index